BASICS *of* AKKADIAN

BASICS *of* AKKADIAN

A GRAMMAR, WORKBOOK, AND GLOSSARY

GORDON P. HUGENBERGER
WITH NANCY L. ERICKSON

ZONDERVAN ACADEMIC

ZONDERVAN ACADEMIC

Basics of Akkadian

Published in Grand Rapids, Michigan, by Zondervan. Zondervan is a registered trademark of The Zondervan Corporation, L.L.C., a wholly owned subsidiary of HarperCollins Christian Publishing, Inc.

Requests for information should be addressed to customercare@harpercollins.com.

Zondervan titles may be purchased in bulk for educational, business, fundraising, or sales promotional use. For information, please email SpecialMarkets@Zondervan.com.

Library of Congress Cataloging-in-Publication Data

Names: Hugenberger, Gordon Paul, author. | Erickson, Nancy L., author.
Title: Basics of Akkadian : a grammar, workbook, and glossary / Gordon P. Hugenberger, Nancy L. Erickson. Other titles: Zondervan language basics
Description: Grand Rapids : Zondervan, 2022. | Series: Zondervan language basics series | Includes bibliographical references and index. Identifiers: LCCN 2022031553 | ISBN 9780310134596 (paperback)
Subjects: LCSH: Akkadian language--Grammar. | Akkadian language. | BISAC: RELIGION / Biblical Reference / Language Study | RELIGION / Biblical Studies / History & Culture
Classification: LCC PJ3251 .H854 2022 | DDC 492/.182421--dc23/eng/20220720
LC record available at https://lccn.loc.gov/2022031553
LC Catalog - No Connections Available

All Scripture quotations, unless otherwise indicated, are the author's own translations.

Cover design: LUCAS Art & Design
Interior design: Kait Lamphere

Printed in the United States of America

HB 08.13.2024

Dedicated to my brilliant, beautiful, and indefatigable wife, Jane, whom I have been chasing ever since I first saw her at a Harvard-Wellesley dance September 20, 1967. By the grace of God we are still dancing, and I am still chasing her, but somehow I have not yet caught her!

—Gordon P. Hugenberger

To Sophie and Paulie—may your faith grow ever rich as you uncover the depths of the ancient Near Eastern world, even as you study Akkadian!

—Nancy L. Erickson

Contents

Acknowledgments

Michel de Montaigne famously said, “My life has been full of terrible misfortunes, most of which never happened.”[1] Many of us can identify with Montaigne in recognizing the boundless creativity of our self-torturing anxieties. The inverse of Montaigne’s admission, however, is surely just as true, even if it is less often acknowledged: my life has been full of all kinds of remarkable blessings, all of which actually happened and ineradicably shaped my life, but most of which I never intended or deserved.

As a major in applied physics at Harvard who had not grown up in a religious home, I decided to attend Gordon-Conwell Theological Seminary for some remedial reading of the Bible before pursuing what I assumed would be a doctorate in physics. Thankfully, the seminary had low enough standards so as to accept a student who made it clear that he had no interest in a career in ministry or biblical studies. What I did not expect, however, was the extent to which its gifted faculty would impact my life through their infectious faith in God, their confidence in the Scriptures, their sincere interest in getting to know and care for each student, inviting them into their homes and lives, and their respect for genuine scholarly competence, whether in those who shared their Evangelical faith or in those who opposed that faith.

With respect to Akkadian, it was there that I was swept off my feet by the biblical-theological genius of Prof. Meredith G. Kline (1922–2007). Kline wrote his doctoral dissertation under Cyrus Gordon on the Habiru, featured prominently in the fourteenth century BCE Akkadian texts from Amarna. Kline’s independence of thought and his passion for discovering fresh insights into the Hebrew Bible, especially supported by a judicious use of Akkadian cultural and literary parallels, was contagious. It was not long before my plan for doctoral studies changed from physics to Hebrew, Akkadian, and related subjects.

Prof. Elmer B. Smick (1921–1994) was another professor whose impact on my life with respect to Akkadian and much else was something I never intended or deserved. He too was a student of Cyrus Gordon and a brilliant linguist in his own right. He never tired of challenging aspiring students and pastors that if they had discovered how deeply satisfying and helpful it is to study the Bible in its original languages, then they should apply this same principle to their study of its cultural background! According to Smick, this made it especially desirable to study the cuneiform languages of Sumerian, Akkadian, Hittite, and Ugaritic because, thanks to the durability of clay tablets, there is a vast supply of original documentary evidence for that cultural background. In 1974, when I was just a third-year student, Prof. Smick shocked me by asking me to teach the course in Ugaritic which he was scheduled to teach. This must have broken some quality standards for faculty, but thanks to his behind-the-scenes tutelage and the kind patience of *my* students, I was now hooked. It was the first course I taught at Gordon-Conwell, where I have been privileged to teach ever since.

Later on I started doctoral studies in a program that was jointly sponsored by the Oxford Centre for postgraduate Hebrew Studies and the College of St. Paul and St. Mary. I immediately registered

1. “Ma vie a été pleine de terribles malheurs dont la plupart ne se sont jamais produits.”

for the first-year Akkadian course at Oxford, but when I showed up for its first class, the professor was visibly disheartened to see me. I was his only student. He explained that since he did not wish to teach such a small class he would arrange for me to take first-year Akkadian at the University of Birmingham. Now it was my turn to be disheartened! I had never heard of the University of Birmingham, nor had I ever heard of Prof. Wilfred G. Lambert (1926-2011), under whom I would be studying.

Ironically, when I showed up for Prof. Lambert's course, I was once again the only student in the class. Thankfully he did not seem to notice! Prof. Lambert taught that year's course as if the room were full of eager, well-prepared students. After each short formal lecture at the chalk board on whatever grammatical matter needed to be covered for the day, he would sit down, and the students were told to remove all papers from their desks. Nothing but an unmarked cuneiform text of the Laws of Hammurabi or, later, the Laws of Eshnunna, and then the Middle Assyrian Laws, was allowed to be in view. For the bulk of the class period, every turn for the students to transliterate, normalize, and translate the text, or to explain any interesting parsing or difficult grammatical feature was my turn! No notes anywhere? Ugh!

It was a terrifying privilege, almost every minute of which I loved. I treasured the many times that Lambert invited me to wait in his office before or after class according to my train schedule, sometimes as he worked correcting galley proofs of CAD or finishing up some paper, and at other times just to allow us to continue our conversation. It was a special treat in a few cases when we were able to extend this into shared meals in his office, or at one of his favorite restaurants (picture an uncouth carnivorous American breaking bread with a refined, vegetarian Brummie). At the time I assumed the reason that Lambert was willing to waste all those hours with just one very average beginning student was that (how can it be put politely?) he must be someone who never made it into the top tier of his field. I could not have been more wrong!

When I took second-year Akkadian at Harvard with Prof. Piotr Steinkeller, whose teaching only deepened my interest in Akkadian, Steinkeller's anecdotes about Lambert and his frequent questions about how Lambert might have explained this or that grammatical point or puzzling feature in one of the laws had a profound effect on me. Knowing how well respected Prof. Steinkeller was and is, I came to appreciate even more how privileged I had been to begin my study of Akkadian under someone whom Steinkeller rightly viewed as one of the foremost Assyriologists of the late twentieth century.

The textbook which is now in your hands is my best effort at summarizing and amplifying what I learned from Prof. Lambert. Clarifications and expansions from Prof. Steinkeller may be mixed in, as is also the case with insights or explanations from other authorities. I have taught first-year Akkadian often over the decades—each time using some combination of what I learned from Lambert and the excellent grammars by Rykle Borger, David Marcus, Richard Caplice, and especially John Huehnergard. Where my dependence on these and others is conscious, I have footnoted that dependency. My own extensive notes, however, on Lambert's lectures and comments, his overall inductive-deductive method, starting with the Laws of Hammurabi, his approach to normalizing vowels, and much else, constitute the backbone of this book. Although I do not wish to blame my former teacher for any of its defects, virtually every page reflects his influence.

It was all from a course taught in a university that I did not wish to attend, studying under one of the most respected Assyriologists of the last seventy-five years, under whom I foolishly did not want to study. My life has been filled with all kinds of blessings, none of which I ever intended or could ever have deserved.

Finally, I want to thank Nancy Erickson, PhD, the Executive Editor for Biblical Languages, Textbooks, Reference Tools, and Seedbed Resources at Zondervan Academic. Dr. Erickson extended to me the kind invitation to write this grammar. Were it not for her many encouragements along the way, this book would not have seen the light of day. I am especially thankful, as its users will be, for her diligent work enhancing its value by going far beyond the usual contributions of a competent editor. Her many recommendations were invaluable, and with great care she managed to condense by one tenth the excessively prolix, sometimes impenetrable, first draft of this grammar. She also wisely eliminated a third of its often-distracting footnotes. Finally, she enriched the result by soliciting, guiding, and editing the inspiring interstitial essays placed at the end of half of its chapters. In addition, she contributed an excellent essay herself. For these reasons, her indispensable contribution is rightly honored on the book's cover through the use of the term "with."

With respect to the other essay contributors, let me express my sincere appreciation here for the insightful and engaging essays that were generously provided by Bill T. Arnold, Christopher B. Hays, Richard S. Hess, Larisa Levicheva, Catherine McDowell, David Musgrave, Sandra L. Richter, and Miles V. Van Pelt. I am especially grateful to Prof. Van Pelt because he also kindly agreed to test drive an earlier draft of this grammar with his 2021 Akkadian course at Reformed Theological Seminary, Jackson, MS. I am similarly thankful to the many brave students in the various Akkadian courses that I have taught through the years, and especially those in my 2018, 2019, and 2020 courses who likewise endured earlier drafts of this grammar. Many of these students kindly offered suggestions for its improvement, encouragement for its publication, as well as a fair amount of good-natured teasing about the many errors and infelicities they discovered. Any mistakes or deficiencies which remain are, regrettably, mine alone. As for anything that may be good and helpful, if it is so it is only because: מִמְּךָ הַכֹּל וּמִיָּדְךָ נָתַנּוּ לָךְ (1 Chr 29:14).

Gordon P. Hugenberger, *June 2022*

Abbreviations

AHw	*Akkadisches Handwörterbuch.* Wolfram von Soden. 3 vols. 2nd ed. Wiesbaden, 1986
ARM	*Archives royales de Mari*
BDB	Brown, Francis, S. R. Driver, and Charles A. Briggs. *A Hebrew and English Lexicon of the Old Testament*
CAD	*The Assyrian Dictionary of the Oriental Institute of the University of Chicago.* Chicago: The Oriental Institute of the University of Chicago, 1956–2010
CANE	*Civilizations of the Ancient Near East.* Edited by Jack M. Sasson. 4 vols. New York, 1995. Repr. in 2 vols. Peabody, MA: Hendrickson, 2006
CDA	*A Concise Dictionary of Akkadian.* Edited by Jeremy Black, Andrew George, and Nicholas Postgate. 2nd rev. ed. Wiesbaden: Harrassowitz, 2000
COS	*The Context of Scripture.* Edited by William W. Hallo. 4 vols. Leiden: Brill, 1997–2016
DCH	*Dictionary of Classical Hebrew.* Edited by David J. A. Clines. 9 vols. Sheffield: Sheffield Phoenix Press, 1993–2014
EA	El-Amarna tablets. According to the edition of Jørgen A. Knudtzon. *Die el-Amarna-Tafeln.* Leipzig: Hinrichs, 1908–1915. Repr., Aalen: Zeller, 1964. Continued in Anson F. Rainey, *El-Amarna Tablets, 359–379.* 2nd rev. ed. Kevelaer: Butzon & Bercker, 1978
ET	English Translation
GAG[3]	*Grundriss der akkadischen Grammatik.* Wolfram von Soden. 3rd ed. Rome: Pontifical Biblical Institute, 1995
HALOT	*The Hebrew and Aramaic Lexicon of the Old Testament.* Ludwig Koehler, Walter Baumgartner, and Johann J. Stamm. Translated and edited under the supervision of Mervyn E. J. Richardson. 4 vols. Leiden: Brill, 1994–1999
HSS	Harvard Semitic Studies
JAOS	*Journal of the American Oriental Society*
JBQ	*Jewish Biblical Quarterly*
KB	*Keilinschriftliche Bibliothek.* Edited by Eberhard Schrader. 6 vols. Berlin: Reuther & Reichard, 1889–1915
KTU	*Die keilaphabetischen Texte aus Ugarit.* Edited by Manfried Dietrich, Oswald Loretz, and Joaquín Sanmartín. Münster: Ugarit-Verlag, 2013
LAOS	*Leipziger Altorientalistische Studien*
LSJ	Liddell, Henry George, Robert Scott, Henry Stuart Jones. *A Greek-English Lexicon.* 9th ed. with revised supplement. Oxford: Clarendon, 1996
NABU	*Nouvelles assyriologiques brèves et utilitaires*
NPN	Gelb, Ignace J., Pierre M. Purves, and Allan A. MacRae. *Nuzi Personal Names.* OIP 57. Chicago: Oriental Institute of the University of Chicago, 1943
OIP	Oriental Institute Publications

PRU	*Le palais royal d'Ugarit*
RA	*Revue d'assyriologie et d'archéologie orientale*
RawlCu	*The Cuneiform Inscriptions of Western Asia.* Edited by H. C. Rawlinson. London, 1891
Rost Tigl.	Rost, Paul. *Die Keilschrifttexte Tiglat-Pilesers III.* Leipzig: Pfeiffer, 1893
RIME	The Royal Inscriptions of Mesopotamia, Early Periods
SAACT	State Archives of Assyria Cuneiform Texts
SBLABS	Society of Biblical Literature Archaeology and Biblical Studies
TDOT	*Theological Dictionary of the Old Testament.* Edited by G. Johannes Botterweck and Helmer Ringgren. Translated by John T. Willis et al. 8 vols. Grand Rapids: Eerdmans, 1974–2006
TLOT	*Theological Lexicon of the Old Testament.* Edited by Ernst Jenni, with assistance from Claus Westermann. Translated by Mark E. Biddle. 3 vols. Peabody, MA: Hendrickson, 1997
Winckler *Sammlung*	Winckler, Hugo. *Sammlung von Keilschrifttexten.* Leipzig: Pfeiffer, 1893

How to Use This Textbook

Basics of Akkadian follows an inductive-deductive approach. It is inductive in that the student will start reading and translating actual cuneiform text from the Laws of Hammurabi in Chapter 2 and will continue to do so in every chapter thereafter. At no point will the student be asked to translate artificially composed or simplified Akkadian sentences, nor will the student be asked to compose Akkadian.

This inductive emphasis explains two other special features of this grammar. First, unlike traditional deductive grammars, where it is typical for students to learn complete paradigms as each grammatical topic is taken up, in this grammar in its early chapters students focus their energies on learning only the most common grammatical forms (such as third-person forms or the non-infixed conjugations), based on what is required for reading the portions of the Laws of Hammurabi that are assigned for a current chapter or a following chapter. Only in later chapters, when the foundational features of Akkadian grammar have been mastered, are students asked to learn the remaining forms of the major paradigms.

A second feature of this grammar, also keeping with its inductive emphasis, is that when a grammatical description or rule is stated, very often examples or lists of examples from the Laws of Hammurabi will be provided that not only illustrate the point but also allow students to infer for themselves the grammatical point.

On the other hand, this book follows a deductive approach in that every grammatical feature will, at some point in the textbook, be explained in detail and the grammatical topic that it involves will be presented in a comprehensive and logical manner. Often, however, this will not happen when the feature is first encountered. At that earlier point, because of the inductive emphasis of this textbook, only the most common or immediately relevant forms or uses are presented.

This book covers all the major features of Akkadian grammar for the Old Babylonian period, which is the classic form of the language. Students will learn all the basic noun, adjective, and verbal paradigms for Old Babylonian. They will acquire a solid working vocabulary of 161 words based on the text of the Laws of Hammurabi, and they will learn 126 cuneiform signs with their most common values in the standard and most frequently encountered Neo-Assyrian script. As such, this book should provide a substantial foundation for any student who aspires to further study in Assyriology and related fields. Since it covers all the essential elements of Akkadian grammar, students should be able to transition successfully into a second semester of Akkadian, regardless of which of the popular teaching grammars is employed.

Similarly, this book should prove very useful even for students who may have no intention to continue formal study in Akkadian, because they will be able to use, as needed, any of the major tools of Akkadian (published lexica, sign lists, and reference grammars), and they will also have sufficient background knowledge to be able to assess and appreciate its benefit for a better understanding of biblical Hebrew and of the wider cultural background for the world of the Hebrew Bible that has been accessed predominately through Akkadian texts.

Although this textbook is, hopefully, accessible to students regardless of their background, it attempts to be particularly helpful to students who have learned some biblical Hebrew and who have an interest in the Hebrew Bible. For those students, its many optional references to cognate Hebrew vocabulary and grammar will assist them in using that knowledge to learn Akkadian while at the same time reinforcing and deepening their knowledge of Hebrew.

The grammar is designed for a one-semester introduction to the language of Akkadian. There are twenty chapters of instruction and exercises. Depending on individual course structure, the last three chapters may be used toward a second-semester class or for additional reading and learning. As noted above, the text base for the grammar is the Laws of Hammurabi. By the end of the grammar, students will have translated laws §§1–20 and 127–149. Each chapter provides essential instruction toward the goal of translation. Signs and vocabulary needed to translate are provided at the end of every chapter. Thorough appendices are also included in the back matter. This includes discussion of Akkadian phonology; major paradigms; a list of cuneiform signs; an alphabetical list of *v*, *cv*, and *vc* cuneiform signs; a glossary; a partial answer key; and a bibliography. An extensive index follows the appendices.

The instruction of some chapters is shorter than others. In these cases, the translation exercises are lengthened. Beginning in Chapter 10, the homework translations grow significantly. Chapters 13, 15, 17, and 19 may at first appear to require much more translation work than other chapters, but this is compensated for by the inclusion of a significant amount of normalized text in each of these chapters. An answer key for Chapters 3–6 and normalization for Chapter 7 is provided in Appendix F (see below for access to a complete answer key).

Throughout the grammar, the author acknowledges views and interpretations of other Assyriologists. Akkadian is unlike Hebrew, Greek, or Latin, for example, where there is virtual unanimity among modern grammars regarding features of the language at the beginner level. These alternative views and interpretations will serve students well as they go on to a second-semester course or consult many of the scholarly references on the Laws of Hammurabi.

Interspersed among the chapters are contributions from esteemed academics in the fields of Hebrew Bible and Assyriology. These articles are rich with connections between the studies of Old Testament and the Akkadian language. They are gems for the student interested in the relationship between the Bible and Akkadian. The contributions are the following: The Genres of Akkadian Literature (Levicheva); Wordplay on "Hammurapi" (Arnold); Takeaways from the First Law of Hammurabi (Hugenberger); Akkadian Cognates and Scripture (McDowell); Akkadian Loanwords and Wordplays in Isaiah (Hays); Two Cognate Features: Verbless Clauses and Reduplication (Musgrave); Akkadian and Deuteronomy's "Centralizing Formula" (Richter); Akkadian Love Literature and the Song of Songs (Van Pelt); The Mari Archive (Erickson); and Akkadian and the Book of Joshua (Hess).

Basics of Akkadian is accompanied by supplementary materials that may be of significant help to self-learners and teachers. This includes a complete answer key with parsings, transliteration, normalization, and translation for each chapter. Also included is a PDF of all cuneiform and vocabulary organized by chapter. This will aid students in easily producing their own physical flashcards for all the assigned cuneiform and vocabulary. These materials may be accessed with an account under Instructor Resources at zondervanacademic.com.

Preface

0.1 Why Study Akkadian?

It is hard to think of a good reason not to learn at least some Akkadian. It is the earliest attested Semitic language and boasts nearly one million texts and fragments, half of which, it is estimated, have not yet been translated.[1] Those that have been translated and studied have supplied a superabundance of meaningful contextual evidence, as is reflected in *The Assyrian Dictionary of the Oriental Institute of the University of Chicago* (*CAD*) with its treatment of 28,000 Akkadian words, most defined with citations of the context for their proposed meanings.[2]

Akkadian is a Semitic language. As such, it belongs to the family of languages, including Hebrew, Aramaic, and Arabic among many others, that is characterized by words mainly built on three root consonants and consisting exclusively of syllables having just one vowel. Most syllables have a single consonant followed by a single vowel (*cv*) or a single consonant followed by a single vowel followed by a single consonant (*cvc*). The Semitic family consists of two language groups: East Semitic (including Akkadian and Eblaite) and West Semitic (including languages such as Hebrew, Ugaritic, Phoenician, Aramaic, and Arabic). Although Hebrew is just one of many West Semitic languages, 53 percent of all Akkadian words or roots have Hebrew cognates, and no language, other than Eblaite, is closer to Akkadian than Hebrew.[3] The close relationship has proven indispensable for illuminating meanings and definitions of Hebrew terms.

Furthermore, although only a few biblical characters, such as the patriarchs Abraham and Sarah, would have had Akkadian as their first language,[4] and a few others, such as Daniel, Hananiah, Mishael, and Azariah, may have acquired Akkadian as a second or third language,[5] Akkadian is, arguably, the most important language for a better understanding of the Old Testament other than the biblical languages themselves.

The vocabulary of biblical Hebrew is rich, with more than 8,300 distinct words.[6] Although philologists consider it ideal to define words based on their use in context, at least 49 percent

1. The observation is offered by Huehnergard and Woods, "Chapter 8: Akkadian and Eblaite," 218.

2. After nine decades of work, which began in the 1920s, *CAD* is now complete with nearly ten thousand pages and published in twenty-six volumes. The volumes are freely available at https://oi.uchicago.edu/research/publications/assyrian-dictionary-oriental-institute-university-chicago-cad. The first three of six proposed supplementary volumes have also been published. Streck, et al., eds., *Supplement to the Akkadian Dictionaries, Vol 1: B, P*; and Streck, et al., eds. *Supplement to the Akkadian Dictionaries, Vol 2: D, T, and Ṭ; Streck, et al., eds., Supplement to the Akkadian Dictionaries, Vol 3: G, K, Q.*

3. So, according to Young, *Diversity in Pre-Exilic Hebrew*, 22–23. Eblaite is almost as old as Akkadian, since it too comes from the third millennium BCE.

4. It is likely that the Proto-Canaanite spoken in the patriarchal period was significantly closer to Akkadian than would be the case for Classical Hebrew, as preserved in the Hebrew Bible from almost a millennium later.

5. Following Hebrew and Aramaic, based on Dan 1:4 and their imposed Akkadian names: Belteshazzar, Shadrach, Meshach, and Abednego.

6. BDB proposes some 8,391 distinct words, according to Clines, *DCH* 9:13. *DCH* estimates 10,500 (p. viii).

of the words in biblical Hebrew occur only once or twice in the Bible. Since very little Hebrew from the biblical period has survived outside the Bible,[7] scholars have no option but to base proposed definitions for the vast number of less common words in Hebrew on evidence other than context, such as the Septuagintal Greek translation of terms and especially the evidence of cognate languages. For this latter purpose, the language of Akkadian has proven to be indispensable.

In addition to its dramatic help with Hebrew lexicography,[8] Akkadian is unquestionably the most important language for an understanding of the history, beliefs, practices, and literary and material culture of much of the ancient Near East from the mid-third millennium BCE down to the mid-first millennium BCE. The discovery since the mid-eighteenth century of those million texts and text fragments, written in the various dialects of Akkadian, and the remarkable decipherment of Akkadian in the mid-nineteen century, has overturned many mistaken assumptions about the ancient Near East and about the Bible. Many longstanding questions have been convincingly answered, and fascinating new ones have been raised about both. Since, as has been mentioned, a majority of these Akkadian texts have not yet been translated or studied, and since new texts are discovered every year, it is likely that for the foreseeable future many of the most important breakthroughs in understanding the Hebrew Bible will come from evidence based on Akkadian texts.

0.1.1 ***Benefits of this Grammar for Students of the Hebrew Bible.*** Although any student should be able to benefit from this grammar and follow all of its explanations, it is especially shaped to meet the needs of those who have some knowledge of Hebrew and are interested in Akkadian for its help in the interpretation of the Hebrew Bible. For these readers, the benefits of Akkadian are very exciting, and plausible examples of those benefits will be provided in many of the chapters of this textbook. Indeed, over the past one hundred fifty years many of the most significant advances in understanding the Hebrew Bible, its contents, language, literary forms, and cultural context, have come from insights based on a study of relevant Akkadian texts.

This applies, for example, to

- our understanding of many details in the opening chapters of Genesis and its anti-idolatry polemic;
- the significance of the "image of God" language in Genesis 1:26–27 and 9:6;
- the legal background for acts of clothing another person, as when God clothes Adam and Eve in Genesis 3:21;
- the literary form of the flood account in Genesis 6–9 and its implication for source critical analysis of that text;
- the rationale for Abram's identification of Sarai as his "sister" in Genesis 12; 20 and Isaac's similar identification of Rebekah as his "sister" in Genesis 26;
- the profound meaning of the covenant-ratifying theophany in Genesis 15;
- the requirement that Israel's altars be made from undressed stones (Exod 20:25; Deut 27:5);
- the expectation of anonymity for the authorship of major literary works, with authors' names retained by tradition;

7. Cf. Davies, *Ancient Hebrew Inscriptions.*
8. See also Tawil, *An Akkadian Lexical Companion for Biblical Hebrew.*

- what made Israel's laws so exceptional, for example regarding marriage, the treatment of aliens or slaves, or the role of a king, that they were expected to impress the surrounding nations, as promised in Deuteronomy 4:5–8;
- the significance of the literary form of the Decalogue and of the book of Deuteronomy in relation to covenants;
- why lenders were tempted to take the cloak of a widow as a pledge (Deut 24:17);
- what is the nature of the "still small voice" (*qôl dəmāmâ daqqâ*, קוֹל דְּמָמָה דַקָּה) of God mentioned in 1 Kings 19:12;
- why God is called a "Great King" (*hammelek haggādôl*, הַמֶּלֶךְ הַגָּדוֹל) in Psalm 95:3 and elsewhere;
- why the expression "thus says" (*kōh-'āmar*, כֹּה־אָמַר) is mainly used by prophets, as in 2 Kings 19:6;
- the meaning of the "seven eyes" of Yahweh that range throughout the earth in 2 Chronicles 16:9; Zechariah 3:9; 4:10;
- what is unique about the theodicy of the book of Job;
- the likelihood of David, as a king, authoring many of the psalms and the authenticity of the early use of psalm titles;
- why earlier prophets like Elijah and Elisha rarely, or never, wrote down their messages, whereas writing down a prophet's message was standard practice with the eighth-century BCE prophets and those who came later;
- the discrepancy between Jeremiah's date for Nebuchadnezzar's siege of Jerusalem in the fourth year of Jehoiakim (Jer 25:1; 46:2) and Daniel's date in the third year of Jehoiakim (Dan 1:1);
- the rationale for Belshazzar's offer in Daniel 5:7 to make anyone who could interpret the handwriting on the wall only the "third highest ruler in the kingdom";
- how historians can offer not just a relative chronology for much of Old Testament history but an absolute chronology; and
- many questions related to unusual forms and grammatical developments in the Hebrew language.

Some of the examples above, as well as others, will be considered in many of the chapters that follow.[9]

0.1.2 ***Social History.*** Modern historians have set a priority on doing history "from the bottom up" by exploring what can be known or inferred about the daily life of ordinary persons. For the history of Israel, the Bible has been the primary source for this work based on occasional and mostly incidental glimpses into the daily life of ordinary individuals. Unfortunately, the kind of direct documentary evidence that scholars prefer for this kind of historiography, such as personal diaries, private letters, commercial contracts, marriage documents, wills, etc., is limited or nonexistent for most of the period of the Hebrew Bible. This is because in the region of Israel, as in Egypt, the preferred media for writing during the biblical period were materials like papyrus, leather, and parchment, all of which prove to be very perishable in the climate of most of Israel.

9. For a scholarly and appropriately cautious overview of the history and current state of comparative studies relating Mesopotamian language and culture to a study of the Bible, see Chavalas and Younger, *Mesopotamia and the Bible, Comparative Explorations*.

Recently, however, some 250 documents from the sixth and fifth centuries BCE have come to light; these have been trumpeted by the media as "the most important ancient Jewish archive since the discovery of the Dead Sea Scrolls."[10] This enthusiastic headline refers to the so-called Al-Yahudu tablets, which are proving to be very significant for the study of the ordinary lives of Jews who were deported in the Babylonian captivity and continued to live there. The documents were preserved because they are all written in Akkadian cuneiform on clay tablets, many of them fired in a kiln. The circumstances of their discovery are unknown, which raises ethical concerns, but despite the lack of provenance, no scholars have questioned their authenticity. They belong to three private collections, and they are still in the process of being published.[11]

Al-Yahudu Tablet
A.D. Riddle/BiblePlaces.com

The Al-Yahudu tablets, each about the size of the palm of a hand and written in Akkadian (Neo-Babylonian, see discussion on dialects in Chapter 1), concern three exiled West Semitic communities who resettled in Babylonia. A portion of these texts follow several generations of one Jewish family from 572 BCE to 477 BCE. Although this Jewish family may have come to Babylon under duress, as did Daniel and his friends, they prospered and lived as free persons in Al-Yahudu ("the city of Judah"), Našar, and other settlements in south-central Babylonia. The Al-Yahudu tablets consist of contracts, tax payments, rental agreements, letters, wills, marriage documents, etc. These provide the kind of evidence that is most prized by social historians. Together they attest to the daily life of this Jewish family and others who appear to exemplify Jeremiah's directive in Jeremiah 29:4–7 and to reflect continuing faith, especially in their personal names. The tablets are one such example of the contribution that Akkadian texts have made to understanding the social history of the ancient Near East.

0.1.3 ***The Advantage of Clay Tablets.*** Although there is a widely held assumption that our knowledge of earlier civilizations and their languages is necessarily less secure than our knowledge of much later ones, the remarkable abundance of primary source material for Akkadian allows it to be a notable exception. Akkadian was written in a cuneiform script. The word "cuneiform" comes from the Latin terms *cuneus*, meaning "wedge," and *forma*, meaning "shape." It is an apt description of the characters used to write Akkadian, which are mainly comprised of a series of wedge-shaped indentations.

Although some Akkadian texts were inscribed on wax, stone, metal, or ivory, among other materials, most extant Akkadian texts were produced by the use of a reed stylus with a triangular tip pressed into moist clay. In preparation for writing, the clay was molded into a variety of shapes, including prisms and cylinders, but most are rectangular, ranging in size from less than a square inch to about 12" x 20". The most popular size is one that fits comfortably into

10. So, according to the headline in the respected Israeli newspaper *Haaretz* on January 29, 2015.

11. See Pearce and Wunsch, *Documents of Judean Exiles and West Semites in Babylonia in the Collection of David Sofer.* For a more recent analysis based on 155 of these tablets that have been published, or will soon be, see Alstola, "Judeans in Babylonia. A Study of Deportees in the Sixth and Fifth Centuries BCE."

The evidence of the Al-Yahudu tablets complements what is known from a number of other primary sources for ordinary Jewish life in the diaspora. See the Murašû archive of 879 documents from the fifth century BCE discovered at the end of the nineteenth century, which relate to an extended Jewish family over three generations who lived and were engaged in banking and other commercial enterprises in Nippur (Provan, Long, and Longman, *A Biblical History of Israel*, 385–86). See also the tablets related to a Jewish family of royal merchants in Sippar, for which see Bloch, "Judeans in Sippar and Susa during the First Century of the Babylonian Exile."

the palm of a hand, like the Al-Yahudu tablet depicted above. Tablets were usually air dried, which was adequate for temporary use, and afterward they could be moistened again and reused as needed.

On occasion, however, tablets were deliberately fired in order to preserve them and thankfully, from our modern perspective, very often they were fired by accidental fires or by ones intentionally set by invading armies. Although fired clay is brittle, it is a nearly permanent medium compared to the perishable materials of papyrus, leather, or parchment normally used for Egyptian, Phoenician, Hebrew, Greek, Latin, and other ancient languages. Consequently, modern scholars have available to them a nearly unequaled abundance of primary source materials in Akkadian–many more, for example, than have been preserved for Classical Latin, even though Akkadian texts are typically much older by up to two millennia.

0.1.4 ***The Achievements of Early Mesopotamian Civilization.*** Although it is often assumed that earlier civilizations were necessarily more primitive or ignorant than much later ones, scholars working on Akkadian texts have discovered one striking example after another of the impressive intellectual, scientific, and cultural accomplishments of the civilizations that flourished in the ancient Near East well before the civilizations of classical Greece and Rome.

0.1.4.1 *Mathematics*—In mathematics, for example, in an eighteenth-seventeenth-century BCE clay tablet known as Plimpton 322, there is evidence that more than a millennium before Pythagoras came up with his celebrated theorem, Babylonian mathematicians had already figured out that the square of the length of the hypotenuse of a right-angle triangle is equal to the sum of the squares of the lengths of each of the remaining sides. Interestingly, the Babylonians used base 60 for their calculations (rather than base 10), and their computations for the fifteen right triangles treated on Plimpton 322 are exact, as opposed to the approximations found in modern trigonometric tables.[12]

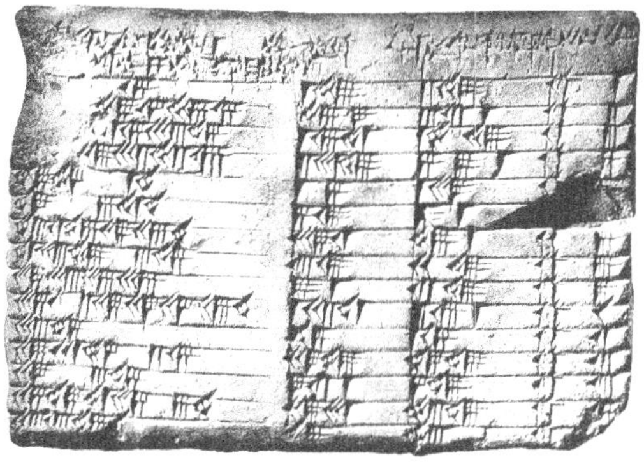

Plimpton 322

0.1.4.2 *Other Intellectual Disciplines*—In addition to mathematics, there were important advances in many other intellectual disciplines. The Babylonians worked out how to predict lunar and solar eclipses with significant accuracy. They discovered effective pharmaceuticals, including the use of cannabis as an antidepressant, and especially the use of anti-inflammatory analgesics from plants rich in salicylate, the chemical antecedent for acetylsalicylic acid otherwise known as aspirin. It is possible that they were the ones who invented the wheel, used at first for the manufacture of pottery and later for wagons and chariots; they constructed the first aqueducts, the first paved roads, and a masonry dam for the Atrush River.

They divided the circle into 360 degrees, each degree into 60 minutes, and each minute into 60 seconds. They developed a system of diatonic scales in music. They measured longitude and latitude for geographical navigation.

12. Mansfield and Wildberger, "Plimpton 322 is Babylonian Exact Sexagesimal Trigonometry."

They had the first postal service. They produced some of the earliest glass work and improved glazes for pottery. They built awe-inspiring step pyramids, temple complexes, and hanging gardens. Finally, thanks to an abundant supply of asphalts and bitumens, prized fuels for achieving the high temperatures required to smelt metals, they made significant advances in metallurgy.

In summary, in almost every area of human endeavor the remarkable discoveries and accomplishments of the ancient Akkadian-speaking inhabitants of Mesopotamia prepared for or anticipated the advances of much later civilizations by many centuries or millennia.

0.1.4.3 *A Cradle of Civilization*—The ancient Near East, or Fertile Crescent, is commonly described as "the cradle of civilization." There are, of course, other significant "cradles of civilization," such as the Yellow River plain in China, or the Ganges plain in India, or much later Mesoamerica and the Norte Chico region of Peru. It appears that important features of civilization developed independently in each of these places.

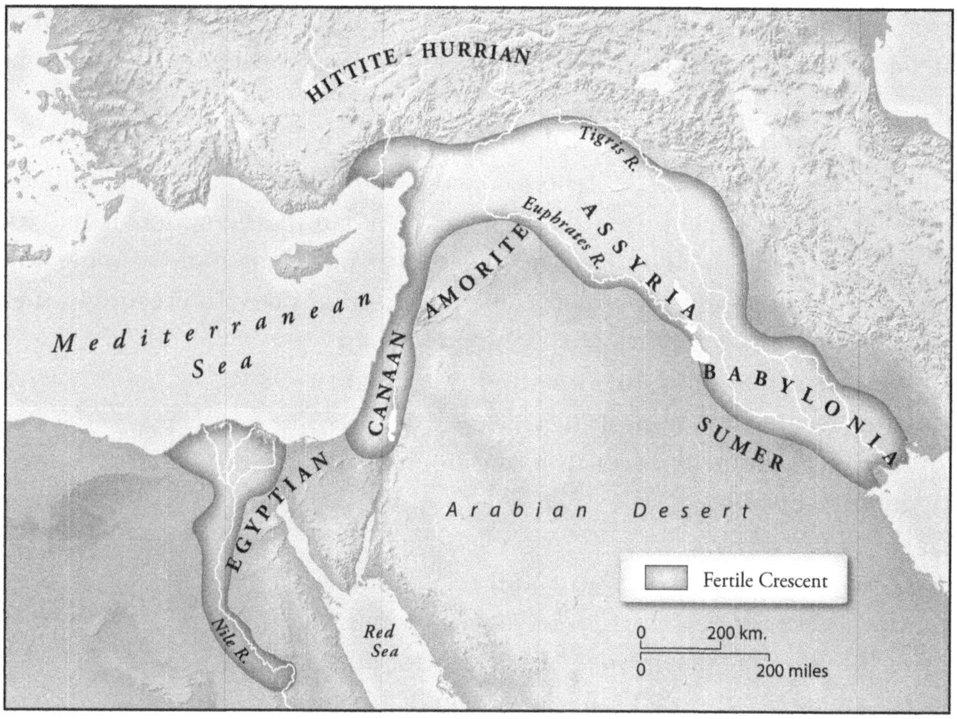

Fertile Crescent

Nevertheless, the ancient Near East has the distinction of being the locale where many of the most important cultural attainments for civilization are first attested. What is in view are those attainments that allowed an increasingly large population to grow and flourish in a relatively stable setting. Necessary for this purpose was the early development of intensive year-round agriculture. This resulted from three crucial innovations: the first attested use of extensive irrigation, the cultivation of a wide variety of crops with varying growing seasons, and the invention of plows that increased productivity. A more consistent and abundant food supply, in turn, supported the establishment of the world's first cities, which were typically temple complexes, starting with the city of Uruk in Sumer. Inextricably linked to urbanization were centralized governments, and with them, the promulgation of laws reflected in their now famous law collections (in Sumerian, the Laws of Ur-Nammu, the Laws of Lipit-Ishtar, and others; in Akkadian, the Laws of Eshnunna, the Laws of Hammurabi, the Middle Assyrian Laws, the Neo-Babylonian Laws, etc.), and the development of a more adequate means for defense (city walls, more effective armies, superior weapons, and political and military alliances).

All of these and many other accomplishments, however, are dwarfed by the one accomplishment that is definitional for any "cradle of civilization" because it is indispensable to the rest, namely the invention of true writing.

1–𒁹

Introduction to Akkadian

The Akkadian language has its origins in the language of Sumer and amidst the rich history of the ancient Near East. Understanding how the Akkadian language developed, including its roots in Sumerian, is important for understanding Akkadian's many features. In this chapter a short history of the language will be covered to provide a broad framework for understanding and acquiring the Akkadian language with ease. The primary dialects of Akkadian will also be addressed, followed by a discussion of the dialect and script taught in this grammar.

1.1 A Short History of True Writing in the Ancient Near East

The ancient Near East is rightly celebrated for a long list of remarkable cultural accomplishments, but all of these are dwarfed by the invention of true writing—writing that is able to represent most of the features of a particular spoken language. This breakthrough was accomplished first by the Sumerians in the mid-fourth millennium BCE. The Sumerians, who were a non-Semitic, non-Indo-European people, lived in southern Mesopotamia in close proximity to Semitic Akkadian speakers. Not surprisingly, their exceptionally useful invention was soon adopted for Akkadian, the earliest attested Semitic language.

1.1.1 ***The Earliest Writing: Pictographs.*** The system used for writing Sumerian was built on earlier proto-writing. Proto-writing is where numbers, objects, and occasionally actions (verbs) are represented by symbols or pictographs (also called "logograms"). These pictographs could be read in any language (similar to the modern use of numerals, signs for disabled seating, or no smoking signs). Not long after true writing was developed in Sumer, another system of true writing was developed in Egypt, perhaps independently. Writing was developed independently in at least two other places: China, at the end of the second millennium BCE, and Mesoamerica, by the middle of the first millennium BCE.[1]

The figure to the right is a photograph of the front of an administrative tablet regarding a distribution of barley from about 3000 BCE.

Jemdet Nasr Tablet,
ca. 3000 BCE

1. See "Introduction" in Woods, Teeter, and Emberling, *Visible Language*, 15.

It was found at Jemdet Nasr but perhaps came from the nearby city of Uruk in ancient Sumer, often said to be the first city.

As was customary in this early period, the cuneiform (wedge-shaped characters) pictographic text begins at the top right. In the box at the upper right are two deep holes; there are two similar holes at the top of the second column. Each hole represents the number 10, which in this context refers to a measure of 10 *gurs* of the item depicted in the pictograph immediately below the holes. One *gur* is an approximate volume measure for what an ass can carry, which is estimated to be 300–350 liters or 10.5–12.25 cubic feet of grain.

The pictographs that follow these numerals, one of which is marked with an arrow, clearly depict an ear of barley. The Sumerian word for this pictograph is ŠE, which is pronounced similar to the English word "she" but with a short *e*, as in the English word "met."[2] The Sumerian language at this time was primarily monosyllabic, meaning words with only one syllable. The common scholarly practice is to represent Sumerian words with all uppercase letters, like ŠE, while words and syllables in Akkadian are printed in lowercase italics, like *še* (see §1.1.2.2 below).

In the second column, also marked with an arrow, there is a pictograph of a foot, which in Sumerian is the word DU. This pictograph may refer to a foot, or, depending on the context, it may be used for some form of the semantically related verb "to stand" (Sumerian GUB), or "to go" (Sumerian GEN), or "to carry" (Sumerian DE_6).[3]

1.1.2 ***Developments in Writing.*** There were six significant developments in cuneiform writing in the centuries that followed its invention.

1.1.2.1 *Fixed Order of Signs*—First, in the earliest period of Sumerian writing, pictographs were not placed in any particular order within their columns or boxes. It was a helpful innovation in the second half of the third millennium BCE when the order of signs within a column began to reflect consistently the word order of the spoken language.

1.1.2.2 *Syllabograms*—Second, and most important, because the Sumerian language is predominantly monosyllabic, it was a tremendously useful step sometime in the mid-third millennium BCE to appropriate pictographs as a means for representing the syllables that name those objects. This is frequently cited as an important example of the rebus principle in linguistics. A playful example of a rebus in English would be to draw a bee next to a leaf in order to represent the word "belief," which otherwise cannot easily be drawn.

When a cuneiform sign is used to represent a syllable, rather than an object, it is called a "syllabogram." For example, the pictograph above that was used to represent a foot, the Sumerian word for which is DU but in Akkadian *šēpum*, now could represent either a foot, as had been the case, or just the syllable *du*. The syllable was usable in either language to write other words or grammatical elements that otherwise were not easily depicted. Since the same pictograph was also used to refer to a number of semantically related verbs, such as "to go," which in Sumerian is GEN but in Akkadian *alākum*, the same sign could also be used to represent the syllable *gen* in

2. For pronunciation guidelines for vowels and consonants, see Appendix A.

3. The subscript 6, which is attached to the Sumerian word DE, is not pronounced. It is written, however, to indicate which of six or more cuneiform signs are intended (in this case the sixth one).

either language as needed.[4] This important shift to syllabograms attests the beginning of syllabic writing.

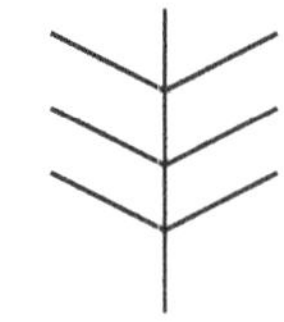

Similarly, the sign for barley could now be used to represent either barley, which in Sumerian is ŠE or in Akkadian *še'um* (a loanword from Sumerian), or just the syllable *še*. This ability to use cuneiform not just for pictographs but also to represent corresponding syllables was a significant advancement in true writing.

1.1.2.3 *Fewer Signs Needed for Literacy*—A third development, related to the introduction of syllabic writing, was a significant reduction in the number of signs that were in common use. In the earlier pictographic writing system, well over a thousand signs were in use, but as signs were increasingly employed to represent syllables, the number of signs in common use dropped to about six hundred. At no time, however, did the use of pictographs cease to be used. Depending on scribal preference or literary genre, texts were written almost entirely with pictographs or, alternatively, almost entirely with syllabograms.

Even with this welcome reduction in the number of signs required to write the language, not many managed to master the use of enough signs to be fully literate. Many scholars estimate ancient Mesopotamian full literacy rates at about 1 percent, and most assume that even kings may have been illiterate in this sense.[5] Even so, since ordinary business records or private letters require only about a hundred and fifty signs, functional literacy rates are likely to have been a good deal higher, rising perhaps as high as 50 percent in some contexts.[6]

1.1.2.4 *Cuneiform*—A fourth development in writing was a shift away from the earlier use of a thin stylus made from bone, metal, wood, or reed with a sharpened point (like a pencil) to a thicker stylus, usually reed, with a beveled wedge-shaped flat tip.

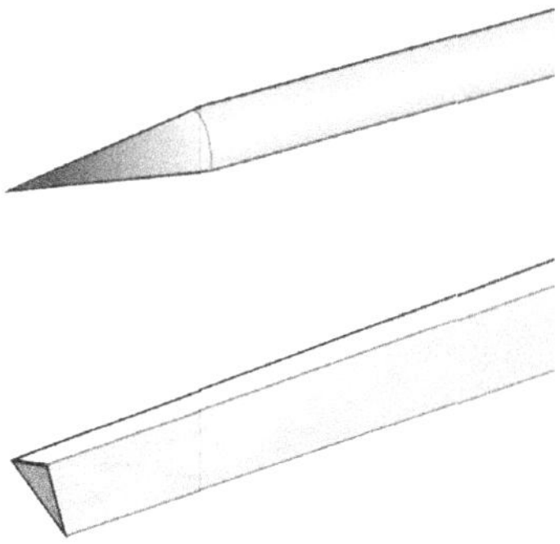

The earlier stylus had the advantage of being able to produce any desired curvilinear shape. As a result, early pictographs were quite realistic. It is uncertain why this earlier mode of writing was abandoned, but perhaps it was related to a growing preference to write on soft clay tablets, an attractive medium in Mesopotamia because of the abundance of clay. When used with clay, a pointed stylus tends to produce raised ridges on both sides of each furrow, which limits how small

4. Long *a*, written *ā*, is pronounced like the *a* in "father." See Appendix A.

5. So Stein, "Foreword," in Woods, Teeter, and Emberling, *Visible Language*, 9. The claim about the illiteracy of kings is based on the famous boast of Assurbanipal (seventh century BCE) that he, unlike the kings before him, could read much earlier inscriptions, including those in Sumerian and "dark Akkadian." This, however, does not mean those earlier kings were actually incapable of reading the Akkadian of their own day, including their own inscriptions.

6. For a generally more optimistic view about early functional literacy, see Finkel and Taylor, *Cuneiform*, 32–37. A very high functional literacy rate seems warranted for the Assyrian merchant families who settled in Karum, a suburb of the early second millennium BCE city of Kaneš in central Anatolia. In the ongoing excavation since 1948, 23,500 clay tablets and envelopes have been recovered from the hundred or so private homes mostly belonging to these Assyrian merchant families but also to some of their non-Assyrian neighbors. It is apparent that these tablets were not, in general, produced by scribes since they often include grammatical errors and numerous simplifications of the cuneiform. This is the largest body of private texts recovered from anywhere in the ancient Near East.

Although it is understandable that merchants would benefit from a higher level of functional literacy than many other individuals, it should be noted that in the Old Babylonian period, at least, a significant level of at least functional literacy is implied by two facts. First, the vast majority of Old Babylonian tablets that have been discovered came from private urban dwellings. Second, of the private dwellings that have been excavated from this period, more than half were found to include cuneiform tablets. See van Koppen, "The Scribe of the Flood Story and His Circle," 140–41.

one can write a complex sign and still have it be legible or how close a sign can be to another without causing destructive interference.

In any case, in the late third millennium BCE scribes started to prefer the thicker reed stylus with its beveled wedge-shaped flat tip, which allowed signs to be made with an action that compressed the clay. As a result, signs could be made very small and still be legible, even when written on tablets the size of a postage stamp. The downside, however, was that it was more difficult to produce curvilinear shapes. Instead, Sumerian writing began to acquire its distinctive linear appearance with each sign composed of wedge-like strokes. It is for this reason that the script came to be called "cuneiform," which, as was mentioned earlier, means wedge-shaped. With this limitation, pictographs became increasingly abstract and less recognizable as depictions. At this stage in the writing, the now abstract signs that represent a word are better termed logograms (or "ideograms"), and those signs that represent syllables, syllabograms.

1.1.2.5 *Direction of Writing*[7]—A fifth development in writing cuneiform concerns a change in the direction of writing. At some point between 3000 BCE and about 1500 BCE the practice of writing cuneiform changed: tablets were rotated ninety degrees counterclockwise, so that writing now began at the top left of a tablet and proceeded across the tablet from left to right in rows. At the same time, the signs themselves were also rotated ninety degrees counterclockwise.

3200 BCE	2500 BCE (?)	1500 BCE (?)	1000 BCE

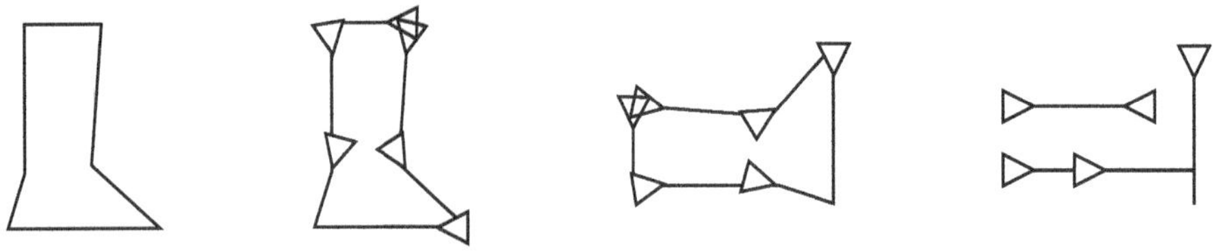

DU	DU/*du*	DU/*du*	DU/*du*

Many scholars favor the view that the change in the direction of writing may have taken place as early as 3000 BCE since this is when writing on clay tablets had become more common and the shapes of cuneiform signs were becoming less curvilinear. Vertical writing works well when cuneiform is scratched or chiseled on hard material, but when a stylus is used to press cuneiform signs into soft clay, it is easier for right-handed scribes to avoid smudging if the writing is in a horizontal direction left to right.

Despite this reasonable explanation, there is little unambiguous evidence that the direction of writing did in fact change as early as 3000 BCE.[8] In the case of cuneiform tablets, usually the original orientation cannot be determined since it is believed that both the direction of writing and the orientation of each character changed at the same time.[9] To make this

7. For more examples of the development in cuneiform writing, see §17.2.

8. For a strong defense of the 3000 BCE date, see Studevent-Hickman, "The Ninety-Degree Rotation of the Cuneiform Script."

9. Cf. Lambert, "Introduction to Akkadian," 92. Lambert argues the change happened between 2000 BCE and 1500 BCE. For recent evidence in favor of a date after 1600 BCE, see Fitzgerald, "pisan dub-ba and the Direction of Cuneiform Script." Fitzgerald marshals evidence based on a special class of tablets that were used as labels or tags for containers. These tablets have two holes with an inside channel between them on one edge of the tablet. Fitzgerald believes these tags were originally attached to the containers and hung like a

point clearer, consider the two photographs below taken of the same tablet from 2350 BCE. If the photograph on the left reflects the original orientation of this tablet, then it would be evidence in support of the theory that the change in the direction of writing took place after 2350 BCE. If the photograph on the right is correct, then it would be evidence in support of the theory that the change took place before 2350 BCE. The only difference between the two photographs, however, is that the tablet has been rotated.

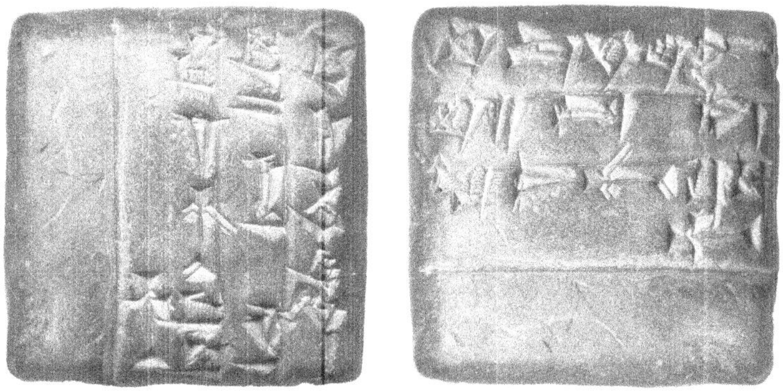

Valdosta 1

"Tablet One," Digital Image UA 2-1-1, Powell Papers, UA 2-1-1, -Box 6, Folder 11, Valdosta State University Archives and Special Collections

The orientation of a tablet when it was originally produced may be ascertained if the cuneiform is combined with some form of artistic representation. There are many such examples of cuneiform combined with art, but they are not on clay tablets.

For example, below are photographs of two cylinder seals.[10] Directly below is a cylinder seal made out of feldspar that is dated to the seventeenth to sixteenth centuries BCE, and to its immediate right is a modern impression made from it. Its cuneiform is in vertical columns starting at the top right.

Cylinder Seal and Modern Impression, ca. 1700–1600 BCE

pendant on a necklace by a string that went through the holes. If that assumption is correct, it implies that the holes are on the top edge of the tablet. If so, they constitute significant evidence that even for ordinary purposes cuneiform was written in a vertical orientation until 1600 BCE.

10. Cylinder seals were highly valued, and in many cases, there is obvious archaizing in the script, including the use of Sumerian, which ceased to be a spoken language around 2000 BCE. Analogously, it is possible that the vertical orientation of Old Babylonian cuneiform is just another kind of archaizing.

Cylinder Seal and Modern Impression, ca. 1400–1300 BCE

The cylinder seal above is made of chalcedony and dated to the fourteenth to thirteenth centuries BCE. On the right is a modern impression made from it. Its cuneiform starts at the top left and is written horizontally.

Similar evidence for a change in the orientation of writing around 1500 BCE is found on vases, sculptures, steles, and other monuments. Because cuneiform script had become thoroughly abstract by 1500 BCE, its rotation would have been unobjectionable–except to lefties. It is virtually impossible to write cuneiform left to right with a stylus held in the left hand.[11]

If the orientation of cuneiform changed around 1500 BCE, what explanation is there for such a dramatic change at that time? The likely stimulus for the change was a result of the remarkable internationalism of the Late Bronze Age (c. 1550–1150 BCE).[12] During this period, Akkadian was the lingua franca of the entire Fertile Crescent (the crescent-shaped region in the Middle East that spans from modern-day Turkey to Syria and down through Israel/Jordan to Egypt). As a result, in the mid-fourteenth century BCE when the city-state kings of Canaan corresponded with Egypt's Pharaoh, both sides did so in Akkadian.[13] Since cursive Egyptian (Hieratic) and all the languages of Canaan were being written in a horizontal direction, it seems plausible that this may have prompted the change in the direction for writing Akkadian from vertical to horizontal. The choice to write Akkadian from left to right, despite the practice of Hieratic and all the Canaanite languages (except Ugaritic), which are written right to left, finds its explanation in the reverse of what was said above about left-handed persons trying to write cuneiform from left to right. It is nearly impossible for right-handed persons, who constitute the majority of human beings, to write cuneiform from right to left. As a result, Akkadian was written from left to right, and for the same reason, Ugaritic was also written left to right. This is because like Akkadian, Ugaritic employs cuneiform wedges pressed into clay tablets (or wax), whereas all the other languages of Canaan and Egypt were written with pigments applied by reed pens and similar implements to the absorbent surfaces of papyrus and parchment, for example.

11. So notes Finkel, *The Ark Before Noah*, 20.

12. This internationalism marked by increased trade, cultural exchange, and the use of Akkadian as a lingua franca is also often mentioned in terms of the Kassite Age (1595–1155 BCE) or the Amarna Age (14th century BCE). Cf. Fitzgerald, "pisan dub-ba and the Direction of Cuneiform Script."

For the internationalism of the period, one need only consider the 1982 discovery off the coast of Turkey of the Uluburun shipwreck and its amazingly diverse cargo from the late fourteenth century BCE. Marine archaeologists have recovered more than seventeen tons of the ship's cargo, which originated from at least eleven far-flung regions: Canaan, Mycenaean Greece, Cyprus, Egypt, Nubia, the southern Baltic, northern Balkans, Kassite Babylonia, Assyria, Central Asia (Afghanistan), and possibly southern Italy or Sicily. Cf. Aruz, Graff, and Rakic, *Cultures in Contact*, and Aruz, Benzel, and Evans, *Beyond Babylon*.

13. See Moran, *The Amarna Letters*.

1.1.2.6 *Standardization of Signs*—Finally, there was a sixth development in writing cuneiform. In earlier periods the general shape and composition of each sign was paramount. Because of this, some variety was allowed in terms of the specific number of wedges or lines that were used to form a sign. By the beginning of the first millennium BCE (the Neo-Assyrian period), however, each sign was comprised of a fixed number of wedges consistently positioned.[14]

1.1.3 ***Sumerian versus Akkadian and Borrowing.*** The cuneiform developed by the non-Semitic Sumerians was adopted for the writing of the Semitic language of Akkadian. In fact, since Sumerian logograms can be read in any language, similar to modern logograms such as numerals like 4 or 5 or symbols like $ or ⊘ and since they were adopted by Akkadian speakers, it is possible that some early texts written entirely in logograms, which many assume were written in Sumerian, were in fact originally written and read as Akkadian. In any case, there was considerable influence and borrowing in both directions between these two languages, which were spoken by peoples who lived in close proximity in southern Mesopotamia for more than a millennium.

1.1.3.1 *Logograms*—One important example of the influence of Sumerian on Akkadian is, as was just mentioned, how Akkadian writers frequently adopted Sumerian logograms to express corresponding Akkadian words.

For example, the Sumerian logogram 𒂍, which was pronounced É in Sumerian, means "house" or "household." When Akkadian speakers used 𒂍 (É) as a logogram in their writing, they pronounced it as *bîtum*,[15] the Akkadian word for "house" or "household." An acute accent is used when transliterating the Sumerian logogram É. This accent does not indicate stress. Instead, it indicates that there are other cuneiform signs that have the value of E and this is the second of them. The first sign with this value is written without any accent, E. The second is usually written with an acute accent, É (or it can be written as E_2), and if there is a third, it is usually written with a grave accent, È (or as E_3). If there is a fourth or fifth sign, etc., these would be indicated by subscripts: E_4, E_5, etc. (much like DE_6 noted above).

1.1.3.2 *Word Order*—A second example of the influence of Sumerian on Akkadian is in the normal word order of Akkadian independent clauses. In most Semitic languages, including Hebrew, the normal word order in independent clauses is verb-subject-object (V-S-O).[16] In Akkadian, however, the normal word order in both main clauses and subordinate clauses is subject-object-verb (S-O-V).[17] Sumerian favors this same word order.

1.1.3.3 *Shared Vocabulary*—A third example of the influence of Sumerian on Akkadian is seen in the many instances where Sumerian words were adopted by Akkadian. Mentioned earlier was one such example: the Akkadian word *še'um* was borrowed from the Sumerian word for "barley,"

14. See Seri, "Adaptation of Cuneiform to Write Akkadian," 85.
15. For the circumflex accent over a vowel ($\hat{v}$), see explanation in Appendix A.
16. Eblaite is an exception in that it allows both S-O-V and S-V-O word order. Imperial Aramaic is also an exception, where the word order is also S-O-V and S-V-O, under the influence of Akkadian. Likewise, Modern Ethiopic is an exception, favoring the S-O-V word order, perhaps because of Cushitic influence.
17. In literary works and poetry, Akkadian allows for more variation in its word order, with the verb often placed before the object and sometimes placed even before the subject.

ŠE. Since Akkadians and Sumerians lived in close proximity for centuries, it is not surprising that some Akkadian words likewise found their way into Sumerian.

1.1.3.4 *Determinatives*—A fourth example of Sumerian influence is that Akkadian, unlike other Semitic languages but like Sumerian, irregularly employs what are called "determinatives" (also called "classifiers"). Determinatives are placed immediately before a word, or in some cases immediately after a word, and they provide a classification for that word. They inform the reader that the word to which they are attached refers to, for example, a female, or to something made of leather, or something made of wood, or that it is a grain, a bird, a fish, an equid, a star, a place name, a river, a mountain, a city, a body part, a pot, a linen garment, or that it is plural, etc. Although there are at least seventy-five determinatives attested for Akkadian, the number in regular use in any one of the dialects (see further discussion below in §1.2) is much smaller.[18] In the Laws of Hammurabi (LH), for example, despite having more than 3,600 lines of text, only eleven different determinatives are used. Because the use of determinatives was borrowed from Sumerian, every determinative is a Sumerian logogram. The most common of these is DINGIR, 𒀭, which is added before the name of any deity.

The use of determinatives may have developed in Sumerian to help readers determine which meaning is intended for an otherwise ambiguous sign. Most scholars assume that determinatives were not pronounced in the spoken language, perhaps because they were less necessary. This would be the case, for example, if spoken Sumerian used tones, which are not represented in the writing, to distinguish one otherwise identical usually monosyllabic word from another.

1.1.3.5 *Common Gender in the Third-Person Singular Prefix Tense*—A final example of the influence of Sumerian on Akkadian is the use of a common gender third-person singular prefix tense form. This is unlike the practice in other Semitic languages which distinguish 3ms forms of the prefix tense from 3fs forms. Compare, for example, the distinction in Hebrew between *yiqṭōl*, יִקְטֹל (3ms), "*he* will kill," and *tiqṭōl*, תִּקְטֹל (3fs), "*she* will kill."

1.2 Major Dialects of Akkadian

As was mentioned previously, Akkadian has the distinction of being the earliest attested Semitic language. The first evidence for Akkadian consists of personal names found in late twenty-seventh century BCE Sumerian texts. The language boasts a long history that demonstrates periods of distinct dialects.

"Akkadian (*akkadû*)" is the name that ancient Babylonians and Assyrians used to refer to their own language. It is a word that derives from the northern Babylonian city of Akkad(e), mentioned in Genesis 10:10 but not yet located. King Sargon of Akkad built up this city as his capital sometime around 2340 BCE, and from it he forged what is thought to be the first real empire, one that lasted a century and encompassed most of Mesopotamia from the Persian Gulf to the Mediterranean. This is when Akkadian, the language that Sargon promoted, emerged as a written language, and it is when it began to function as a bridge language, first for the region and later well beyond. Old Akkadian (OAkk) is the term used by scholars to refer to the Akkadian of this earliest period (2350–2000 BCE).

18. Miller and Shipp, *An Akkadian Handbook*, 257–59.

After Old Akkadian, the language divided into two major dialectical streams based on geography: Babylonian, the dialect of southern Mesopotamia, and Assyrian, the dialect of northern Mesopotamia. Babylonian was in many respects the prestige version of the language. For example, in the latter second millennium and first millennium BCE, a strictly literary form of Akkadian emerged. Scholars term it "Standard Babylonian" (SB). It was a purely written dialect (not spoken) employed by both Babylonian and Assyrian scribes. They were seeking, not always with great success, to imitate the features of Old Babylonian when writing or copying important literary texts such as the Gilgamesh Epic and Enuma Elish. Similarly, because of the prestige of Babylonian, Neo-Assyrian kings chose to have their royal inscriptions written in Babylonian rather than in the Neo-Assyrian vernacular for their region.

Below are the major dialects and periods of Akkadian:

Old Akkadian (OAkk) 2350–2000 BCE		
Old Babylonian (OB)	2000–1600 BCE	Old Assyrian (OA)
Middle Babylonian (MB)	1600–1000 BCE	Middle Assyrian (MA)
Neo-Babylonian (NB)	1000–600 BCE	Neo-Assyrian (NA)
Late Babylonian (LB)	600 BCE–100 CE	
Standard Babylonian (SB) 1500–100 BCE		

In the period of Middle Babylonian, when Akkadian became the lingua franca of the entire Fertile Crescent, a number of peripheral dialects of Akkadian emerged. Each is characterized by some level of language mixing between Akkadian and the native language of the region. The Canaanite-Akkadian of the Amarna letters in the fourteenth century BCE is one such example.

1.3 The Focus of This Textbook

Each of the above dialects and periods of Akkadian witnessed developments in the grammar, vocabulary, morphology, and phonology of the language, as well as modifications in the values and shapes of the cuneiform utilized for its writing. This introductory grammar, however, will follow the wise and longstanding practice of introductory Akkadian grammars by focusing almost exclusively on the grammar and vocabulary of Old Babylonian and on the cuneiform of Neo-Assyrian.

There are many good reasons for this odd-sounding practice. As mentioned earlier, Old Babylonian was viewed by later Akkadian speakers as the classical form of their language. In part, this is because Old Babylonian was when the grammar of the language was its most regular and consistent. It was also a period of exceptional creativity when many significant works in Akkadian were composed, including the Laws of Hammurabi, which provide the text base for this grammar.

As a practical matter, once one has learned Old Babylonian, it is not difficult to learn any of the other dialects as needed. The most important difference between any of them and Old Babylonian can be summarized in a half-dozen pages or so.[19]

19. See Chapter 20 where significant differences between Old Babylonian and the other major Akkadian dialects and periods are briefly summarized.

The reason for choosing to learn the cuneiform of the Neo-Assyrian period is that its signs are the most regular and the simplest in shape and composition. In fact, it is generally acknowledged that it is virtually impossible to devise a means for arranging the cuneiform from any other period in a consistent and predictable manner. As a result, catalogues of cuneiform signs for all periods are typically arranged according to their Neo-Assyrian shape.

Furthermore, knowledge of the Neo-Assyrian script is of direct benefit because the great majority of extant Akkadian texts are written in the Neo-Assyrian script. Furthermore, Neo-Assyrian signs bear significant resemblance to the cuneiform of most of the other periods of both Assyrian and Babylonian, although not with the archaized Old Babylonian script used on monuments, such as the famous stele of the Laws of Hammurabi (LH). Nevertheless, there were later scribes who copied portions of LH in their own Neo-Assyrian script, apparently as student exercise tablets. Their copies, among others, have provided important textual evidence allowing scholars to correct some mistakes in the famous stele that is housed in the Louvre and to fill in some damaged portions, especially a large section of erased text between LH §65 and §100. Their example, copying LH in Neo-Assyrian script, provides a good precedent for the practice of this textbook.[20]

1.4 Homework

1.4.1 *Signs*

Learn the following cuneiform signs so that you can recognize them and draw them, and learn the values of each. (Early forms of the cuneiform and comparisons with Hebrew do not need to be learned.)

𒁹 1

𒀀 *a* (in Sumerian around 3200 BCE this sign had the form ≈ and is pronounced A, which means "water")

𒀭 there are three possible meanings for this sign depending on the context (around 3200 BCE this sign depicted a star, ✳)

1. DINGIR, *ilum*, "god" (cf. *'ēl*, אֵל)[21]

   DINGIR is a Sumerian word, which is why it is written in all uppercase letters, and it means "god." In Akkadian this logogram is read as *ilum*, the Akkadian word for "god" (see Vocabulary below in §1.4.2)

2. ^{d}

   This use of 𒀭 is a determinative. The superscripted d is an abbreviation for DINGIR and is not pronounced. It is placed immediately before the name of a god.

20. Old Babylonian Monumental (Lapidary) cuneiform will be introduced in the last four chapters of this book. For a convenient list and brief characterization of the extant copies of portions of LH especially from the Neo-Assyrian period and with less detail from the Old Babylonian, Middle Babylonian, Middle Assyrian, and Neo-/Late Babylonian periods, see Wright, *Inventing God's Law*, 106–10, 118–20.

21. Throughout this grammar many comparisons with Hebrew will be given. They will always be given first in English transliteration and then in Hebrew characters.

3. *an*

The most common use of  is as a syllabogram for *an*. This value came about because in Sumerian the sign  (its earlier form, , depicting a star) had another meaning in addition to DINGIR, namely the Sumerian word AN, which is the name of the god of the sky, *Anu*. *Anu* is the father of all the gods. He is mentioned in both the prologue and epilogue of LH. When the sign for AN is used as a syllabogram, rather than a logogram, it represents the syllable *an*.

 *du, ṭù* (these are two alternative syllabic values for this sign; 3200 BCE form , "foot")

 É, *bîtum,* "house, household" (cf. *bayit,* בַּיִת)

 *ma*

 this sign has two options depending on the context

1. ŠE, *še'um,* "barley" (perhaps cf. *šay,* שַׁי, "tribute"; 3200 BCE form )[22]

2. *še*

Congratulations! If you have learned the seven cuneiform signs above, you will be able to read 13 percent of all the cuneiform signs in LH §§1–20, 127–149, which are the laws that will be translated and studied in this textbook.

1.4.2 *Vocabulary*

bîtum = house, household (cf. *bayit,* בַּיִת)
ilum = god (cf. *'ēl,* אֵל)
še'um = barley

22. In support of ŠE being read as *ūm,* see Cavigneaux ("Le nom akkadien du grain") who was the first to propose the reading based on certain lexical texts in "Le nom akkadien du grain." This proposal was widely accepted and is reflected in the first edition (1997) of Huehnergard's *A Grammar of Akkadian* (p. 115) and more recently in Worthington, *Complete Babylonian* (p. 104). The proposed Akkadian word *ūm* is borrowed from the Sumerian word Ú for "grass, food."

In support of the traditional view that ŠE may still be read as *še'um,* see Kouwenberg, Review of *A Grammar of Akkadian,* by John Huehnergard, 815. See also Streck, Review of *Letters in the British Museum,* by W. H. van Soldt, 147–48. *CDA* (p. 369) likewise prefers *še'um,* though it allows *ūm* as possible. Similarly, Huehnergard, in the third edition of *Grammar of Akkadian* (pp. 115 and 528) acknowledges that *še'um* "may in fact be the more common word for 'grain' in Akk." He cites in support Weeden, "The Akkadian Words for 'Grain' and the God 'Ḫaya,'" 77–107.

The Genres of Akkadian Literature

Larisa Levicheva

Akkadian literature includes numerous literary genres: epics and myths, royal inscriptions, wisdom texts, hymns, prayers to gods, incantations against evil spirits, law codes, prophetic texts, and love songs among others. At times, genres come together in a single composition and it is up to the interpreter to determine its appropriate reading. Below is a summary of some of the types of texts in Akkadian literature. The intent is to supply a framework for the breadth of documents attested in the Akkadian language.

Epics and Myths

The cosmic order and the subjugation of chaos was of primary importance for ancient Mesopotamians. Among the most significant literary texts was the religious epic that dealt with cosmology, known as the Enuma Elish, meaning "When on high," after the first two words of the composition. The work dates to the end of the second millennium BCE and consists of several tablets. It is a creation myth and reveals insight into an ancient perspective of how the world began. Another significant religious myth is the Gilgamesh epic, dating to the first millennium BCE. The epic deals with the issue of eternal life. The Atrahasis epic from the same time period gives an account of creation and includes a flood story. The legend of Adapa, dating to the mid-fourteenth century BCE, provides an explanation on the origins of death. The Descent of Ishtar to the Underworld comes from the twelfth century BCE and explains seasonal changes in the world as they relate to the fertility cult. These compositions, among others, are considered religious epics and myths because they offer explanations about how the world functions through stories about the gods. The stories offered meaning for their ancient hearers, grounding them in the past and offering a way into the future.

Royal Epics, Royal Inscriptions, and Fictional Royal Autobiographies

Royal ancient Mesopotamian epics and inscriptions served to establish and reinforce the power and authority of the king. Royal courts employed scribes to document great deeds of the king and preserve his name and fame through the ages. The Birth Legend of Sargon of Akkad (ca. 2300 BCE) celebrates the king's birth, upbringing, and reign. The Black Obelisk of Shalmaneser III (827 BCE) documents the events of the king's reign in both relief and inscription. A significant number of royal inscriptions detail military campaigns of Assyrian and Babylonian kings. For example, the inscription titled Sennacherib's Siege of Jerusalem (700 BCE) describes the kings and accompanying cities that were defeated by the Assyrian king, including Hezekiah of Judah.

Fictional royal autobiographies functioned as propaganda pieces to support and endorse a new king who just came to power or was about to take the throne. These literary documents described the new monarch as superior to his predecessors in wisdom, achievements, and greatness. The Adad-Guppi

Autobiography (sixth century BCE) and the Autobiography of Idrimi (1200 BCE) present the kings as surpassing the earlier kings and bettering the life of their subjects.

Hymns, Prayers, Incantations, Rituals

Ancient Near Eastern literature teaches that gods must not only be served, they must be praised. Every event in human life was ordered by the actions of a particular god or several gods. Thus, petitions and requests were brought to deities via cultic rituals in places of worship. Rituals outlined procedures to be followed and prayers to be said during temple services, which regulated the relationship between the human and divine worlds. Omens were used to advise the king and incantations were used to ward off evil. Hymns to Shamash, Ishtar, and Marduk (all first millennium BCE) extoll the gods' great powers and attributes and include petitions for protection from enemies and blessing on the holy cities of the empire. Documents also describe different divination practices including omens and incantations. For example, Maqlu offers incantation on neutralizing evil spells and the people who offered them. The Old Babylonian Incantation against Cattle Disease protects animals, and the Installation of the Storm God's High Priestess describes the ritual and festivities of the occasion.

Wisdom Texts

Works that belong to this genre in Akkadian literature generally offer advice on daily living and ethics. The genre of didactic and wisdom literature includes the subgenres of fables, proverbs, admonitions, and instructions. The Babylonian Theodicy and a Dialogue between a Man and His God address the issue of theodicy, righteous suffering, illness as a sign of divine punishment, and restoration to good health as a sign of divine favor. The Instructions of Shuruppak are written in a form of teaching passed from father to son and concern the ways of life. The Counsels of Wisdom provide situational advice on the issues of improper speech and bad company, kindness to the needy and avoidance of prostitutes, importance of religion, and temptations common to a public officer. Mesopotamian fables differ from traditional Aesopic ones and contain contest literature that typically describe a dialogue between two entities competing for supremacy. The Tamarisk and the Palm and The Ox and the Horse are good examples of this subgenre. Popular Assyrian and Babylonian sayings and proverbs present moral lessons about human nature and behavior.

Chronicles, Law Documents, and Treaties

There are multiple documents that span a significant time that belong to these subgenres in Akkadian literature. The Laws of Hammurabi, written in the second millennium BCE, contains at least 275 laws and offers an insight into the Old Babylonian culture. The Edict Ammisaduqa, written two centuries later, proclaims an act of justice at the beginning of the king's reign, outlining remission of debts and reversal of property to original owners. The Weidner Chronicles (second millennium BCE) and Babylonian Chronicles (seventh century BCE) are good examples of historical material from those times. Abbael's Gift of Alalakh (second millennium BCE) records a gift of a city as part of a treaty between two kingdoms. The Agreement between Ir-Addu and Niqmepa (first millennium BCE) outlines the stipulations concerning the extradition of fugitives.

An important resource for the breadth of Akkadian texts (as well as others from the ancient Near

East) available in English translation is the four-volume set *The Context of Scripture,* edited by William W. Hallo (Leiden: Brill, 1997–2016). For the summary above, see also the following works:

Lambert, W. G. *Babylonian Creation Myths.* Winona Lake, IN: Eisenbrauns, 2013.
Lambert, W. G. *Babylonian Wisdom Literature.* Winona Lake, IN: Eisenbrauns, 1996.
Pritchard, James B., ed. *The Ancient Near East: An Anthology of Texts and Pictures.* Princeton: Princeton University Press, 2011.
Walton, John H. *Ancient Near Eastern Thought and the Old Testament: Introducing the Conceptual World of the Hebrew Bible.* 2nd ed. Grand Rapids: Baker Academic, 2018.

2–𒐖

Hammurabi, Cuneiform, and Noun Declension

This chapter provides a short history of Hammurabi and his laws, and it offers steps to begin reading the first law (LH §1 V:26). These steps include learning how to transcribe cuneiform signs, transliterate, normalize, and translate. Noun declension and definiteness will also be explained.

2.1 Introduction to Hammurabi's Laws

King Hammurabi, who ruled from about 1792 BCE to 1750 BCE, began his remarkable career as the ruler of the city of Babylon and its environs. Starting in the thirtieth year of his reign, however, through a combination of native genius, patient diplomacy, and military success, he expanded his kingdom in stages to the point where it included most of Mesopotamia.

Toward the end of his reign, Hammurabi issued a list of at least 275 laws, which is conventionally called "the Code of Hammurabi" (= CH). It is widely recognized, however, that this collection of laws is not a "code" in the proper sense of the term. In other words, it makes no pretense at exhaustive completeness even over any single area of law. Furthermore, there is no clear evidence that the CH was ever consulted or cited as an authoritative basis for any legal decision, as is expected for a true "code" of laws. Accordingly, in this book the "Code of Hammurabi" will be called the "Laws of Hammurabi" (LH), as is increasingly the scholarly convention.[1]

Based on the evidence of other extant collections of law from the period before Hammurabi, his famous laws reflect a long tradition of law, whether or not there was any direct literary dependence. That tradition is represented by the Sumerian Laws of Ur-Nammu (2100 BCE), the Laws of Lipit-Ishtar (1930 BCE), and also by the near-contemporary Old Babylonian Laws of Eshnunna (1770 BCE). Nevertheless, LH is by far the most extensive, most detailed, and most carefully structured collection of laws of any from the ancient Near East.

Hammurabi Stele
jsp/Shutterstock.com

In Hammurabi's day, many copies of LH were made, including at least three that were engraved on stone monuments. One of these

1. Cf., e.g., Bottéro, "The 'Code' of *Ḫammurabi*" in *Mesopotamia*; and Roth, "Mesopotamian Legal Traditions and the Laws of Hammurabi."

was engraved on a seven-foot, five-inch-high black diorite stele and placed in Sippar, or some other equally important city within his kingdom. Six centuries later that stele was plundered by Elamite armies, who brought it to their capital, Susa. In 1901–02 French archaeologists working at Susa found it, and it is now kept in the Louvre as an incalculably valuable work of art and history.

Although this stele offers the most complete copy of LH, portions are damaged, making them difficult to read, and there is a section at the bottom of the front of at least twenty-five laws (five to seven rows of text), starting in the middle of law 65, that was deliberately erased and smoothed over by the Elamites. It is possible that they were planning to add a dedicatory inscription of their own, but for whatever reason failed to do so. Thankfully, however, many other copies of LH, whether partial or complete, were made, both at the time of Hammurabi and over the next thousand years. Portions of dozens of these copies have survived, and these have allowed scholars to fill in many of the missing parts.

2.2 Transcribing Signs

A lengthy and impressive introduction begins at the upper right front of the Hammurabi stele. The first of the laws appears in the fifth row down (out of sixteen) and in the twenty-sixth column (out of sixty-eight) from the right. The arrow in the previous photograph points to the first law. There are twenty-eight additional rows of text on the reverse side of the stele.

The rows and columns are well defined by grooves that form little rectangular boxes which contain about three to eight cuneiform signs each. There are no spaces between words, but words are generally not divided between boxes.

Depicted in the photograph to the right is a closeup of the first eight cuneiform signs for the beginning of the first law. Within the box five signs go down on the right followed by three signs that go down on the left. The script is a special archaic style of Old Babylonian cuneiform that was reserved for formal monuments.

First Eight Signs of LH §1

2.2.1 ***Right Justified.*** Notice that the cuneiform in both columns within the box to the right are bottom justified. In other words, although the signs at the top of the two columns within the box start at different levels (the second column often starts below the first) they end up firmly planted on the bottom.

Scholars normally transcribe these signs following the later convention that rotates the text by ninety degrees counterclockwise. This allows the cuneiform to be read from left to right, with the text right justified:

LH §1 V:26

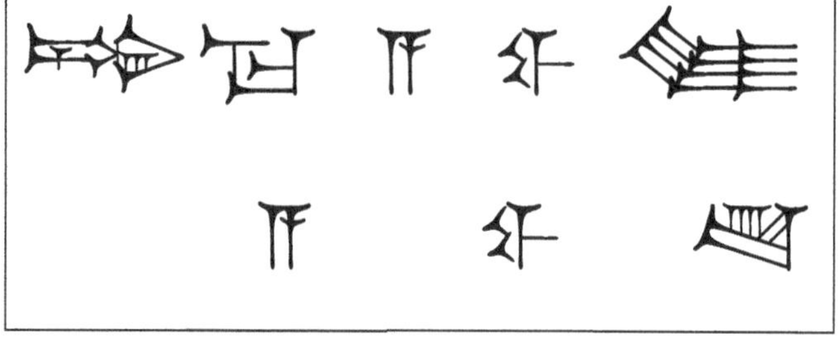

A designation like LH §1 V:26 above will be found next to each box of cuneiform text in this grammar. Here, the Roman numeral V and the number 26 represent the location of the text on the stele: this box came from the fifth row down and the twenty-sixth column from the right. Interestingly, because of the mentioned ninety-degree rotation, Assyriologists (scholars who specialize in Akkadian) conventionally refer to this as the fifth column and the twenty-sixth row. The designation §1 refers to the first law in LH.

2.2.2 ***Usually No Spaces.*** If one compares the original cuneiform with the transcription on the previous page, one major difference will be readily apparent. In the original, especially in the first column where there are five signs, there are no spaces between the signs. This may not seem like a major problem, but it is a challenge for modern readers of Akkadian because it means that there are no spaces between words, even if, in general, words do not continue onto a following line. This scribal practice of having each sign touch its neighbors is typical, especially in later periods. Scribes accomplish this not only by placing signs adjacent to each other, but also by stretching, compressing, or otherwise modifying each individual sign.

Despite the convenience of modern computer fonts for Akkadian, where the same sign always has the same size and shape, virtually every time a cuneiform sign is employed in an inscription, it has a slightly different shape. Accordingly, in scholarly contexts, the practice is to use photographs and hand drawings for a more accurate representation.[2]

2.2.3 ***Neo-Assyrian Script.*** The Laws of Hammurabi was composed around 1750 BCE. Appropriate to that period, it was written in a special Old Babylonian script reserved for monuments that is now called "Old Babylonian Monumental" or "Old Babylonian Lapidary." Modern students, however, normally learn the cuneiform script of the much later Neo-Assyrian period (1000–600 BCE), as mentioned in §1.3 above. At least nineteen copies of segments of LH have been recovered from the Neo-Assyrian period which were, apparently, exercise tablets for scribal practice. This is the case, for example, with a broken tablet found at Nineveh, which is now housed in the British Museum and designated as K4223+. This tablet, which combines four contiguous fragments, parallels much of LH §§23–33.[3]

Neo-Assyrian Reconstructed Tablet, K4223+

2. Even these representations fall short because the original cuneiform signs are actually three dimensional. As a result, for much scholarly work, three dimensional images of the text are increasingly being used. Cf., e.g., The Cuneiform Digital Paleography Project at The University of Birmingham (http://etana.org) and The West Semitic Research Project at The University of Southern California (http://www.inscriptifact.com).

3. See Borger (*Babylonisch-Assyrische Lesestücke*, 1:2) in his comments on what he identifies as source J. K4223+ is comprised of K4223, K9054, K11795 and K13979 [+ Sm 1008a]). Cf. K4223+ on p. 116 fig. 17 in Parpola, *Letters from Assyrian and Babylonian Scholars*. Interestingly, in a few cases the readings in this and other late copies of LH are more likely to be original than that which is on the stele.

Below are how the eight Old Babylonian signs, reproduced above on the previous page in §2.2.1, appear when transcribed into the simpler, more standardized Neo-Assyrian script:

LH §1 V:26

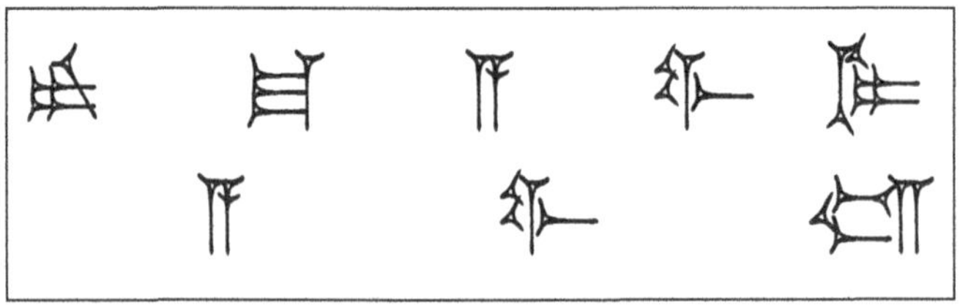

2.3 Transliterating Signs: Step One (Finding Values)

After producing a transcription of the cuneiform of a text, such as the eight signs on the previous page (§2.2.3), the next challenge is to transliterate each sign with its appropriate value (indicating how it was read). This is expressed in Roman alphabetical characters. In order to accomplish this, two things need to be done. First, the alternative values, which changed over time, need to be considered for each sign; and second, it has to be determined which value results in a plausible translation with appropriate vocabulary and grammar. This second step will be discussed below in §2.4.

For the first step, unless the value of a particular sign is known by heart, it has to be looked up in a reference list that summarizes the shapes and values of each sign for each period of Akkadian.[4] In order to look up a sign, it is necessary to know how such a list is organized.

There are two ways to order a list of signs. One is to order the list alphabetically according to a characteristic phonetic value for each sign (see Appendix D). This kind of list is useful for some purposes, but not for transliterating a cuneiform text like the one above. If the purpose is to transliterate signs, what is needed is a list not of values but of the signs themselves with their values. This list needs to be ordered in some logical way by the physical characteristics of each sign.

It is conventional for lists of signs to be based on their appearance in Neo-Assyrian script because of its greater standardization, simplicity, and prevalence. The signs are then ordered based on the type and number of the wedges that comprise each sign starting from the left.

In sign lists published before 2010, the general order of the type of wedges is as follows:

1. horizontal
2. upward oblique
3. downward oblique
4. angled (also called *Winkelhaken*)
5. vertical

Reflecting the above order, sign lists start with all the signs that have just one horizontal wedge on the far left. This group of signs is then ordered by the type and number of the wedges in a position immediately to the right of the one horizontal wedge, following the order of the above list. Groups of signs with one kind of wedge at any position will be listed before those

4. Appendix C includes all the needed signs for this textbook. For much more complete lists, see Labat, *Manuel d'épigraphie akkadienne*; and Borger, *Mesopotamisches Zeichenlexikon*.

with two wedges of the same kind in the same position. Those with two wedges of the same kind in the same position will be listed before those with three wedges, and so on.

Many recent lists of signs, including the list in Appendix C, employ the general principles discussed above, but instead of applying them to the ordered five major types of wedges listed above, they apply them to a much more detailed and serviceable list of thirty-one wedges, as proposed by Rykle Borger in 2010 (*Mesopotamisches Zeichenlexikon*). His list inverts the order for upward and downward oblique wedges, but it specifies in a far more complete manner the order of frequently occurring sign elements as follows:

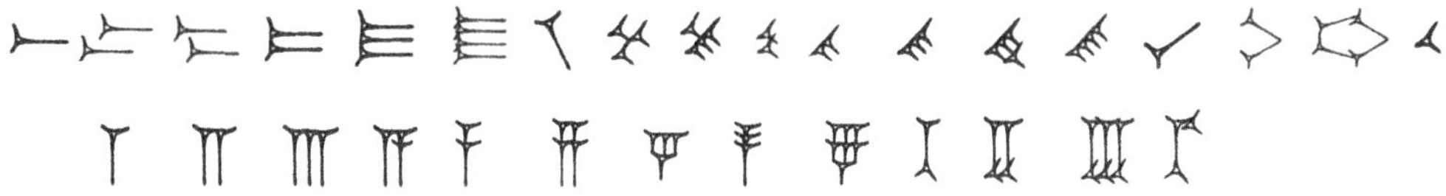

Spend some time reviewing Appendix C to become familiar with how signs are ordered in this grammar.

2.3.1 ***Ambiguity of Signs.*** There are two surprising oddities about how cuneiform and its syllabic transliteration work. The first oddity is what is called "polyphony." This term refers to the fact that the same sign often has more than one possible value. An example of this is seen in the sign , which in LH normally represents either the sound *wi* or, less commonly, the sound *wa*. In more exhaustive sign lists, ones that cover all periods of the language, an individual cuneiform sign may have a half dozen or more alternative syllabic values in addition to having one or more values as logograms. Nevertheless, the number of values in any individual period and dialect of Akkadian, or in any particular genre of literature, is much more limited.

The second oddity is termed "homophony." This refers to the fact that often two or three and sometimes many more different signs can represent the same syllable. Again, this issue is less problematic in actual practice because the number of identical values for different signs is much more limited in any particular period and dialect of Akkadian or in any particular genre of literature.

2.3.2 ***Transliteration of LH §1 V:26: Step One.*** The following is a preliminary transliteration of the eight signs that begin Law #1 of LH. Refer to §2.2.3 for the text box.

 *šum*

 *ma*

 *a*

 *wa, wi* (*we, wu, pe, pi*) (*Note:* Only *wa* and *wi* appear in the portions of LH that are treated in this textbook, and *wi* is three times more common than *wa*.)

 *lum*

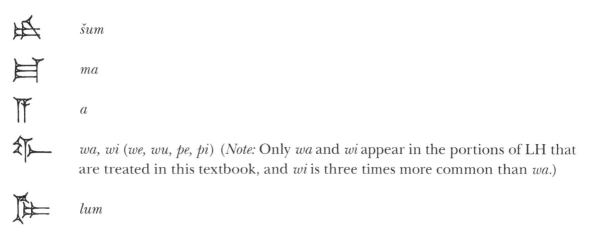

 *a*

 *wa, wi,* (*we, wu, pe, pi*)

 *lam*

None of the above signs functions by itself as a logogram in LH.[5]

2.4 Transliterating Signs: Step Two (Grouping Values)

The next step of transliteration is to group sign values into words. If the above list is put into a continuous and more readable form, it yields the following sequence of syllograms:

-šum-ma-a-wa/wi-lum-a-wa/wi-lam-

In order to group these signs into words, two rules apply:

1. Scribes generally avoid dividing a word over two lines or columns.[6] In the text above, then, it is likely that there is a break between words that occurs between the sign for *lum* and the second sign for *a*. Likewise, since the first word is unlikely to have begun in the previous column, the first word begins with *šum*, and because it is unlikely to be carried over into the following column, the last word probably ends with *lam*. This yields:

šum-ma-a-wa/wi-lum | *a-wa/wi-lam*

2. Because Akkadian is a Semitic language, some words have two root consonants, but most words have three. Very few words (usually loanwords from other languages) have more than three root consonants. This makes it unlikely that the sequence *šum-ma-a-wa/wi-lum* is just a single word.

In order to divide correctly this five-sign sequence or any sequence into words, a knowledge of Akkadian grammar and vocabulary is necessary. Educated guesses, however, can be checked by consulting a glossary, such as Appendix E, or a more definitive Akkadian lexicon, such as *A Concise Dictionary of Akkadian* (*CDA*) to confirm whether the resulting words do, in fact, exist in Akkadian.

For example, since Akkadian has relatively few monosyllabic words, it is unlikely that the five signs in the first line should be divided into one word comprised of four signs and another word comprised of just one sign.[7] A quick check of the glossary confirms that neither *šum* nor *lum* are words in Akkadian. So a good guess is to divide the first line into either *šum-ma-a*

5. The cuneiform sign for *a* can function as part of a logogram, as happens in LH §2, but only when it is immediately followed by certain other signs. The same is true for the sign for *ma*, as happens in LH §139.

6. There are notable exceptions where a word is split between two lines, often at a morphological break in the word (such as between a word and its suffix, as in the case of *maḫri-*|*-šunu*, "before them," in LH §9), or at a break between syllables (such as *ḫul-*|*-qum*, "lost property," in LH §9). Note, however, the rare and infelicitous division made within a single syllable, such as *innaddi-*|*-inma*, "shall be given and," in LH §29.

7. There are only nine monosyllabic words that occur in the portions of LH that are treated in this book: *id, lâ, lû, ša, šī, šu, u, û,* and *ul*. If one includes the whole of LH, then there are ten more monosyllabic words. To this list should be added seven disyllabic words but which have the following monosyllabic forms: *bêl, bît, dîn, mâr, nîš, qât,* and *sar*. If one includes the whole of LH, then there are five more monosyllabic forms of disyllabic words.

followed by *wa/wi-lum* or *šum-ma* followed by *a-wa/wi-lum*. Only a glossary or lexicon can decide which option yields attested Akkadian words.

Likewise, in the second line, the three signs could all belong to one word, *a-wa/wi-lam*, or to two words. Since monosyllabic words are rare, however, the best guess is that all three signs represent one word.

2.4.1 ***Alphabetical Order.*** Modern glossaries and lexica for Akkadian use the following alphabetical order:

a, b, d, e, g, ḫ, i, j(y), k, l, m, n, p, q, r, s, ṣ, š, t, ṭ, u, w, z

This list summarizes all the phonemes of Akkadian, which include nineteen consonants and four vowels.[8] There is one more consonantal phoneme, the ʾ, which is well established for Akkadian, even though there is no explicit cuneiform sign for ʾ in the period of Old Babylonian.[9] In any case, no word begins with an ʾ in Akkadian and in cases where an ʾ may be inferred within a word, it is ignored when alphabetizing.[10]

2.4.2 ***Transliteration of LH §1 V:26: Step Two.*** The glossary in Appendix E of this grammar follows the alphabetic ordering noted above. Spend some time looking at the glossary and become familiar with its ordering. Notice that the glossary attests Akkadian words for *šumma* and *awīlum*. This helps to solve where to divide the first transliterated line, *šum-ma-a-wa/wi-lum*, and which value for the ambiguous sign *wa/wi* is correct. Thus, the transliteration of the first four signs that begin Law #1 of LH is as follows:

šum-ma a-wi-lum

The second line of text, *a-wa/wi-lam*, looks similar to the word *awīlum* above. Its ending, however, is different. Both words are in fact related, and the distinction will be discussed below (see §2.6). The complete transliteration, then, of LH §1 V:26 is

šum-ma a-wi-lum | *a-wi-lam*

2.5 Normalization

Once a cuneiform text has been properly transliterated, then it has to be "normalized." Normalization refers to rewriting the text in Roman letters in a manner that no longer informs the reader how words were spelled in cuneiform, whether with logograms or syllabograms, but rather how they are pronounced. Accordingly, there are no hyphens used to distinguish cuneiform syllabograms (or periods used to distinguish cuneiform logograms). Normalization

8. The *h* with a breve under it (*ḫ*) is similar in pronunciation to Hebrew *ḥ*. Whereas *ḥ* is a voiceless pharyngeal fricative—the sound of a breath being forced through a constricted throat (like a person who is being strangled)—*ḫ* has more of a slight rasping sound. It is described by linguists as a voiceless velar fricative. This means that the sound is produced by the friction of air moving against the parts of the vocal apparatus in the top back of the mouth, not in the throat. It is the sound of the German pronunciation of the *ch* in a word like *doch*. See Appendix A for the International Phonetic Alphabet (IPA) symbol for each phoneme and for the relationship between these phonemes and those in Hebrew and other Semitic languages.

9. This letter corresponds to the *aleph* in the Hebrew alphabet and is pronounced as a glottal stop.

10. For a more detailed discussion of ʾ in Akkadian, see §3.4.

does, however, indicate more adequately how an ancient Akkadian speaker would have pronounced the text. Note that double consonants are written as double, whether doubled in the cuneiform or not, and long vowels are clearly indicated. Normalizing a Sumerian logogram into the correct Akkadian form depends on context.

To normalize a text requires knowledge of the vocabulary and grammar of Akkadian. Below are a few rules explaining how syllables are represented in cuneiform as well as a discussion of vowel length, shortening, syncope, and accentuation. These principles help determine how to normalize a text.

2.5.1 ***Syllable Writing in Cuneiform.*** Ancient scribes had a variety of ways to spell words using cuneiform signs, with four syllable types in Akkadian writing where *c* stands for consonant and *v* stands for vowel: *cv*, *cvc*, *v*, and *vc*.[11] A few rules on syllable writing are addressed here along with an illustrative example.

2.5.1.1 *Syllable Splitting*—Although scribes could represent a *cvc* syllable with a cuneiform sign having the value *cvc*, scribes often chose, for no particular reason, to split syllables and represent them with two signs, cv_1-v_1c, using the same vowel in both signs (a subscript is used with the vowel to indicate that the two vowels are identical), rather than with one sign, *cvc*. This practice is called "syllable splitting."

2.5.1.2 *Double Consonant*—In Old Babylonian, scribes normally represented a doubled consonant with two signs showing explicitly that the consonant is doubled. Sometimes, however, they chose, for no particular reason, to indicate only one consonant, and the reader is expected to know to normalize and pronounce the word with two consonants if that is what the grammar or vocabulary requires. This practice is termed "defective spelling," but this expression should not be misunderstood as having a pejorative implication.

2.5.1.3 *False Plene*—In Old Babylonian, a vowel that is long because of contraction is normally expressed through an additional sign, especially at the end of words, such as cv_1-v_1. Occasionally, however, a vowel that is *not* long is also spelled out in this manner. This is termed a "false plene" spelling.

2.5.1.4 *Historical Spellings*—Words that once began with an ʾ lost the ʾ without any other change (such as compensatory lengthening) to the following vowel. In Old Babylonian, such words are often spelled in cuneiform with an extra initial vowel sign, v_1-v_1c. This initial vowel does *not* mean that the vowel is long. It is, instead, simply a "historical spelling," which indicates that the word once began with an ʾ.[12]

2.5.1.5 *Example*—The following example illustrates the rules above. The Akkadian word *ubbirma*, meaning "he accused and," appears later in this first law of LH. Since only four syllable types are allowed in Akkadian, it is a simple matter to check the possible patterns (*cv*, *cvc*, *v*, and *vc*) and divide *ubbirma* into its constituent syllables: *ub-bir-ma*. It might be assumed that *ub-bir-ma*

11. See §4.1 for discussion on Akkadian syllables and syllabification rules.

12. A helpful analogy in English is the "historical" spelling of the word "island." Earlier in its Middle English form it lacked the unpronounced "s," but later in the fifteenth century the "s" was added, perhaps as an acknowledgment of its apparent derivation from either Old French or Latin.

would always be written with exactly three cuneiform signs corresponding to the three syllables: *ub-bir-ma*. That is certainly one correct way to spell the word in cuneiform signs. Nevertheless, scribes often chose to spell words by splitting up closed syllables ("syllable splitting") and occasionally by using spellings that fail to indicate doubling ("defective spellings") or by using false plene spellings or historical spellings.

Accordingly, a scribe could write the word *ubbirma* with cuneiform signs in any of the following five ways:

1. *ub-bir-ma*
2. *ub-bi-ir-ma*
3. *u-ub-bi-ir-ma*
4. *u-ub-bir-ma*
5. *u-bir-ma*

Although the first option reproduces more clearly in cuneiform the actual syllable structure of the word, *ubbirma*, the splitting of one *cvc* syllable into two, as in the second and third options above (*bi-ir*) is common and does not indicate a long vowel. An extra vowel that is *not* combined with a consonant *may* indicate a long vowel, especially one lengthened through vowel contraction. In Old Babylonian (the period of LH), however, when an extra vowel is at the beginning of a word and followed by the same vowel in a *vc* syllable, as in the case of the third and fourth options above (*u-ub*), it is usually a historical spelling indicating that the word once began with an ʾ, not that this initial vowel is actually long. Finally, although double consonants are normally indicated in an explicit way, the fifth option above, which has only one *b*, sometimes occurs as an optional "defective spelling."

2.5.2 *Vowels*

2.5.2.1 *Vowel Length*—Unfortunately, no one method for indicating vowel length has gained general acceptance among Assyriologists. Some scholars normalize a text without any indications of vowel length. Others mark all long vowels with a macron (*v̄*) or, in the case of many French scholars, with a circumflex accent (*v̂*). Still others use a circumflex accent (*v̂*) only to distinguish vowels that have become long through contraction, where two vowels combined to produce the resulting long vowel, while they mark all other long vowels with a macron (*v̄*).

This textbook will follow the practice of a fourth approach, advocated by Albrecht Goetze and Wilfred G. Lambert.[13] According to this approach, there are four kinds of vowel length: *ṽ*, *v̂*, *v̄*, and *v*. All vowels lengthened by contraction of two vowels will be indicated with a tilde, *ṽ*. Vowels lengthened because of compensatory lengthening, due to the quiescing of an earlier ʾ, will be indicated with a circumflex, *v̂*. All other long vowels, in other words those lengthened due to morphological considerations because of paradigms, noun patterns, and the like, will be marked with a macron, *v̄*. Short vowels will have no additional marking, *v*. It is likely that there was no difference in the pronunciation of the three kinds of long vowels. So, for example, *ā*, *â*, and *ã*, would all have been pronounced identically (perhaps something like the *a* in the English word "father," while short *a* was perhaps pronounced like the *a* in the word "that").

13. Lambert, "Class Notes."

2.5.2.2 *Vowel Shortening*—If the final syllable of a word has a macron long vowel ($\bar{v}$) or circumflex long vowel ($\hat{v}$) in an open syllable, it may have been shortened in actual speech. Accordingly, some Assyriologists normalize some or all non-tilde long vowels in final open syllables as short.[14] Other Assyriologists normalize these vowels as long. This is the practice of the grammar here. In support of this practice is the recognition that the length of these vowels is clearly retained whenever a suffix is added.[15]

2.5.2.3 *Vowel Syncope*—In general, Akkadian does not permit two or more non-final open syllables with short vowels in a row (*cvcv-*). It resolves this by syncope of (omitting) the last vowel (*cvcv-> cvc-*).[16] Exceptions occur if the next syllable begins with a vowel or with the consonant *r*, or less commonly the consonant *l*. Vowel syncope is also avoided if the *cvcv-* sequence precedes a pronominal suffix like *-šunu*, meaning "their" (see Chapter 8).

2.5.3 ***Accentuation (Stress).*** Some Assyriologists hold that no definitive rules for accentuation in Akkadian have yet been established.[17] Others, including the author of this grammar, maintain that there is at least suggestive evidence in support of the following ordered rules:[18]

1. If the final syllable (the ultima) has a tilde long vowel, $\tilde{v}$, it is accented.
2. If the final syllable (the ultima) is closed and has any long vowel in it, it is accented.
3. If the next-to-final syllable (the penult) is closed, or if it has a long vowel, or if it is the first syllable in the word, it is accented.
4. Otherwise, the third to last syllable (the antepenult) is accented.

2.5.4 ***Normalization of LH §1 V:26.*** The transliteration of the first line was noted above: *šum-ma a-wi-lum* | *a-wi-lam*. Based on the glossary in Appendix E and the discussion above related to rules of syllabification and vowel length, the normalization of the transliteration is as follows: *šumma awīlum awīlam*. Before proposing an English translation of the normalization and for a fuller understanding of the long *i* vowels in *awīlum awīlam*, noun declension and definiteness must be addressed.

2.6 Declension of the Noun

Compare the word in the second line of the first law, *awīlam*, to the similar word in the first line, *awīlum*.[19] To understand the difference between these, it is necessary to introduce some important features of the grammar of the noun in Akkadian.

Akkadian nouns are declined in the Old Babylonian period (declension broke down in

14. This is the practice, for example, of *CAD*. For the argumentin support of reducing long vowels in final open syllables, see *GAG*³ §105 and, more recently, applied to III-weak verbs, Kouwenberg, *The Akkadian Verb and Its Semitic Background*, §16.7.2.1.

15. Cf. Huehnergard, *A Grammar of Akkadian*, Appendix C, §2(k), 593.

16. The rule of syncope applies equally to situations where the first syllable is just a vowel, which comes about when a word-initial ʾ quiesces.

17. Cf. Reiner (*A Linguistic Analysis of Akkadian*, §3.2, "Stress," 38–39), who discusses alternative proposals, though she favors a view that has found few supporters, namely that stress was typically on the first syllable of words. Cf. also Worthington, *Complete Babylonian*, §3.1.

18. Cf., e.g., Ungnad, *Akkadian Grammar*, §§23–24; Caplice, *Introduction to Akkadian*, §4.8; Huenhergard, *A Grammar of Akkadian*, §1.3.

19. The vowel pattern of *awīlum* is a common noun pattern for persons and professions. See §14.2.4. Interestingly, this same noun pattern (*a-ī*) exists in Hebrew for persons and professions.

later periods).[20] Like Hebrew, Akkadian nouns have two genders, masculine and feminine. Masculine nouns are generally unmarked, while most feminine nouns are marked by a suffix *-t* or less often *-at*. The longer *-at* suffix is used with geminates (words that have two identical final consonants) like *šarr*. Dual forms are relatively uncommon in Akkadian, and they are used mostly for nouns that come in natural pairs, like eyes (*înān* in Akkadian).[21]

The following noun paradigm should be memorized. The word *šarrum* means "king," and *šarratum* means "queen."

		Masculine	Feminine
Singular	Nominative	*šarrum*[22]	*šarratum*
	Genitive	*šarrim*	*šarratim*
	Accusative	*šarram*	*šarratam*
Dual	Nominative	*šarrān*	*šarratān*
	Genitive-Accusative	*šarrīn*	*šarratīn*
Plural	Nominative	*šarrū*	*šarrātum*[23]
	Genitive-Accusative	*šarrī*	*šarrātim*

The nominative case is used for the subject of a verb and as the predicate nominative of a verbless clause. The genitive case is used for the object of a preposition and to express the "of" relationship in a clause (e.g., "king *of* Babylon"). The accusative case is used for the direct object of a verb and for a wide variety of adverbial clauses, including, especially, prepositional phrases.[24]

2.7 Definiteness

Akkadian has neither a definite nor an indefinite article. Based on context, a noun like *šarrum* can be translated as "king," "a king," "the king," "some king," or "any king."

2.8 Translation of LH §1 V:26

The normalization for the first eight signs of LH §1 was noted above: *šumma awīlum awīlam*. Based on the declensional pattern for nouns set out above in §2.6, *awīlum* is a nominative masculine singular form, while *awīlam* is an accusative masculine singular form. As the glossary indicates, *awīlum* means "man, person, citizen (a free man)" and *šumma* means "if." A translation, then, of LH §1 V:26 is "If a man . . . a man. . . ." This expression is not yet a complete

20. See Chapter 20.

21. The only dual noun that appears in LH is the word *kilallān*, which means "both." It is found in LH §152 and §157.

22. Based on the rules of accentuation in §2.5.3, the accent is on *šar* in all six singular forms and also the two mp forms. In dual forms it is on the ultima (the final syllable), and in feminine plural forms it is on the penult (the syllable right before the final syllable).

23. The feminine plural with *-āt-* parallels the Hebrew feminine plural *-ôt*. An original long *a*-vowel shifted to *ô* in Hebrew because of what is called the Canaanite Shift. This shift took place before the fourteenth century BCE Amarna Letters, which offer many examples. These letters were written by Canaanite kings to the Pharaoh using Akkadian, the lingua franca of the period. Because the authors were not native Akkadian speakers, there are many examples of Canaanite vocabulary, spelling, and grammar mixed in.

24. The genitive-accusative case is also sometimes referred to as the "oblique case."

sentence but based on the nominal endings it is clear that *awīlum* is the subject and *awīlam* is an object. More of LH §1 will be uncovered and explained in the next chapter.

2.9 Homework

Before you move on, be sure to understand how to transcribe signs, the steps of transliteration, and normalization. The process of transcription, transliteration, and normalization is an essential building block toward translation. Also, be sure to understand and recognize the paradigm for noun declension.

2.9.1 *Signs*

 2

 *bi, bé, pé, pí*

 *lum*

 *šum*

 *ú*

 *wa, wi* (*we, wu, pe, pi*)

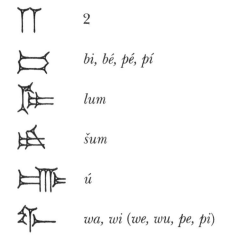

Congratulations! If you have learned the seven cuneiform signs in Chapter 1 and the six signs in this chapter, you will be able to read 24 percent of the cuneiform signs in LH §§1–20, 127–149.

2.9.2 *Vocabulary*

abārum = D: to accuse (pin on), bind[25]
awīlum = man, person, citizen (a free man) (cf. *'ĕwîl*, אֱוִיל)
lâ = not (a negative particle used only in subordinate clauses; cf. *lō'*, לֹא)
šarratum = queen (cf. *śārâ*, שָׂרָה)
šarrum = king (cf. *śar*, שַׂר)
šumma = if

25. This is a verb. The D refers to its verbal stem. See §3.1.

3–𒐗

Introduction to the Verbal System

In the previous chapter, a translation of LH §1 V:26 was provided: "If a man . . . a man. . . ." This expression, however, does not yet make sense because it lacks a verb. Based on the normal word order of S-O-V in Akkadian (see §1.1.3.2), the next word in the text of LH §1 is likely to be a verb, and sure enough that is the case (see Exercises below). Before one can identify the verb or look it up in a glossary, it is necessary to gain an overview of the verbal system in Akkadian. In this chapter, the Akkadian verb will be introduced. The four main verb stems will be explained, along with the three prefix tenses. In order to understand the particular verb in the next part of LH §1 (V:27), a brief discussion of I-ʾ weak verbs is included.

3.1 The Four Main Verb Stems

In Akkadian there are just four common stems or conjugations. This is unlike Hebrew, which has seven common stems (*qal, niphal, piel, pual, hiphil, hophal, hithpael*) in addition to a dozen or so less common stems. The four stems in Akkadian are designated by the four letters G, D, Š, and N, or alternatively by the four Roman numerals I, II, III, IV.[1] The overview here is more detailed than may be easily mastered. Do not worry, however, because much of this material will be reviewed again and again in succeeding chapters. In the meantime, it will prove helpful to gain a sense of the big picture of the verbal system, and the chapter will be useful for future reference because it puts much of the detail together in one place.

3.1.1 ***G-Stem* (I).** The G-stem is so designated because it is the "Ground stem" (in German, the *Grundstamm*), which is the simplest and most frequent stem for verbs. This corresponds to the *qal* conjugation in Hebrew.

3.1.1.1 *Lexical Forms of Verbs and Mimation*—Verb paradigms in Akkadian traditionally use the three root consonants *p-r-s*. The G-stem infinitive of this verb is *parāsum*, which means "to divide, separate, cut (off), to decide." The verb *parāsum* is a strong verb, which means that it maintains all three of its visible consonants in all of its forms. The G-stem infinitive is used as the normal lexical form of any verb that exists in the G-stem.

The final *-m* in the G-stem infinitive is called "mimation." It is part of the suffix and not a root consonant. It also appears at the end of all singular nouns (like the *-m* in *awīlum*), feminine plural nouns, and all adjectives as well as on dative pronouns and a special verbal form called the ventive.[2] Mimation, however, began to disappear early in the Old Babylonian period,

1. The system of Roman numerals is used, for example, in *CAD*.
2. The ventive will be covered in Chapter 7.

and it is entirely missing in all later dialects of Akkadian. For this reason, Akkadian lexica and glossaries that seek to cover all periods of the language rather than just Old Babylonian often omit the final *-m* in their spelling of the G-stem infinitive, or they place the final *-m* in parentheses, as in *parāsu(m)*.

3.1.2 ***D-Stem* (II).** The D-stem is so designated because it involves a characteristic doubling (hence, "D") of the middle root consonant of the verb. The D-stem, which corresponds to the *piel* conjugation in Hebrew, sometimes has a factitive or causative meaning when applied to verbs that are adjectival in the G-stem. So, for example, *šalāmum* (LH §2; cf., *šālôm*, שָׁלוֹם), which in the G-stem means "to be well, whole, safe," in the D-stem (*šullumum*) means "to make whole; make restitution; heal; pay back in full." At other times the D-stem has an intensifying effect on the meaning. Sometimes the intensifying reflects the fact that the action represented by the G-stem is applied to a plurality of direct objects, or it is the result of a plurality of subjects, or it is repeatedly or more thoroughly effectuated. In the D-stem, the infinitive of *parāsum* is spelled *purrusum*, and it means "to chop off, to dismember (the parts of a body)" or "to investigate."

3.1.3 ***Š-Stem* (III).** The Š-stem is so designated because the consonant *š* is prefixed before the first root consonant of the verb. This stem often adds a causative idea to the meaning of the verb, and as such it corresponds to the *hiphil* conjugation in Hebrew. In the Š-stem, the infinitive of *parāsum* is spelled *šuprusum*, and it means "to cause to be cut off, to block," or "to cause to be stopped."

3.1.4 ***N-Stem* (IV).** The N-stem is so designated because the consonant *n* is prefixed before the first root consonant of the verb. The N-stem often expresses the passive, or less commonly, the middle of verbs that are active and transitive in the G-stem. As such, it corresponds to the *niphal* in Hebrew.[3] In the N-stem, the infinitive of *parāsum* is spelled *naprusum* and means "to be cut off, to be stopped," or "to be decided."

Below are the infinitive forms of all four stems.

	Infinitive	Translation
G	*parāsum*	to divide
D	*purrusum*	to chop off
Š	*šuprusum*	to cause to be cut off
N	*naprusum*	to be cut off

3.1.5 ***Notes on Meaning.*** Although the above-mentioned nuances of meaning for each of the stems are typical and useful guidelines for guessing or remembering the meaning of a verb in a particular stem, in many cases the meaning cannot be predicted. It must be determined by context and a careful comparison with occurrences of the verb in the same stem found elsewhere. In other words, as a practical matter, it is wise to consult a glossary, like Appendix E, or better still, an up-to-date scholarly lexicon to confirm the meaning of a verb in a particular stem.[4]

3. Seventy-three percent of all the verb forms appearing in the texts from LH covered in this textbook are G-stem forms; 10 percent are D-stem; 5 percent are Š-stem; and 12 percent are N-stem.

4. The three best reliable scholarly lexica are: *CAD*; *AHw*; and *CDA*.

3.2 The Three Prefix Tenses

There are three finite prefix tenses for the verb: durative, perfect, and preterite. Each of these verbal forms is inflected for person, gender, and number and each appears in the four stems addressed above. Much like Hebrew, the prefix tenses in Akkadian are formed with prefixes in each case and suffixes half of the time. Second- and first-person verbal forms are rare in the casuistic laws of LH, so for now learn the third-person forms (see Appendix B for a complete paradigm).

3.2.1 ***Durative.*** The durative tense, which is sometimes called the present or the present-future, is the verbal form that describes action as incomplete, potential, ongoing, or occurring over a period of time. Depending on the context, it is sometimes translated into English with a present tense, but it is more often rendered as a future tense.[5] It may also be translated into English with almost any modal auxiliary verb including "would," "could," "should," "must," "may," or "might."[6] Among these many uses of the durative, by far its most common use in LH is as a modal past tense, best translated "would." In the G-stem the 3cs durative of *parāsum* is *iparras*, which, depending on the context, could be translated "he/she will divide," "he/she could divide," or "he/she would divide."

Form: In the durative, the second consonant is typically doubled. Also, the vowel between the first and second root consonants is *a* (see §4.4 for the "theme" vowel between the second and third root consonants). The 3cs conjugations of the durative are below.

	Durative	English
G	*iparras*	he/she would/will decide/divide
D	*uparras*	he/she would/will chop off
Š	*ušapras*	he/she would/will cause to be cut off
N	*ipparras*[7]	he/she/it would/will be decided/cut off

3.2.2 ***Perfect.***[8] The primary use of the perfect tense is similar to the present perfect in English, usually rendered "have/has" + past participle. The perfect refers to an action that took place in the past with an implication for the present but without specifying when the action took place. In Old Babylonian letters, the perfect often refers to recently completed action or action in the present moment. For example, "I have just x," or even "I am now doing x." In such cases the perfect has a focusing implication and refers to a crucial action or a major point that provides the basis for some instruction. In subordinate clauses the perfect can refer to the future.

5. Alternatively, Kouwenberg (*The Akkadian Verb and Its Semitic Background*, xxii and 91–95) prefers to designate this form the "imperfective." He defines the imperfective as a tense that expresses the fact that an action is not yet finished or has not yet begun at a given moment, whether that moment is at the time when the statement is made or at some referenced moment in the past.

6. When a negative particle such as *lā* is used with the durative, the durative typically has the meaning "would not," "should not," or "must not." For more on negative particles, see §5.6.

7. For the doubling of the initial root consonant here and in other N-stem forms, see Notes on *n*, §3.3.1, below.

8. The perfect tense was at first overlooked by Assyriologists since it is not found in any other Semitic language and because many of its forms are ambiguous. Thanks to the work of Benno Landsberger and his student Wolfram von Soden in the mid-twentieth century, however, its existence and uses are now well established. See Goetze, "The *t*-Form of the Old Babylonian Verb." Marcus, for example, does not recognize the perfect tense in *A Manual of Akkadian*.

For example, "When they have done x. . . ." In the G-stem the 3cs perfect of *parāsum* is *iptaras*, which, depending on the context, could be translated "he/she has divided."

Form: The perfect form takes the same prefixes and suffixes as the durative. However, its primary feature is the infix *-ta* after the first consonant. The 3cs conjugations of the perfect are below.

	Perfect	Translation
G	*iptaras*	he/she has decided/divided
D	*uptarris*	he/she has chopped off
Š	*uštapris*	he/she has caused to be cut off
N	*ittapras*	he/she/it has decided/cut off

In LH the most common use of the perfect is within the protasis (the "if" clause), where typically the main verbs are in the preterite (see below), but where the last clause or the last two are often in the perfect. As such, the perfect again has a focusing implication as it marks the action that provides the critical basis for the judgment that is given in the apodosis (the "then" clause).

3.2.3 ***Preterite.*** The preterite tense expresses completed action or action that the speaker views as having occurred at a single point of time. It is normally translated in English by a simple past tense, or, depending on the context, by a pluperfect. In the G-stem, the 3cs preterite of *parāsum* is *iprus* (from a hypothetical earlier form **yaprus*[9]) which, depending on the context, could be translated, "he/she divided."[10]

Form: The preterite form takes the same prefixes and suffixes as the durative and perfect. The 3cs conjugations of the preterite are noted below.

	Preterite	English
G	*iprus*	he/she decided/divided
D	*uparris*	he/she chopped off
Š	*ušapris*	he/she caused to be cut off
N	*ipparis*	he/she/it was decided/cut off

Within LH, the preterite, as with the perfect, is often used to describe a situation or offense for which the law stipulates a punishment. Since these are case laws that are meant to be widely applicable, many English translations use a generalizing present tense. So, for example, LH §22 is often translated something like: "If a man *commits a robbery* [*iḫbutma*, which is a preterite] and *then is seized* [*ittaṣbat*, which is a perfect], that man shall be killed."[11] Nevertheless, if we pay attention to the literary context of these case laws, which are sandwiched between a lengthy prologue (Pro) and epilogue (Epi) that explain their purpose, it is clear that Hammurabi was not legislating, whether for his own generation or for future generations. Instead, he was

9. An asterisk (*) is used by linguists to mark an unattested hypothetical form.
10. See §3.4.2 and §3.4.4 below for rules related to how the consonant *y* was lost at the beginning of words.
11. So, e.g., Roth, *Law Collections from Mesopotamia and Asia Minor*, 85.

claiming that these "laws" are a report of what were, in fact, his own praiseworthy judicial responses to a long list of challenging offenses that he had adjudicated over the years. In keeping with this context, the last phrase of the prologue that introduces the first law and applies to all the others that follow is: "At that time [*inūmīšu*]." In other words, the laws are descriptions of what happened in the past. Accordingly, any preterite or perfect tense in the protasis of the first law and in all the following laws should be translated as past tense. Likewise, any durative found in the apodosis of the first law and in any following law should be translated as a modal past tense. For example, "If a man *committed robbery* [*iḫbutma*] and then *was caught* [*ittaṣbat*],[12] that man would be killed [*iddāk*]."

3.3 Major Verbal Paradigm

The verbal paradigm below is built on the 3cs verb form of *parāsum*. The following should be learned:

	Durative	Perfect	Preterite	Infinitive
G	*iparras*	*iptaras*	*iprus*	*parāsum*
D	*uparras*	*uptarris*	*uparris*	*purrusum*
Š	*ušapras*	*uštapris*	*ušapris*	*šuprusum*
N	*ipparras*	*ittapras*	*ipparis*	*naprusum*

3.3.1 ***Notes on* n.** The consonant *n* in Akkadian often assimilates to a following juxtaposed consonant. For example: **inparras* > *ipparras*. This characteristic of *n* is observed in other Semitic languages, including Hebrew. It should be noted, however, that in Akkadian *n* is less likely to assimilate if it is the final root consonant in a word. For example: *uktīnšu* in LH §1, *dînšu* in LH §5, and *ḫarrānša* in LH §141. In each of these three examples, the final syllable, -*šu* and -*ša*, is a pronominal suffix that has been added to words that have -*n* as their final root consonant.

3.4 Weak Verbal Roots: *'aleph*

In Akkadian, as in the other Semitic languages, some verbs have one or more root consonants that are weak. These weak verbs have an ', *w*, *y* (often written as *j* by Assyriologists of German background), or *n* among their root consonants. In this section, the discussion of weak verbs is limited to those involving ' because the first verb encountered in LH §1 (*abārum*) has as its first root consonant an '. This causes the verb to behave somewhat differently than the strong verb paradigms introduced above.

3.4.1 ***The Writing of 'aleph.*** Akkadian in the period of Old Babylonian does not explicitly represent ' in its script even though there is ample evidence for its existence in the language.[13] This apparent inadequacy of the cuneiform script may be a result of the fact that cuneiform was invented to

12. See, e.g., Richardson, *Hammurabi's Laws*, 49.
13. In Middle Babylonian and later periods, Akkadian had a special sign for ' with an adjacent vowel, , which was developed from the sign for *aḫ*, .

meet the needs of Sumerian, which is generally thought to lack an '.[14] Nevertheless, at times Akkadian indicates the presence of an ' by using signs involving *ḫ*.[15] In most cases, however, no special sign is used to indicate the presence of an '. Instead, the ' is merely implied by the use of an extra vowel sign (as in the case of *la-a-bu-um* for *la'bum* in LH §148) or simply by the juxtaposition of two different vowels (as in the case of *šu-a-ti*, which represents *šu'āti* in LH §2).[16]

3.4.2 ***The Sources of 'aleph in Akkadian.*** The ', whether explicitly written, implied, or quiescent, is frequently encountered in Akkadian because the Akkadian ' originates from seven different Proto-Semitic consonants (out of twenty-nine).[17] This fact can be inferred from comparisons with Hebrew and other cognate languages that retain some or all of those consonants. Akkadian grammars distinguish these seven different origins by using the following subscripts:

' = $'_1$
h = $'_2$
ḥ = $'_3$
ʿ = $'_4$
ǵ = $'_5$ (sometimes, however, an original *ǵ* became *ḫ* instead of $'_5$)[18]
w = $'_6$
y = $'_7$

By about 2000 BCE, probably under the influence of Sumerian, the first five Proto-Semitic guttural consonants listed above had all become a simple glottal stop in Akkadian, the '. The only exceptions are a few cases where an original *ǵ* became *ḫ*. The consonants *w* and *y* also became *'aleph*'s but only in situations where they are immediately followed by a consonant. These will be explained further in §4.5.

3.4.3 ***Vowel Attenuation and Babylonian Vowel Harmony.*** The expression "vowel attenuation" refers to cases where an original *a* or *ā* shifted to *e* or *ē*. This happens when an *a*-vowel is in close proximity to an original consonant *ḥ* ($'_3$) or ʿ ($'_4$), or sometimes *ǵ* ($'_5$).

For example, the Akkadian word for "father-in-law" was originally **ḥamum* (cf. *ḥām*, חָם).

14. It is generally recognized that the Sumerian origin of cuneiform analogously explains, for example, why Akkadian cuneiform at first failed to have any sign to represent the consonant *w*, since this phoneme also did not exist in Sumerian. Instead, Akkadian scribes used the signs for the other labial consonants to represent *w*. Ultimately, they settled on the sign for PI, , which was used from the period of Old Babylonian on to represent a *w* followed by any vowel. See above, §2.3.1. See also Jagersma, *Descriptive Grammar of Sumerian*, 33.

Some Sumerian scholars, especially Jagersma, have recently argued for the presence of a glottal stop in Sumerian. Foxvog (*Introduction to Sumerian*), appears to accept Jagersma's proposal. Similarly, Zólyomi (*An Introduction to the Grammar of Sumerian*, p. 10) builds on Jagersma but notes that the glottal stop was lost in Sumerian during the second half of the third millennium BCE.

15. In particular, the cuneiform sign that is used for *aḫ*, *eḫ*, *iḫ*, or *uḫ* can also represent *a'*, *e'*, *i'*, or *u'* as needed. Likewise the three signs for *ḫa*, , *ḫe*/*ḫi*, , and *ḫu*, can be used to represent *'a*, *'e*/ *'i*, and *'u* respectively. In such cases, some scholars transliterate these signs with their normal *ḫ* values, but they use uppercase letters to indicate the special use of this sign for '. For example, they write ḪA for the sign *ḫa* () when it represents *'a*. When *ḫa*, , *ḫe*/*ḫi*, , and *ḫu*, , are so used, it is customary to transliterate these signs as $'a_4$, *'i*, and $'u_5$. Examples of these uses are uncommon in LH but see a case of ḪA used in LH §221, ḪI in LH §39, and AḪ in LH §148.

16. Another means by which Akkadian in the period of Old Babylonian can imply the presence of an ' is through the use of "broken writing," although there are no examples of this practice in LH. Broken writing refers to a case where the cuneiform signs appear to imply that a non-initial syllable starts with a vowel. This happens when a (*c*)*vc* sign is immediately followed by a *v*(*c*) sign. See Huehnergard, *A Grammar of Akkadian*, §21.4.

17. Proto-Semitic refers to the hypothetical reconstructed ancestral language of Semitic languages.

18. These consonants, or others, may be unfamiliar to the reader. For their likely pronunciation see Appendix A.

By vowel attenuation *ḥamum >*ḥemum. Then, when most gutturals were lost in Akkadian, *ḥemum > *'$_3$emum. Then, by quiescing of all word-initial *'aleph*'s, *'$_3$emum > *emum.*

An original *a* or *ā* vowel elsewhere in a word that contains an *e* or *ē* likewise shifts to an *e* or *ē*. This attenuation of the *a*-vowel is termed "Babylonian vowel harmony." Babylonian vowel harmony does not apply, however, to the *a*-vowels in pronominal suffixes and in certain other suffixes when they are added to words that have an *e*-vowel.[19]

For example, the original feminine nominative plural word for "female owners" or "mistresses" was **ba'lātum* (cf. *ba'al*, בַּעַל). Because of vowel attenuation, the first *a* shifted to *e* because of the adjacent ': **ba'lātum* > **be'lātum*. Later, the original ' was lost and became an ': **be'lātum* > **be'$_4$lātum*. Subsequently, the ' quiesced causing compensatory lengthening of the adjacent *e*-vowel: **be'$_4$lātum* > **bêlātum*. Finally, by Babylonian vowel harmony, the *a*-vowel elsewhere in the word likewise shifts to an *e*-vowel: **bêlātum* > *bêlētum*.

3.4.4 ***Loss of Word-Initial 'aleph.*** In Akkadian an original ', regardless of its origin, is lost at the beginning of a word without any lengthening effect on the following vowel. For example, an original **'abum*, the Akkadian word for "father" (cf. *'āb*, אָב), had become *abum* by the time of Old Babylonian.[20]

The one exception to this rule about loss of an original word-initial ', is an initial *w* ('$_6$), which was usually maintained in Old Babylonian. So, for example, a word-initial *w* is observed in the verb *waṣûm*, "to go out," which appears in LH §4 (cf. *yāṣā'*, יָצָא—in Hebrew all I-*w* verbs became I-*y*).

Even though these word-initial original *'aleph*'s were lost, if they were '$_3$ (an original *ḥ*) or '$_4$ (an original '), before they disappeared they caused any proximate *a*-vowel to shift to an *e*-vowel.

As an example of this, consider the preposition *elî*, which means "on, upon, over, against" and which will appear later in LH §1. The word *elî* came about through at least the following five stages:[21]

'alay, the hypothesized original preposition meaning "on, upon, over, against," etc. (cf. *'al*, עַל, which came from the III-*y*/III-*h* verb *'ālâ*, עָלָה, "to go up," which has forms that preserve the original final *y*, such as *'ālîtî*, עָלִיתִי, "I went up."). *'alay* then became:

'elay (through vowel attenuation, as described in §3.4.3), which in turn became:

'$_4$elay (through the early loss of most of the Proto-Semitic guttural consonants, as described in §3.4.2), which in turn became:

elay (through the loss of word-initial ', as described in §3.4.4), which in turn became:

elî (through contraction of an original *ay* diphthong at the end of the word, which became *î*, as will be explained in §4.5).[22]

---

19. Among the other suffixes where Babylonian vowel harmony does not apply are the conjunctive or topicalizing suffix *-ma* (see §3.5 below), the ventive suffix *-am* (see §7.3), and the helping or linking *a*-vowel that is sometimes employed to attach a word to a pronominal suffix (see §8.2).

20. Most of these initial *'aleph*'s were present and acted as strong consonants in the period of Old Akkadian. See Gelb, *Old Akkadian Writing and Grammar.*

21. Similar to the negative particle *lâ*, which is sometimes written as *la-a* rather than *la*, probably as a historical spelling but perhaps as an indication of a final long vowel in some settings. Note that *elî* also has an attested variant spelling of *e-li-i*.

22. Most Assyriologists assume that this final long *î*, regardless of its origin, had become a short *i* in ordinary speech. Nevertheless, most are agreed that the *i*-vowel's original length is consistently restored when pronominal suffixes are added. Cf., e.g., Huehnergard, *A Grammar of Akkadian*, §10.3 and his Appendix C, §2(k), 593. The decision to mark this *i*-vowel as long or not whether it precedes a pronominal suffix or not is a matter of taste. In this textbook, for pedagogical reasons, it is consistently represented as long.

3.4.5 ***Vowel Contractions from Loss of an Intervocalic 'aleph.*** In Akkadian, elision of an intervocalic ' is frequent. Hence $v_1'v_2$ often becomes v_1v_2, and v_1v_2 often results in vowel contraction, where the two vowels combine into a tilde long vowel.

There are only four vowels in Akkadian (*a, e, i, u*), which can be long or short, so in theory there are sixty-four possible permutations for vowel contraction.[23] Thankfully, the vast majority of these vowel contractions follow three simple rules:

1. *ā/ē + i/ī > ẽ*. This contraction of the *a-i* vowel sequence is analogous to what is observed in Hebrew with a word like *bayit*, בַּיִת, "house," which in construct becomes *bêt*, בֵּית, "house of." So, for example, *ā + i > ẽ*.
2. (*e/ē* or *i/ī*) + (*a/ā*) > *e/i + a/ā*. In other words, if a short or long *e* or a short or long *i* is followed by a short or long *a*-vowel, the first vowel shortens, but the two vowels remain uncontracted. Although Assyriologists agree that the two vowels remain uncontracted and that the first vowel is always shortened, it is a matter of taste whether to assume, as does this textbook, that whenever juxtaposed vowels remain uncontracted, the original intervocalic ' is preserved. So, for example, *i + a > i'a*.[24]
3. In every other case, $v_1/\bar{v}_1 + v_2/\bar{v}_2 > \tilde{v}_2$. So, for example, *ā + u > ũ*.

3.4.5.1 *I-'aleph Verbs and Vowel Contraction*—Exceptions to the above patterns will be noted as they occur. One of the most significant exceptions, however, concerns I-' verbs. In these verbs, any time the original ' would be expected to appear between two vowels, the ' and the vowel that follows it are lost without lengthening the preceding vowel. Presumably, the reason for this otherwise unexpected exception is that it preserves the opening preformative vowel, which in verbal forms has crucial grammatical significance.

3.4.6 ***The Quiescing of 'aleph and Compensatory Lengthening of an Adjacent Vowel.*** As mentioned in §3.4.4 above, an original word-initial ' normally quiesces without any lengthening effect on the following vowel. This is not the case, however, in most other situations where an original ' immediately follows or precedes a vowel. In these cases, when an original ' quiesces within a word, or at its end, it results in compensatory lengthening of the adjacent vowel, which is then marked with a circumflex: *v̂*.[25]

3.5 The Enclitic *-ma*

In Akkadian, a suffix *-ma* is at times attached to a word. When present, it lengthens the vowel of any word ending in a short vowel. As a result, the syllable before the *-ma* is invariably accented. If the last syllable of the word ends with the consonant *-n* or *-b* (less often *-p*) these final consonants assimilate to the *m* of the enclitic, resulting in *-mma*.[26]

23. For the purpose of these rules of contraction, the source of vowel length does not matter.

24. Other Assyriologists, however, assume that the intervocalic ' has quiesced but without the expected compensatory lengthening of the preceding vowel: *ī'a > ia*.

25. See §2.5.2.1.

26. In such cases, the scribes sometimes choose to spell the word with a historical spelling or what is sometimes called a "morphographemic" spelling, as if this assimilation had not taken place.

The enclitic *-ma* has two main alternative functions. Either it functions as a conjunction that connects clauses, or it is a topicalizing particle that emphasizes the word to which it is attached.

3.5.1 If *-ma* is attached to a finite verb, it normally functions as a conjunction that connects clauses. In this situation it is usually translated "and," "but," "and so," or "and then," according to the context. In other words, the suffix *-ma* marks the verb of a clause that is logically subordinate to or temporally prior to the clause that follows. In some cases, the clause that follows may be a purpose or result clause.[27]

3.5.2 If *-ma* is attached to a non-verb, it is typically not a conjunction. Instead, it functions as a topicalizing particle that places emphasis on the non-verb to which it is attached. In a verbless clause, for example, an enclitic *-ma* may be used to mark the predicate nominative.

Occasionally an enclitic *-ma* is attached to a verb for the purpose of topicalizing the verb, rather than having its more usual function with verbs as a conjunction. This emphasizing purpose is most obvious when the clause to which it belongs is not followed by a related clause, and as such a conjunction is unexpected.

3.6 Conjunction *u*

The coordinating conjunction *u*, like *-ma*, may be translated "and" or "but." The difference between *u* and *-ma* is that *-ma*, when used as a conjunction, is only used to connect clauses, whereas *u* can be used to connect either clauses or noun phrases. Furthermore, when clauses are connected with *-ma* there is a logical or temporal order between them, with the first clause logically subordinated to or temporally prior to the following clause. When clauses are connected with *u*, on the other hand, they have equal weight, and they could be reversed in their order without changing the meaning.

3.7 Homework

Before you move on, be sure to understand the four main verb stems (G, D, Š, and N) and the three finite prefix tenses (durative, perfect, and preterite). Weak verbs, such as I-', are not uncommon and deviate from the strong verb paradigms. As such, rules associated with I-' verbs should become familiar and learned early on in order to properly parse and translate LH. Finally, learn to recognize enclitic *-ma* and conjunction *u*.

Note: In this chapter, and in each succeeding chapter, it is assumed that you have either already learned or you will be learning in the current chapter all the grammar, cuneiform signs, and vocabulary that are needed in order to transliterate, normalize, and accurately translate the assigned readings. At any point where additional information may be needed, it will be given.

27. The suffix *-ma* when used as a conjunction is curiously similar in its effect to the *wa* + doubling prefix on the consecutive preterite in Hebrew. The Hebrew prefix is likewise translated "and" or "and then," etc. and is used to mark logical or chronological consecution.

3.7.1 *Signs*

 3

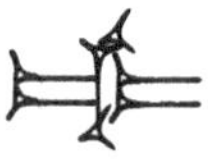 *ub, up*

 *ud, ut, uṭ, tam*

 KÙ.BABBAR, *kaspum*, "silver"; KÙ means "pure, holy," referring to a precious metal, and BABBAR means "white"; BABBAR is the same sign as UD, which means "day"

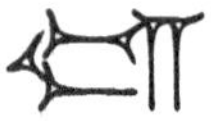 *lam*

 *er, ir*

 *šu* (ŠU is the Sumerian word for "hand." This sign originally depicted a hand. Can you see it?)

3.7.2 *Vocabulary*

abum = father (cf. *'āb*, אָב, "father")
elî = on, upon, over, against, beyond, than (in comparisons) (cf. *'al*, עַל, "on, upon, over, against," from the III-*y* and III-*h* verb *'ālâ*, עָלָה)
kaspum = silver (cf. *kesep*, כֶּסֶף)
-*ma* = an enclitic particle; when attached to a verb, "and (then), but, so"; when attached to a noun, it topicalizes the noun
nêrtum = (f) murder
parāsum = to divide, separate, cut (off); to decide (cf. *pāras*, פָּרַס, *qal*: "to break [bread]"; *hiphil*: "to divide, split [hoofs]")
u = and, but (cf. *wə/û*, וְ/וּ)

Congratulations! If you learn the six words (not counting the suffix -*ma*) in this chapter and each of the nine words in the preceding chapters, you will be able to read 21 percent of all the Akkadian words that appear in LH §§1–20, 127–149.

3.7.3 *Exercises*

1. Identify Signs: Using the signs that have already been learned, identify the five signs below. If a sign has been forgotten, see the sign list in Appendix C. Provide all possible values for each sign, then check your answer in Appendix F.

LH §1 V:27

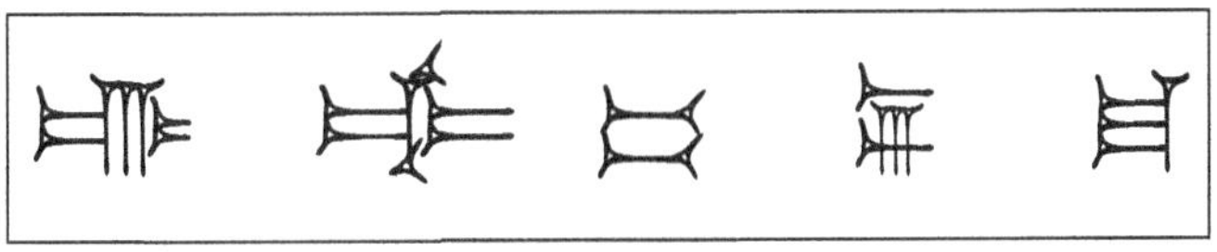

2. Transliterate and Normalize: As was noted above, the signs here are expected to form a verb (following S-O-V word order). The *-ma* ending the verb is the enclitic *-ma*. This implies that the first four signs represent the verb itself. Based on the learned vocabulary thus far, it is likely that the verb is *abārum* (from Chapter 2). Give the correct transliteration for the five signs. In other words, in the case of signs that have more than one value, decide which is the correct value here. Then, using this information, normalize the signs, and check your answer in Appendix F.

3. Parse and Translate: Only two root letters are apparent in the normalization of the signs above, *b* and *r*. The missing root letter is an original first ʾ, but the ʾ has quiesced without further vowel lengthening. Using the rules of Akkadian verbs introduced above, parse and translate the verb. Note the doubling of the middle root consonant. Indicate the verb stem, tense, person, and number. Check your answer in Appendix F.

4. LH §1 V:26–27: Provide a translation of the text learned thus far. See Appendix F to check your answer.

4–

Syllabification, Pronominal Suffixes, Vowel Classes for Verbs, and Weak *w* and *y*

This chapter will introduce rules of syllabification in Akkadian, classes of consonants, and pronominal suffixes for nouns and verbs. Vowel classes and theme vowels for verbs will also be explained. Finally, weak verb forms with *w* and *y* will be further explained in order to continue translating the text in LH §1 V:28 and 29.

4.1 Syllabification

In Proto-Semitic it is assumed that every syllable had one and only one vowel (*a*, *i*, or *u*—each of which could be either short or long), and that every syllable began with one and only one consonant, and that every syllable was either an open syllable, *cv*, or a closed syllable, *cvc*.

Hebrew only rarely deviates from these patterns. One deviation is seen in those instances where a syllable is doubly closed at the end of a word (cvc_1c_2#).[1] For example, the Hebrew verb שָׁאַלְתְּ, *šāʾalt*, "you (fs) asked" in 1 Samuel 1:17, has a doubly closed final syllable. This exception came about because of the loss of an earlier unaccented final short vowel. In this case, the form originally ended in an unaccented short *i*. The original *i*-vowel is restored and lengthened, however, when object suffixes are added.[2]

In Akkadian, similarly, there are three rules for syllabification.

1. Every syllable has one and only one vowel: *a*, *e*, *i*, or *u*—each of which can be either long or short. Although the *e*-vowel is phonemic in Akkadian, in each case it arose from either an original *a* or an *i*.
2. Every syllable begins with a single consonant, with only one exception. At the beginning of a word a syllable may begin with a vowel, but only because it lost an original word-initial ʾ. See §3.4.4.

   Some scholars, however, recognize another exception. Accordingly, a syllable may begin with a vowel within a word if that vowel is juxtaposed with a different vowel in a situation like $cv_1v_2(c)$. Others, including the author of this book, assume that in cases like this an ʾ is present between the two juxtaposed different vowels even though it is not explicitly indicated in cuneiform.

1. The character # is commonly used in linguistics to mark the end of a word.

2. Also compare, for example, יְלִדְתִּנִי, *yəlidtīnî*, "you bore me," in Jeremiah 15:10. Other rare exceptions in Hebrew include the form of the conjunction וּ, *û*, "and," found before bilabial consonants and any consonant followed by *šəwa*. A still less common exception is the Hebrew word for "two," שְׁתַּיִם, *štayim*, and related forms that begin with a consonantal cluster.

For example, some Assyriologists normalize the demonstrative pronoun *šuāti* ("that"), but others, along with this textbook, normalize the pronoun as *šu'āti.*

3. Finally, every syllable in Akkadian is either open (*cv*) or closed with a single consonant (*cvc*). There are no cases where a cluster of two or more consonants comes at the beginning of a syllable or at its end.

4.2 Akkadian Consonants

As has already been observed, cuneiform signs frequently have multiple values, such as 𒁉, which may mean *bi, bé, pé,* or *pí.* These different values of one sign follow predictable phonetic categorization. Review the chart below and notice that all the values of 𒁉 begin with a labial.

	Voiced	Voiceless	Emphatic/Glottalic
Dentals	d	t	ṭ
Velars	g	k	q (= ḳ)
Sibilants	z	s	ṣ
Labials	b	p	

In the Old Babylonian cuneiform representation for these consonants, the same sign is often used to represent syllables that begin with a voiced, voiceless, or emphatic variant of the same type of consonant, and the same sign is invariably used with syllables that end with a voiced, voiceless, or emphatic variant of the same type of consonant.

For example, although *ba* (𒁀) and *pa* (𒉺) are consistently distinguished in cuneiform, *bu* (𒁍) and *pu* (𒁍) are not. On the other hand, *ad* (𒀜), *at* (𒀜), and *aṭ* (𒀜) all employ the same sign.

4.3 Pronominal Suffixes

Pronominal suffixes may be attached to a verb, a noun, or a preposition. When attached to a verb, they may function as a direct object (accusative) or as an indirect object (dative). When pronominal suffixes are attached to a noun, they often express possession (genitive). In other contexts, however, they can be used as an objective or subjective genitive where they function either as the implied object of the verbal idea or the implied subject. Finally, when pronominal suffixes are attached to a preposition, they are the object of the preposition.

The full paradigm for pronominal suffixes is below. The vast majority of cases in LH, however, are third-person forms. So for now, learn the third-person forms marked in bold below.

	Genitive (with nouns and prepositions)	Dative (with verbs)	Accusative (with verbs)
1cs	*-ī, -ya, 'a*	*-am, -m, -nim*	*-ni*
2ms	*-ka*	*-kum*	*-ka*

(continued)

	Genitive (with nouns and prepositions)	Dative (with verbs)	Accusative (with verbs)
2fs	*-ki*	*-kim*	*-ki*
3ms	***-šu***	***-šum***	***-šu***
3fs	***-ša***	***-šim***	***-ši***
1cp	*-ni*	*-ni'āšim*	*-ni'āti*
2mp	*-kunu*	*-kunūšim*	*-kunūti*
2fp	*-kina*	*-kināšim*	*-kināti*
3mp	***-šunu***	***-šunūšim***	***-šunūti***
3fp	***-šina***	***-šināšim***	***-šināti***

In the case of the genitive 1cs pronominal suffix, the *-ī* form is normal. The *-ya* alternative form is found after nouns in the genitive singular or oblique (genitive-accusative) plural. For example, *ḫulqiyami*, "my lost property," in LH §9. In these cases *-ya* is normally written with the cuneiform sign for *i'a*, 𒅀. After the *-ū* of the nominative plural of a noun or adjective, the *-ya* suffix sometimes becomes an *-'a*. For example, *mârū'a*, "my children," in LH §170.

In the case of the dative 1cs pronominal suffix, the *-am* form is normal. After a 2fs verb that ends in *-ī*, the dative suffix is just *-m*, and after *-ū* or *-ā* suffixes of the 3p and 2p forms of the verb, the dative suffix is *-nim*. When *-nim* is added it causes the final long *-ū* or *-ā* to be preserved, just as happens when pronominal suffixes are added to words ending in these vowels (see §7.3).

Verbs can have both a dative and an accusative pronominal suffix. When they do, the dative always comes first. When a 1cs dative form is used, however, the final *-m* assimilates to the following consonant. Since the consonant *m* does not normally assimilate, this case of assimilation supports the assumption that the final *-m* of the dative 1cs suffix was in fact originally an *-n*.

4.3.1 ***Reciprocal Assimilation of Dental and Sibilant Consonants before š.*** When a pronominal suffix starting with *š* is added to a word ending in a consonant that is a dental (*d, t, ṭ*) or a sibilant (*s, ṣ, š, z*), both the final consonant and the *š* of the suffix each assimilate to produce *-ss-*.[3] This is termed "reciprocal assimilation."

For example, in LH §117 there is a reference to "his wife." The word for "wife" is *aššatum* (cf. *'iššâ*, אִשָּׁה). To write "his wife," one first removes the case ending *-um* (see §8.1 for further explanation on removing case endings as it relates to "bound" or "construct" forms of the noun). After the case ending is removed the genitive pronominal suffix for "his" is added, *-šu*. This would result in **aššatšu*, but according to this rule for the reciprocal assimilation of dentals and sibilants before *š*, the correct result for "his wife" is *aššassu*.

3. There are no exceptions to this rule within LH. Elsewhere, however, there are cases where the scribes chose to write the word as if assimilation had not yet taken place. These are termed "historical spellings." For more on this practice, see §2.5.1.4.

4.3.2 ***Pronominal Suffixes Attached to a Preposition.*** Only certain prepositions take pronominal suffixed forms. For example, this is the case for the preposition *elî* learned in Chapter 2, but it is not the case for *ana*, "to, for," which will be learned in the present chapter.[4]

Since prepositions in Akkadian govern words in the genitive case, those which employ pronominal suffixes understandably use genitive forms for those suffixes, as listed in §4.3.[5] When a pronominal suffix is added to a preposition that ends in a short vowel, that vowel is lengthened (or its earlier length is restored). So, for example, if an Akkadian author wants to write "upon him," using the preposition *elî*, all that is needed is to add the correct suffix taken from the chart in §4.3, *šu*.[6]

Since cuneiform does not usually or consistently reflect vowel length, the evidence for this assertion that the final vowel of the preposition *elî* is long, at least before a pronominal suffix, is necessarily indirect. One argument in support, however, is based on the rule of vowel syncope presented in §2.5.2.3. The rule of vowel syncope states that Akkadian normally does not permit two or more non-final open syllables with short vowels in a row. Whenever this happens, the problem is resolved by elision of the second short vowel. As applied to the present case, if the final *i* in *elî* were short after a pronominal suffix is added, as in *elišu*, the rule of vowel syncope would require the second vowel to quiesce, resulting in *elšu*.

This predicted form, however, is unattested. Instead, in every appearance of *elî* with a pronominal suffix, the cuneiform writing proves that its *i*-vowel continues to be present. There are only two ways to explain this. Either the *i*-vowel is long and therefore the rule of vowel syncope is inapplicable, or this must constitute a surprising exception to the rule of vowel syncope.

If the evidence is stated this way, it may seem like this is a very strong argument. Unfortunately, there are other undisputed examples of situations where, for little or no apparent reason, the rule of vowel syncope does not apply. So pronominal suffixes on prepositions ending in a short vowel could be just one more such exception.

This textbook, however, follows those Assyriologists who hold that the final vowels of prepositions are in fact lengthened, or that they have an earlier length restored before a pronominal suffix.[7] As a matter of consistency, it should be noted that the same approach to vowel lengthening before a suffix was taken earlier in §3.5, where it is stated that when the enclitic *-ma* is added to a form ending in a short vowel, that vowel is lengthened (or has its length restored). Likewise, a similar approach will be taken in a number of analogous situations in the following chapters.[8]

Finally, it needs to be mentioned that Babylonian vowel harmony (see §3.4.3), by which *a*

---

4. Of the prepositions that appear in LH, the following can be used with a pronominal suffix: *aššum*, "because of, concerning" (*Note:* A long *ī* is added between the preposition and its pronominal suffix, as in *aššumīšu*.); *balūm*, "without" (*Note:* The final *-m* acts like *-n*, and as such it assimilates with the suffix, as in *baluššu*.); *elî*, "on, upon, over, against"; *itti*, "with," and *warki*, "after."

5. As with all other prepositions, the preposition *ana*, "to, for," governs nouns in the genitive case. Unexpectedly, however, when it governs an independent pronoun, the pronoun is in the dative case. There are no instances of this in LH.

6. Assyriologists typically normalize this preposition as *eli* because there is reason to believe that final vowels like this had become short in ordinary speech. Nevertheless, there is general agreement that a final short vowel like this was in fact lengthened, or had its length restored, before pronominal suffixes (whether one chooses to normalize this *i*-vowel as long or not). Cf., e.g., Huehnergard (*A Grammar of Akkadian*, §10.3), who marks it with a macron, *ī*.

7. Cf., e.g., Caplice, *Introduction to Akkadian*, §84i, and Huehnergard, *A Grammar of Akkadian*, §10.3.

8. As will be discussed in §7.3, a similar case of vowel lengthening (or the restoration of the length a vowel had at a prior stage in the language) occurs when the so-called "ventive" suffix *-nim* is added to a verbal form ending in a vowel. Additionally, a similar need for vowel lengthening before pronominal suffixes will be seen with nouns and verbs in §8.2 and §19.1. Finally, in §13.3 there will be vowel lengthening before the suffix *-mi*, a particle that indicates direct discourse.

or *ā* vowels, when in a word that contains *e* or *ē*, shift to *e/ē*, does not apply to the *a*-vowels in pronominal suffixes when they are added to a word having an *e*-vowel.

4.4 The Four Main Vowel Classes (*a/u, a, i, u*) of Verbs

In the vocabulary for this chapter there are a number of verbs that have vowels after them that are placed in parentheses. Consider, for example, *šalāmum* (*i,i*), which means "to be well, whole, safe." These vowels within parentheses identify the vowel class of each verb—in this case it is a verb belonging to the *i*-class. The vowel class of each verb does not need to be memorized. Most verbs belong to the so-called ablaut class, or *a,u*-vowel class of the paradigm verb *parāsum*. This means that their theme vowel (the vowel after the middle consonant) in the G-durative and G-perfect tenses is *a*, while their theme vowel in the G-preterite is *u*. It likewise means that the theme vowel for their N-durative and N-perfect is also *a*. If a verb belongs to one of the other vowel classes, it will have, according to its class, either an *a, i,* or *u* as its theme vowel in all three G prefix tenses and also in two of the N prefix tenses, namely the durative and perfect.

The chart below summarizes this. Students should begin to memorize this chart in order to become familiar with the various forms.

Stem	Class	Durative 3cs	Perfect 3cs	Preterite 3cs
G	*a,u*	*iparras*	*iptaras*	*iprus*
	a	*iṣabbat*	*iṣṣabat*[9]	*iṣbat*
	i	*išallim*	*ištalim*	*išlim*
	u	*iballuṭ*	*ibtaluṭ*	*ibluṭ*
D		*uparras*	*uptarris*	*uparris*
Š		*ušapras*	*uštapris*	*ušapris*
N	*a,u*	*ipparras*	*ittapras*	*ipparis*
	a	*iṣṣabbat*	*ittaṣbat*	*iṣṣabit*
	i	*iššallim*	*ittašlim*	*iššalim*
	u	*ibballuṭ*	*ittabluṭ*	*ibbaliṭ*

Notes:

1. The vowel classes apply only to the G-stem and N-stem. In the case of the N-stem, they apply only to the durative and perfect, since all verbs are, in effect, *i*-class for N-stem preterite.
2. The *a*-theme vowel appears in the durative and perfect for the *a,u*-class verbs in the G-stem and N-stem, while the *u*-theme vowel appears only in the preterite. On the other hand, all verbs are, in effect, *a,i* class in both the D-stem and Š-stem, but the *a*-theme vowel applies only to the durative, while the *i*-theme vowel applies to both the perfect and preterite.

9. *iṣṣabat* < **iṣtabat*. See §13.5 for the explanation for why an infixed *-t-* assimilates to an adjacent dental or sibilant (other than *š*) and partially assimilates to an adjacent *g* by becoming *d*.

These observations are summarized in the following chart:

Stem	Class	Durative 3cs	Perfect 3cs	Preterite 3cs	
G	*a,u*	*iparras*	*iptaras*	*iprus*	
	a	*iṣabbat*	*iṣṣabat*	*iṣbat*	
	i	*išallim*	*ištalim*	*išlim*	
	u	*iballuṭ*	*ibtaluṭ*	*ibluṭ*	
D	(*a, i*) class	*uparras*	*uptarris*	*uparris*	
Š		*ušapras*	*uštapris*	*ušapris*	
N	*a,u*	*ipparras*	*ittapras*	*ipparis*	
	a	*iṣṣabbat*	*ittaṣbat*	*iṣṣabit*	(*i*)-class
	i	*iššallim*	*ittašlim*	*iššalim*	
	u	*ibballuṭ*	*ittabluṭ*	*ibbaliṭ*	

4.5 Semi-Vocalic Consonants *w* and *y*

As was mentioned in Chapter 3 (§3.4.2), five of the Proto-Semitic guttural consonants had already coalesced into ’ and had nearly disappeared by the time of Old Babylonian. Two additional non-guttural consonants, *w* and *y*, were also well on their way to a similar result. This is why these two consonants are also often identified as varieties of the ’:

w = ’$_6$
y = ’$_7$

In general, the consonants *w* and *y* had become *’aleph*’s within words by the period of Old Babylonian. Word-initial *w*, however, was often preserved, such as in the case of *waṣûm* (*i,i*), “to go out” (cf. *yāṣā’*, יָצָא), although sometimes word-initial *w* is lost even in the period of Old Babylonian. Note that word-initial *w* is almost entirely lost in Hebrew except in the case of the conjunction *wə* (וְ), and a few rare words.

Word-initial *y, on the other hand, was regularly lost like ’ without compensatory lengthening of the initial vowel. For example, the D-stem durative 3ms of *parāsum* was originally **yuparras*, but this had become *uparras* by the period of Old Babylonian. Word-initial **ya*-, however, became *i*. For example, the G-stem preterite 3ms of *parāsum* was originally **yaprus*, which then became *iprus*. It is worth noting that the earlier form **yaprus* relates directly to the Hebrew *qal* imperfect 3ms form *yiqṭōl*, יִקְטֹל. This parallel may not be immediately apparent, but the *ō*-theme vowel in Hebrew is categorized as the normal *u*-type changeable vowel for accented or near-open syllables. As for the preformative *i*-vowel, it is known that it was originally an *a*-type vowel (Barth-Ginsberg Law), which then shifted to *i*.[10] The original *a*-vowel is preserved when it is in an open syllable, as in *yāqûm*, יָקוּם, or before a guttural, as in *ya‘ămōd*, יַעֲמֹד.

Both *w* and *y* quiesced in situations where they were immediately followed by another consonant (see §3.4.2). In such situations, again exactly like ’, *w* and *y* cause the previous vowel to experience compensatory lengthening. For example, a syllable that originally ended with

10. Hasselbach, “Barth-Ginsberg Law,” 258–59.

**-ew* or **-ey* became a syllable ending with *-ê*. If, however, the vowel before the *w* or *y* happens to be *a*, the following changes result:

**ay* > *î* (cf., e.g., how **baytum*, "house," became *bîtum*)
**aw* > *û* (cf., e.g., how **mawtum*, "death," became *mûtum*)

Finally, although in most situations *w* and *y* became *'aleph*'s and as such either disappeared without a trace or quiesced with compensatory lengthening, in a few situations these consonants were preserved at least during the Old Babylonia period.

There are two situations where, for example, *w* is often preserved. One has already been mentioned, namely word-initial *w*. The second situation in which *w* is regularly preserved is when it is immediately followed by another *w*, as in *nuwwurim*, "to illumine," in LH §Pro 1:44.[11] Finally, the consonant *w* is sometimes preserved within words, but only when it starts a syllable, such as in the words *awīlum*, "man, person, citizen (a free man)" and *awâtum*, "word."

There are also two situations where the consonant *y* is often preserved. The first situation is when one *y* is immediately followed by another *y*. The sequence *-yy-* is expressed in the cuneiform by *-a-a-*,  (cf., e.g., *dayyānum*, "a judge," in LH §5). The second situation where the consonant *y* is occasionally preserved is when it appears before the vowel *a*. This happens especially in the case of the pronominal suffix *-ya*, "my." In these situations, *ya* is expressed by the cuneiform combined sign for *ia*, .

4.6 Homework

Before you move on, be sure to understand the three syllabification rules of Akkadian. Be able to recognize pronominal suffixes, especially third-person forms, and understand the rules of assimilation and vowel lengthening. Also, become familiar with the four main vowel classes for verbs. And finally, continue to become comfortable with weak verbs in Akkadian.

4.6.1 *Signs*

 4, *ṣa, za, sà*

 *e*

 *de, di, ṭe, ṭi* (values with *e* or *ṭ* are less common)

 *ed, et, eṭ, id, it, iṭ* (values with *e* or *ṭ* are less common)

 *le, li*

 *em, im*

 *ne*

11. As commonly happens, the cuneiform in this line explicitly indicates only one of the *w*'s with the sign for *wu*, .

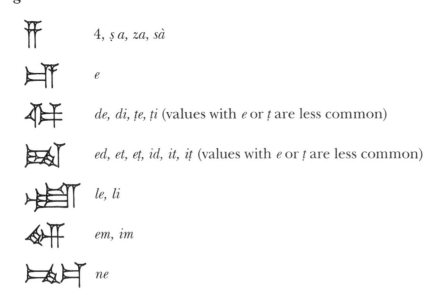

Congratulations! If you have learned the seven cuneiform signs in this chapter and each of the preceding twenty signs, you will be able to read 41 percent of all the cuneiform signs in LH §§1–20, 127–149.

4.6.2 *Vocabulary*

ana = to, for
dākum (< *d-w-k*) (*a,u*) = to kill, execute (outside LH also: to crush; cf. *dûk*, דּוּךְ, "to pound"; *dākā'*, דָּכָא, *piel*: "to crush"; *dākâ*, דָּכָה, *piel*: "to crush")
kānum (< *k-w-n*) (*u,u*) = G: to be firm; D: to establish, make secure, prove, have proof, convict (cf. *kûn*, כּוּן, *niphal*: "to be firm"; *polel*: "to make firm, establish")
kišpū (always plural) = witchcraft, sorcery (cf. *kāšap*, כָּשַׁף, *piel*: "to practice sorcery")
nadûm (< *n-d-y*) (*i,i*) = throw, hurl, accuse (lay a charge of), leave (cf. *nādâ*, נָדָה, *piel*: "to throw out, to exclude")
šalāmum (*i,i*) = to be well, whole, safe; D: to make whole, make restitution; heal; pay back in full (cf. *šālēm*, שָׁלֵם, "to be complete, sound")

4.6.3 *Exercises*

1. Identify Signs: Using the signs that have already been learned, identify each of the nine signs below and include all the listed possible values of each. If a sign has been forgotten, see the sign list in Appendix C. Check your answer using Appendix F.

LH §1 V:28

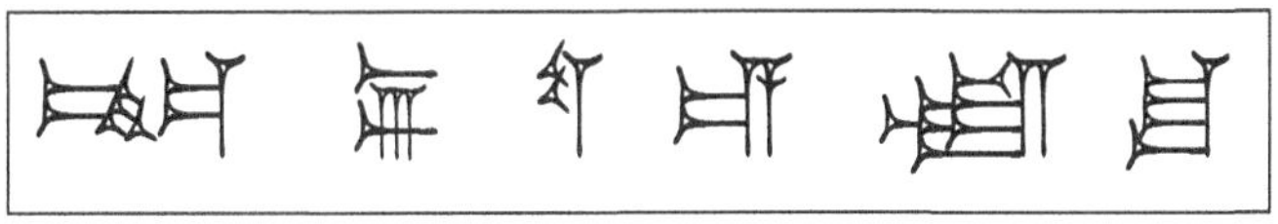

LH §1 V:29

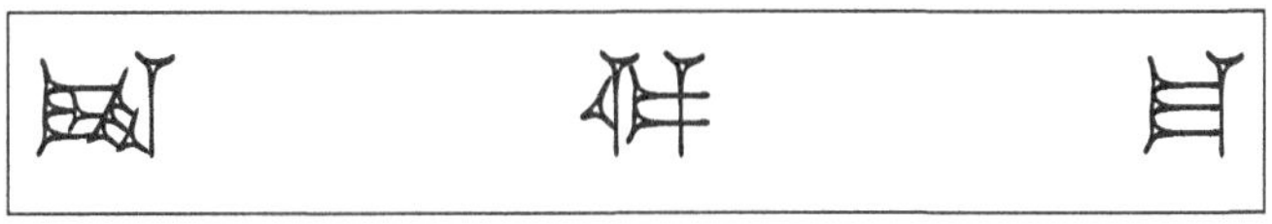

2. Transliterate: In order to offer a correct transliteration, it is necessary to know the relevant vocabulary and grammar introduced thus far. See the notes below for additional help. After working through the notes below and attempting your own transliteration, check your answer in Appendix F.

Note: The first two signs in V:28, 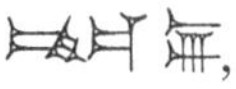, have adjacent vowels. In §2.5.1.1 the scribal practice of syllable splitting was discussed. The reader needs to undo this practice of syllable splitting and put together any split syllables. In this case, it is straightforward. Since the first sign is transliterated as *ne* with an ending *e*-vowel, what vowel must the second sign begin with?

Note: In the signs above,  could be transliterated as either *ud, ut, uṭ* or *tam*. Based on §4.1 above, however, no syllable within a word can begin with a vowel. Hence, in this situation where the previous sign is a *vc*-sign and ending in a consonant, what is the only value that  can have in this context?

Note: The three signs in V:29 constitute a verb + the enclitic *-ma*. The verb is a G-stem preterite 3cs of *nadûm*. The verb belongs to a type of verb that is called III-weak because the third root of its original root consonants, *n-d-y*, quiesced into an ʾ. III-weak verbs will be studied in detail in Chapter 16.

Using the transliteration of this verb and the enclitic *-ma* suffix, and using what you know about the G-stem preterite 3cs of the paradigm verb *parāsum*, try to normalize the verb. Try to explain in detail how a verb with the original root consonants *n-d-y* came to be spelled in the way that you are normalizing. Check your answer in Appendix F.

3. Normalize: Normalize the transliteration. Check your answer in Appendix F.

4. Translate: Translate V:28–29. Add your translation of V:26–27.

Wordplay on "Hammurapi"[1]

Bill T. Arnold

The etymological specifics of Hammurapi's name are famously obscure.[2] The two components are most likely *ḫammu-* and *-rap/bi*, both of which present problems of interpretation. Assuming a West Semitic or Amorite origin for the name (by no means a certainty), we may also assume that the first element is "paternal uncle" or "kinsman," meaning "Divine Kinsman," an element occurring in more than two hundred Amorite personal names[3] and often in Israelite personal names, such as Moses's father Amram, Jeroboam, and Rehoboam.[4] The second element of Hammurapi's name is "he/it heals" if read with *p* but "mighty" if read with *b*. If the royal name *ʿmrp* attested at Ugarit is cognate (again, not a certainty), then we may conclude that Hammurapi's name is *ʿammu* + *rapi*, "The (Divine) Kinsman Heals."[5]

While we may never know the specifics of the personal name, I propose here a subtle soundalike play on the name, hidden in plain sight in the prologue to the famous LH. The introduction marches relentlessly along, listing the royal attributes and praiseworthy accomplishments of the great king, reaching a triumphant climax in the claim that Hammurapi established truth and justice as the rule of the land (V:20–23). Along the way to this conclusion, Hammurapi claims *mušēpī kīnātim mušūšir ammi*, "[I am the king] who proclaims truth, who puts the people in order" (IV:53–54). The rare term *ammu*, "people," is clearly a West Semitic loanword appearing only in Old Babylonian (*AHw* 44; *CAD* A 2:77). Although we will never be certain how the ancient Amorite phonemes might have been heard and understood by Old Babylonian speakers, this particular spelling of the noun *ammu* (*am-mi*, LH IV:54) most likely reflects an initial voiced pharyngeal ʿ, and therefore represents the West Semitic "people" or "uncle, kinsman." On the other hand, a textual variant preserved on a clay tablet at the Louvre uses a different sign than that found on the stela, where we find *ḫa-am-mi* for *am-mi*,[6] sounding even closer to the pronunciation of the king's name on the stela: *ḫa-am-mu-ra-pí* (I:50).

Perhaps the scribes devoted to satisfying so megalomaniacal a patron as Hammurapi used this quaint turn of phrase to aver that even the king's name adumbrated the way he would put "the people in order" by providing truth and justice. We have other examples of puns embedded in colophonic types of paronomasia in which scribes or authors form a pun upon a name when the personage in view is not mentioned in the near context but stands in the background or at a distance in the text.[7] More broadly, these might be thought of as appellative puns because they can occur on proper nouns

1. The essay here is derived with permission from an earlier publication. See Bill T. Arnold, "Wordplay on 'Hammurapi' in CH iv 54," *NABU* 2016.2 §43.

2. The present grammar follows the majority of current Assyriologists who choose to use the spelling "Hammurabi" while recognizing the evidence is still indecisive. In support of the spelling "Hammurabi," see *CANE* 2, 902.

3. Ignace J. Gelb, *Computer-Aided Analysis of Amorite*, Assyriological Studies 21 (Chicago: University of Chicago Press, 1980), 92–95 and 260–264; Edward Lipínski, "*ʿam*," *TDOT* 11:164–70.

4. A. R. Hulst, "*ʿam/gôy* people," *TLOT* 2:896–919.

5. Bill T. Arnold, *Who Were the Babylonians?* SBLABS 10 (Leiden: Brill, 2005), 42; Jack M. Sasson, "King Hammurabi of Babylon," in *CANE* 2, 901–15.

6. J. Nougayrol, "Le prologue du code Hammourabien d'après une tablette inédite du Louvre," *RA* 45 (1951): 66–79.

7. Moshe Garsiel, "Puns upon Names: Subtle Colophons in the Bible," *JBQ* 23 (1995): 182–87.

more generally, not just personal names.[8] In a similar way, this line of the prologue (LH IV:54) may be cleverly avowing that the great "Kinsman-Heals" has himself healed his people by ordering them with truth and justice. And we should assume that listeners to an oral presentation of this prologue would have immediately caught the phonemic affiliation.

8. Scott B. Noegel, private communiqué.

5–

Verbal Nouns, Participles, Verbal Adjectives, and Statives

In addition to the three prefix tenses that were presented in Chapter 3, namely the durative, the perfect, and the preterite, there are five other verbal forms in Akkadian. This chapter will introduce four of those five.[1] Three of the verbal forms that will be introduced in this chapter, the infinitive, the participle, and the verbal adjective, are verbal nouns or adjectives. Because none of these is a finite verb, they are not inflected to agree with their subject in terms of person, and they do not have tense or aspect. The fourth verbal form treated in this chapter, the stative, is a finite verb. Unlike the three prefix tenses presented in Chapter 3, the stative is a suffix tense. The exercises in this chapter will conclude LH §1 with V:30, 31, and 32.

5.1 Infinitives (Verbal Nouns)

As mentioned earlier, the infinitive is traditionally the form of the verb used in Akkadian lexica. When a verb is attested in the G-stem, lexica use the G-stem infinitive, for example, *parāsum*, "to divide, separate, cut (off); to decide."[2] Otherwise, as is the practice of the *Chicago Assyrian Dictionary* (*CAD*), verbs are typically listed under the infinitive of whichever stem is most characteristic for the verb, while a cross reference to that form is provided from a hypothetical G-stem infinitive.

Akkadian infinitives are masculine singular verbal nouns. Although they do not have plural forms, they are declinable, and they operate like any other noun in terms of the overall grammar of the sentences in which they appear. For example, just as nouns can be the object of a preposition, so also infinitives can be the object of a preposition, and when they are, they will be in the genitive case (*parāsim*), as would be true for any other noun.

On the other hand, since infinitives are *verbal* nouns, their meanings normally suggest a verbal idea, and, as with other verbs, the action or state they describe can have an explicit or implied subject, or a direct object, or both.

Although infinitives can often be translated with English infinitives, in some contexts it is preferable to translate them with English gerunds. For example, while *parāsum* may be translated "to decide," sometimes it is preferable to translate it as "deciding," as in the clause, "deciding is hard."

1. The fifth verbal form is the injunctive and will be introduced in Chapter 13.

2. The Akkadian G-stem infinitive has essentially the same vowel pattern as the Hebrew infinitive construct, *qəṭôl*, and the infinitive absolute, *qāṭôl*. The *ô* in each form would have been an original long *a*-vowel that shifted to *ô* in the Canaanite Shift. See also footnote 23 in Chapter 2.

G-Stem Infinitive

Nominative	*parāsum*
Genitive	*parāsim*
Accusative	*parāsam*

5.2 Participles (Verbal Adjectives) and Adjectives

Whereas the infinitive is a verbal noun, the participle is a verbal adjective. Its basic form is the same as the adjective.

G-Stem Participle

		Masculine	Feminine
Singular	Nominative	*pārisum*	*pāristum*
	Genitive	*pārisim*	*pāristim*
	Accusative	*pārisam*	*pāristam*
Plural	Nominative	*pārisūtum*	*pārisātum*
	Genitive-Accusative	*pārisūtim*	*pārisātim*

The above chart should be learned. The same set of suffixes are used for participles in any stem (G, D, Š, or N) and for all adjectives. Likewise, the suffixes are identical to those learned for nouns in §2.6 with two important exceptions:

1. Participles and adjectives have no special forms for the dual.
2. The masculine plural suffixes differ. For participles and adjectives, the suffixes are *-ūtum* and *-ūtim* for the nominative and genitive-accusative, while the corresponding suffixes for nouns are *-ū* and *-ī*.

Any transitive verb may form a participle. Verbs that are stative in their meaning, however, such as the verb *damāqum*, "to be good," lack a participle. Instead there is usually a corresponding adjective. In the case of the verb *damāqum*, the related adjective is *damqum*, "good."

Since a participle is a *verbal* adjective, it always carries a verbal sense. For transitive verbs, the participle is active in its meaning. So *nadānum*, which means "to give, pay" or "to sell," has a participle, *nādinum*, which means "one who sells" or "a seller." For intransitive verbs, the participle is imperfective in its meaning.[3] So, for example, the verb *ḫalāqum* is an intransitive verb, "to lose, go/be missing." Accordingly, its participle, *ḫāliqum*, has an imperfective meaning, "fleeing."

Unlike the practice in Hebrew, Akkadian participles are not used predicatively in place of a progressive tense or to express some action in the present or immediate future. For example, with a clause such as "the king is deciding," Akkadian would use its durative tense, as in *šarrum iparras* but not a participle, *šarrum pārisum*. If *šarrum pārisum* were used, it would mean "a (the) deciding king." Attributive adjectives follow the nouns they modify.

3. "Imperfective" means that the action described is incomplete or ongoing.

As this last example illustrates, the Akkadian participle is invariably used to describe not an action by itself but the person or thing that does the action. An alternative way to translate a phrase like *šarrum pārisum* is with a relative clause, "a king who decides."

Since a participle is a verbal *adjective*, it can be substantivized, as can any adjective, and as such it can function as a noun.[4] So, if the participle *pārisum* appears by itself, it could be translated as "one who decides" or "a decider," or, to be more idiomatic in English, "a decision-maker."[5] Because of this substantivized use of participles, at times participles in the masculine plural take normal noun endings (*-ū* and *-ī*) rather than the characteristic adjectival endings (*-ūtum* and *-ūtim*).[6]

5.2.1 ***Excursus: Hebrew and Akkadian Participles.*** The vowel pattern of the Hebrew participle, *qôṭēl* (קוֹטֵל), may help fix in one's mind the similar vowel pattern observed in the Akkadian participle *pārisum*. In order to appreciate this similarity, however, one has to be aware of three developments in Hebrew related to vowels.

1. Originally the Hebrew participle was presumably **qāṭilu* (exactly like the Akkadian participle, *pārisum*, but without the final *-m*). At some point in the mid-second millennium BCE, Hebrew words lost final short vowels, which resulted in the loss of all case endings. Accordingly, at that time **qāṭilu* became **qāṭil*.
2. At about the same time, an original long *ā*-vowel shifted to become an unchangeable long *ô*, so the Hebrew participle became **qôtil*. This early vowel change in Hebrew of *ā* to *ô* is termed the Canaanite Shift, since it is observed in each of the Canaanite Semitic languages (Phoenician, Edomite, Moabite, etc.).[7] The same vowel change also applies to the feminine plural suffix, which earlier had been *āt* but became *ôṯ*.
3. Finally, a short *i*-vowel in Hebrew shifted to *ē* when it was in an accented syllable or in an open pretonic syllable.[8] Thus **qôtil* became *qôṭēl* (קוֹטֵל).

5.3 Verbal Adjectives

All verbal roots have, at least in principle, a form that is explicitly termed a "verbal adjective."

G-Stem Verbal Adjective

		Masculine	Feminine
Singular	Nominative	*parsum*	*paristum*
	Genitive	*parsim*	*paristim*
	Accusative	*parsam*	*paristam*
Plural	Nominative	*parsūtum*	*parsātum*
	Genitive-Accusative	*parsūtim*	*parsātim*

4. Substantivize means that the adjective can be made into a noun, or substantive. An example in English is the way the word "good," which is usually an adjective, can be substantivized just by adding a definite article: "the good."

5. Akkadian has no definite article so each of these examples could be construed as definite rather than indefinite.

6. See Worthington, *Complete Babylonian*, §35.5.

7. The Amarna Tablets from about 1350 BCE provide evidence that the Canaanite Shift had taken place by that time.

8. The earliest evidence for this change is seen in the Septuagint's representation in Greek of Hebrew names (third-second century BCE) and Origen's *Secunda*. See Reymond, *Intermediate Biblical Hebrew Grammar*, 77–83.

The masculine singular form *parsum* derives from an original longer form, **parisum*. This longer form with an *i*-vowel, which is the theme vowel for this verb form, is preserved in feminine singular forms such as *paristum*. The forms of *parsum* that lack the *i*-vowel are explained by the rule of vowel syncope discussed in §2.5.2.3. Most verbal adjectives follow the above paradigm for *parsum* with an *i*-vowel in the feminine singular forms, but some verbs have either *a* or *u*.

Interestingly, most adjectives in Akkadian are verbal adjectives in their form—they follow the *parsum* paradigm. As their name implies, all verbal adjectives (*parsum*-form) are verbal adjectives in the general sense of this expression in that they have a verbal meaning, but within the larger grammar of their clause, they function like an adjective. In this respect they resemble participles. The meaning of a verbal adjective, however, differs from the participle in important respects. For transitive verbs, whereas the participle is active in its meaning and what it describes is the person or object that is performing the action, in the case of a verbal adjective, the meaning is passive and what is described is the action itself not the subject of the action.[9]

For example, the masculine singular verbal adjective of the transitive verb *parāsum*, "to divide, separate, cut (off); to decide," is *parsum*, and it is used for something that is "decided," rather than referring to the one who is "deciding" or the "decider."

For intransitive verbs, whereas the participle is imperfective in its meaning, the verbal adjective is perfective. So, the verbal adjective of *ḫalāqum*, "to lose, go/be missing," is *ḫalqum*, "lost" or "missing," whereas the participle, *ḫāliqum*, means "fleeing."

5.4 Statives

The stative, sometimes called the predicative verbal adjective,[10] is used to express a state or condition rather than an action or process. When applied to action verbs the stative is normally passive in its sense, since the verbal idea is applied to the subject. For example, the verb *qerēbum* normally means "to be near, draw near," but in its stative form, as in LH §13, it means "to be present" or "to be available." The stative is tenseless and as such may be translated with a past, present, or future tense based on the context.

5.4.1 ***Form.*** The stative is normally built on a verbal adjective base to which pronominal suffixes are then attached (there is no suffix for the 3ms form). Less frequently, non-verbal adjectives, or even a noun, can be used to produce a stative.

1. The stative is formed from the verbal adjective of the verb *parāsum*, "to divide, separate, cut (off); to decide" in the following way:
   a. **parisum* > *parsum*—This is the G-stem verbal adjective of *parāsum*, and it reflects the application of vowel syncope.
   b. *parsum* > **pars*—This is the result of removing the declensional ending *-um* from *parsum*.

9. Since the participle is also a verbal adjective, it has been suggested that a more descriptive name for the verbal adjective, to distinguish it more clearly from the ordinary participle, would be the resultative participle. Cf. Kouwenberg, *The Akkadian Verb and Its Semitic Background*, 200, n.14.

10. See Huehnergard, *A Grammar of Akkadian*, §§22.1, 33.2. The advantage of the label "predicative verbal adjective" is that it avoids confusion with the other use of the term "stative" as a description of a class of verbs that, instead of being active (whether transitive or intransitive), are adjectival in their meaning (like *ebēbum*, "to be clean" in LH §2).

c. **pars* > *paris*—Since Akkadian does not allow a doubly closed syllable, one needs to restore the original *i*-vowel to break up the consonantal cluster.
d. *paris*—This is the G-stem stative 3ms form of *parāsum.* It can be translated, depending on the context, "it is (was/will be) divided."

2. The stative is formed from the noun *šarrum* (or what could be called a predicative use of the noun) in the following way:
   a. *šarrum*—This is a ms noun that means "king."
   b. **šarr*—This is the result of removing the declensional ending *-um* from *šarrum.*
   c. *šar*—Since Akkadian does not allow a doubly closed syllable and since there is no original vowel that can be restored between the doubled *r* in the geminate root of this noun, the final *r* drops out.
   d. *šar*—This is the G-stem stative 3ms form of the noun *šarrum.* It can be translated, depending on the context, "he is (was/will be) king."

Note: In Old Babylonian, the three prefix verbal tenses (durative, perfect, and preterite) have a common gender form in the third-person singular ("he" and "she" forms are not distinguished). In the stative, however, the 3ms form differs from the 3fs form. Under the increasing influence of Aramaic starting from the early seventh century BCE, Neo-Babylonian in this later period acquired a distinct 3fs form (with prefix *t-*) for the prefix tenses, resulting in 3fs forms that are identical to the corresponding 2ms forms.

In Chapter 18 we will consider the rest of the paradigm for the G-stem stative (forms for "she," "you," "I," "they," etc.).

5.5 Major Verbal Paradigms

The following expanded list of paradigmatic verbal forms should now be learned.

Stem	Durative 3cs	Perfect 3cs	Preterite 3cs	Participle ms	Verbal Adjective ms	Stative 3ms	Infinitive ms
G	*iparras*	*iptaras*	*iprus*	*pārisum*	*parsum*	*paris*	*parāsum*
D	*uparras*	*uptarris*	*uparris*	*muparrisum*	*purrusum*	*purrus*	*purrusum*
Š	*ušapras*	*uštapris*	*ušapris*	*mušaprisum*	*šuprusum*	*šuprus*	*šuprusum*
N	*ipparras*	*ittapras*	*ipparis*	*mupparsum*	*naprusum*	*naprus*	*naprusum*

5.6 The Negative Particles

The particle *ul* (cf. *ʾal*, אַל) is the negative adverb "not" that is used in independent clauses. In verbal clauses it comes immediately before the verb; in verbless clauses it comes before the predicate nominative.

The particle *lâ* (cf. *lōʾ*, לֹא) is the negative adverb "not" that is used in dependent clauses, such as the protasis of a conditional, relative clauses, etc. It is also used to negate interrogative sentences that have an interrogative particle ("who," "what," "where," "why," etc.). The particle usually comes immediately before the verb. It is also used to negate nouns, including infinitives.

5.7 Homework

Before you move on, be sure to understand infinitives (verbal nouns), participles (verbal adjectives), verbal adjectives, and statives, including their forms. Also, become familiar with the negative particles *ul* and *lâ*.

5.7.1 *Signs*

 5

 *da, ṭa* (less often)

 *ag, ak, aq*

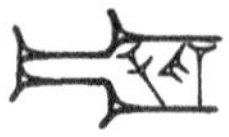 *ug, uk, uq*

 *la*

 *mu*

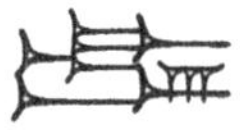 *in*

 *ti*

5.7.2 *Vocabulary*

ina = in, from, among, with, by (means of), some of; *time*: in, on, at; *with verb*: when, while, by (*ina* is never used as a conjunction)
qâtum[11] = hand
šalūm (< *š-l-y*) (*i,i*) = plunge, immerse
tabālum (*a,a*) (related to *wabālum*) = take, remove, confiscate, bring (away)
ul = not (independent clauses) (cf. *'al*, אַל)
wabālum (*a,i*) = bring (away), carry

Congratulations! If you learn the six words above and have learned each of the twenty-one words in the vocabulary lists of the preceding chapters, you will be able to read 35 percent of all the words in LH §§1–20, 127–149.

5.7.3 *Exercises*

The following three boxes of text constitute the conclusion of LH §1.

11. Supportive of the posited compensatory length of the *a*-vowel through metathesis of a lengthening consonant or metathesis of the two hypothesized earlier final root consonants (*q-t-'*), cf. *AHw*, ad loc. and Gelb, *Glossary of Old Akkadian*, ad loc. See especially Huehnergard, *A Grammar of Akkadian*, §6.1(b) for a discussion of examples of compensatory lengthening like *mârum* < **mar'um*, "son."

1. Identify Signs: Using the signs that have already been learned, identify each of the thirteen signs below and include all the listed possible values of each. If a sign has been forgotten, see the sign list in Appendix C. Check your answer using Appendix F.

LH §1 V:30

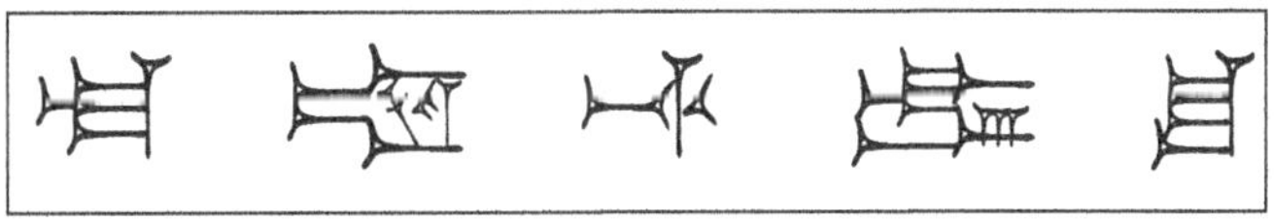

LH §1 V:31

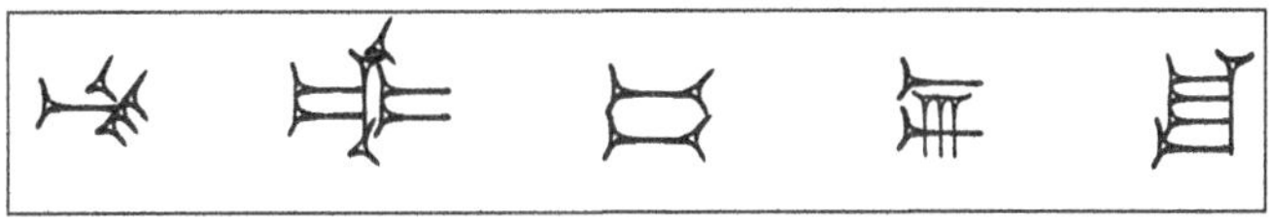

LH §1 V:32

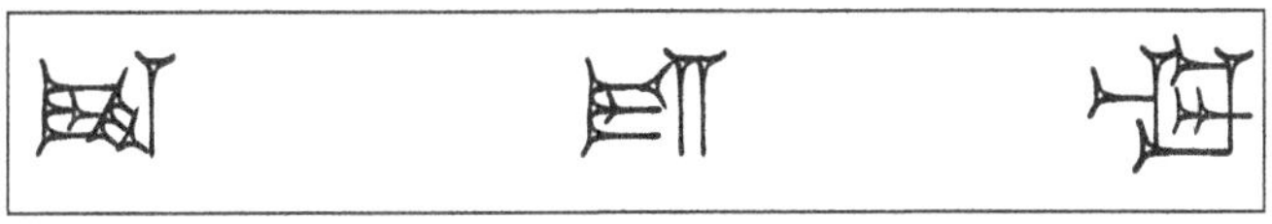

2. Transliterate: Using the vocabulary learned thus far, transliterate the signs. If a word has been forgotten, consult the glossary in Appendix E. See the notes below for additional help. After working through the notes below and attempting your own transliteration, check your answer in Appendix F.

Note: The verbs in V:30 and V:32 are II-*w* verbs and have not yet been fully addressed (see Chapter 11 for further explanation). The verb in V:30 is from *kānum* and will appear again in future laws. This verb belongs to a type of verb that is called II-weak because the second root of its original root consonants, *k-w-n*, quiesced into an ʾ.

The form of *kānum* that is here is a D-stem perfect 3cs + 3ms suffix. Using the transliteration of this verb and the suffix, and using what you know about the D-stem perfect 3cs of the paradigm verb *parāsum* and what a 3ms object suffix looks like, try to normalize the verb. Try to explain in detail how a verb with the original root consonants *k-w-n* came to be spelled in the way that you are normalizing. Check your answer in Appendix F.

The verb in V:32 is from *dākum* and will appear again in future laws. Like *kānum*, this verb is a II-weak verb because the second root of its original root consonants, *d-w-k*, quiesced into an ʾ. Again, II-weak verb types will be studied in detail in Chapter 11.

The form of *dākum* that is here is a N-stem durative 3cs. Using the transliteration of this verb, and using what you know about the N-stem durative 3cs of the paradigm verb *parāsum*, try to normalize the verb. Try to explain in detail how a verb with the original root consonants *d-w-k* came to be spelled in the way that you are normalizing. Check your answer in Appendix F.

Note: The form in V:31 is a participle from *abārum* + 3ms suffix.

3. Normalize: The correct vowel lengths for some of the verbal forms here and in the next few chapters may not always be possible to predict based solely on inference from the strong verb *parāsum*. This is especially the case because of irregularities in verbs that are hollow or have a second weak root consonant. For now, normalize as best you can and check your answer in Appendix F.

4. Translate: Translate V:30–32, and then provide a full translation of LH §1.

Takeaways from the First Law of Hammurabi

Gordon P. Hugenberger

There are at least six major takeaways from LH §1, each of which has some relevance for a more adequate understanding of biblical law.

1. **The Laws of Hammurabi is not a "code" of laws in the modern sense.** One of the most important observations about the first law of LH is what is not said. LH §1 takes for granted the fact that a murderer deserves to be executed. This assumption can be inferred from those laws that authorize execution in what are more difficult, marginal, or unusual cases of murder, such as in LH §153, where a wife is complicit in the murder of her husband, although she does not commit the actual act. Accordingly, unlike modern law, which since the time of the Napoleonic Code seeks to be explicit and exhaustively complete in its coverage, ancient Near Eastern law collections like LH and those found in the Hebrew Bible often leave unstated laws that could be assumed. Instead, they often focus on difficult, borderline, and unusual cases to establish the desired legal principles. For this reason, despite the practice of earlier scholars, the term "code" is no longer applied to the Laws of Hammurabi.

A parade example of this issue of incompleteness in biblical law occurs in Leviticus 18 and 20, both of which condemn various forms of incest, among other offenses. What is surprising to modern readers is that while sexual acts between rather distant relatives are singled out for explicit prohibition, left unstated is a prohibition of father-daughter incest. This, however, is not because father-daughter incest was approved, but because it was universally abhorred and condemned as antithetical to the accepted protective responsibility of a father for his daughter and who, in that role, was expected to secure a husband for his virginal daughter (cf. e.g., LH §154 and Gen 19:30–35).

2. **Law is embedded in a historical narrative.** A second important takeaway from LH §1 is its literary context. Prior to the first law is a lengthy historical prologue. Similarly, after the last law, LH §282, there is a lengthy epilogue. Before the discovery of LH, it was common for biblical scholars to assume that the legal texts of the Bible derived from a literary source other than its current context. While these source-critical theories are still possible, ancient Near Eastern law collections, such as LH, and numerous covenant (treaty) documents imply that the legal portions within the Exodus-Leviticus sequence and in Deuteronomy and the historical materials that introduce them, as well as the blessings and curses and other narrative elements that follow them, all belong together.[1]

3. **The laws in LH are framed as statements summarizing the judicial decisions of the king.** A third important takeaway of LH §1 is that these laws are not so much prescriptions as they are descriptions by Hammurabi toward the end of his reign of what were allegedly his own legal decisions. He shares these first and foremost to commend himself to the gods but also to posterity, as a king who secured justice

1. Cf. Kenneth A. Kitchen and Paul J. N. Lawrence, *Treaty, Law, and Covenant in the Ancient Near East*. 3 vols (Wiesbaden: Harrassowitz, 2012).

and protected the needs of the disadvantaged. His lengthy prologue concludes: "I am Hammurabi, the shepherd selected by the god Enlil. . . . I established truth and justice as the declaration of the land. I enhanced the well-being of the people. At that time: [LH §1] If a man accused another man and charged him with murder, but did not convict him, his accuser would be executed."[2]

When read in its immediate context, this first law and the laws that follow should not be translated with present tenses, as they often are, but with past tenses, "if x happened [verb in the preterite or perfect], then y would happen [verb in the durative]."

Hammurabi's self-congratulatory claims concerning his judicial practice or laws is similar to what is found in earlier Sumerian law collections, which set the pattern of law embedded in a largely historical narrative. Interestingly, in Israel's practice, nowhere does one find a collection of "the laws of David" or "the laws of Solomon," for example. Instead, in the radically counter-cultural Israelite conception, it is the LORD God alone who is the ultimate king of his people (e.g., Deut 33:5; Judg 8:23; 1 Sam 8:7; Pss 10:16; 24:8; 95:3; Isa 6:5; 43:15; 44:6; Jer 10:10), and as such, the LORD alone is Israel's true lawgiver (Isa 33:22). Consistent with this perspective is Deuteronomy 17:18–20, which explains that when Israel's earthly kings take the throne, they must first write for themselves a copy of the law given by the LORD, so they can read it all the days of their lives. This is because they, like their brother Israelites, are not above the law, but must live under it.

4. **Casuistic law is prevalent in both LH and the Bible, but apodictic law is seemingly unimportant in LH versus the Bible.** Apodictic laws are those that are absolute and are expressed with unqualified imperatives or prohibitions, such as, "love your neighbor as yourself. I am the LORD" (Lev 19:18). Casuistic laws, on the other hand, are expressed with a qualifying protasis. They start with a conditional clause, such as, "If a man steals an ox or a sheep and slaughters it or sells it, he must pay back five head of cattle for the ox and four sheep for the sheep" (Exod 22:1). The vast majority of laws in the ancient Near Eastern law collections are casuistic in form. Consider the expression *šumma awīlum*, "if a person," which introduces LH §1 and reappears 120 times elsewhere in LH. There are five random apodictic laws in LH, but they have no special significance. Although many of Israel's casuistic laws find helpful parallels in the ancient Near Eastern law collections like LH, perhaps the law collections are not the right place to look for a more adequate parallel to explain Israel's dramatic use of apodictic laws. Rather, when it comes to the placement and use of apodictic laws, and also a number of other distinctive features in the biblical accounts, there are much closer and far more illuminating parallels in the ancient Near Eastern treaty (covenant) documents, especially those of the Hittites in the late second millennium BCE. These parallels were first pointed out by Donald J. Wiseman in an unpublished paper read in 1948 at the Society for Old Testament Study, and since then many other scholars have studied them in much greater detail.[3]

5. **The Principle of Lex Talionis.** Although execution is the explicitly required punishment for murder in the law collections prior to LH, such as the Laws of Ur-Nammu §1,[4] none of these law collections

2. Translation of LH prologue and epilogue come from Martha T. Roth, *Law Collections from Mesopotamia and Asia Minor* (Atlanta: Scholars Press, 1995), 133.

3. Cf. G. E. Mendenhall, "Covenant Forms in Israelite Tradition," *The Biblical Archaeologist* 17:3 (1954): 50–76; Dennis J. McCarthy, *Treaty and Covenant: A Study in Form in the Ancient Oriental Documents and in the Old Testament.* 2nd ed. (Rome: Biblical Institute Press, 1978); and Meredith G. Kline, *Treaty of the Great King: The Covenant Structure of Deuteronomy* (Grand Rapids: Eerdmans, 1963) and *The Structure of Biblical Authority.* 2nd ed. (Grand Rapids: Eerdmans, 1989). More recently, see the monumental work of Kitchen and Lawrence, *Treaty, Law, and Covenant in the Ancient Near East.*

4. Lex Talionis, which literally means "law of retaliation," refers to laws where the punishment matches the crime. So, if a man commits a murder, he is to be executed ("life for life"), and if he blinds an eye, his eye is blinded ("eye for eye"), etc.

is characterized by the principle of lex talionis as a whole. LH §1 is, however, a fitting introduction to a law collection that does feature talionic punishments, even if this emphasis sometimes gives way to compensatory punishments (especially when the victims are of lower status). In the Hebrew Bible, many divinely arranged adverse consequences for disapproved behavior consist of mirror punishments that are often literalistic examples of lex talionis, much like those found in LH.[5] When it comes to the actions of human courts, however, there are at least four significant differences between the literalistic application of lex talionis as attested in LH and punishments authorized in the Hebrew Bible. First, the Hebrew Bible rejects vicarious liability of family members based on a literalistic lex talionis (Deut 24:16; cf. 2 Kgs 14:6; 2 Chron 25:4; Jer 31:30; Ezek 18:20). Second, the Hebrew Bible rejects instrumental talion based on a literalistic lex talionis.[6] Third, the Hebrew Bible rejects a social status-based application of lex talionis. Fourth, the lex talionis laws in the Hebrew Bible are likely intended to be understood figuratively, as an aphorism for punishments that fit the crime, rather than literally, other than in the case of murder.[7]

6. **The Laws of Hammurabi demonstrate organized law.** A sixth take-away with respect to LH §1 becomes apparent as one reads subsequent laws. As will be seen, there is often a logical coherence in the grouping of laws based on their topics and shared vocabulary. In other words, LH §1 does not just introduce a random list of precepts. Furthermore, adjacent smaller groups of laws are often organized under larger unifying topics. On the other hand, there is not an obvious tight logical organization that explains all the laws as a whole or why some practical topics were never included (such as arson, although theft at a fire is covered in LH §25).

5. For examples cf. Deut 32:21; Judg 1:6–7; 1 Sam 15:33; 2 Sam 12:11; 16:21–22; 1 Kgs 21:19; Ps 57:6; Prov 26:27; 30:17; Esth 7:9–10; Isa 5:8–9; Jer 32:19; Ezek 16:59; Hos 4:6; Obad 16; Hab 2:8.

6. Accordingly, there are no biblical laws similar to LH §218 where a physician whose surgery kills his patient has his hand cut off.

7. An interpretation of the relevant biblical texts requiring literal mutilation is argued by many scholars including Baruch A. Levine, *The JPS Torah Commentary: Leviticus* (Philadelphia: Jewish Publication Society of America, 1989) 268–70; William H. C. Propp, *Exodus 19–40*, Anchor Bible (New York: Doubleday, 2006) 227–32; and Jacob Milgrom, *Leviticus 23–27*, Anchor Bible (New York: Doubleday, 2001), 2133–40.

In support of a figurative understanding, reflected already in early rabbinic interpretation, cf., e.g., Umberto Cassuto, *A Commentary on the Book of Exodus* (Jerusalem: Magnes, 1967), 276–77; Nahum M. Sarna, *The JPS Torah Commentary, Exodus* (Philadelphia: Jewish Publication Society of America, 1991), 125–27; Raymond Westbrook, *Studies in Biblical and Cuneiform Law*, Cahiers de la Revue Biblique, 26 (Paris: Gabalda et Cie, 1988), 39–64; and T. Desmond Alexander, *Exodus* (Downers Grove, IL: InterVarsity Press, 2017), 485–89.

6–𒐋

The Determinative Relative Pronoun, the Subordinative Suffix, and Verb Conjugation

In this chapter the determinative relative pronoun *ša* and the subordinative suffix *-u* will be introduced. The pronoun *ša* is an important grammatical feature found frequently throughout LH and Akkadian literature. Its first appearance in LH is in the second law, which will be introduced below (LH §2 V:33–40). The second law concerns the issue of unsubstantiated allegations (the theme of LH §1–5). This time the alleged offense is witchcraft, rather than murder as in LH §1. In addition, all third-person verb forms will be introduced.

6.1 The Determinative Relative Pronoun *ša*

The determinative relative pronoun *ša*, which is translated "who, whom, which, he who, the one who, that which" and "of" is an undeclined word. It corresponds to the relative pronoun in Hebrew that is spelled *ša*, שֶׁ + doubling, "which," and perhaps also to the less common relative pronoun *zû*, זוּ, "which."[1]

The indeclinable particle *ša* in Old Babylonian and later forms of Akkadian derives from an earlier Old Akkadian determinative relative pronoun *šu*, normally translated "he of," which had the accusative form *ša*. This earlier declined determinative relative pronoun mostly fell out of use by the time of Old Babylonian. This history, however, explains the root meaning of *ša* as "(the) one of."

There are two common uses of *ša*: (1) paraphrastic and (2) as a relative pronoun.

6.1.1 ***ša in a Genitival Paraphrasis.*** The paraphrastic use of *ša* is where it expresses a genitival relationship, especially possession, with a following noun. In Akkadian, as in Hebrew, nouns may be put in a construct or bound state when they are connected very closely to a following noun. In Hebrew, the second noun is in the absolute state. In Akkadian the second noun is in the genitive case. The combination of a noun in the bound state with a following noun in the genitive case is termed "a construct chain" or a "genitive chain." A construct chain in either language can permit a series of nouns to be strung together.

The bound state of nouns will be presented in greater detail in a subsequent chapter (§8.1). For the purpose at hand it is enough to know that typically the construct form of a noun is the noun with its case ending removed. Sometimes, however, this removal requires a slight

1. Both Akkadian *ša* and Hebrew *ša*, שֶׁ + doubling, may have derived from the Proto-Semitic phoneme *ḏ*. This Proto-Semitic consonant was realized in a variety of ways in the subsequent Semitic languages such as Akkadian and Hebrew. The best attested correspondences are to *z* in Hebrew but to *d*, *ḏ*, or *z* in Ugaritic, *ḏ* (pronounced as *ḏ*, but written with the grapheme *d*) in Aramaic, and *ḏ* in Arabic. In support of the derivation of Akkadian *ša* and Hebrew *ša*, שֶׁ + doubling, from the Proto-Semitic phoneme *ḏ*, see Pope, *Song of Songs*, 33. For the more regular correspondences, see Reymond, *Intermediate Biblical Hebrew Grammar*, 36–37.

modification in the spelling of the noun base in order to avoid a consonantal cluster at the end of the bound form.

For example, the Akkadian word for "female slave" is *amtum* (cf. *'āmâ*, אָמָה). Based on what has just been said, one expects that the bound form of *amtum* should be **amt*, since that is what is left when the case ending is removed. The problem, however, with this result is that *amt* ends with a consonantal cluster. Akkadian solves this problem by inserting an anaptyctic *a*-vowel between the two final consonants.[2] So, the actual construct form of *amtum* is *amat.*

There are two options for how to say "a female slave of a man." One option is *amat awīlim*, where *amat* is the bound state of *amtum* and *awīlim* is in the genitive case. Alternatively, one can express the same idea with the more paraphrastic expression, *amtum* (or *amtim* or *amtam*) *ša awīlim*. The phrase, *amtam ša awīlim*, appears in LH §280. This could be literally translated, "a female slave, one of a man," where *ša awīlim* is interpreted as being in apposition to *amtam*. The more customary translation, however, of an expression like this is "a female slave of a man."

There is a potential advantage in using this second option to express some genitival relationships, such as possession, rather than using a construct chain. That potential advantage is that the longer expression with *ša* preserves the case ending on the first noun. This is seen in the example taken from LH §280, *amtam ša awīlim*: the term *amtam* retains its accusative suffix. As a result, the reader knows unambiguously that this is the direct object of the verb. The immediate context in LH §280 is: "If a man purchased a female slave of a(nother) man [*amtam ša awīlim*]. . . ."

6.1.2 ***ša as a Relative Pronoun.*** The other common use of *ša* is as a relative pronoun. In this use the pronoun is normally translated as "who(m)" or "which." For example, in LH §25 we read, "If a fire broke out in a man's house, and a(nother) man who [*ša*] came to put out the fire . . . stole some goods of the owner of the house. . . ."

In the example above the particle *ša* has an explicit antecedent noun, "a(nother) man." Frequently, however, *ša* appears without an antecedent noun. In a situation like this, it is translated, "the one who(m)," or "that which." An example of this usage is seen in LH §30 where *ša iṣṣabtūma* is rendered, "*the one who* has seized it."

Unlike English where a preposition can immediately precede and modify a relative pronoun, as in the expressions "to whom" or "by which," such phrases in Akkadian are expressed by an appropriate preposition, noun, or verb coming later in the clause and modifying a resumptive pronoun. For example, LH §265 says literally, "If a shepherd, *who* [*ša*] cattle . . . were given *to him*, acts criminally. . . ." This should be translated, "If a shepherd, *to whom* [*ša*] cattle . . . were given, acts criminally. . . ."

6.2 Subordinate Clauses and the Subordinative Suffix

In Akkadian there are, in effect, two different kinds of subordinate clauses. One kind is the conditional subordinate clause, namely any clause that is introduced by *šumma*, "if." The other kind consists of all other subordinate clauses, such as relative, temporal, causal, purpose, circumstantial, or explanatory.[3]

2. An anaptyctic vowel is one that is added inside a word to assist in pronunciation by breaking up a consonantal cluster, which is avoided in Akkadian.

3. It is worth noting that these other subordinators are normally a preposition being used as a conjunction, or a noun in the construct

As was mentioned in §5.6, the negative particle *lâ* is used with both categories of subordinate clauses, as opposed to the particle *ul* that is used only in independent clauses. An important difference between these two kinds of subordinate clauses is the observation that while ordinary verb forms are used in conditional clauses, there are some special verbal forms that are used in non-conditional subordinate clauses. Some Akkadian grammars describe these special verbal forms as being subjunctive. This modal term, however, is misleading because these verbal forms do not carry any kind of subjunctive meaning. Other grammars describe these special verbal forms as having a "subordinative suffix" or a "subordination marker."[4] This textbook uses this alternative terminology.

The subordinative suffix is the vowel *-u*. This is added to any verb tense form (durative, perfect, preterite, or stative) that ends in a consonant, with only a few exceptions which will be mentioned below. When used with a verb that has any additional suffix, such as an object suffix or a *-ma* suffix, it comes before that suffix. This grammatical form is unique to Akkadian and is found in no other Semitic language.[5]

For example, one meaning of the verb *maḫārum* is "to receive," and the G-stem preterite 3cs form is *imḫur*, "he received." In LH §254, there is a subordinate relative clause, *ša imḫuru*, meaning, "[the grain] which he received." The verb *imḫuru* has the subordinative suffix *-u*. This is why this verb is not translated, "the grain which *they* received," as if the closing *-u* vowel were the 3mp suffix (presented in §6.3 below).

6.2.1 ***Important Exceptions.*** If a verb is in a non-conditional subordinate clause where a subordinative *-u* suffix is expected, but if it already ends in a vowel from a pronominal suffix or if it ends with the 3fs stative suffix *-at* or has a ventive suffix *-am* (which will be explained in §7.3), the subordinative *-u* suffix will not be added. The first exception does not apply to cases of III-weak verbs, where in some forms the verb ends with a vowel that is part of its root rather than part of a pronominal suffix.

Finally, one possibly helpful way to think of the subordinative *-u* suffix is to view it as a means of "nominalizing" an entire clause. Just as nouns end with *-u(m)*, the addition of a final *-u* on a verb at the end of a clause suggests that the clause as a whole functions as if it were a single noun. This explanation is appealing since these clauses do in fact typically fill a slot in the larger grammar of the sentence that could be filled by a noun. It is, however, far from certain that this interesting possibility is a correct explanation either for how ancient Akkadian speakers understood the subordinative *-u* suffix or for how this form actually developed.[6]

---

state, or the determinative relative pronoun *ša*. What is common about each of these subordinators, unlike *šumma*, is that in their other uses they are normally followed by a noun in the genitive case. For example, the preposition *ina*, which means "in," "at," or "on," when governing a noun in the genitive can mean "while" when it functions as a subordinating temporal conjunction.

4. Worthington, *Complete Babylonian*, §30.12 calls it simply "the verbal suffix *-u*."

5. It is similar, however, to the use in Sumerian of a nominalizing *-a* suffix on verb forms in subordinate clauses. See, e.g., Jagersma, *Descriptive Grammar of Sumerian*, §27.3.3.

6. This interesting suggestion, with an appropriate warning that it lacks clear support, comes from Worthington, *Complete Babylonian*, §30.12. Whether Worthington's suggestion has merit or not, it is hypothesized that this final *-u* is a residual form that preserves an original final *-u* that existed in the Proto-Semitic imperfective form **yiqtulu*. In support, see Kouwenberg, *The Akkadian Verb and Its Semitic Background*, §9.3.3.

6.3 Verb Conjugation

Until now attention has only been given to prefix and suffix tense forms of the verb in the third-person common singular. See below:

	Durative	Perfect	Preterite	Stative
G	*iparras*	*iptaras*	*iprus*	*paris*
D	*uparras*	*uptarris*	*uparris*	*purrus*
Š	*ušapras*	*uštapris*	*ušapris*	*šuprus*
N	*ipparras*	*ittapras*	*ipparis*	*naprus*

It is now time to learn all third-person forms. Since the prefixes and suffixes are the same for the conjugation of each of the prefix tenses (the durative, perfect, and preterite), the strong verb paradigm for the preterite will be sufficient to represent the conjugation of all three tenses.[7]

		Preterite	Stative
Singular	**3m**	***iprus***	***paris***
	3f	***iprus***	***parsat***
	2m	*taprus*	*parsāta*
	2f	*taprusī*	*parsāti*
	1c	*aprus*	*parsāku*
Plural	**3m**	***iprusū***	***parsū***
	3f	***iprusā***	***parsā***
	2m	*taprusā*	*parsātunu*
	2f	*taprusā*	*parsātina*
	1c	*niprus*	*parsānu*

First- and second-person forms are rare in LH, so at this point it will be sufficient to memorize only the third-person forms that are in bold font below. The remaining forms are presented here for reference.

6.4 Homework

Before you move on, be sure to understand and recognize the two common uses of *ša*: in a genitival relationship and as a relative pronoun. Also be sure to understand subordinate clauses and be able to recognize the subordinative suffix *-u*, which can be added to any verb tense form. Finally, commit to memory the third-person verb forms in the prefix tenses.

7. Verb conjugations in all tenses may be found in Appendix B.

6.4.1 *Signs*

 6

 *i*

 *bu, pu*

 ÍD (this sign begins with the A sign, which in Sumerian is a logogram for *nârum,* "river")

 *ke, ki, qé, qí*

 *il*

 *lim, ši*

 *na*

 *ša*

 *iš*

Congratulations! If you have learned the ten cuneiform signs in this chapter and each of the preceding thirty-five signs, you will be able to read 67 percent of all the cuneiform signs in LH §§1–20, 127–149.

6.4.2 *Vocabulary*

alākum (*a,i*) = to go (cf. *hālak,* הָלַךְ)

^{d}ID = Id (the god of the river ordeal). Id, as a deity, always has before it the determinative DINGIR for deity (cf. *'ēd,* אֵד, "stream, spring," as in Gen 2:6). ^{d}ID may also be rendered *nârum,* "river" (cf. *nāhār,* נָהָר).

kašādum (*a,u*) = to overcome, reach

maḫārum (*a,u*) = to receive, acquire, be comparable; Št: to make oneself equal to (cf. *məḥîr,* מְחִיר, "money, recompense")

ša = who, whom, which, he who, the one who, that which, of; *ša* is an undeclined determinative relative pronoun (cf. *ša,* שֶׁ + doubling, "which")

-*u* = a subordinative suffix used on a final verb to mark a subordinate clause other than a protasis (a *šumma,* "if," clause); subordinative -*u* may be used on any verbal form ending in a consonant—not including a ventive -*am* or a 3fs stative suffix -*at*—or a vowel, but only if it is the root vowel of a III-weak verb

6.4.3 *Exercises*

1. Identify Signs: You have now learned in Chapters 1–6 all the signs that appear in LH §2. Throughout the rest of this textbook, whenever you are asked to transliterate signs, these will always be signs that you learned in the current chapter or in preceding chapters. The same is true for any vocabulary that is involved. If some sign or word has not yet been taught, you will be told the sign's value or a word's lexical form and meaning. If at any time you need to find a sign's values, it can be found in Appendix C. Similarly, any needed vocabulary can be found in the Glossary in Appendix E. Identify each of the signs below and include all the listed possible values of each. Check your answer using Appendix F.

LH §2 V:33

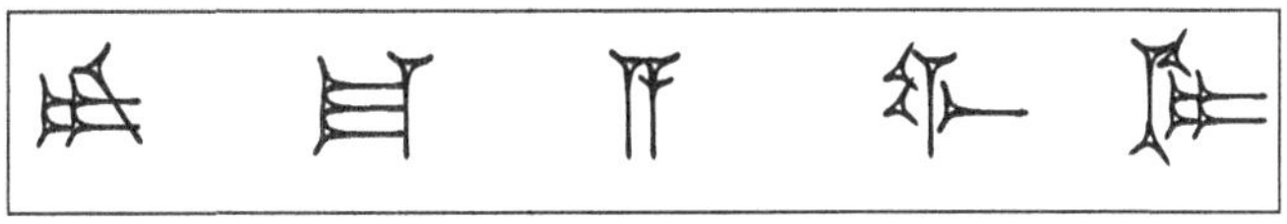

LH §2 V:34

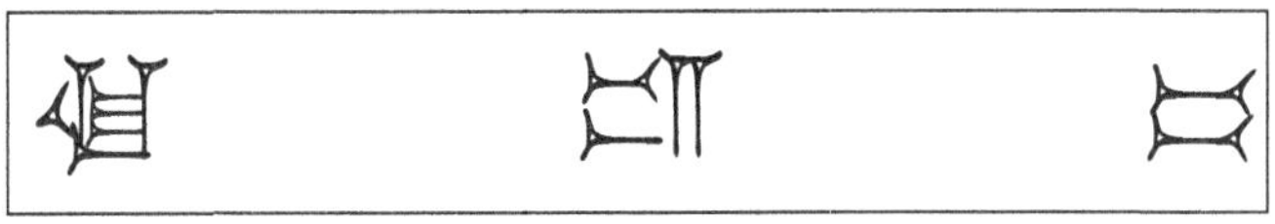

LH §2 V:35

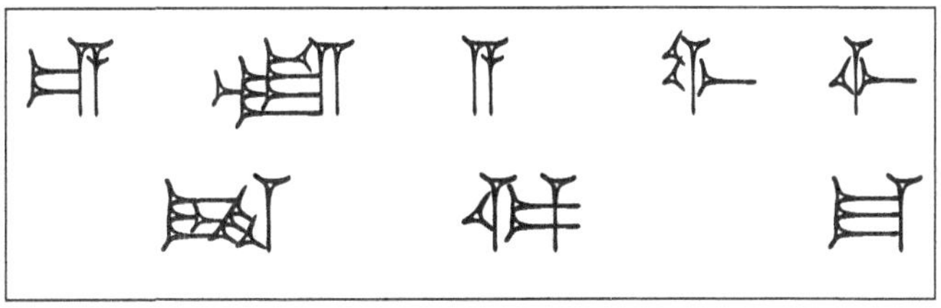

LH §2 V:36

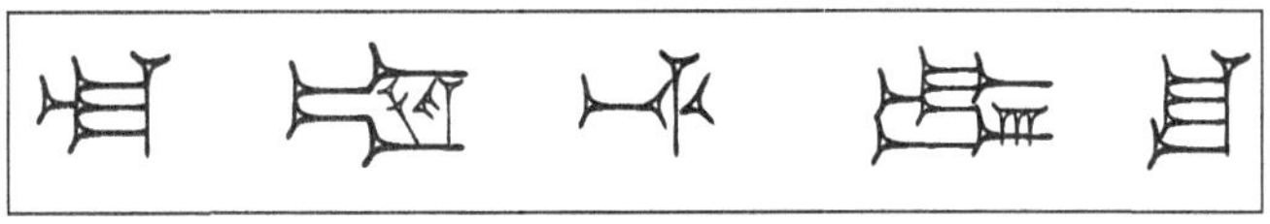

LH §2 V:37

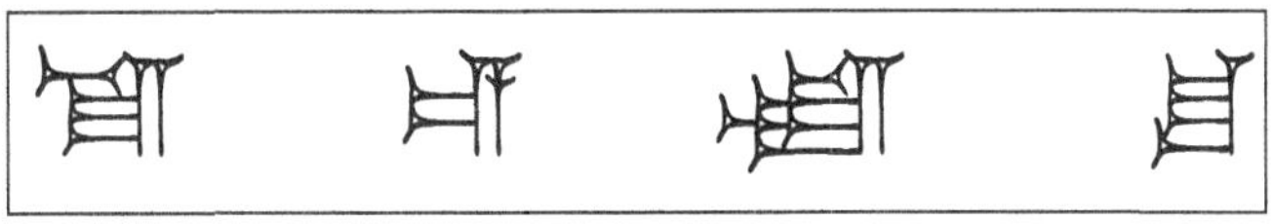

LH §2 V:38

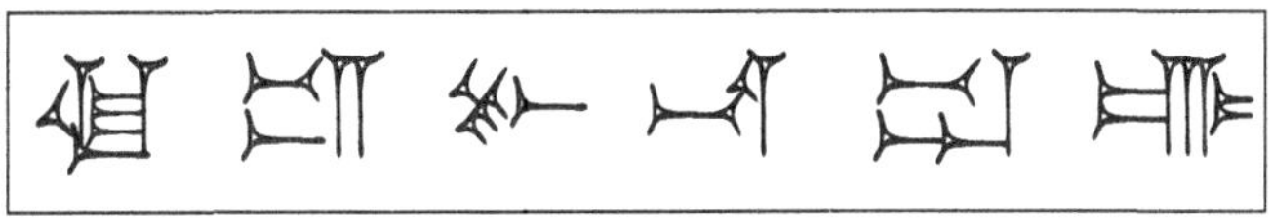

LH §2 V:39

LH §2 V:40

2. Transliterate: See the note below for additional help. After working through the note below and attempting your own transliteration, check your answer in Appendix F.

Note: The verb in V:40 is from the I-' root *alākum*. In the scribal practices of LH an extra vowel sign at the beginning of a word is most often a historical spelling indicating an original '. As expected with I-' verbs (like *abārum* from Chapter 3) the ' has been lost without any compensatory lengthening of the following vowel. (For further explanation of I-' verbs, see Chapter 14.)

3. Normalize: Normalize your transliteration and check your answer in Appendix F. See the note below for additional help.

Note: ÍD, , can refer to the god Id. But ÍD is also a logogram for *nârum*, "river," and in the immediate context ÍD refers to the literal Euphrates river or one of its tributaries into which the accused individual has to go. The determinative sign for deity, ^{d}, is used because the god Id is identified with the river, especially in a case where the river is being employed in a judicial ordeal.

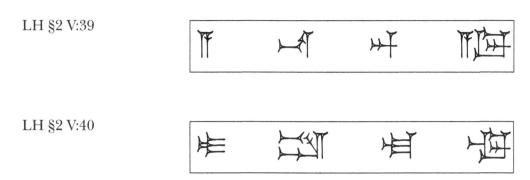

4. Grammatical Analysis: Answer the questions below by identifying grammatical features in LH §2 V:33–40 and check your answers in Appendix F.

   a. Parse the four verbs in the lines above. See the notes below for additional help.

Note: Note the appearance of the III-*y* verb *nadûm* in V: 35 and 38. This weak verb has already been learned and explained in §4.6.

Note: The II-*w* verb in V: 36 should be familiar from §5.7.

b. Provide the case and number of the five nouns.

5. Translate: Translate LH §2 V:33–40.

7–

Scribal Practices, Phonetic Complements, and the Ventive

This chapter will explain scribal habits, practices in writing, and phonetic complements in order to learn to anticipate certain grammatical constructions when transliterating, normalizing, and translating. The ventive suffixes will also be explained. The exercises continue with the second law, LH §2 V:41–43.

7.1 Scribal Practices

The scribal practices reflected in LH as copied on the stele now housed in the Louvre are generally consistent and very helpful for readers.

For example, the scribe observes helpful spelling patterns, such as restricting the use of the ù-sign almost exclusively for spelling the two conjunctions "and, but" (*u*) and "or" (*û*), while using the ú-sign in all other situations.[1]

Also, although initial or internal long vowels are generally unmarked, tilde long final vowels are generally indicated with an extra vowel sign. On the other hand, short vowels are almost never written with an extra vowel sign. The most common exceptions to this rule are historical spellings, where an extra initial vowel sign reflects the earlier presence of an initial ʾ that has quiesced. This is especially common in monosyllabic words like the negative particle *ul*, which is invariably written as ú-ul, (cf. *ʾal*, אַל). There are, however, many other examples, such as the verb *illāk*, written as i-il-la-ak in text box LH §2 V:40, as was discussed in the previous chapter.[2]

In the case of doubled consonants within a word, most of the time these are explicitly indicated. Nevertheless, so-called "defective spellings" (§2.5.1.2) are not uncommon where a doubled consonant is written with only one consonant in the cuneiform text. For example, LH §47 has the defective spelling i-le-qé for the verb *ileqqê*, "he shall take," the G-stem durative 3cs of *leqûm*.

Furthermore, as long as there is adequate space, short phrases are typically kept together on the same line or within the same box. Most boxes contain just one line, but about 15 percent include two lines. If there is a conjunction other than the suffix *-ma*, it is written with at least one word following it. For example, the term *šumma*, "if," which introduces a protasis, invariably appears as the first word on a line, and it is always followed by at least one word.[3] Likewise, the negative particle *lâ* is written on the same line before the verb, noun, or predicate adjective that

1. There are only four exceptions in LH, all within the prologue: ú-šar-bí-ù-šu (*ušarbiʾūšu*), ib-bi-ù (*ibbiʾu*), ib-ni-ù-šu (*ibniʾūšu*), and ú-šu-pí-ù (*ušūpiʾu*).

2. See §6.4

3. Strangely, the *šumma* that introduces LH §154 heads the second line in a box with two lines rather than starting a new box.

it negates. Similarly, prepositions are kept with the words they modify, and the determinative relative pronoun *ša* is kept with at least one word of the clause it introduces or with a noun in the genitive case with which it forms a genitive construction.

Finally, as has been mentioned before, words are normally written without being divided between lines or boxes.

There are two notable exceptions to the scribal tendencies summarized above. First, when there is insufficient space for a word the scribe divides it as necessary, usually between morphemes (such as between the verb or noun base and a possessive suffix or an object suffix, which then starts the next line), or at least between syllables, but not always.[4] There is one such divided word in the portion of LH §2 that is examined in this chapter.

A second notable exception concerns nouns that are in construct with either another noun in the genitive or with a verb. Despite the fact that the noun in construct has lost its primary accent to the following noun or verb (in effect, a substantivized clause), there is surprisingly little concern to keep the noun in construct on the same line as the word that follows.[5]

7.2 Phonetic Complements

In the first chapter it was explained that cuneiform signs are typically used in three ways. First, they are sometimes used as logograms to represent entire words, such as 𒂍, which is pronounced É in Sumerian but *bîtum* in Akkadian (meaning "house" or "household"). Second, they are used as syllabograms to represent syllables in Akkadian, such as 𒋳, which represents the syllable *šum*. Third, sometimes cuneiform signs can be used as determinatives. For this use most signs are placed immediately before words but some signs are placed after words. In either case, they identify classes of items to which the attached words belong. For example, the sign 𒀭, normalized as a raised *d* (^{d}) for the Sumerian word DINGIR (meaning "a god") is placed immediately before the name of any deity.

There is a fourth and final use of cuneiform signs that now needs attention: their use as phonetic complements. In this use, the sign is a syllabogram but it operates in combination with an attached logogram. It is not difficult to imagine that a logogram by itself could easily be ambiguous when read. For example, although the cuneiform sign 𒂍 is transliterated É and can be readily normalized in Akkadian as *bîtum*, the cuneiform sign 𒂍 by itself does not inform the reader whether *bîtum* should be read in the nominative, genitive, or accusative, or whether it should be read as plural, or even whether it should be read with a pronominal suffix.

To eliminate these ambiguities, Akkadian often uses an additional sign, a syllabogram, connected to the logogram that is called a phonetic complement. This sign specifies how the ending of the Akkadian normalization for the logogram should be read.

For instance, if an author has written 𒂍, É, but wants it to be read in Akkadian in a particular case not simply as *bîtum*, "house," but perhaps as *bîssu*, "his house," the writer can accomplish this by writing 𒂍 𒋢. This is transliterated É-sú, and it is normalized and read in Akkadian as *bîssu*, "his house."

4. Cf. the last two lines of LH §48 where the line break comes unexpectedly in the middle of an example of syllable splitting: *-na-*|*-ad-*. This syllable belongs to the final word of LH §48, *i-na-ad-din*, *inaddin*, "he shall give."

5. Cf. LH §7 where there is a line break between *qât* and *mâr* in the phrase, *ina qât mâr awīlim*, "from the hand of the son of a man." Since *mâr*, "son [of]," is represented by a logogram, this division could have been easily avoided by having five signs on the first line instead of four.

Interestingly, there are analogous uses of "phonetic complements" in English. For example, if an author writes the English logogram, 2, it is usually read in English as "two." If, however, the author follows the same logogram, 2, with the phonetic complement *-nd*, in other words, when he or she writes 2nd, it is read in English as "second."

7.3 The Ventive

Pronominal suffixes were introduced in §4.3. The genitive suffixes are applicable to nouns and prepositions, and the dative and accusative suffixes are applicable to verbs. The focus in §4.3 was on learning just the third-person forms. For the present purpose, however, it is helpful to be aware of the 1cs dative forms that are listed in that section: *-am, -m, -nim.* In LH §9, for example, there is a verbal form, *iddinam,* which is a G-stem preterite 3cs of *nadānum (i,i)* "to give, pay" or "sell," with the *-am* 1cs dative suffix. Hence, *iddinam* can be translated, "he sold to me." These first-person common dative suffixes acquired four special non-dative uses that no longer have the translation "to me":

1. The first of these non-dative uses is to mark a verb of motion as being motion toward or for the benefit of, or of relevance to the speaker (comparable to an "ethical dative").[6] For example, if a 1cs dative suffix is added to *illik* (*alākum*), "he went," the result is *illikam.* While this could be translated, "he went to/for me," in most cases it can be translated simply, "he came." For this reason, the more general non-dative use of these 1cs dative suffixes is called "ventive," based on the Latin verb *venire,* "to come." It is important to stress that when one of these 1cs dative suffixes is used as a ventive, it is no longer translated "to me."
2. Often the ventive suffix is used in a second way, one that is still dative in its general meaning but no longer reflective of the first-person origin of the suffix. In this second use, the ventive marks or highlights motion or action toward or for the benefit of, or of relevance to, the person who is being addressed or about whom a statement is made.
3. A third use of the ventive is an attractional use. Curiously, if two verbs are connected with the conjunctive suffix *-ma,* usually translated "and (then)," and if the second verb is ventive, then the first verb will often also be ventive, even if there is no apparent ventive implication for the first verb.
4. Finally, there is a fourth use of the ventive where the suffix is purely stylistic and has no lexical significance. It is common, for example, to add a ventive suffix before the conjunction *-ma,* and also to add a ventive suffix before any of the dative or accusative pronominal suffixes, other than the dative 1cs suffix (since this would be a needless duplication).

   When another suffix follows the ventive, as often happens, the final *-m* of the ventive assimilates to the initial consonant of the suffix that follows. Since the consonant *m* does not normally assimilate elsewhere, this case of assimilation supports the assumption that the final *-m* of the dative 1cs suffix was, in fact, originally an *-n.* For example, the verb *ipṭuraššuma,* "he redeemed him, and (then) . . . ," appears in LH §32. This verbal form is comprised of four elements:

6. See Kouwenberg, *The Akkadian Verb and Its Semitic Background,* §9.4.2.

ipṭurassšuma < *ipṭur* + *-am* + *-šu* + *-ma*

First, there is the verb *ipṭur,* which is a G-stem preterite 3cs (*iprus* form) of *paṭārum,* which means "to redeem." Added to *ipṭur* is a ventive suffix, *-am,* which is purely stylistic and has no ventive implication. As mentioned, a stylistic ventive suffix is often found before pronominal suffixes. After the ventive comes the 3ms accusative pronominal suffix *šu,* "him."[7] Notice that the *-m* of the ventive suffix assimilates to the *š* of the pronominal suffix. Finally, there is an enclitic *-ma* suffix, which means "and (then)."[8]

7.4 Homework

Before you move on, become familiar with the scribal practices discussed above, including typical spelling patterns. Also, be sure to understand and recognize the use of phonetic complements. Finally, become comfortable with recognizing the ventive suffix and its four special non-dative uses.

7.4.1 *Signs*

 7

 *eg, ig, ek, ik, eq, iq*

 É.GAL, *ekallum,* "palace" (lit. "great house"; cf. *hêkāl,* הֵיכָל)

 *al*

 *am*

 *ta*

 *zu, sú, ṣú*

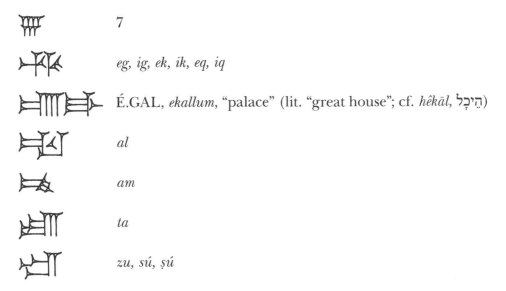

7.4.2 *Vocabulary*

-am = marks a ventive
dînum (plural is fem.: *dînātum*) = legal case, trial; decision (cf. *dîn,* דִּין; tribe of Dan, דָּן)
ebēbum (i,i) = G: to be(come) clean; D: to clean, purify; to declare innocent
ekallum = palace (cf. *hêkāl,* הֵיכָל)
sarrātum (always plural) = lies, deception, fraud (cf. *sārār,* סָרַר, "to be stubborn")
šībum = old man; witness (cf. *śêbâ,* שֵׂיבָה, "old age")
šībūtum = testimony

7. See §4.3.
8. See §3.5.

šumum = name (cf. *šēm*, שֵׁם)
waṣûm (*i,i*) = to go out (cf. *yāṣā'*, יָצָא; almost all I-*w* verbs became I-*y* in Hebrew)

Congratulations! If you learn the eight words above and have learned each of the thirty-two words in the vocabulary lists of the preceding chapters, you will be able to read 44 percent of all the words in LH §§1–20, 127–149.

7.4.3 *Exercises*

1. Identify Signs: Identify each of the signs below and include all the listed possible values of each.

LH §2 V:41

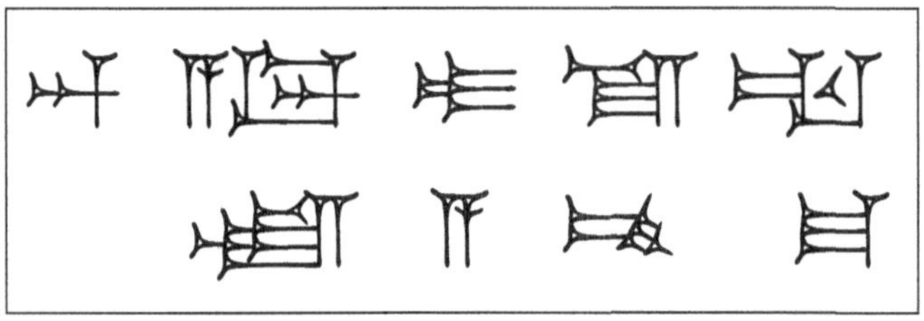

LH §2 V:42

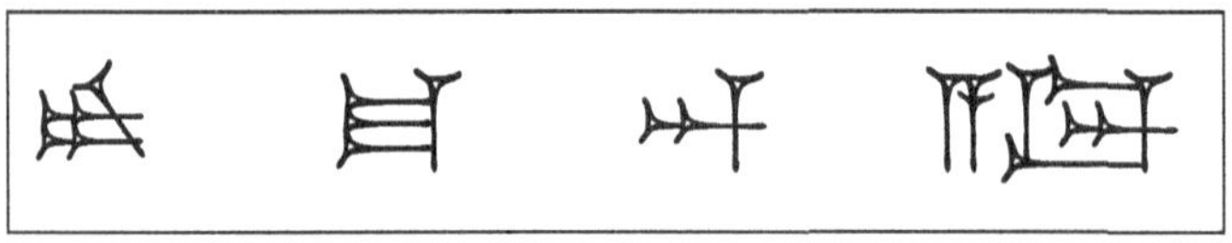

LH §2 V:43

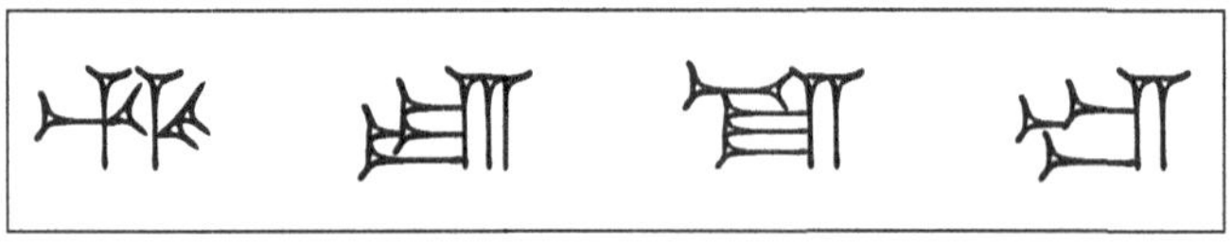

2. Transliterate: See the notes below for additional help.

   Note: The sign 𒀀, *a*, in V:41, which seems redundant, is used in this verb to indicate the preservation of an ʾ between the two vowels *i* and *a*. This demonstrates the helpful scribal practice in LH that confirms the presence of the ventive *-am*.

   Note: In V:43, the final *d* of the verb and the initial *š* of the suffix partially assimilate to each other resulting in *-ss*.

3. Normalize: Normalize your transliteration and check your answer in Appendix F.

4. Grammatical Analysis: Parse all verb forms.

5. Translate: Translate LH §2 V:41–43. Add to this your previous translation of LH §2.

Akkadian Cognates and Scripture

Catherine McDowell

You may be surprised to learn that about 50 percent of biblical Hebrew vocabulary has cognates in Akkadian. These cognates can be very helpful in determining the meaning of rare biblical Hebrew vocabulary or words whose meanings may differ from their typical Old Testament use. Exodus 19:5 is a case of the former. At the top of Mount Sinai, God gives Moses a message for Israel, "You yourselves have seen what I did to the Egyptians, and how I bore you on eagles' wings and brought you to myself. Now, therefore, if you will indeed obey my voice and keep all my covenant, you shall be my *səg̱ullâ* among all the peoples, for all the earth is mine" (Exod 19:4-5). *Səg̱ullâ* occurs only eight times in the Old Testament. Twice it refers to a king's treasure of silver and gold (Eccl 2:8, 1 Chr 29:3). The other six occurrences (Exod 19:5; Deut 7:6, 14:2, 26:18; Mal 3:17; and Ps 135:4) describe Israel's relationship to the LORD. She is his "treasured possession" (ESV, NRSV, NIV, JPS), his "own possession" (HCSB, NASB), a "peculiar treasure" (KJV), and the LORD's "own special treasure" (NLT) whom he has chosen from among all the peoples on earth. The LXX translates *səg̱ullâ* as λαὸς περιούσιος, "a special people," whereas the Latin Vulgate renders it as *peculium* ("private property"). The Aramaic Targum translates it as חֲבִיבִין ("beloved"). Despite the Targum's interpretive approach to translation, the meaning seems clear enough—Israel was the LORD's personal treasure.

While the meaning of the cognate Akkadian term, *sikiltu*, overlaps with Hebrew *səg̱ullâ* in terms of private property[1] and special treasure,[2] an Akkadian text from Alalakh designates King Abban-AN as a god's *sikiltu*, that is, as the god's "special, personal property," and as his worshipper.[3] This is significant because it suggests that Israel would have recognized *səg̱ullâ* as defining a privileged and unique relationship between a king and his god. By applying this term to Israel, God declares them to be not only his personal treasure, but a holy people set apart for a special relationship with him (Exod 19:6), contingent on their obedience (Exod 19:5). What an extraordinary moment it must have been for this band of bedraggled and homeless Hebrews to hear God identify them as his *səg̱ullâ*![4]

Akkadian cognates can also help us recognize that some common Hebrew words have a broader semantic range than what their typical Old Testament use indicates. One such example is the well-known term "image" (*ṣelem*). Hebrew lexicons define *ṣelem* as "statue, image, likeness, resemblance, idol," with "idol" being its most frequent meaning in the Old Testament. In Genesis 1:26–27, nearly all English Bibles translate *ṣelem* as "image": "Let us make humanity in our <u>image</u>," and, "So God created humanity in his <u>image</u>, in the <u>image</u> of God he created them." Many scholars rightly conclude that in Genesis 1, *ṣelem* refers to humanity's function as God's representative, his "living statuette," but they do so with the support of Semitic cognates, especially Akkadian. The Akkadian cognate *ṣalmu* shares a similar

1. HSS V, 71:17ff.

2. Daniel David Luckenbill, *Annals of Sennacherib*, ed. James Henry Breasted. OIP 2 (Chicago: Oriental Institute of the University of Chicago, 1924), 55 line 61.

3. *TLOT* 2:791.

4. In addition to this Akkadian parallel, there is a Ugaritic cognate, *sglt*, that describes Ammurāpi, the king of Ugarit, as the servant and *sglt* (possession) of the king of Hatti, his master (RS 18.038 lines 11–16). Given the covenant context of Exodus 19–20ff., Ugaritic *sglt* suggests that *səg̱ullâ* designates not only "treasured possession" but also "covenant partner," specifically, "vassal."

semantic range to Hebrew *ṣelem* and frequently refers to a statue of a god (what the Old Testament calls an "idol") or even the god itself. However, like *ṣelem, ṣalmu* occurs in the context of creation to define the relationship between a king and his patron deity. A hymn from the Epic of Tukulti-Ninurta (1243–1207 BCE) describes the king's birth as "successfully engendered through/cast into the channel of the womb of the gods." He alone is "the eternal image (*ṣalmu*) of (the god) Enlil" whom "Enlil raised . . . like a natural father, after his firstborn son." Using metallurgical imagery, the poet depicts the king's body as a statue that represents the god. In this context, however, *ṣalmu* is likely a double entendre. Not only is Tukulti-Ninurta a "living statue" of Enlil, but he is also Enlil's *son.* I suggest that he can only be a living image of Enlil *because* he is first Enlil's son. Function proceeds from ontology. Could *ṣelem* in Genesis 1 also be a double entendre?

Genesis 5:3 demonstrates that *ṣelem* can indicate a father-son relationship. Seth was created in the image (*ṣelem*) and likeness of his father, Adam, as Adam was created in the likeness and image (*ṣelem*) of God. Hence, in addition to the statuary connotations *ṣelem* carries, Genesis 1 also defines the divine-human relationship in kinship terms. *Humans are God's representatives because we are first his sons and daughters.* This has profound implications for understanding our identity as human beings and our mission in this world, which Akkadian has helped us uncover!

8

The Four States of Nouns, Pronominal Suffixes on Nouns, and the Demonstrative Pronouns and Adjectives

This chapter addresses the four states of nouns with special emphasis on the construct state and its formations. Pronominal suffixes will also be addressed (see §4.3). Interest here is on the use and formation of pronominal suffixes with nouns and substantive adjectives. Finally, determinative pronouns and adjectives will be introduced. The exercises below (§8.4.3) introduce a second legal case within the second law of LH. Keep in mind that the division of laws is the result of decisions made by modern scholars; it is not something that is explicitly indicated by the original text. Scholars could have decided to designate this as the beginning of a third law in LH, rather than a continuation of the second.

8.1 The Four States of Nouns

Akkadian nouns and adjectives appear in one of four states: free, absolute, predicative, and construct.

1. The free form, also called the normal state or the *status rectus,* is the form of the word with its case ending, such as *šarrum,* "king," or *šarrātum,* "queen."

2. The absolute state, also called the *status absolutus,* is a form of the word where it is stripped of its case ending. If the word is feminine, it is sometimes also stripped of the feminine marker *t* and a preceding short vowel if there is one. This state is relatively rare, and it is mostly limited to numbers and units of measure or fixed prepositional and adverbial expressions.

3. The predicative state, or predicate state, changes the noun into a stative or an equative verb. Like the absolute state, it is formed by stripping the free form of the noun of its case ending. In place of that ending, the pronominal suffixes that are used on stative verbs are then added.

For example, if the case ending is removed from *šarrum* (nominative, singular), the result is a hypothetical form **šarr.* Since Akkadian does not allow a final doubled consonant, it resolves this by eliminating the doubling: *šar.* This form appears as either the predicative state of the noun or as the G-stem 3ms form of a stative verb meaning "he is king." The predicative noun or stative is placed last in its clause since that is the expected position for the verb in Akkadian (S-O-V). The predicative state will be studied in more detail in the next chapter (see §9.2.2).

4. The construct state is sometimes called the bound form or *status constructus*. When a noun or adjective (or participle as a substantivized verbal adjective) is in the construct state it loses its primary accent. It is, in effect, bound to a noun in the genitive case or a substantivized verb that immediately follows and with which it forms a "construct chain" or "genitive chain." Only two things can come between a noun in the construct state and the noun in the genitive case or substantivized verb with which it is bound: the negative *lâ* or the suffix *-mi*, which is used to mark direct discourse (this suffix will be discussed in Chapter 13).

8.1.1 ***Formation of the Construct State (or Bound State).*** To form the construct of a noun, the general rule is for the noun to be stripped of any short vowel case ending (*-um*, *-im*, or *-am*, whether on singulars or plurals) and also any final *-n* (from the nunation of dual endings).[1] For example, the construct of *awīlum* (ms nominative) is *awīl*, "man of." The construct of *kišpī* (mp oblique), however, is *kišpī*, "witchcraft of." The construct of *šarrātim* (fp oblique) is *šarrāt*, "queens of." Accordingly, only the construct forms of masculine plural nouns and dual nouns maintain the final vowels that indicate case.

There are five rules outlined below to help identify any words from LH when they are in construct. Nevertheless, not every construct form of a word can be predicted on the basis of these rules. Accordingly, at times it is necessary to check a reliable lexicon to confirm what construct form is, in fact, attested for a particular word.

1. For words with a biconsonantal root, such as *abum*, "father," the construct is often formed by removing a short vowel case ending (such as *-um*), as indicated above, but then adding a final *-i*, as a paragogic vowel, to yield the construct form *abi*, "father of," as in LH §159.[2]

Some biconsonantal words, such as *mutum*, "husband," may have two alternative forms of the construct. They may have a form with a paragogic *-i*, like *muti*, "husband of," but in other contexts the same word may appear without a paragogic *-i*, as happens with *mut*, "husband of," in LH §172.[3]

2. Words that have a final double consonant usually have a construct form with both consonants followed by a paragogic *-i*. For example, the word for "heart" is *libbum* (cf. *lēb*, לֵב). To form the construct, the short vowel case ending is removed, resulting in **libb*. Since Akkadian does not permit a doubly closed syllable, however, the construct is formed by adding to the word base a paragogic *-i*. Hence, the construct form is *libbi*, meaning "heart of."

Less commonly a final doubled consonant in the construct can be simplified by the retention of only one final consonant. This option is seen in the construct for *šarrum*, "king," which is invariably *šar* in LH, although elsewhere it is often *šarri* with a paragogic *-i*.

3. Similar to the situation with a final doubled consonant, when the case ending of a word is removed, the result may be a syllable that ends with a consonantal cluster of dissimilar consonants. Once again, since a consonantal cluster is not permitted in Akkadian, an anaptyctic

1. For rare dual forms, see §2.6. Like mimation, nunation is part of the suffix and not a root consonant.

2. Paragogic is a term used by scholars of Semitic languages to describe a letter that has been added to the end of a word. This may be done in order to help pronunciation, and it may or may not indicate a change in the word's meaning or grammatical function.

3. In LH §137 a rare alternative construct form for *mutum* appears, namely *mutu*. This form reflects an archaic *-u* suffix that is used for singular nouns in construct. See Driver and Miles, *The Babylonian Laws*, 2: 220, and Worthington, *Complete Babylonian*, §10.9.

vowel is added to break up the cluster.[4] Usually the vowel identical to whatever other vowel is present earlier in the root word is added; in such cases it is termed a harmonizing anaptyctic vowel. The only exceptions to this practice are words where the original free form of the word came about through vowel syncope (§2.5.2.3). In these instances, the original vowel that was elided is restored.

For example, the noun *maḫrum* means "front" or "presence." The construct of *maḫrum* is produced by removal of the short vowel case ending, resulting in **maḫr.* The cluster is broken up with a harmonizing anaptyctic vowel. Hence, the construct of *maḫrum* is *maḫar,* meaning "the presence of," which appears in LH §9. For the constructs of adjectives, however, the anaptyctic vowel is not always a harmonizing vowel.

For another example, the noun *šubtum* (< **w-š-b*) means "seat, dwelling" (cf. *yāšab;* יָשַׁב, "to dwell"). To form the construct, the short vowel case ending *-um* is removed resulting in **šubt.* Normally one expects the use of a harmonizing anaptyctic vowel, in this case the vowel *-u-*, to break up the *-bt* consonantal cluster. Since, however, the consonant *t* in this word comes from an original feminine ending *-at* rather than being a root consonant for the word and since that original *a* vowel was then reduced because of vowel syncope (*šubat* < *šubtum* < **šubatum*), the *a* vowel is restored for the construct: *šubat,* "dwelling of," found in LH §Pro II:31.

4. Some feminine nouns that, after short vowel case endings are removed, end with a consonantal cluster may produce a construct form with a restored feminine *a*-vowel, as illustrated in the example above of *šubat.* Alternatively, however, they may instead produce a construct form by adding a paragogic *-i* after the *t.*

For example, the construct of *amtum,* "female slave," is *amat,* "female slave of," in LH §213, with the restored feminine *a*-vowel. On the other hand, the construct of *šaluštum,* "a third," is *šalušti,* "a third of," with a paragogic *-i* after the *t,* as in LH §29.

5. The construct of a noun or adjective with a stem that ends in a vowel (which originally was a vowel followed by an ') is formed in one of two alternative ways. Either the construct consists simply of the word with the short vowel case ending removed, or it is formed by adding the vowel of the case ending, with or without vowel contraction of the stem vowel with the case vowel.

For example, the Akkadian word for "physician" is *asûm* (< **asi'um*). The construct of *asûm,* as found in LH §224, is *asî,* "a physician of." Since *asî* functions as the subject of its clause and so is an unmarked nominative, we know that the long *i* vowel here is the result of compensatory lengthening, *asî* < **asi'* < **asi'um,* rather than contraction, since *i* + *u* contracts to *û* according to §3.4.5.

Alternatively, an example of a noun whose base ends with a vowel followed by ' but whose construct is formed by vowel contraction with the stem vowel and the case vowel (here, a genitive-accusative plural) is *rugummê* < **rugummā'ī,* "a legal claim; a penalty assessed or awarded in a lawsuit" in LH §12.

4. An anaptyctic vowel is one that is added inside a word to assist in pronunciation by breaking up a consonantal cluster, which is avoided in Akkadian.

8.2 Nouns and Substantivized Adjectives with a Pronominal Suffix

In general, when a pronominal possessive suffix is added to a noun or to a substantivized adjective (including a participle), the noun or adjective is first put into the construct state. Sometimes a linking vowel, which is normally the vowel *a*, is added, and finally the desired pronominal suffix is added. Note that the rule of vowel syncope (§2.5.2.3) does not apply to pronominally suffixed nouns and neither does the rule of Babylonian vowel harmony (§3.4.3).

The detailed rules and examples presented below will be sufficient for correctly analyzing an Akkadian noun or adjective with a pronominal suffix, which is the purpose in this textbook for learning these forms. These rules may not suffice for predicting the exact form of a noun or adjective with a pronominal suffix in any given case because, at times, there is more than one possible option.

8.2.1 ***Singular Nouns in the Nominative or Accusative.*** For a singular noun in the nominative or accusative, the general rule is to take the construct form of the noun and add the desired suffix.

For example, *šībum* means "old man" or "witness." If one wants to place a 3ms pronominal suffix on the noun so that it will mean "his old man/witness," the first step is to produce the construct form. Based on the five rules set out in §8.1.1 the most likely construct state for this word is *šīb*, regardless of whether it is nominative or accusative.[5] Following the procedure described above, the nominative/accusative of "his witness" is *šībšu* < *šīb* + -*šu*.

If the construct of a noun ends in *t*, as in feminine nouns, a pronominal suffix that begins with *š* will experience reciprocal assimilation so that *tš* becomes *ss*. For example, the Akkadian word for "woman" or "wife" is *aššatum* (cf. *'iššâ*, אִשָּׁה). The construct of this word in the nominative or accusative is *aššat*. Accordingly, "his wife" would seem to be **aššatšu*, except that by reciprocal assimilation this form with *tš* becomes *aššassu*. This form appears in LH §134.

If the construct of a singular noun in the nominative or accusative has a paragogic -*i*, then the suffixed form will replace the paragogic -*i* vowel with an -*a* linking vowel before pronominal suffixes. For example, the word for "heart" in Akkadian is *libbum* (cf. *lēb*, לֵב). The construct of *libbum* (or *libbam*) is *libbi* with a paragogic -*i*. Accordingly, the form of *libbum* or *libbam* with a 3ms pronominal suffix meaning "his heart" is *libbašu* (< *libba* + *šu* < *libbi* + *šu*), as seen in LH §264.

8.2.2 ***Singular or Dual Nouns in the Genitive.*** For singular or dual nouns in the genitive, the rule for adding a pronominal suffix is straightforward: remove the mimation (the -*m*), or in the case of dual nouns the nunation (-*n*), from the genitive case ending but retain the case vowel, which is *i* (or, with some III-weak roots, *ē*), and then add the desired pronominal suffix.

For example, the genitive of *libbum* is *libbim*. When mimation is removed, the result is *libbi*. Accordingly, this base with a 3fs pronominal suffix meaning "her heart," is *libbiša* (< *libbi* + *ša*), as seen in LH §237.

5. The construct of *šībum* also sometimes appears as *šībi*.

8.2.3 ***Plural Nouns.*** For plural nouns, regardless of the case, the rule for adding a pronominal suffix is straightforward: remove mimation (the *-m*), if there is mimation, from the case ending of the noun in the nominative or genitive-accusative, and then add the desired suffix.

For example, if one wants to write "his witnesses," it is necessary to start with the nominative plural form for "witnesses," which is *šībū*.[6] Therefore, "his witnesses" is *šībūšu* < *šībū* + *šu*.

8.2.4 ***Less Common Forms of Nouns.*** Some nouns and adjectives like *abum*, "father," the construct of which is *abi*, replace the paragogic *-i* not with the expected linking vowel *-a-* but with the vowel from the appropriate case ending. So "his father" in the nominative is *abušu* (cf. *abuša*, "her father" in LH §178), in the genitive, *abišu* (so LH §28), and in the accusative, *abašu* (so LH §186). The nouns for "father-in-law," *emum*, "brother," *aḫum*, and "son," *mârum* often follow a similar pattern.

Similarly, there are other singular nouns and adjectives that retain, as needed, all three short case vowels, *-u-*, *-i-*, and *-a-*, before pronominal suffixes. This especially applies to nouns and adjectives from III-weak roots such as *mimmûm* (< **mimma'um*), "whatever; property." Accordingly, "his property" in the nominative is *mimmûšu* (< **mimma'u* + *šu*), as is attested in LH §125 and elsewhere in LH, *mimmîšu* in the genitive, and *mimmâšu* in the accusative (as attested in LH §240, and elsewhere in LH).

The same applies to *kalûm* (< **kala'um*), "entirety, all," (cf. *kôl*, כּוֹל), although this common word does not happen to appear in LH. Nevertheless, "his entirety" or "all of it" is *kalûšu* in the nominative, *kalîšu* in the genitive, and *kalâšu* in the accusative.

8.2.5 ***Secondary Lengthening of Final Short Vowels.*** When pronominal suffixes (see §4.3) are added to a word ending with an original long vowel that was shortened, the original long vowel is restored. When pronominal suffixes are added to a word that ends with an original short vowel, that vowel (excluding paragogic vowels) is, in the opinion of many Assyriologists, secondarily lengthened.[7] It seems likely that this lengthening may reflect actual pronunciation in the Old Babylonian period. Such lengthening would explain, for example, why syncope of vowels does not apply with these vowels. Many Assyriologists, however, prefer to normalize these vowels as short (this is the practice of *CAD*, for example).[8] The advantage of this practice is that it allows singular nouns with pronominal suffixes to be more consistently distinguished from plural nouns. Accordingly, in this textbook all original short case vowels will be written as short. For example, *mârišu*, "of his son," is clearly distinguished in its normalization from *mârīšu*, "of his sons."

8.2.6 ***The Pronominal Suffixes.*** The paradigm for pronominal suffixes was provided in §4.3, but for the benefit of review, they are repeated here. The genitive forms are the ones used on nouns:

6. See §2.6.

7. Recall that this same kind of lengthening of final short vowels occurs to words when the enclitic *-ma* suffix is added. See §3.5. Cf., e.g., Huehnergard, *A Grammar of Akkadian*, 86; Worthington, *Complete Babylonian*, §§11.3, 11:5.

8. Cf., e.g., Caplice, *Introduction to Akkadian*, §18.4 and §84i; Worthington, *Complete Babylonian*, §11.5.

	Genitive (with nouns and prepositions)	**Dative (with verbs)**	**Accusative (with verbs)**
1cs	*-ī, -ya, 'a*	*-am, -m, -nim*	*-ni*
2ms	*-ka*	*-kum*	*-ka*
2fs	*-ki*	*-kim*	*-ki*
3ms	*-šu*	*-šum*	*-šu*
3fs	*-ša*	*-šim*	*-ši*
1cp	*-ni*	*-ni'āšim*	*-ni'āti*
2mp	*-kunu*	*-kunūšim*	*-kunūti*
2fp	*-kina*	*-kināšim*	*-kināti*
3mp	*-šunu*	*-šunūšim*	*-šunūti*
3fp	*-šina*	*-šināšim*	*-šināti*

8.3 Demonstrative Pronouns and Adjectives

Demonstrative pronouns and adjectives have the same form. They agree with their antecedent or the noun they modify in gender and number, and, when they are used attributively, they also agree in their grammatical case. When demonstratives function as adjectives, they follow the noun they modify.

The following set of demonstratives are commonly translated as "that" or "those," but since they are used anaphorically (referring to something that has just been mentioned), they can also be rendered "this" or "these." The singular forms in bold should be memorized. There are not examples of the nominative plural forms in LH and each of the genitive-accusative forms occurs only once, so they do not need to be learned.

		Masculine	**Feminine**
Singular	Nominative	***šū***	***šī***
	Genitive-Accusative	***šu'āti***	***šu'āti***
Plural	Nominative	*šunu*	*šina*
	Genitive-Accusative	*šunūti*	*šināti*

Following the consistent spelling conventions of LH, the independent demonstrative pronoun *šū*, "that," is always spelled in cuneiform as *šu-ú*, whereas the 3ms pronominal suffix *-šu* is always spelled just with the sign for *šu*.

8.4 Homework

Before you move on, be sure to understand the four states of nouns: free, absolute, predicative, and construct. Also, be familiar with the rules associated with identifying and understanding construct forms. Rules about adding pronominal suffixes on nouns and substantivized adjectives should also be learned. Finally, be able to recognize the demonstrative pronouns and understand how they appear in texts and how to translate them.

8.4.1 *Signs*

 8

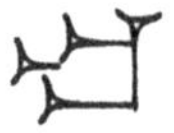 *ba*

 *eb, ib, ep, ip*

 *re, ri*

 *aš*

 *te*

 *tab, tap*

Congratulations! If you have learned the seven cuneiform signs in this chapter and each of the preceding fifty-two signs, you will be able to read 76 percent of all the cuneiform signs in LH §§1–20, 127–149.

8.4.2 *Vocabulary*

arnum = penalty, guilt
awâtum = word (a feminine noun from the root *awũm*).
napištum = life (cf. *nepeš*, נֶפֶשׁ, "life")
qabũm (*q-b-y*) (*i,i*) = to speak, declare, order
šī = that, this (nom fs)
šũ = that, this (nom ms)
šu'āti = that, this (gen-acc cs)

8.4.3 *Exercises*

1. Identify Signs: Identify each of the signs below and include all the listed possible values of each.

LH §2 V:44

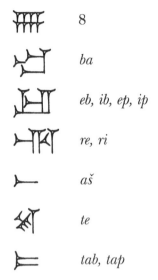

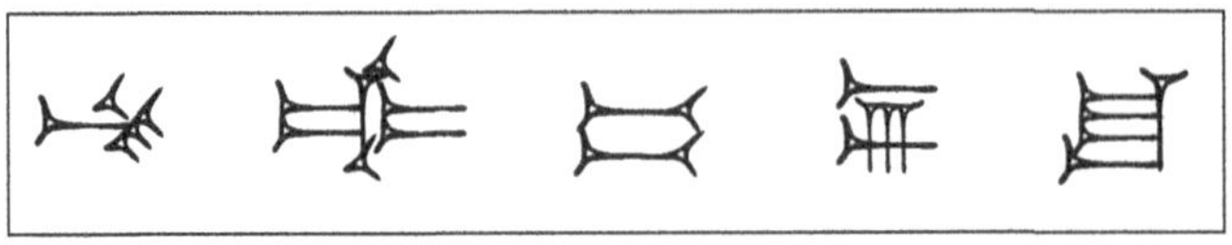

LH §2 V:45

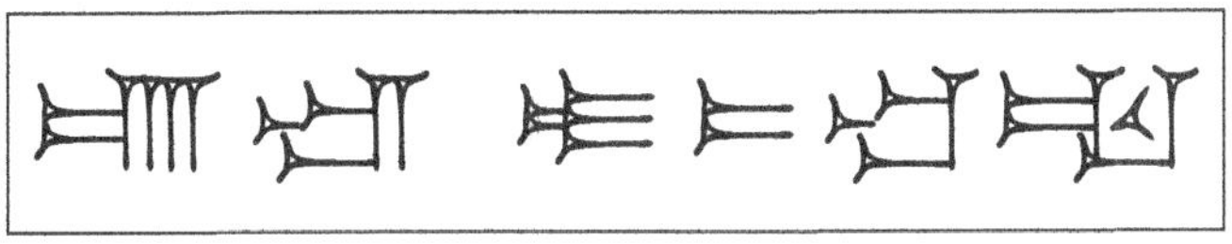

LH §2 V:46

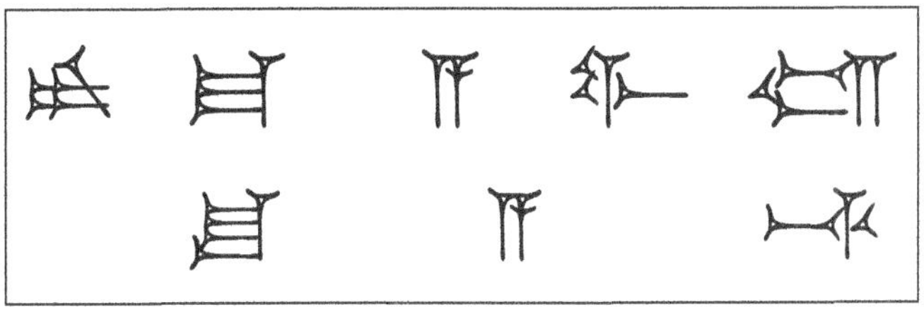

LH §2 V:47

LH §2 V:48

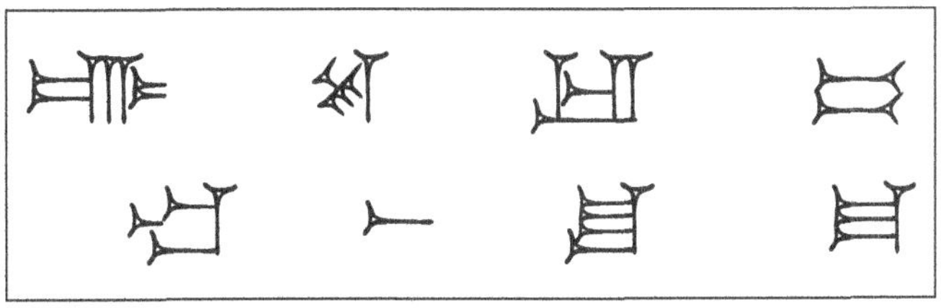

LH §2 V:49

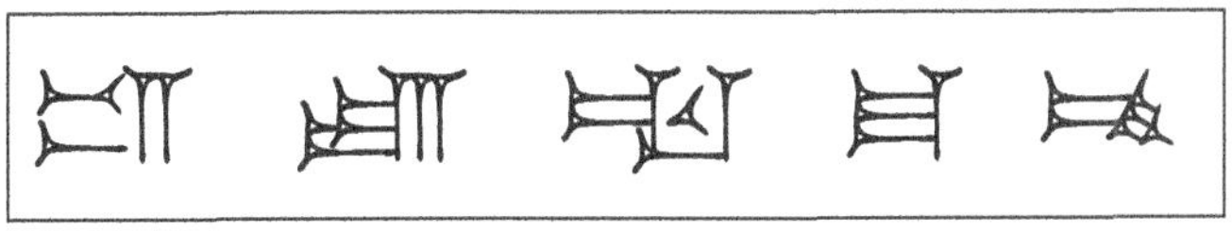

2. Transliterate: See the note below for additional help.

   Note: What is the term used to describe the special use of the sign  in V:45?

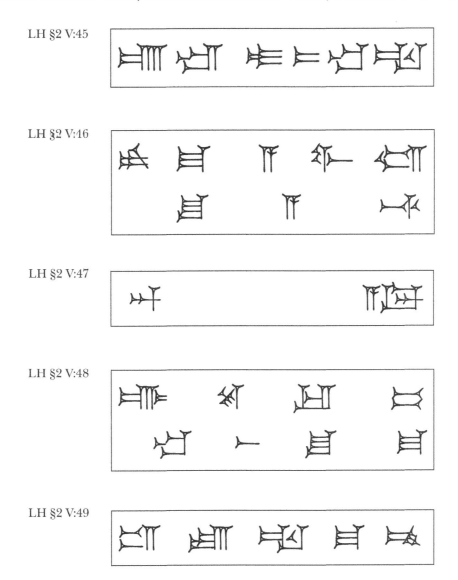

3. Normalize: Normalize your transliteration.

4. Grammatical Analysis: Parse the first form in V:44 and all verb forms. See the notes below for additional help.

   Note: The verb in V:48 is I-' *ebēbum* and has three attached suffixes.

   Note: The verb in V:49 experiences vowel syncope reduction with the ventive suffix *-am*.

5. Translate: Translate LH §2 V:44–49. See the note below for additional help. Add to this your previous translation of LH §2.

   Note: What is unusual about the word order in V:46–48?

Akkadian Loanwords and Wordplays in Isaiah

Christopher B. Hays

If we could not read Akkadian texts, our understanding of the book of Isaiah would be greatly impoverished. This is not only because they illuminate the book's historical and cultural contexts; even at the level of word choice, it seems clear that Isaiah ben Amoz and later Isaianic authors were aware of and played with Akkadian terms. As the great H. W. F. Saggs said of the eighth-century prophet: "His interests appear to have extended beyond Theology to Comparative Semitic Philology, for we find the prophet making a pun based on cross-correspondences between Hebrew and Akkadian vocabulary."[1]

Perhaps the most overt Hebrew-Akkadian wordplay in the book is a boast attributed to the Assyrian king: "Are not my commanders (*śāray*) all kings?" (10:8). The comment plays on the divergent meanings of cognate terms— Hebrew *śar* ("commander") and Akkadian *šarru*, ("king"). The Hebrew term is used for an array of high officials subordinate to the king (Heb. *melek*; see, for example, 2 Sam 18:5). The force of the boast in Isaiah 10:8 seems to have been that the Assyrian emperor's officials were as powerful as kings—which was true, since they were assigned to govern regions larger than many sovereign nations of earlier periods. The claim also echoes the Assyrian royal epithet *šar šarrāni*, "king of kings." But Isaiah went on to promise that there was a surprise in store for Assyria.

Speaking of Assyrian commanders, the imperial representative who comes to speak at the wall of Jerusalem in Isaiah 36–37 (and its parallel in 2 Kgs 18–19) bore a title (*rab šaqê*) with a direct Akkadian cognate. The phrase translates as "chief cupbearer," but there is no evidence that this was more than a vestigial title. What we do know is that he was commander of the empire's northern armies and a governor of large territories.[2] Not surprisingly, the speeches that the Bible attributes to him echo actual diplomatic language used by the Assyrians.[3]

Another wordplay on an Akkadian meaning is the use of *s-k-r* in Isaiah 19:4a, which is consistent with the use of the Akkadian verb *sekēru*, meaning "dam up/stop up." The half-verse should be translated, "I will dam up Egypt by the hand of a harsh overlord." Because the idea of "damming up Egypt" neatly introduces the Nile-Curse section of the oracle in verses 5–10, this also clarifies that the whole passage is a unified composition. Most translations render it, "I will *hand over* Egypt into the hand of a harsh overlord," as if the Hebrew verb were *s-g-r* instead of *s-k-r*. And it may well be that Isaiah was playing with that similar-sounding verb![4] The use of paronomasia, or double entendre, was characteristic of the prophet.

Wordplay with Akkadian might also explain why Jerusalem is called "Ariel" in Isaiah 29:1, 7. In this case, the Great Isaiah Scroll from Qumran instead reads ארואל, suggesting the reading *'Ūrû'ēl*,

1. H. W. F Saggs, *Assyriology and the Study of the Old Testament: An Inaugural Lecture Delivered at University College, Cardiff, Tuesday December 3rd, 1968* (Cardiff: University of Wales Press, 1969), 4–5.

2. Raija Mattila, *The King's Magnates: A Study of the Highest Officials of the Neo-Assyrian Empire*, SAAS 11 (Helsinki: Neo-Assyrian Text Corpus Project, 2000), 163.

3. Peter Machinist, "Assyria and Its Image in the First Isaiah," *Journal of the American Oriental Society* 103 (1983): 719–37; Shawn Zelig Aster, *Reflections of Empire in Isaiah 1–39: Responses to Assyrian Ideology*, SBL Ancient Near East Monographs 19 (Atlanta: SBL Press, 2017).

4. Christopher B. Hays, "Damming Egypt / Damning Egypt: The Paronomasia of *skr* and the Unity of Isa 19:1–15," *Zeitschrift für die Alttestamentliche Wissenschaft* 120 (2008): 612–16.

"City of God." The first element in the name Jerusalem was consistently vocalized with *u*-sounds, both in Akkadian (Amarna Letters: *Ú-ru-sa-lim*; Sennacherib inscriptions: *Ur-sa-lim-mu*) and other Semitic languages. The Akkadian forms seem to absorb phonetically the Sumerian logogram URU, "city" (e.g., URU Salimmu="City of Shalem"; cf. Gen 14:18; Ps 76:3[ET 76:2]).[5] The Šal(i)mu from which Jebusite Jerusalem took its name was a Canaanite deity known from Ugaritic texts. Thus, Isaiah would be playing on the meaning "City of God" as well as a term for an altar-hearth known from Ezekiel 43:15–16 and the Mesha inscription. Jerusalem, the city of God, was threatened with being a place where blood flowed and flesh was burned.

There are other words in Isaiah that we could not be sure we understood if we did not recognize them as Akkadian loanwords. For example, Isaiah 9:5 [9:4 MT] promises that Judah will be delivered from the Assyrians and that "every sandal tramping (*sāʾôn sōʾēn*) like an earthquake . . . will be burned as fuel for the fire." These terms that share the root s-ʾ-n occur nowhere else in the Hebrew Bible, but the term *šēnu* is a relatively common term for "sandal" in Akkadian. (The associated verb *šênu* also exists but was less common.)

The interconnected nature of the ancient Near East and Akkadian's role as a lingua franca are also in view in Isaiah. When describing the Egyptians' proclivity for consulting the dead in Isaiah 19:3, the prophet uses an Akkadian loanword: "they will consult the idols and the spirits of the dead (אטים)." This term also occurs nowhere else in the Bible but is clearly recognizable as a loanword from Akkadian *eṭimmu*, which has the same meaning.

Isaiah ben Amoz, then, had picked up at least a few words of Akkadian. Beyond that, the degree to which Judahite officials and scribes would have learned or understood Akkadian remains contested, partly because of the relatively small number of cuneiform tablets that have been discovered in the Iron Age Levant in the territory of preexilic Israel and Judah. Certainly, Aramaic was already on the rise as an administrative language in the late eighth century BCE, as Isaiah 36:11||2 Kings 18:26 reflects. Nonetheless, the discovery of Assyrian cuneiform tablets, including a treaty-tablet, in the ruins of the Syrian temple in Tell Tayinat is a provocative indication that it would have been highly desirable for Levantine nations to have some understanding of the language of their imperial masters.

When one looks ahead at Second Isaiah, the mechanism of Akkadian influence is even easier to understand. The author of Isaiah 40–48 probably had once lived in Babylon. Images of Babylonian divine statues in 46:1 are often cited as proof of this (e.g., "Bel bows down, Nebo stoops, their idols are on beasts and cattle"). The term *Bēl* ("Lord") refers to the Babylonian chief deity Marduk; it is cognate with Baal, the Levantine deity who appears much more often in the Hebrew Bible.

More striking still is Second Isaiah's use of unusual vocabulary. For example, despite all the terms for trees and wood in the Bible, *ʾōren*, referring to a specific type of cedar, occurs only in Isaiah 44:14. This was indeed a tree sacred to Babylonian deities and used for magical figurines.

Finally, certain verb choices in Second Isaiah also have to be understood in light of Akkadian influence. For example, the Lord says to Cyrus, "I call you by your name, I honor you by title (*ʾăkannĕkā*), though you do not know me" (45:4). This is an unusual verb in Hebrew, but its cognate *kunnû* is a relatively common one in Akkadian where it means "to honor, show respect" and can be used to refer to honoring both humans and deities.

This is only a small sample of the relevance of Akkadian to the study of Isaiah. The scholar who wants to understand the language of the prophets does well to study the language of the Mesopotamians.

5. Ronald Youngblood, "Ariel, 'City of God,'" in *Essays on the Occasion of the Seventieth Anniversary of the Dropsie University*, ed. Abraham Isaac Katsh and Leon Nemoy (Philadelphia: Dropsie University, 1979), 458–59.

9—

Asyndeton, Verbless Clauses, and the Predicative State

The exercises in this chapter conclude the final lines of LH §2. Asyndeton, verbless clauses, and the predicative state will be explained.

9.1 Asyndeton

Asyndeton is when clauses are juxtaposed and have some implied semantic relationship to each other but lack an expected conjunction. Asyndeton is relatively common in LH.[1] There is an example in the earlier portion of LH §2 where the clause, *ša elīšu kišpū nadû ana Id illak,* "the one against whom charges of sorcery were hurled would go to the river (Id)," is followed directly by the clause, *Id išalli'amma,* "He would plunge into the river (Id). . . ." The second clause presupposes the first and is necessarily subsequent to it, so the two clauses cannot be interpreted as a simple example of apposition or a case where the second clause is merely a restatement or explication of the first. In such a case, it is a translator's choice whether to start a new sentence with the second clause or to separate the clauses with a semicolon, a comma, or an added conjunction like "and," as in LH §183.

Based on semantic considerations, sometimes the clauses are clearly not in chronological order but are presented as alternatives. In such cases, the translator often needs to add the conjunction "or," as in LH §264. In other cases, if the clauses are contrastive in meaning, as in LH §144, the translator needs to add a contrastive conjunction such as "but" or "however."

9.2 Verbless Clauses and the Predicative State

Akkadian lacks any verb meaning "to be." Instead, for such purposes, it employs one of two options: (1) Either it uses a verbless clause, sometimes called a nominal clause, or (2) it turns the predicate noun or adjective into a stative, also called the predicative state of the noun or adjective.

9.2.1 ***Verbless Clauses.*** A verbless clause is a clause that lacks a finite verb (durative, perfect, preterite, or stative). Instead of employing an explicit verb, the subject (noun or pronoun) and the predicate (a noun, pronoun, or adjective) both appear within the same clause in the nominative case. Alternatively, a verbless clause may consist of a subject that is a noun or pronoun in the nominative case followed by a prepositional phrase.

1. Cf. Patterson, "Old Babylonian Parataxis as Exhibited in the Royal Letters of the Middle Old Babylonian Period and in the Code of Hammurapi."

If the subject is a noun, it will be first in its clause with the predicate nominative at the end (S-P). For example, in LH §177 the clause, *mârūša ṣeḫḫerū*, appears, meaning "her children are young."[2]

If the subject is a pronoun, it is normally placed last in its clause (P-S). For example, in LH §Pro I:50–53 "I am . . . . Hammurabi" is written, *Ḫammurabi . . . anāku.*[3]

If the predicate is a prepositional phrase, the word order is normally the subject (noun or pronoun) first followed by the prepositional phrase (S-P). If the prepositional phrase comes first, however, this may transform it into an existential clause, which may be translated, "there is/are. . . ."[4]

If the predicate of a verbless clause is a *ša* phrase, as in *šeriktaša ša bît abišama* in LH §163, it expresses possession: "her dowry *is that which is of* the house of her father," or better, "her dowry *belongs to* the house of her father."[5]

9.2.2 ***Predicative State.*** The predicative state is the noun or adjective with its case ending removed (identical to the absolute state) but with the pronominal suffixes of the stative verb added to it. Since the stative verb has no suffix in the 3ms form, this means that no suffix is added to a predicative state.[6]

For example, one can express "that man is a thief" using the predicative state of the word "thief," *šarrāqum*, which is *šarrāq*. Hence, "that man is a thief" as it appears in LH §7 is *awīlum šū šarrāq*. Notice that the normal word order here is subject first and predicate second (S-P).

Alternatively, one can say in Akkadian "that man is a thief" with a verbless clause by juxtaposing two nouns in the nominative in the expected word order of subject first and predicate second (S-P). So, the subject, "that man" is *awīlum šū*, and the "predicate nominative" is *šarrāqum*, "a thief," hence, *awīlum šū šarrāqum*, "that man is a thief."

---

2. Cf. also LH xlviii:99, *awâtū'a nasqā*, "my words are special."

3. Cf. also LH §192, *ul abī atta*, "you are not my father," or LH xlvii:79-80, where we find *šarrum anāku*, "I am the king." The reverse word order appears in LH xlvii:42-43, *anākuma rē'um*. This reversed word order may be explained as the result of the emphatic *-ma* suffix on *anāku*. Accordingly, the unexpected fronting of *anākuma* reinforces the emphatic or contrastive implication of the *-ma* suffix.

4. See Huehnergard, *A Grammar of Akkadian*, §2.5. In LH, existential clauses are typically expressed with the explicit verb *bašûm*, "to exist, be." Cf., e.g., LH §§32, 133a, 134, 135, 139.

5. These rules for the word order of verbless clauses in Akkadian are similar to the rules for verbless clauses in Hebrew. In Hebrew with the early loss of declension, it is widely accepted among Hebraists that the word order of verbless clauses is generally consistent and semantically meaningful, especially in prose. There is some debate, however, about the particulars. According to Andersen (*The Sentence in Biblical Hebrew*), for example, in a "clause of identification" in Hebrew prose where both the subject and the verbless predicate are definite, the normal word order is S-P, where S is more definite than P (pronouns like "he" are more definite than proper nouns like "David," which are more definite than common nouns like "the king"). If the expected order is inverted, this is because P is contrastive (emphasized) or the reversal is for rhetorical effect. On the other hand, in a "clause of classification" in Hebrew prose, where S is definite but P is indefinite (an adjective, for example), the normal word order is P-S, unless the clause is circumstantial or explanatory or inverted for a rhetorical effect. For a more recent assessment of Andersen's proposals, see Miller, *The Verbless Clause in Biblical Hebrew, Linguistic Approaches*.

A more recent summary of the word order of verbless clauses suggests simply that the normal word order in Hebrew verbless clauses is S-P, where P can be a noun phrase, an adjective phrase, or a prepositional phrase. When the order is P-S, the predicate is "marked." Often an adjunct of the clause or some constituent is also fronted. So, according to van der Merwe, Naudé, and Kroeze, *A Biblical Hebrew Reference Grammar*, §46.2.3.

6. Some grammars consider the predicative state not as the state of a noun or adjective but as, in fact, a stative verb. This is the view, for example, of Marcus, *A Manual of Akkadian*, §8.3; and Ungnad, *Akkadian Grammar*, §52. Favoring the view that these forms represent the state of a noun or adjective (most frequently that of a verbal adjective), see Huehnergard, *A Grammar of Akkadian*, §22.1. For a fuller discussion, cf. Kouwenberg, "Nouns as Verbs: the Verbal Nature of the Akkadian Stative." Kouwenberg argues that while historically these forms derived from the predicative use of the verbal adjective (and subsequently, other adjectives and nouns more generally), with the addition of a pronominal suffix, these forms are true finite verbal forms (statives) on par with any of the prefix tenses.

9.3 Homework

Before you move on, be sure to understand asyndeton as it relates to LH, verbless clauses, and the predicative state.

9.3.1 *Signs*

 9

 GÉME, *amtum*, "female slave" (cf. *'ămâ*, אָמָה)

 *ad, at, aṭ*

 DUMU, *mârum*, "son"

 *mi*

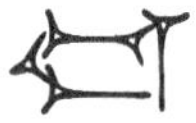 *nim*

 *ra*

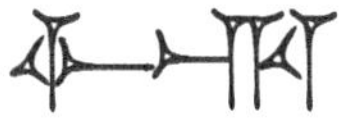 *ar*

 *ṣe, ṣi, zé, zí*

 *tim*

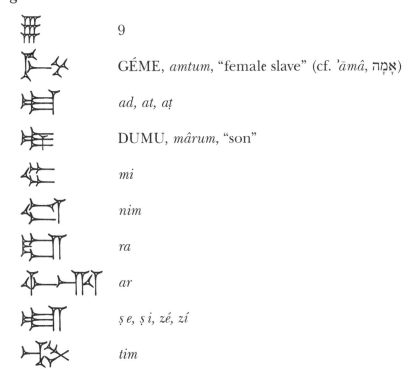

9.3.2 *Vocabulary*

dânum (*d-y-n*) (*a,i*) = to try (conduct a trial), judge (cf. *dîn*, דִּין, "to judge," *dān*, דָּן, "Dan")
dayyānum = a judge (a common *nomen agentis* form for D-stem nouns).
kunukkum = seal; sealed clay tablet (This word is built on the verb *kanākum*, "to seal." This noun type doubles the third radical—sometimes called the R-stem, or "Reduplicated stem"—but it lacks a sufformative.)
mârum = son (cf. Hebrew *mərî'*, מְרִיא, "fatling"; Aramaic *mārē'*, מָרֵא, "lord," related to *maranatha*)[7]
našûm (*n-š-'*) *i*-class = to lift, carry, bear; to support (cf. *nāśā'*, נָשָׂא, "to bear").
purussûm = decision (a common Old Akkadian noun type with a doubled final consonant [an example of the R-stem], followed by a sufformative -*a'*; cf. *pāras*, פָּרַס, "to break [bread]"; "to divide [hoofs]")

Congratulations! If you learn the six words above and have learned each of the forty-seven words in the vocabulary lists of the preceding chapters, you will be able to read 51 percent of all the words in LH §§1–20, 127–149.

7. Supportive of the posited length of the *a*-vowel through metathesis of a lengthening consonant or metathesis of the two earlier final root consonants, cf. Old Akkadian and Assyrian *mar'um* and lexical texts with readings such as *ma-a-ru-um*. See *AHw*, ad loc. See especially Huehnergard, *A Grammar of Akkadian*, §6.1(b) for the example of compensatory lengthening in *mârum* < **mar'um*, "son."

9.3.3 *Exercises*

1. By way of review of LH §2, translate the following:
   šumma awīlum kišpī elî awīlim iddîma lâ uktînšu ša elîšu kišpū nadû ana Id illak Id išalli'amma šumma Id iktašassu mubbiršu bîssu itabbal šumma awīlam šu'āti Id/nârum ûtebbibaššūma ištalmam

The remaining lines of LH §2 constitute the apodosis (the "then" clause) for the second case in this law. In other words, they describe what would be done if the man accused of sorcery was determined by the river ordeal to be innocent. Not only would the false accuser be executed, but there was also an additional requirement.

2. Identify Signs: Identify each of the signs below and include all the listed possible values of each.

LH §2 V:50

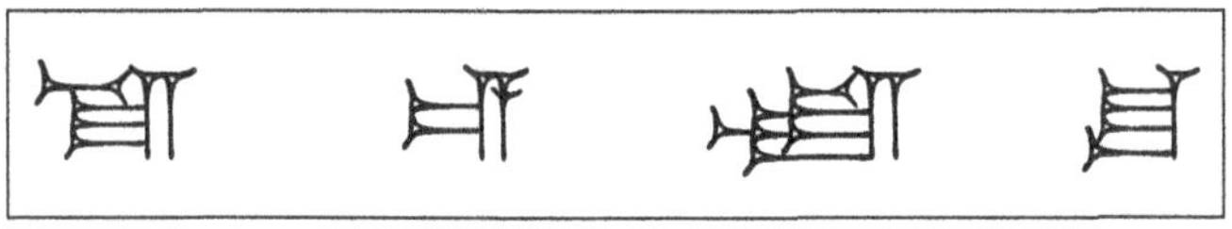

LH §2 V:51

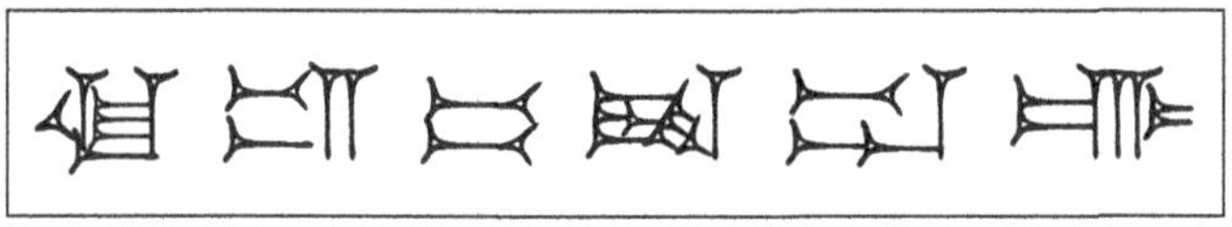

LH §2 V:52

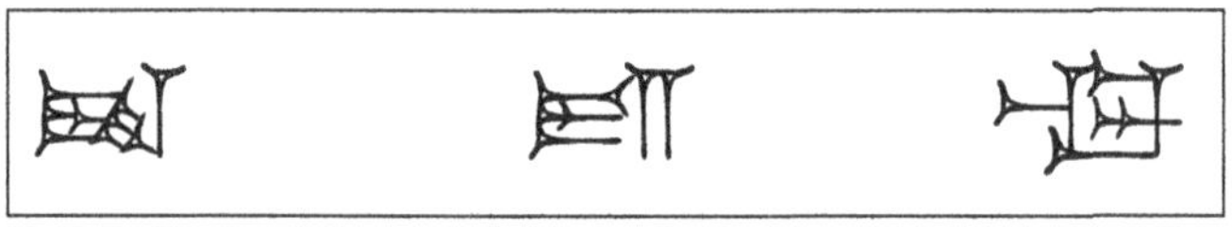

LH §2 V:53

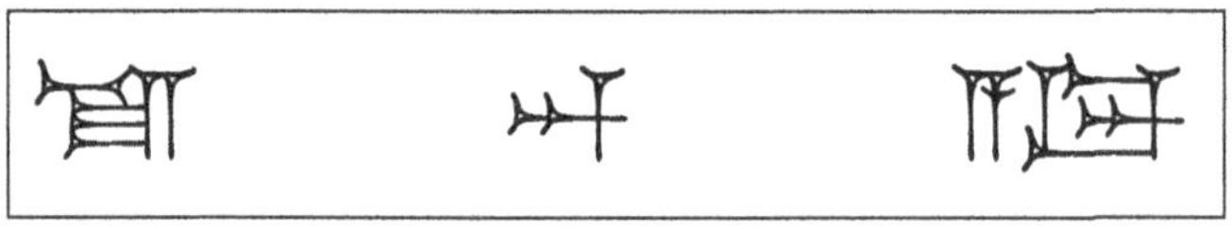

LH §2 V:54

LH §2 V:55

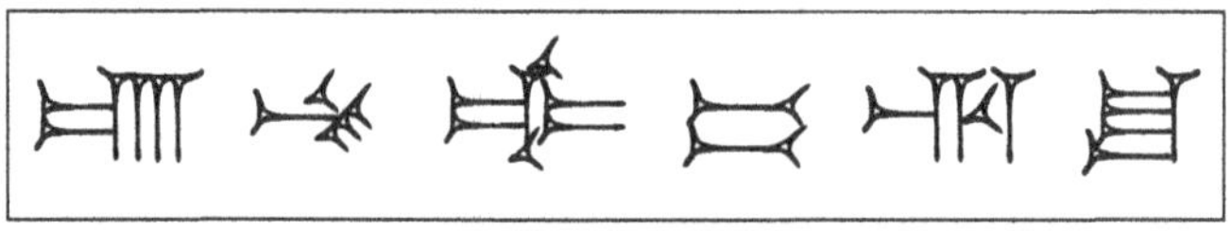

LH §2 V:56

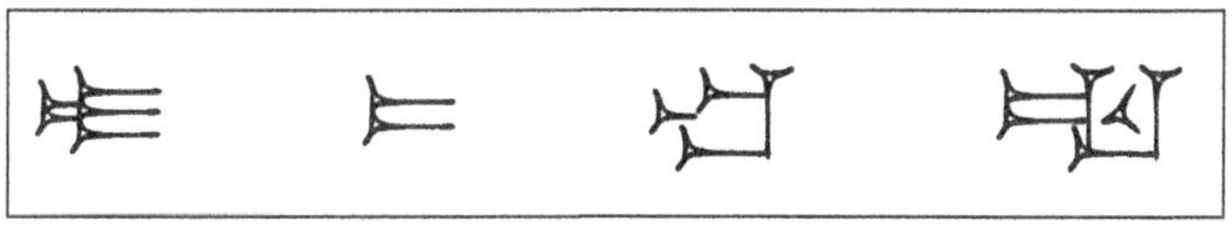

3. Transliterate: See the note below for additional help.

   Note: Why is there no subordinative *-u* suffix in V:54? The verb here is III-*y* *šalūm*.

4. Normalize: Normalize the text in LH §2 V:50–56.

5. Grammatical Analysis: Parse the verbs above.

6. Translate: Translate LH §2 V:50–56, and then provide a full translation of LH §2. Also answer the question below.

   a. Where in all of LH §2 is there a plausible example of asyndeton?

10–𒌋

Derived Stems, Prepositions, and Independent Personal Pronouns

The four basic and most common verb stems were learned in Chapter 3: the G-stem, D-stem, Š-stem, and N-stem. There are, however, two additional sets of verb forms that will be explained here. These are called the derived stems because each is related to corresponding forms in the G, D, Š, and N stems. Prepositions and independent personal pronouns will also be explained. The remaining portion of this chapter will cover the entirety of LH §3.

10.1 Derived Stems

The first set of derived forms is created by the addition of an infixed *-t(a)-* immediately following the first root consonant of each verb in the G-stem and D-stem and immediately following the prefixed *š* of each verb in the Š-stem. The only exception to this rule is with verbs in the perfect where the infixed *-t(a)-* follows the infixed *-ta-* of the perfect. Because of the infixed *-t(a)-* the derived stems are designated as Gt, Dt, Št, and Nt. The Nt-stem, however, is hypothetical. It is either unattested or at best exceedingly rare.

The second set of derived forms is created by the addition of an infixed *-tan-* immediately following the first root consonant in each verb in the G-stem and D-stem and immediately following the prefixed *š* in each verb in the Š-stem and the prefixed *n* in each verb in the N-stem. There are two exceptions to these rules. The first exception occurs with verbs in the perfect where the infixed *-tan-* immediately follows the infixed *-ta-* of the perfect. The second exception is that all infixed *-tan-* forms other than those in the G-stem or in the durative are identical to the corresponding infixed *-t(a)-* forms. Only their meaning as determined by the context allows one to parse these ambiguous forms as either an infixed *-tan-* or infixed *-t(a)-*. Because of the infixed *-tan-* the derived stems are designated as Gtn, Dtn, Štn, and Ntn.

Other Akkadian sources, such as *CAD*, designate these stems and derived forms using the following numerical system:

G = I/1	D = II/1	Š = III/1	N = IV/1
Gt = I/2	Dt = II/2	Št = III/2	[Nt = IV/2]
Gtn = I/3	Dtn = II/3	Štn = III/3	Ntn = IV/3

In this textbook only the most common of these derived stems will be considered in any detail, but it needs to be added that none is very common.[1]

1. Only 3 percent of all the verb forms appearing in the texts from LH covered in this textbook are these infixed forms.

10.1.1 ***Derived Stems with Infixed -t(a)-.*** For Gt, Dt, and Št derived stems, as mentioned above, the required modification consists of adding a *-t(a)-* infix to each verb form. For example, if the G-stem durative 3cs of *parāsum* is *iparras,* the Gt-stem durative 3cs is *iptarras.*

The derived forms do not change the temporal reference or aspect of a verb, such as when a verb is changed from one tense, like the durative, to another, like the preterite. Instead, these Gt, Dt, and Št derived stems change the meaning of the verb itself. With most verbs this involves adding a reflexive sense to the verb, so it will be translated with "himself, herself," etc., or a reciprocal sense to the verb, so that it will be translated with an expression like "each other." In the case of verbs of motion, however, the derived stems add a separative sense, which may require translating the verb with "away."

For example, if the G-stem infinitive *ni'ālum (i)/nālum (a)* means "to lie down, sleep" then the Gt-stem infinitive *itûlum/utûlum* means "to lie down/sleep together," as in LH §129. Alternatively, if a verb of motion like G-stem *alākum,* means "to go," then Gt-stem *atlukum* means "to go out," or "to go away," as in LH §191. The use of an infixed *-t(a)-* derived stem is relatively uncommon in LH.[2]

When an infix *-t(a)-* is added to preterite forms in each of the modified stems, Gt, Dt, and Št, the resulting forms are, unfortunately, identical in appearance to the corresponding perfect forms in the unmodified stems, G, D, and Š. Nevertheless, they are different in their meaning, so they should not be confused.

10.1.1.1 *Derived Stems with Infixed -t(a)- and the Perfect*—Recall from Chapter 3 that the perfect tense is formed by adding an infix *-ta-* immediately after the first root consonant of the verb. This modification does not change the tense of the verb but its aspect. For example, whereas the preterite expresses action as taking place at a single point in time, usually in the past, and is best translated with a simple past tense in English (such as *iprus,* "he decided"), the perfect with its infixed *-ta-* views an action or state in relation to something else. In general, the perfect expresses an action or state that is prior to the present but with ongoing important implications for the present, or it expresses an action or state that is prior to the action or state expressed by a subsequent main verb (usually a durative in LH) and it provides the crucial basis for the action or state expressed by the main verb. In keeping with these uses, the perfect is often translated in English with a simple past tense (such as *iptaras,* "he decided") or a present perfect (such as *iptaras,* "he has decided").

In the context of LH, it is notable that when there is a series of conditions in the protasis of a law, the first conditions are expressed with preterites, but the last one or two conditions is frequently expressed with perfects. This is because the conditions expressed with perfects are the decisive basis for the assertions that are made in the apodosis, which will be expressed with duratives. As such, the typical order of main verbs for each of the laws of LH is as follows:

preterite—(preterite)—(perfect)—perfect—durative

Akkadian is unique among the Semitic languages for having a perfect tense. This uniqueness is one reason why earlier Assyriologists failed to recognize the existence of the perfect tense. It is an intriguing question how Akkadian developed this particular innovation.

2. For example, in LH §§1–20, 127–149 there are only eight examples of an infixed *-t(a)-* derived stem vs. fifty-one perfects.

Although Akkadian owes much else to the influence of Sumerian, there is no clear evidence that Sumerian was the source of the Akkadian perfect. Instead, the consensus of Assyriologists is that the perfect tense marked by an infix *-ta-* developed from the derived stems with their use of an infixed *-t(a)-*.

The derived stems are reasonably assumed to be a feature of Proto-Semitic. This is why a similar use of an infixed *-ta-* to express reflexive or reciprocal ideas is found in many other Semitic languages, including Hebrew. For example, in Hebrew consider the fairly common *hithpael* conjugation, the related *hithpolel* conjugation, as well as the rare *hištaphel* conjugation.

As these examples show, the effect of an infixed *-ta-* in the derived stems is not to change the tense of the verb but its meaning. In Hebrew, for example, if a *piel* perfect 3ms verb, *gillâ*, גִּלָּה, "he uncovered," is turned into a *hithpael* perfect 3ms, *hitgallâ*, הִתְגַּלָּה, "he uncovered himself," it is still a past tense. What is different is that the infixed *-ta-* form, the *hithpael*, adds a reflexive meaning.

Although there is no direct evidence for how or when Akkadian first developed the perfect tense, it is clear that the effect of its infixed *-ta-* is similar: it changes the meaning of the preterite but not its time reference.

10.1.2 ***Derived Stems with Infixed -tan-.*** For Gtn, Dtn, and Štn derived stems, as mentioned above, the required modification consists of adding a *-tan-* infix to each verb form. The *n* of the *-tan-* infix is visible only in the durative form. Otherwise the *n* assimilates to a following single consonant, or it is deleted when it would produce a cluster of three consonants.[3]

In the D-stem system, Š-stem system, and probably N-stem system, infixed *-tan-* forms are indistinguishable from infixed *-t(a)-* forms except in the durative. Hence these ambiguous verbal forms can only be determined based on their meanings.

Regarding their meanings, infixed *-tan-* forms of the verb add an iterative or repetitive sense to the verb or a sense of continuity of action or protraction (graduality) of the action. Infixed *-tan-* stems are uncommon in LH.[4]

For example, LH §125 treats the case of a householder whose negligence resulted in the loss of property entrusted to his care, as well as loss of his own property. In such a situation, the householder is required to make restitution and "the householder shall *continue to search* [*ištene'îma*] for whatever was lost. . . ." The verb *ištene'îma* is a Gtn durative 3cs of *še'ûm*, "to search," + *-ma*.[5]

Occasionally, an infixed *-tan-* verbal form may have none of the above usual implications for its meaning. At times, if the infixed *-tan-* form is a durative, it is possible that the use of an infixed *-tan-* reflects the author's desire to imitate a common Sumerian durative verb form called a *marû* formation, which involves complete or partial repetition of the verb stem.[6] Stated differently, in most cases this means extending the verb by one syllable. At other times, an infixed *-tan-* may have no discernable implication.

10.1.3 ***The Strong Verb Paradigms for the Derived Stems.*** The following paradigm forms for derived stems is intended mainly for reference. The infixed *-t(a)-* forms that should be learned are in bold print. They are the durative, perfect, preterite, and infinitive forms for the Gt, Dt, and Št stems.

3. Cf., e.g., Ungnad, *Akkadian Grammar*, §70c.
4. Only three instances of an infixed *-tan-* stem appear in LH §§1–20, 127–49.
5. The hypothetical original *iptanarras* form of *še'ûm* (*š-'-y*) (*e,i*) is **ištene''iy*.
6. So W. Lambert, "Class Notes." For the alternative ways to put a Sumerian verb into the *marû* formation, see Hayes, *A Manual of Sumerian Grammar and Text*, 166–67.

Stem	Durative	Perfect	Preterite	Participle	Verbal Adjective	Stative	Infinitive
G	*iparras*	*iptaras*	*iprus*	*pārisum*	*parsum*	*paris*	*parāsum*
Gt	***iptarras***	***iptatras***	***iptaras***	*muptarsum*	*pitrusum*	*pitrus*	***pitrusum***
Gtn	*iptanarras*	*iptatarras*	*iptarras*	*muptarrisum*	*pitarrusum*	*pitarrus*	*pitarrusum*
D	*uparras*	*uptarris*	*uparris*	*muparrisum*	*purrusum*	*purrus*	*purrusum*
Dt	***uptarras***	***uptatarris***	***uptarris***	*muptarrisum*	*putarrusum*	*putarrus*	***putarrusum***
Dtn	*uptanarras*	*uptatarris*	*uptarris*	*muptarrisum*	*putarrusum*	*putarrus*	*putarrusum*
Š	*ušapras*	*uštapris*	*ušapris*	*mušaprisum*	*šuprusum*	*šuprus*	*šuprusum*
Št	***uštapras/ uštaparras***[7]	***uštatapris***	***uštapris***	*muštaprisum*	*šutaprusum*	*šutaprus*	***šutaprusum***
Štn	*uštanapras*	*uštatapris*	*uštapris*	*muštaprisum*	*šutaprusum*	*šutaprus*	*šutaprusum*
N	*ipparras*	*ittapras*	*ipparis*	*mupparsum*	*naprusum*	*naprus*	*naprusum*
Nt	unattested or exceedingly rare						
Ntn	*ittanapras*	*ittatapras*	*ittapras*	*muttaprisum*	*itaprusum*	*itaprus*	*itaprusum*

10.1.4 ***Unexpected Spellings.*** Some unexpected and unusual spellings occur with the derived stems. Below are two such scenarios that should be recognized.

1. I-*n* verbs lose the *n* in Gt, Dt, Gtn, and Dtn stems in all the forms where *n* would be the first letter, such as the infinitive.

For example, *ni'ālum* is a verb that means "to lie down, sleep." The Gt infinitive, based on the strong verb paradigm form of *pitrusum*, would be **nit'ulum*. This rule about I-*n* verbs, however, implies that the correct form would be **it'ulum* instead. The rule about non-initial *'aleph*'s and how they quiesce before a vowel resulting in compensatory lengthening explains why the final form of the Gt infinitive of *ni'ālum* is *itûlum*.

2. If a verb starts with either one of the dentals, *d* or *t* (not *ṭ*), or one of the sibilants, *s*, *ṣ*, or *z* (not *š*), this initial consonant metathesizes with the infix *-t-* in any of the Gt or Gtn forms that would otherwise start with that dental or sibilant.[8]

Although there are a number of verbs in LH that begin with one of the listed dentals or sibilants and appear in the Gt stem, for the purpose of illustrating this rule, none of them happens to appear in one of the verbal forms (the verbal adjective, stative, or infinitive) where the dental or sibilant would have come first and therefore would have metathesized with the infix *-t-*.

The common verb *ṣabātum*, which means "to seize, catch, find" and in the Gt, "to grasp one other" or "to take away," appears frequently in LH. Outside LH, however, the Gt infinitive (the *pitrusum* form) is attested, and it illustrates this rule of metathesis: **ṣitbutum* > *tiṣbutum*.

7. The *uštapras* form is often identified as a "Št durative passive," since it is typically used for the passive of the Št verb. On the other hand, *uštaparras* is called a "Št durative lexical" form because its meaning is so often unpredictable. As a result, verbs in this form require one to consult a reliable lexicon to learn their attested meanings. For example, in LH §145 is *uštamaḫḫar*, a Št durative lexical form which in context translates, "she would make herself equal to," based on *maḫārum*, G: "to face; receive; acquire"; Š: "to cause to meet; to receive."

8. Metathesis refers to the transposition of sounds or syllables in a word.

A similar metathesis occurs in the Hebrew infixed *-t-* conjugations, especially the *hithpael*, between the infixed *-t-* and the first root consonant of verbs that begin with a sibilant. As a result, for example, an expected **hitšammēr*, הִתְשַׁמֵּר, "he guarded himself," becomes *hištammēr*, הִשְׁתַּמֵּר.

10.2 Prepositions

Most prepositions in Akkadian are two syllables and end in a short vowel. The following prepositions are those that are found in LH. These need to be learned only as they come up in the listed vocabulary of each chapter. They are listed here for easy reference. A few general rules follow below.

adî = up to, until, so long as; *with numerals*: exactly, -times, -fold (< *'adiy*; cf. *'ad*, עַד)
ana = to, toward, into, for (the purpose of), at, in accordance with; time: for; with verb: in order to
ašar = at, on; conjunction: where (cf. *'ăšer*, אֲשֶׁר)
aššum = because of, concerning; with infinitive: in order that (< **an*[*a*] *šum*, "for the name of"[9])
balūm = without (the *-ūm* suffix is an old locative suffix hence literally, "in lack of") (cf. *bal*, בַּל; *bəlî*, בְּלִי)
elî = on, upon, over, against, beyond, than (in comparisons) (cf. *'al*, עַל, "on, upon, over, against," from the III-*y* and III-*h* verb *'ālâ*, עָלָה)
ina = in, from, among, with, by (means of), some of; *time*: in, on, at; *with verb*: when, while, by (*ina* is never used as a conjunction)
ištu = from, out of; *time*: since, after
itti = with, from (cf. *'ēt*, אֵת)
kīma = like, in the same way as (preposition); that (conjunction to introduce indirect discourse) (cf. *kə*, כְּ, *kî*, כִּי, *kəmô*, כְּמוֹ)
maḫar = in front of, before (bound form of *maḫrum*: front, presence)
mala = all, as much as; full amount (cf. *mālē'*, מָלֵא)
qadūm = besides, together with (locative *-ūm*) (cf. *qedem*, קֶדֶם)
qerbūm = within (locative *-ūm*) (cf. *qerbum*, "inside") (cf. *qereb*, קֶרֶב)
warki = "after"

General Rules:

1. Any noun that is the object of a preposition must be in the genitive case.
2. Some prepositions, like *elî* and *itti*, employ the same set of suffixes as are used on nouns:

1cs	*-ya*	1cp	*-ni*
2ms	*-ka*	2mp	*-kunu*
2fs	*-ki*	2fp	*-kina*
3ms	**- *šu***	**3mp**	**- *šunu***
3fs	**- *ša***	**3fp**	**- *šina***

9. Huehnergard, *A Grammar of Akkadian*, 606.

The third-person forms, printed in bold, should be memorized. When suffixes are added to *itti*, its final vowel is lengthened (*ittīšu*). The final vowel of *elî* is already long and retains its length when suffixes are added. For example, in LH §48 we read how a man has a "debt lodged against him," where "against him" is expressed by *elîšu*.

3. Most prepositions govern the independent form of the personal pronoun in the genitive case. For example, in LH §203 we read "who is like him," where "like him" is expressed as *kīma šu'āti*.
4. Finally, almost any preposition can be used as a subordinating conjunction that introduces a clause.

10.3 Independent Personal Pronouns

Although general familiarity with all these pronominal forms is helpful, the third-person forms (printed in bold) should be learned.

	Nominative		Genitive-Accusative	Dative
1cs	*anāku*	I	*yāti*	*yāšim*
2ms	*atta*	you	*kāta*	*kāšim*
2fs	*atti*	you	*kāti*	*kāšim*
3ms	***šū***	**he, it**	***šu'āti, šu'ātu***	***šu'āšim***
3fs	***šī***	**she, it**	***šu'āti***	***šu'āšim***
1cp	*nīnu*	we	*ni'āti*	*ni'āšim*
2mp	*attunu*	you	*kunūti*	*kunūšim*
2fp	*attina*	you	*kināti*	*kināšim*
3mp	***šunu***	**they**	***šunūti***	***šunūšim***
3fp	***šina***	**they**	***šināti***	***šināšim***

10.4 Homework

Before you move on, be sure to understand and recognize the derived stems, especially the forms of the durative, perfect, preterite, and infinitive in the Gt, Dt, and Št stems. The derived forms do not change the temporal reference or aspect of a verb but instead change the meaning of the verb itself. Stay attuned to how the *-t(a)-* and *-tan-* infixes impact translation and meaning. Also, become familiar with the general rules associated with prepositions. Finally, commit to memory the third-person independent personal pronouns and become familiar with the first- and second-person forms.

10.4.1 *Signs*

 10, *u*

 *ku, qú*

 *um*

 *nam*

 *nu*

 *ru*

 *uš, ús*

 *ù*

Congratulations! If you have learned the eight cuneiform signs in this chapter and each of the preceding sixty-eight signs, you will be able to read 86 percent of all the cuneiform signs in LH §§1–20, 127–149.

10.4.2 *Vocabulary*

adî = up to, until, so long as; *with numerals*: exactly, - times, -fold (< **adiy*; cf. ʿ*ad*, עַד)
bašûm (*i,i*) = to exist, be (in the sense of, to exist); Š: to produce (cf. *bə*, בְּ, "in" + *šû*, "it")[10]
enûm (*i,i*) (< ʿ-*n*-*y*) = to change, exchange (cf. ʿ*ānâ*, עָנָה, "to answer")
ezēbum (*i,i*) = G: to abandon, leave behind, divorce; Š: to cause to leave behind, deposit (cf. ʿ*āzab*, עָזַב).
nadānum (*i,i*) = to give, pay; sell (cf. *nātan*, נָתַן)
rugummûm = complaint
û (< *'*u*) = or (cf. '*ô*, אוֹ)
warkānūm < **warki* + *ān* (common noun ending) + -*ūm* (locative/adverbial ending) = afterwards (cf. *yərēkâ*, יְרֵכָה, "rear [portion], most distant part")
warki = after (preposition and conjunction) (cf. *warkānum*) (cf. *yərēkâ*, יְרֵכָה, "rear [portion], most distant part")

10.4.3 *Exercises*

1. Transliterate and Normalize.

LH §3 V:57

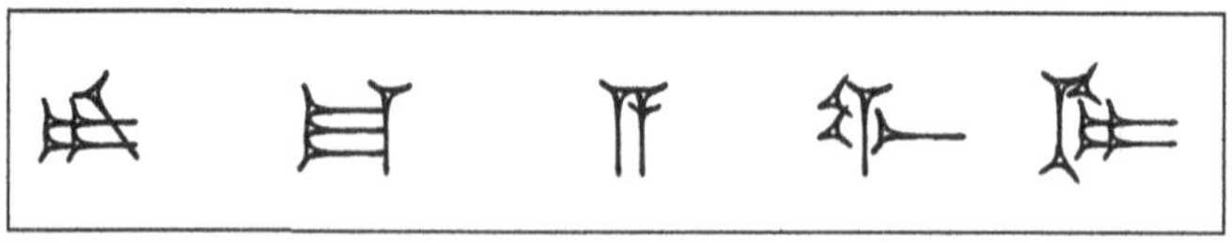

10. This proposed etymology of *bašum* is favored by Huehnergard, "Hebrew and Other Semitic Cognates to the Lesson Vocabularies" in *A Grammar of Akkadian*, 606.

LH §3 V:58

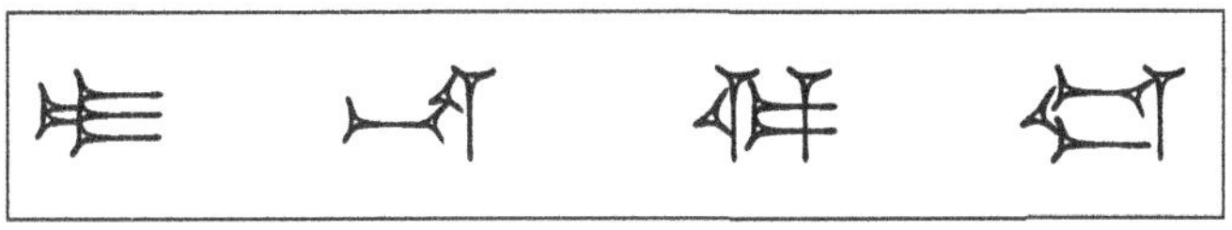

LH §3 V:59

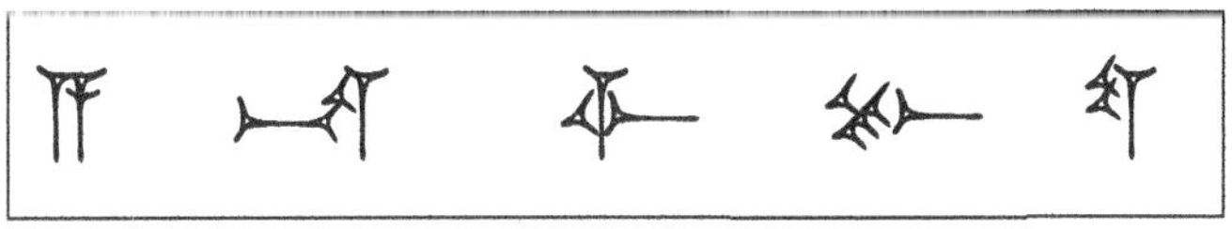

LH §3 V:60

LH §3 V:61

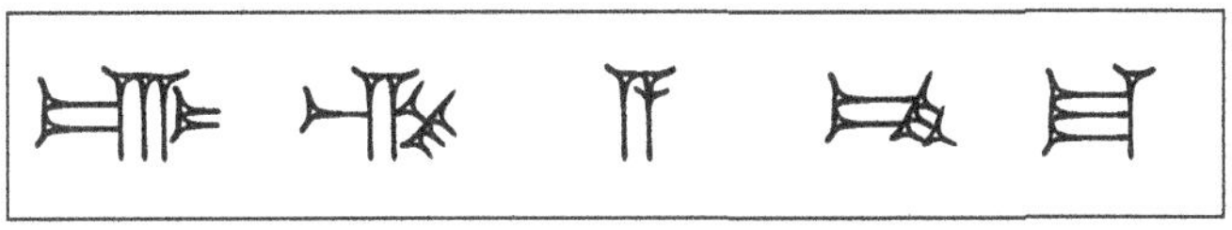

LH §3 V:62

LH §3 V:63

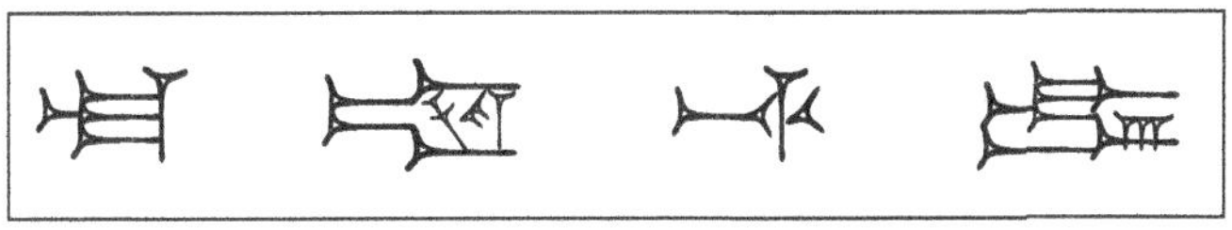

LH §3 V:64

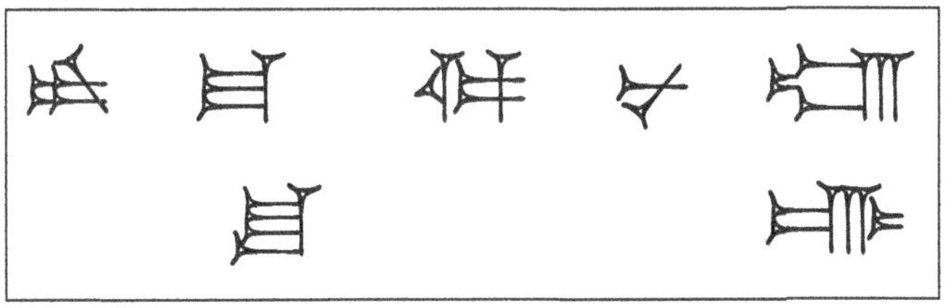

LH §3 V:65

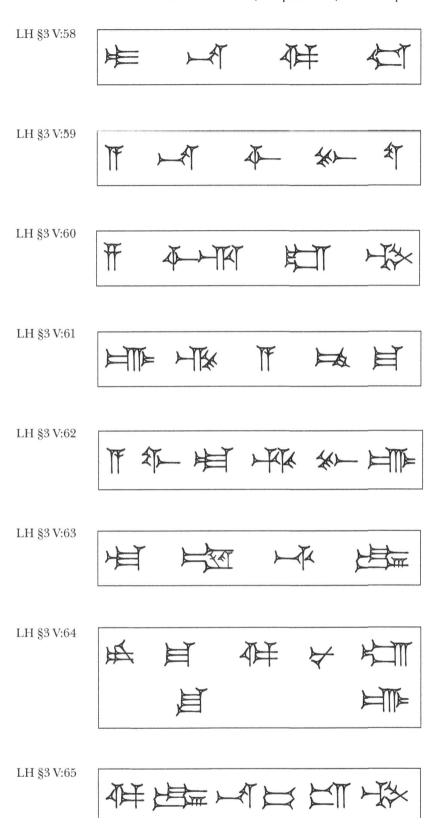

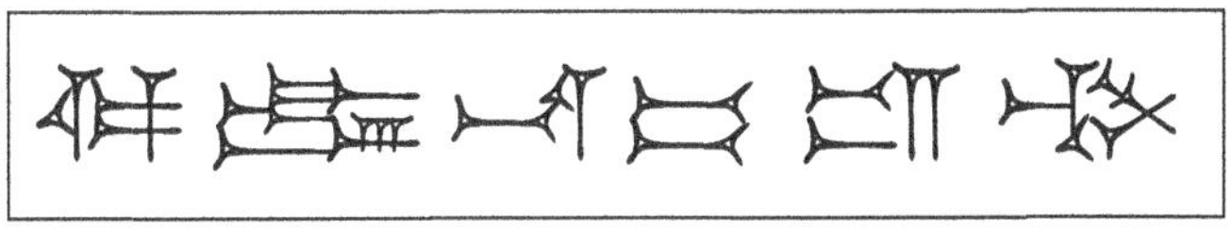

LH §3 V:66

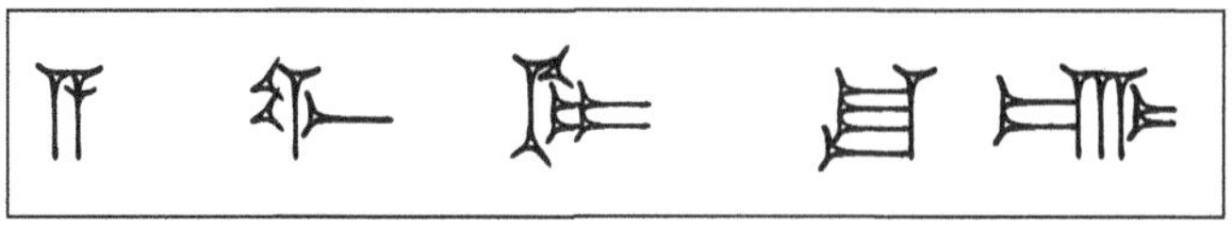

LH §3 V:67

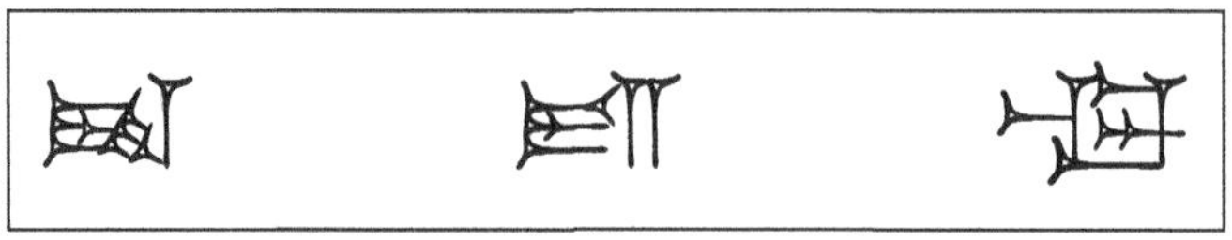

2. Grammatical Analysis: Answer the questions below.

   a. Parse all verb forms. See the note below for additional help.

   Note: The verb in V:61 is a I-*w* verb from *waṣûm*. I-*w* verbs will be examined in detail in Chapter 12. For the present purpose it will help to know that an original *iw*-prefix in I-*w* verbs became *u* (no lengthening). See the chart in Appendix B.

   b. Explain the form of the noun in V:62.

3. Translate LH §3.

Two Cognate Features: Verbless Clauses and Reduplication

David Musgrave

To view any language from the perspective of a related language can often give the scholar an insight into the target language that perhaps otherwise cannot be gained. The prominence of Akkadian as a lingua franca of the ancient Near East as well as its relationship with biblical Hebrew suggests that such a comparison and contrast can provide unique insights into each.[1] The approach of this essay will be to offer examples and accompanying observations in two specific areas—verbless clauses and reduplication—in order to demonstrate the value of Akkadian as a basis for elucidating such features.

The first example is the position of the independent personal pronoun subject as last in a verbless clause. This construction has been recognized as a feature of Akkadian[2] and can also be observed in other Semitic languages.[3] Some biblical Hebrew examples of this feature include: *hăšōmēr ʾāḥî ʾānōkî*, "Am I my brother's keeper?" (Gen 4:9); *ʾiššāh qəšat-rûaḥ ʾānōkî*, "I am a bitter woman" (1 Sam 1:15); and *ʿibrî ʾānōkî*, "I am a Hebrew" (Jon 1:9). A biblical Aramaic example includes *ḥelmāk wəḥezwê rēʾšāk ʿal miškəbāk dənāh hûʾ*, "your dream and the visions of your head upon your bed, were these" (Dan 2:28). Akkadian examples include: *ul abī atta ul ummī atti*, "you are not my father; you are not my mother" (LH §192); *ul ṣīt uriya atta*, "you are not my offspring" (*Gilgamesh* III: 123 in SAACT I [SB]); and *bêlet rabītu anāku*. "I am a great queen" (RawlCu IV: 61 vi 11 [NA]). Consistent with the biblical examples, the pronoun is understood in the Akkadian examples to be the subject.[4]

The extent of the feature described above in the other Semitic languages will depend upon further textual studies. Yet this introduction demonstrates a correlation of the use between Akkadian and biblical Hebrew and Aramaic.

Another shared syntactic feature is that of "reduplication,"[5] here defined as a couplet consisting of a word (root) appearing twice in succession to indicate plurality or other comprehensive meaning. Some biblical Hebrew nominal examples include *šālôm šālôm*, "perfect peace" (Isa 26:3); *hămônîm hămônîm*, "multitudes, multitudes" (Joel 4:14 [MT]); and *ʾāmēn ʾāmēn*, "amen, amen" (Num 5:22).[6] J. Motyer limits the meaning of reduplication in biblical Hebrew to the superlative (citing 2 Kgs 25:15) or totality (citing

1. Inasmuch as there are likely many influences on every language as they come into contact. See Stephen A. Kaufman, *The Akkadian Influences on Aramaic*, Assyriological Studies 19 (Chicago: University of Chicago, 1974), 15ff. Furthermore, the transition from one language to the other is not seamless.

2. Huehnergard, *A Grammar of Akkadian*, 12. Huehnergard also points out that "when the subject is a personal pronoun, the word order is usually inverted in most dialects, the pronoun standing at the end of its clause, although again in OA both orders, Predicate-Subject and Subject-Predicate, are common." John Huehnergard, "On Verbless Clauses in Akkadian," *Zeitschrift für Assyriologie* 76 (1986): 223.

3. Including Targumic Aramaic, *ʾrwm ṭb hw'*, "that it was good" (Gen 1:4) in Neophyti. See Aaron Michael Butts, "Observations on the Verbless Clause in the Language of Neophyti I," *Aramaic Studies* 4.1 (2006): 63. The feature also appears in Ugaritic, *ʿbdk an*, "your servant am I." See KTU 1.5.ii.12. It is not, however, observable in Hittite.

4. These examples also all have to do with an aspect of identification or a "clause of identification," as termed by Nauff Zakaria, "The Verbless Clause in Genesis," (academia.edu), 6.

5. This terminology follows Dietz Otto Edzard, *Sumerian Grammar* (Atlanta: Society of Biblical Literature, 2003).

6. Cf. David Musgrave, "Making Application of Biblical Hebrew," in *Living and Active Word* (Montgomery, AL: Amridge University Press, 2020), 43 n104.

Gen 14:10).[7] However, other idiomatic expressions in the Hebrew Bible seem to reflect that reduplication can be more flexible. For example, *yôm yôm*, "day by day," in Genesis 39:10 is a quotidian use. Consider also *dōr lədōr*, "each and every generation," in Exodus 3:15 as a distributive use. Akkadian examples include "DINGIR.DINGIR," "gods" (Ee I 52, 57), "KUR.KUR," "lands" (Rost Tigl 29´); and "EN.EN," "lords" (Winckler Sammlung 2 1:9). Interestingly, in reduplication the Sumerian noun may bear a comprehensive or distributive force.[8]

This feature is also not limited to either Akkadian or biblical Hebrew, but the extent to which it is observable in other Semitic languages requires further investigation.[9] In addition to demonstrating the cognate nature of reduplication, the few examples noted above also demonstrate the varied nuances contained therein, and thereby perhaps elucidate our understanding of the two languages under consideration.

The two syntactic features highlighted here demonstrate the importance of the features themselves, but they also emphasize the nature of this type of material as cognate between Akkadian and biblical Hebrew. While neither feature is unique to either language, and both features have been previously recognized, that which has seemingly remained unemphasized is the affinity of these features between Akkadian and biblical Hebrew. Perhaps this study may serve as preliminary for other studies that may further elucidate these and other matters. Who knows what other treasures lie underneath the surface, the value of which could further enhance our understanding of both languages?

7. J. Alec Motyer, *Isaiah*, TOTC (Downers Grove, IL: InterVarsity Press, 1999), 70

8. Cf. Daniel A. Foxovg, *Introduction to Sumerian Grammar*, rev. ed. (no other publication information, 2014), 24.

9. For a modern example (albeit utilizing an adjective), compare the stereotypical salesperson utilizing the phrase "for the low, low price of . . ." (cf. Musgrave, "Making Application," 43 n106).

11—𒌋𒁹

Adverbial Suffixes, Nominative Absolute, and II-Weak Verbs

This chapter, which may require a little more time than some, treats LH §4 and LH §5. LH §4 considers the case of false testimony offered in a property offense, as opposed to false testimony offered in a capital crime, which was the concern of LH §§1–3. Clearly there is a logical order governing all four laws: LH §1 concerns false testimony in a murder case; LH §2 concerns false testimony in a case of sorcery; LH §3 concerns false testimony in a more general capital case; and LH §4 concerns false testimony in a property crime.

Alternatively, it is apparent that the first five laws of LH are linked by their common concern to address aberrations in judicial process: LH §§1–4 focus on the problem of false testimony and LH §5 focuses on the problem of double jeopardy. Examples like this of careful logical organization here and elsewhere within LH make it reasonable to expect that there may be similar patterns of deliberate organization within the other law collections from the ancient Near East, including the Hebrew Bible.

In addition to the work of translating LH §4 and LH §5 below, this chapter will address locative and terminative adverbial suffixes, the nominative absolute, and II-weak verbs.

11.1 Locative and Terminative Adverbial Suffixes

In place of the usual case endings on nouns and adjectives, there are other suffixes that are sometimes encountered. Already mentioned in previous chapters are pronominal suffixes and predicative suffixes. In this chapter, two more suffixes are introduced: the locative *-ūm* and terminative *-iš*.

11.1.1 ***Locative -ūm.***[1] The locative adverbial suffix *-ūm* is occasionally found on the end of nouns. This suffix carries the meaning of "at" or "in." It is normally added to a singular noun with its case ending removed. Although this suffix resembles the nominative masculine singular suffix *-um*, it is, nevertheless, a distinct suffix. One clear evidence for this distinction is observed when the word in question is in construct. Whereas the *-um* case ending is dropped when a word is in construct, the locative *-ūm* suffix is retained.

When a pronominal suffix is added to a word ending with a locative *-ūm* suffix, the final *-m* assimilates to the first consonant of the suffix, as is the case with the final *-m* of the ventive. For example, the noun *qerbum* means "center," but this word with the *-ūm* locative adverbial suffix, *qerbūm*, means "in the center of" or "in the midst of." This locative form appears in the phrase *qerbūm bâbilim*, "in the midst of Babylon," in LH §Pro IV:42 (see also *qerbūm* in IV:50).

1. Many Assyriologists assume that the *u*-vowel is short in the locative *-ūm* suffix. For evidence in support of a long vowel, see Buccellati, *A Structural Grammar of Babylonian*, 152.

Below are examples of locative *-ūm* in LH. These do not need to be learned until they come up in a vocabulary list.

balūm = without (the locative *-ūm* suffix suggests an original literal meaning such as, "in lack of") (cf. *bal*, בַּל; *bəlî*, בְּלִי)
qadūm = besides, together with (cf. *qedem*, קֶדֶם)
qerbūm = within (cf. *qerbum*, inside) (cf. *qereb*, קֶרֶב)
warkānūm (< **warki* + *ān* [common noun ending] + *-ūm* [locative *-ūm*]) = afterwards (cf. *yərēkâ*, יְרֵכָה, "rear [portion], most distant part")

11.1.2 ***Terminative -iš.*** The terminative adverbial ending *-iš* carries the meaning of "to, toward" or with infinitives, "in order to." For example, *šaplum* means "low" and thus *šapliš*, which appears three times in the epilogue of LH, means "toward what is low" or "downward" (XLVII:31; XLVIII:30; L:37).

This *-iš* suffix is also used to make an adverb out of an adjective. For example, in the epilogue of LH the adverb *arḫiš*, "quickly," appears twice (L:32 and XXVIII:90). This word is built on the adjective *arḫum*, "quick."

Similar to the locative suffix, the terminative adverbial suffix *-iš* is normally placed on a singular noun (often an infinitive) or an adjective with its case ending removed.

11.2 Nominative Absolute

As in Hebrew and other Semitic languages, Akkadian makes frequent use of a nominative absolute (also variously termed dangling words, *casus pendens*, a hanging case, or extrapositional words). This describes a situation where a noun, or noun phrase, is fronted in a clause in order to emphasize that it is the focus of some assertion. What follows then is a clause in which a resumptive pronoun is used to refer back to the initial emphasized noun. Despite the name nominative absolute, the fronted noun is often in the accusative case, although the nominative case appears to be more common (see e.g., LH §8, line V:46).[2] An effective way to translate the nominative absolute is with the expression, "as for."

For example, a nominative absolute appears at the beginning of LH §13: *šumma awīlum šū šībūšu*, "As for that man, if his witnesses . . . ." The phrase *awīlum šū*, "that man," which happens to be in the nominative, is a nominative absolute.

11.3 II-Weak Verbs (Hollow Verbs and II-*'aleph* Verbs)[3]

In Akkadian, as in Hebrew, there are essentially two kinds of II-weak verbs. One kind consists of those verbs that originally had either *w* or *y* as their middle radical. These are often called Hollow Verbs. A complementary, more recent understanding of these verbs is that they had biconsonantal roots with a medial long vowel *û* (associated with Proto-Semitic *w*) or *î* (associated

2. So Worthington, *Complete Babylonian*, §11.12. Huehnergard (*A Grammar of Akkadian*), in his treatment of *casus pendens* in §21.5, only mentions the use of the nominative case for this purpose. Marcus (*A Manual of Akkadian*, §§6.11; 9:9) on the other hand, surprisingly states that *casus pendens* normally employs the oblique case and only exceptionally the nominative case.
3. For a detailed analysis of II-weak verbs, see Kouwenberg, *The Akkadian Verb and Its Semitic Background*, §16.5.

with Proto-Semitic *y*), or less commonly *â*.[4] According to this view, these verbs may be called II-vowel verbs, where the second root letter is a vowel rather than a consonant.

The other kind of II-weak verb consists of II-’ verbs, also called II-guttural verbs. These verbs originally had one of the five guttural consonants as their middle radical. These guttural consonants subsequently quiesced to an ’ (’$_1$ = ’; ’$_2$ = *h*; ’$_3$ = *ḥ*; ’$_4$ = ‘; ’$_5$ = *ǵ*).[5] Those verbs that had an original ’ or *h* as their middle consonant are *a*-class. Those verbs that had an original *ḥ*, ‘, or *ǵ* as their middle consonant were also originally *a*-class, but because of vowel attenuation they all became *e*-class.[6]

Below are the major forms of II-weak verbs. These should be memorized. The corresponding forms of the strong verb, *parāsum*, are included for reference. Following the paradigms and observations below, individual forms will be examined and discussed systematically, and some general principles will be considered that will help one understand and learn how to produce most of these forms based on the strong verb paradigm.

11.3.1 *Paradigms for II-Weak Verbs*

Stem	Class	Durative 3cs/3mp	Perfect 3cs/3mp	Preterite 3cs/3mp	Infinitive
G		*iparras/iparrasū*	*iptaras/iptarasū*	*iprus/iprusū*	*parāsum*
	u	***ikān****/ikunnū*	***iktûn****/iktûnū*	***ikûn****/ikûnū*	***kânum***
	i	***iqî’aš****/iqiššū*	***iqtîš****/iqtîšū*	***iqîš****/iqîšū*	***qi’āšum***[7]
	a	***irām****/irammū*	***irtâm****/irtâmū*	***irâm****/irâmū*	***rāmum***[8]
	e	***imēš****/imeššū*	***imtêš****/imtêšū*	***imêš****/imêšū*	***mēšum***[9]
D		*uparras/uparrasū*	*uptarris/uptarrisū*	*uparris/uparrisū*	*purrusum*
	II-v[10]	***ukân****/ukannū*	***uktîn****/uktinnū*	***ukîn****/ukinnū*	***kunnum***
Š		*ušapras/ušaprasū*	*uštapris/uštaprisū*	*ušapris/ušaprisū*	*šuprusum*
	II-v[11]	***ušmât****/ušmattū*	***uštamît****/uštamittū*	***ušmît****/ušmittū*	***šumuttum***[12]
N		*ipparras/ipparrasū*	*ittapras/ittaprasū*	*ipparis/ipparisū*	*naprusum*
	u	***iddāk****/iddukkū*	unattested	unattested	unattested
	i	***iqqî’aš****/iqqiššū*	unattested	*iqqîš* (rare)	unattested
	a	***irrām****/irrammū*	unattested	*irrâm* (rare)	unattested
	e	***immēš****/immeššū*	unattested	*immêš* (rare)	unattested

4. This interpretation, that II-weak verbs in Akkadian are best thought of as deriving from biconsonantal roots rather than triconsonantal roots, has become the dominant view among Assyriologists since von Soden, *GAG*^{3}. In favor is the recognition that the supposed weak middle-root consonant never appears in any form of the verb in Babylonian.

The distribution of biconsonantal root verbs among the three vowel classes resembles what is also observed in Hebrew. In Hebrew, as in Akkadian, hollow verbs with a middle *w* radical, or *û*-theme vowel, are the most common (cf. *qûm*, קוּם, "to arise"). Less common are those with a middle *y* radical, or *î*-theme vowel (cf. *śîm*, שִׂים, "to put, place"). Least common in Hebrew are those with an original *â*-theme vowel, or middle *w* radical, representing the Hebrew long *ô* vowel that derives from an earlier long *â* vowel (cf. *bôš*, בּוֹשׁ, "to be ashamed").

5. See §3.4.2.

6. See §3.4.3.

7. *qâšum* (or *qi’āšum*) (< *q-y-š*) (*i*) = G: "to give." See §11.3.5 below.

8. *rāmum* (< *r-’-m*) (*a*) = G: "to love." See §11.3.5 below.

9. *mēšum* (*e*) = G: "to despise, neglect, scorn" (cf. *m-’-s*, מאס, "to reject"). See §11.3.5 below.

10. II-guttural verbs may follow an alternative paradigm either with a tilde long theme vowel or with an explicit doubled ’ mirroring the strong verb paradigm (see Huehnergard, *A Grammar of Akkadian*, §29.1; Worthington, *Complete Babylonian*, §25.4).

11. II-guttural verbs may follow an alternative paradigm with a tilde long theme vowel reflecting vowel contraction (see Huehnergard, *A Grammar of Akkadian*, §29.1; Worthington, *Complete Babylonian*, §25.4).

12. The G-stem is *mâtum* (*m-w-t*), "to die." Š-stem: "to cause to die, to kill."

11.3.1.1 *Observations*

1. In most forms of II-weak verbs (all preterites and perfects in all stems, as well as D-stem and Š-stem duratives), the theme vowel has compensatory lengthening (*v̂*).
2. In forms where the theme vowel is long (*v̂* or *ṽ*), if a suffix is added that begins with a vowel (such as the 3mp suffix *-ū*) then the final root consonant is often doubled instead of the theme vowel being lengthened. This is called resolutory doubling.
3. II-weak verbs in the D-stem have a compensatorily lengthened *â*-theme vowel in the durative, which marks the durative as a durative, and a compensatorily lengthened *î*-theme vowel in both the preterite and the perfect. These D-stem forms are unexpected based on the strong verb paradigms, which would predict tilde long vowels (from vowel contraction).
4. There are two forms where vowel syncope takes place: in the Š-stem durative and Š-stem preterite. In each case, the expected *a* immediately after the *š* is lost.
5. In the N-stem preterite, rather than an expected *i*-theme vowel, the theme vowels for II-weak verbs appear to be the same as they are in the G-stem preterite. Unfortunately, however, there are too few examples to be sure, and there are no examples of a II-*w* verb.

In summary, every form of II-weak verbs can be derived from the strong verb paradigm except for four:

a. the G-stem perfect, which is built directly on the preterite;[13]
b. the D-stem prefix forms where the theme vowels are compensatorily lengthened (*v̂*) rather than tilde long (*ṽ*);
c. the N-stem preterites of II-weak verbs, which use their vowel class;
d. and cases where there is resolutory doubling of the third root consonant.

11.3.2 ***Additional Explanation of II-Weak Forms.*** This section includes explanations for some key II-weak forms, including II-weak infinitives, II-weak vowel classes, II-weak preterites in the G-stem (and probably N-stem), II-weak prefix tenses in the D-stem, II-weak prefix tenses in the Š-stem, and II-weak perfects.

11.3.2.1 *II-Weak Infinitives*—As is the case with all verbs, the lexical form of any II-weak verb is ordinarily the G-stem infinitive. If a verb is unattested in the G-stem, lexica may offer a hypothetical G-stem infinitive with a cross-reference to the main entry for the verb, which is its infinitive form in the stem in which it appears most frequently.

1. Most G-stem infinitives of hollow verbs are a simple result of vowel contraction. For example, based on the paradigm form of *parāsum*, a verb with the roots *k-w-n* will have a G-stem infinitive *kãnum*, "to be firm"; D: "to establish, make secure, prove, have proof, convict," based on the following assumed historical sequence: **kawānum* > **kûānum* (since the diphthong *aw* contracts to *û*) > *kãnum* (since the vowel sequence *û* + *ā* contracts to *ã*).

13. Another way to state this is that II-weak verbs form their G-stem perfect with an infix *-t-* rather than *-ta-*, since, unlike the strong verb, they do not need the added *a*-vowel in order to avoid an unallowed cluster of three consonants (**iptras* vs. *iptaras*).

2. Some *i*-class hollow verbs act like strong verbs in the G-stem infinitive. In other words, their original II-*y* ('$_7$) root is maintained. For these verbs, their G-stem infinitive is a form like *qi'āšum*, "to give."

The form *qi'āšum* is explained by two considerations. First, the short *a*-vowel in the strong verb paradigm form *parāsum* partially contracts with the semi-vocalic consonant *y*. Rather than resulting in the expected circumflex long vowel *î* (**ay* > *î*), however, the result is an intermediate form, namely a short *i* followed by an ' ('$_7$): **ay* > **i'*$_7$ > *î*. This ' is the immediate result of a reduction of the *y*. Second, unlike most juxtaposed vowels *i* followed by *a* normally does not contract in Old Babylonian (see §3.4.5).

3. II-' verbs are normally *a*-class, but those that derive from an original *ḥ*, ', or *ġ* as their middle consonant are *e*-class verbs rather than *a*-class. For example, with a verb like *mēšum* (< **m-'-š*), "to despise, neglect," the G-stem infinitive would have developed from the strong verb paradigm form *parāsum* as follows: **ma'āšum* > *me'ēšum* (by vowel attenunation[14]) > *mēšum*.

11.3.2.2 *II-Weak Vowel Classes*—II-weak verbs exhibit four vowel classes: *u* and *i* for hollow verbs, which are verbs that were originally II-*w* and II-*y*, and *a* and *e* for II-' verbs. Based on what has been presented about regular verb forms for the paradigmatic strong verb *parāsum*, if one knows the vowel class of a particular II-weak verb, one can predict, or at least identify, most of its verbal forms.

The key principle for II-weak verbs, whether in the preterite, the durative, or the perfect, is to recognize that while II-weak verbs follow the strong verb paradigm in terms of their prefixes and suffixes, they follow their own paradigm with respect to the second root consonant of the strong verb and adjacent vowels.[15] As already mentioned, this is particularly so with respect to the D-stem, the N-stem preterite, and any form where resolutory doubling takes place.

11.3.2.3 *II-Weak Preterites in the G-Stem (and Probably N-Stem)*—To form II-weak preterites in the G-stem (and probably N-stem) replace the middle consonant and any adjacent vowel(s) of the strong verb paradigm with a compensatorily lengthened theme vowel reflecting the II-weak verb's distinctive vowel class (*v̂*).

Consider the following steps in order to form the G-stem preterite 3cs (*iprus*) form of *kānum* (< *k-w-n*), a *u*-class hollow verb meaning in the G-stem, "to be firm," and in the D-stem, "to establish, make secure, prove, have proof convict" (cf. *kûn*, כּוּן, *niphal*: "to be firm, be established").

Step 1: Start with the relevant paradigm form of the strong verb, in this case *iprus*.
Step 2: Replace the first and third root consonants of the paradigm verb *iprus* with the corresponding consonants of the II-weak verb in question, and replace the second root consonant of the paradigm either with the likely original second root consonant of the II-weak verb or with an ': **ikwun*.
Step 3: Since a *w* inside a word in Akkadian typically reduced to ' and then was elided, resulting in compensatory lengthening of any adjacent vowel, the form of **ikwun* becomes *ikûn*.

14. See §3.4.3.
15. It is this fact that provides key support for the consensus that II-weak verbs are best thought of as II-vowel verbs. Cf., e.g., Kouwenberg, *The Akkadian Verb and Its Semitic Background*, §2.3.3, especially 41 n27.

11.3.2.4 *II-Weak Prefix Tenses in the D-Stem*—The commonly attested forms of D-stem prefix tenses for II-weak verbs follow their own paradigm. This should not be surprising since, after all, the D-stem is characterized by doubling of the second root consonant, whereas II-weak verbs by definition no longer have a second root consonant.

In particular, the D-stem prefixes and suffixes all mirror the strong verb paradigm, and their theme vowel also mirrors the strong verb paradigm. Nevertheless, in place of the second root consonant (whether doubled or not) of the strong verb paradigm and in place of any vowel that immediately precedes the second root consonant of the strong verb paradigm, the prefixed verbal forms of II-weak verbs in the D-stem employ a compensatorily lengthened (*v̂*) *a*-theme vowel for the durative and *i*-theme vowel for both the perfect and the preterite.

Consider the following example of the D-stem preterite 3cs (*uparris*) of *kânum*.

Step 1: Start with the relevant paradigm form of the strong verb, in this case *uparris*.
Step 2: Replace the first and third root consonants of the relevant strong verb paradigm form *uparris* with the corresponding consonants of the II-weak verb in question: **uk*[*arr*]*in*
Step 3: Contrary to the strong verb paradigm for the D-stem, which doubles the second root consonant, II-weak verbs do not have a second root consonant to double and follow their own paradigm. Replace the doubled second root consonant of the strong verb paradigm form as well as the immediately preceding vowel, the [*arr*] in **uk*[*arr*]*in* above, with compensatory lengthening of the *i*-theme vowel (for all D-stem and Š-stem perfects and preterites): *ukîn*, "he firmly established."

11.3.2.5 *II-Weak Prefix Tenses in the Š-Stem*—Š-stem durative and preterite forms of II-weak verbs can be derived directly from the strong verb paradigm, but it is necessary as a last step to apply the rule of vowel syncope.[16]

For example, to form the Š-stem durative 3cs (*ušapras*) of *mâtum*, a *u*-class hollow verb (< *m-w-t*), meaning in the G-stem "to die" and in the Š-stem "to kill," do the following.

Step 1: Start with the relevant strong paradigm form, in this case *ušapras*.
Step 2: Replace the first and third root consonants of the strong verb paradigm form with the corresponding consonants of the II-weak verb in question: **ušam*[*r*]*at*.
Step 3: Replace the second root consonant(s) of the strong verb paradigm form with the assumed original second root consonant or an ʾ. In the case of *mâtum* (< *m-w-t*), replace with the semi-vowel *w*: **ušamwat*.
Step 4: Since an original *w* within words usually reduced to ʾ, this results in **ušamʾat*.
Step 5: Since an internal ʾ normally quiesced, this results in compensatory lengthening of the final *a*-theme vowel, **ušamât*.
Step 6: The form **ušamât* requires the application of the rule of vowel syncope since this form has two non-final unaccented open syllables with short vowels ([c]*v-cv-*). Accordingly, the second short vowel is elided and the form **ušamât* becomes *ušmât*, "he will/would kill."

16. See §2.5.2.3.

11.3.2.6 *II-Weak Perfects*—II-weak verbs form the perfect in any stem based directly on the preterite by infixing a *-t-* immediately after the first root consonant of the preterite. For example, the G-stem preterite 3cs of *a*-class *šāmum* (< *š-'-m*), which means "to purchase, buy," is *išâm*. Accordingly, the G-stem perfect 3cs of *šāmum* is *ištâm*, "he purchased/bought."

In the Š-stem, this rule for forming the perfect still applies, but it is necessary first to undo any vowel syncope that affects the preterite. For example, the Š-stem preterite 3cs of *mātum*, "to die," is *ušmît*. The word *ušmît*, however, derives from **ušamît* based on vowel syncope. Accordingly, the Š-stem perfect 3cs is *uštamît*, "he caused to die."

11.3.3 ***Resolutory Doubling: II-Weak Verb Forms with a Vocalic Suffix.*** A surprising feature of the chart for II-weak verbs above (§11.3.1) is the number of examples where instead of a theme vowel that is compensatorily lengthened or lengthened by vowel contraction, the final root consonant is doubled (resolutory doubling).

This doubling of the final root consonant occurs only under two conditions. First, a suffix that begins with a vowel has to be added to the II-weak verb, such as a 3mp *-ū* or ventive *-am*. Otherwise, the verb form in question would end with a consonantal cluster, which is not allowed in Akkadian.

Second, resolutory doubling is observed only in those forms of the II-weak verb where there is normally doubling of the II-root consonant in the strong verb paradigm. It is as if an attempt was made to rectify the inability to double the second root consonant (since in II-weak verbs it is either a root vowel or an ' that has quiesced) by doubling the third root consonant. Naturally, the third consonant could not double unless a suffix beginning with a vowel is added, since, as mentioned above, no word in Akkadian ends with a doubled consonant. On the other hand, there was no ability to double the first root consonant, instead of the (missing) second, or the result would lead to confusion with N-stem forms. So, the paradigms that are set out in the chart are the best solution to this challenge![17]

11.3.3.1 *Excursus on the Lengthening Consonant*—It will be useful at this point to introduce a formalism that is used in certain linguistic contexts called the "lengthening consonant."[18] The lengthening consonant is an imaginary consonant that is symbolized as a colon (:). It functions by lengthening a vowel that immediately precedes it (or follows it), turning a vowel, *v*, into a long vowel, *v̂* (compensatory lengthening) or *ṽ* (length due to vowel contraction). If a consonant immediately precedes the lengthening consonant, it doubles the consonant. What is written and pronounced is not the lengthening consonant itself but the results of its invisible presence: either a circumflex long vowel or a doubled consonant.

An alternative, perhaps more elegant explanation for what is involved in "resolutory doubling" is offered by Erica Reiner. She notes simply that II-weak verbs can be described as verbs whose second "consonant" is the lengthening consonant. Then, as often elsewhere in Akkadian, in these II-weak verbal forms there is a metathesis of the lengthening consonant that constitutes a free variant (resulting in no difference in meaning). In other words, the sequence */v:cv/* and */vc:v/* are free variants.[19]

---

17. Cf. Worthington, *Complete Babylonian*, §25.6.
18. See Reiner, *A Linguistic Analysis of Akkadian*, §4.1.2.
19. Reiner, *A Linguistic Analysis of Akkadian*, §4.1.2.5.

11.3.4 ***Hollow Verb Participles and Verbal Adjectives.*** The participle of G-stem hollow verbs follows the strong verb, *pārisum*. For example, the participle of *dâkum* (< *d-w-k*) (*a,u*), "to kill, execute," is *dā'ikum*. There is also, however, a less common irregular *mupîsum*-form, *mudîkum*.

The verbal adjective of the G-stem hollow verbs generally have a *pîsum* form, as would be expected (*pîsum* < **pa'isum*). For example, *kînum* is the verbal adjective for *kânum*, G: "to be firm"; D: "to establish, make secure, prove, have proof, convict." Some *a*-class verbs, however, have a *pâsum* form and some *e*-class verbs have a *pêsum* form.

11.3.5 ***II-Weak Verbs in LH.*** Below are all of the II-weak verbs in LH. These do not need to be learned, except as they may come up in the required vocabulary for each chapter. They are provided here for easy reference.

bârum (< *b-w-r* < **b-'-r*) (*u*) = D: to declare, affirm (cf. *bi'ēr*, בֵּאֵר, "to make plain")
dâkum (< *d-w-k*) (*u*) = G: to kill, execute (outside LH also: to crush); Š: to cause to die (the only example of a II-weak verb in the Š-stem in LH); N: to be killed (*iddâk* < **indû'ak* < **indûwak* < **indawwak*) (cf. *dāk*, דָּךְ < *d-w-k*, דוך, "to pound, crush"; *dākâ*, דָּכָה, *piel*: "to crush")
dânum (or *di'ānum*) (< *d-y-n*) (*i*) = G: to try (conduct a trial), judge (cf. *dîn*, דִּין)
dâṣum (< *d-'-ṣ*) (*a*) = G: to trick, treat with disrespect
dâšum (or *di'āšum*) (< *d-y-š*) (*i*) = G: to thresh (cf. *dûš*, דּוּשׁ, "to thresh")
ḫârum (or *ḫi'ārum*) (< *ḫ-y-r*) (*i*) = G: to choose for marriage, seek out for marriage
ḫâṭum (or *ḫi'āṭum*) (< *ḫ-y-ṭ*) (*i*) = G: to supervise, discover
kânum (< *k-w-n*) (*u*) = G: to be firm; D: to establish, make secure, prove, have proof convict (cf. *k-w-n*, כון; *niphal*: "to be firm, be established"; *hiphil*: "to determine"; *polel*: "to make firm, establish")
le'ûm (< *l-'-y*) (*i*) = to be able (cf. Ugaritic, *l'w/y* "to prevail")
mâtum (< *m-w-t*) (*u*) = G: to die (cf. *m-w-t*, מות, "to die")
mêšum (*e*) = G: to despise, neglect, scorn (cf. *m-'-s*, מאס, "to reject")
nâḫum (< *n-w-ḫ*) (*u*) = G: be still, at rest; D: to calm, soothe (cf. *n-w-ḥ*, נוח, "to rest")
pâḫum (< *p-'-ḫ*) = D: to exchange
qâlum (< *q-w-l*) (*u*) = G: to heed, pay attention to
qâpum (or *qi'āpum*) A (*i*) = G: to entrust
qâpum (< *q-w-p*) B (*u*) = G: to collapse, crumble
qâšum (or *qi'āšum*) (< *q-y-š*) (*i*) = G: to give
râbum (or *ri'ābum*) (< *r-y-b*) (*i*) = G: to compensate, make restitution
râmum (< *r-'-m*) (*a*) = G: to love
re'ûm (< *r-'-y*) (*i*) = G: to tend (small animals) (cf. *r-'-h*, רעה, "to shepherd")
ṣênum (*e*) = G: to load (cargo)
šâmum I (< *š-'-m*) (*a*) = G: to purchase, buy; N: to be purchased
šâmum II (or *ši'āmum*) (*i*) = G: to assign, determine, establish
târum (< *t-w-r*) (*u*) = to return; *in hendiadys*: to do again (intransitive in G and transitive in D) (cf. *t-w-r*, תור, "to explore")
ṭâbum (or *ṭi'ābum*) (< *ṭ-y-b*) (*i*) = D: to improve (cf. *ṭ-w-b*, טוב, "to be good")
(w)ârum (< *w-y-r* < **w-'-r*) (*i*) = G: to advance against; D: to send, direct, lead
zâzum I (< *z-w-z*) (*u*) = to share
zêrum (*e*) = to hate, dislike; to reject

11.4 Homework

Before you move on, be sure to recognize the locative *ūm* and terminative *-iš* suffixes and understand their uses. Also, become familiar with the placement and function of the nominative absolute in Akkadian. In addition, familiarize yourself with the many rules associated with II-weak verbs. These forms appear regularly in LH. Finally, review the list above of all the II-weak verbs that appear in LH so that you can easily pick them out, assess their form, and translate.

11.4.1 *Signs*

 11

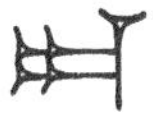 *ab, ap*

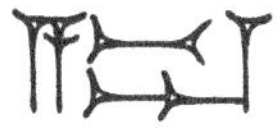 A.RÁ, *adî* (< *'*adiy*) (cf. *'ad*, עַד)

 GIŠ (= ^{iš} < *iṣum;* determinative for wood) (cf. *'ēṣ*, עֵץ); *is, iṣ, iz*

 *gu*

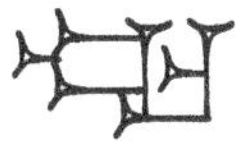 *ka*

 *kam;* ^{KAM} (postpositive determinative for numbers)

 *ul*

 *lí, ni*

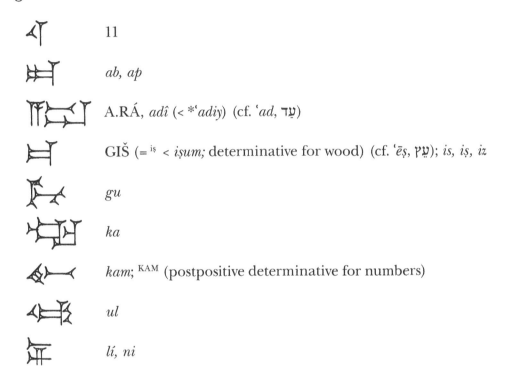

11.4.2 *Vocabulary*

dayyānūtum = judgeship (cf. *dayyān*, דַּיָּן, "judge")
-iš = terminative adverbial suffix added to nouns with the meaning "to" or "toward," or with infinitives, "in order to"; when added to adjectives, it turns them into adverbs
itti = with (cf. *'ēt*, אֵת, "with")
kussûm = seat (cf. *kissē'*, כִּסֵּא, "seat, throne")
puḫrum = assembly, council
-šu (a suffix on some number x) = x-fold
târum (*t-w-r*) (*u*) = to return; *in hendiadys*: to do again (intransitive in G and transitive in D) (cf. *t-w-r*, תור, "to explore")
tebûm (*i,i*) = to rise up, depart; Š: to remove
-ūm = locative-adverbial suffix added to a noun stripped of its case ending with the meaning "at" or "in"
wašābum (*a,i*) = to sit, dwell (cf. *yāšab*, יָשַׁב, "to sit, dwell")

Congratulations! If you learn the seven words above (not counting the suffixes) and have learned each of the sixty-two words in the vocabulary lists of the preceding chapters, you will be able to read 60 percent of all the words in LH §§1–20, 127–149.

11.4.3 *Exercises*

Laws 4 and 5 are treated separately below. LH §5 is significantly longer than §4.

1. Transliterate and Normalize: See the note below for additional help.

LH §4 V:68

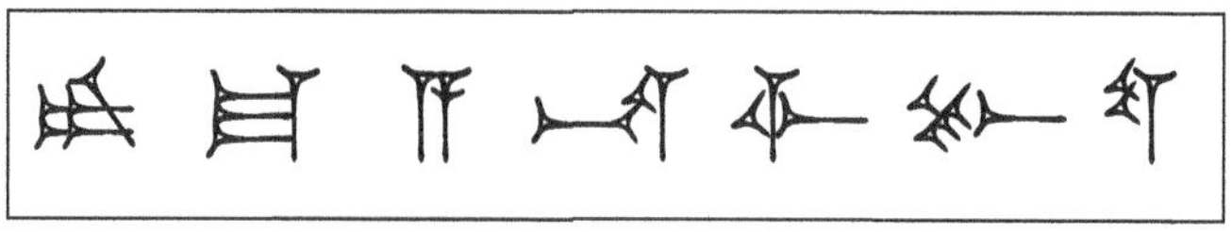

LH §4 VI:1

Note: The  sign in VI:1 helps determine which of the possible values for  is correct.

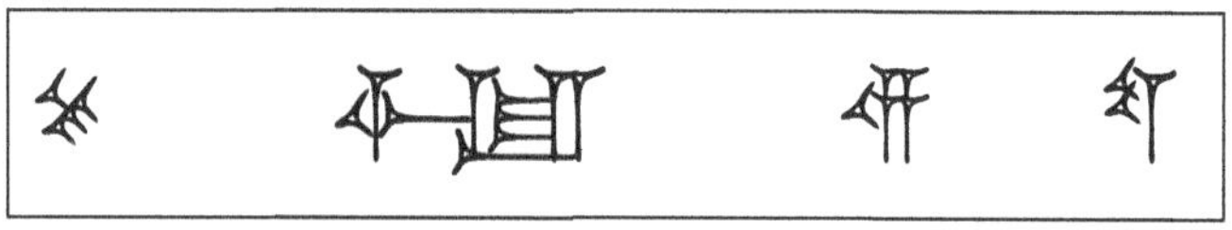

LH §4 VI:2

LH §4 VI:3

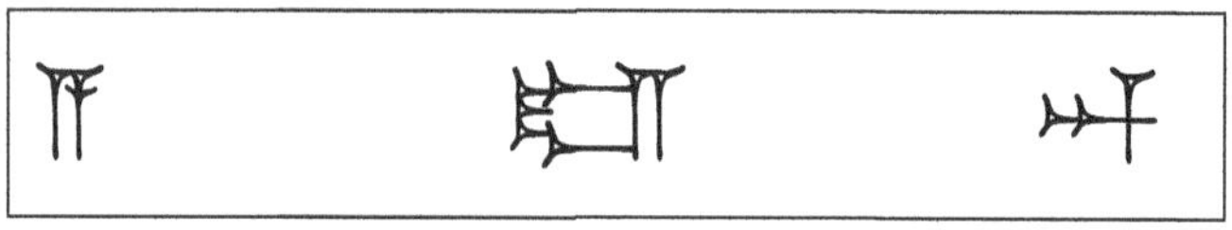

LH §4 VI:4

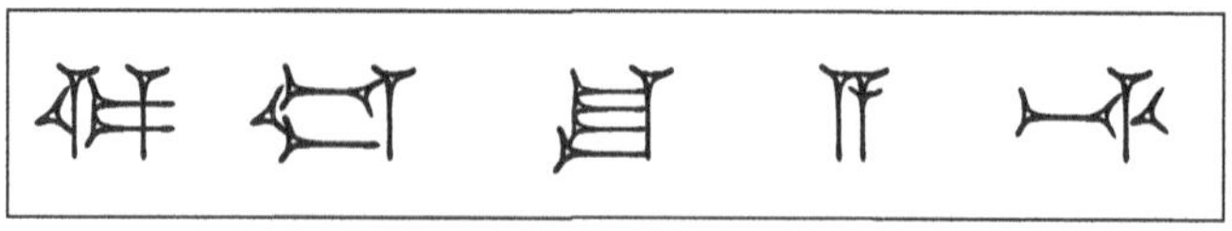

LH §4 VI:5

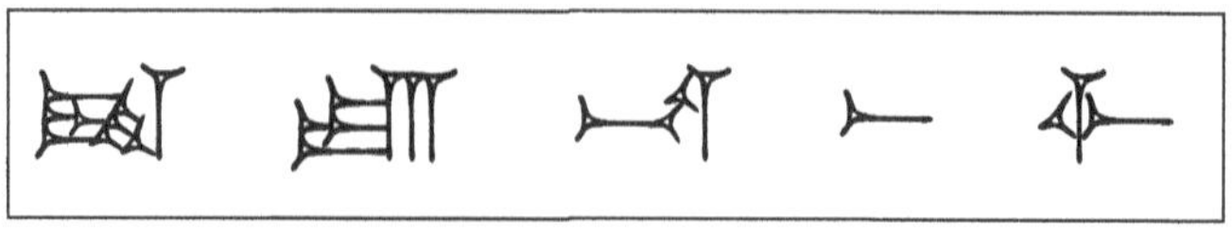

2. Grammatical Analysis: Parse all verb forms.

3. Translation: Translate LH §4. When rendering Akkadian, try to translate as literally as possible and into idiomatic English in terms of normal word order and grammar.

---

1. Transliterate and Normalize: See the notes below for additional help.

LH §5 VI:6

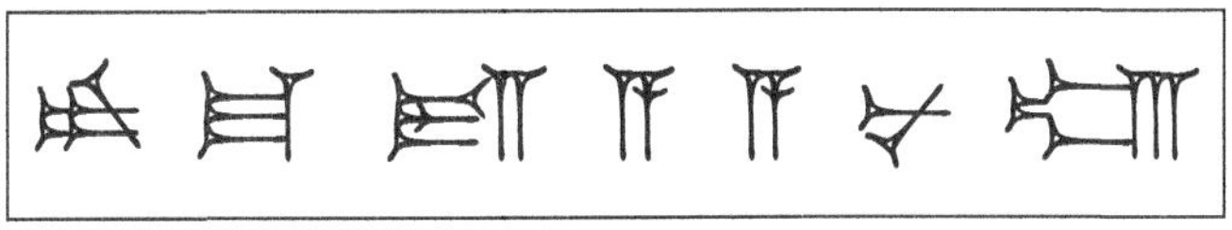

LH §5 VI:7

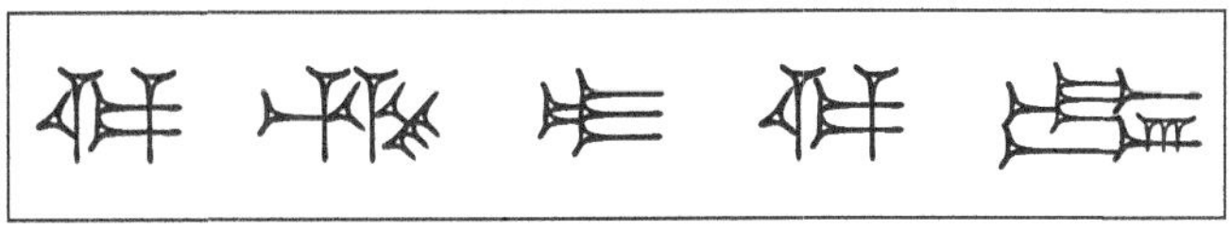

LH §5 VI:8

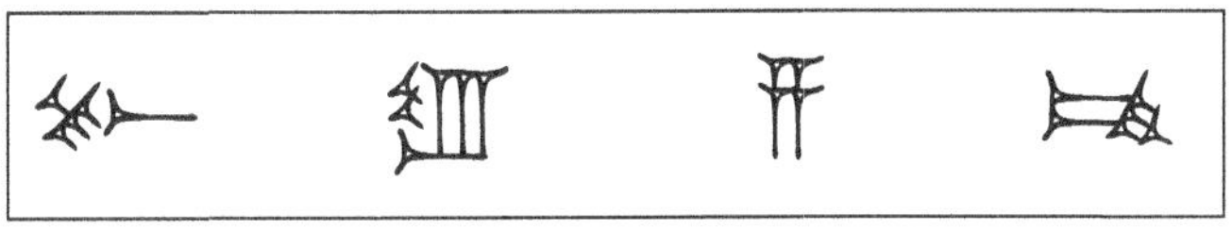

LH §5 VI:9

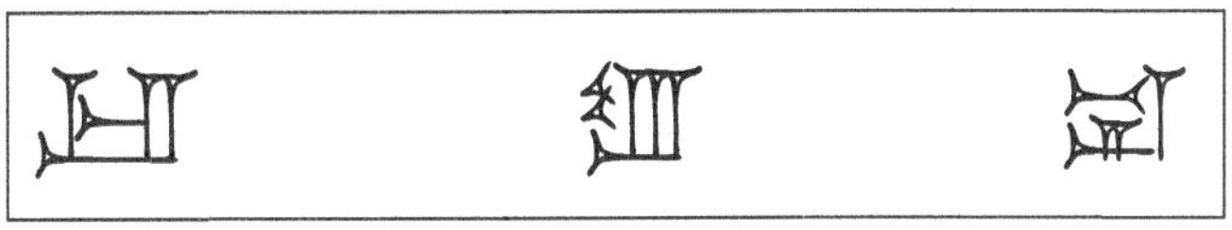

LH §5 VI:10

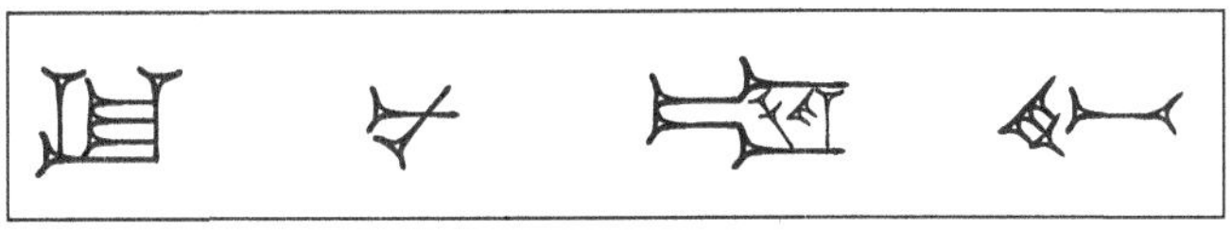

LH §5 VI:11

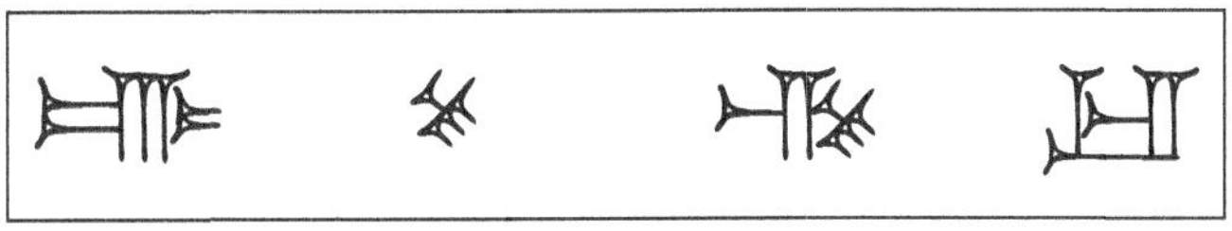

LH §5 VI:12

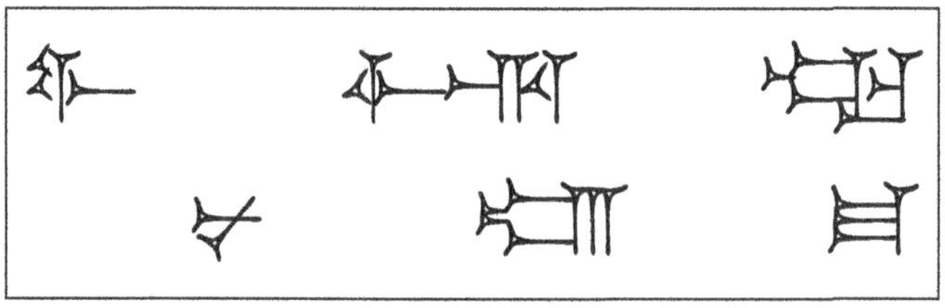

LH §5 VI:13

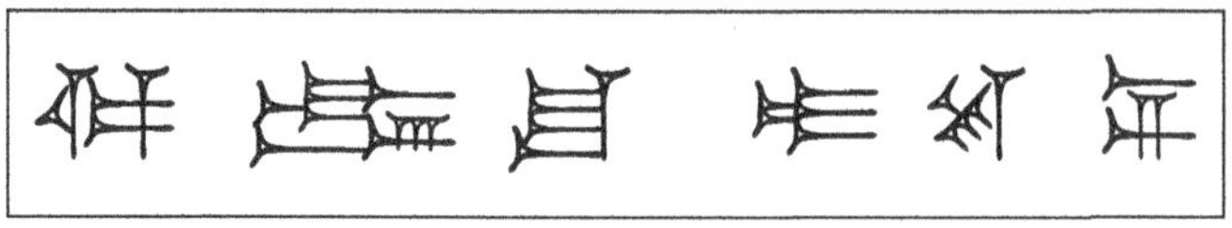

LH §5 VI:14

LH §5 VI:15

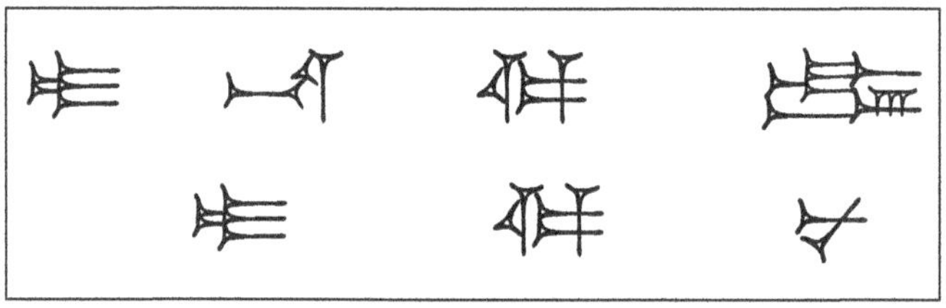

LH §5 VI:16

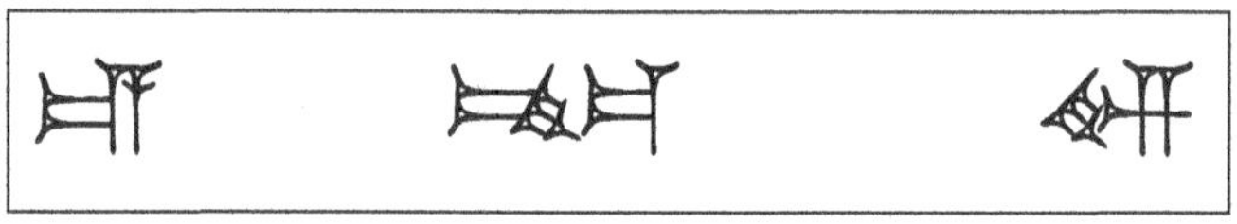

LH §5 VI:17

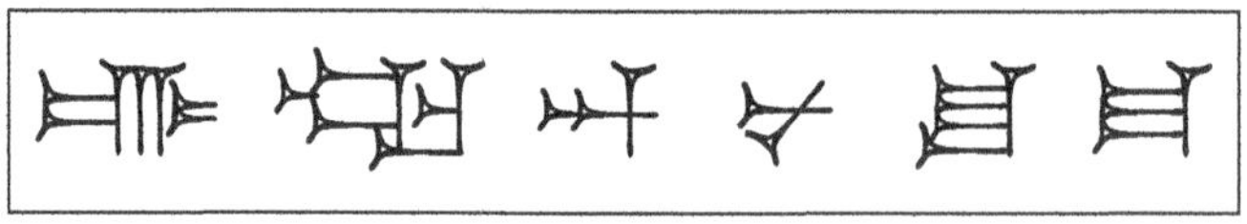

LH §5 VI:18

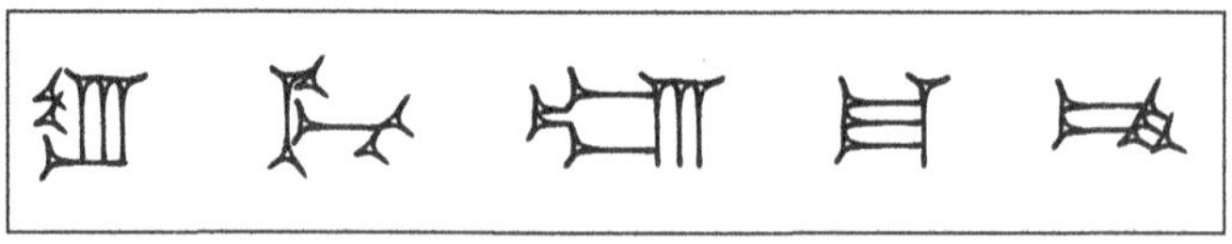

LH §5 VI:19

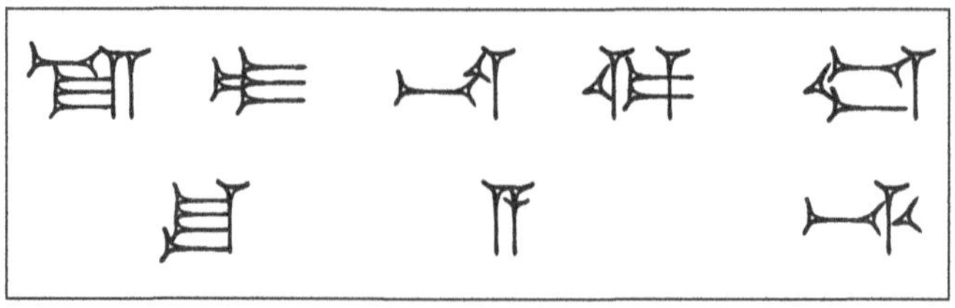

LH §5 VI:20

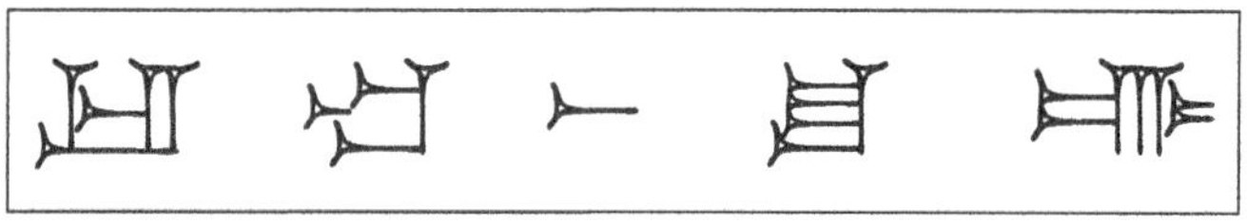

LH §5 VI:21

LH §5 VI:22

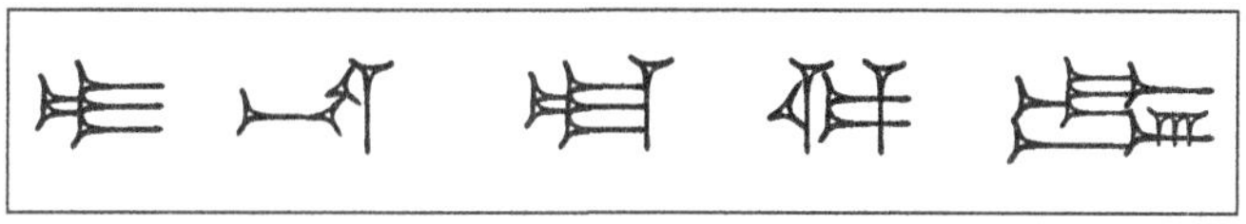

LH §5 VI:23

Note: The sign  in VI:23 is *úḫ*. This does not need to be learned.

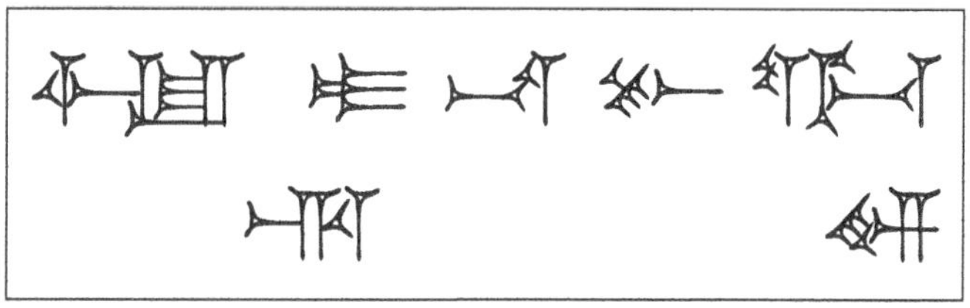

LH §5 VI:24

Note: The signs  in VI:24 should be read GU.ZA, *kussûm*, "seat, throne." This expression does not need to be learned.

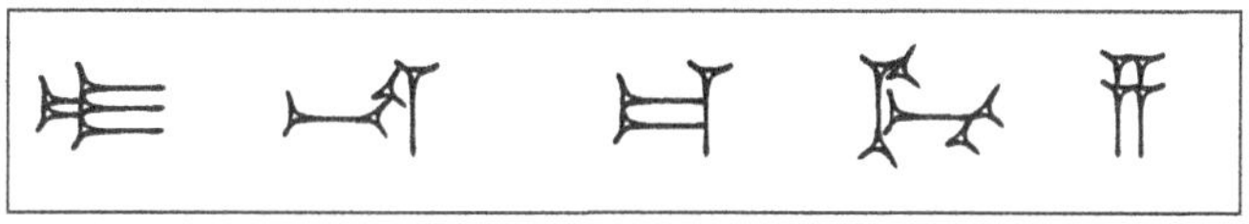

LH §5 VI:25

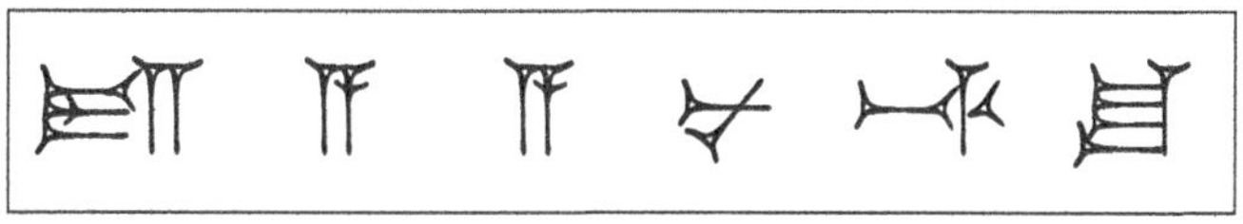

LH §5 VI:26

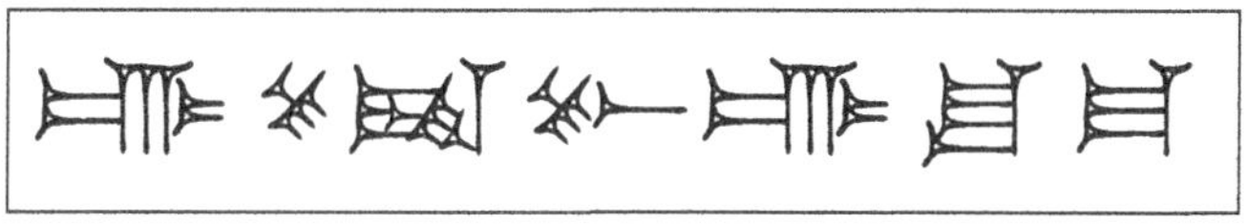

LH §5 VI:27

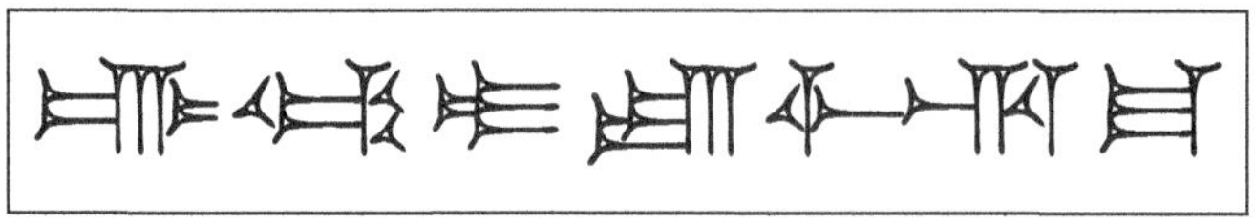

LH §5 VI:28

LH §5 VI:29

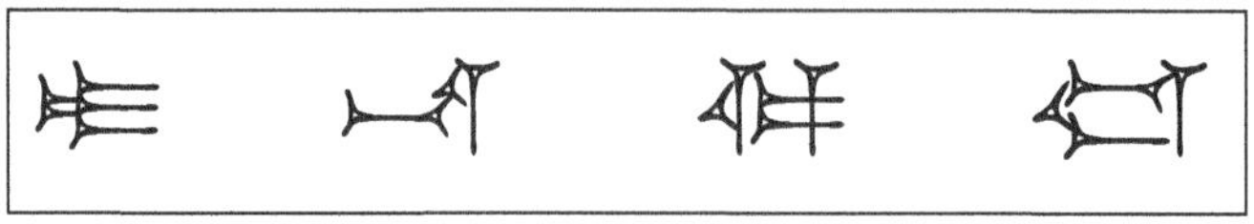

LH §5 VI:30

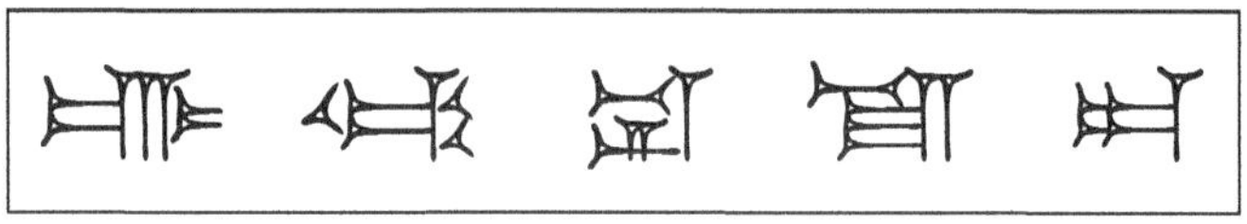

2. Grammatical Analysis: Parse all verb forms and answer the question below. See the note below for additional help.

   a. Analyze and explain the elements of *warkānūmma.*

   Note: The morphology of the I-*w* verb in VI:30 will be treated in the next chapter. For the present purpose it is enough to know that it is a G-stem durative 3cs of *wašābum* (*a,i*), which means "to sit" or "dwell." Cf. *yāšab,* יָשַׁב. The initial *u* vowel in the durative form is short.

Commentary: Although in general this textbook will not consider most of the text critical issues related to LH, this last text box does offer one illustrative example. On the stele housed in the Louvre, rather than the *ša*-sign, 𒊭, in box LH §5 VI:30, what is actually written is a *ta*-sign, 𒋫. Most Assyriologists who have studied the matter agree that the correct reading in this text should be the *ša*-sign.

The prime directive for text criticism with Akkadian texts, or with the Bible, is not simply for a scholar to provide what are thought to be "better" readings of a text. Instead, the prime directive is to recover the most likely original text based on plausible explanations for how any and all erroneous later copies arose based on that posited original text. Normally, the most convincing explanation is one that assumes an unintentional accident rather than a deliberate alteration. In the present case, that accidental error came about because, although these two signs sound quite different and they also appear quite different in the Neo-Assyrian script taught in this textbook, they appear very similar in the Old Babylonian monumental script that was used in the days of Hammurabi. Compare the Old Babylonian sign for *ta*, 𒋫, with the sign for *ša*, 𒊭.

3. Translation: Translate LH §5.

12–

I-*w* Verbs

This chapter addresses I-*w* verbs. The exercises below include LH §6–7. These two laws start a lengthy section of LH, LH §§6–25, all of which concern the illicit acquiring of property or persons. There are three major subdivisions of this larger section:

LH §§6–13: theft of property
LH §§14–20: illicit taking of person
LH §§21–25: offenses of robbery and looting

12.1 I-*w* Verb Forms

I-*w* verbs need to be distinguished from I-weak (I-ʾ) verbs, even though the consonant *w* often reduces to an ʾ, sometimes designated as $ʾ_6$.[1] Both verb types have many features in common, such as those forms where the original I-weak or I-*w* consonant has quiesced with compensatory lengthening or is deleted along with the following vowel when intervocalic. Nevertheless, there are many significant differences in the paradigms of these two types of verbs. I-weak (I-ʾ) verbs will be examined in detail in Chapter 14; here the focus is on I-*w* verbs.

12.1.1 ***Paradigm Chart for I-w Verbs.*** Forms in bold are explained in more detail below and should be learned. I-*w* verbs also appear in the derived stems, but their forms are predictable based on those offered here.

Stem	Class	Durative 3cs	Perfect 3cs	Preterite 3cs	Participle ms	Verbal Adjective ms	Stative 3ms	Infinitive ms
G		*iparras*	*iptaras*	*iprus*	*pārisum*	*parsum*	*paris*	*parāsum*
	Active	***uššab***	***ittašab***	***ušib (ûšib)***	*wāšibum*	*(w)ašbum*[2]	*(w)ašib*	*(w)ašābum*[3]
	Stative	***ittir***	***îtatir/ îtetir***	***îtir***		*(w)atirum*	*(w)atar*	*(w)atārum*
D		*uparras*	*uptarris*	*uparris*	*muparrisum*	*purrusum*	*purrus*	*purrusum*
		uwatter	***ûtatter***	*uwaššir*[4]	*muwašširum*	*(w)uššurum*	*(w)uššur*	***(w)ulludum***[5]

1. See §4.5.
2. The use of parentheses means that sometimes there is a *w* and sometimes not. This variation can apply to the same verb. For example, the D-stem infinitive of *walādum* sometimes appears as *wulludum*, "to beget," but at other times it appears as *ulludum*.
3. *wašābum* (*a,i*) = to sit, dwell (cf. *yāšab*, יָשַׁב). See §12.2 below.
4. *wašārum* = D: to prove innocent; Dt: to be proved innocent, exonerated, allowed to go free (cf. *yātar*, יָתַר, *niphal*: "to be left over"). See §15.3 below.
5. *walādum* (*a,i*) = to bear, give birth to (cf. *yālad*, יָלַד). See §17.3.

Stem	Class	Durative 3cs	Perfect 3cs	Preterite 3cs	Participle ms	Verbal Adjective ms	Stative 3ms	Infinitive ms
Š		*ušapras* *ušabbal*	*uštapris* *uštâbil*	*ušapris* *ušâbil*	*mušaprisum* *mušâbilum*	*šuprusum* *šûbulum*	*šuprus* *šûbul*	*šuprusum* *šūbulum*[6]
	e-type	*ušerred*	*uštêrid*	*ušêrid*	*mušêridum*	*šûrudum*	*šûrud*	*šûrudum*[7]
N		*ipparras* *iwwallad*	*ittapras*	*ipparis* *iwwalid*	*mupparsum* *muwwaldum*	*naprusum*	*naprus*	*naprusum*

12.1.2 ***Main Features of the Paradigms for I-w Verbs.***[8] Many aspects of the paradigms for I-*w* verbs are predictable based on the paradigm of the strong verb *parāsum*, but the following irregularities must be kept in mind.

1. There are two main categories of I-*w* verbs that need to be distinguished for G-stem forms: active-meaning verbs, which are more common and which some Assyriologists believe were mostly derived from original biconsonantal roots (this now seems doubtful[9]), and stative-meaning verbs ("to be X"), which are less common and were originally triconsonantal.

In the D, Š, and N-stems as well as in their derived infix stems, both kinds of verbs have the same forms.

2. I-*w* verbs, whether active-meaning or stative-meaning, have a number of forms that treat the *w* as a strong consonant. This happens in three situations that will be addressed below: when *w* is the first letter of the word, when *w* is doubled, and when *w* is protected by the sequence *uwa*.

a. **When *w* is the first letter of the word.** This occurs only in the G-stem participle and the G-stem and D-stem verbal adjective, stative, and infinitive. See, for example, the G-stem infinitive ms (*parāsum*) of *walādum* (*a,i*), "to bear, give birth to," in the chart below.

Stem	Class	Durative 3cs	Perfect 3cs	Preterite 3cs	Participle ms	Verbal Adjective ms	Stative 3ms	Infinitive ms
G		*iparras*	*iptaras*	*iprus*	*pārisum*	*parsum*	*paris*	*parāsum*
	Active	***uššab***	***ittašab***	***ušib (ûšib)***	*wāšibum*	*(w)ašbum*	*(w)ašib*	*(w)ašābum*
	Stative	***ittir***	***îtatir/îtetir***	***îtir***		*(w)atirum*	*(w)atar*	*(w)atārum*
D		*uparras*	*uptarris*	*uparris*	*muparrisum*	*purrusum*	*purrus*	*purrusum*
		uwatter	***ûtatter***	*uwaššir*	*muwašširum*	*(w)uššurum*	*(w)uššur*	***(w)ulludum***
Š		*ušapras* *ušabbal*	*uštapris* *uštâbil*	*ušapris* *ušâbil*	*mušaprisum* *mušâbilum*	*šuprusum* *šûbulum*	*šuprus* *šûbul*	*šuprusum* *šūbulum*
	e-type	*ušerred*	*uštêrid*	*ušêrid*	*mušêridum*	*šûrudum*	*šûrud*	*šûrudum*
N		*ipparras* *iwwallad*	*ittapras*	*ipparis* *iwwalid*	*mupparsum* *muwwaldum*	*naprusum*	*naprus*	*naprusum*

6. *wabālum* (*a,i*) = to bring (away), carry.
7. *werēdum/warādum* (*a,i*), "to go down."
8. After Old Babylonian, word-initial *w* was lost. As a result, Akkadian lexica usually list I-*w* verbs using their more prevalent later spelling, for example, *ašābu(m)* instead of *wašābum*.
9. Cf., e.g., Riemschneider, *Lehrbuch des Akkadischen*, §12.7; Caplice, *Introduction to Akkadian*, §73. Although it is possible that some I-*w* verbs arose from biconsonantal roots, the claim that this was common seems increasingly doubtful based on the evidence of comparative Semitics and other considerations. For a thorough discussion, see Kouwenberg, *The Akkadian Verb and Its Semitic Background*, §16.2.4.

b. **When *w* is doubled.** This occurs only in any N-stem form. See, for example, the N-stem durative 3cs (*ipparras*) of *walādum* (*a,i*), "to bear, give birth to," *iwwallad* in the chart below.

Stem	Class	Durative 3cs	Perfect 3cs	Preterite 3cs	Participle ms	Verbal Adjective ms	Stative 3ms	Infinitive ms
G		*iparras*	*iptaras*	*iprus*	*pārisum*	*parsum*	*paris*	*parāsum*
	Active	***uššab***	***ittašab***	***ušib (ûšib)***	*wāšibum*	*(w)ašbum*	*(w)ašib*	*(w)ašābum*
	Stative	***ittir***	***îtatir/îtetir***	***îtir***		*(w)atirum*	*(w)atar*	*(w)atārum*
D		*uparras*	*uptarris*	*uparris*	*muparrisum*	*purrusum*	*purrus*	*purrusum*
		uwatter	***ûtatter***	***uwaššir***	*muwašširum*	*(w)uššurum*	*(w)uššur*	***(w)ulludum***
Š		*ušapras*	*uštapris*	*ušapris*	*mušaprisum*	*šuprusum*	*šuprus*	*šuprusum*
		ušabbal	*uštâbil*	*ušâbil*	*mušâbilum*	*šûbulum*	*šûbul*	*šūbulum*
	e-type	*ušerred*	*uštêrid*	*ušêrid*	*mušêridum*	*šûrudum*	*šûrud*	*šûrudum*
N		*ipparras*	*ittapras*	*ipparis*	*mupparsum*	*naprusum*	*naprus*	*naprusum*
		iwwallad		*iwwalid*	*muwwaldum*			

c. **When *w* is protected by the sequence *uwa*.** This occurs only in the D-stem durative, preterite, and participle.[10] See, for example, the D-stem preterite 3cs (*uparris*) *uwaššir* in the chart below.

Stem	Class	Durative 3cs	Perfect 3cs	Preterite 3cs	Participle ms	Verbal Adjective ms	Stative 3ms	Infinitive ms
G		*iparras*	*iptaras*	*iprus*	*pārisum*	*parsum*	*paris*	*parāsum*
	Active	***uššab***	***ittašab***	***ušib (ûšib)***	*wāšibum*	*(w)ašbum*	*(w)ašib*	*(w)ašābum*
	Stative	***ittir***	***îtatir/îtetir***	***îtir***		*(w)atirum*	*(w)atar*	*(w)atārum*
D		*uparras*	*uptarris*	*uparris*	*muparrisum*	*purrusum*	*purrus*	*purrusum*
		uwatter	***ûtatter***	*uwaššir*	*muwašširum*	*(w)uššurum*	*(w)uššur*	***(w)ulludum***
Š		*ušapras*	*uštapris*	*ušapris*	*mušaprisum*	*šuprusum*	*šuprus*	*šuprusum*
		ušabbal	*uštâbil*	*ušâbil*	*mušâbilum*	*šûbulum*	*šûbul*	*šūbulum*
	e-type	*ušerred*	*uštêrid*	*ušêrid*	*mušêridum*	*šûrudum*	*šûrud*	*šûrudum*
N		*ipparras*	*ittapras*	*ipparis*	*mupparsum*	*naprusum*	*naprus*	*naprusum*
		iwwallad		*iwwalid*	*muwwaldum*			

3. In other situations, whenever a *w* is followed immediately by another consonant, it behaves like an ʾ. The *w* then quiesces and produces one of two results: compensatory lengthening or resolutory doubling.

a. **compensatory lengthening.** Lengthening of an adjacent vowel occurs in the G-stem preterite for stative-meaning I-*w* verbs, perfect forms in each stem, and in all forms of the Š-stem, except the durative. See, for example, the G-stem preterite 3cs (*iprus*) of *watārum*, (*i,i*), "to be exceeding," in the chart below: *îtir* < **iʾtir* < **iwtir*. See also the Š-stem participle ms (*mušaprisum*) of *wabālum* (*a,i*), "to bring, carry": *mušâbilum* < **mušaʾbilum* < **mušawbilum*.

10. This vowel sequence, *u-a*, may not be arbitrary for its protective effect. The articulation of the semivowel *w* closely approximates that of the combined vowels *ua*.

Stem	Class	Durative 3cs	Perfect 3cs	Preterite 3cs	Participle ms	Verbal Adjective ms	Stative 3ms	Infinitive ms
G		*iparras*	*iptaras*	*iprus*	*pārisum*	*parsum*	*paris*	*parāsum*
	Active	***uššab***	***ittašab***	***ušib (ûšib)***	*wāšibum*	*(w)ašbum*	*(w)ašib*	*(w)ašābum*
	Stative	***ittir***	***îtatir/îtetir***	***îtir***		*(w)atirum*	*(w)atar*	*(w)atārum*
D		*uparras*	*uptarris*	*uparris*	*muparrisum*	*purrusum*	*purrus*	*purrusum*
		uwatter	***ûtatter***	*uwaššir*	*muwašširum*	*(w)uššurum*	*(w)uššur*	***(w)ulludum***
Š		*ušapras*	*uštapris*	*ušapris*	*mušaprisum*	*šuprusum*	*šuprus*	*šuprusum*
		ušabbal	*uštâbil*	*ušâbil*	*mušâbilum*	*šûbulum*	*šûbul*	*šūbulum*
	e-type	*ušerred*	*uštêrid*	*ušêrid*	*mušêridum*	*šûrudum*	*šûrud*	*šûrudum*
N		*ipparras*	*ittapras*	*ipparis*	*mupparsum*	*naprusum*	*naprus*	*naprusum*
		iwwallad		*iwwalid*	*muwwaldum*			

b. **resolutory doubling.** This occurs in the G-stem perfect and the Š-stem durative.[11] See, for example, the G-stem perfect 3cs (*iptaras*) of *warādum*, "to go down": *ittarad* < **îtarad* < **i'tarad* < **iwtarad.*

Stem	Class	Durative 3cs	Perfect 3cs	Preterite 3cs	Participle ms	Verbal Adjective ms	Stative 3ms	Infinitive ms
G		*iparras*	*iptaras*	*iprus*	*pārisum*	*parsum*	*paris*	*parāsum*
	Active	***uššab***	***ittašab***	***ušib (ûšib)***	*wāšibum*	*(w)ašbum*	*(w)ašib*	*(w)ašābum*
	Stative	***ittir***	***îtatir/îtetir***	***îtir***		*(w)atirum*	*(w)atar*	*(w)atārum*
D		*uparras*	*uptarris*	*uparris*	*muparrisum*	*purrusum*	*purrus*	*purrusum*
		uwatter	***ûtatter***	*uwaššir*	*muwašširum*	*(w)uššurum*	*(w)uššur*	***(w)ulludum***
Š		*ušapras*	*uštapris*	*ušapris*	*mušaprisum*	*šuprusum*	*šuprus*	*šuprusum*
		ušabbal	*uštâbil*	*ušâbil*	*mušâbilum*	*šûbulum*	*šûbul*	*šūbulum*
	e-type	*ušerred*	*uštêrid*	*ušêrid*	*mušêridum*	*šûrudum*	*šûrud*	*šûrudum*
N		*ipparras*	*ittapras*	*ipparis*	*mupparsum*	*naprusum*	*naprus*	*naprusum*
		iwwallad		*iwwalid*	*muwwaldum*			

4. When *w* is between two vowels it acts like the ' of a I-' verb;[12] the *w* and the following vowel are deleted without compensatory lengthening. This happens with stative-meaning I-*w* verbs in the G-stem durative 3cs (*iparras*).[13] See, for example, the G-stem durative 3cs (*iparras*) of stative-meaning *watārum*, *(i,i)* "to be exceeding" in the chart below: *ittir* < **i'attir* < **iwattir.*

11. An alternative, perhaps less convincing explanation, is that I-*w* verbs in these instances are acting like I-*n* verbs. Cf. Huehnergard, *A Grammar of Akkadian*, §19.1.

12. See §3.4.5.1.

13. Kouwenberg (*The Akkadian Verb and Its Semitic Background*, §16.2.2) marks the *i* of *ittir* as long; Huehnergard (*A Grammar of Akkadian*, 15.1§) marks the *i* as short. Worthington (*Complete Babylonian*, §26.3) offers both, noting that the short vowel reflects a "later" practice. There are no examples of stative-meaning I-*w* verbs in the durative in LH.

Stem	Class	Durative 3cs	Perfect 3cs	Preterite 3cs	Participle ms	Verbal Adjective ms	Stative 3ms	Infinitive ms
G		*iparras*	*iptaras*	*iprus*	*pārisum*	*parsum*	*paris*	*parāsum*
	Active	***uššab***	***ittašab***	***ušib (ûšib)***	*wāšibum*	*(w)ašbum*	*(w)ašib*	*(w)ašābum*
	Stative	***ittir***	***îtatir/îtetir***	***îtir***		*(w)atirum*	*(w)atar*	*(w)atārum*
D		*uparras*	*uptarris*	*uparris*	*muparrisum*	*purrusum*	*purrus*	*purrusum*
		uwatter	***ûtatter***	*uwaššir*	*muwašširum*	*(w)uššurum*	*(w)uššur*	***(w)ulludum***
Š		*ušapras*	*uštapris*	*ušapris*	*mušaprisum*	*šuprusum*	*šuprus*	*šuprusum*
		ušabbal	*uštâbil*	*ušâbil*	*mušâbilum*	*šūbulum*	*šûbul*	*šūbulum*
	e-type	*ušerred*	*uštêrid*	*ušêrid*	*mušêridum*	*šûrudum*	*šûrud*	*šûrudum*
N		*ipparras*	*ittapras*	*ipparis*	*mupparsum*	*naprusum*	*naprus*	*naprusum*
		iwwallad		*iwwalid*	*muwwaldum*			

5. All the forms of I-*w* verbs discussed above are understandable, if not predictable, based on the strong verb paradigm of *parāsum* and an awareness that *w* in many situations reduced to an ʾ. There are two remaining verb forms, however, that are unexpected and unique to I-*w* verbs: the G-stem preterite (*iprus*) and durative (*iparras*) for active-meaning I-*w* verbs. These verbs, which are all *a-i* class, depart from the strong verb paradigm. Rather than having an *i*-vowel for their prefix vowel followed by the *w* or *wa* of the verb root, they have just a short *u* as a prefix vowel with the expected *w* or *wa* deleted.

For example, the G-stem preterite 3cs (*iprus*) of *wašābum* (*a,i*), "to sit, dwell," is *ušib* > **iwšib*. That the performative *u*- is short is confirmed by the addition of a ventive ending. Often when a ventive ending is added to a form like *ušib*, the *i*-vowel is elided based on vowel syncope (§2.5.2.3): **ušibam* > *ušbam*.

This change in the prefix vowel, from *i* to *u*, deserves some explanation. One plausible explanation is that this change occurred in the period of Proto-Semitic when, in the view of most scholars, the original prefix vowel was *a* (the original Proto-Semitic 3ms prefix was *ya*-).[14] Accordingly, an original *aw* diphthong in these forms may have contracted to *û* and later shortened in most of its occurrences: **yawšib* > **yûšib* > **ûšib* > *ušib*, "he dwelt."

Less often, however, the G-stem preterite of I-*w* active verbs retains the assumed earlier compensatory lengthening of the *u*-prefix. As a result, a G-stem preterite form like *ûšib* sometimes occurs. One evidence for this alternative form is the fact that these preterites are often written with an extra vowel sign. Also, when a ventive ending is added in these cases, the *i*-vowel is not elided, as would otherwise be required by vowel syncope: *ûšibam*.[15]

14. Against the widely held view regarding the Proto-Semitic verbal prefix vowel being *a*, Kouwenberg (*The Akkadian Verb and Its Semitic Background*, §16.2.4) tentatively suggests that it may have been -*u*. If so, then I-*w* verbs merely preserve that original vowel in the G-stem.

15. Cf. Worthington, *Complete Babylonian*, §26.1; Kouwenberg, *The Akkadian Verb and Its Semitic Background*, §16.2.4.

Stem	Class	Durative 3cs	Perfect 3cs	Preterite 3cs	Participle ms	Verbal Adjective ms	Stative 3ms	Infinitive ms
G		*iparras*	*iptaras*	*iprus*	*pārisum*	*parsum*	*paris*	*parāsum*
	Active	***uššab***	***ittašab***	***ušib (ûšib)***	*wāšibum*	*(w)ašbum*	*(w)ašib*	*(w)ašābum*
	Stative	***ittir***	***îtatir/îtetir***	***îtir***		*(w)atirum*	*(w)atar*	*(w)atārum*
D		*uparras*	*uptarris*	*uparris*	*muparrisum*	*purrusum*	*purrus*	*purrusum*
		uwatter	***ûtatter***	*uwaššir*	*muwašširum*	*(w)uššurum*	*(w)uššur*	***(w)ulludum***
Š		*ušapras*	*uštapris*	*ušapris*	*mušaprisum*	*šuprusum*	*šuprus*	*šuprusum*
		ušabbal	*uštâbil*	*ušâbil*	*mušâbilum*	*šûbulum*	*šûbul*	*šûbulum*
	e-type	*ušerred*	*uštêrid*	*ušêrid*	*mušêridum*	*šûrudum*	*šûrud*	*šûrudum*
N		*ipparras*	*ittapras*	*ipparis*	*mupparsum*	*naprusum*	*naprus*	*naprusum*
		iwwallad		*iwwalid*	*muwwaldum*			

6. Finally, some I-*w* verbs in the G-stem and Š-stem have an unexpected vowel attenuation of an *a*-vowel to an *e*-vowel. In these cases, however, vowel attenuation is not based on proximity to one of the usual elided gutturals (*ḫ*, ʿ, or *ĝ*) that foster this vowel change.[16] There are no rules for determining which I-*w* verbs are *e*-type.

For example, the G-stem perfect of *watārum* may be either *îtetir* < (**iʾtetir*) or *îtatir* (< **iʾtatir*). Likewise, the Š-stem durative (*ušapras*) for *e*-type (*a,i*) *wašābum*, "to sit, dwell," is *ušeššeb*.

12.1.2.1 *Excursus: On the History of I-w Active-Meaning Verbs*—I-*w* verbs have one form that lacks any evidence of there ever having been an initial *w*: the G-stem imperative. Imperatives will be examined in Chapter 13, but for the verb *warādum*, "to descend, go down" (cf. *yārad*, יָרַד) the ms imperative is *rid*. This form offers no hint that there is or ever was a missing root consonant, and yet it was understood to mean "go down!" This seems to imply that the meaning of this verb inheres in just two root consonants, in this case *r-d*.

Another evidence for original biconsonantal roots for active I-*w* verbs is the presence of a fair number of I-*w* verbs that have related byforms. "Byforms" refer to related verbal roots with the same or similar meaning. In the case of I-*w* verbs, these have another initial consonant rather than *w*, which is typically a full or partial assimilation to the second root consonant. For example, the verb *wabālum*, "to bring (away), carry" (cf. *y-b-l*, יבל, *hiphil*: "to bring, carry"), has two byforms: *babālum*, "to carry," and *tabālum*, "to take, remove, confiscate, bring (away)."

Both of these lines of argument, however, admit other explanations. Although there may be some I-*w* verbs that originated from biconsonantal roots, it now seems unlikely that the majority did, especially since there is so much supportive evidence for original I-*w* roots based on cognates for many of these verbs and related nouns attested in the other Semitic languages. For example, *wašābum*, "to sit, dwell," finds a close cognate in Hebrew *yāšab*, יָשַׁב,

16. See §3.4.3.

"to sit, dwell."[17] Nevertheless, the theory of an original biconsonantal root may help beginning students remember some of the unique features of I-*w* active verbs over against I-weak (I-') verbs.

12.2 I-*w* Verbs in LH

For reference, below are the I-*w* verbs in LH. These do not need to be learned except as they may come up in the required vocabulary. They are listed here for easy reference.

wa'ārum, ārum = D: to lead, direct
wabālum (*a,i*) = to bring (away), carry (cf. *y-b-l*, יבל, *hiphil*: "to bring, carry")
walādum (*a,i*) = to bear, give birth to (cf. *yālad*, יָלַד)
wapā'um = Š: to make visible (cf. *y-p-'*, יפע, *hiphil*: "to shine")
waqārum = Š: to value, hold in esteem (cf. *yāqar*, יָקַר, "to be precious")
waṣûm (*i,i*) = to go out (cf. *yāṣā'*, יָצָא)
wašābum (*a,i*) = to sit, dwell (cf. *yāšab*, יָשַׁב)
wašārum = D: to prove innocent; Dt: to be proved innocent, exonerated, allowed to go free
watārum (*i,i*) = to be exceeding, be much; D: to exceed; Š: to make supreme (cf. *y-t-r*, יתר, *niphal*: "to be left over")

12.3 Homework

Before you move on, be sure to understanding the rules associated with I-*w* verbs and become familiar with the list of I-*w* verbs that appear in LH.

12.3.1 *Signs*

 *ga, qá*

 *ḫu*

 *lu*, UDU, *immerum*, "sheep" (cf. *'immēr*, אִמֵּר)

 ÌR, *wardum*, "slave" (cf. *yārad*, יָרַד, "to descend")

 *šar*, KIRI$_6$, *kirûm*, "orchard"

 *ze, zi, sé, sí, ṣé, ṣí*

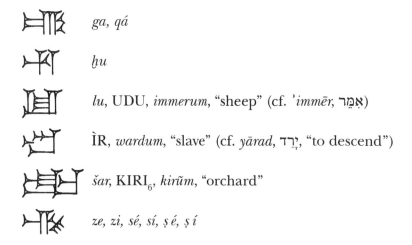

Congratulations! If you have learned the seven cuneiform signs in this chapter and each of the preceding eighty-five signs, you will be able to read 92 percent of all the cuneiform signs in LH §§1–20, 127–149.

17. In Hebrew, virtually all initial *w* consonants became *y*. For more examples of Hebrew cognates, see §12.2.

12.3.2 *Vocabulary*

amtum = female slave (cf. *'āmâ*, אָמָה)
lû = either, or (cf. *lû*, לוּ, "if only")
mimma = something, anything, whatever, all that; property (cf. *mə'ûmâ*, מְאוּמָה)
mimmūm – whatever, property (the form of *mimma* used with pronominal suffixes)
riksum (fp: *riksātum*) = contract, covenant (cf. *rākas*, רָכַס, "to bind")
šâmum (*a,a*) (< *š-y-m*) = to purchase, buy
šarāqum (*i,i*) = to steal
šarrāqum = thief
šurqum = stolen property
û lû = or (cf. *lû*, לוּ, "if only")
wardum = slave (cf. *yārad*, יָרַד, "to descend")

12.3.3 *Exercises*

Laws 6 and 7 are treated separately below.

1. Transliterate and Normalize: See the notes below for additional help.

LH §6 VI:31

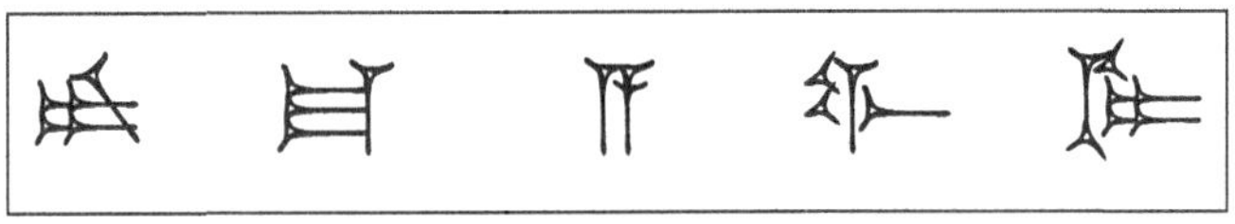

LH §6 VI:32

Note: The signs  in VI:32 should be read as NÍG.GA, *makkūrum*, meaning "property" (cf. *mākar*, מָכַר, "to sell"). This does not need to be learned.

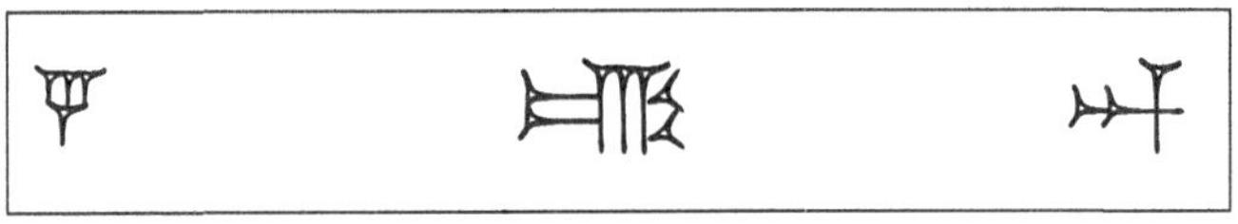

LH §6 VI:33

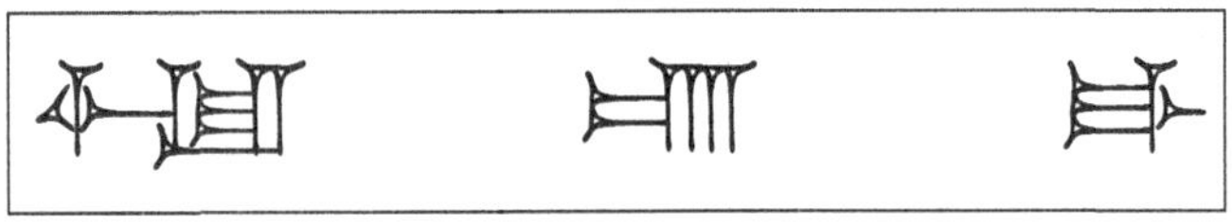

LH §6 VI:34

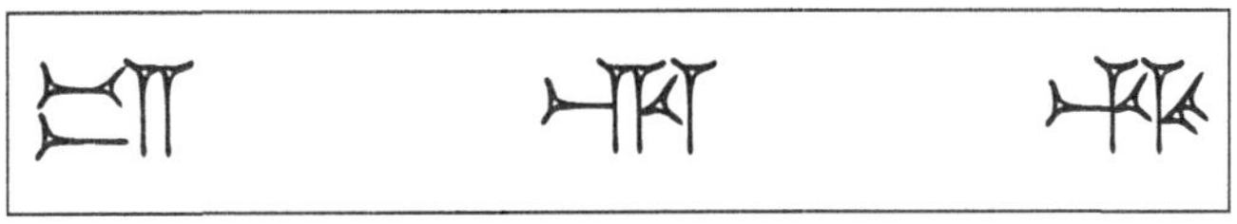

LH §6 VI:35

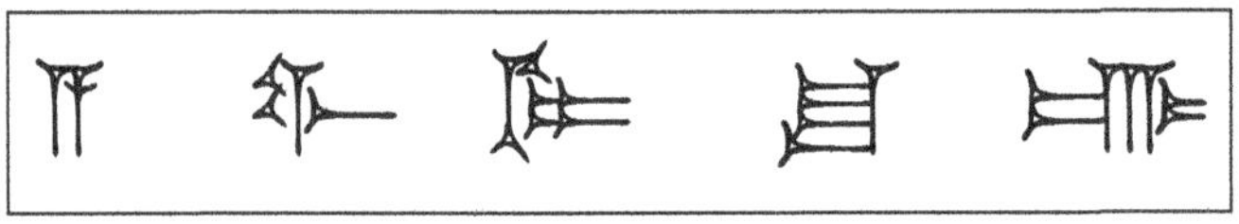

LH §6 VI:36

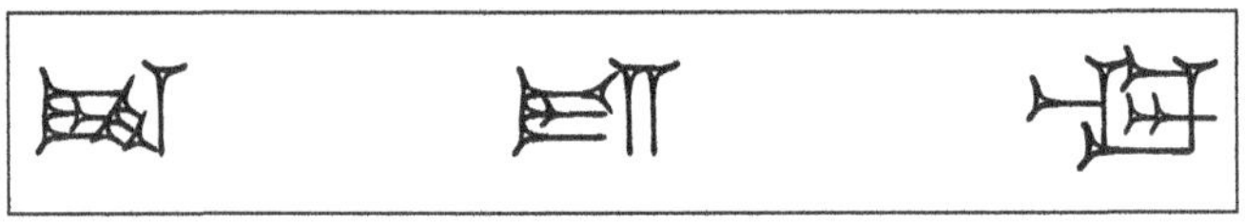

LH §6 VI:37

Note: The sign 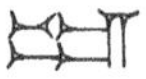 in VI:37 is *úr*. This does not need to be learned.

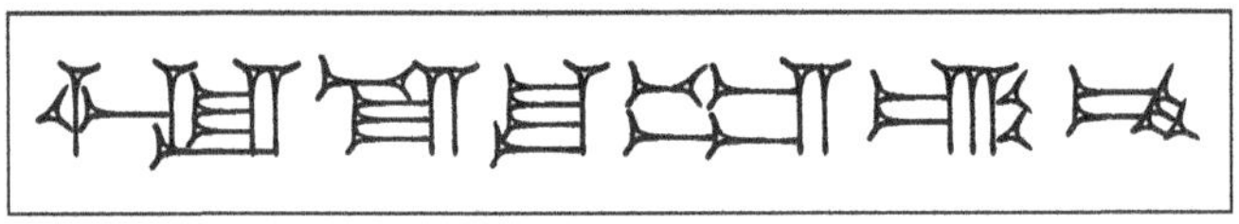

LH §6 VI:38

LH §6 VI:39

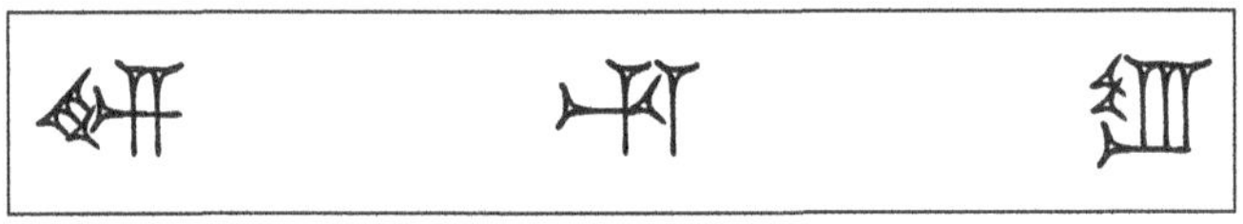

LH §6 VI:40

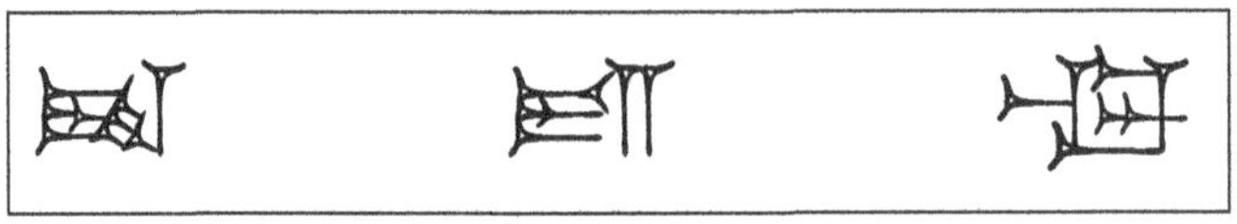

2. Grammatical Analysis: Parse all verb forms.

3. Translation: Translate LH §6.

---

1. Transliterate and Normalize: See the notes below for additional help.

LH §7 VI:41

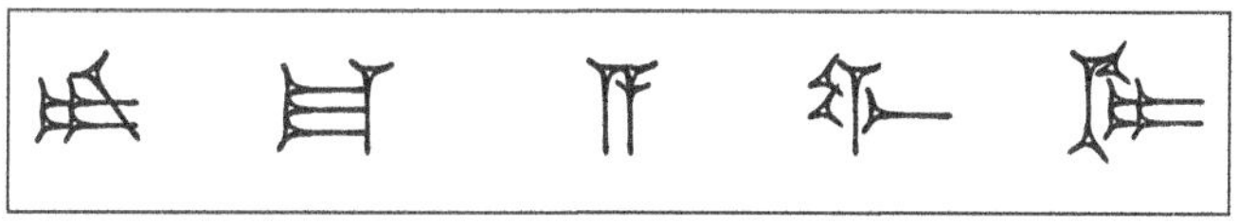

LH §7 VI:42

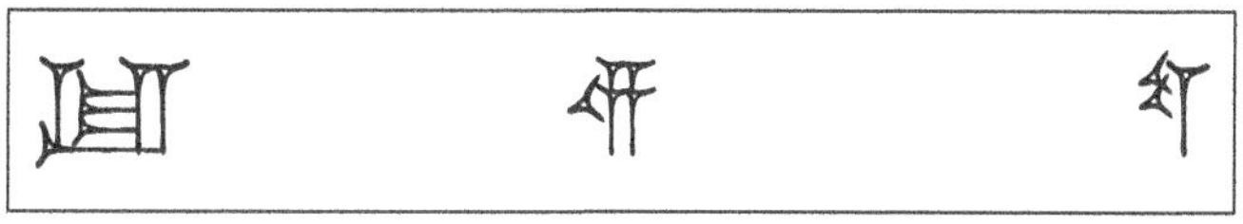

LH §7 VI:43

Note: The sign 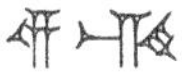 in VI:43 is GUŠKIN, *ḫurāṣ um*, meaning "gold." GUŠKIN is represented by KÙ.GI (logograms for "precious metal" and "yellow"). In Sumerian final consonants drop unless a suffix is attached, although for our purposes they will usually be included. This sign and the word *ḫurāṣum* (cf. *ḥārûṣ*, חָרוּץ) do not need to be learned.

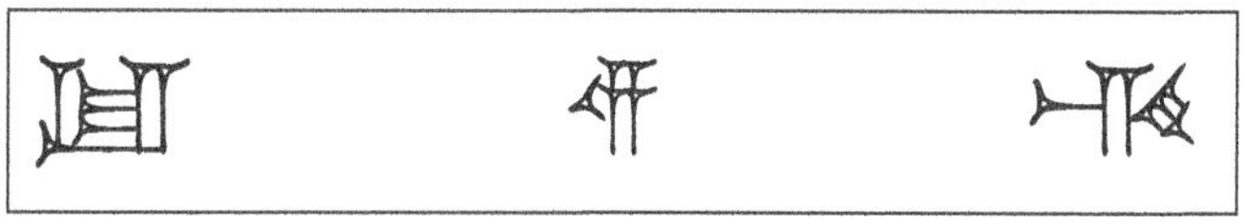

LH §7 VI:44

LH §7 VI:45

Note: The sign 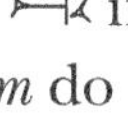 in VI:45 is GUD, *alpum*, meaning "ox" (cf. *'elep*, אֶלֶף). This sign and the word *alpum* do not need to be memorized but be aware that the sign appears in the next chapter in LH §8.

LH §7 VI:46

Note: The sign  in VI:46 is ANŠE, *imēram*, meaning "donkey, ass" (cf. *ḥămôr*, חֲמוֹר). This sign and the word *imēram* do not need to be memorized but be aware that the sign appears in the next chapter in LH §8.

LH §7 VI:47

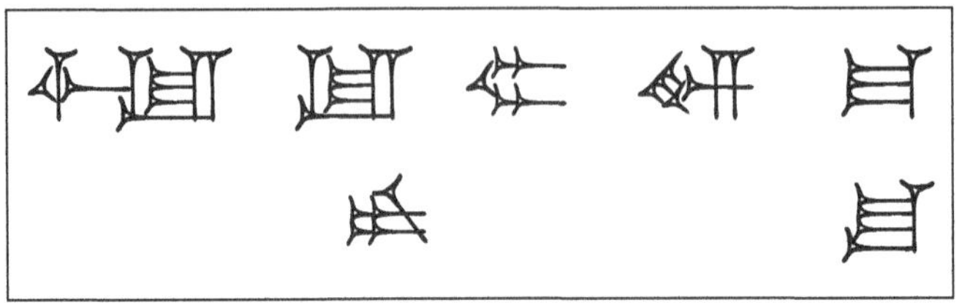

LH §7 VI:48

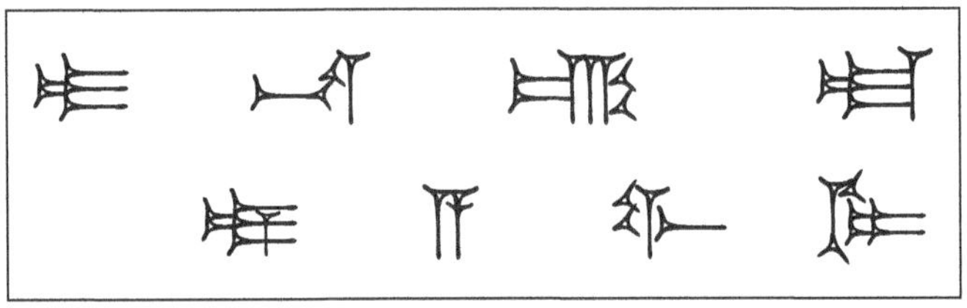

LH §7 VI:49

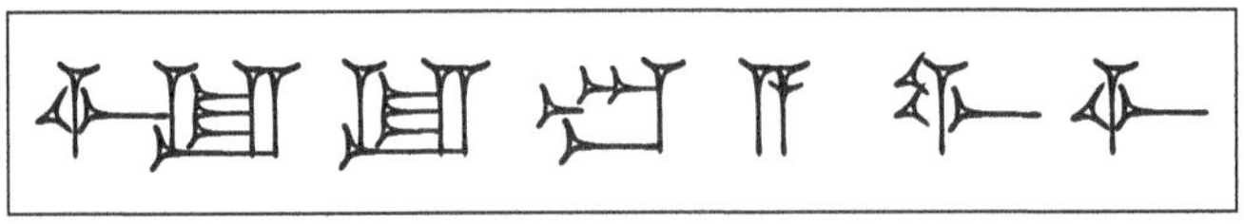

LH §7 VI:50

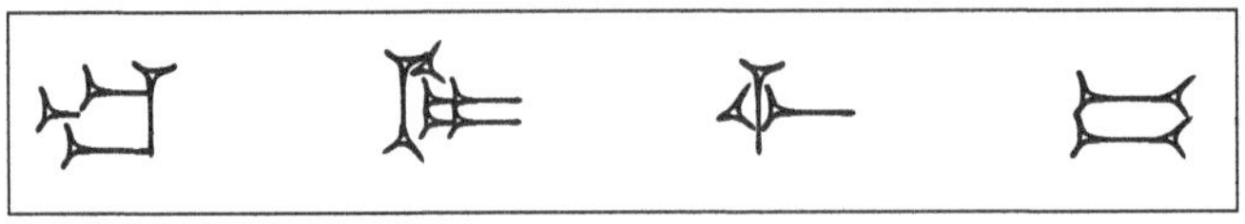

LH §7 VI:51

Note: The sign  in VI:51 is *sa*. This does not need to be learned at this point (it will be learned in Chapter 19).

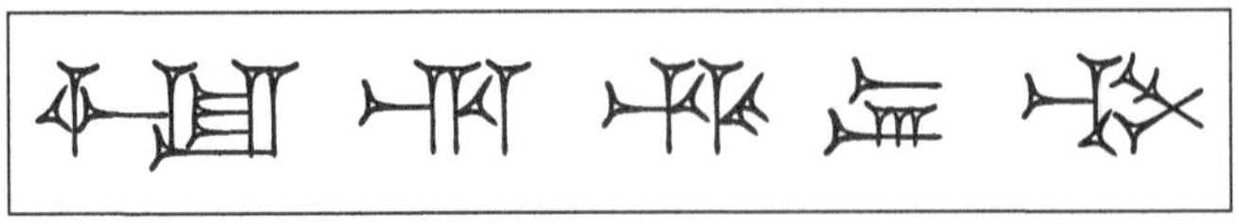

LH §7 VI:52

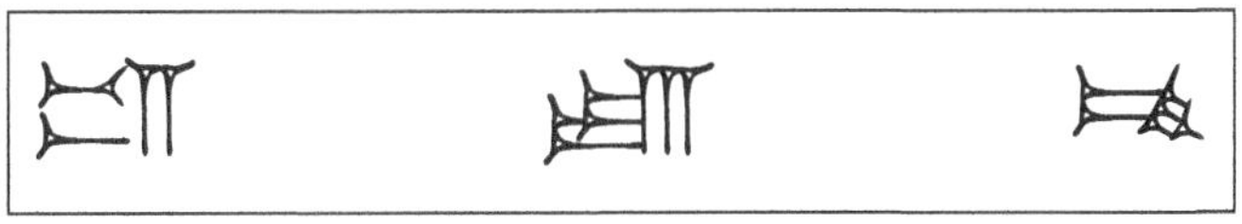

LH §7 VI:53

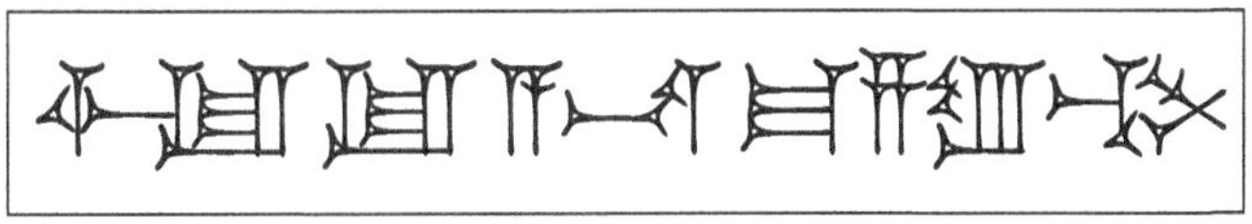

LH §7 VI:54

Note: The sign  in VI:54 is *ur*. This does not need to be learned at this point. It will be learned in Chapter 19.

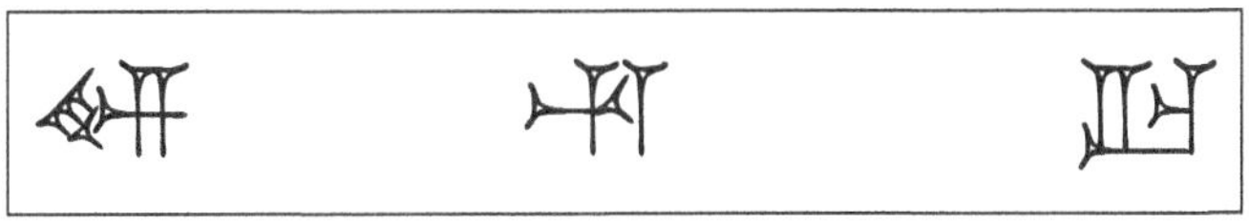

LH §7 VI:55

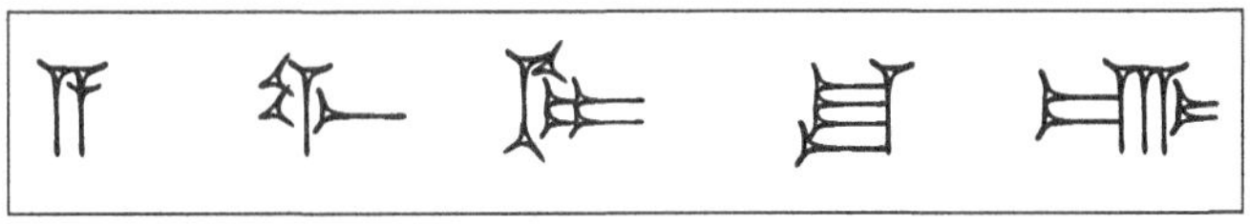

LH §7 VI:56

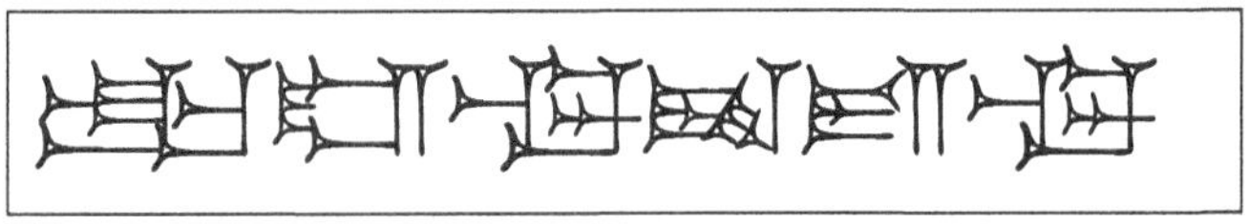

2. Grammatical Analysis: Parse all verb forms. See the notes below for additional help.

   a. The scribe made an error of assimilation to the many examples of "if a man" in VI:48. What is the mistake?

b. Explain the grammatical function of the noun in §7 VI:56.

Note: VI:50 includes the word *balūm*, meaning "without." This does not need to be learned.

Note: VI:53 includes the word *maṣṣarūtum* (< *n-ṣ-r*), meaning "watch, guard, safekeeping" (cf. *nāṣar*, נָצַר). This word does not need to be learned.

3. Translation: Translate LH §7 and add your translation of LH §6.

Akkadian and Deuteronomy's "Centralizing Formula"

Sandra L. Richter

Twenty-one times the book of Deuteronomy speaks of "the place Yahweh your God will choose" as Israel's future site of worship in the promised land (e.g., Deut 12:5, 11, 14, 18, 21, 26; 14:23, 24, 25; 14:23, 24, 25). In modern scholarship this oft-repeated phrase has come to be known as the "centralizing formula." Here the twelve tribes of Israel are commanded to gather and acknowledge their allegiance to the Sinai covenant and to each other. Here and here only may this newly monotheistic nation offer legitimate sacrifice to their God. Deuteronomy speaks of this place as a future, anonymous location chosen by Yahweh himself, from "among your tribes"—*one* place for one God.

Six times the centralizing formula in Deuteronomy is augmented by the phrase: *lĕšakkēn šĕmô šām* (Deut 12:11; 14:23; 16:2, 6, 11; 26:2; cf. Jer 7:12, Ezra 6:12, and Neh 1:9). And three times it is augmented by: *lāśûm šĕmô šām* (Deut 12: 5, 21; 14:24; cf. 1 Kgs 9:3; 11:36; 14:21; and 2 Kgs 21:4, 7). Whereas the latter is easily translated, "[the place Yahweh your God will choose] *to place his name*," the first has proven to be quite a challenge for biblical scholarship. And the fact that the ancient translators viewed these two phrases as synonymous further muddies the water.[1]

For those conversant in biblical Hebrew, the verbal form *lĕšakkēn* is transparently a *piel* (D-stem) infinitive construct. As is typical for the D-stem, the form has been translated as a factitivization (causation of state) of the common, intransitive *qal* (G-stem) *škn*: "to dwell." Thus, the infinitive construct, "to cause to dwell" or more technically "to settle for a certain period of time."[2] The end result of this translation for the centralization formula is: "the place where Yahweh your God will choose to cause his name to dwell." This translation can be found in the KJV, RSV, and the ASV versions of the Old Testament, as well as the dynamic equivalent translation of the 2011 NIV. Too often a further interpretive step is taken and the centralizing formula is written, "the place where Yahweh your God will choose to cause his Name to dwell," communicating that the "name" in this passage is some sort of hypostasized aspect of Yahweh himself.[3]

1. In Deuteronomy 12:21 and 14:24 where the MT has *lāśûm šĕmô šām*, the Samaritan Pentateuch utlilizes *lĕšakkēn šĕmô šām*. In these same instances, the LXX translates *lāśûm šĕmô šām* with the same collocation it uses for *lĕšakkēn šĕmô—epiklēthēnai* (the aorist passive infinitive of *'epikaleō*, "to invoke"; cf. LSJ, s.v., "*epikaleō*"). This demonstrates that at an early point in the Hebrew Bible's transmission, these formulae were considered interchangeable.

2. "שכן," *HALOT* 2:1496; "שכן," BDB 1015. See Ernst Jenni, *Das hebräische Pi'el* (Zurich: Evz-Verlag, 1968], 9–15 and Bruce Waltke and Michael O'Connor, *An Introduction to Biblical Hebrew Syntax* (Winona Lake, IN: Eisenbrauns, 1990), §24.2b (401); cf. §§24.1d–24.2e (398–402).

3. This translation helped to birth the turn-of-the-century theological paradigm known as the Name Theology. Here the "name" in Deuteronomy's formula is understood as a persona, a newly hypostatized aspect of Yahweh, who will now live in the temple. The original Name Theologians saw this move on the part of the Deuteronomist as an intentional correction of J and E's theology in which the god of Israel was anthropomorphic, limited, and immanent; and a movement toward P's theology in which Israel's god was now inaccessible, transcendent, and therefore in need of mediation. See Sandra L. Richter, *The Deuteronomistic History and the Name Theology: lĕšakkēn šĕmô šām in the Bible and the Ancient Near East*, BZAW 318 (Berlin: de Gruyter, 2002), 7–35 for a full discussion.

How to Read "*škn*"?

But Akkadian has a different tale to tell. Whereas in biblical Hebrew *qal* (G-stem) *škn* means "to dwell" (an intransitive fientive, i.e. a verb that shows continued or progressive action on the part of the subject), in Akkadian the G-stem verb *škn* means "to put, to place" (an active transitive verb with a subject and a direct object).[4] More importantly, Akkadian has an idiom with all the essential elements of *lĕšakkēn šĕmô šām*. This idiom can be found throughout Mesopotamian literature—victory stelae, correspondence, building inscriptions, and even songs. The idiom is Akkadian *šuma šakānu* and, like *lāśûm šĕmô šām* in the biblical text, it means "to place a name." It is best known for its use in the Mesopotamian royal monumental tradition. What does "to place a name" mean in the royal monumental tradition? It means to write one's inscription on a monument and thereby claim the monument as one's own. Here "name" signifies "inscription" and "to place" means "to inscribe." Eventually, *šuma šakānu* came to communicate installing an inscribed monument or claiming the territory marked by the monument, or even to become famous because of the heroic deeds reported on the monument. One example is Iahdun-Lim of Mari (ca. 1830 BCE) and his victory monument:

> But Iahdun-Lim, the son of Iaggid-Lim, the mighty king, a wild ox among kings, marched to the shore of the sea in irresistible strength. To the 'Great Sea' he offered a multitude of royal sacrifices and his army washed in the waters of the 'Great Sea.' To the Cedar and Boxwood Mountain, the great mountains, he penetrated . . . He set up a monument, **placed his name** [*šu-mi-šu iš-ta-ka-an*] and made known his might.[5]

Another would be Gilgamesh and his quest for eternal fame:

> I will conquer him in the Forest of Cedar: let the land learn Uruk's offshoot is mighty! Let me start out, I will cut down the cedar, **I will place a name** eternal [*šu-ma ša da-ru-ú a-na-ku lu-uš-tak-nam*].[6]

In sum, Deuteronomy's *lĕšakkēn šĕmô šām* is a loan adaptation of Akkadian *šuma šakānu*. And Deuteronomy and the Deuteronomistic History's *lāśûm šĕmô šām* is the NW Semitic version of this same Akkadian idiom. The ninth century BCE, bilingual Tell Fakhariyeh inscription proves the point. Here Akkadian *šuma šakānu* is translated into Aramaic as *wšmym lšem bh/šumīma liškun*—"Whoever comes afterwards, should it [the inscribed statue] become dilapidated, may he restore it, may he put my name on it." As the Masoretes recognized, these phrases in the book of Deuteronomy *are* synonymous, and they are synonymous because they both derive from the same Akkadian idiom: *lĕšakkēn šĕmô šām*.

So What?

In the Mesopotamian tradition, the Akkadian idiom *šuma šakanu* is always found in the mouths of kings, conquering kings. A hero would "place his name" to declare his mighty acts to the world, and often to claim new territory as his own. Reading Deuteronomy's *lĕšakkēn šĕmô šām* in light of the Akkadian evidence helps us to understand that the biblical writers were presenting Yahweh as the mighty champion,

4. "*šakānu*," *CAD Š* 1:116, meaning 1.

5. *Iaḫdun*-Lim, E4.6.8.2:51–59 (RIME 4:606) and Georges Dossin, "L'inscription de fondation de *Iaḫdun*-Lim, roi de Maria," *Syria* 32 (1955), 1–28, see 14, ii:20.

6. Andrew George, *The Epic of Gilgamesh: The Babylonian Poem and Other Texts in Akkadian and Sumerian* (London: Penguin Books, 1999), 20, 112, Y183–87.

who "personally brought you from Egypt by his great power, driving out from before you nations greater and mightier than you, to bring you in, to give you their land for an inheritance, as it is today" (Deut 4:37 b–38). Thus, when the Deuteronomist records Yahweh's command that "You shall do thus and such in the place I choose *to place my name* . . ." he is marshalling thousands of years of royal monumental imagery to inform the statement. Like Iahdun-Lim and Gilgamesh, Yahweh is "placing his name" in the territory he has conquered. He is commanding that the altars and statues of Baal and Asherah—the previous sovereigns of Canaan—be torn down and their names chiseled off their monuments (Deut 12:1–5). Yahweh then commands that his own inscribed monument be set up at a new (singular) place of worship (Deut 27:1–8). These ideas and idioms, although perhaps foreign to us, would have been expressly familiar to the Israelites. And they all served to communicate that Yahweh had won the right to demand Israel's unrivaled obedience in the singular place of worship he would approve.

13–𒌋𒐈

Injunctive Verb Forms, Irregular Verbs *išûm* and *idûm*, and Direct Discourse

This chapter explains injunctive verb forms and how to identify direct discourse. The stylistic *-ān* suffix will also be explained, as will the rules of infix *-t-* assimilation. The exercises for this chapter include LH §§8–9, a continuation of the section of laws (LH §§6–13) that concern the theft of property. There are many lines of translation below. To aid translation, normalization of LH §9 is provided in the exercises below.

13.1 Injunctive Verb Forms

In Akkadian there are three kinds of positive injunctives: jussives (third-person injunctions), cohortatives (first-person injunctions), and imperatives (second-person injunctions). Jussives and cohortatives are often combined under the designation "precatives." These are usually translated with "let," "may," or "should." There are also two corresponding negative injunctives: prohibitives (negative exhortations) and vetitives (negative wishes). Both express something that should not be done or not be the case.

Injunctive forms are well attested in the prologue and epilogue of LH, but they are relatively rare in the laws themselves, appearing in only five: LH §§9, 15, 16, 49, 172. Four of these, however, are laws that happen to be treated in this book. Below are further explanations of the forms.

13.1.1 ***Precatives.*** Precative (third- and first-person) forms of verbs are usually produced by adding the precative prefix *l(u)-* directly onto a corresponding preterite form.[1] The first-person plural form is the only exception (see below under Cohortative). The *l-* prefix is used with third-person forms (jussives), and *lu-* is used with first-person singular forms (cohortatives). Precatives are attested in LH only for third-person forms, singular or plural, and first-person singular forms.

13.1.1.1 *Jussives*—A jussive is a third-person form expressing a wish or an indirect command. Its form corresponds to the preterite 3cs *iprus*, "he decided," by adding the precative prefix *l-*, *liprus*, "may he decide."[2]

1. The cognate Hebrew term, לוּ, "if only," provides some indirect evidence in support of the assumption the vowel in *lû* is, or at least was originally, long. Other possible evidence is seen in the many examples where *lû* is regularly written in the cuneiform of LH as *lu-ú*. On the other hand, the cognate evidence for this vowel length is indecisive for the related prefix *lu-*, which in some forms loses the vowel altogether. Accordingly, some Assyriologists (e.g., *CAD*, ad loc., *lu*) regularly mark the vowel as short, *lu*, while others mark it as long (e.g., Caplice, *Introduction to Akkadian*; Huehnergard, *A Grammar of Akkadian*; Worthington, *Complete Babylonian*).

2. Precatives can also be formed by placing the precative particle *lû* before a stative verb. These precatives can be in any person, singular or plural. There are, however, no examples in LH of this kind of precative based on a stative verb.

The following chart summarizes the jussive forms and should be learned:

Third Person	Singular	Plural
Masculine	*liprus*	*liprusū*
Feminine	*liprus*	*liprusā*

13.1.1.2 *Cohortatives*—Cohortatives are first-person forms expressing exhortations. The form of the cohortative corresponds to the first-person singular preterite with the prefix vowel *a*- replaced with the precative particle *lu*-. For example, *aprus*, "I decided," is the first-person singular preterite from of the verb *parāsum*. The cohortative, then, is *luprus*, "let me decide."

On the other hand, the cohortative first-person plural, though unattested in LH, is formed by placing the cohortative particle *i* before the first-person plural preterite form. For example, the first-person plural preterite of the verb *parāsum* is *niprus*, "we decided." The cohortative, then, is *i niprus*, which means "let us decide," "may we decide," or "we should decide."[3]

The following cohortative forms should be learned:

	Singular	Plural
First Common	*luprus*	*i niprus*

13.1.2 ***Imperatives.*** Imperatives are second-person forms expressing exhortations. They are built on the preterite form of the verb with its prefix stripped off. When the prefix is removed, this often produces a consonantal cluster, such as *iprus* < **prus*. This initial consonantal cluster is resolved by inserting a harmonizing vowel (one that is the same as the theme vowel). In the case of the 3cs form *iprus*, this yields the imperative 2ms form *purus*, "decide!" For some *a*-class verbs, however, the inserted vowel is *i*.

Imperatives appear in the following forms for gender and number. These forms should be learned:

Second Person	Singular	Plural
Masculine	*purus*	*pursā*
Feminine	*pursī*	*pursā*

13.1.3 ***Prohibitives.*** Negative commands are normally confined to second- and third-person forms only. They are formed by preposing the negative particle *lâ* to the corresponding durative tense form of the verb.

For example, "do (ms) not decide," is *lâ taparras*. This differs from a simple negative, "you will not decide," or "you are not deciding," which is expressed by *ul taparras*.

3. The "should" translation of cohortative forms is especially useful following an interrogative, as in *ana mīnim luprus*, "why should I decide?"

13.1.4 ***Vetitives (Negative Precatives).*** A negative precative, or vetitive, is formed by preposing the vetitive particle *ay* before a corresponding preterite form or *ê* if the corresponding preterite begins with a consonant. For example, preterite 3cs *iprus*, "he decided," becomes *ay iprus*, meaning, "may he not decide!" Vetitives are attested in all three persons.

13.2 Irregular Verbs *išûm* and *idûm*

The verbs *išûm*, "to have," and *idûm* (also spelled *edûm*) "to know," are not only doubly weak verbs with their first and last root consonants *'aleph*'s, but they are also irregular. Since they appear quite frequently, they need to be learned.

For no apparent reason, *išûm* and *idûm* exist only in preterite, infinitive, and participial forms. In the preterite, however, they can refer to the past, the present, or the future, depending on the context. In the case of *išûm*, it is even more limited: it is unattested as a participle.

Rather than listing all of their irregularities, here it is only necessary to note the following forms.

		išûm	**idûm/edûm**
G-Stem Preterite	3cs	*îšû*	*îdê*
	3mp	*îšû*	*îdû*
G-Stem Participle	ms		*mûdûm* (<**mûde'um*)
	mp		*mûdûtum*

Notes:

1. *Idûm/edûm* often uses a derived noun, *mûdûm*, "knowing, wise; knower, expert," as a substitute for the participle. Accordingly, instead of the bound form of mp *mûdûtum*, namely *mûdût*, one regularly finds the oblique mp form, *mûdê*, "knowers of."[4] This parallels the bound form of the singular *mûdûm* (<**mûde'um*), "knower of," which is *mûdê*.[5]
2. *Idûm/edûm* occurs in the D-stem where it acts like a I-*w* verb. For example, the D-stem preterite 3cs *uweddîma*, "he identified with, recognized," appears in LH §193.

13.3 Direct Discourse

Direct discourse in Akkadian is often unmarked. In these cases context alone (such as an explicit reference to speaking or informing or some other introductory formula) is usually sufficient to determine whether a text is intended to be understood as a quotation. Sometimes, however, a special *-mi* suffix is used to indicate direct discourse. It can be found on any one word in a quoted clause. It may also be repeated in subsequent clauses of the discourse. When it is attached to a word, it causes an immediately preceding vowel to lengthen, or it preserves the original length of that vowel.

---

4. Borger, *Babylonisch-Assyrische Lesestücke*, 2:§106(q).

5. Alternatively, as pointed out in §5.2, at times mp participles take normal noun endings (*-ū* and *-ī*) rather than the characteristic adjectival endings (*ūtum* and *ūtim*). Cf. Worthington, *Complete Babylonian*, §35.5.

13.4 Stylistic *-ān* Suffix

Akkadian nouns and adjectives, including participles and sometimes plural forms of these words, often appear with a suffix *-ān*, which is placed immediately before case endings. Earlier Assyriologists described this as a "particularizing *-ān*." It was thought that the *-ān* suffix was intended to draw attention to a particular instance of the item or quality to which the noun or adjective refers. For example, if *šarrum* means "king," *šarrānum* was thought to mean "*that* king" or a particular king.

Now, however, most Assyriologists believe that the *-ān* suffix has no significance for the meaning of a word. Instead, the *-ān* suffix appears to be nothing more than a stylistic variation in spelling. In some cases, it became the normal spelling for the plurals of certain nouns and adjectives. Likewise, its frequent use with some nouns and adjectives resulted in the formation of substantially synonymous derivative nouns and adjectives.

13.5 The Rule of Infix *-t-* Assimilation

The *-t-* that is infixed in the perfect tense and the *-t(a)-* that is infixed in the derived stems (*-t[a]-* and *-tan-*) assimilate to adjacent dentals such as *d* and *ṭ* and sibilants (other than *š*) *s*, *ṣ*, and *z*. The infixed *-t-* also partially assimilates into *d* when it is adjacent to the consonant *g*.

For example, in LH §18 the G-stem perfect 3cs of *zakārum* (*a,u*) "to speak, say, name, swear," appears. It is *izzakar* from **iztakar*, "he declared." On the other hand, in LH §227 the D-stem perfect of *galābum*, "to shave, cut off," appears. It is *ugdallib* from **ugtallib*, "he has shaved off" and attests partial assimilation.

13.6 Homework

Before you move on, be sure to understand the injunctive forms, both positive and negative, and become familiar with the irregular verbs *išûm* and *idûm*. Also, learn to recognize the discourse marker *-mi*. Be able to recognize the stylistic *-ān* suffix, and become comfortable with the assimilation of the *-t-* infix.

13.6.1 *Signs*

 *i'a, i'e, i'i, i'u, ya, ye, yi, yu*

 *be, bat*

 *ḫal*

 *el*

 MAŠ.EN.KA(K) (= *muškēnum*, "royal servant, civil servant")

 *tu*

13.6.2 *Vocabulary*

-ān = a stylistic suffix added to nouns or adjectives that does not change their meaning
bêlum = lord, owner, master (cf. *ba'al*, בַּעַל)
ḫalāqum (*i,i*) = to lose, go/be missing
ḫalqum = lost, missing
ḫulqum = lost property
idûm (*edûm*) = to know (cf. *yāda'*, יָדַע)
išûm (< *i-š-y*) (*u/i* alternates in preterite, *u* is older) = to have (cf. *yēš*, יֵשׁ, "there is")
leqûm (*e,e*) = to take, receive (cf. *lāqaḥ*, לָקַח)
maḫrum = front, presence; *construct*: before (cf. *maḫārum*; *məḥîr*, מְחִיר, "equivalent value, price, recompense")
-mi = a suffix sometimes used to mark direct discourse that can be placed on any word within the discourse
mûdûm (<**mûde'um*) = knowing, wise; knower, expert (cf. *yāda'*, יָדַע).
muškēnum (< *m-š-k-'*) = royal servant, civil servant (cf. *miskēn*, מִסְכֵּן, "poor")
ṣabātum (*a,a*) = to seize, catch, find; N: to be found, be captured (cf. *ṣābaṭ*, צָבַט, "to reach, hold")
šayyāmānum (< *šâmum*) = buyer
šîmum (< *šâmum*) = purchase

Congratulations! If you learn the thirteen words above and have learned each of the eighty words in the vocabulary lists of the preceding chapters, you will be able to read 74 percent of all the words in LH §§1–20, 127–149.

13.6.3 *Exercises*

Laws 8 and 9 are treated separately below. LH §9 is significantly longer than §8.

1. Transliterate and Normalize: Answer the question below. See also the notes below for additional help.

LH §8 VI:57

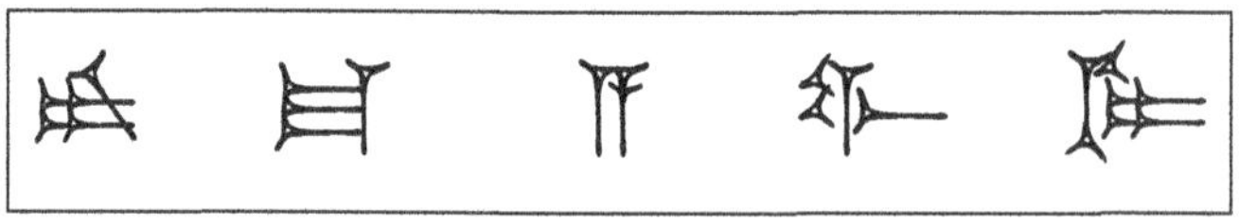

LH §8 VI:58

Note: Signs  and 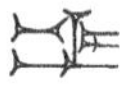 in VI:58 also appeared in LH §6. The sign 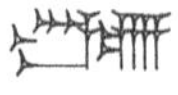 in VI:58 is ŠAḪA, *šaḫûm*, meaning "pig." This sign and the word *šaḫûm* do not need to be memorized.

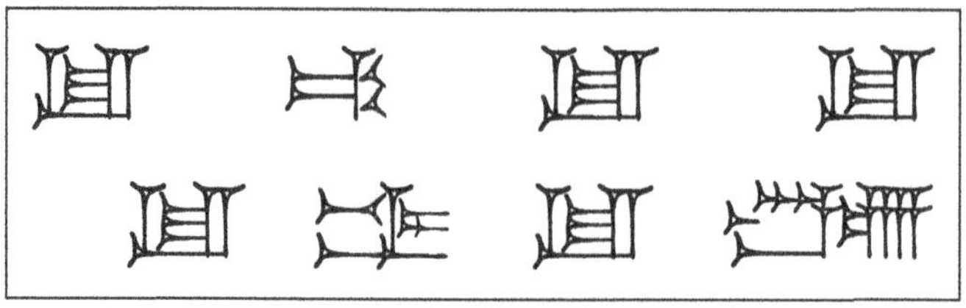

LH §8 VI:59

Note: The sign  in VI:59 is MÁ, *eleppum*, meaning "boat." This sign and the word *eleppum* do not need to be memorized.

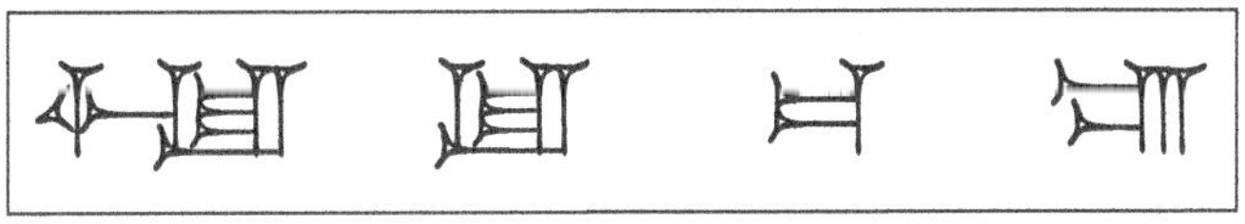

LH §8 VI:60

LH §8 VI:61

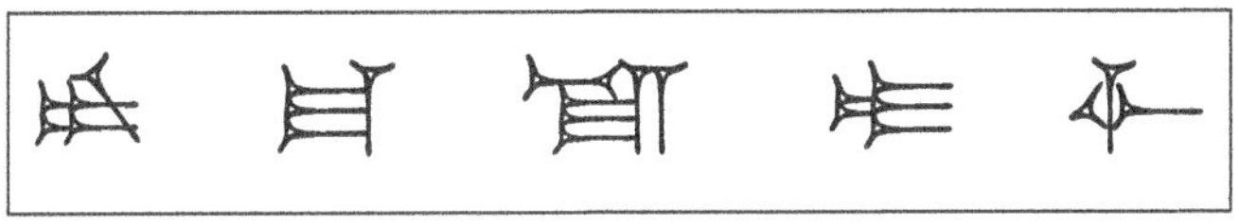

LH §8 VI:62

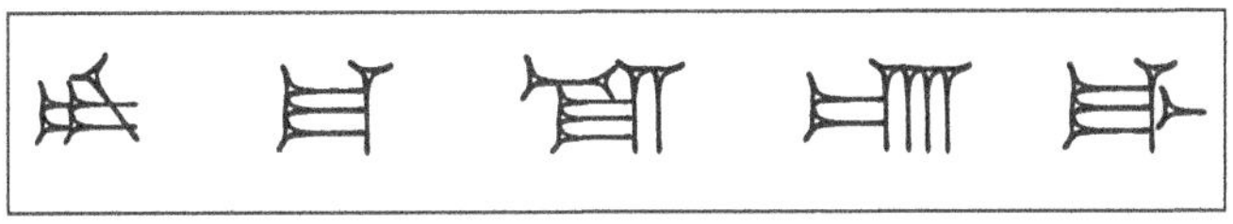

LH §8 VI:63

LH §8 VI:64

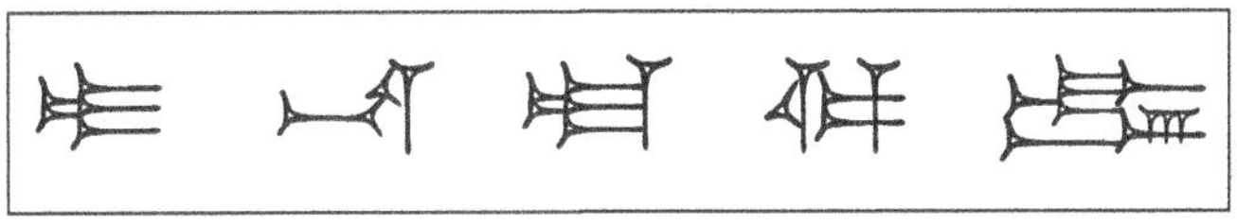

LH §8 VI:65

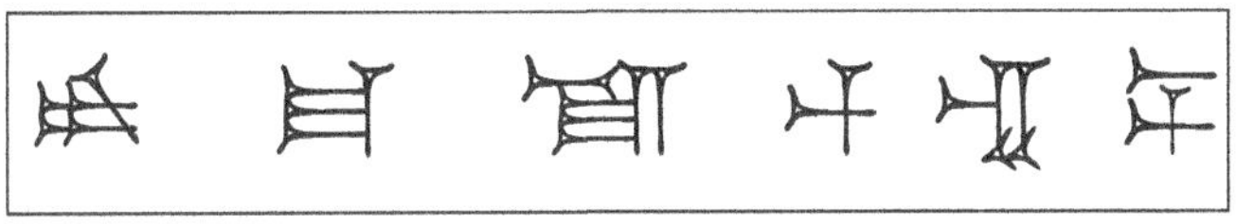

LH §8 VI:66

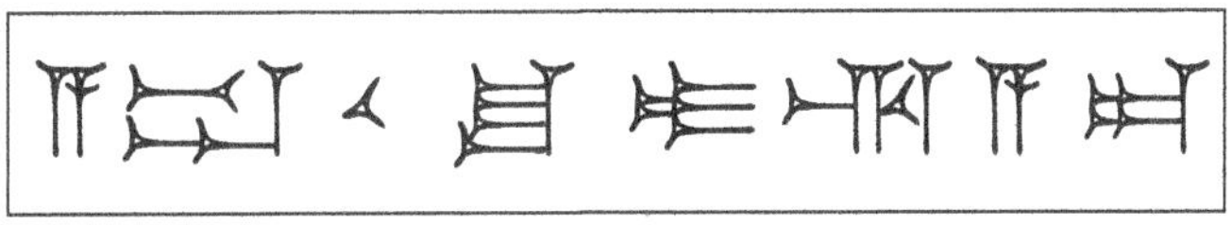

LH §8 VI:67

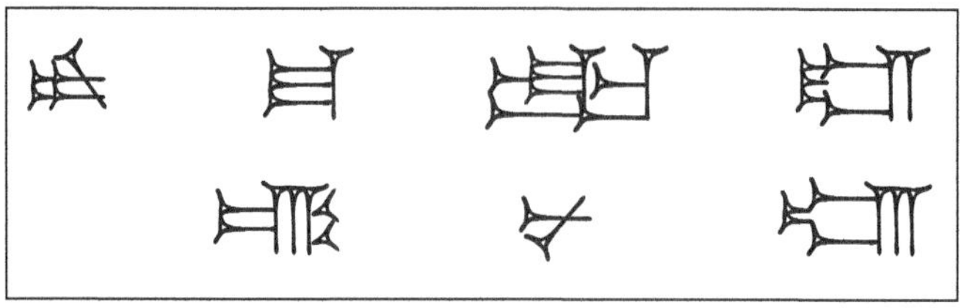

a. What is the significance of the *-ān* suffix on the noun in VI:67?

LH §8 VI:68

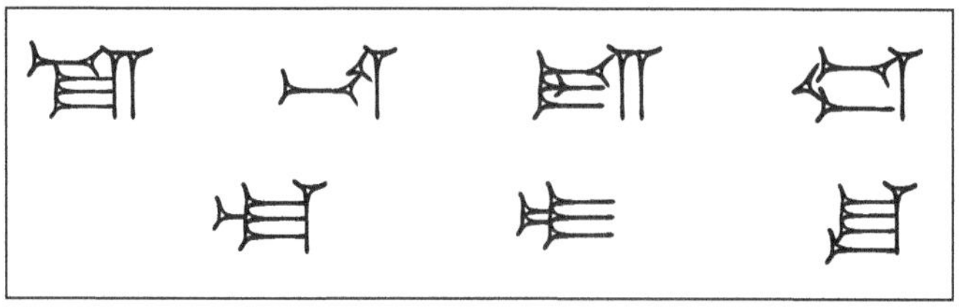

LH §8 VI:69

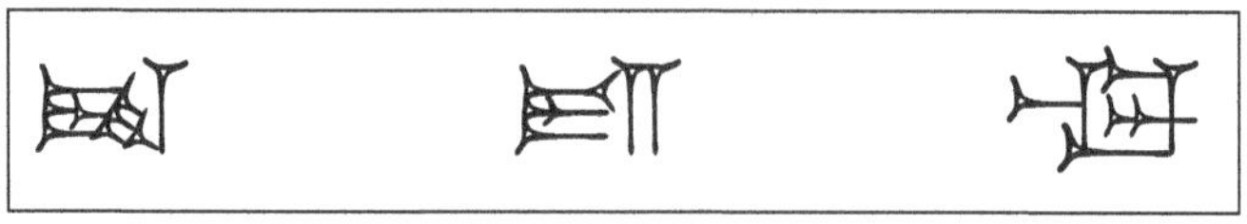

2. Grammatical Analysis: Parse all verb forms. See the note below for help.

   Note: VI:66 includes the word *rābum* (or *ri'ābum*) (*a,i*), "to compensate, make restitution." This word and meaning do not need to be learned.

3. Translation: Translate LH §8. See the note below for help.

   Note: *šumma . . . šumma . . .* is often better translated, "whether . . . or. . . ."

The forty-eight text boxes labeled VI:70–VII:47 comprise the rather lengthy LH §9. LH §9 takes up the issue of what happened when stolen goods were fenced. If the original owner of some property that was stolen could establish his ownership by producing witnesses and if the buyer of that stolen property could establish that his purchase was lawfully made by producing witnesses to the purchase, and if both sets of witnesses swore to these facts before a god, then the seller of the stolen property would be executed. In addition, the property would be returned to its rightful owner, and the purchase price for the fenced property would be returned to the buyer out of the estate of the executed thief.

Normalization for LH §9 is provided below each text box. Be sure to review signs as you work through parsings and translation.

LH §9 VI:70

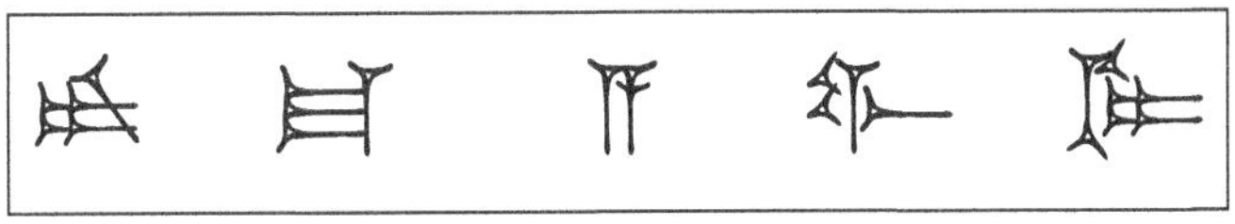

[VI:70]*šumma awīlum*

LH §9 VII:1

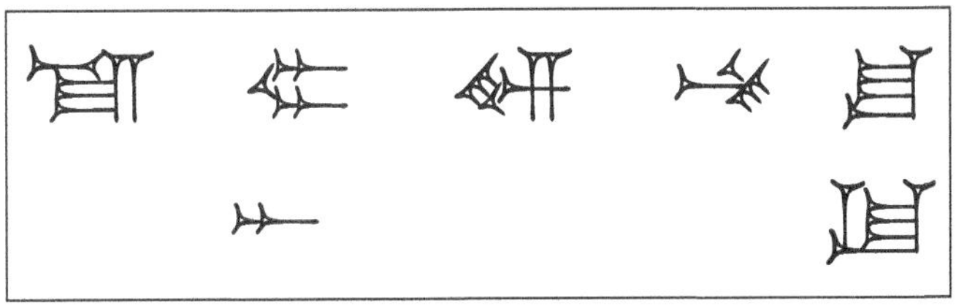

[VII:1]*ša mimmûšu ḫalqu*

LH §9 VII:2

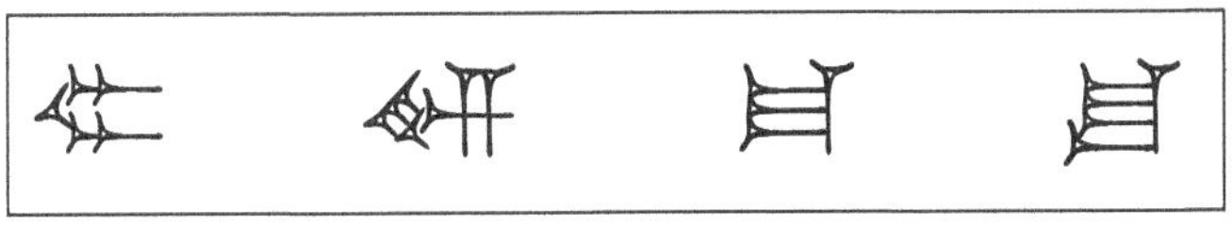

[2]*mimmâšu*

LH §9 VII:3

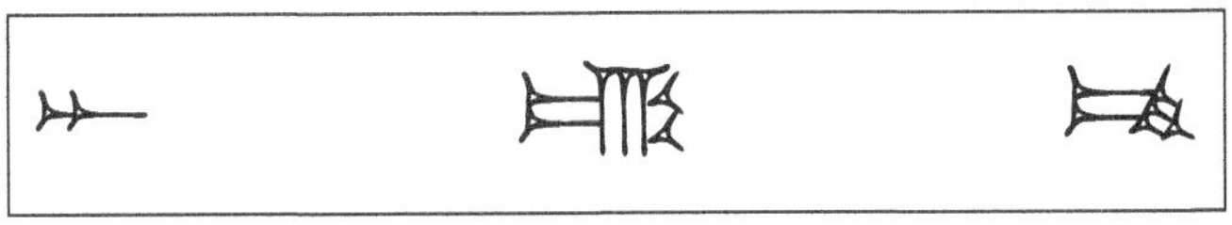

[3]*ḫalqam*

LH §9 VII:4

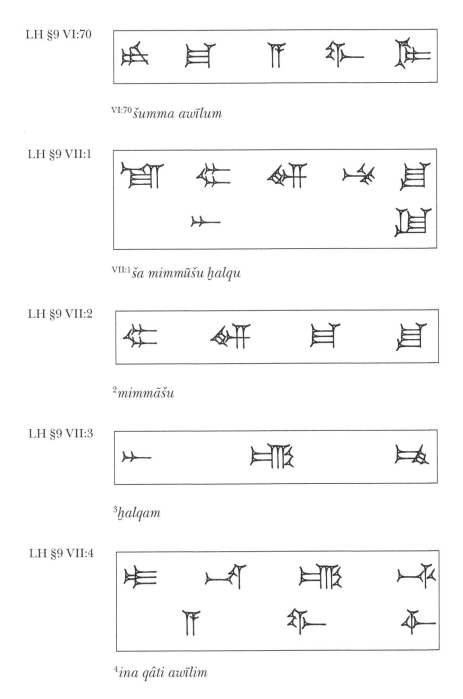

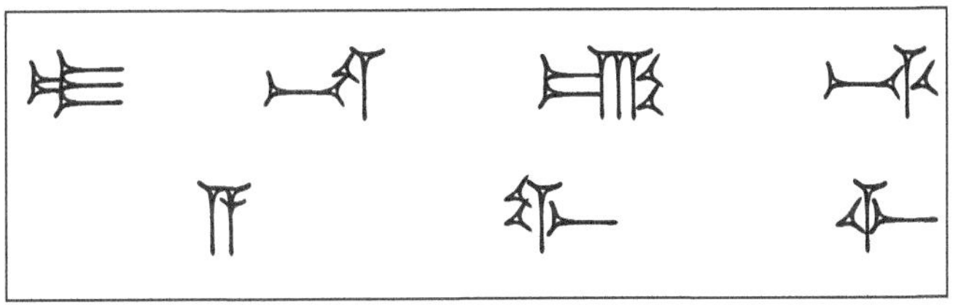

[4]*ina qâti awīlim*

LH §9 VII:5

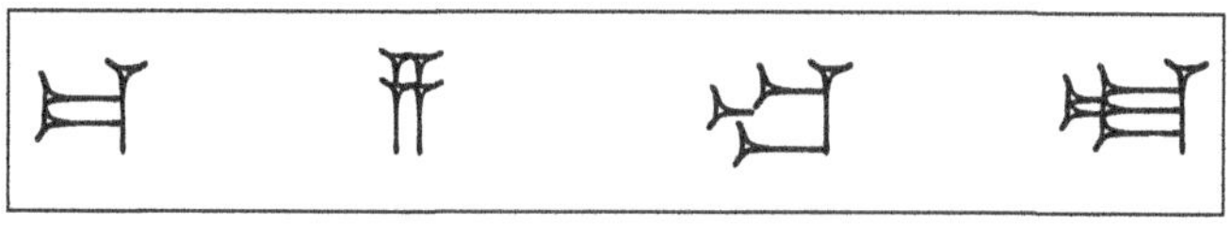

[5]*iṣṣabat*

LH §9 VII:6

Note: The sign  in VII:6 is *qu, qum*. This does not need to be memorized now but will be learned in Chapter 20.

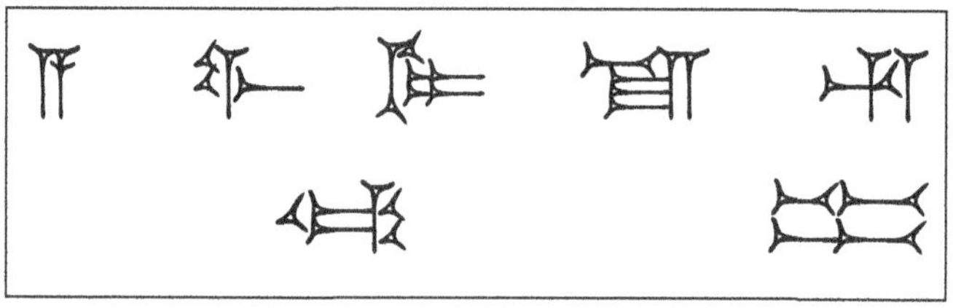

[6]*awīlum ša ḫulqum*

LH §9 VII:7

[7]*ina qâtišu*

LH §9 VII:8

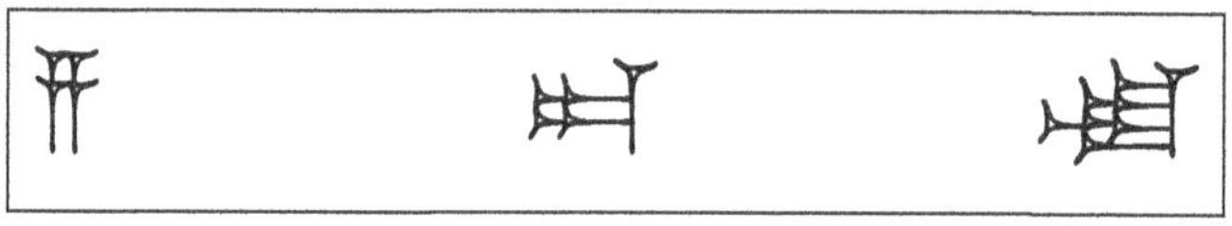

[8]*ṣabtu*

LH §9 VII:9

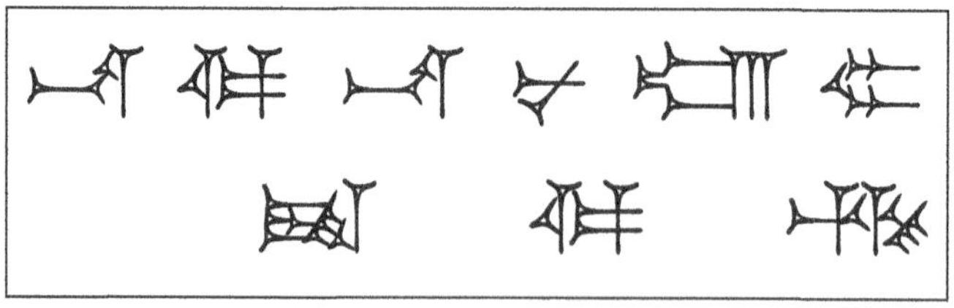

[9]*nādinānummi iddinam*

LH §9 VII:10

Note: The sign  in VII:10 and 36 is *ḫar*. It does not need to be memorized. The sign  in VII:22, 30, and 51 is *maḫ*. This does not need to be learned.

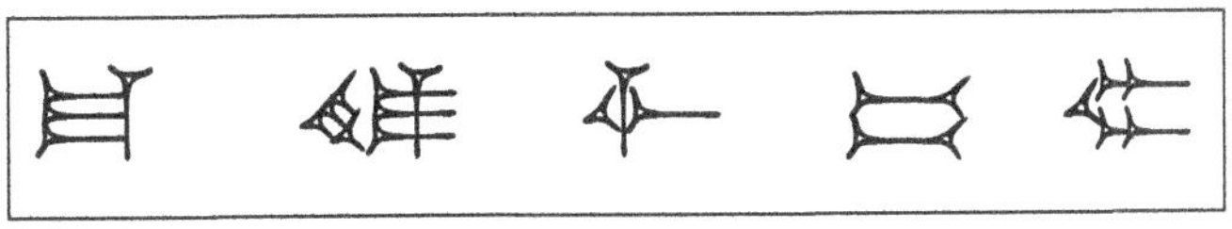

[10]*maḫar šîbīmi*

LH §9 VII:11

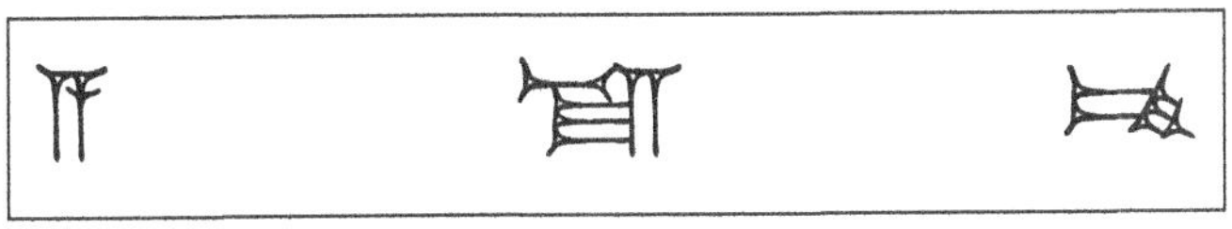

[11]*ašâm*

LH §9 VII:12

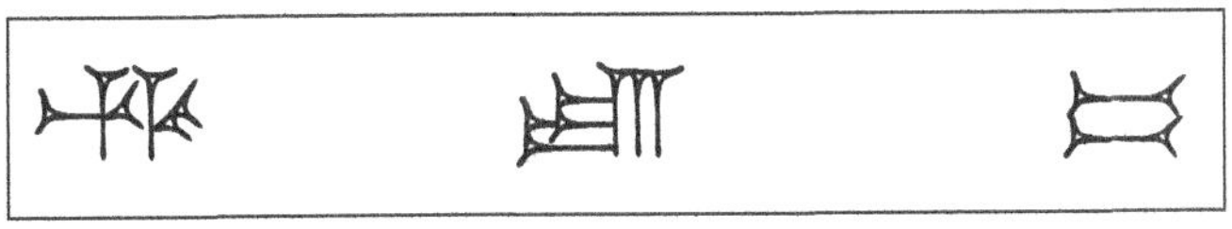

[12]*iqtabî*

LH §9 VII:13

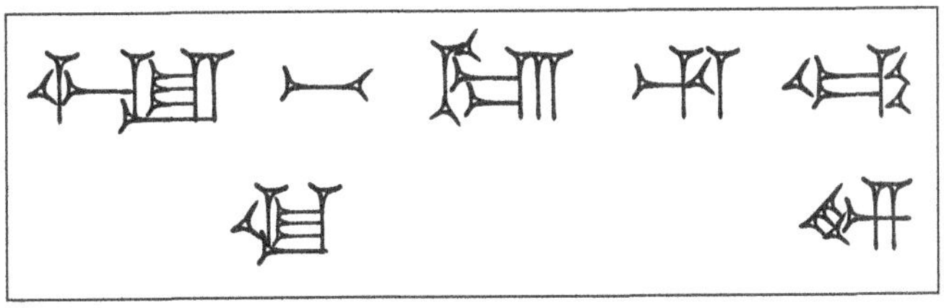

[13]*u bêl ḫulqim*

LH §9 VII:14

[14]*šîbī mûdē*

LH §9 VII:15

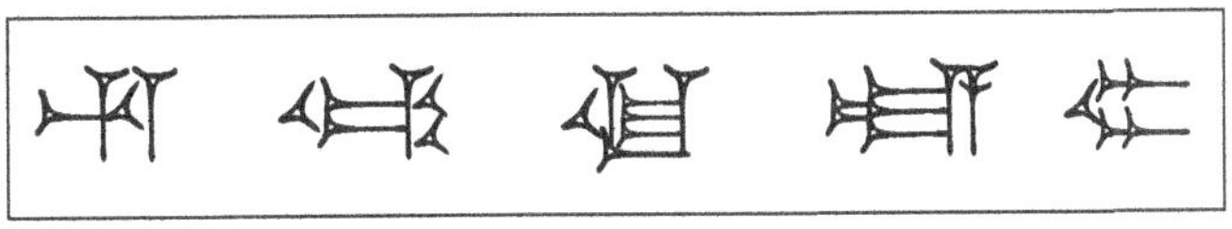

[15]*ḫulqiyāmi*

LH §9 VII:16

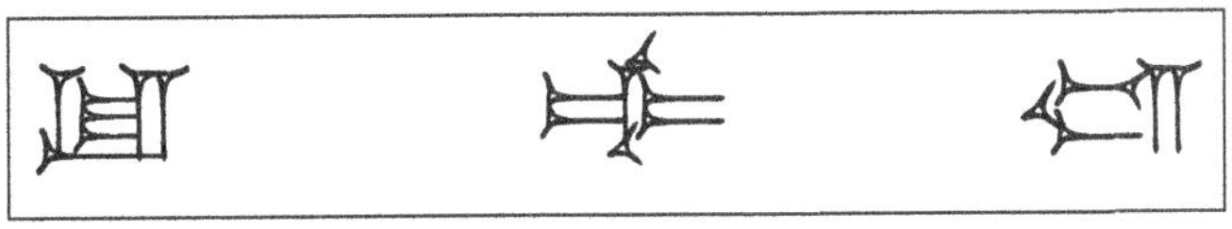

[16]*lublam*

LH §9 VII:17

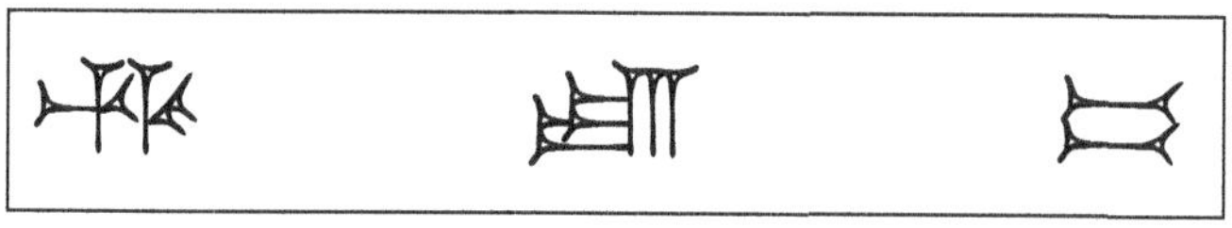

[17]*iqtabî*

LH §9 VII:18

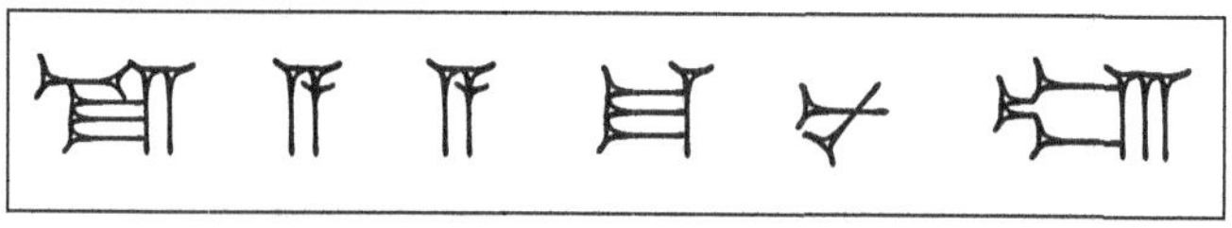

[18]*šayyāmānum*

LH §9 VII:19

[19]*nādin*

LH §9 VII:20

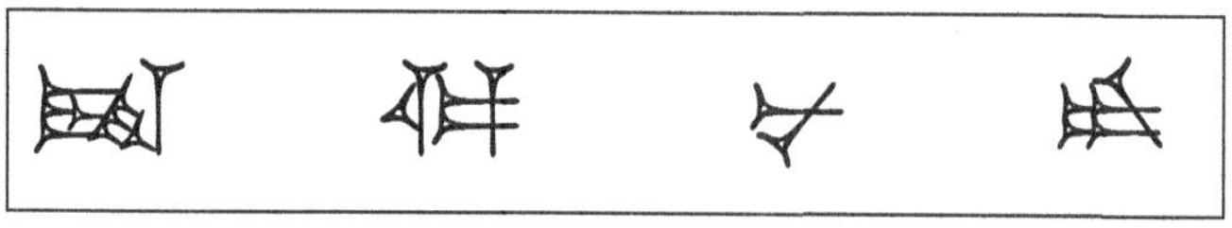

[20]*iddinūšum*

LH §9 VII:21

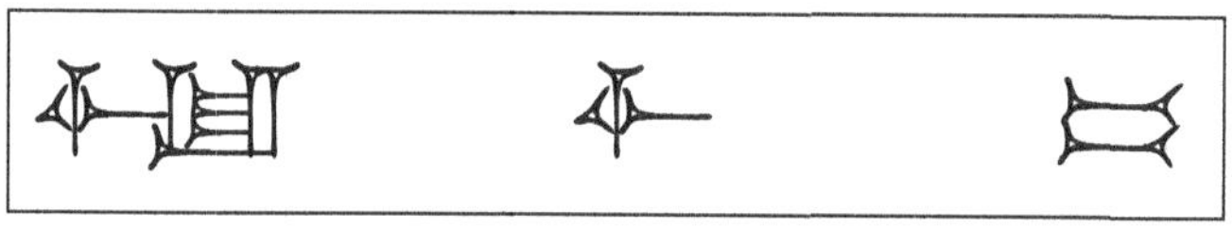

[21]*u šîbī*

LH §9 VII:22

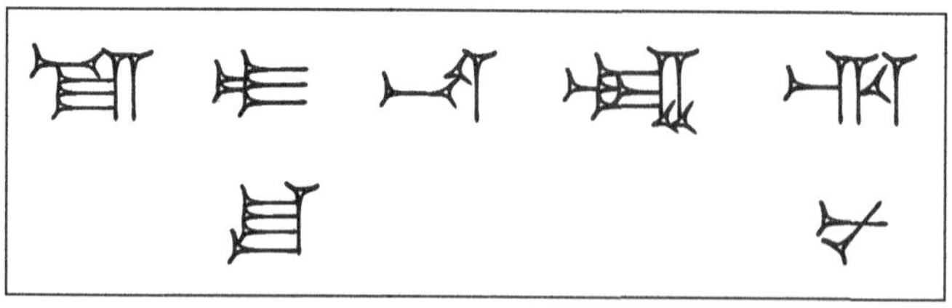

[22]*ša ina maḫrišunu*

LH §9 VII:23

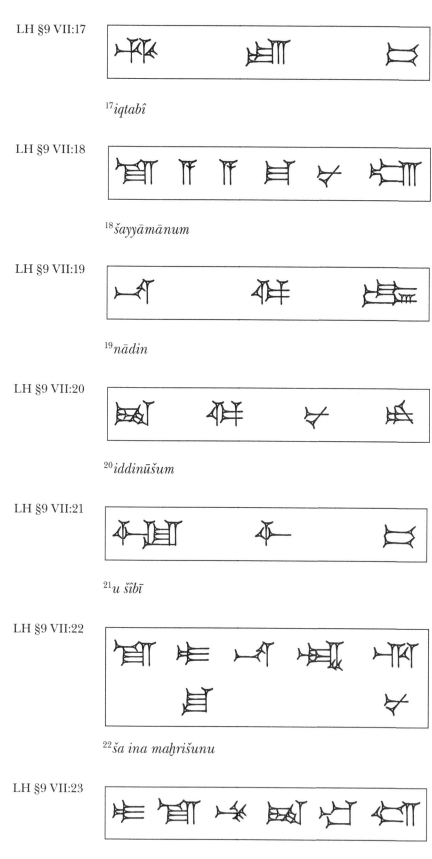

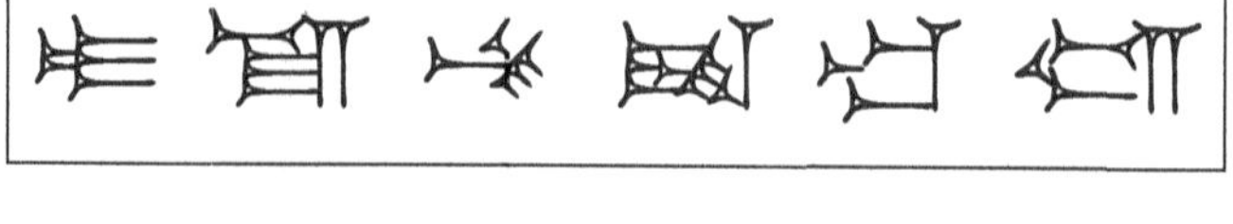

[23]*išâmu itbalam*

LH §9 VII:24

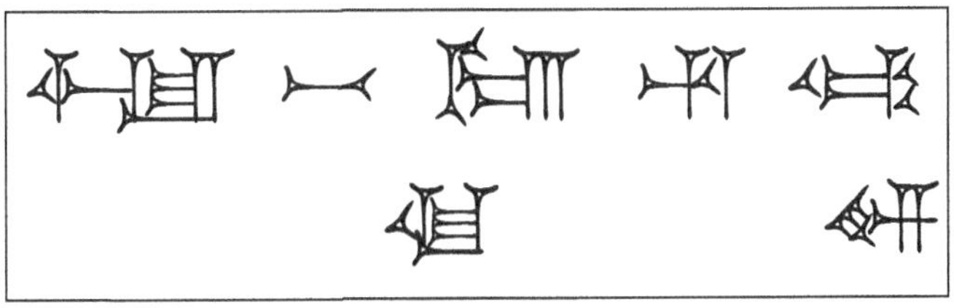

[24]*u bêl ḫulqim*

LH §9 VII:25

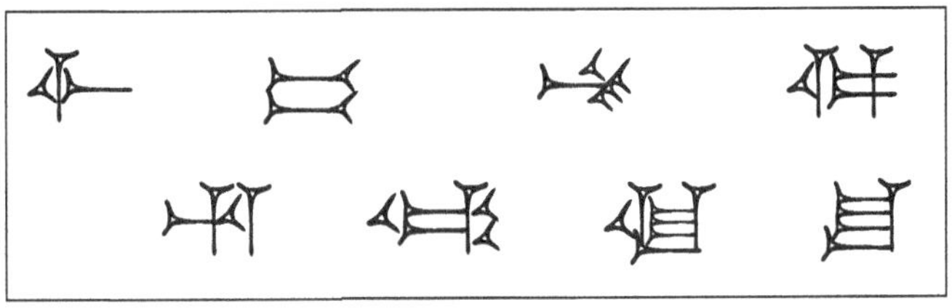

[25]*šībī mûdē ḫulqišu*

LH §9 VII:26

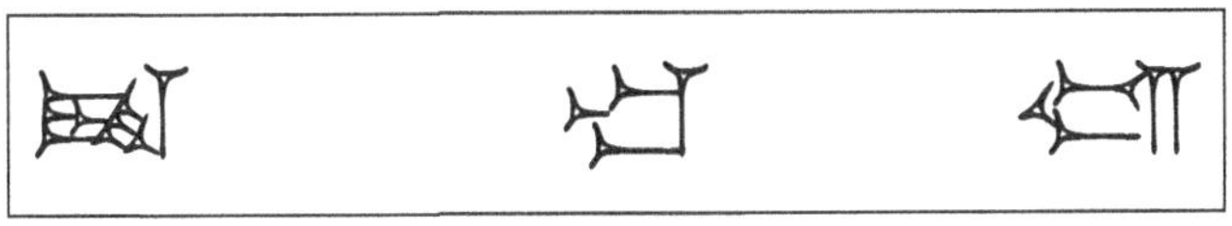

[26]*itbalam*

LH §9 VII:27

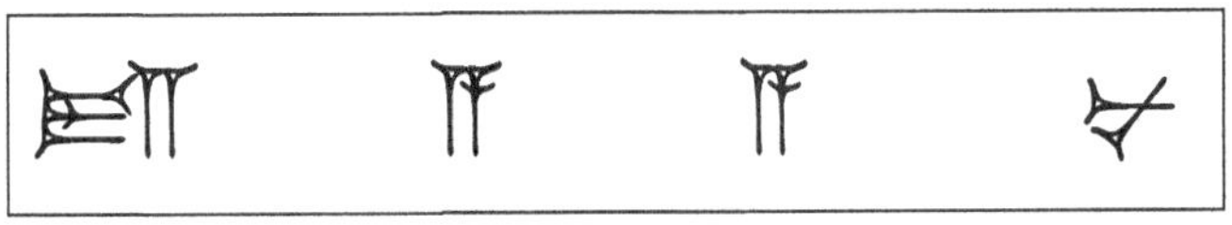

[27]*dayyānū*

LH §9 VII:28

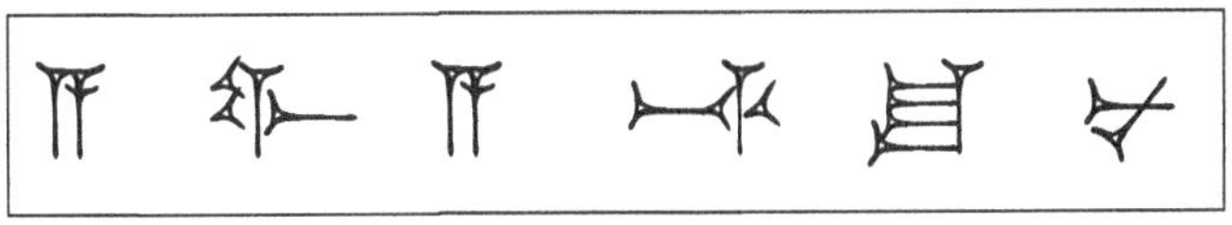

[28]*awātišunu*

LH §9 VII:29

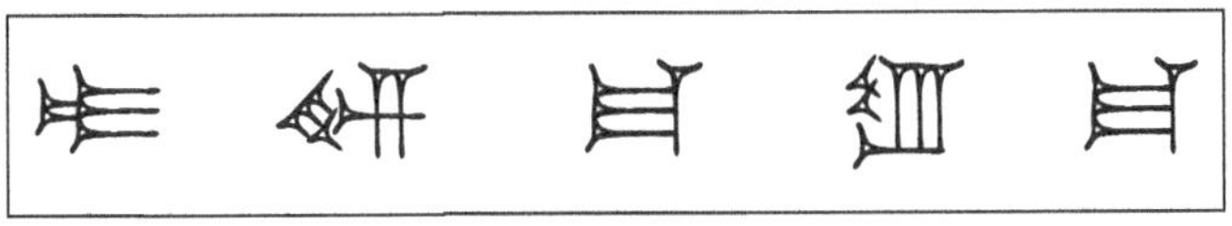

[29]*immarūma*

LH §9 VII:30

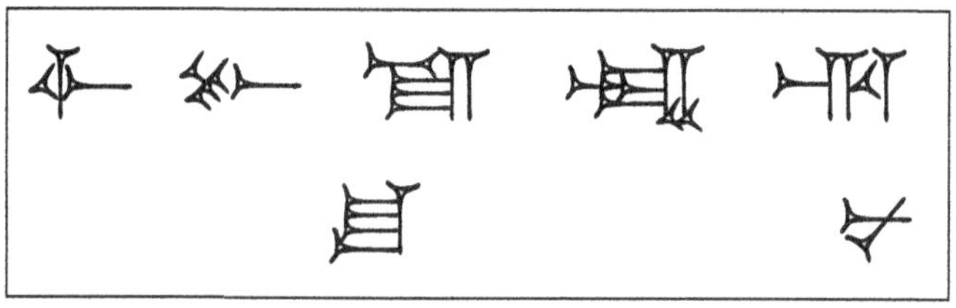

[30]*šĩbū ša [ina]*[6] *maḫrišunu*

LH §9 VII:31

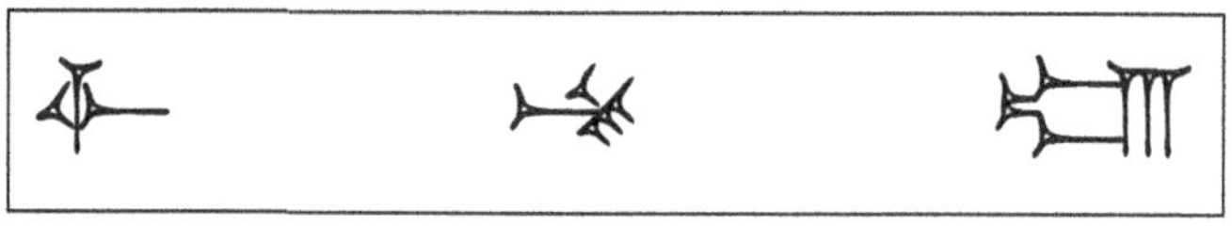

[31]*šĩmum*

LH §9 VII:32

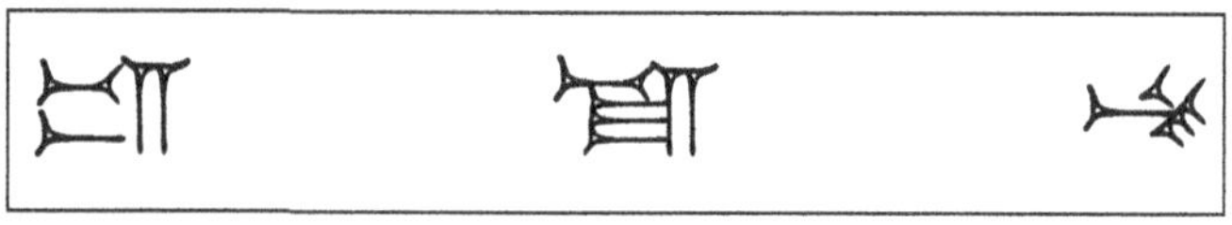

[32]*iššâmu*

LH §9 VII:33

[33]*u šĩbū mûdẽ*

LH §9 VII:34

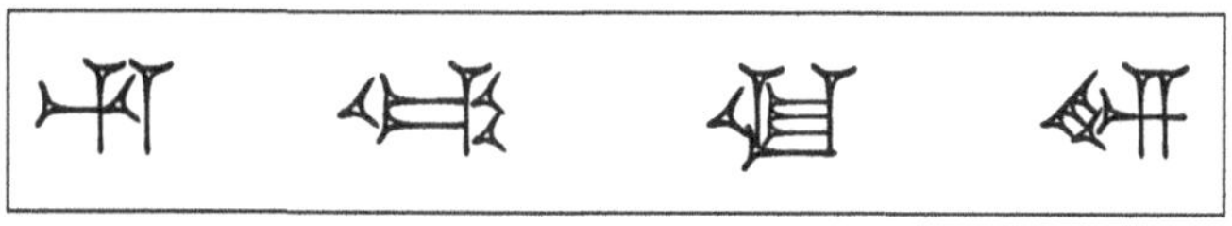

[34]*ḫulqim*

LH §9 VII:35

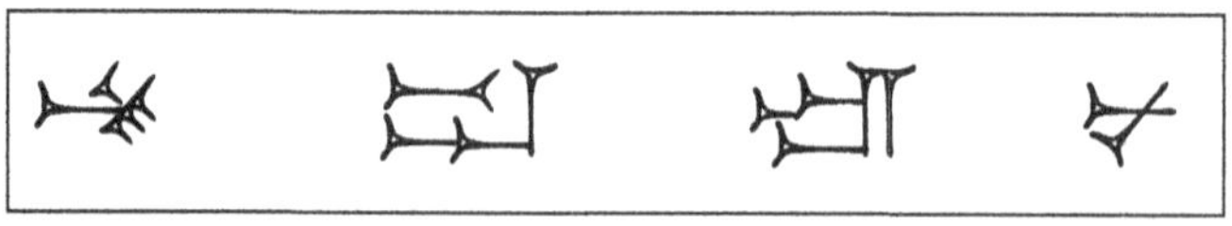

[35]*mûdũssunu*

LH §9 VII:36

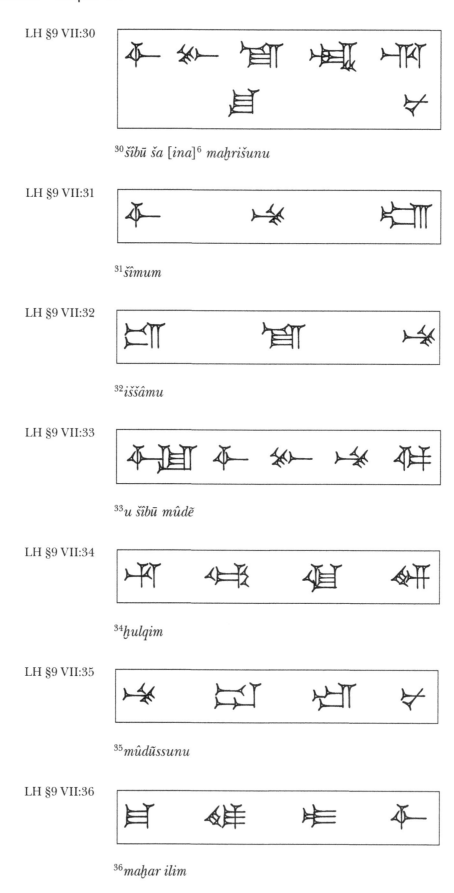

[36]*maḫar ilim*

6. With Borger, *Babylonisch-Assyrische Lesestücke*, 2:290, this *ina* should be restored to the text.

LH §9 VII:37

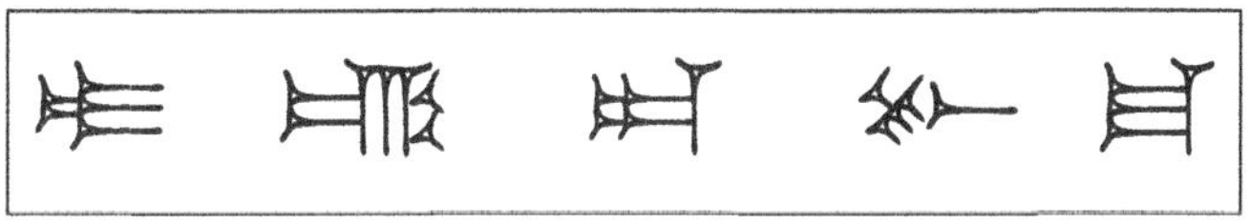

[37]*iqabbūma*

LH §9 VII:38

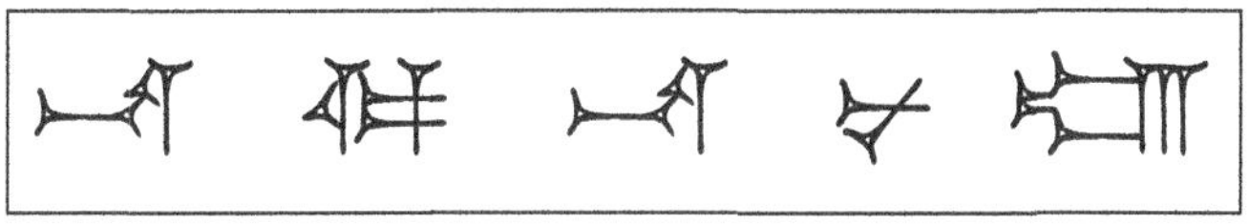

[38]*nādinānum*

LH §9 VII:39

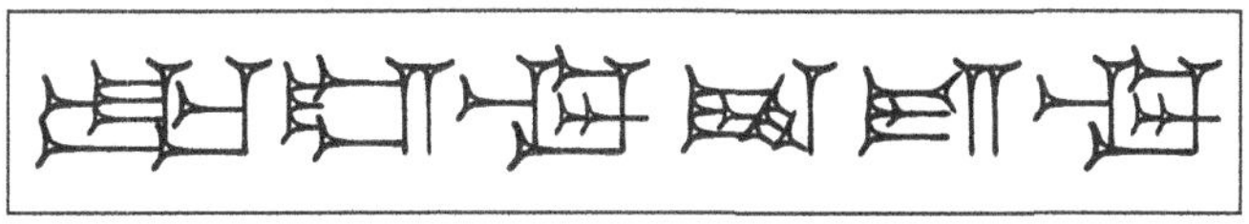

[39]*šarrāq iddāk*

LH §9 VII:40

[40]*bêl ḫulqim*

LH §9 VII:41

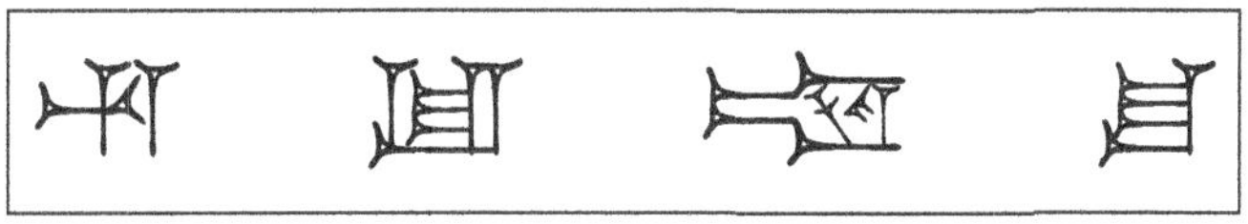

[41]*ḫuluqšu*

LH §9 VII:42

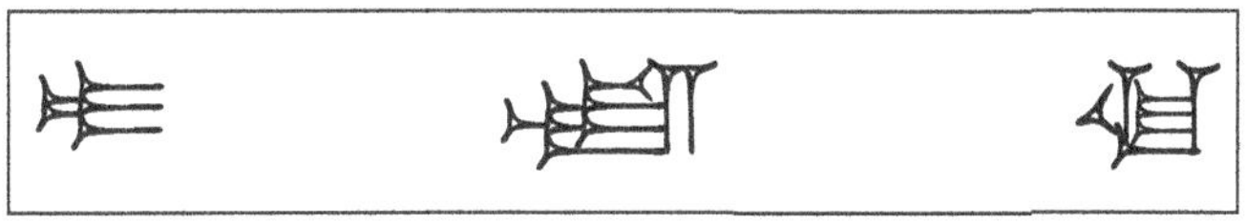

[42]*ileqqê*

LH §9 VII:43

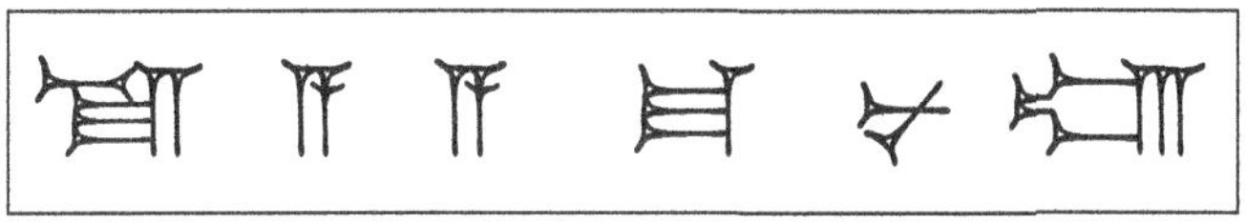

[43]*šayyāmānum*

LH §9 VII:44

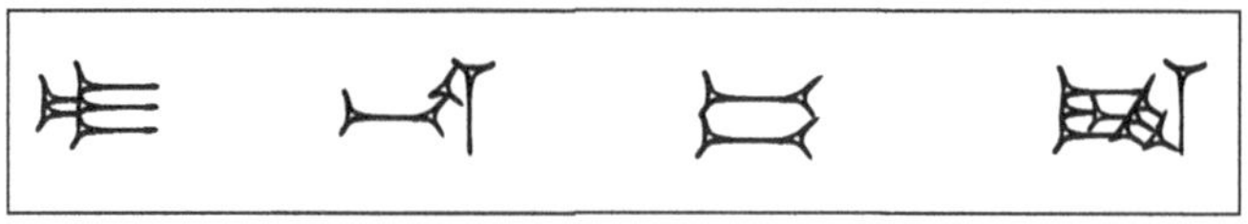

[44]*ina bît*

LH §9 VII:45

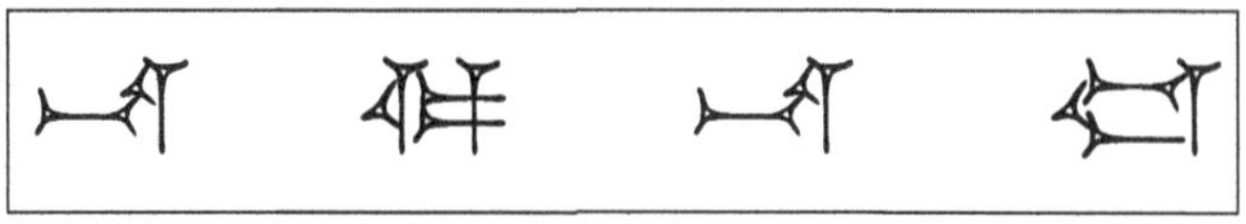

[45]*nādinānim*

LH §9 VII:46

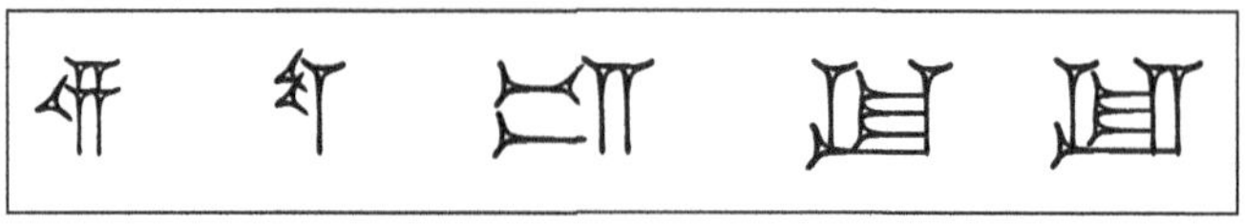

[46]*kasap išqulu*

LH §9 VII:47

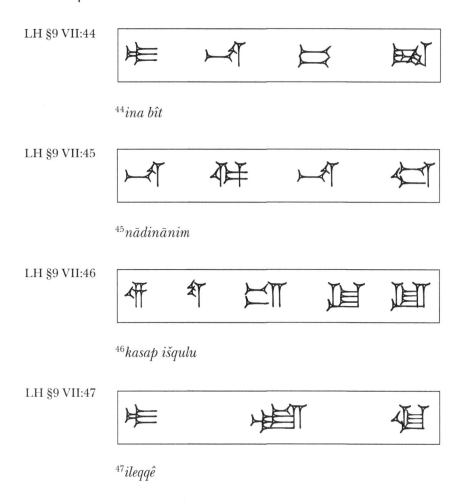

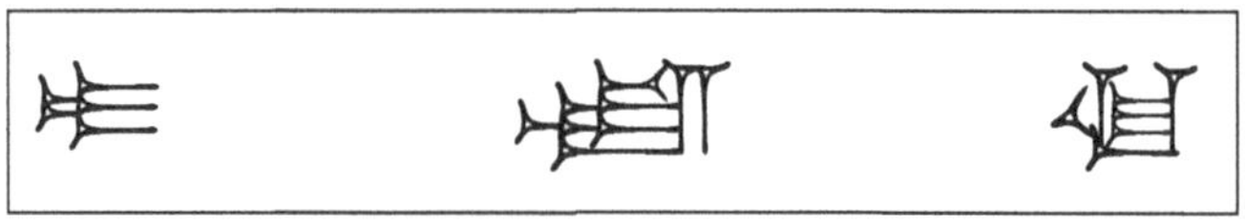

[47]*ileqqê*

1. Grammatical Analysis: Parse all verb forms and answer the questions below. See the notes below for help.

   a. In terms of its spelling, the verb in VII:5 could be correctly parsed in two distinct ways. What are they? Based on the meaning that is expected for this verb in this context, which of these two possible parsings is correct?

   b. Explain the form *nādinānummi* in VII:9.

   c. What is unusual about the scribal practice in LH §9 VII:13?

d. Explain each element of the word in VII:15.

e. Explain each element of the word in VII:18.

Note: The word *mûdē* in VII:14 can be parsed in two ways. What are the two possibilities? Is there a correct or better parsing for this word in this context?

Note: VII:29 includes the word *amārum* (*a,u*), "to see, examine (cf. *ʾāmar*, אָמַר, "to say"). This does not need to be learned.

Note: VII:35 includes the word *mûdûtum*, "knowledge" (cf. *yādaʿ*, יָדַע). This does not need to be learned.

Note: VII:46 includes the word *šaqālum* (*a,u*), "to weigh out" (cf. *šāqal*, שָׁקַל). This does not need to be learned.

2. Translate: Translate LH §9.

14–

I-'*aleph* Verbs, Common Noun Formations, and Numbers

This chapter explains I-' verbs in more depth (see also §3.4) and addresses the irregular verb *alākum*. Common noun formations and numbers will also be introduced. The exercises in this chapter begin LH §§10–13, which are a part of a larger group, LH §§6–25, that treats the illicit acquisition of property or persons. Each of the four laws in this chapter consider additional variations on the situation described in LH §9, where stolen property has been sold to a buyer.

In LH §10 the buyer cannot produce witnesses to the sale, by which he allegedly received the stolen property. Because of this failure, the supposed "buyer," who was caught with the stolen goods in his possession, is shown to be the thief himself. As a result, he is condemned to execution, while the stolen property is returned to its rightful owner.

In LH §11 the original supposed owner of the disputed property fails to produce witnesses to confirm his ownership. As a result, he is shown to be a liar who has spread calumny against the new legitimate owner. In a court proceeding, where oaths before the gods were taken, this may constitute criminal perjury. As a result, he is condemned and executed.

In LH §12 if the seller has already died a natural death, the presumably deceived buyer of the stolen goods is compensated from the estate of the deceased five-fold for the claim made.

In LH §13 if the alleged deceived buyer cannot produce witnesses attesting to his purchase, the judges are to grant him a six-month extension. If he still fails to produce any witnesses, then the buyer is deemed to be a liar, and he shall be assessed whatever penalty is appropriate for the case (presumably, some level of restitution, as in LH §12, and death, as in LH §10).

14.1 I-'*aleph* Verbs

Attention has already been given to some matters regarding the conjugation of I-' verbs.[1] This chapter will summarize those comments and augment them with additional comments and forms that will help explain the I-' verb forms in the portion of LH on which this textbook is based.

14.1.1 ***Two Kinds of I-'aleph Verbs.*** The first matter that needs to be considered is the origin of the initial '. As mentioned in §3.4.2, at least by 2000 BCE and probably because of the influence of Sumerian, five of the original Proto-Semitic guttural consonants had reduced to a simple glottal stop. The following list summarizes this and uses subscripts for convenience to distinguish the origin of each ':

1. See §3.4.4 and §3.4.5.1.

' = $'_1$
h = $'_2$
ḥ = $'_3$
' = $'_4$
ǵ = $'_5$ (sometimes an original *ǵ* became *ḫ* instead of $'_5$)

One important aspect in the development of these gutturals concerns the vowel attenuation of *a*-vowels (§3.4.3). Specifically, an original *a*-vowel of any length in proximity to any of the last three kinds of ', namely $'_3$ (*ḥ*), $'_4$ ('), or $'_5$ (*ǵ*), shifted to an *e*-vowel of corresponding length. Later on, any other *a*-vowel in the base of these words (not in their suffixes) likewise shifted to *e* in a process that is called Babylonian vowel harmony (see §3.4.3). This is so named because while this shift took place in the Babylonian dialects of Akkadian, it did not take place in the Assyrian dialects (see §20.2.2). As a consequence of these vowel changes, there are two classes of I-' verbs: those that feature *a*-vowels because their initial ' was originally ' ($'_1$) or *h* ($'_2$) and those that feature *e*-vowels because their initial ' was originally *ḥ* ($'_3$), ' ($'_4$), or *ǵ* ($'_5$).

14.1.2 *Summary of Four Spelling Rules for I-'aleph Verbs*

14.1.2.1 *Disappearance (Quiescence) of Initial 'aleph*—Normally, any word-initial ' in Akkadian completely disappears. If, however, the ' in question is one of the last three ', namely $'_3$ (*ḥ*), $'_4$ ('), or $'_5$ (*ǵ*), any *a*-vowel in its proximity attenuates into an *e*-vowel.

The following sequence illustrates the effects of vowel attenuation, Babylonian vowel harmony, and loss of original guttural consonants in the example of the verb *ezēbum*, "to abandon, leave behind, divorce":

*'*azābum* = presumed to be the earliest form of this verb (cf. *'āzab*, עָזַב)
> *'*ezābum* = through vowel attenuation of *a* to *e* in the presence of an original *ḥ* ($'_3$), ' ($'_4$), or *ǵ* ($'_5$).
> *'*ezēbum* = through Babylonian vowel harmony
> *'*ezēbum* = through the loss of original guttural consonants, each of which became a glottal stop (an ').
> *ezēbum* = because of the disappearance of word-initial '

In the Old Babylonian script of LH, these word-initial vowels are often indicated by an extra vowel sign. This extra vowel sign does not indicate vowel length; it is, instead, a historical spelling that indicates the earlier presence of the ' (see §2.5.1.4).

14.1.2.2 *Loss of Intervocalic 'aleph*—In §3.4.5 it was mentioned that in Akkadian elision of intervocalic ' is frequent. In other words, $v_1 ' v_2$ frequently becomes $v_1 v_2$, which typically results in contraction of the two vowels into a tilde long vowel. Nevertheless, as §3.4.5.1 stresses, I-' verbs are an important exception to this rule. In their case, both the intervocalic ' and the following vowel disappear without any effect on the preceding vowel.

14.1.2.3 *Quiescing of an 'aleph at the End of a Syllable with Compensatory Lengthening*—Within a word when an ' is at the end of a syllable, the ' quiesces and the preceding vowel experiences compensatory lengthening (see §2.5.2.1 and §10.1.4).

14.1.2.4 *Resolutory Doubling/Assimilation to the Pattern of I-n Verbs*—As was observed earlier with respect to II-weak verbs (see §11.3.3), often in place of compensatory lengthening of a vowel due to the quiescing of an ' that immediately follows, there are instances of resolutory doubling of a following consonant. This regularly occurs with I-' verbs in the Š-stem durative.

Another way to describe this resolutory doubling is to recognize that I-' verbal forms often follow the pattern of I-*n* verbs, where the *n* assimilates to an immediately following consonant. In the N-stem, I-' verbal forms are patterned on I-*n* verbal forms to an even greater degree since the I-*n* regularly appears in place of the expected I-'.

14.1.3 ***Paradigm Chart for I-'aleph Verbs in LH.***[2] The following chart illustrates the typical results of the patterns discussed above as applied to I-' verbs. Forms in bold should be learned. I-' verbs also appear in the derived stems, but their forms are predicable from those offered here. It should be kept in mind that, in addition to being found in the *a/e,u*-class, I-' verbs may also be *i*-class or *u*-class.

Stem	Class	Durative 3cs	Perfect 3cs	Preterite 3cs	Participle ms	Verbal Adjective ms	Stative 3ms	Infinitive ms
G		*iparras*	*iptaras*	*iprus*	*pārisum*	*parsum*	*paris*	*parāsum*
	a,u	***iḫḫaz***	***îtaḫaz***	***îḫuz***	***āḫizum***	***aḫizum***	***aḫiz***	***aḫāzum***
	e,u	***ippeš/ ippuš***	***îtepeš/ îtepuš***	***îpuš***	***ēpišum***	***epišum***	***epiš***	***epēšum***
Gt		*iptarras*	*iptatras*	*iptaras*	*muptarsum*	*pitrusum*	*pitrus*	*pitrusum*
Gtn		*iptanarras*	*iptatarras*	*iptarras*	*muptarrisum*	*pitarrusum*	*pitarrus*	*pitarrusum*
D		*uparras*	*uptarris*	*uparris*	*muparrisum*	*purrusum*	*purrus*	*purrusum*
		uḫḫaz	***ûtaḫḫiz***	***uḫḫiz***	***muḫḫizum***	***uḫḫuzum***	***uḫḫuz***	***uḫḫuzum***
Dt		*uptarras*	*uptatarris*	*uptarris*	*muptarrisum*	*putarrusum*	*putarrus*	*putarrusum*
Dtn		*uptanarras*	*uptatarris*	*uptarris*	*muptarrisum*	*putarrusum*	*putarrus*	*putarrusum*
Š		*ušapras*	*uštapris*	*ušapris*	*mušaprisum*	*šuprusum*	*šuprus*	*šuprusum*
		ušaḫḫaz	***uštâḫiz***	***ušâḫiz***	***mušâḫizum***	***šûḫuzum***	***šûḫuz***	***šûḫuzum***
Št		*uštapras/ uštaparras*	*uštatapris*	*uštapris*	*muštaprisum*	*šutaprusum*	*šutaprus*	*šutaprusum*
Štn		*uštanapras*	*uštatapris*	*uštapris*	*muštaprisum*	*šutaprusum*	*šutaprus*	*šutaprusum*
N		*ipparras*	*ittapras*	*ipparis*	*mupparsum*	*naprusum*	*naprus*	*naprusum*
	a,u	***innaḫḫaz***	***ittanḫaz***	***innaḫiz***	***munnaḫzum***	***nanḫuzum***	***nanḫuz***	***nanḫuzum***
	e,u	***inneppeš***	***ittenpeš***	***innepiš***	***munnepšum***	***nenpušum***	***nenpuš***	***nenpušum***
Nt		unattested or exceedingly rare						
Ntn		*ittanapras*	*ittatapras*	*ittapras*	*muttaprisum*	*itaprusum*	*itaprus*	*itaprusum*

2. In addition to forms of the strong verb *parāsum*, which are offered for comparison, this chart uses forms of the following I-' verbs: *aḫāzum* (*a,u*), "to take, take in marriage" (used only of the man), "take sexually"; *alākum*, "to go"; and *epēšum*, "to do, make, build."

14.1.4 ***Irregular Verb alākum.*** The irregular verb *alākum* follows the pattern of I-' verbs discussed above with two exceptions. First, it is an *a,i*-class verb rather than either an *a,u*-class or *i*-class (*i,i*). Second, when its first root consonant, ', would close a syllable, rather than compensatory lengthening of the prefix vowel *i* there is resolutory doubling of the following consonant. Alternatively, though perhaps less convincingly, this is often described as assimilation to the I-*n* paradigm. This irregularity also applies to *alākum* when it is in the Gt and Gtn derived forms.

Stem	Class	Durative 3cs	Perfect 3cs	Preterite 3cs	Participle ms	Verbal Adjective ms	Stative 3ms	Infinitive ms
G		*iparras*	*iptaras*	*iprus*	*pārisum*	*parsum*	*paris*	*parāsum*
	(a,i)	***illak***	***ittalak***	***illik***	***ālikum***	***alkum***	***alik***	***alākum***

14.2 Noun Formations

As in many other languages, including Hebrew and for that matter English, there are a variety of common noun formations in Akkadian that carry somewhat predicable meanings. Several of these have already been encountered, but they now merit being summarized and highlighted.

14.2.1 ***Abstract -ūt Sufformative.***[3] Many abstract nouns in Akkadian are formed by adding a feminine singular *-ūt* sufformative to a noun, adjective, or verbal base. The effect of this sufformative is to make a word that is often translated in English with suffixes such as: *-y, -ity, -ing, -ship, -ness, -ude, -ion, -ance.*

Notice that this feminine *-ūt* sufformative results in nouns that have endings in the nominative and genitive singular (*-ūtum* and *-ūtim*) that happen to be identical in appearance to the masculine nominative plural and genitive-accusative plural suffixes respectively for participles and other adjectives (see §5.2.1).

Consider the following examples:

aplūtum, "inheritance" (cf. *aplum*, "heir, son")
awīlūtum, "humanity" (cf. *awīlum*, "man, person, citizen (a free man)")
errēšūtum, "cultivation" (cf. *errēšum*, "a cultivator, tenant farmer," or *erēšum*, "to plow")
mârūtum, "sonship" (cf. *mârum*, "son")
maṣṣarūtum, "watch, guard, safekeeping" (cf. *maṣṣarum*, "guard, watchman")
mûdûtum, "knowledge" (cf. *mûdûm* [<**mûde'um*], "knowing, wise; knower, expert")
rîqūtum, "emptiness" (cf. *rîqum*, "empty")
šībūtum, "testimony" (cf. *šībum*, "old man; witness")
wardūtum, "servitude, slavery" (cf. *wardum*, "slave")

Although it is less common, an analogous *-ūt* sufformative is employed in Hebrew. Compare *malkût*, מַלְכוּת, "kingship"; *'ēdût*, עֵדוּת, "precept"; *'abdût*, עַבְדוּת, "servitude"; *bākût*, בָּכוּת, "weeping."

3. The term "sufformative," which contrasts with the term "preformative," is often used as a near synonym of "suffix," but it stresses the fact that this suffix does not have an independent meaning. It is more a part of the word or verb form where it is found, and it cannot be removed without changing the meaning of the word to which it is attached.

14.2.2 ***Abstract pursum Noun Pattern.*** Abstract nouns are also frequently formed for verbs with stative meanings by using the noun pattern of *pursum*. The following are some examples of this abstract noun formation found in LH:

bulṭum, "life" (cf. *balāṭum*, "to live")
dumqum, "goodness, favor" (cf. *damāqum*, "to be good")
ḫubtum, "robbery" (cf. *ḫabātum*, "to rob")
ḫulqum, "lost property," (cf. *ḫalāqum*, "to lose, go/be missing")
puḫrum, "assembly, council" (cf. *paḫārum*, "to assemble, to come together")
ṭuḫdum, "abundance" (cf. *ṭaḫādum*, "to flourish")

14.2.3 ***Professional parrāsum Noun Pattern.*** There is a common form of nouns, *parrāsum*, which is used for persons who customarily perform an action or are engaged in an occupation. This form is often designated as a *nomen agentis*. Below are some examples of this pattern.

dayyānum, "a judge" (cf. *dânum*, to try [conduct a trial], judge)
errēšum, "cultivator, tenant farmer" (cf. *erēšum*, "to plow")
šarrāqum, "thief" (cf. *šarāqum*, "to steal")
šayyāmum, "buyer" (cf. *šâmum*, "to purchase, buy")

An analogous *parrās* noun pattern for persons who customarily perform an action or are engaged in an occupation is employed in Hebrew. Compare *dayyān*, דַּיָּן, "judge"; *ḥārāš* (< **ḥarrāš*), חָרָשׁ, "engraver, one who plows"; *gannāb*, גַּנָּב, "thief"; *ḥaṭṭā'*, חַטָּא, "sinner."

14.2.4 ***Professional parīsum Noun Pattern.*** There is another less common vowel pattern, namely *parīsum*, which is also used for professions and persons. The following are some examples attested in LH:

awīlum, "man, person, citizen (a free man)"
awīltum, "woman"
nadîtum, "devotee; high priestess (one who must remain childless)" (< **nadī'tum*)
talīmum, "devoted follower, favorite brother"

This same noun pattern (*a-ī*) also exists in Hebrew for professions: *māšîaḥ*, מָשִׁיחַ, "anointed one"; *pālîṭ*, פָּלִיט, "refugee"; *nābî'*, נָבִיא, "prophet."

14.2.5 ***Legal purussā'um Noun Pattern.*** There is a common quadrilateral form of nouns, **purussā'um*, which is used for various legal activities.

purussûm, "(legal) decision" (cf. *parāsum*)
rugummûm, "(legal) complaint" (cf. *ragāmum*)
uzubbûm, "divorce settlement" (cf. *ezēbum*).

14.2.6 ***Prefix m- Pattern for Place Where or Time When.*** There are various patterns of nouns with an *m*-prefix, mostly without meanings that are easily summarized. One such pattern, namely *maprasum/maprastum*, is worth learning because it is often associated with the place where an action is done or the time when it is done.

> *maškanum*, "threshing floor" (cf. *šakānum*, "to set, appoint, arrange, provide")
> *mašqîtum*, "watering place" (cf. *šaqûm*, "to give drink to")
> *mêreštum*, "arable land" (cf. *erēšum*, "to plow")
> *mirîtum*, "pasture" (cf. *re'ûm*, "to shepherd")

If the root word contains a labial consonant (*b, m, p*), then the prefix *n-* is used in place of *m-*.

> *našpakum* "storage area" (cf. *šapākum*, "to store")

A similar *m*-prefix form is attested in Hebrew: *môšāb*, מוֹשָׁב, "dwelling place" (cf. *yāšab*, יָשַׁב, "to dwell"); *mizbēaḥ*, מִזְבֵּחַ, "altar" (cf. *zābaḥ*, זָבַח, "to sacrifice"); *māqôm*, מָקוֹם, "place" (cf. *qûm*, קוּם, "to arise"); *mišteh*, מִשְׁתֶּה, "banquet" (cf. *šātâ*, שָׁתָה, "to drink").

14.3 Numbers: Logographic and Determinative KAM

14.3.1 ***Logographic Writing of Numbers.*** In Akkadian, numbers are almost always written logographically, just as they are often written in English: for example, "2" rather than "two." As a result, the Akkadian vocabulary for some numbers is uncertain. Because non-logographic numbers are uncommon, the details of their vocabulary and the grammar of their uses goes beyond the needs of the present textbook.

It is sufficient for most uses to be aware of just a few matters. First, the practice of writing logographic numbers in Akkadian combines a decimal system (base 10) with a sexagesimal system (base 60), which was inherited from the Sumerians.[4]

Numbers 1 through 9 all make sense in terms of a pattern of adding vertical cuneiform wedges to each other: 𒁹, 𒈫, 𒐈, 𒐉, 𒐊, 𒐋, 𒐌, 𒐍, 𒐎.

The following somewhat random list of larger numbers illustrates how the combination of decimal and sexagesimal systems worked:

> 10: 𒌋 The fact that this single character represents 10 shows that the later sexagesimal system was built on an earlier decimal system.
> 15: 𒌋𒐊
> 20: 𒎙
> 51: 𒐐𒁹
> 60: 𒁹 (= 1 × 60). As mentioned earlier, although Akkadian used a decimal system for numbers from 1 to 59, this is combined with the larger framework of a sexagesimal system, which determines the values of each of the imaginary columns in which numbers are placed. This cuneiform sign for the number 1, when it is positioned to the far right in the 1's column, represents the number 1. But if it is in the 60's

4. No one knows why the Sumerians chose a base 60 number system. It is possible that the reason is an extension of the common speculation for why the early British chose 12 as a base for measurements (twelve pence to a shilling; twelve inches to a foot; twelve months in a year, twelve dozen to a gross, etc.). That choice was apparently for pragmatic reasons since 12 is the smallest number divisible by 1, 2, 3, and 4. The number 60, on the other hand, is the smallest number divisible by 1, 2, 3, 4, and 5. So perhaps, for a culture that wanted the convenience of larger measures that were easily divisible, the number 60 was a reasonable choice.

column, which is imagined to be immediately to the left of the 1's column, then it represents the number 60. Unfortunately, Akkadian has no zero to put in the 1's column, so here the reader can only know that a cuneiform sign for "1" represents 60 (= 1 × 60) rather than 1 based on context, whether because of another appropriate number (from 1 to 59) to its right in the 1's column or because extra space is given to its right, intended to represent, in effect, a zero.

61: 𒁹 𒁹 (= 1 × 60 + 1). These two signs closely resemble the signs for the number 2, 𒈫, but they are positioned slightly further apart to let the reader know that the right one is in the 1's column (for all numbers from 1 to 59) and the left one is in the 60's column (for all numbers from 1 × 60 to 59 × 60).

70: 𒁹 𒌋 (= 1 × 60 + 10). The sign for 10 on the right is in the 1's column and the sign for 1 on the left is in the 60's column.

100: 𒁹 𒐏 (= 1 × 60 + 40) or 𒈨, a single cuneiform sign representing the number 100 from the earlier decimal system.

120: 𒈫 (= 2 × 60) This represents a 2 in the 60's column.

151: 𒈫 𒌍𒁹 Note the slight space between the signs for 31 (in the 1's column on the right) and the signs for 2 (in the 60's column on the left).

300: 𒐈𒈨 (= 3 × 100) The fact that the 3, a smaller number, is to the left of the 100, shows that this is 3 × 100, rather than 3 + 100, which would be 𒈨𒐈.

600: 𒁹𒌋 (= 60 × 10)–Unlike the earlier use of 𒁹 𒌋 above, where its elements are slightly separated and represent 1 × 60 (1 in the 60's column) + 10 (in the 1's column), in this case the elements are closer together. This implies that they are in the same column (the 60's column, with a space to the right with nothing in it) so the sign for 1 represents 1 × 60, and the fact that the sign for 10 follows this without any space between them represents a multiplication (1 × 60 × 10).

1000: 𒌋𒈨 (= 10 × 100)

3000: 𒐈𒌋𒈨 (= 3 × 1000)

3600: 𒊹

3,661: 𒁹 𒁹 𒁹 (= $1 \times 60^2 + 1 \times 60^1 + 1 \times 60^0$). These three signs closely resemble the signs for number 3, 𒐈, but they are positioned slightly further apart to let the reader know that the right one is in the 1's column (or the 60^0 column, for all numbers from 1 to 59), and the middle one is in the 60's column (or the 60^1 column, for all numbers from 1 × 60 to 59 × 60), and the one on the far left is in 3600's column (or the 60^2 column).

This method of writing numbers, much like our modern system of writing numbers, uses the relative position of each sign to assist the reader in determining its intended value. The example above of 151, 𒈫 𒌍𒁹, is a good example. The normal practice is, as in English, to start on the right with the smallest unit in the number (the 1's column, or to use exponential numbers, the column for 60^0). The single vertical wedge represents the number 1. To the immediate left but still in the 1's column are 3 *Winkelhaken* wedges, each representing 10. So, these four signs together represent the number 31 in the 1's or the 60^0 column. To the left are two closely positioned vertical wedges representing the number 2, but these are in the 60's column, or the 60^1 column, so they represent 120 (= 2 × 60). Adding 120 to 31 produces the result: 151.

As mentioned, Akkadian has no zero as a place holder, so although a small space was typically used for this purpose, in actual practice context is often what is most decisive. For example, apart from any other contextual indication, the cuneiform sign  in isolation could represent "2" or "61," or "120." Thankfully, the context of each sign and number is usually sufficient to determine what is intended. It is a significant help, however, that Akkadian often marks numbers with a postpositive determinative (§14.3.2).

For the sake of completeness, in cases where there was a need to refer to fractions, Akkadian has some explicit terms that it uses in LH for common fractions but in mathematical texts, it often uses columns that were located to the right of the 60^0 column in a manner that is analogous to our modern decimal system. In these texts, the first column to the right was the 60^{-1} (=1/60) column and the next column further to the right was the 60^{-2} (= 1/3600) column, etc. For example, the number 72.5 was written as  = (1 × 60) + (12 × 1) + (30 × 1/60). The sign for 1 on the far left is in the 60's (= 60^1) column; the three signs for 12 are in the 60^0's (= 1) column; and the 30 that is in the 60^{-1} (= 1/60) column on the right represents 30/60, or 1/2. Since there is no sign for a decimal point, only context can allow the reader to know for sure the value of each column. In other words, the same cuneiform in another context could be read as 4,350 = (1 × 3,600) + (12 × 60) + (30 × 1).

14.3.2 ***The Determinative KAM for Numbers.*** The postpositive determinative for numbers is KAM, . It is used both with ordinal and cardinal numbers. In Sumerian, KAM means "it is of." KAM is postpositive, which means that it is written immediately after the number rather than before it. In transliteration it is indicated by writing the Sumerian value, KAM, often as a superscript (^{KAM}), but as with all other determinatives, it is typically omitted in the normalization of the text.

A determinative KAM will be omitted, however, with multiplicatives. These numbers are expressed in Akkadian by placing a pronominal suffix *-šu* on the number. For example,  represents the number 2 followed by a phonetic complement *-šu*. This indicates that it should be read in Akkadian as *šinâšu*, meaning literally "two of it," or in more idiomatic English, "twofold" or "twice." Although sometimes a number like  is transliterated by indicating the exact phonetic value of the Sumerian logogram, MIN-*šu*, it is more common and much simpler to transliterate  as 2-*šu*.

14.3.3 ***Logographic Writing around Numbers.*** When numbers are used in various expressions, just as the numbers themselves are normally written with logograms, any close modifiers also tend to be written with logograms.

In LH §5, for example, there is a multiplicative expression where a penalty of twelve-fold restitution is imposed. This is expressed in cuneiform as , which may be transliterated as A.RÁ U.MIN-šu, or more simply, A.RÁ 12-šu. A.RÁ is the Sumerian logogram for the Akkadian *adî*, normally translated "until," or "up to." In this usage, however, where *adî* appears before a number followed by a pronominal suffix, it is an idiomatic introduction to a multiplicative expression, and it is best translated as "times." Hence, A.RÁ 12-šu is rendered "12 *times* it."

14.4 Homework

Before you move on, be sure to understand the complexities of I-' verbs and become familiar with anticipated spellings. Likewise, become comfortable with the verb *alākum* and how it deviates from the expected I-' spellings. Make sure to familiarize yourself with the common noun formations in Akkadian. This will greatly help your acquisition of vocabulary. Finally, understand how numbers are written in Akkadian so that you can accurately render them in context.

14.4.1 *Signs*

60 (This is the same sign as the sign for 1, but it can have the value of 60 if it is located one column to the left of the 1's column in an Akkadian number.)[5]

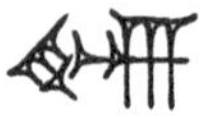

aḫ, eḫ, iḫ, uḫ, á', é', í', ú'

me

Congratulations! If you have learned the three cuneiform signs in this chapter and each of the preceding ninety-eight signs, you will be able to read 95 percent of all the cuneiform signs in LH §§1–20, 127–149.

14.4.2 *Vocabulary*

ištu = *place*: out of, from; *time*: since, after
kīma = like, in the same way as (preposition); that (conjunction to introduce indirect discourse) (cf. *kə*, כְּ, *kî*, כִּי, *kəmô*, כְּמוֹ)
qerēbum (i,i) = to be near, draw near; to be available (irregular stative ms is *qerub*) (cf. *qārab*, קָרַב)
redûm (e,e)/(i,i) [*(e,e)* is more likely for LH] = to lead, send; *ventive*: to bring (cf. *rādâ*, רָדָה, "to rule")
sarārum (a,u) = to lie, be criminally dishonest
sarrum = false, dishonest; *substantive use:* liar
šakānum (a,u) = set, appoint, arrange, provide (cf. *hiphil* of *kûn*, כּוּן)[6]
šīmtum = destiny, fate (literally, "that which is appointed or set") (cf. *śîm*, שִׂים)
-ūt = a sufformative, feminine singular ending; when placed on a noun, it turns it into an abstract noun
warḫum = month (cf. *yeraḥ*, יֶרַח)

14.4.3 *Exercises*

The fourteen text boxes labeled VII:48–61 comprise LH §10.

1. Transliterate and Normalize: Transliterate the signs below and then answer the questions below. Normalize your transliteration. See the note below for help.

5. See §14.3.1.
6. A probable Hebrew cognate, according to Huehnergard, *A Grammar of Akkadian*, 613.

LH §10 VII:48

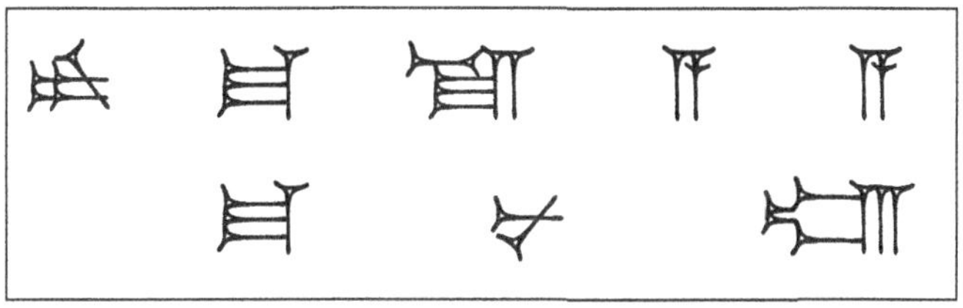

LH §10 VII:49

LH §10 VII:50

a. How does the word in VII:49 relate to the word in VII:50?

LH §10 VII:51

b. The first sign in LH §10 VII:51 can be normalized and then translated in one of two different ways. What are they? Give some justification, based on the context, for which is the preferable option here.

Note: The sign  in VII: 51 is *maḫ*. This does not need to be learned.

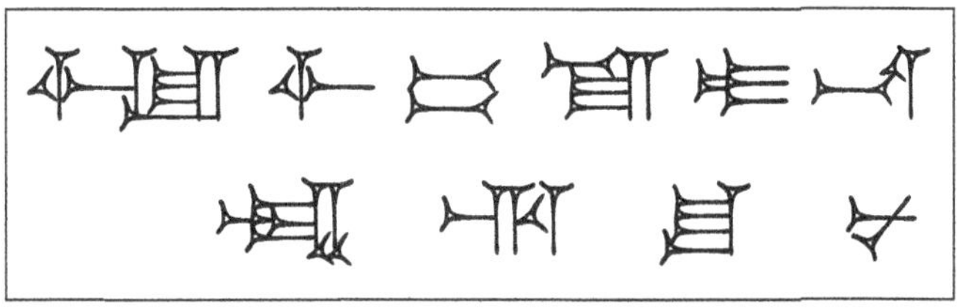

LH §10 VII:52

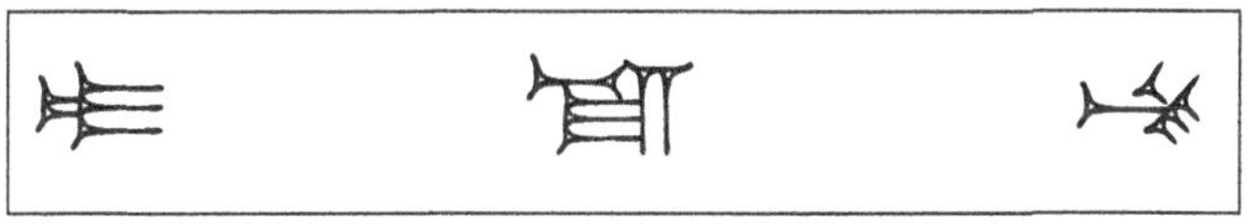

LH §10 VII:53

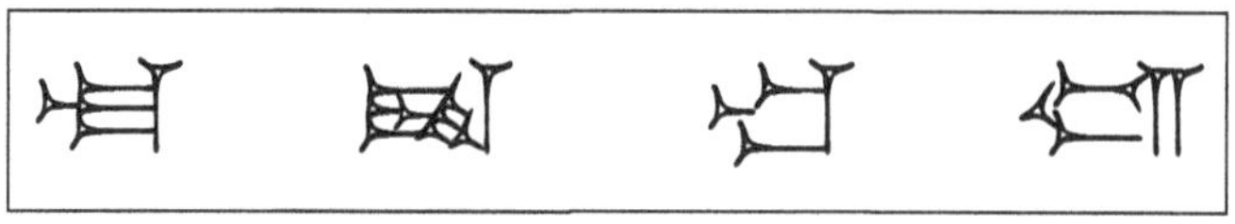

LH §10 VII:54

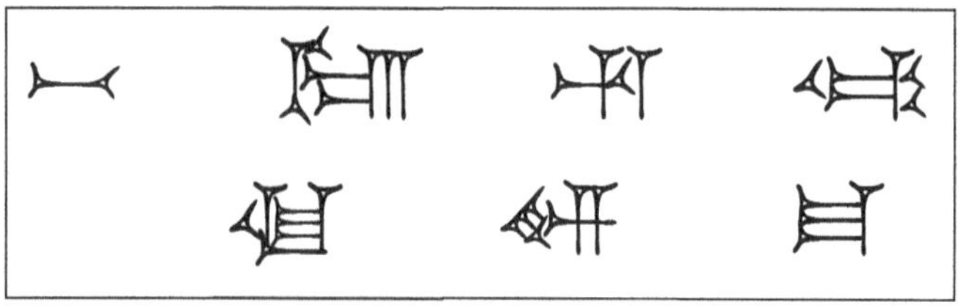

LH §10 VII:55

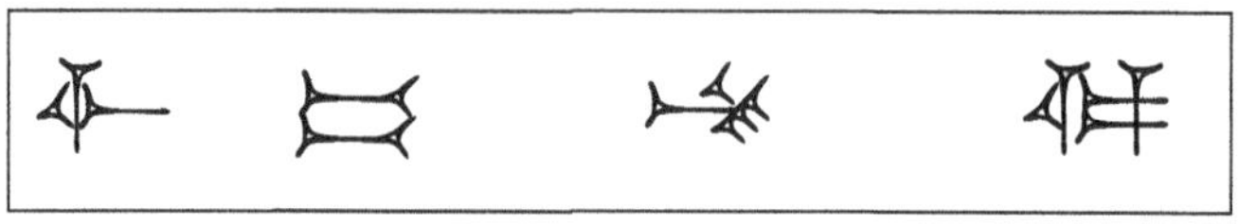

LH §10 VII:56

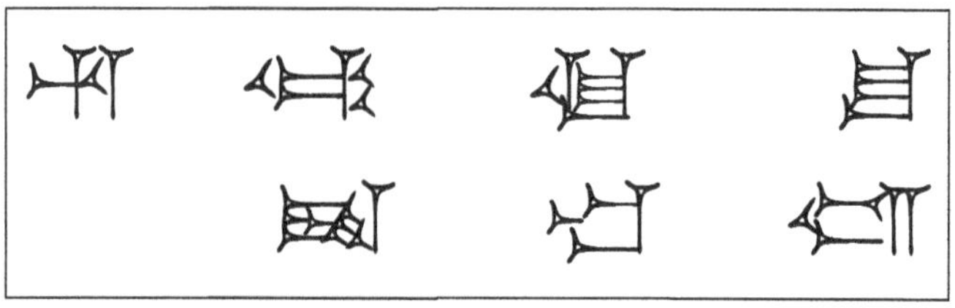

LH §10 VII:57

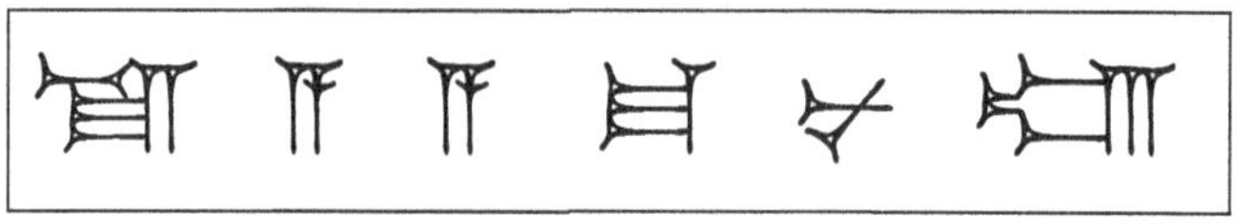

LH 10 VII:58a

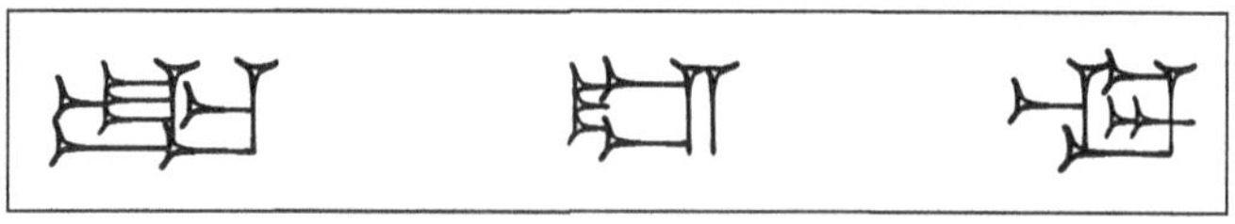

LH §10 VII:58b

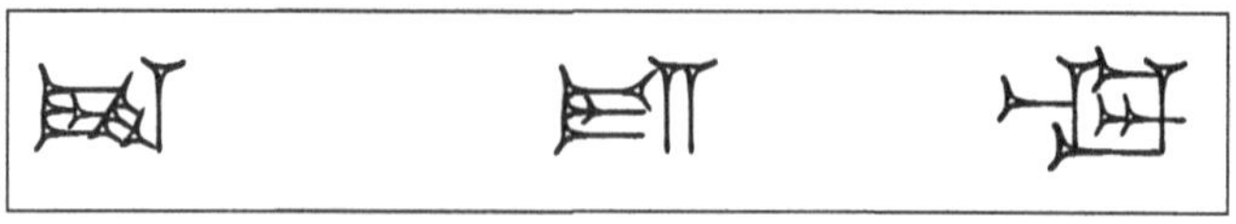

LH §10 VII:59

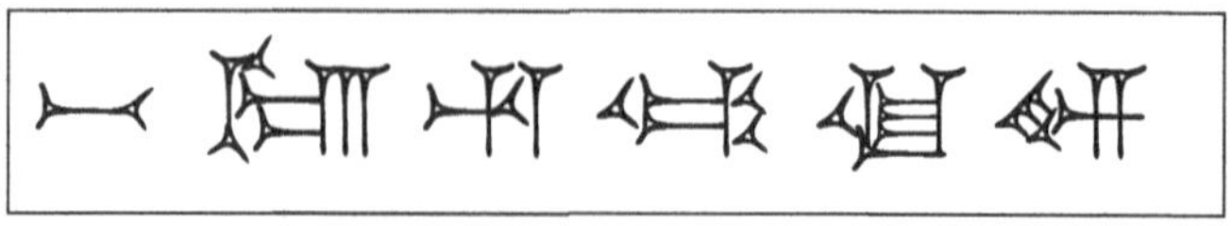

LH §10 VII:60

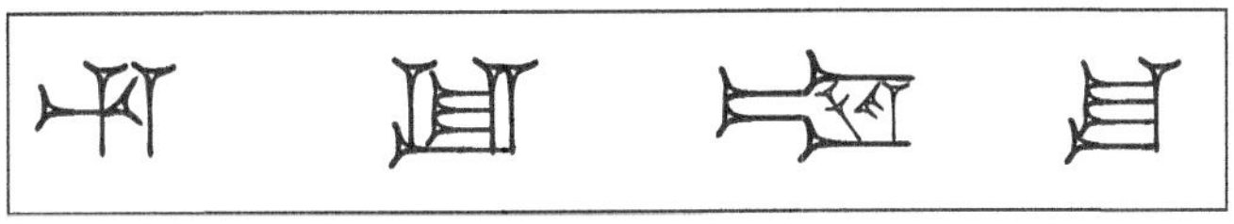

LH §10 VII:61

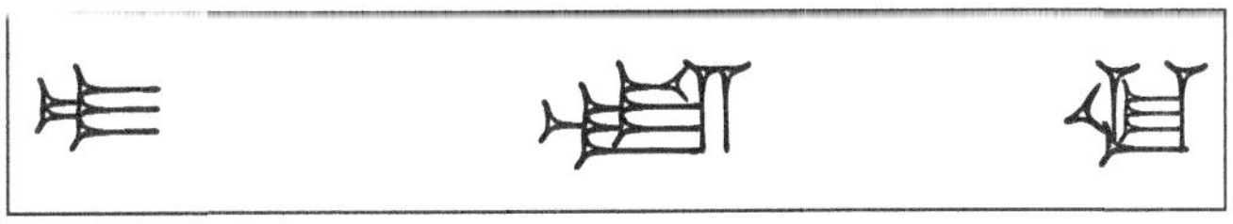

2. Grammatical Analysis: Parse all verb forms.

3. Translation: Translate LH §10.

The seven text boxes labeled VII:62-VIII:3 comprise LH §11.

1. Transliterate and Normalize.

LH §11 VII:62

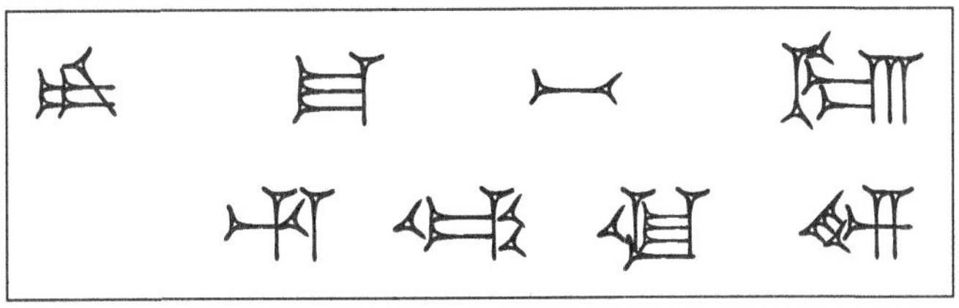

LH §11 VII:63

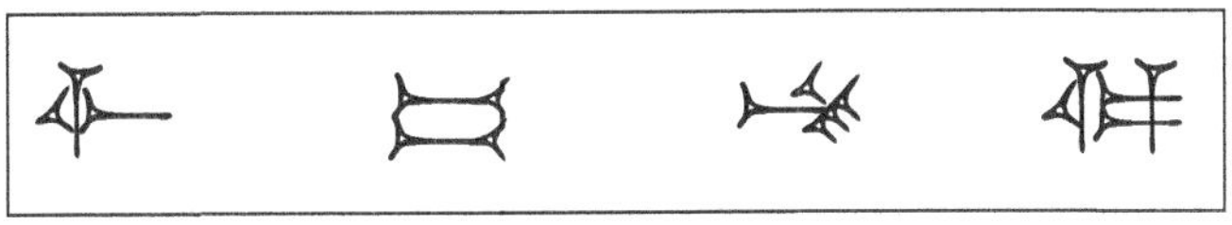

LH §11 VII:64

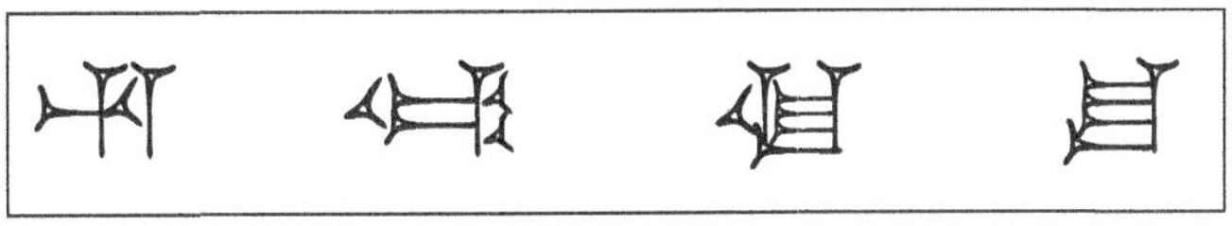

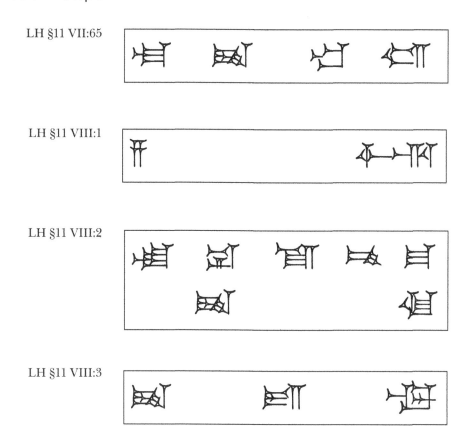

LH §11 VII:65

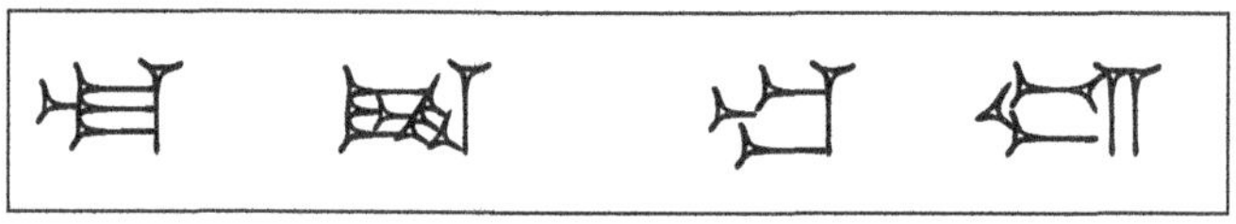

LH §11 VIII:1

LH §11 VIII:2

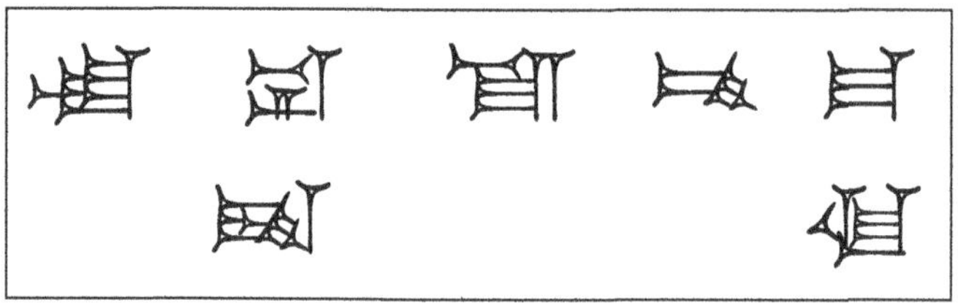

LH §11 VIII:3

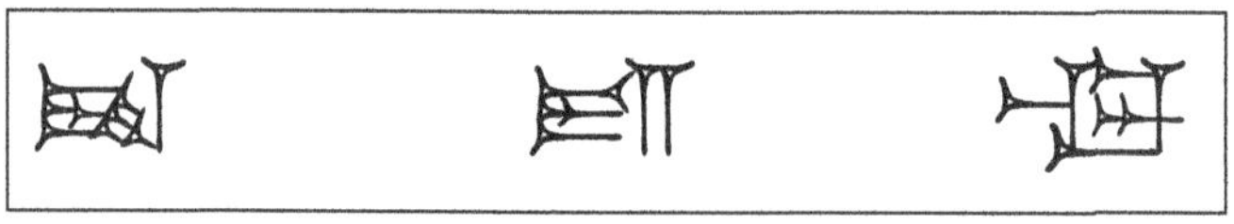

2. Grammatical Analysis: Parse all verb forms and answer the questions below. See the note below for help.

   a. What are two equally correct ways that one could analyze the word in VIII:1?

   b. The text box in VIII:2 includes the following words: *tuššum*, meaning "slander, calumny, malicious talk," and *dekûm* (*e,e*), meaning "to stir up, raise." These words do not need to be learned.

c. Although it goes beyond the concerns of this textbook, some scholars suggest emending the last sign in VIII:2 to . In Old Babylonian script these signs are even more similar: *ke* is  and *di* is . Parse and translate the new verb that is formed based on this proposed textual emendation.

3. Translation: Translate LH §11.

The ten text boxes labeled VIII:4–13 comprise LH §12.

1. Transliterate and Normalize.

LH §12 VIII:4

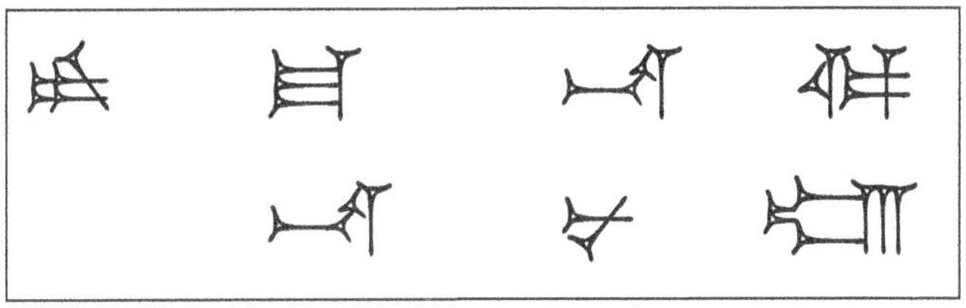

LH §12 VIII:5

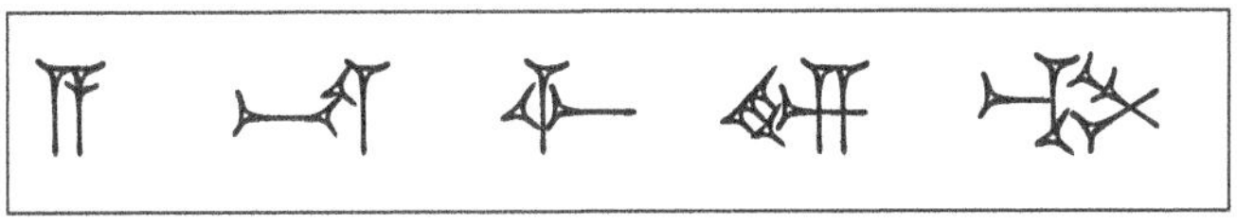

LH §12 VIII:6

LH §12 VIII:7

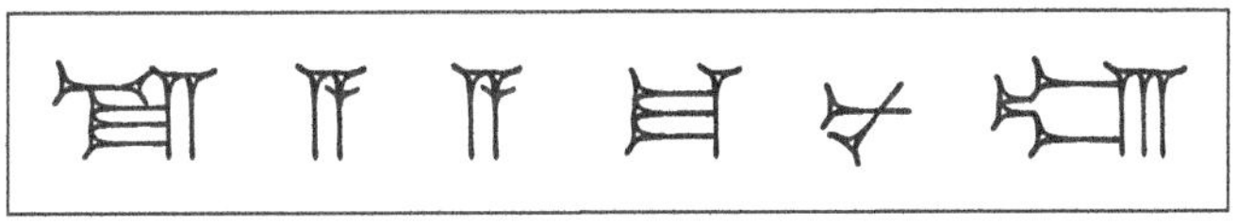

LH §12 VIII:8

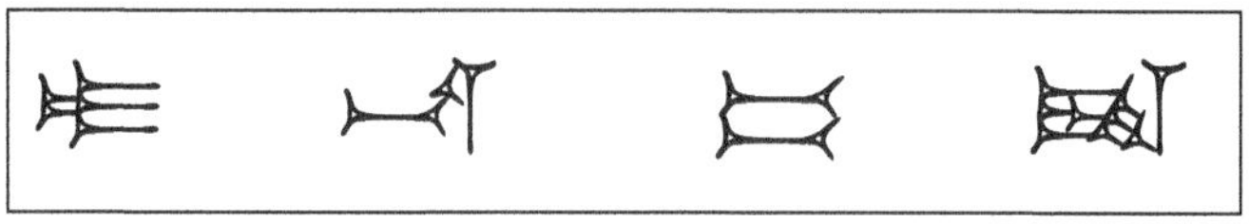

LH §12 VIII:9

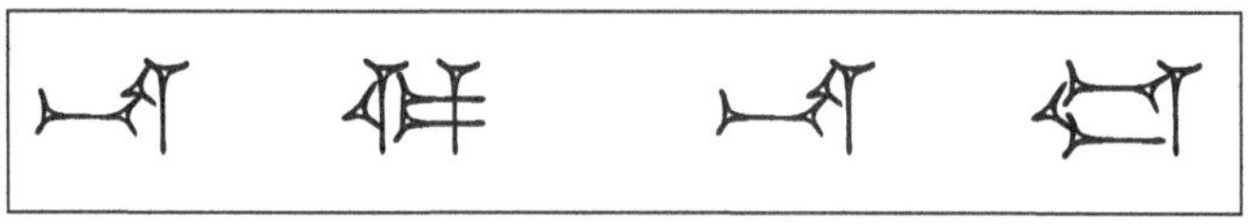

LH §12 VIII:10

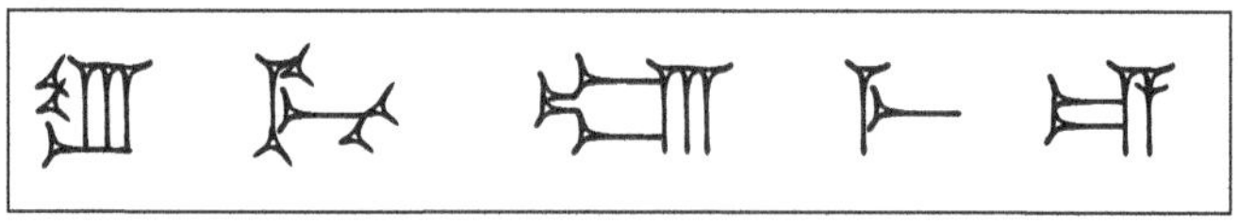

LH §12 VIII:11

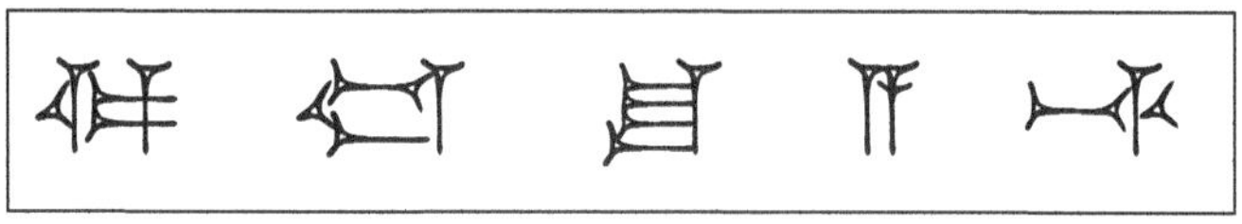

LH §12 VIII:12

LH §12 VIII:13

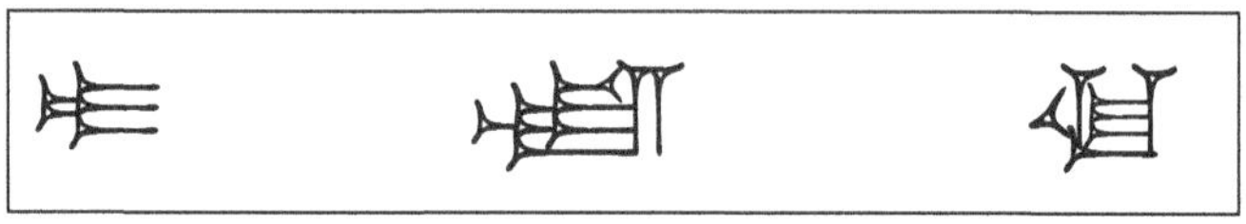

2. Grammatical Analysis: Parse all verb forms.

3. Translation: Translate LH §12.

The eleven text boxes labeled VIII:14–24 comprise LH §13.

1. Transliterate and Normalize: See the notes below for additional help.

LH §13 VIII:14

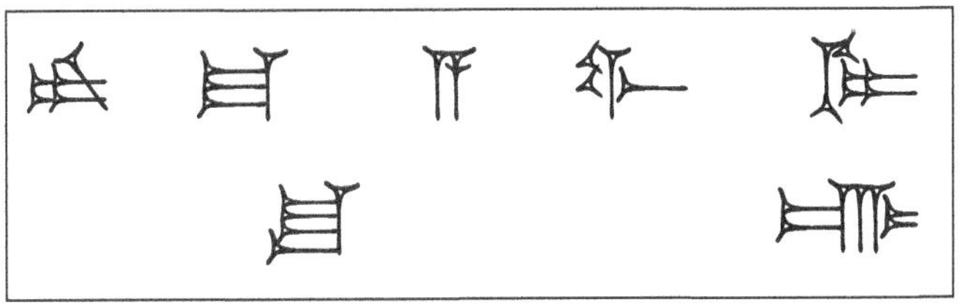

LH §13 VIII:15

Note: The sign  in VIII:15 is *qer*. This does not need to be learned.

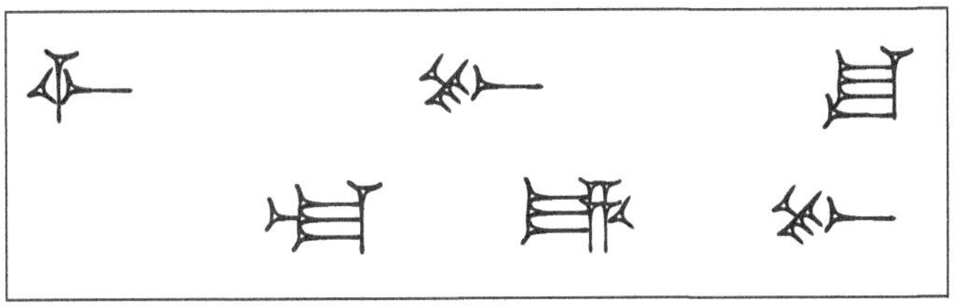

LH §13 VIII:16

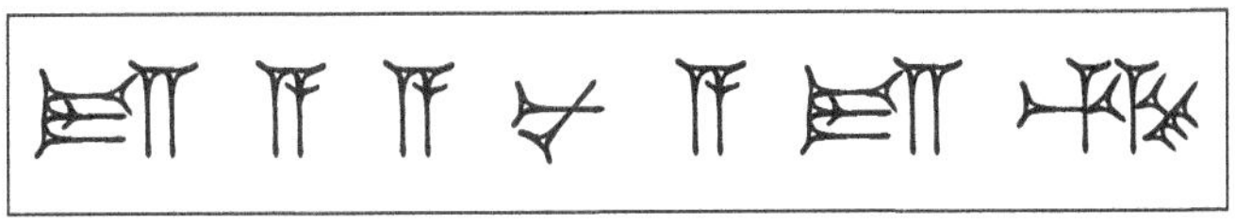

LH §13 VIII:17

Note: The sign, 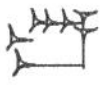 in VIII:17 and 19 is ITI, *warḫum*, meaning "month." This sign does not need to be learned.

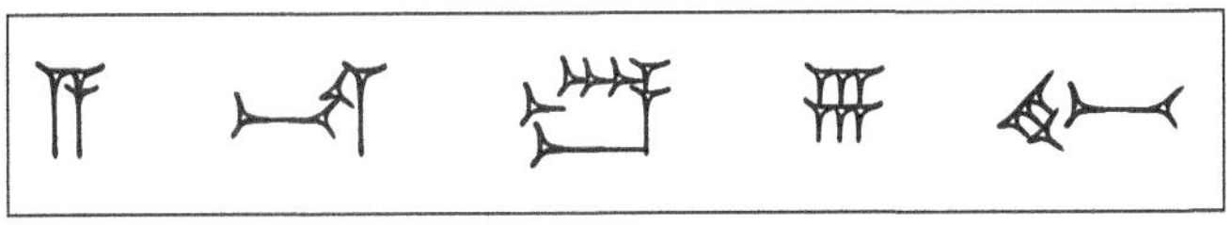

LH §13 VIII:18

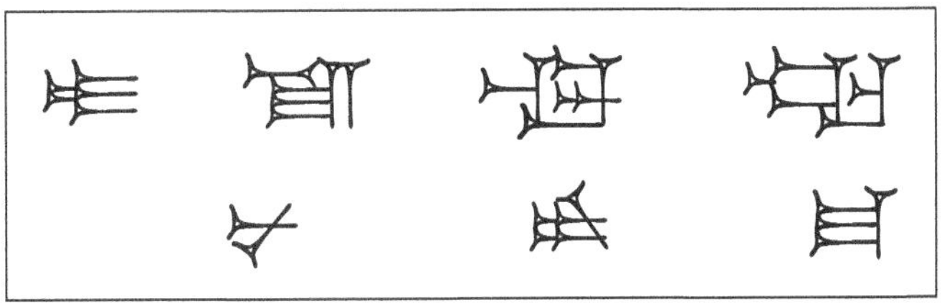

LH §13 VIII:19

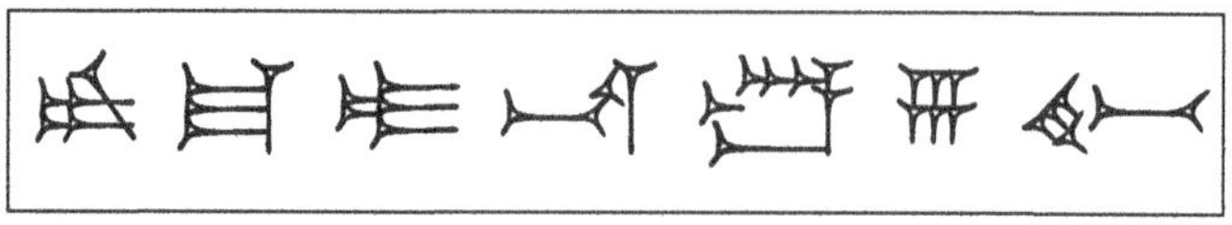

LH §13 VIII:20

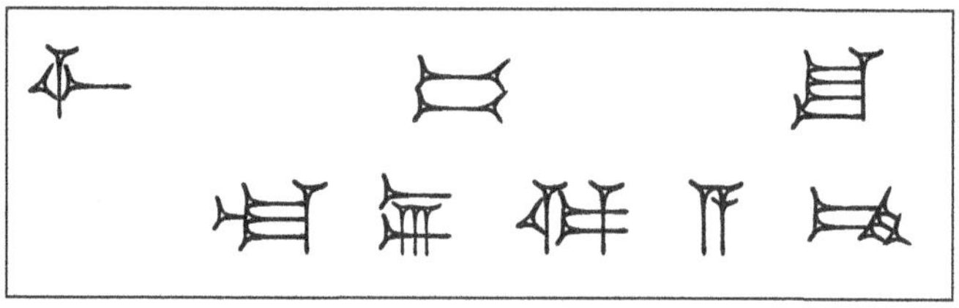

LH §13 VIII:21

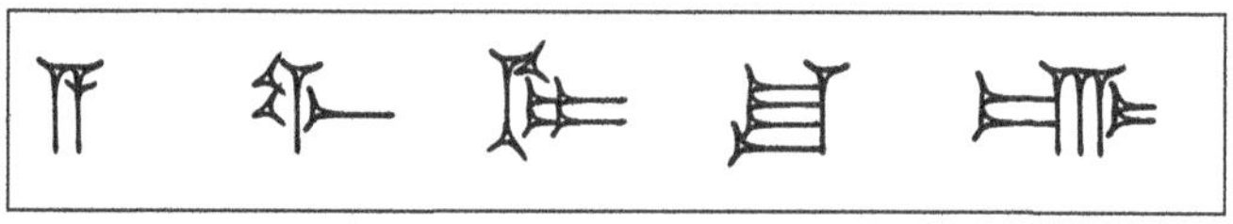

LH §13 VIII:22

LH §13 VIII:23

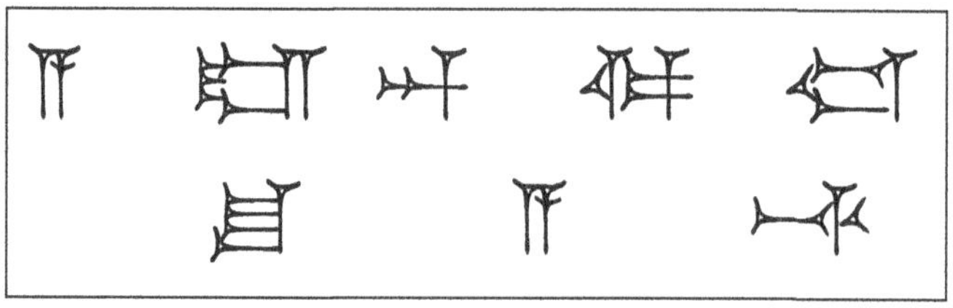

LH §13 VIII:24

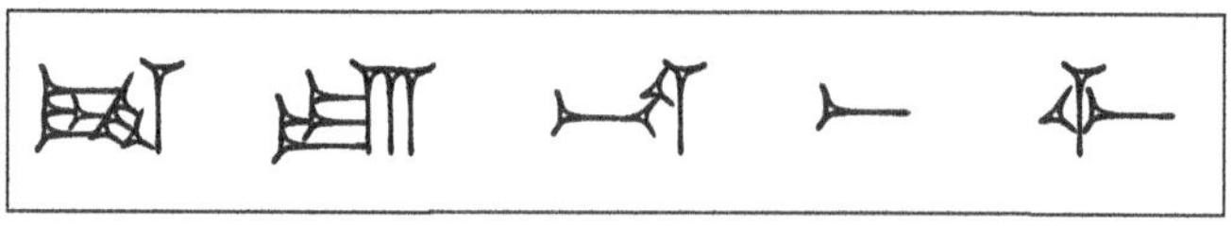

2. Grammatical Analysis: Parse all verb forms. See the notes below for help.

   Note: The verb in VIII:20 is in the vocabulary for this chapter. See Chapter 16 for explanation of III-weak verbs as needed.

   Note: VIII:16 includes the word *adânum* (or *adannum*), "appointed time." This does not need to be learned.

3. Translation: Translate LH §13. Add to this translation your translation of LH §§10–12.

15–𒌋𒐊

The Verb-Limiting Accusative and Adjectives

This chapter addresses the three forms of the verb-limiting accusative case. The three uses of adjectives are also explained, namely attributive adjectives, predicative adjectives, and substantive adjectives.

The exercises for this chapter include seven laws, LH §§14–20, all of which concern the theft or loss of persons, whether this was accomplished through kidnapping a non-slave (LH §14) or through offering assistance to a fugitive slave (LH §15) or harboring a fugitive slave (LH §16). The law stipulates a bounty to encourage the extradition of a fugitive slave (LH §17) and then proceeds to deal with two major impediments to the return of a fugitive slave. LH §18 treats the case of a slave who does not divulge the identity of his owner, while LH §19 prohibits keeping such a slave, despite the practical impossibility of extradition caused by ignorance of the slave's rightful owner. LH §20, on the other hand, treats the case of a fugitive slave who runs away from the person who caught him who, presumably, would have returned him to his owner. Because of the substantial combined length of the laws covered in this chapter, normalized text is provided for the last three laws, LH §§18–20.

15.1 Verb-Limiting Accusative

The function of the accusative case may be defined in general terms as the case that limits the action of the verb. In practice, this limiting function appears in the following three forms: (1) accusative for a direct object, (2) double accusative to complete the meaning of a verb, and (3) adverbial accusative of time, place, or specification.

15.1.1 ***Accusative for a Direct Object.*** The main use of the accusative case, which is to mark the direct object of a verb, is well attested and has been encountered numerous times in LH laws that have been translated up to this point. Normally, the direct object (in the accusative) follows the subject of the clause and precedes the verb: S-O-V. Any marginal qualifiers (M), such as an indirect object, a prepositional phrase, or an adverb, are usually placed between the direct object and the verb: S-O-M-V.

For example, LH §2 reads, *šumma awīlum <u>kišpī</u>* [genitive-accusative] *elî awīlim iddîma*, "If a man hurled (charges of) *sorceries* against a man, but. . . ."

15.1.2 ***Double Accusative to Complete the Meaning of the Verb.*** A second important use of the accusative is seen in cases where two nouns are required to complete the meaning of a verb. Typically, the first noun in the accusative is the direct object of the verb, while the second noun in the accusative normally requires a preposition before it when translated into English, such as "with," "in," "at," "for," or "from" in order to express the nature of its relationship to the verb.

For example, in LH §§43, 44 there is the repeated clause, *u eqlam . . . mayyāri imaḫḫaṣ*, "and he shall break up the field *with* mattocks." Similarly, LH §163 has the clause, *mārī lâ ušaršīšu*, "she did not provide him *with* children. LH §154, on the other hand, has, *awīlam šu'āti âlam ušeṣṣūšu*, "as for that man, they shall expel him *from* the city."

15.1.3 ***Adverbial Accusative of Time, Place, or Specification.*** A third important use of the accusative is what is often described as an adverbial use for time, place, or specification. This kind of accusative is often found even with stative verbs, which cannot take a direct object. This usage is similar in meaning to the second use of the accusative mentioned above in that translations involving virtually any English preposition are likely to be used, including "with," "in," "at," "for," or "from." Sometimes, when translating, it helps to begin with a wooden translation such as "regarding . . ." or "with respect to. . . ." Afterward, however, that wooden translation should be improved with whatever constitutes more idiomatic English according to the context.

For example, in LH §31, *šumma šattam išti'atma uddappirma* may be rendered, "If he has kept away *for* only one year. . . ." On the other hand, LH §191 has *mârum šū rîqūssu ul ittallak,* which can be translated as "that son shall not go out *empty-handed.*" This is a more idiomatic translation for the wooden rendering: "*with respect to* his emptiness" or "*in* his emptiness."

15.2 Adjectives

In Akkadian, adjectives, including participles, can be used attributively, predicatively, or substantively.

15.2.1 ***Attributive Adjective.*** When an adjective is used attributively it immediately follows the noun it modifies.[1] For example, LH §3 has the phrase *awīlum šū*, "*that* man."

When an adjective is used attributively, it agrees with the noun it modifies in gender, number, and case. For reference, the declensional suffixes for demonstrative adjectives are given in §8.3, and the declensional suffixes for adjectives more generally are in §5.2.1. As may be inferred from both sets of paradigms, adjectives do not have a special dual form; the plural form is used instead.[2]

In the above-mentioned phrase from LH §3, *awīlum šū*, *šū* is a ms nominative form of the demonstrative adjective to agree with the ms nominative *awīlum.*

If an adjective modifies a noun that is in construct with another word, it will be placed immediately after the construct chain. If it modifies the noun that is in the construct state, which has lost its case ending, the attributive adjective will be in the implied case of the noun in construct. For example, the phrase *bêl bîtim šū* appears in LH §16. Since *šū* is the demonstrative adjective in the ms nominative and not *šu'āti*, the same demonstrative adjective but in the genitive-accusative case, the phrase should be rendered "*that* owner of the house," and not "the owner of *that* house."

If an attributive adjective simultaneously modifies two nouns, it will follow the second of those nouns. If the nouns are in the singular but are linked by "or," the adjective will be in the singular. If the nouns are singular but are linked by "and," the attributive adjective will

1. The one regular exception to this rule is that of ordinals. For example, *rebūtim*, "fourth," precedes the noun it modifies in LH §44 and LH §117.

2. Dual nouns are uncommon in Old Babylonian. The only dual noun in LH, which appears in LH §152 and §157, is the word *kilallān*, which means "both."

be in the plural. For example, LH §16 has *lû wardam lû amtam ḫalqam*, "either a *fugitive* male slave or a female slave. . . ." This example of a ms attributive adjective in the accusative case also shows that with two nouns of mixed gender, the attributive adjective will be masculine.

15.2.2 ***Predicative (or Predicate) Adjective.*** An adjective can also be used predicatively. When an adjective is so used, it is found at the end of its clause. If it is a verbal adjective (*parsum* < **parisum*, by vowel syncope), as most adjectives are, it will be the corresponding stative of the verb (usually a *paris*-form, but sometimes a *paras*- or *parus*-form). For the conjugation of the stative verb, see §6.4.[3]

If the predicative adjective is not built on a verb form, it will be the adjective with its case endings removed and replaced with the pronominal suffixes of the stative verb. For example, in LH §Epi XLVII:81, *awātūya nasqā*, "my words are special," where *nasqā* is the adjective *nasqum*, "special," with the *-um* suffix removed and replaced with the *-ā* feminine plural suffix of the stative verb.

15.2.3 ***Substantive Adjective.*** When an adjective is used substantively, it usually refers to one who is described by the adjective. This is the case, for example, in LH §Pro I:37–38, where the text reads, *dannum enšam ana lâ ḫabālim*, "the strong should not exploit the weak."[4]

Sometimes a feminine singular adjective may be used as an abstract noun.

15.2.4 ***List of Adjectives.*** Except for participles, ordinals, and pronouns (demonstrative and possessive), the following are all the adjectives found in LH. These need to be learned only as they come up in the vocabulary of each chapter. They are listed here for easy reference.

aḫûm, "(an)other"
annûm, "this"
aštum, "hard"
atrum, "extra"
baltum, "living"
damqum, "good"
dannum, "strong"
dārûm, "everlasting"
ellum, "pure, sacred"
elûm, "upper"
emqum, "wise"
eršum I, "wise"
eršum II, "planted"
eššum, "new"
ezzum, "angry, violent"
gamrum, "complete"
gašrum, "mighty"
gitmālum, "perfect"
ḫablum, "exploited"
ḫabṭum, "robbed"
ḫalqum, "lost"
ḫassum, "intelligent"
îṣum, "insufficient"
kabtum, "serious"
kînum, "firm"
lemnum, "bad"
maḫrûm, "former"
malûm, "full"
marṣum, "diseased"
maṭûm, "light, small"
na'dum, "devout"
nasqum, "special"
pānûm, "former"
rabûm, "large, great"
raggum, "evil"
rēštûm, "oldest, first"
rîqum, "empty"
rûqum, "distant"
sarrum, "false, dishonest"; *substantive use:* "liar"
ṣalmum, "black"
ṣeḫḫerum, "young"
ṣeḫrum, "small, young"
ṣēnum, "wicked"
šaknum, "placed, provided"
šanûm, "another, a second"
šaṭrum, "inscribed"
šûqurum, "precious"
ṭābum, "good"
telîtum, "uplifted"
warkûm, "subsequent, rear, later"
wašrum, "humble"

3. Some Assyriologists, such as Huehnergard, prefer to term the stative verb a "predicative adjective."

4. This expression is also repeated in LH §Epi XLVII:59–60. In Akkadian, as in Hebrew, at times the feminine singular form of the adjective can be used to express abstract ideas, so, for example, *ṭābtum* is "goodness."

As the list above illustrates, the vast majority of adjectives in Akkadian are verbal adjectives—in the G-stem, following the paradigm form of *parsum*. For example, the G-stem ms verbal adjective of *ḫalāqum*, "be missing, to escape, to flee," is *ḫalqum*, "lost" or "fugitive." Some, however, have undergone vowel attenuation of the expected *a*-vowel to an *e*-vowel based on an elided guttural (*ḥ*, ʿ, or *ǵ*).

15.3 Homework

Before you move on, be sure to understand the three uses of the verb-limiting accusative case. Also, be able to recognize the three uses of the adjective (attributive, predicative, and substantive) and translate them accordingly.

15.3.1 *Signs*

 *ge, gi*

 *pa*

 *se, si*

 *as, aṣ, az*

 *ás, áš*

15.3.2 *Vocabulary*

kalûm = to retain, detain, withhold (cf. *kālāʾ*, כָּלָא, "withhold, keep back")
nîšum = life (cf. *nāšîm*, נָשִׁים, "women")
raqûm (*i,i*) = to hide, give refuge to
ṣābitānum = one who finds, captor
ṣeḫrum = small, young (cf. *ṣāʿîr*, צָעִיר)
ṣêrum = open country (beyond cultivated areas)
šiqlum [GÍN] = shekel (cf. *šeqel*, שֶׁקֶל)
warka = after, afterwards (cf. *warki*; cf. *yərēkâ*, יְרֵכָה, "rear [portion], most distant part")
warkatum = back, inheritance, background (cf. *yərēkâ*, יְרֵכָה, "rear [portion], most distant part")
wašārum = to be free; D: "to prove innocent"; Dt: "to be proved innocent, exonerated, allowed to go free" (cf. *yātar*, יָתַר, *niphal*: "to be left over")
zakārum (*a,u*) = speak, say, name, swear + *nîš ilim* = swear by a god (cf. *zākar*, זָכַר, "to mention, remember")

Congratulations! If you learn the eleven words above and have learned each of the 102 words in the vocabulary lists of the preceding chapters, you will be able to read 78 percent of all the words in LH §§1–20, 127–149.

15.3.3 *Exercises*

The five text boxes labeled VIII:25–29 comprise LH §14.

1. Transliterate and Normalize.

LH §14 VIII:25

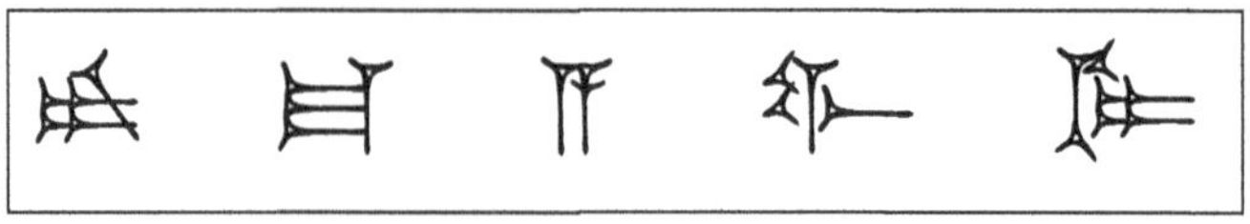

LH §14 VIII:26

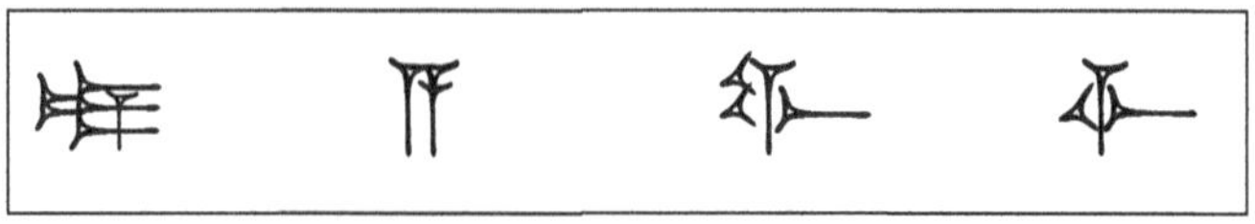

LH §14 VIII:27

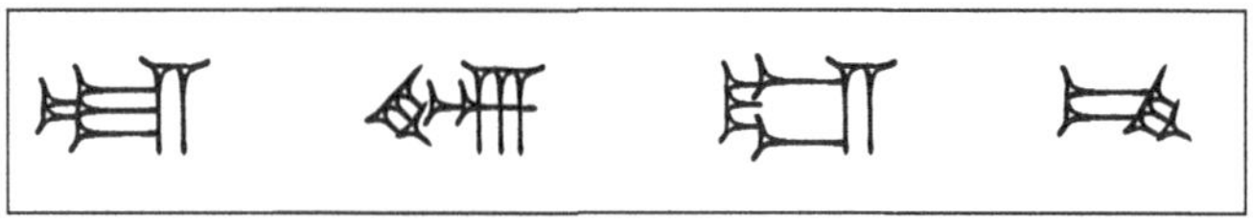

LH §14 VIII:28

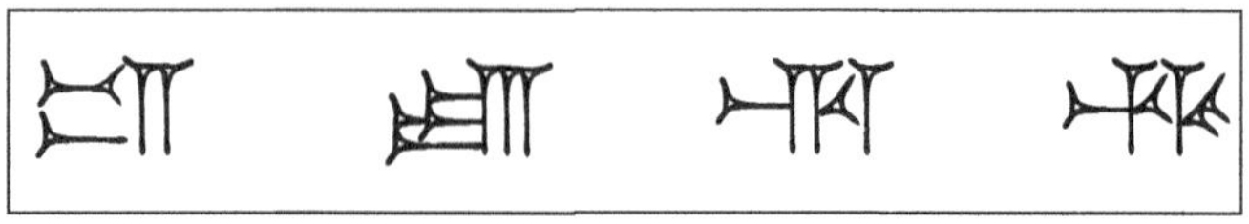

LH §14 VIII:29

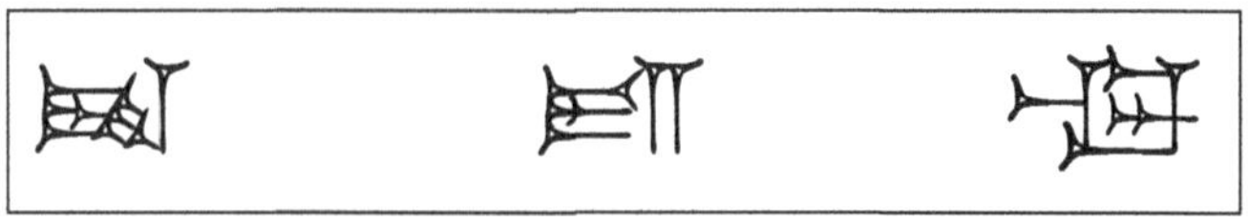

2. Grammatical Analysis: Parse all verb forms and answer the question below.

   a. Notice the case of the adjective in VIII:27. Explain why it is in this case.

   Note: The *ḫ* in VIII:27 may represent a historical spelling that may have been pronounced ʿ (Akkadian had no other clear way to represent this sound). Compare, for example, Hebrew צָעִיר. Presumably, later this distinct pronunciation would have been forgotten. The historical spelling is similar to what may be the case for the last king of Ugarit whose name was in Ugaritic, *ʿmrpi*, "Hammurapi." In Ugaritic, however, an original *b* was often interchanged with *p*.[5] So the spelling of the name *ʿmrpi*, which is generally held to be the Ugaritic equivalent of the Akkadian name, Hammurabi, is not necessarily evidence for an original spelling with *-pi*, as is sometimes suggested.

3. Translation: Translate LH §14.

The seven text boxes labeled VIII:30–36 comprise LH §15.

1. Transliterate and Normalize: See the note below for additional help.

LH §15 VIII:30

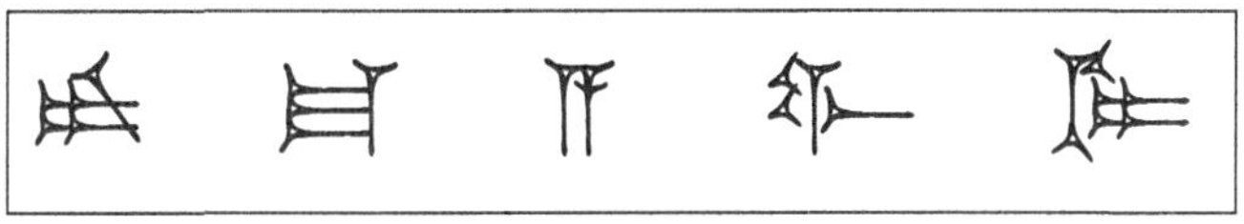

LH §15 VIII:31

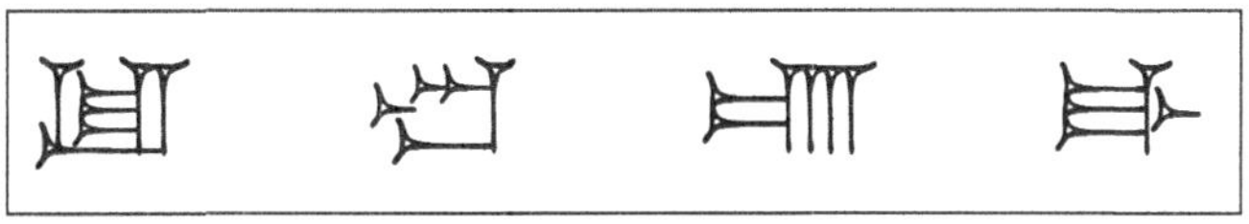

LH §15 VIII:32

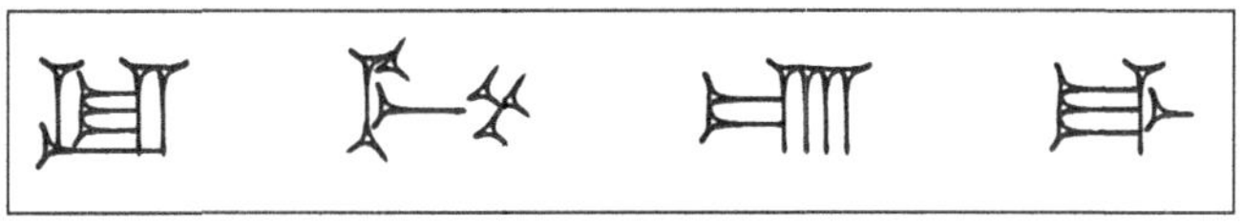

LH §15 VIII:33

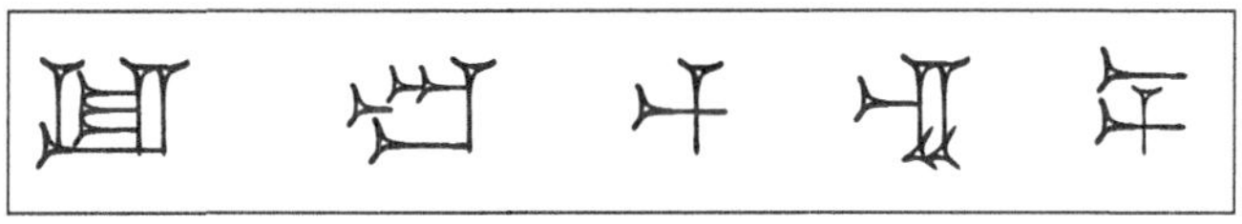

5. In support, see Garr, "On Voicing and Devoicing in Ugaritic," 45.

LH §15 VIII:34

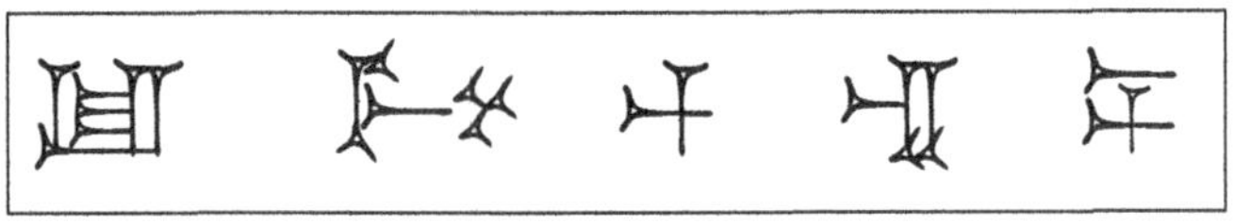

LH §15 VIII:35

Note: In VIII:35 the sign 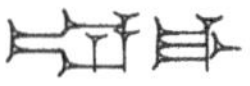 is KÁ.GAL, *abullum*, meaning "city gate." This sign and the word *abullum* do not need to be learned.

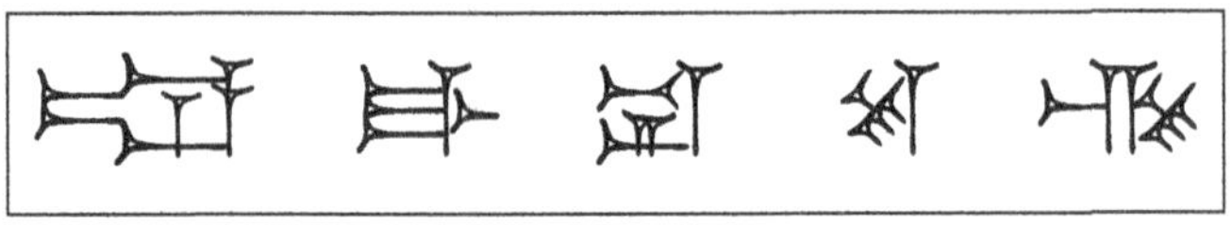

LH §15 VIII:36

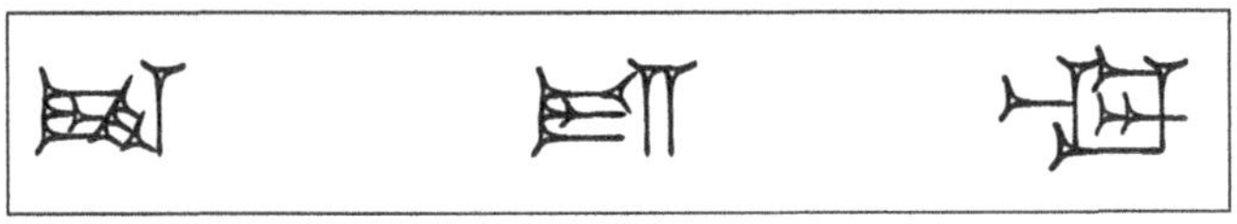

2. Grammatical Analysis: Parse all verb forms.

3. Translation: Translate LH §15.

The twelve text boxes labeled VIII:37–48 comprise LH §16.

1. Transliterate and Normalize.

LH §16 VIII:37

LH §16 VIII:38

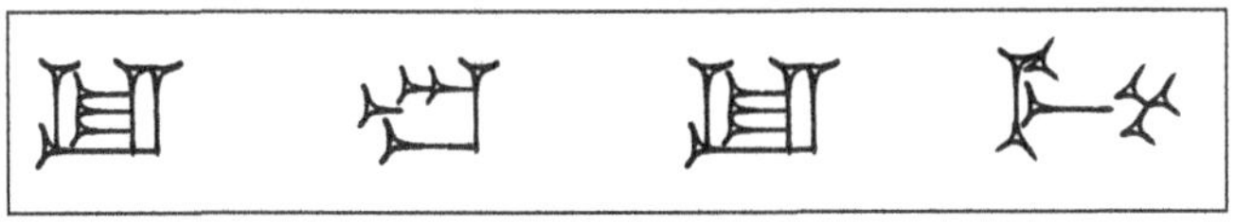

LH §16 VIII:39

LH §16 VIII:40

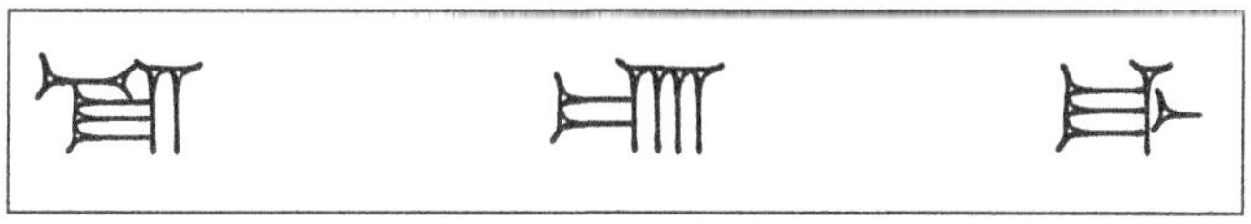

LH §16 VIII:41

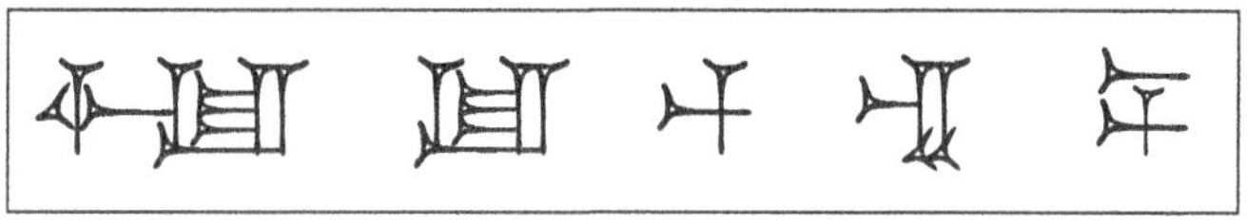

LH §16 VIII:42

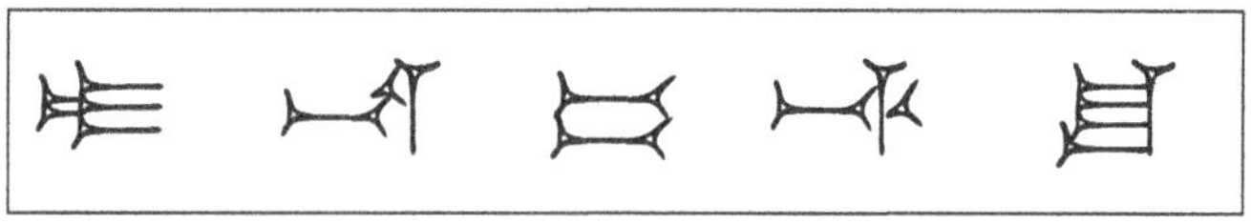

LH §16 VIII:43

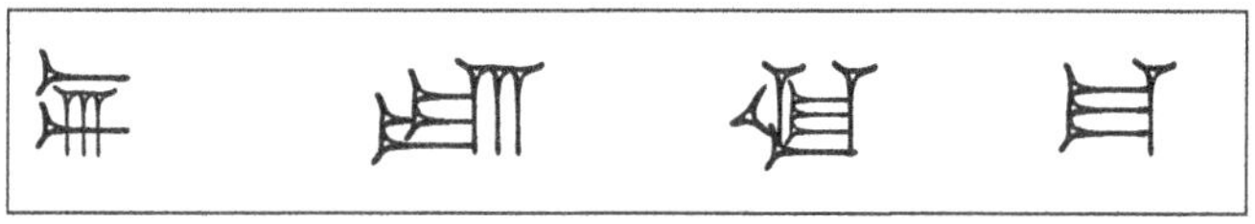

LH §16 VIII:44

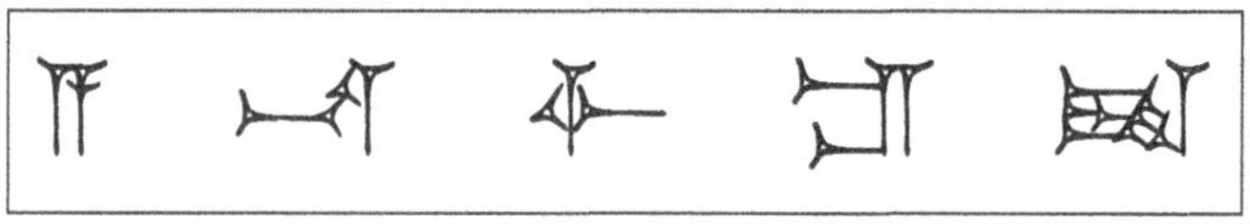

LH §16 VIII:45

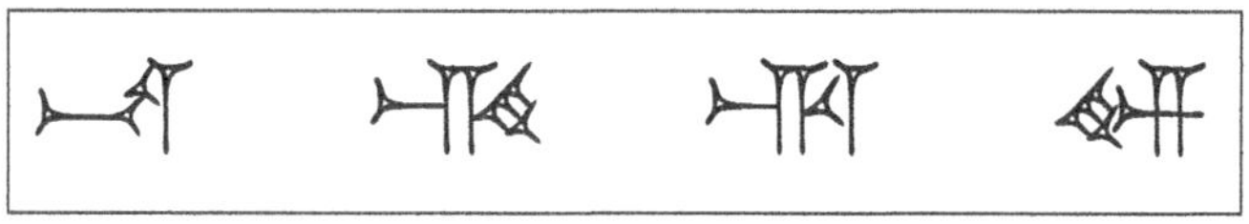

LH §16 VIII:46

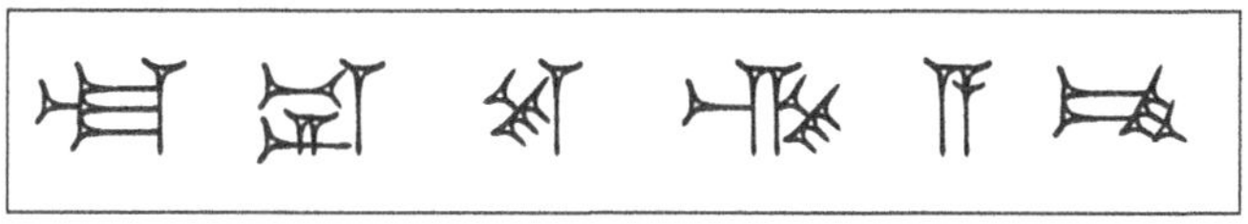

LH §16 VIII:47

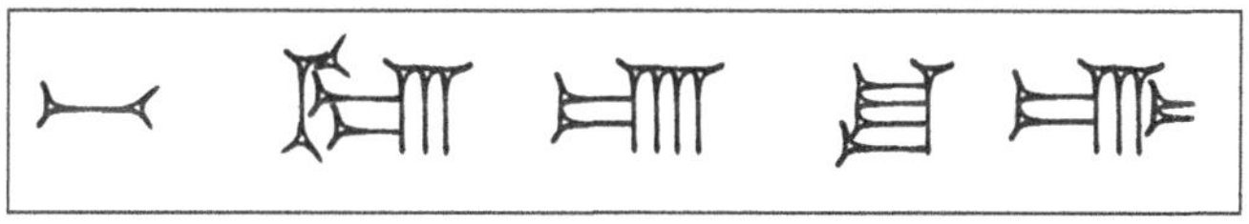

LH §16 VIII:48

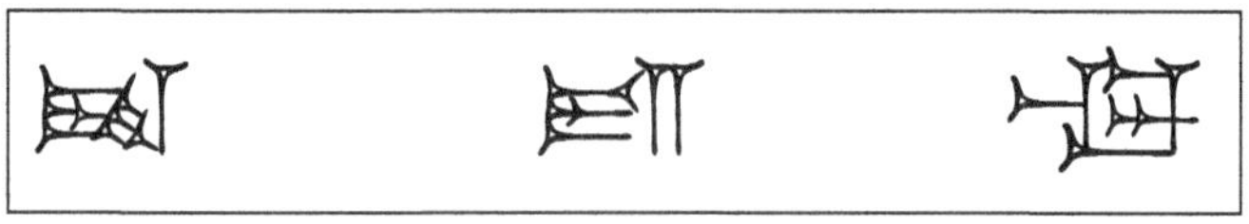

2. Grammatical Analysis: Parse all verb forms and answer the question below. See the notes below for help.

   a. There are two nouns in VIII:47. How do you know which noun is modified by the demonstrative?

   Note: Text box VIII:43 includes a III-weak verb. See Chapter 16 for explanation of III-weak verbs.

   Note: VIII:44 includes the word *šisîtum*, meaning "summons, call." This word does not need to be learned.

   Note: VIII:45 includes the word *nāgirum*, meaning "herald, (town) crier." This word does not need to be learned.

3. Translation: Translate LH §16.

The ten text boxes labeled VIII:49–58 comprise LH §17.

1. Transliterate and Normalize: See the notes below for additional help.

LH §17 VIII:49

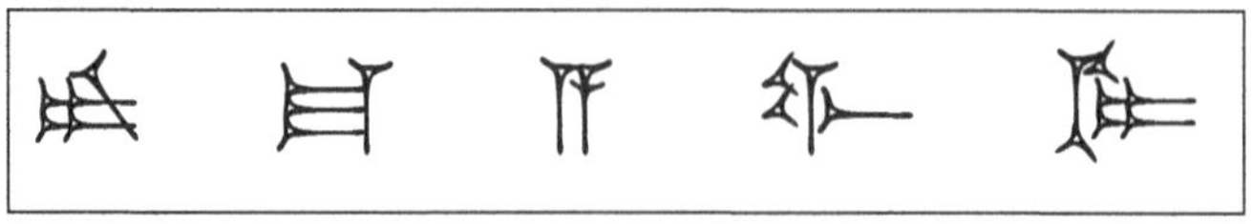

LH §17 VIII:50

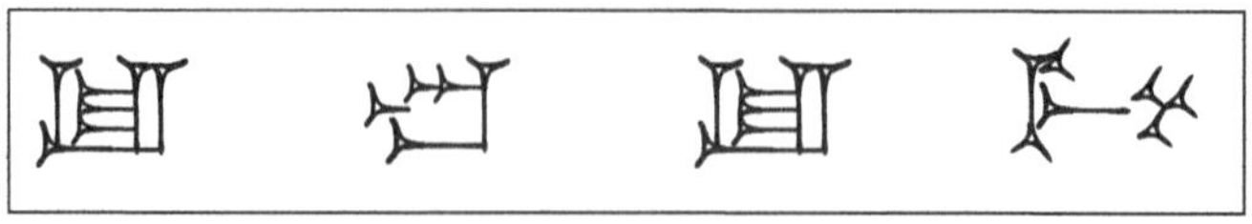

LH §17 VIII:51

LH §17 VIII:52

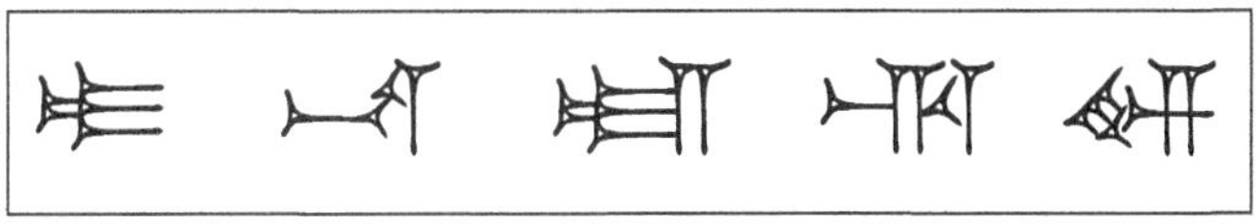

LH §17 VIII:53

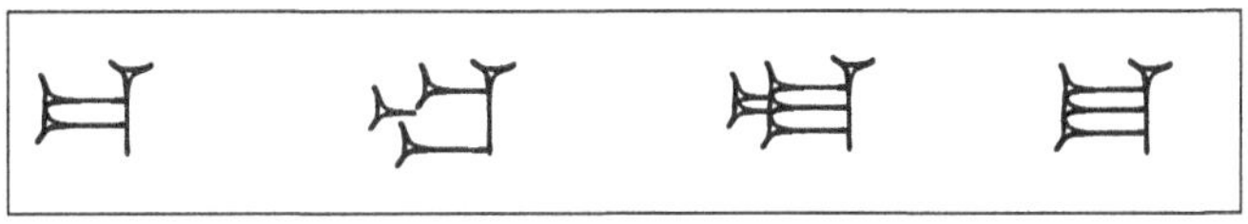

LH §17 VIII:54

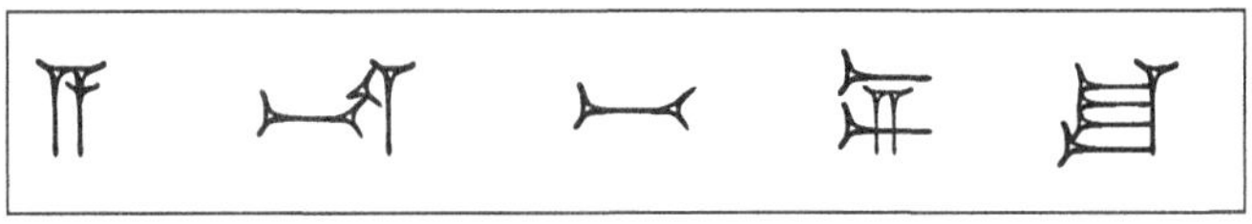

LH §17 VIII:55

Note: How do we know whether to transliterate the third sign in VIII:55 as *-de-* rather than *-di-*? We don't know for sure! The *CDA* lists both (*e,e*) and (*i,i*) as the vowel class for this verb. John Huehnergard, however, lists only (*e,e*), and he vocalizes the forms of this verb in both LH §17 and LH §18 with *e*-vowels. Everyone agrees that before Old Babylonian in the period called Old Akkadian, the vowel class for this verb was (*a,a*). It is also agreed that *a*-vowels shifted to *e*-vowels in the presence of certain guttural consonants because of vowel attenuation. It is also generally agreed that with III-weak verbs there was a tendency over time for many verbs to assimilate to the increasingly popular (*i,i*)-vowel class, as was mentioned in §16.1.2. Unfortunately, however, we do not know whether the shift to the (*i,i*)-vowel class had already taken place for this verb by the time of LH, or if it had whether the author of LH may have intended to retain earlier (*e,e*)-class forms for this verb, given the conservative spelling tendencies of LH elsewhere (such as is witnessed in its consistent retention of mimation).

Although it is, accordingly, just a taste preference, it seems best to go with both Borger and Huehnergard and vocalize the forms of this verb in both LH §17 and LH §18 with the earlier (*e,e*)-vowel class. If, however, one prefers the slightly later (*i,i*)-vowel class for this verb, this may be correct, and one could appeal to the Assyriologists Martha T. Roth and Martin Worthington in support.

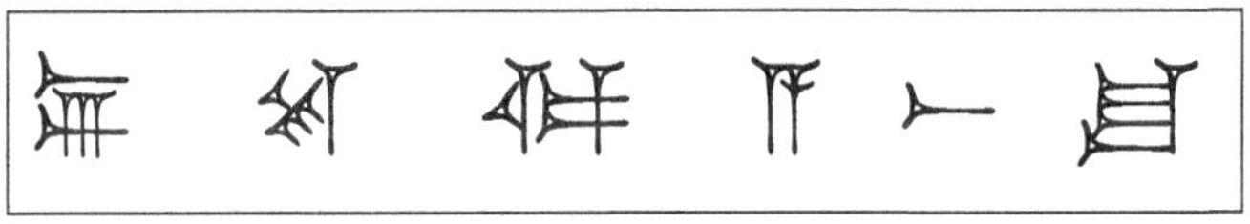

LH §17 VIII:56

Note: The sign  in VIII:56 is GÍN, *šiqlum*, meaning "shekel"; or *ṭu*. This sign does not need to be learned yet. It will be learned in Chapter 19.

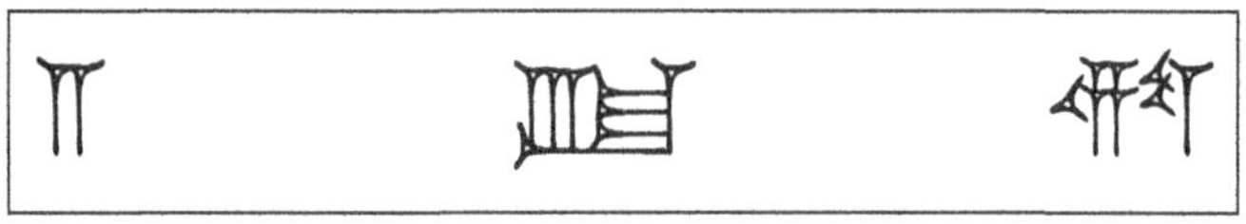

LH §17 VIII:57

LH §17 VIII:58

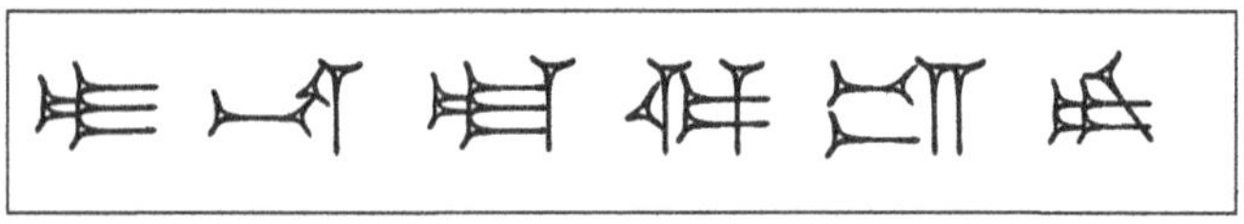

2. Grammatical Analysis: Parse all verb forms.

3. Translation: Translate LH §17.

The nine text boxes labeled VIII:59–67 comprise LH §18. Normalization is provided below each text box. Be sure to review signs as you work through parsings and translation.

LH §18 VIII:59

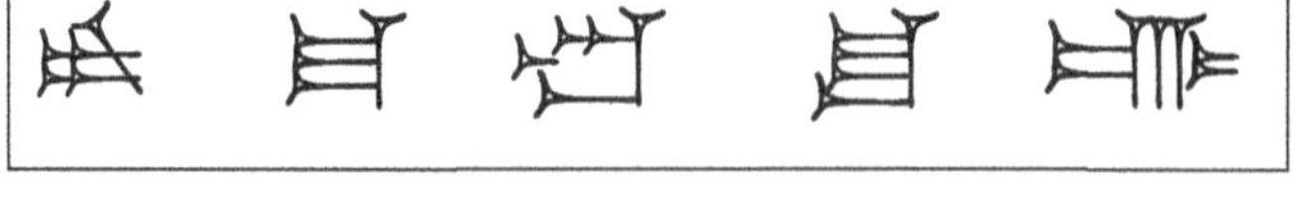

VIII:59 *šumma wardum šū*

LH §18 VIII:60

[60]*bêlšu*

LH §18 VIII:61

Note: The sign  in VIII: 61 is *kar.* This sign does not need to be learned.

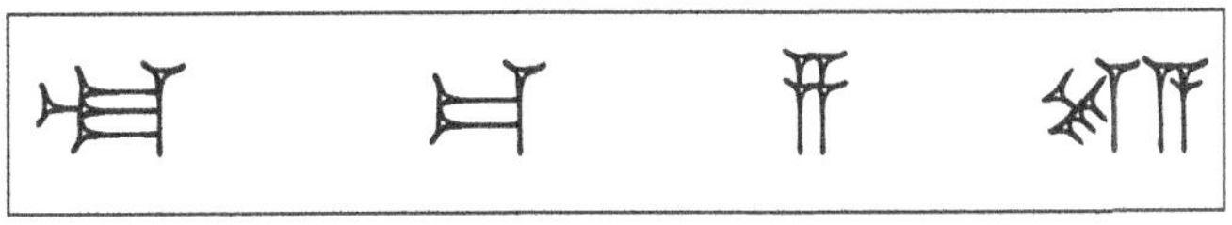

[61]*lâ izzakar*

LH §18 VIII:62

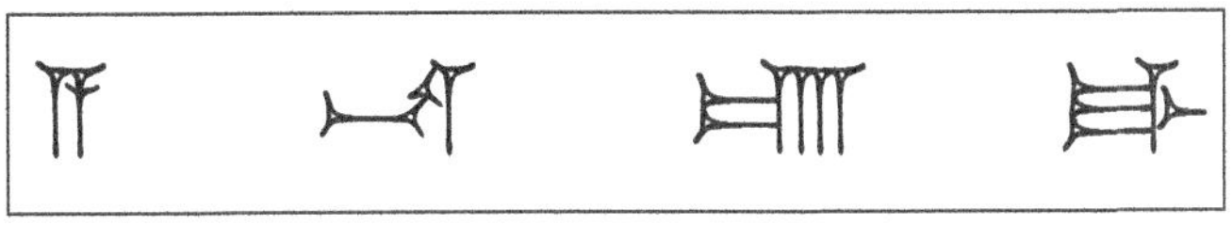

[62]*ana ekallim*

LH §18 VIII:63

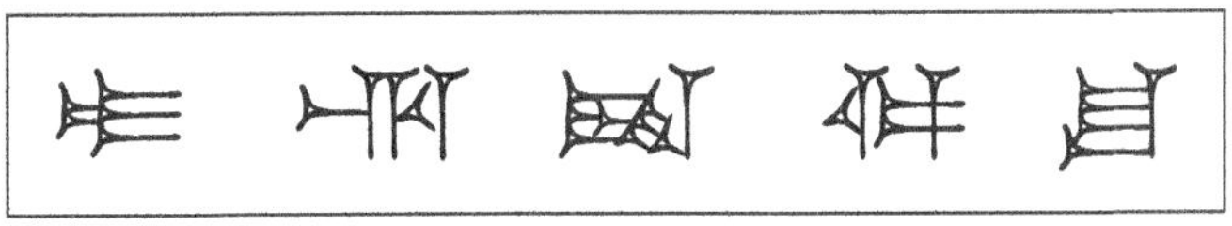

[63]*ireddêšu*

LH §18 VIII:64

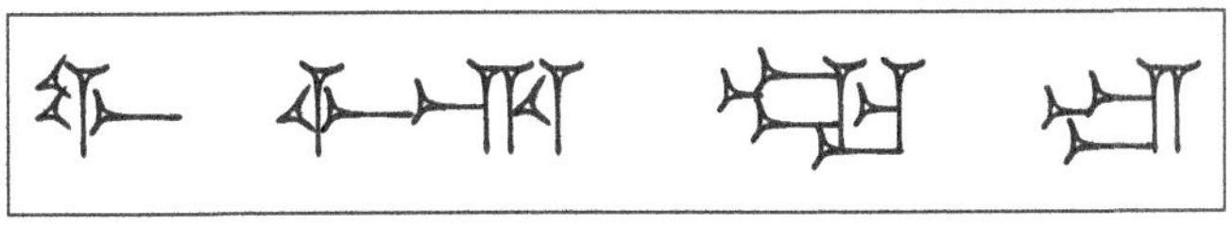

[64]*warkassu*

LH §18 VIII:65

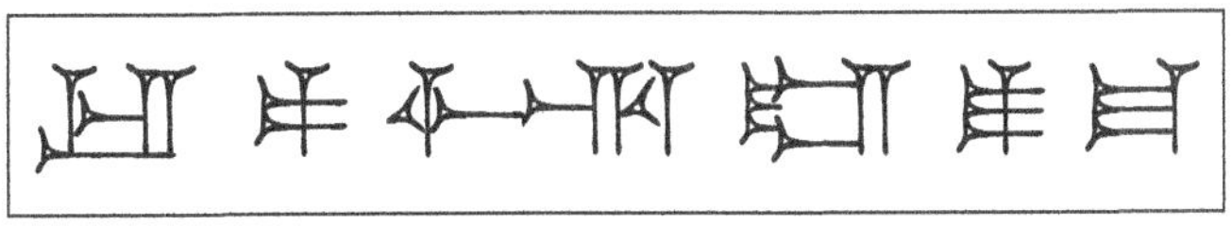

[65]*ipparrasma*

LH §18 VIII:66

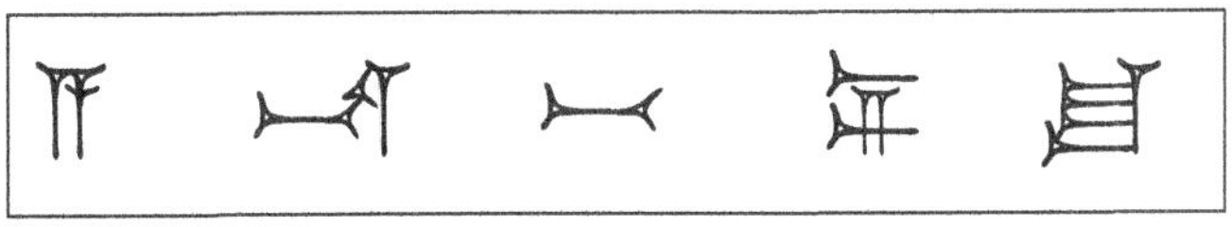

[66]*ana bêlišu*

LH §18 VIII:67

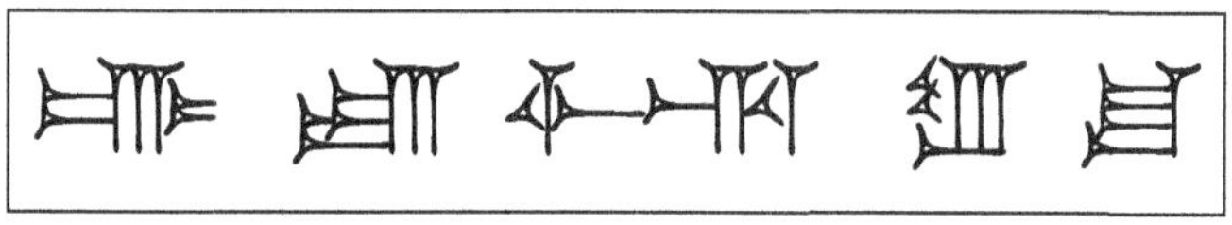

[67]*utarrūšu*

1. Grammatical Analysis: Parse all verb forms.

2. Translation: Translate LH §18.

The nine text boxes labeled §19 VIII:68-IX:4 comprise LH §19. Normalization is provided below each text box.

LH §19 VIII:68

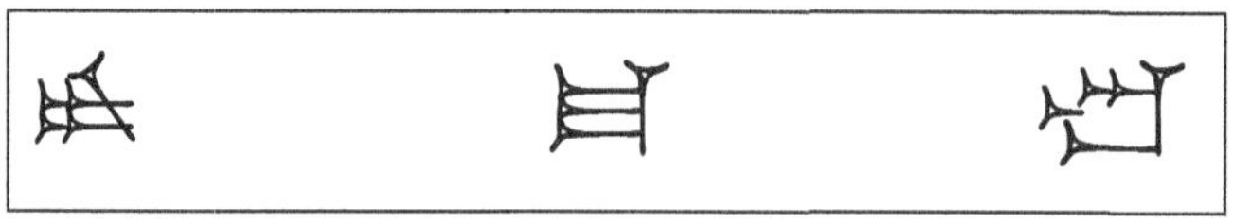

[VIII:68]*šumma wardam*

LH §19 VIII:69

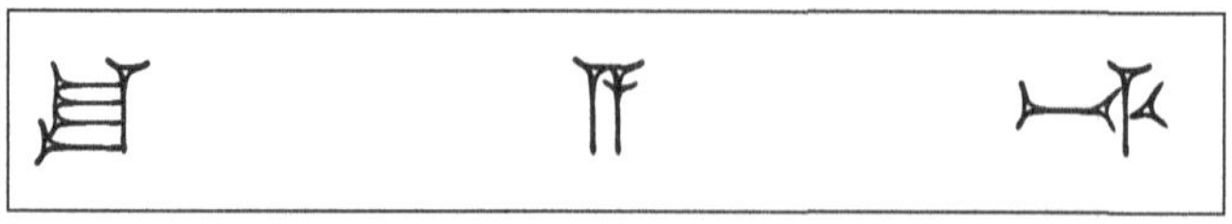

[69]*šu'āti*

LH §19 VIII:70

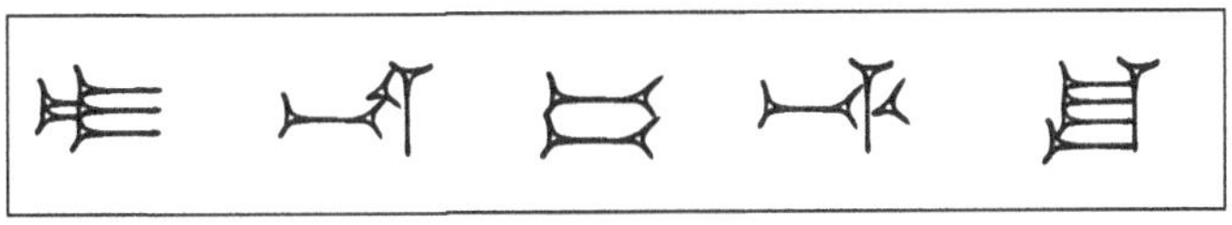

[70]*ina bîtišu*

LH §19 VIII:71

[71]*iktalâšu*

LH §19 VIII:72

[72]*warka wardum*

LH §19 IX:1

[IX:1]*ina qâtišu*

LH §19 IX:2

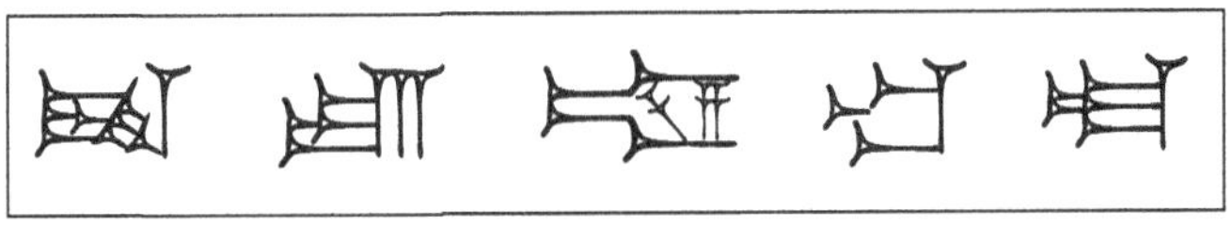

[2]*ittaṣbat*

LH §19 IX:3

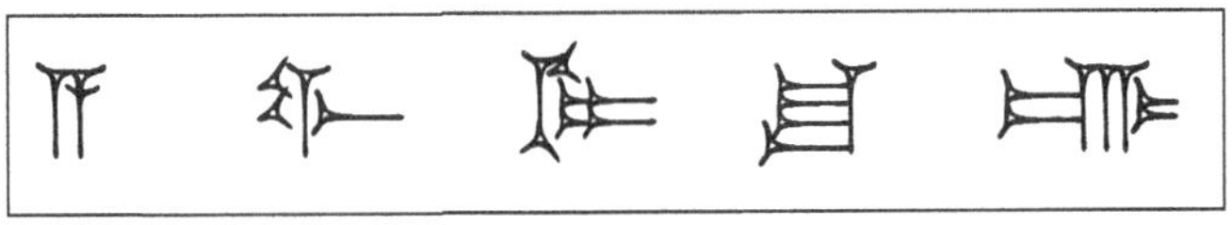

[3]*awīlum šū*

LH §19 IX:4

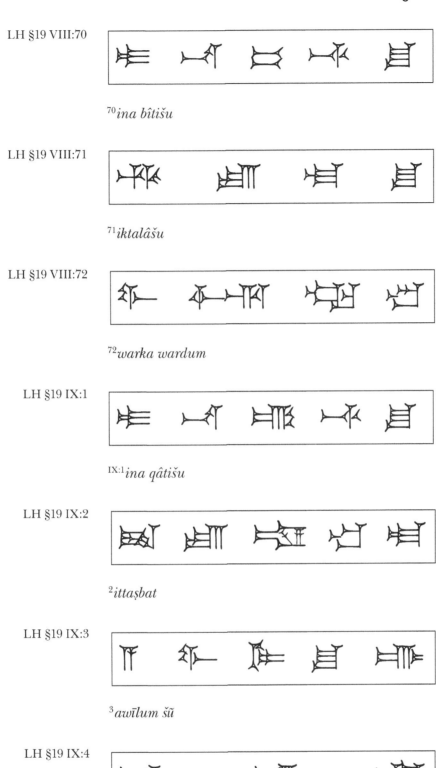

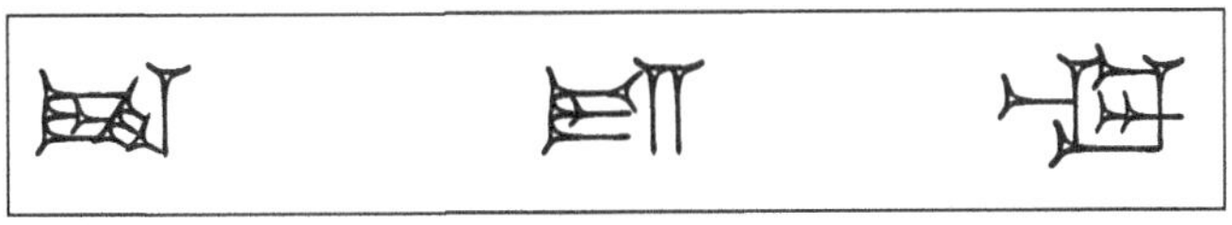

[4]*iddāk*

1. Grammatical Analysis: Parse all verb forms. See the note below for help.

   Note: The word in VIII:71 is a G-stem perfect 3cs III-weak verb from *kalūm*. (See Chapter 16 for explanation of III-weak verbs.)

2. Translation: Translate LH §19.

The nine text boxes labeled LH §20 IV:5–13 comprise LH §20. Normalization is provided below each text box.

LH §20 IX:5

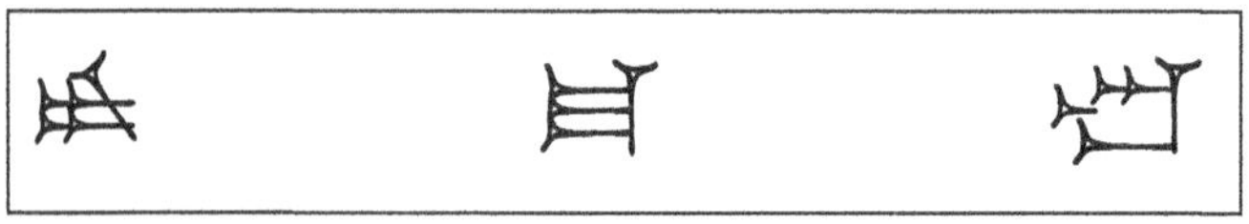

[5]*šumma wardum*

LH §20 IX:6

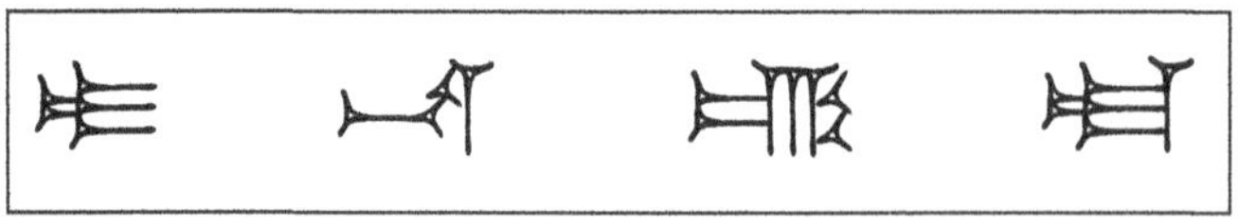

[6]*ina qât*

LH §20 IX:7

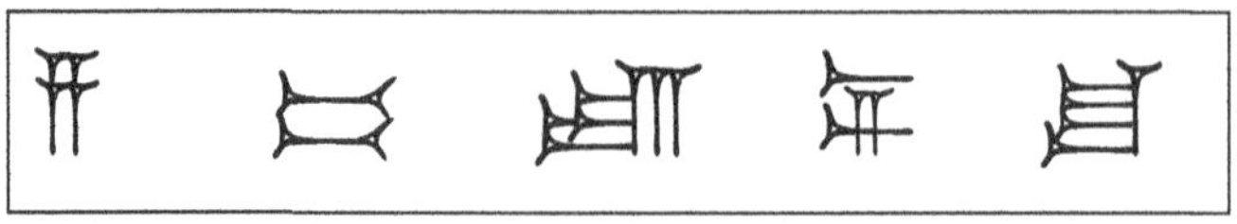

[7]*ṣābitānišu*

LH §20 IX:8

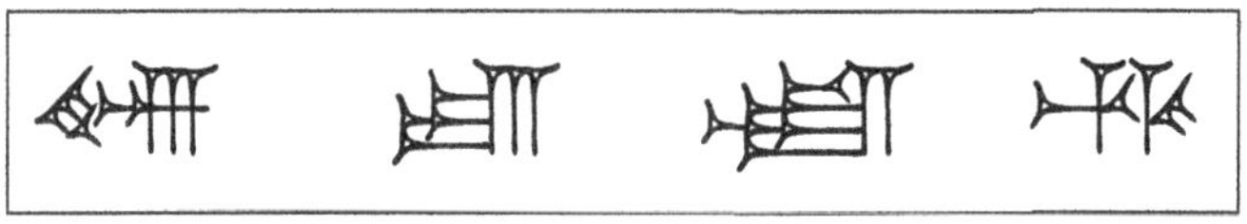

[8]*iḫtaliq*

LH §20 IX:9

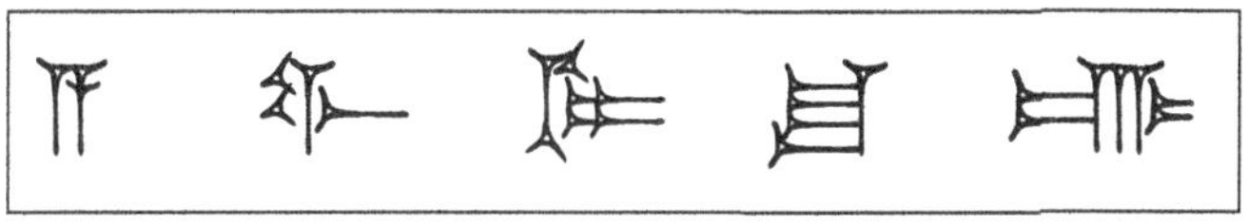

[9]*awīlum šū*

LH §20 IX:10

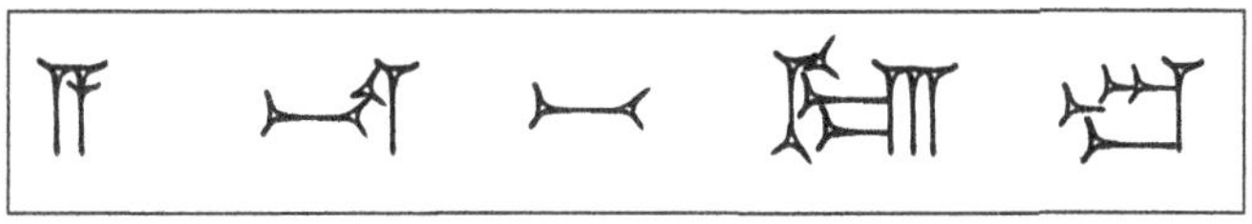

[10]*ana bêl wardim*

LH §20 IX:11

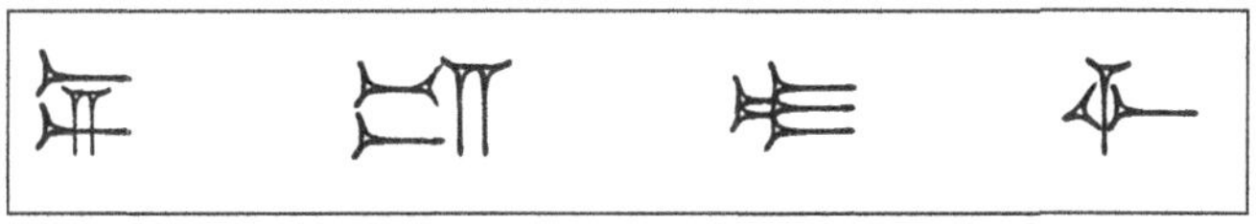

[11]*nîš ilim*

LH §20 IX:12

Note: The sign  in IX:12 is *kar*. This sign also appeared in LH §18 VIII: 61 but does not need to be learned.

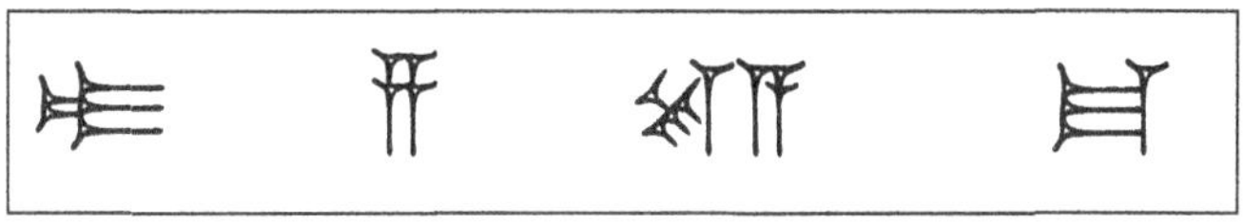

[12]*izakkarma*

LH §20 IX:13

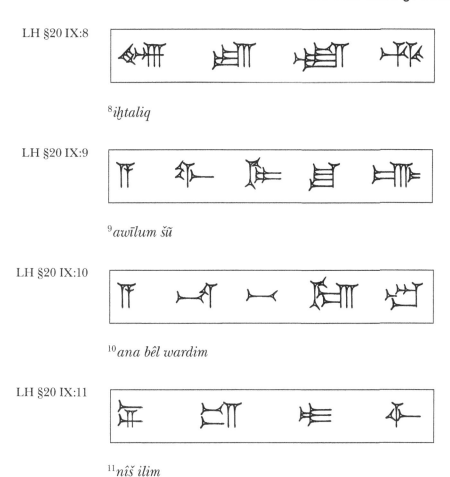

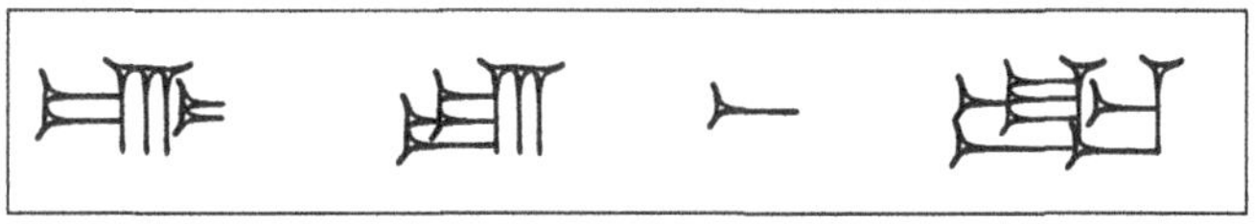

[13]*ûtaššar*

1. Grammatical Analysis: Parse all verb forms.

2. Translation: Translate LH §20.

16–𒌋𒐋

III-Weak Verbs and Conditionals

Following the laws in LH that concern false charges or a judge who changes his verdict (LH §§1–5) and the laws that concern the theft or misappropriation of property (LH §§6–13) or persons (LH §§14–20), there are the following groups of laws that will be skipped in this textbook:

LH §§21–25: Robbery, unsolved murder, and looting
LH §§26–41: Obligations of soldiers and other officials
LH §§42–56: Obligations of agricultural tenants
LH §§57–66: Obligations of shepherds, gardeners, and merchants
LH §§67–77(?): Obligations related to houses and land (neighbors, homeowners, landlords, merchants, and business partners)[1]
LH §§100–111: Additional obligations of merchants, brewers, and priestesses (with respect to taverns and the selling of alcohol)
LH §§112–26: Obligations of those who are entrusted with the property of others and loans.

It should be noted that the laws that came between the end of LH §65 and the beginning of LH §100 were deliberately erased by the Elamites from the stele now housed in the Louvre. The Elamites had taken the stele as booty from its original site, probably Sippar, and transported it to Susa in the twelfth century BCE. The Elamites erased about seven rows of columns on the front bottom of the stele, apparently in preparation for a new dedicatory inscription that was never added. It is estimated that approximately thirty laws were erased. Thankfully, many of these missing laws have now been reconstructed from surviving ancient copies of various portions of LH. Since, however, the exact number of missing laws is unknown, it is purely conventional to start the laws on the reverse side of the stele with LH §100.

The remaining chapters of this textbook will cover LH §§127–149, all of which involve laws regarding the family, especially women, sexual behavior, marriage, divorce, and inheritance. After this section, the remaining groups of laws that will be skipped in this textbook are as follows:

LH §§150–184: Additional familial themes regarding inheritance, a wife's debt, assaults and murder of family members, prohibited sexual relationships, estates, disinheritance, support for priestesses by brothers, etc.
LH §§185–195: Adoption and rebellious children
LH §§196–214: Injury and assault
LH §§215–240: Various professionals (physicians, veterinarians, barbers, builders, boatmen)
LH §§241–252: Farm animals
LH §§253–273: Agricultural labor and equipment

1. The enumeration of the laws between LH §65 and LH §100 is somewhat arbitrary, and many of the recovered laws (or portions of laws) are quite fragmentary.

LH §§274–277: Rates for tradesmen and for boats
LH §§278–282: Slaves unable to work

The grammar of this chapter covers III-weak verbs and conditionals.

16.1 III-Weak Verbs

Like I-weak and II-weak verbs, III-weak verbs can be described in historical terms based on the evidence of cognate Semitic languages. III-weak verbs are those that originally (in the Proto-Semitic period) had either *ʾ*, *h*, *ḥ*, *ʿ*, *ǵ*, *w*, or *y* as their third root consonant. All of these consonants became glottal stops, or *ʾaleph*'s, which in turn quiesced, resulting in compensatory lengthening.

As pointed out in §2.5.2.2, many Assyriologists stress how final non-tilde long vowels normally lose their length in a final open syllable. Other Assyriologists normalize these vowels as long, as is the practice of this textbook, since the length of these vowels is clearly retained when a suffix is added, such as *-ma*.[2] So, even if only for didactic purposes, it will be a useful practice to mark these vowels as long. In the case of III-weak verbs, this means that these vowels will usually be circumflex long (*v̂*) because of compensatory lengthening, even if it appears likely that in actual pronunciation these vowels were shortened when in final open syllables.

16.1.1 ***III-Weak Verb Examples.***[3] III-weak verbs are categorized according to the four vowel classes: *-i*, which is the most common option, but also *-u*, *-a*, and *-e*. III-weak verbs are also attested in the various derived stems, but the paradigm examples below should be sufficient for working out the remaining forms as needed.

Stem	Class	Durative 3cs	Perfect 3cs	Preterite 3cs/3mp	Participle ms	Verbal Adjective ms	Stative 3ms	Infinitive ms
G		*iparras*	*iptaras*	*iprus/iprusū*	*pārisum*	*parsum*	*paris*	*parāsum*
	i	***ibannî***	***ibtanî***	***ibnî/ibnû***	***bānûm***	***banûm***	***banî***	***banûm***
	u	***imannû***	***imtanû***	***imnû/imnû***	***mānûm***	***manûm***	***manî/û***	***manûm***
	a	***imallâ***	***imtalâ***	***imlâ/imlû***	***mālûm***	***malûm***	***malî***	***malûm***
	e	***ileqqê***	***ilteqê***	***ilqê/ilqû***	***lēqûm***	***leqûm***	***leqî***	***leqûm***
Gt		*iptarras*	*iptatras*	*iptaras*	*muptarsum*	*pitrusum*	*pitrus*	*pitrusum*
Gtn		*iptanarras*	*iptatarras*	*iptarras*	*muptarrisum*	*pitarrusum*	*pitarrus*	*pitarrusum*
D		*uparras*	*uptarris*	*uparris*	*muparrisum*	*purrusum*	*purrus*	*purrusum*
		ubannâ	***ubtannî***	***ubannî***	***mubannûm***	***bunnûm***	***bunnû***	***bunnûm***
Dt		*uptarras*	*uptatarris*	*uptarris*	*muptarrisum*	*putarrusum*	*putarrus*	*putarrusum*
Dtn		*uptanarras*	*uptatarris*	*uptarris*	*muptarrisum*	*putarrusum*	*putarrus*	*putarrusum*

(continued)

2. Kouwenberg (*The Akkadian Verb and Its Semitic Background*, §16.7.2.1) normalizes these final vowels as long in "the original paradigm" and argues that they are long for both structural and historical reasons. He summarizes the evidence for the subsequent shortening of these final vowels when in open syllables "if only to create a contrast with vowels that are long through vowel contraction." This textbook accomplishes the same objective through its practice of distinguishing three forms of vowel length.

3. Although the particular verbs used in this chart are attested in some of the forms as indicated, they are not attested in all of them. Other III-weak verbs, however, confirm the remaining forms.

Stem	Class	Durative 3cs	Perfect 3cs	Preterite 3cs/3mp	Participle ms	Verbal Adjective ms	Stative 3ms	Infinitive ms
Š		*ušapras*	*uštapris*	*ušapris*	*mušaprisum*	*šuprusum*	*šuprus*	*šuprusum*
		ušabnâ	***uštabnî***	***ušabnî***	***mušabnûm***	***šubnûm***	***šubnû***	***šubnûm***
Št		*uštapras/ uštaparras*	*uštatapris*	*uštapris*	*muštaprisum*	*šutaprusum*	*šutaprus*	*šutaprusum*
Štn		*uštanapras*	*uštatapris*	*uštapris*	*muštaprisum*	*šutaprusum*	*šutaprus*	*šutaprusum*
N		*ipparras*	*ittapras*	*ipparis*	*mupparsum*	*naprusum*	*naprus*	*naprusum*
	i	***ibbannî***	***ittabnî***	***ibbanî***	***mubbanûm***	***nabnûm***	***nabnû***	***nabnûm***
	u	***immannû***	***ittamnû***	***immanî***	***mummanûm***	***namnûm***	***namnû***	***namnûm***
	a	***immallâ***	***ittamlâ***	***immalî***	***mummalûm***	***namlûm***	***namlû***	***namlûm***
	e	***illeqqê***	***ittelqê***	***illeqî***	***mulleqûm***	***nelqûm***	***nelqû***	***nelqûm***
Nt		unattested or exceedingly rare						
Ntn		*ittanapras*	*ittatapras*	*ittapras*	*muttaprisum*	*itaprusum*	*itaprus*	*itaprusum*

16.1.2 ***Parsing III-Weak Verbs.*** Students do not need to memorize the verb forms above, but they do need to remember the main patterns and understand how these III-weak verbs were formed so that they can correctly produce or parse any of the forms in bold. The following practical observations should enable students to accomplish this goal.

1. There are four vowel classes of III-weak verbs that affect their forms in the G-stem and N-stem only.

As mentioned earlier, at least from a historical perspective, the original vowel classes of III-weak verbs were likely derived from a particular III-weak consonant that quiesced. In general:

III-*y* verbs became *i*-class
III-*w* verbs became *u*-class
III-ʾ or -*h* verbs became *a*-class
III-*ḥ*, ʿ, or *ġ*, verbs became *e*-class.

Unfortunately, this reasonable and attractive picture breaks down at many points. While the theory explains all the *a*-class and *e*-class verbs for which we have a reliable etymology, and while it likely explains all the verbs that were III-*y*, it does little to help explain the vowel class of a majority of the verbs. This is the case because of two factors. First, for many verbs there is no reliable evidence for their original III-root consonant.[4] Second, it is apparent that many III-weak verbs, whatever their original vowel class, assimilated to the increasingly dominant *i*-class paradigm. As will be seen in the list below of all III-weak verbs attested in LH, the majority (almost two-thirds) are *i*-class.

4. In the accompanying list (§16.4.1), attention is limited mainly to Hebrew cognates for these III-weak verbs. More evidence is available from other cognate languages, but unless the student knows these they will be of no help remembering or determining the vowel class of any particular III-weak root.

2. The vowel class of a III-weak verb determines the final vowel of the 3cs form of the G-stem and N-stem durative, perfect, preterite, and stative forms. The vowel class of a III-weak verb has no influence on its D-stem or Š-stem forms.

3. Nearly all forms of III-weak verbs can be generated from the corresponding forms of the strong verb paradigm (*parāsum*) if two things are kept in mind:

a. One can often guess the vowel class of a verb, but because of many exceptions it needs either to be learned as a part of vocabulary acquisition or confirmed by consulting a lexicon.

b. If the III-root consonant of the appropriate form of the strong verb (*parāsum*) closes a syllable, the vowel that reflects it in the corresponding III-weak verb form will be circumflex long (v̂) because of compensatory lengthening. If the III-root consonant of the strong verb has a vowel following it, the vowel that reflects it in the corresponding III-weak verb form will be tilde long (ṽ) because of vowel contraction.

4. There are two additional issues to watch out for. First, the G-stem stative (*paris*) for a III-weak verb like *banũm* is normally *banî* (< **bani'* < **baniy*). The one exception occurs in some *u*-class verbs, like *manũm*, where the G-stem stative (*paris*) is *manû*.[5] Second, because of Babylonian vowel harmony (§3.4.3), every *a*-vowel in the strong verb paradigm will be, with only few exceptions, an analogous form of an *e*-vowel for *e*-class verbs. For example, the G-stem infinitive (*parāsum*) of *e*-class *leqũm*, "to take, receive," is *leqũm*, rather than *laqũm*, as would otherwise be the case.

16.1.3 *Parsing Examples of III-Weak Verb Forms*

Example 1: G-stem 3cs durative of *tamũm* (*a*-class), "to swear"

Step 1: Start with the G-stem 3cs durative of the strong verb *parāsum*. The desired form is *iparras*, "he would decide."

Step 2: Substitute the three root consonants of the III-weak verb *tamũm* for the form *iparras*. For the missing third root use '. The result is **itamma'*.

Step 3: In the G-stem and N-stem, replace the second vowel of the strong verb paradigm (*a*) with the vowel of the vowel class of the III-weak verb. In this case, the vowel class of *tamũm* is *a*-class. The result is, again, **itamma'*.

Step 4: Allow the ' to quiesce, which will cause compensatory lengthening of the theme vowel: **itamma'* > *itammâ*, "[the man] would swear," which is found in LH §206.

Example 2: N-stem 3cs durative of *ḫepũm* (*e*-class), "to smash, destroy"

Step 1: Start with the N-stem 3cs durative of the strong verb *parāsum*. The desired form is *ipparras*, "it was destroyed."

Step 2: Substitute the three root consonants of the III-weak verb *ḫepũm* for the form *ipparas*. For the missing third root use '. The result is: *iḫḫappa'*.

5. This may reflect the fact that of all the weak root consonants, *w* seems to have been the last to quiesce, so its influence is stronger.

Step 3: In the G-stem and N-stem, replace the second vowel of the strong verb paradigm (*a*) with the vowel of the vowel class of the III-weak verb. In this case, the vowel class of *ḫepûm* is *e*-class. The result is **iḫḫappe'*. Since this is an *e*-class verb, there will also be Babylonian vowel harmony for any *a*-vowel nearby. As a result, **iḫḫappe'* becomes **iḫḫeppe'*.

Step 4: Allow the ' to quiesce, which will cause compensatory lengthening of the theme vowel: **iḫḫeppe'* > **iḫḫeppê*, "it [the tablet] would be smashed," which is found in LH §37.

16.1.4 ***III-Weak Verbs in LH.*** The following is a list of III-weak verbs attested in LH. These do not need to be learned except as they appear in the required vocabulary in this and other chapters. They are listed here for easy reference.

apûm/wapûm (*i*) = to be visible, appear (cf. *hiphil* of *yp*', יפע, "to cause to shine [forth])

arum/warûm (*u*) = (<**u*"*rum*) to lead

aṣûm/waṣûm (*i*) = to go out (cf. *yāṣā'*, יָצָא)

balûm/ belûm (*i*) = to be extinguished (cf. *bālâ*, בָּלָה, "to be worn out")

banûm (*i*) = to make, build (cf. *bānâ*, בָּנָה)

bašûm (*i*) = to exist, be (cf. *bə*, בְּ, "in" + *šû*, "it")

dekûm (*e*) = to stir up, raise

egûm (*i/u*) = to be careless, negligent (cf. *yāga*', יָגַע, "to toil, be weary")

elûm (*i*) = to go up, ascend (cf. '*ālâ*, עָלָה)

enûm (*i*) = to change, exchange (cf. '*ānâ*, עָנָה, "answer")

ešûm (*i*) = to confuse

ḫepûm (*e*) = to smash, destroy

idûm/edûm (*e*) = to know (cf. *yāda*', יָדַע)

kalûm (*a*) = to retain, detain, withhold (cf. *kālā'*, כָּלָא, "to restrain, withhold")

kasûm (*u/i*) = to bind (cf. *kəsût*, כְּסוּת, "covering")

leqûm (*e*) = to take, receive (cf. *lāqaḥ*, לָקַח)

le'ûm (*i*) = to be able

malûm (*a*) = to be full (cf. *mālē'*, מָלֵא)

manûm (*u*) = to count, reckon, recount (cf. *mānâ*, מָנָה)

maṣûm (*i*), = to be equal to, be sufficient for (cf. *māṣā'*, מָצָא, "to find")

maṭûm (*i*) = to be small (cf. *mə'aṭ*, מְעַט, "little")

nabûm (*i*) = to name, invoke (cf. *nābî'*, נָבִיא, "prophet")

nadûm (*i*) = to throw, hurl, accuse (lay a charge of), leave (cf. *niddâ*, נִדָּה; *piel*: "to push away")

našûm (*i*) = to lift, carry, bear; to support (cf. *nāśā'*, נָשָׂא)

naṭûm (*u*) = to hit, beat

nepûm (*e*) = to take as pledge, seize

ni'ālum (*i*)/ *nālum* (*a*) = to lie down, sleep; Gt: *itūlum/utūlum*, to lie down together, sleep together

peḫûm (*e*) = to close, shut, caulk

petûm (*e*) = to open (cf. *pātaḥ*, פָּתַח)

qabûm (*i*) = to speak, declare, order

qalûm (*i*) = to burn (down), roast, refine (cf. *qālâ*, קָלָה, "to roast")

qamûm (*i*) = to set on fire

qatûm (*i*) = to come to an end, finish

rabûm (*i*) = to be great (cf. *rābâ*, רָבָה)

raqûm (*i*) = to hide, give refuge to

rašûm (*i*) = to have, own, acquire; Š: to provide

redûm (*e,e*)/(*i,i*) = to lead, send; *ventive*: bring (cf. *rādâ*, רָדָה, "to rule")

re'ûm (*i*) = to tend, pasture, graze (cf. *rā'â*, רָעָה)

ṣamûm (*u*) = to thirst (cf. *ṣāmā'*, צָמָא)

ṣebûm (*i*) = D: to observe, inspect, check; Roth: to make conform to specifications

šalûm (*i*) = to plunge, immerse

šanûm (*i*) = to do again, repeat; Š: to double (cf. *šānâ*, שָׁנָה)

šapûm (*u*) = to be silent

šaqûm (*u*) = to be high, tall

šasûm (*i*) = to shout, cry out
šemûm (*e*) = to hear (cf. *šāma'*, שָׁמַע)
še'ûm (*i/e*) = to search (cf. *šā'â*, שָׁעָה, "to gaze, look at")
tamûm (byform of *wamûm*) (*a*) = to swear
tebûm (*i*) = to rise up, revolt (cf. Ugaritic *tb'*)
ṭebûm (*u*) = to sink (cf. *ṭāba'*, טָבַע, "to sink down")
ṭeḫûm (*e*) = to go near

16.2 Conditionals

As is now familiar, conditional sentences have a protasis, an "if" clause. Outside LH, protases are often unmarked and linked to their apodoses by semantics and especially by the enclitic *-ma*, which is used to imply logical consecution (if . . . then).

Within LH, however, protases are almost invariably introduced with the explicit conditional particle *šumma*, "if." Normally, any subsequent conditions before the apodosis (within the same law) are unmarked. A plausible example of this practice was encountered earlier in LH §9: VI:70 "If a man found his lost property in the hand of [another] man, [and if] the man in whose hand the lost property was found declared 'a seller sold it to me. . . .'"

There are many exceptions to this, however. Most of these involve instances where the protasis is long, complicated, or interrupted, and the use of one or more additional *šumma*s provides needed clarity. An important variation on this are laws where a general condition is first introduced by *šumma*, and this then is followed by a series of alternative subsidiary conditions, which may be linked to alternative protases.

For example, in LH §8 *šumma* is repeated five times. In its first appearance *šumma* introduces a case where a man has stolen any one of five valuable items. This is then followed by a series of important qualifications: "if [*šumma*] this (stolen item) belonged to a god or if [*šumma*] this belonged to the palace, he would repay thirtyfold." After this an alternative situation is taken up: "if [*šumma*] it belonged to a civil servant, he would repay tenfold." The law concludes by taking up the case where no repayment is possible: "if [*šumma*] the thief has nothing with which to repay, he would be executed."

Conditional sentences also have an apodosis, a "then" clause," which in LH is usually unmarked (there is no word for "then"). Nevertheless, grammatical considerations reinforced by semantics leave little room for doubt about what is the protasis and what is the apodosis. Most conditionals in LH have preterite verbs in their protases. In a sequence of such clauses, which are usually linked to each other with an enclitic *-ma* that implies logical or chronological order, the last one or two verbs are often perfects. In this context the perfect is chosen to imply that the clause is the most decisive condition or an immediate past condition on which the apodosis crucially depends.

Although apodoses in LH tend to be unmarked, the last verb in each protasis that is introduced with *šumma* stands out because it lacks a *-ma* suffix.[6] Furthermore, any finite verbs in an apodosis tend to be duratives, which express what would or should happen as a

6. This is curiously in contrast to the practice with unmarked conditionals (ones that lack *šumma*), as mentioned earlier. There is one notable exception to the rule about *šumma* clauses not ending with an enclitic *-ma*. This apparent exception appears in Roth gap ¶ v, *Law Collections from Mesopotamia and Asia Minor*, 98. In that law the verb that closes the protasis is *ilteqêma*, "he took (then)," which is followed by the apodosis. Not much weight should be placed on this one exception, however, since the original text was erased on the stele, and this term appears in a reconstruction from later copies which remain, for this law, demonstrably incomplete. Furthermore, it is possible that the enclitic *-ma* in this case may not have been intended as a conjunction but as a topicalizing particle. See §3.4.

consequence of the conditions that are stipulated in the protasis. If there is a durative in the protasis, it usually expresses not future or stipulated action but repetitive or habitual action or action that is merely potential, intended, or wished. For example, LH §274 begins, "If a man *was intending to* hire [*iggar*, G-stem durative of *agārum*, "to hire"] a craftsman. . . ."[7]

Finally, rarely an apodosis may be marked by the conjunction *u*, which in this circumstance can be translated "then."[8] Interestingly, this use of *u* reflects what is a common practice in Hebrew, where *w*, ו, often introduces an apodosis.[9]

It is notable that within LH, *u* as a conjunction between clauses is most often found within apodoses. The implication of this is, in contrast to the use of the conjunction *-ma*, that the listed consequences are not necessarily specified in chronological order. In LH §5, for example, the guilty judge would pay a twelve-fold fine and (*u*) he would be removed from office, but these penalties could be accomplished in either order.

16.3 Homework

Before you move on, be sure to understand the general rules associated with the formation of III-weak verbs. Also, familiarize yourself with the III-weak verb list and learn the vowel class of each verb. Finally, be aware of marked and unmarked conditional sentences and how to translate them.

16.3.1 *Signs*

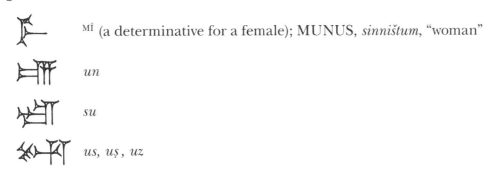

 MÍ (a determinative for a female); MUNUS, *sinništum*, "woman"

 *un*

 *su*

 *us*, *uṣ*, *uz*

Congratulations! If you have learned the four cuneiform signs in this chapter and each of the preceding 106 signs, you will be able to read 96 percent of all the cuneiform signs in LH §§1–20, 127–149.

16.3.2 *Vocabulary*

aḫāzum (*a,u*) = to take, take in marriage (used only of the man), take sexually (cf. *ʾāḥaz*, אָחַז, "to grasp, take")
aššatum (< *ʾ-*n*-*š*) = wife (cf. *ʾiššâ*, אִשָּׁה)
balāṭum (*u,u*) = to live; D: let live, spare (through dissimilation, cf. *pālaṭ*, פָּלַט, "to escape")

7. Outside LH, conditionals are frequently expressed without the use of *šumma*, and often they employ a durative in both the protasis, where it expresses a modal sense, and the apodosis, where it expresses the consequence: "*should* x happen or be the case, then y *will* happen." Cf. Huehnergard, *A Grammar of Akkadian*, §17.3.

8. This use of *u* occurs only once in LH (LH §129), but it is more common elsewhere according to Driver and Miles, *The Babylonian Laws*, 2:214.

9. Cf. Joüon-Muraoka, "The *Waw* of Apodosis" in *A Grammar of Biblical Hebrew*, §176d.

mūm (*plurale tantum*); *mē* (< **ma'i*) (oblique and construct) = water (cf. *mayim*, מַיִם)
muttatum = half (of hair)
ni'ālum (*i*), *nālum* (*a*) = to lie down, sleep; Gt: lie down together, sleep together (cf. possible cognates with dissimilation: *lîn*, לִין, "to spend the night"; *laylâ*, לַיְלָה, "night")
sinništum [MUNUS] = woman, female; MÍ, a determinative for a female
šanūm = another, a second (cf. *šēnî*, שֵׁנִי, "second")
tarāṣum (*a,u*) = to extend, stretch out; Š: point
ubânum (< *'-*b*-*h*-*n*) = finger (cf. *bōhen*, בֹּהֶן)
zikarum = man, a male (cf. *zākār*, זָכָר)

16.3.3 *Exercises*

The ten text boxes labeled XXVIII (Rv. V): 25–34 comprise LH §127. The law treats the matter of someone who makes a false charge of infidelity against a priestess or a wife. The penalty for such a false charge is corporal punishment and public humiliation.

1. Transliterate and Normalize: See the notes below for additional help.

LH §127 XXVIII (Rv. V):25

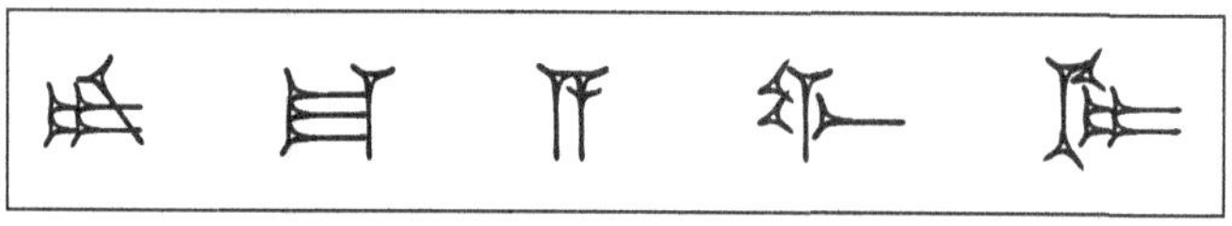

LH §127 XXVIII (Rv. V):26
Note: The sign 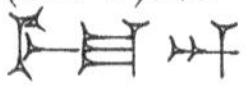 in XXVIII (Rv. V):26 is NIN.DINGIR, *ugbabtum*, meaning "priestess." An *ugbabtum* was often a daughter of a king or other socially ranked person. This sign and the word *ugbabtum* do not need to be learned.

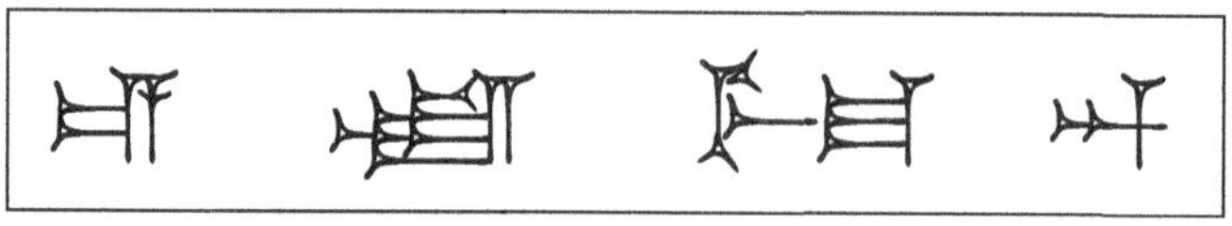

LH §127 XXVIII (Rv. V):27

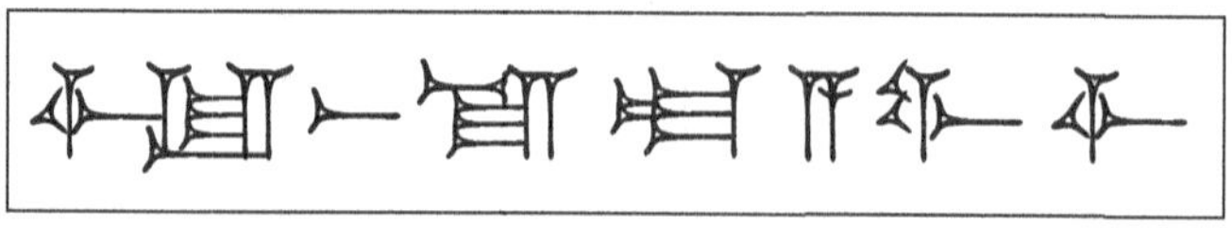

LH §127 XXVIII (Rv. V):28

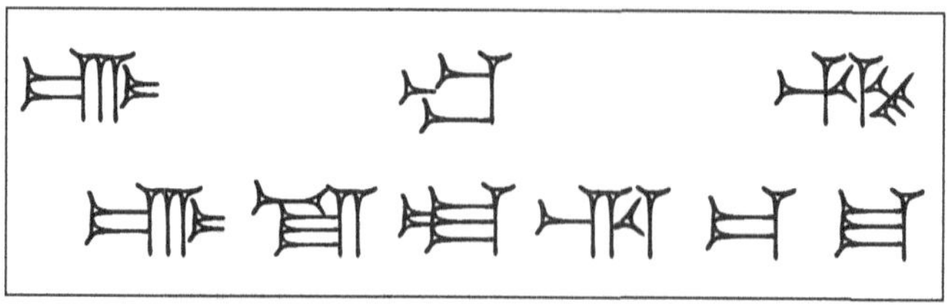

LH §127 XXVIII (Rv. V):29

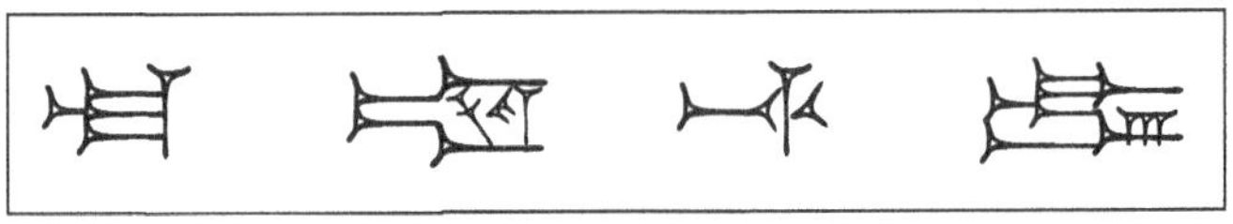

LH §127 XXVIII (Rv. V):30

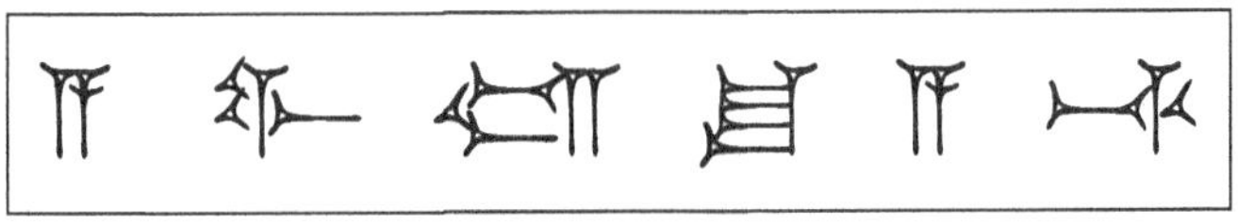

LH §127 XXVIII (Rv. V):31

Note: The sign  in XXVIII (Rv. V):31 is *ḫar*. This does not need to be learned.

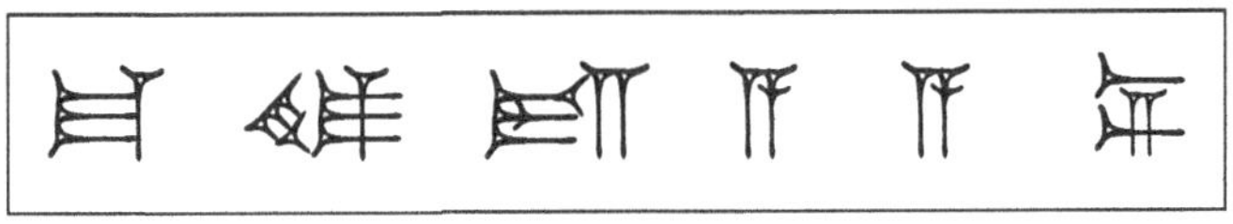

LH §127 XXVIII (Rv. V):32

Note: The sign 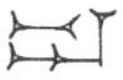 in XXVIII (Rv. V):32 is normally used for *du*, but perhaps here (and in LH §72) it is used for *ṭù*. For now, maintain both readings, as well as *ad* and *aṭ* for 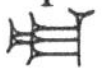 in the same text box. Be sure to answer the related question below while analyzing the grammar.

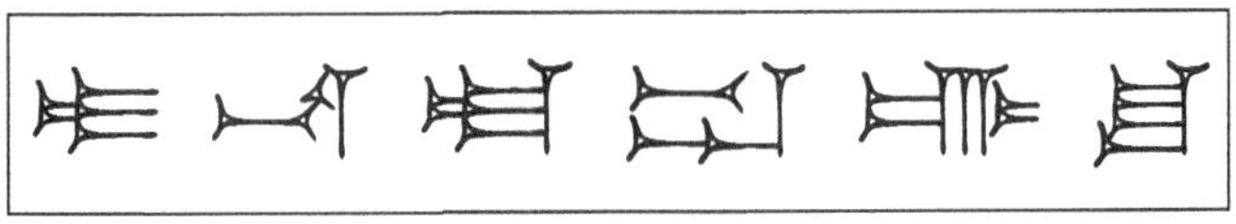

LH §127 XXVIII (Rv. V):33

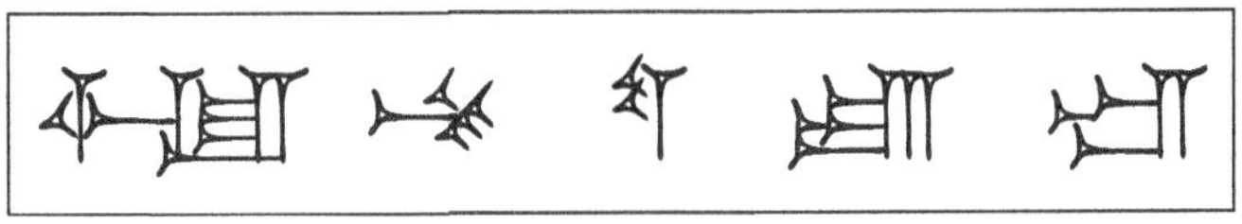

LH §127 XXVIII (Rv. V):34

Note: The sign  in XXVIII (Rv. V):34 is *gal*. This sign does not need to be learned.

2. Grammatical Analysis: Parse all verb forms. See the notes below.

   Note: Text box XXVIII (Rv. V):32 may represent two different verbs. One form may be from the II-weak verb *naṭūm* (*i,i*) (*u,u*), meaning "to beat." The other word has already been learned in the vocabulary lists of this grammar. What is it? Parse both verbs. What contextual considerations are there that might favor one verb over the other?

   Note: The form in XXVIII (Rv. V):34 is from *galābum*. In the D-stem it means "to shave, cut off" (cf. *gallāb*, גַּלָּב, "barber"). This word does not need to be learned.

3. Translation: Translate LH §127.

The seven text boxes labeled XXVIII (Rv. V): 35–41 comprise LH §128. The law implicitly prohibits common law marriage. A woman is not a "wife" apart from a legal marriage contract.

1. Transliterate and Normalize: See the note below for additional help.

LH §128 XXVIII (Rv. V):35

LH §128 XXVIII (Rv. V):36

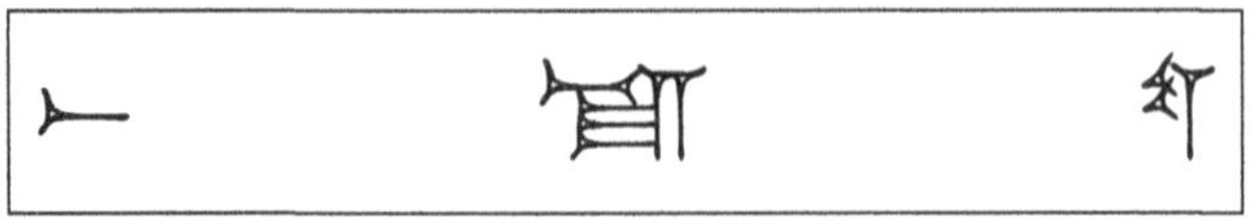

LH §128 XXVIII (Rv. V):37

LH §128 XXVIII (Rv. V):38

Note: The sign  in XXVIII (Rv. V):38 is *sa*. This does not need to be learned at this point. It will be learned in Chapter 19.

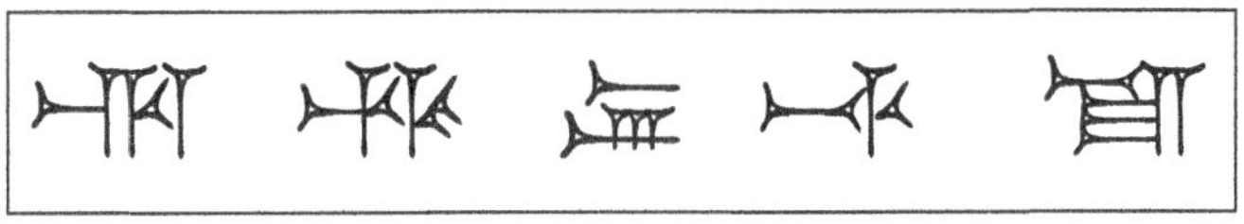

LH §128 XXVIII (Rv. V):39

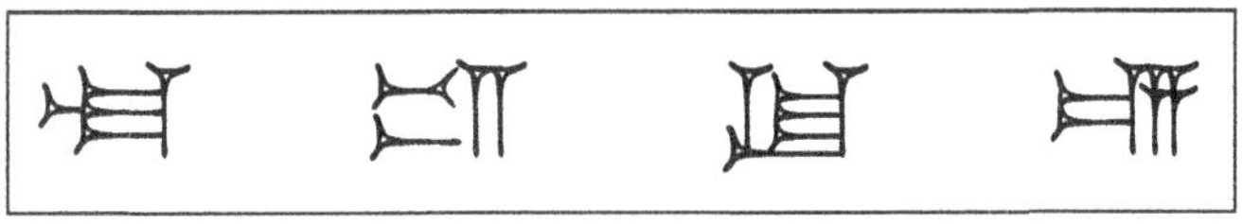

LH §128 XXVIII (Rv. V):40

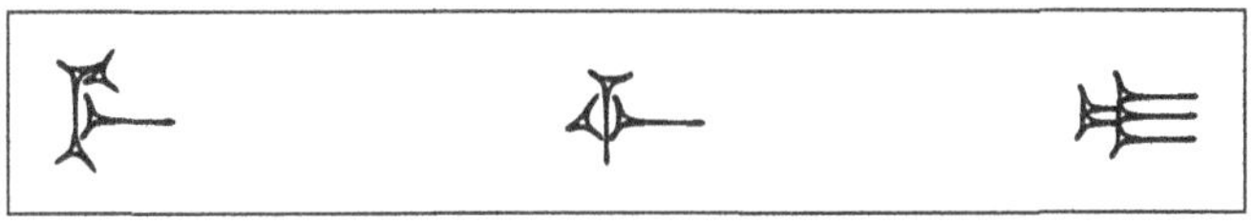

LH §128 XXVIII (Rv. V):41

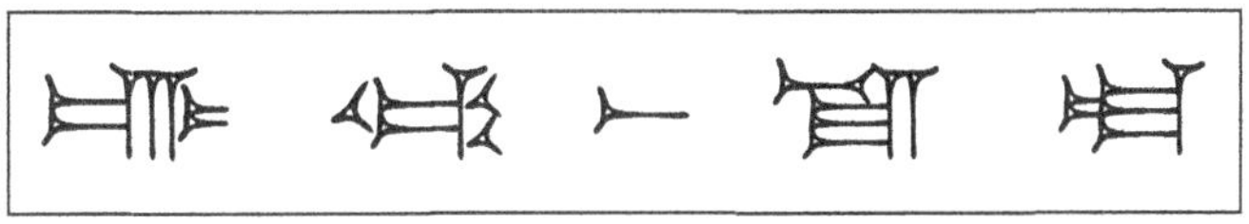

2. Grammatical Analysis: Parse all verb forms and answer the questions below.

    a. What is surprising about the negative particle in XXVIII (Rv. V):41, and how can this be explained?

    b. Identify the form of the last word in XXVIII (Rv. V):41.

3. Translation: Translate LH §128.

The twelve text boxes labeled LH §129 XXVIII (Rv. V): 42–53 comprise LH §129. The law establishes what is to be done to adulterers who are caught in the act: they are to be drowned together. The law, however, allows the offended husband the right to spare his wife's life, but it insists on the same leniency toward the offending man.

1. Transliterate and Normalize.

LH §129 XXVIII (Rv. V):42

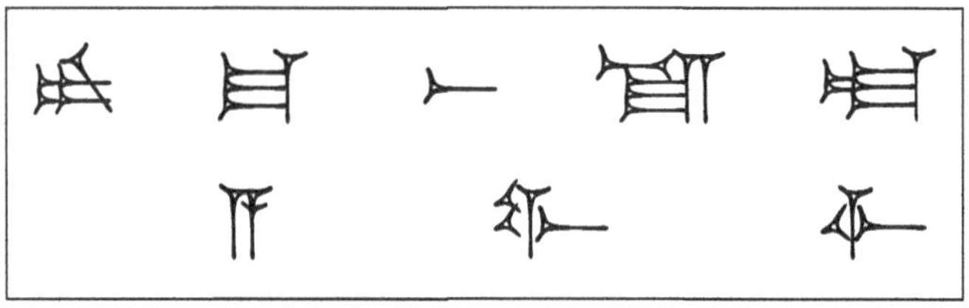

LH §129 XXVIII (Rv. V):43

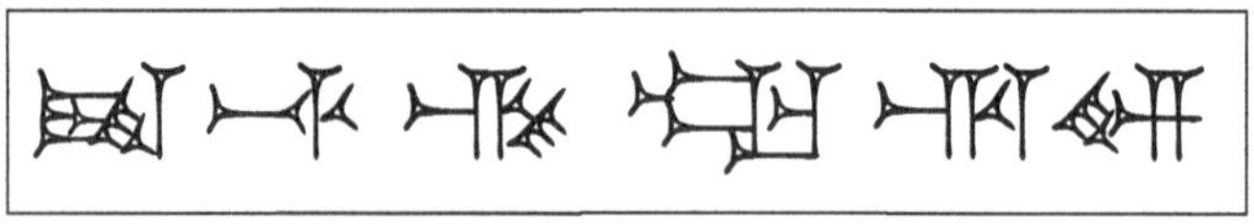

LH §129 XXVIII (Rv. V):44

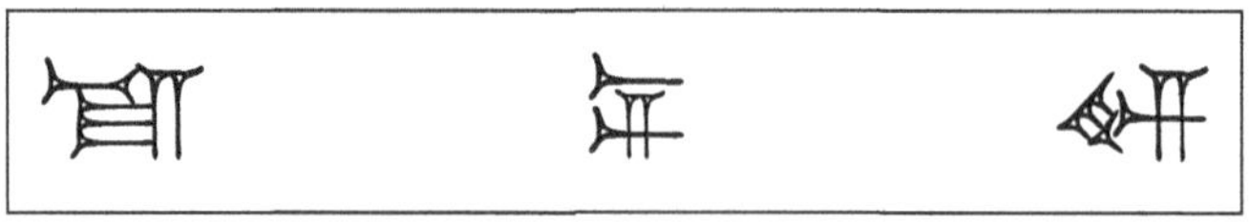

LH §129 XXVIII (Rv. V):45

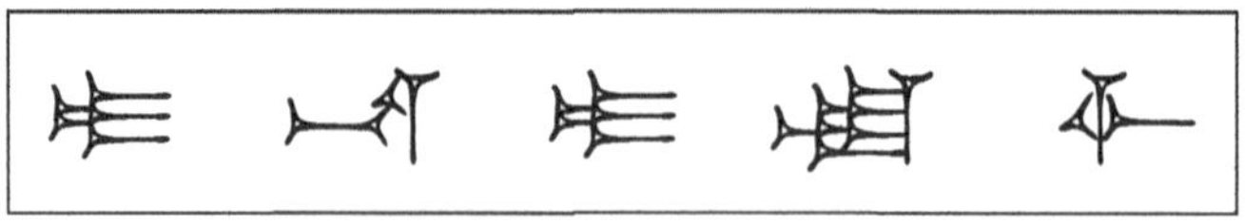

LH §129 XXVIII (Rv. V):46

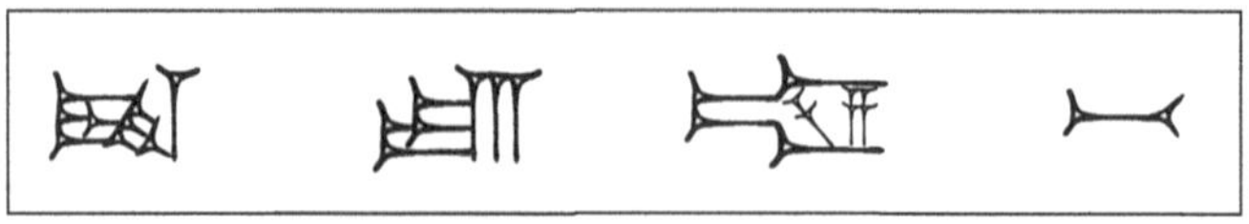

LH §129 XXVIII (Rv. V):47

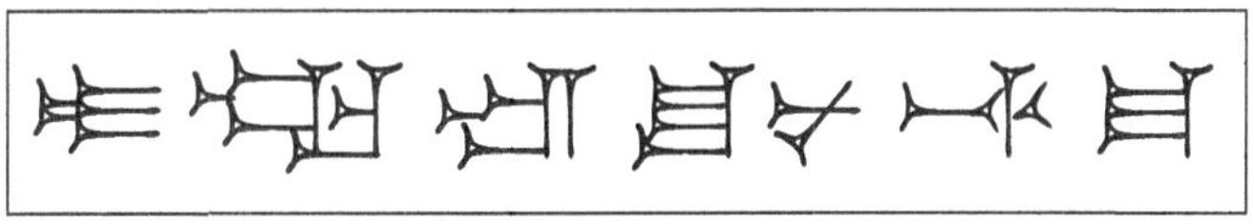

LH §129 XXVIII (Rv. V):48

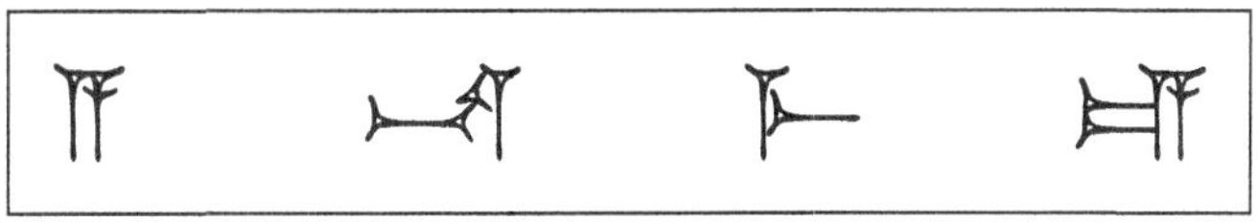

LH §129 XXVIII (Rv. V):49

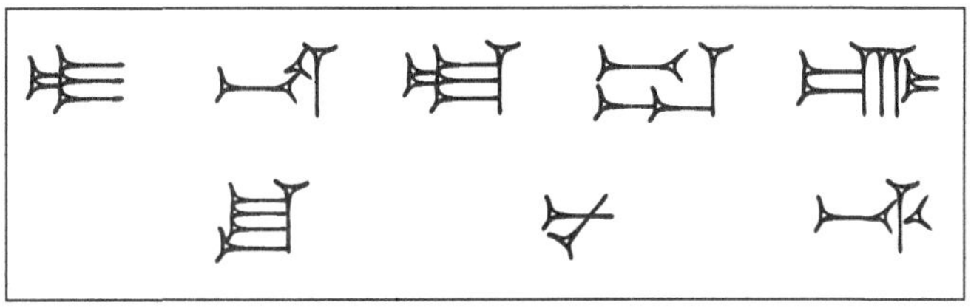

LH §129 XXVIII (Rv. V):50

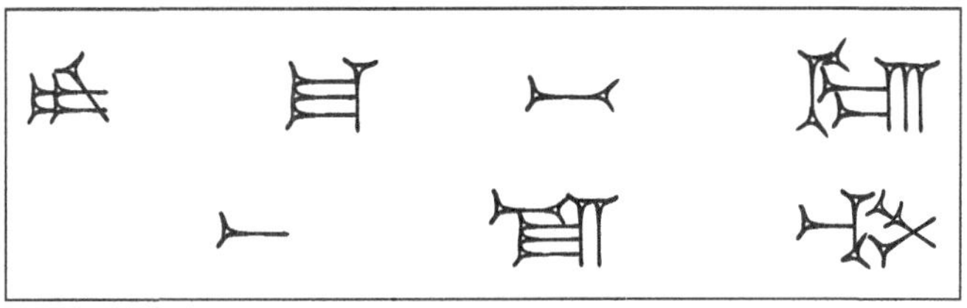

LH §129 XXVIII (Rv. V):51

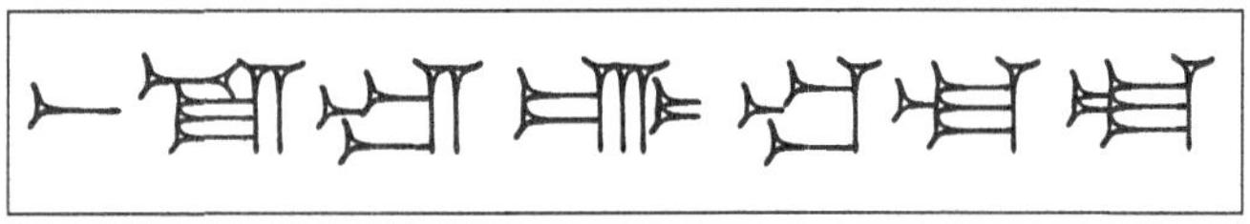

LH §129 XXVIII (Rv. V):52

LH §129 XXVIII (Rv. V):53

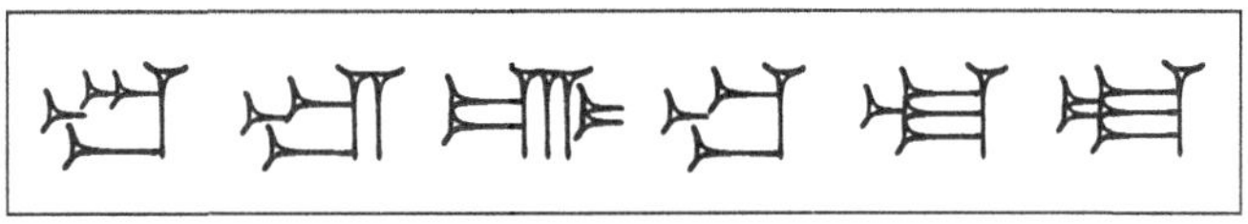

2. Grammatical Analysis: Parse all verb forms and answer the questions below. See the note below for help.

   a. What is unusual about the spelling of the noun in XXVIII (Rv. V):43, and how may it be explained?

   b. What is the function of the conjunction in XXVIII (Rv. V):52?

   Note: The form in XXVIII (Rv. V):47 is from *kasûm* (*u/i*), meaning "to bind" (cf. *kəsût*, כְּסוּת, "covering, clothing"). This word does not need to be learned.

3. Translation: Translate LH §129.

The fourteen text boxes labeled XXVIII (Rv. V): 54–67 comprise LH §130. The law demands execution for a man who rapes an inchoately married woman and stipulates that the victim is innocent of all charges.[10]

1. Transliterate and Normalize: See the note below for additional help.

LH §130 XXVIII (Rv. V):54

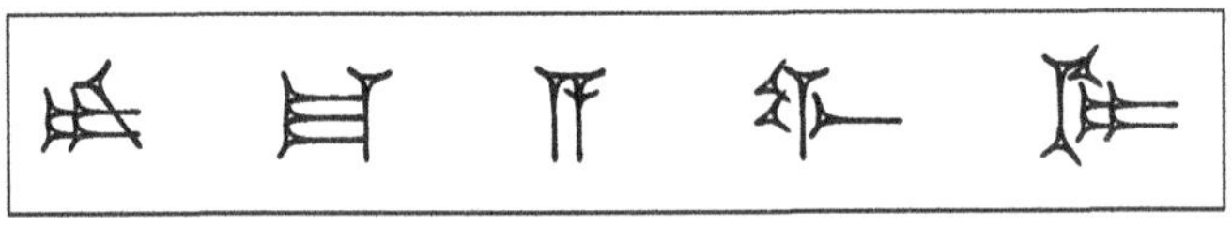

LH §130 XXVIII (Rv. V):55

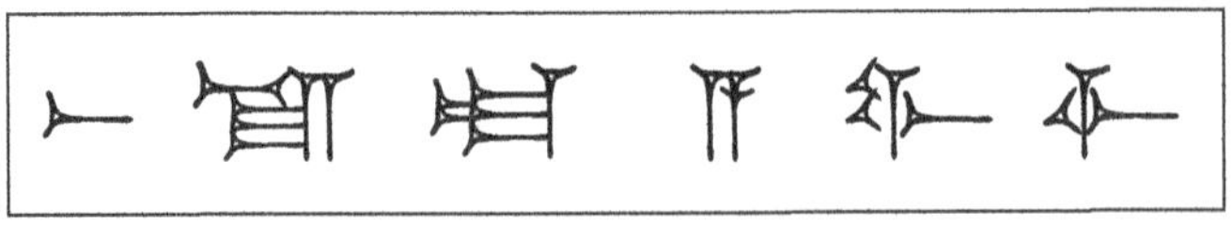

10. "Inchoately married" is a term introduced by G. R. Driver and J. C. Miles (*The Babylonian Laws*, vol. 1 [Oxford: Clarendon Press, 1952; 245–65] to describe a common first stage of marriage in the ancient Near East. This term refers to when a man and a woman are solemnly promised to each other in marriage, often by means of written contracts between the groom and the father or guardian of the bride and/or by the groom giving a *terḫatu(m)/mōhar* [מֹהַר], a "betrothal present" (often incorrectly rendered as "bride-price"), to the guardian or father of the bride. An inchoate marriage frequently took place before the bride was sexually mature and while still living in her father's home. Nevertheless, although the marriage was not yet consummated in sexual union and the couple was not yet living together, they were already described as husband [*bêl aššatim*] and wife [*aššatum*] (LH §161). Consequently, any sexual infidelity, especially on the part of the wife (the concern of the ancient Near Eastern texts), was viewed as an act of adultery. For more details, cf. §18.4 below.

LH §130 XXVIII (Rv. V):56

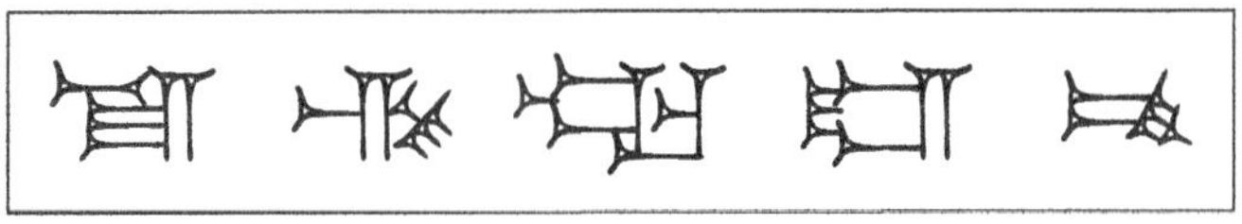

LH §130 XXVIII (Rv. V):57

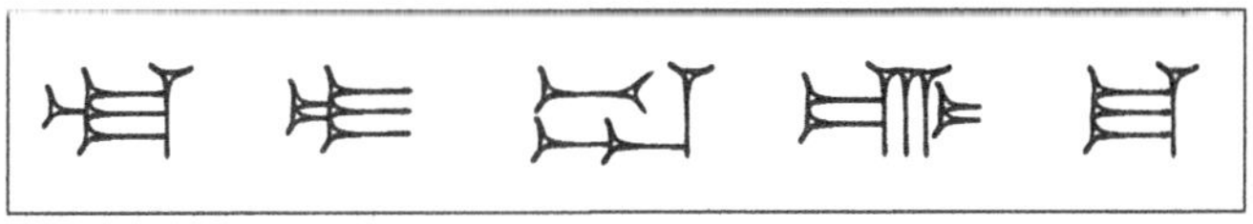

LH §130 XXVIII (Rv. V):58

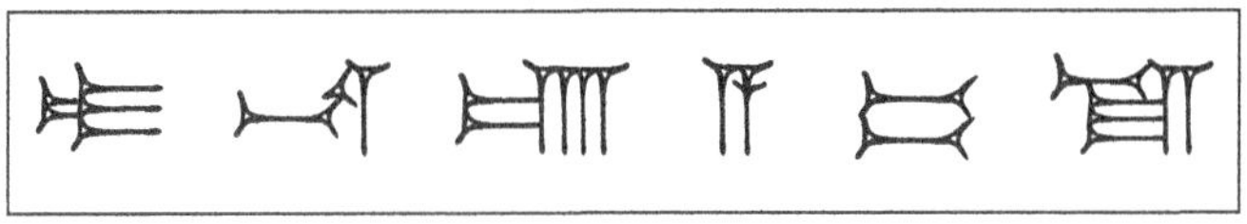

LH §130 XXVIII (Rv. V):59

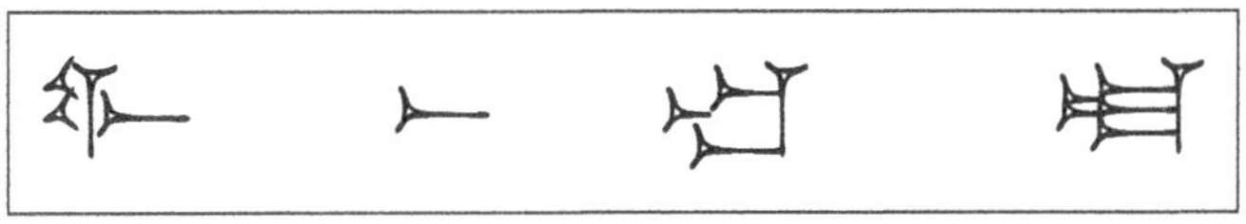

LH §130 XXVIII (Rv. V):60

Note: The signs  and 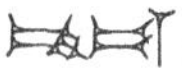 in XXVIII (Rv. V):60 are *kab* and *bíl* respectively. These signs do not need to be learned.

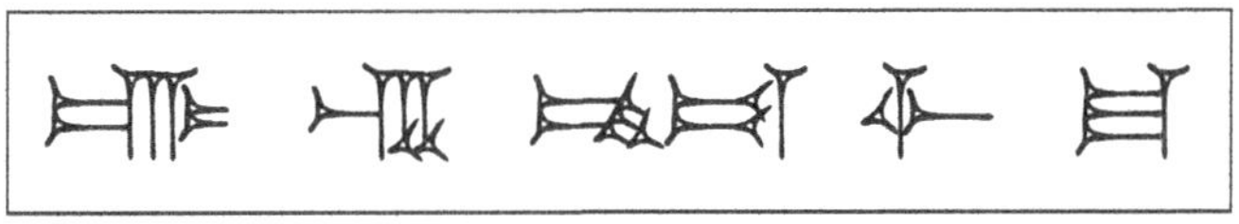

LH §130 XXVIII (Rv. V):61

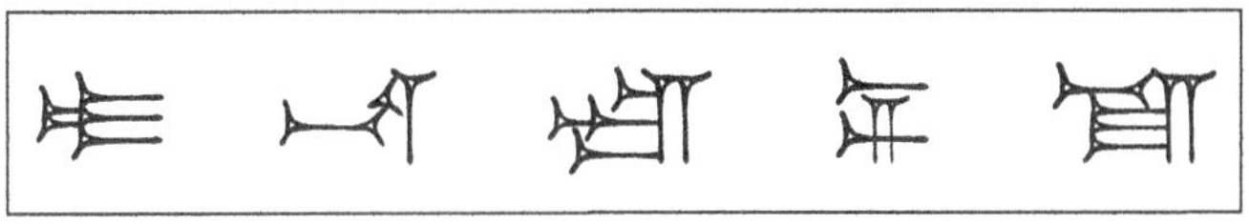

LH §130 XXVIII (Rv. V):62

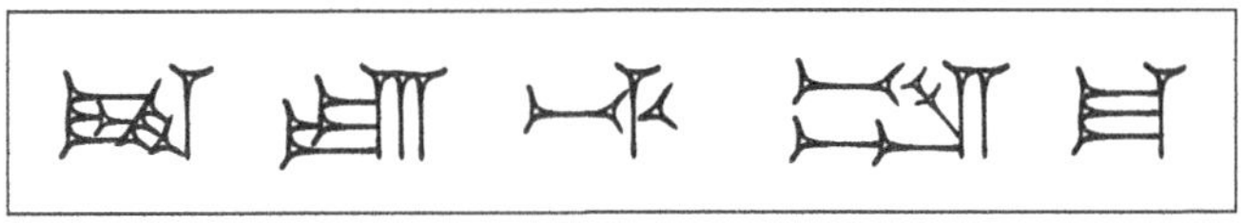

LH §130 XXVIII (Rv. V):63

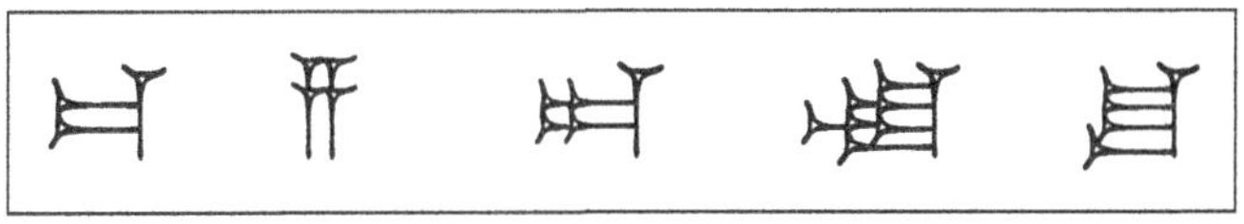

LH §130 XXVIII (Rv. V):64

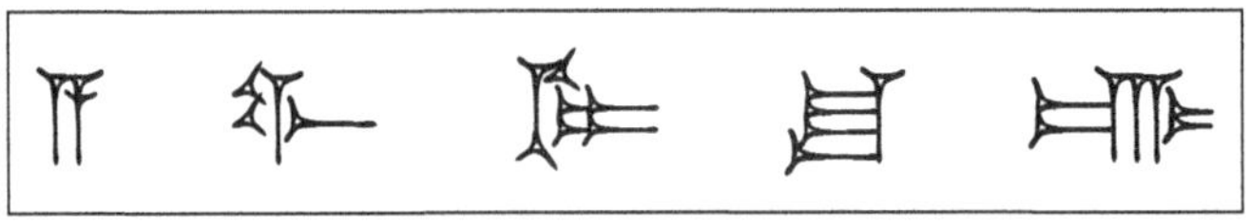

LH §130 XXVIII (Rv. V):65

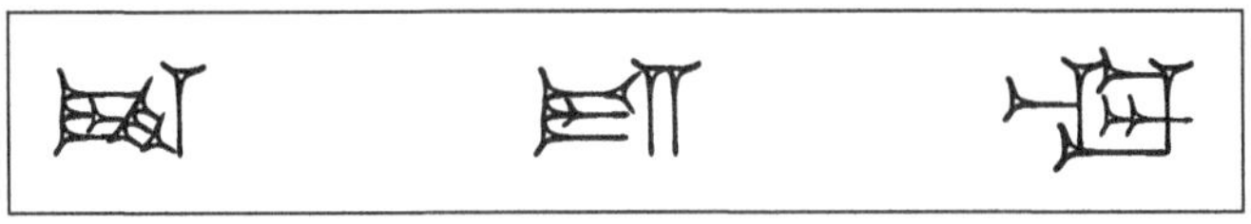

LH §130 XXVIII (Rv. V):66

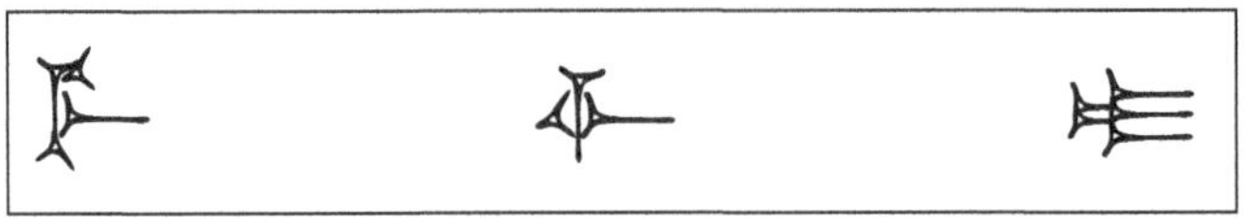

LH §130 XXVIII (Rv. V):67

2. Grammatical Analysis: Parse all verb forms. See the notes below for additional help.

   Note: XXVIII (Rv. V):60 includes the word *kabālum*, meaning "to be paralyzed." In the D-stem it means "to bind, make immobile" (cf. *kebel*, כֶּבֶל, "fetters"). This word does not need to be learned.

   Note: XXVIII (Rv. V):61 is from the word *sûnum*, meaning "loin, lap, genital area." This word does not need to be learned.

3. Translation: Translate LH §130.

Akkadian Love Literature and the Song of Songs

Miles V. Van Pelt

After decades of teaching the biblical languages to undergraduate and graduate students, I still receive the same question each year: Why study the original languages when English translations are so readily available? And what about cognates like Ugaritic, Aramaic, or the Akkadian language of this grammar? I usually give two answers to questions of this sort.

The first answer is linguistic in nature. Like ancient Hebrew, Akkadian is a Semitic language, and it can aid in our understanding of other Semitic languages like the Hebrew and Aramaic found in the Hebrew Bible. For example, the short prefix conjugation (preterite, *waw* consecutive) in Hebrew finds a correlate in the *iprus* conjugation of Akkadian. Also, the Akkadian ventive affix –*am* helps to explain the function of the lengthened imperative. Another example includes the Akkadian Š-stem borrowed by Aramaic and appearing as the *shaphel* stem (also Š-stem) in Biblical Aramaic. By studying other Semitic languages, apparent irregularities or oddities in Biblical Hebrew or Aramaic become interesting and intelligible points of contact with similar languages of the same family and period.

The second answer to the question posed is contextual in nature. The content and world of Akkadian literature overlaps the content and world captured in biblical literature. For example, it is well known that LH appearing in this grammar connect in significant ways with the legal material that appears in Exodus through Deuteronomy of the biblical corpus. Though perhaps less well known, the collection of Akkadian literature available to us also contains an impressive stock of love literature that shares both linguistic and contextual features in common with the enigmatic Song of Songs appearing in the third and final section of the Hebrew Bible known as the Writings.

For example, like the Song of Songs, Akkadian love literature[1] contains frequent references to a royal figure. N. Wasserman comments, "No less significant is the royal presence in the corpus. The king holds a special place in [Akkadian love literature]: *šarrum* is mentioned explicitly 14 times, and is probably referred to indirectly elsewhere."[2] Six different kings are mentioned in the corpus, including Hammurabi and Shalmaneser.[3] A similar reality occurs in the Song of Songs. King Solomon is explicitly mentioned seven times (Song 1:1, 5; 3:7, 9, 11; 8:11–12), from the beginning to the end of the song. Furthermore, the noun "king" (Song 1:4, 12; 3:9, 11; 7:6) occurs five additional times in reference to the king's chambers, bed, crown, and other such royal accoutrements. The presence of a shepherd and shepherding, perhaps also a royal connection, is also common to both sources.

In addition to the presence of a royal figure, Akkadian love literature and the Song of Songs share the themes of lovemaking, lovesickness, and the separation of lovers. There are frequent references to body parts, both explicit and suggestive. The use of flora and fauna, both descriptively of the human body and contextually of the environment for love, also pervades both corpora. In Akkadian love literature,

1. For photos, transliteration, translation, and commentary on Akkadian love literature from the third and second millennium BCE, see Nathan Wasserman, *Akkadian Love Literature of the Second and Third Millennium BCE*, LAOS 4 (Wiesbaden: Harrassowitz, 2016). All of the following references to Akkadian love literature come from this source.

2. Wasserman, *Akkadian Love Literature*, 24.

3. Ibid.

the affectionate designation *dādum* for "beloved" or "darling" is very common, corresponding to the Hebrew *dôd*, דּוֹד, meaning the same thing in Hebrew and appearing (in the singular) twenty-seven times in the Song of Songs (Song 1:13–14, 16; 2:3, 8–10, 16–17; 4:16; 5:2, 4–6, 8–10, 16–6:3; 7:10–12, 14; 8:5, 14). Interestingly, the plural forms also have related but distinctive meanings. In the plural, the Akkadian *dādū* means "sexual attractiveness," but the plural *dôdîm*, דּוֹדִים, in Hebrew refers to the act of lovemaking itself (Song 1:2, 4; 4:10; 5:1; 7:13).

Another compelling connection is the theme of sleeping, dreaming, and waking. In Song of Songs 5:2, the woman of the song explains, "I was asleep, but my heart was awake" as she waited to be united to her beloved. In one Akkadian text, we find something similar, "I avoid talking, my eyes are drawn, my heart is awake (though) I am sleeping."[4] Wasserman astutely comments, "The [b]iblical parallel 'I was asleep, but my heart was wakeful. Hark, my beloved knocks!' (Songs 5: 2) is remarkable, proving that Mesopotamian and biblical love literature drew from a common pool of stock-phrases."[5]

Though the Song of Songs may be considered unique in the context of biblical literature, it is certainly not unique in the context of the literature of the ancient Near East with strong connections to both Egyptian[6] and Akkadian love literature. The Song of Songs has suffered the weight of various interpretations like no other book in the Hebrew Bible. Perhaps this Akkadian love literature will help future generations of interpreters find the key to unlock its original meaning.

4. Ibid., 135. The Akkadian text comes from The Moussaieff Love Song, "My Heart is Awake Though I am Sleeping."

5. Wasserman, *Akkadian Love Literature*, 137.

6. For a transcription, translation, and commentary of the Egyptian love literature, see Michael V. Fox, *The Song of Songs and the Ancient Egyptian Love Songs* (Madison, WI: University of Wisconsin Press, 1985).

17–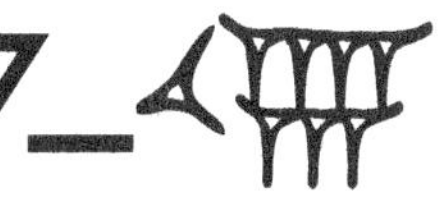

Doubly Weak Verbs and Old Babylonian Monumental Cuneiform

The laws that will be covered in this chapter, LH §§131–136, continue to relate to the themes of marriage, sexuality, and family. In particular, they concern responses to the suspected sexual infidelity of a wife (LH §§131–132) and the absence of a husband, both involuntary and voluntary, namely desertion (LH §§133–136).

Starting with this chapter and continuing in succeeding chapters, each text box will include the Old Babylonian Monumental script (also called Old Babylonian Lapidary) in a smaller font above the Neo-Assyrian script. Students are not expected to learn the Old Babylonian Monumental script; it is included for reference and for the benefit of those students who may wish to go on in their study of Akkadian. Doubly weak verbs will also be explained in this chapter.

17.1 Doubly Weak Verbs

There are three kinds of doubly weak verbs:

1. The first kind consists of those verbs that are conjugated in an entirely predictable manner based on a combination of the familiar effects of each weak root consonant.
2. The second kind are those doubly weak verbs with a second weak root consonant that acts like a strong root consonant.
3. The third type of doubly weak verb are those that are truly irregular.

17.1.1 ***Doubly Weak Verbs: Two Weak Root Consonants.*** Doubly weak verbs that are conjugated in a predictable manner based on the familiar effects of each weak root consonant are typically those that have a weak first root consonant and a weak third root consonant. For example, the G-stem preterite 3cs of the I-*n* and III-' verb *nadûm* (*i,i*), "to throw hurl, accuse [lay a charge of], leave" is easily produced by combining the characteristic changes of I-*n* verbs (see §10.1.4) and III-' verbs (see §16.1).

Step 1: Begin with the appropriate form of the paradigmatic strong verb, *parāsum*. For the G-stem preterite 3cs this is *iprus* (see §10.1.3).

Step 2: Replace each of the three root consonants of *iprus* with the corresponding (original) root consonants of the doubly weak verb, in this case *nadûm* (< **n-d-'*). This results in **indu'*.

Step 3: Treat the influence of the I-weak consonant as appropriate. In this case, one needs to recall that the consonant *n* tends to assimilate to a juxtaposed consonant, hence **indu'* < **iddu'*.

Step 4: Treat the influence of the III-weak consonant as appropriate. This requires noting the vowel class of the verb, which in the case of *nadûm* is *i*. In both the G-stem and also the N-stem, the paradigm theme vowel (in this case from *iprus*), which is a *u*, will be replaced with the vowel of the vowel class of any III-weak verb, which in the case of *nadûm* is *i*, hence **iddu'* > **iddi'*.

Step 5: Finally, the final ' quiesces, resulting in compensatory lengthening of the theme vowel or, in other situations where there are vowels on either side of the ', resulting in contraction of adjacent vowels, hence: **iddi'* > *iddî*, "he threw down."[1]

17.1.2 ***Doubly Weak Verbs: Middle Weak Consonant Acts Strong.*** The doubly weak verbs that are more challenging, though less common in LH, are a subset of verbs where one of the weak consonants is the second root consonant (II-weak verbs). Normally, these verbs are conjugated based on a combination of the expected characteristics that have been presented in earlier chapters of this textbook for each pattern. At other times, however, they are conjugated as if the II-weak root consonant is, in effect, a strong root consonant. There are no firm rules for predicting which approach applies to a given verb.

For example, verbs that are I-*n* or I-*w* and II-' frequently treat the second root consonant as if it were a strong consonant. This is observed at the end of LH §Pro V:19 with the verb *uwa''eranni*, "directed me." This is a D-stem preterite 3cs (*uparris*) of *wa'ārum*, G: "to advance"; D: "to direct." (The verb *uwa''eranni* happens to have a ventive *-am* suffix before the accusative 1cs pronominal suffix *-ni*).

Another example of this second type of doubly weak verb is the verb *le'ûm*, (*i*), "to be able, capable." Below are the steps to determine the G-stem durative 3cs of this verb.

Step 1: Begin with the appropriate form of the paradigmatic strong verb, *parāsum*. For the G-stem durative 3cs this is *iparras* (see §10.1.3).

Step 2: Replace each of the three root consonants of *iparras* with the corresponding (original) root consonants of the doubly weak verb, in this case *le'ûm* (< **l-'-y*). This results in **ila''ay*.

Step 3: Based on the *e*-vowel in the infinitive *le'ûm*, the original middle guttural (before it became a glottal stop [']) was, presumably, either *ḥ*, ', or *ǵ* (see §3.4.3). This third step results in **ile''ay*.

Step 4: Because the vowel class of *le'ûm* is *i*, the theme vowel of the verb changes from the *a*-vowel in the strong verb paradigm of *iparras* to an *i*-vowel. This fourth step results in **ile''ay* > **ile''iy*.

Step 5: The final *y* becomes an ' and then results in compensatory lengthening of the adjacent vowel: **ile''iy* > *ile''î*, "he is able." This form appears four times in LH (LH §§28, 29, 54, Epi XLVIII:77). Borger notes that whenever *le'ûm* occurs in a *šumma* clause, it is always in the durative, as is also the case with the verb *bašûm*, "to exist, be."[2]

1. Other Akkadian authorities would add one additional step: shorten any non-tilde final vowel. It is likely that this is how final non-tilde long vowels were pronounced in contemporary speech, but it is less clear that this reflects the intention of the somewhat archaizing and formal grammar of LH.

2. Borger, *Babylonisch-Assyrische Lesestücke*, 1:116.

17.1.3 ***Doubly Weak Verbs: Irregular.*** The third type of doubly weak verbs are those that are truly irregular. See §13.2 to review two of the most common doubly weak irregular verbs: *išûm*, "to have," and *idûm* (also spelled *edûm*), "to know."

Another common irregular doubly weak verb is *itūlum* (< *'-'-*l*), "to lie down together, sleep together," which is also sometimes spelled *utūlum* (the result of an irregular vowel harmony where the initial *i*-vowel assimilates to the following *u*-vowel).[3] It seems preferable, however, to argue that all of the examples of the hypothesized verb *itūlum* are actually Gt-stem (reflexive/passive) forms of the doubly weak verb *ni'ālum/nālum*, which means "to lie down, sleep."[4]

In this case, the paradigm of the doubly weak I-*n*, II-*y* verb *ni'ālum* (*i*-class)/*nalūm* (*a*-class) (< *n-y-l*) is as follows:

Stem	Class	Durative 3cs	Perfect 3cs	Preterite 3cs	Participle ms	Verbal Adjective ms	Stative 3ms	Infinitive ms
G		*iparras*	*iptaras*	*iprus*	*pārisum*	*parsum*	*paris*	*parāsum*
	i/a	*ini''al/ inãl*	*ittîl*	*inîl*	*nîlum*	*nîlum*		*ni'ālum/ nālum*
Gt		*iptarras*	*iptatras*	*iptaras*	*muptarsum*	*pitrusum*	*pitrus*	*pitrusum*
		itti''al/ittãl	***ittatîl***	***ittîl***	***muttîlum***	***itûlum***	***utûl***	***itûlum/ utûlum***[5]
Gtn		*iptanarras* *ittanayyal*	*iptatarras*	*iptarras*	*muptarrisum*	*pitarrusum*	*pitarrus*	*pitarrusum*
D		*uparras*	*uptarris*	*uparris*	*muparrisum*	*purrusum*	*purrus*	*purrusum*
Š		*ušapras* *ušnâl*	*uštapris* *uštanîl*	*ušapris* *ušnîl*	*mušaprisum*	*šuprusum* *šunullum*	*šuprus* *šunûl*	*šuprusum* *šunullum*

Note: The Gt forms are the only forms that in bold since they are the only ones that the student needs to learn based on their appearance in LH. Note also that 3cs forms ending in a long vowel followed by a single consonant experience resolutory doubling in other forms, like the 3mp where the vowel is short and followed by a doubled consonant, such as *ittilū* (Gt-stem durative 3mp).[6]

17.2 Babylonian Monumental Cuneiform

The Old Babylonian Monumental script (also called Old Babylonian Lapidary) is the script that is employed on the stele commissioned by Hammurabi about 1750 BCE, which is now housed in the Louvre. It is an impressive, archaizing style of writing that was reserved for formal inscriptions, such as stone monuments during the Old Babylonian period

3. Huehnergard, *A Grammar of Akkadian*, §33.1.
4. *AHw*, ad loc.; and *CDA*, ad loc., which is based on *AHw*, favor the existence of the verb *itūlum*. Cf. also Worthington, *Complete Babylonian*, §28.3, although Worthington acknowledges that *itūlum* may derive from *ni'ālum*. In support of the view that *itūlum* arose as a lexicalized form of the Gt of *ni'ālum*, cf., e.g., Huehnergard, *A Grammar of Akkadian*, §§21.3b; 33.1; p. 646; and Kouwenberg, *The Akkadian Verb and Its Semitic Background*, §16.5.53.1. Cf. also Borger, *Babylonisch-Assyrische Lesestücke*, 2:§§107 i–m.
5. Both forms of the infinitive are attested in LH §§129, 131, and 132.
6. See §11.3.3.

(2000–1600 BCE).[7] This period of the language represents its classic stage, as was the view of later Akkadian speakers.

The Old Babylonian Monumental script does not need to be learned at this point. It should be looked at, however, in order to gain some familiarity with it. This will enable the student to learn it with greater ease at some point in the future, should she or he wish to do so.[8] An incidental benefit of some awareness of the Old Babylonian script is that it is closer to the earlier pictographic script that depicted objects or activities that were referred to by those signs. Knowing this history can, at least in a few cases, help fix in one's mind the logographic or syllabic values of the signs. Consider the table below:

	ca. 3000 BCE	**ca. 1750 BCE** ***OB Lapidary***	**ca. 1750 BCE** ***OB Cursive***	**ca. 700 BCE** ***Neo-Assyrian***	**value**
water					a
star, sky					an
to go, foot				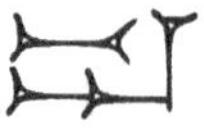	du
arm		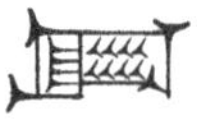			ed, id
sun, day					ud
canal					e
female servant (= foreign woman)	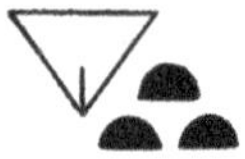	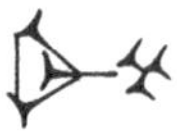			GÉME
ox					GUD, gu_4
fish					ḫa
bird, duck					ḫu

7. The vast majority of documents, however, that have survived from the Old Babylonian period were written not on stone monuments but on clay tablets. These employ a less formal script, often called "Old Babylonian cursive," which closely resembles Old Babylonian Monumental script.

8. Some students may choose to take a second semester of Akkadian. If so, in many academic settings this will require transitioning to some midpoint in Huehnergard's exceptionally fine *A Grammar of Akkadian*. If so, the main challenge for students making this transition will be that students who used Huehnergard's grammar for their first semester will have learned not only Neo-Assyrian cuneiform, as taught in this textbook, but also cuneiform in the Old Babylonian Monumental script and the related Old Babylonian cursive script. On the other hand, students using this textbook for their first semester are likely to know a greater number of cuneiform characters, and they will have covered more grammar, although in some cases in less detail. To make this transition easier, students are encouraged to learn to recognize the Old Babylonian Monumental script as it comes up in this chapter and in those that follow.

	ca. 3000 BCE	ca. 1750 BCE *OB Lapidary*	ca. 1750 BCE *OB Cursive*	ca. 700 BCE *Neo-Assyrian*	value
mouth	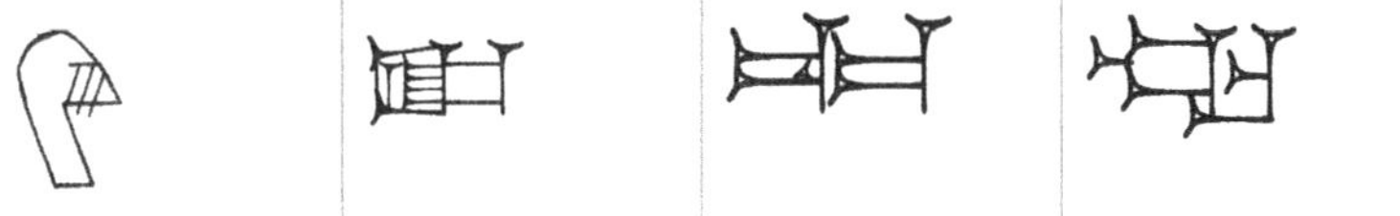				ka
earth, land					ki
mountain,foreign					kur
sheep, sheepfold					lu, UDU
man					lú
bread, food					NINDA, gar, šá
head, person	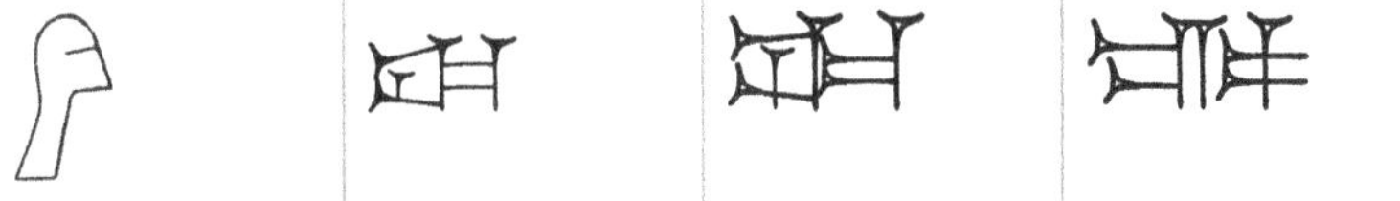				sag
woman					sal, MUNUS
net					sa
barley, grain					še
eye, to see					lim, ši
hand	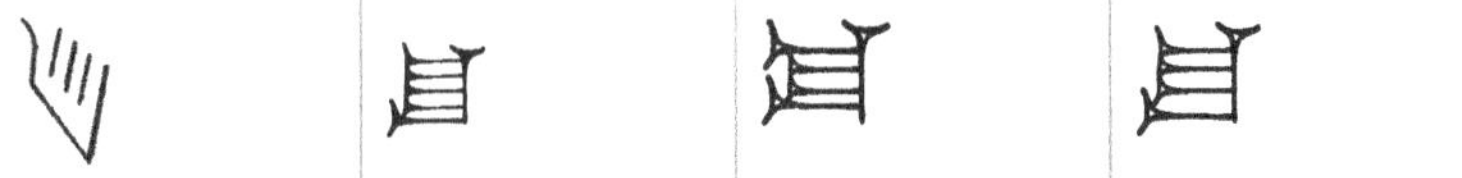				šu
piece of wood	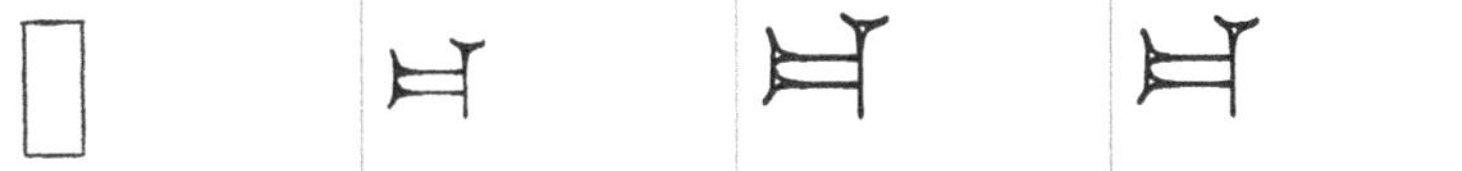				*iṣ*

17.3 Homework

Before you move on, be sure to understand the three types of doubly weak verbs and become comfortable with their irregularities. Also, review the table above to become familiar with the development of signs from their pictographic to Neo-Assyrian forms.

17.3.1 *Signs*

 *ḫa*

 MEŠ (postpositive determinative for plural, mostly of persons); this cuneiform sign is comprised of two parts: *me* () + *eš* ()

 URU, *âlum*, "city"

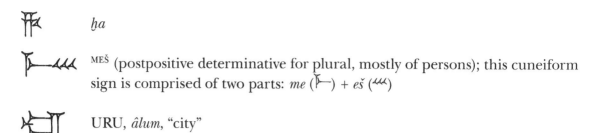

17.3.2 *Vocabulary*

abātum (*a,u*) = to destroy [*Note:* Some Assyriologists do not distinguish *abātum* from *nabātum.*[9]] (Cf. homologous forms of *'ābad*, אָבַד, which also means "to be lost, be a fugitive," as well as "to perish, to destroy.")
akālum (*a,u*) = to eat (cf. *'ākal*, אָכַל)
âlum = city (cf. *'ōhel*, אֹהֶל, "tent")
aššum = because of, concerning; *with infinitive*: in order that (< **an*[*a*] *šum*, "for the name of")[10]
erēbum (*u,u*) = to enter (cf. *'ereb*, עֶרֶב, "evening")[11]
mutum = husband (cf. *mətîm*, מְתִים, "men"; *mətûšelaḥ*, מְתוּשֶׁלַח, "Methuselah")
nabātum (< **n-'-b-t*) (*i,i*) = N: "to flee, escape; to be a fugitive." *Note: nabātum* has irregular forms suggesting that it derives from an original quadraliteral root, *n'bt*. (Cf. homologous forms of *'ābad*, אָבַד, which also means "to be lost, be a fugitive," as well as "to perish, to destroy.")
naṣārum (*a,u*) = to watch over, guard, keep; *stative*: to be careful (cf. *nāṣar*, נָצַר)
pagrum = body, self (cf. *peger*, פֶּגֶר)
pânum = face; *ina pâni* = because of, in front of; *ana pâni* = previously, in front of, before (cf. *pānîm*, פָּנִים)[12]
šalālum (*a,u*) = to take captive; N: to be captured (cf. *šālal*, שָׁלַל, "to plunder")
walādum (*a,i*) = to bear, give birth to (cf. *yālad*, יָלַד)
zêrum (*e,e*) = to hate, dislike; to reject

Congratulations! If you learn the thirteen words above and have learned each of the 124 words in the vocabulary lists of the preceding chapters, you will be able to read 91 percent of all the words in LH §§1–20, 127–149.

---

9. *CDA* lists the two meanings, "to destroy" and "to run away, flee," under two distinct but identically spelled roots, *abātum* I and *abātum* II.
10. So, according to Huehnergard, *A Grammar of Akkadian*, 606.
11. So, according to Huehnergard, *A Grammar of Akkadian*, 607.
12. The *a* in *pânum* is marked with a circumflex reflecting compensatory lengthening because of the loss of a final root consonant. Cf. Huehnergard, *A Grammar of Akkadian*, §6.1(b), for a discussion of the analogous compensatory lengthening in *mârum* < **mar'um*, "son."

17.3.3 *Exercises*

LH §131 stipulates what is to be done if a husband charges his wife with sexual infidelity, but she and her supposed lover were not caught in flagrante delicto.

1. Transliterate and Normalize. See the note below for additional help.

LH §131 XXVIII (Rv. V):68

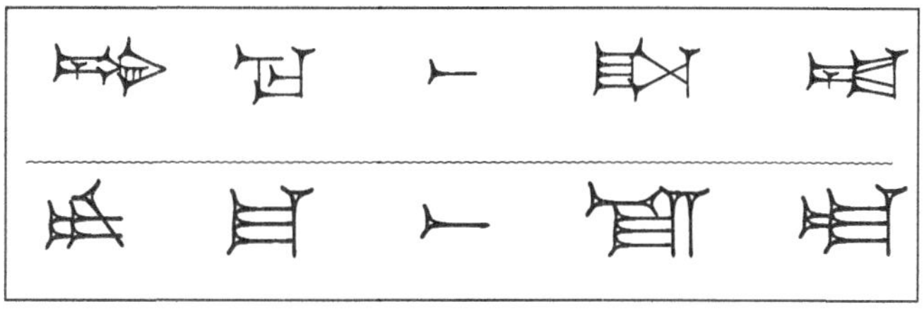

LH §131 XXVIII (Rv. V):69

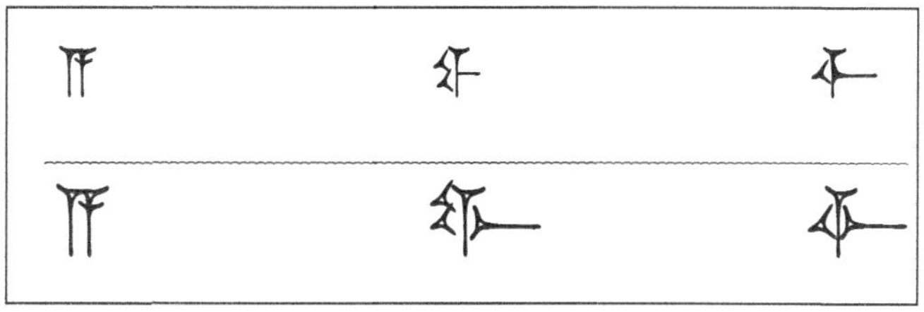

LH §131 XXVIII (Rv. V):70

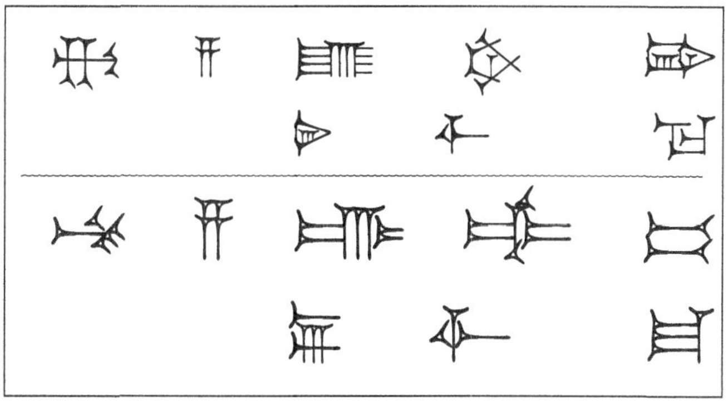

LH §131 XXVIII (Rv. V):71

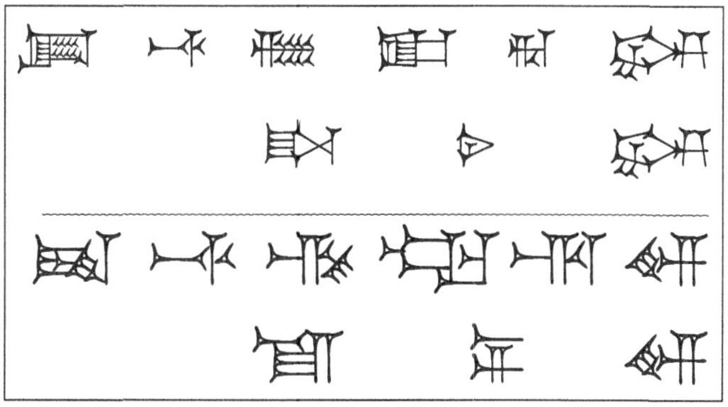

LH §131 XXVIII (Rv. V):72

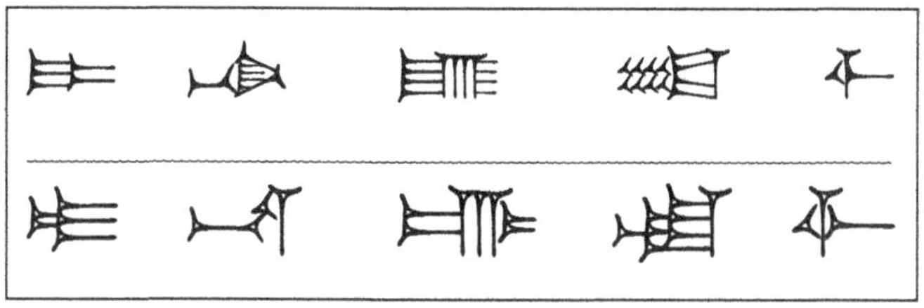

LH §131 XXVIII (Rv. V):73

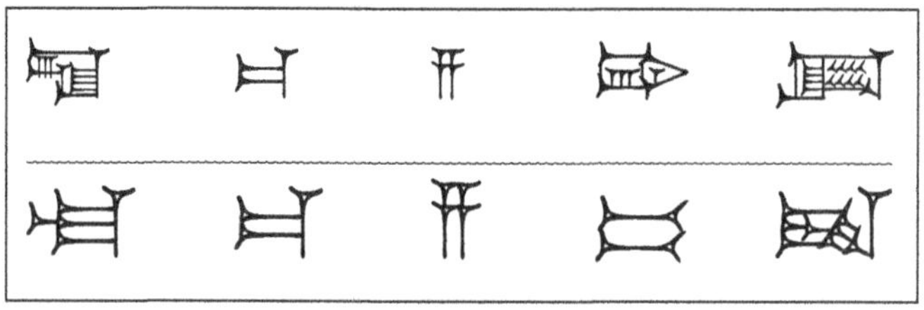

LH §131 XXVIII (Rv. V):74

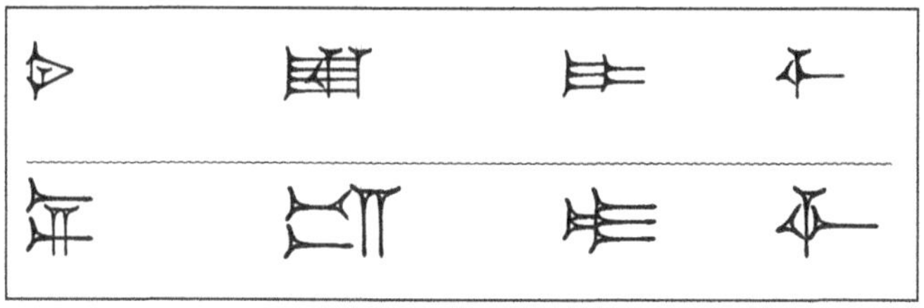

LH §131 XXVIII (Rv. V):75

Note: The sign  in XXVIII (Rv. V):75 is *kar*. This sign does not need to be learned.

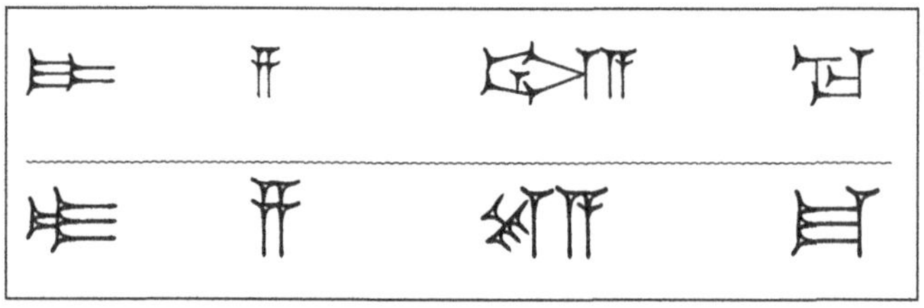

LH §131 XXVIII (Rv. V):76

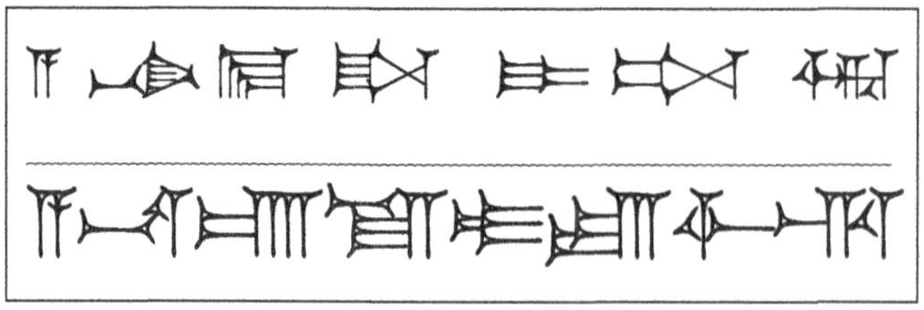

2. Grammatical Analysis: Parse all verb forms and answer the question below.

   a. Explain the implication of the stem used by the verb in LH §131 XXVIII (Rv. V):72.

3. Translation: Translate LH §131.

LH §132 resembles LH §131, only this time it is some outside person, rather than her husband, who has accused a wife of sexual infidelity. Once again, the wife and her supposed lover were not caught in flagrante delicto.

1. Transliterate and Normalize.

LH §132 XXVIII (Rv. V):77

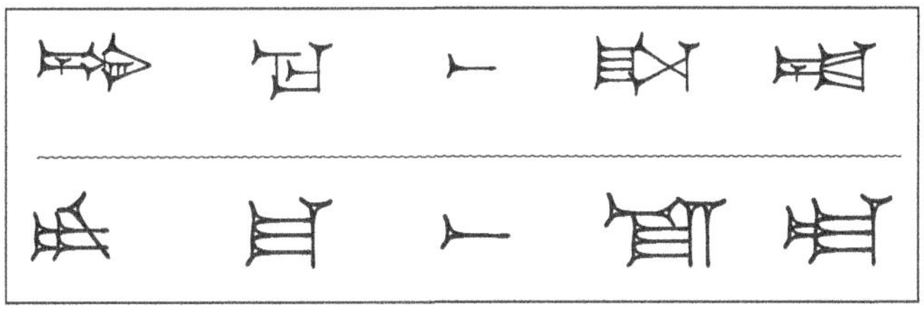

LH §132 XXVIII (Rv. V):78

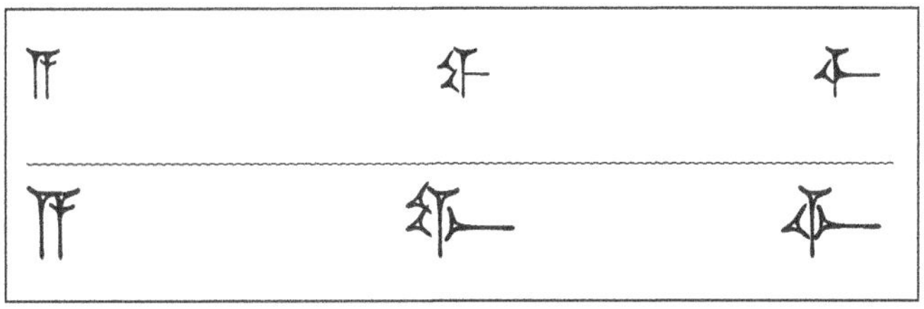

LH §132 XXVIII (Rv. V):79

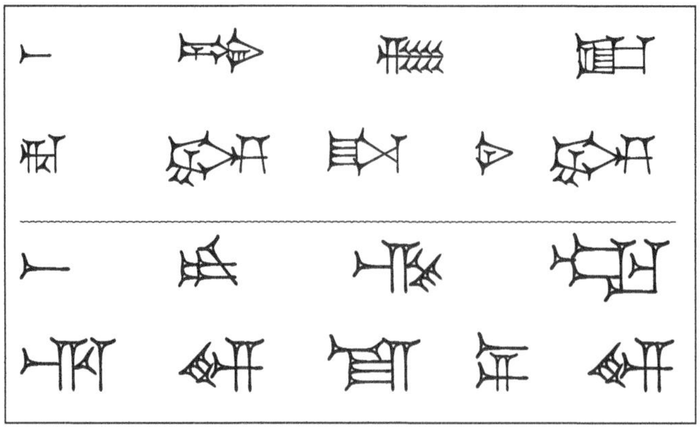

LH §132 XXVIII (Rv. V):80

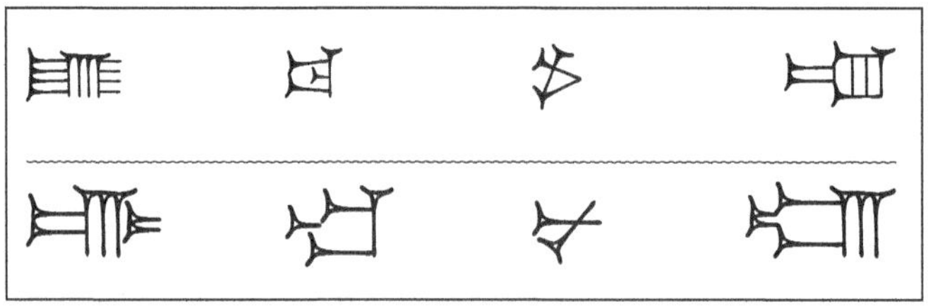

LH §132 XXVIII (Rv. V):81

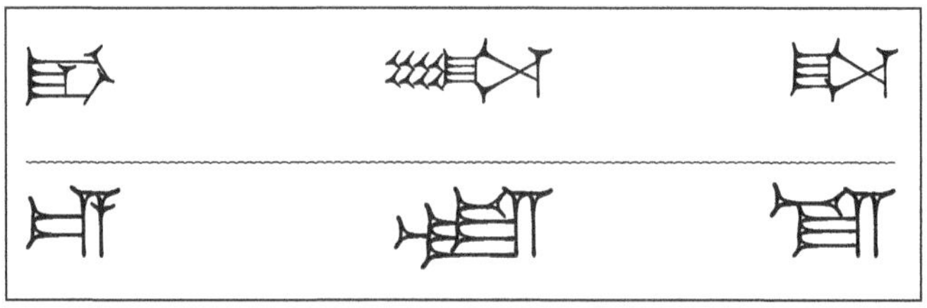

LH §132 XXVIII (Rv. V):82

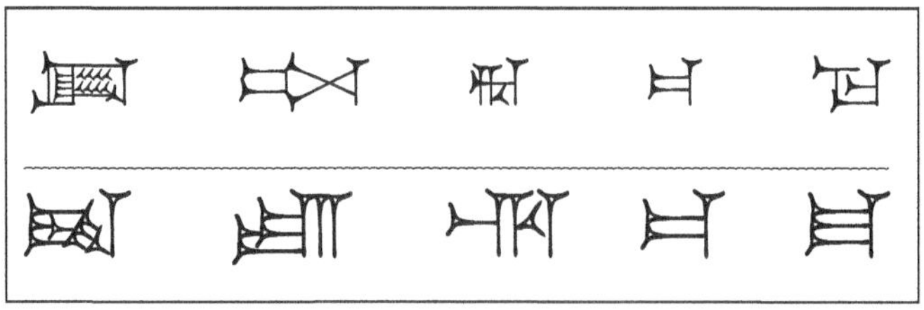

LH §132 XXVIII (Rv. V):83

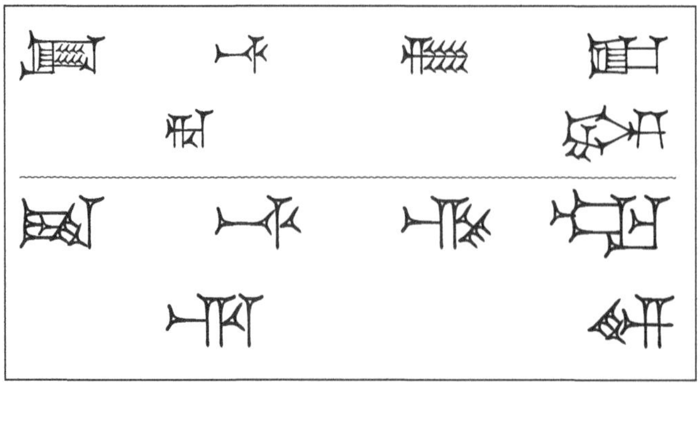

LH §132 XXIX (Rv. VI):1

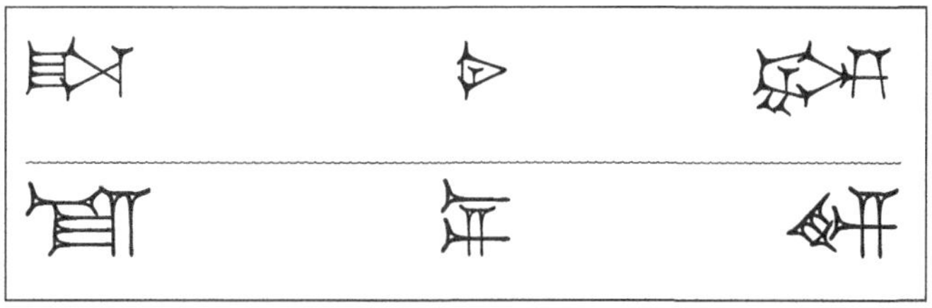

LH §132 XXIX (Rv. VI):2

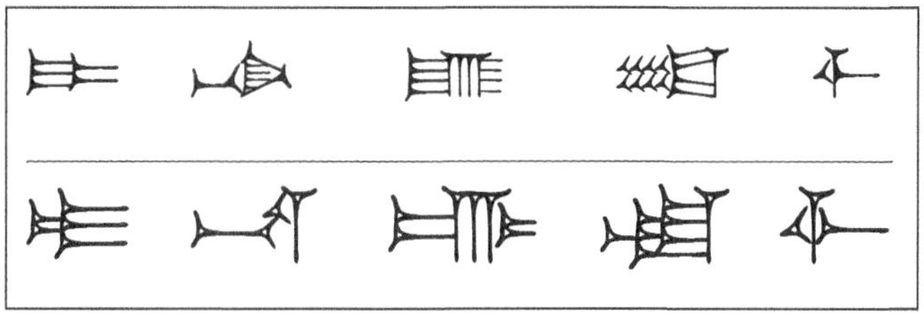

LH §132 XXIX (Rv. VI):3

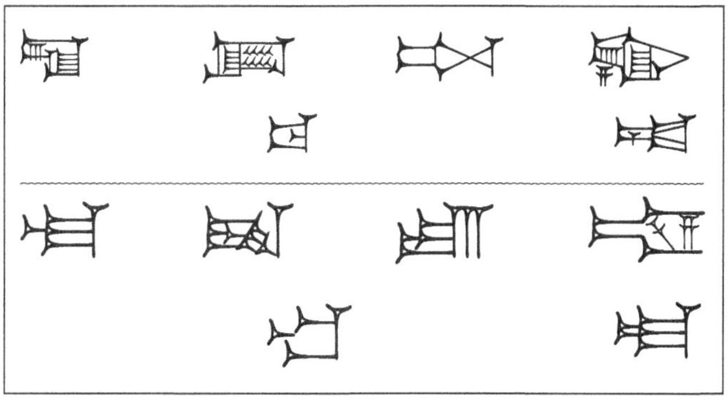

LH §132 XXIX (Rv. VI):4

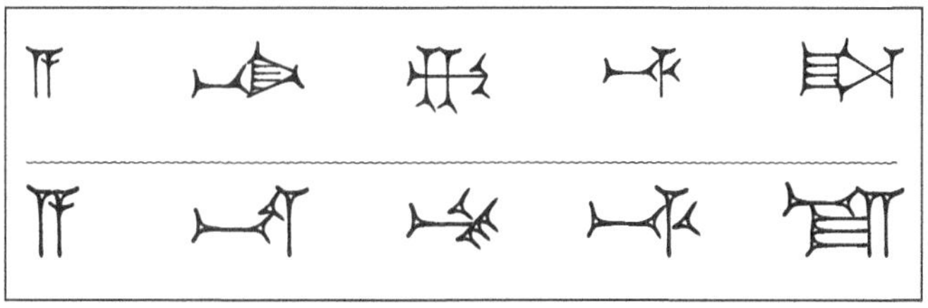

LH §132 XXIX (Rv. VI):5

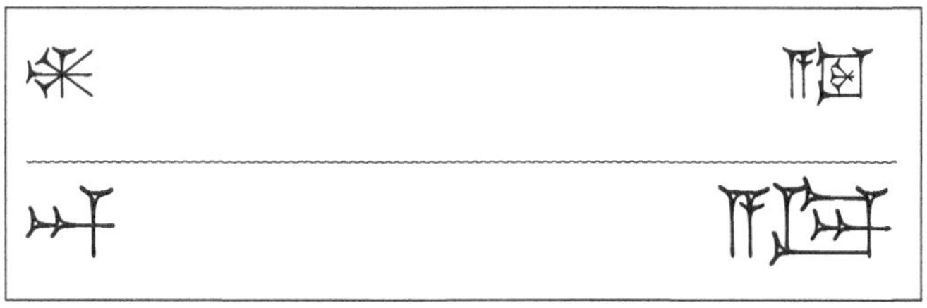

LH §132 XXIX (Rv. VI):6

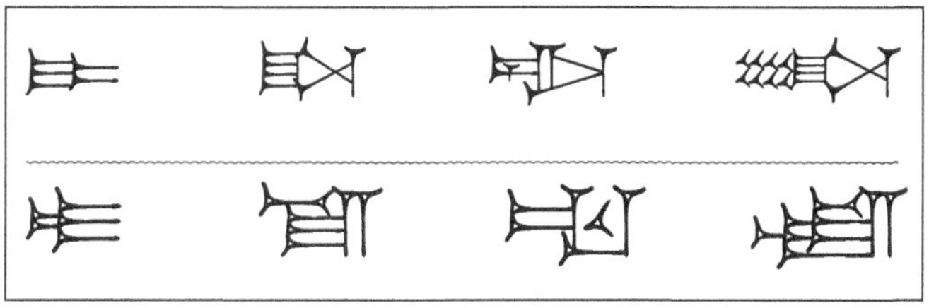

(Transliterate and normalize in the space provided here.)

2. Grammatical Analysis: Parse all verb forms and answer the question below. See the note for additional commentary.

   a. Check a lexicon for the preposition in XXIX (Rv. VI):4. What are two significant alternative options for its meaning that might fit in the present context? Offer some support for the option you have chosen.

   Note: It is unclear what significance, if any, should be attached to the observation that the verb in XXIX (Rv. VI):6 is not a ventive, as it was in LH §2. The most likely explanation for this difference is the fact that the use or nonuse of the ventive is generally optional or stylistic. A supplemental explanation may be the observation that there is a tendency in Akkadian (especially Akkadian poetry) to end sentences with a stressed-unstressed accentual pattern.

3. Translation: Translate LH §132.

LH §133a and the next, LH §133b, are very fragmentary on the stele, for which reason they are sometimes omitted.[13] These laws have been reconstructed, however, based on the evidence of other ancient copies of LH. LH §133a concerns the involuntary absence of a husband during which a wife is prohibited from another marriage as long as there are suitable provisions for her in her husband's home.

13. It is omitted, for example, from Borger, *Babylonisch-Assyrische Lesestücke*, 2:298.

Because of the substantial combined length of the laws covered in this chapter, normalized text is provided after each text box for laws, LH §§133a-134. As time permits, students may find it helpful to use this combination of cuneiform and normalized text, once again, to practice more rapid recognition of the appropriate values for each combination of signs.

LH §133a XXIX (Rv. VI):7

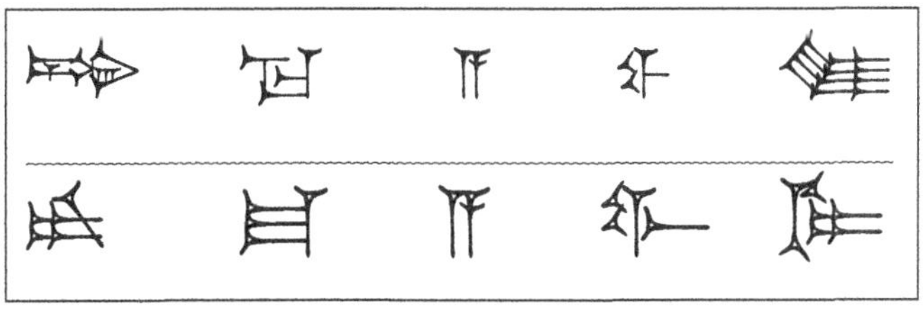

XXIX (Rv. VI):7 *šumma awīlum*

LH §133a XXIX (Rv. VI):8

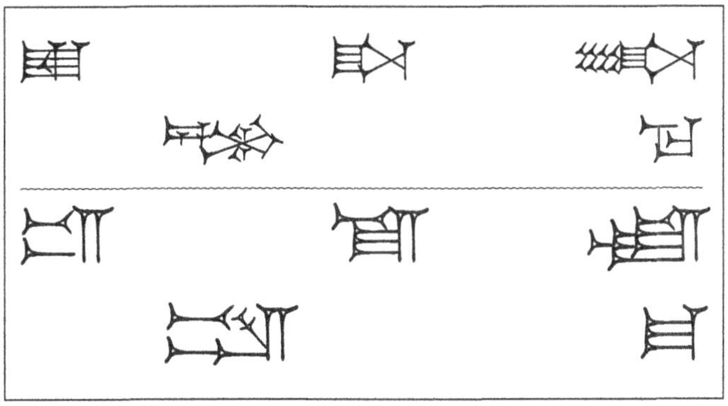

8 *iššalilma*

LH §133a XXIX (Rv. VI):9

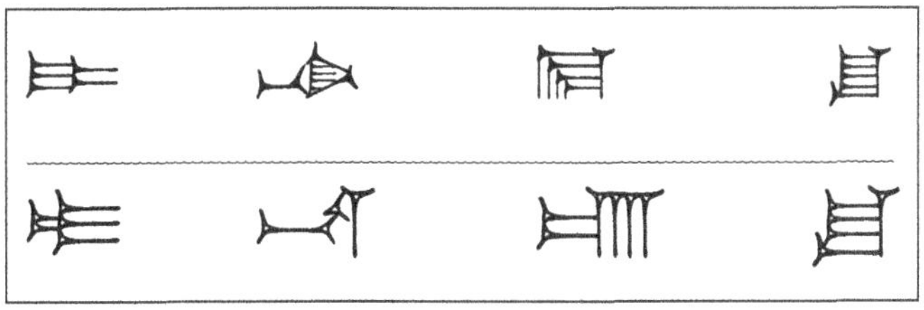

9 *ina bîtišu*

LH §133a XXIX (Rv. VI):10

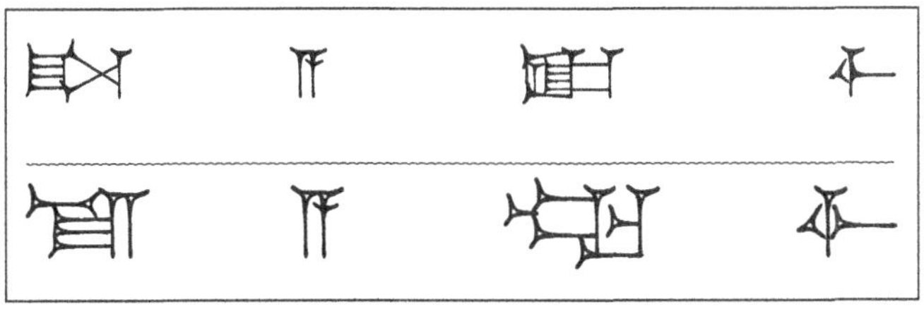

10 *ša akālim*

LH §133a XXIX (Rv. VI):11

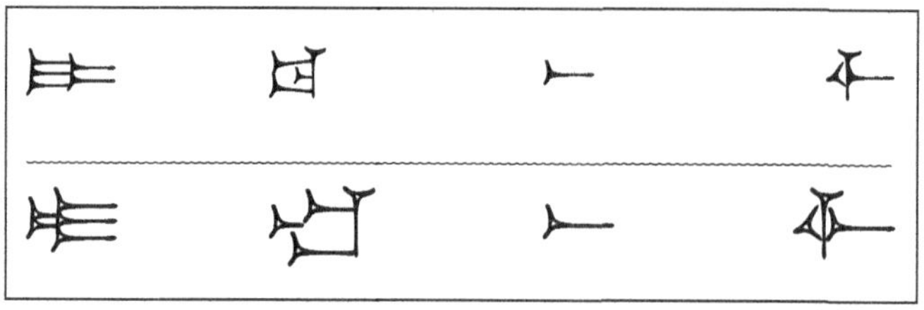

[11]*ibaššî*

LH §133a XXIX (Rv. VI):12

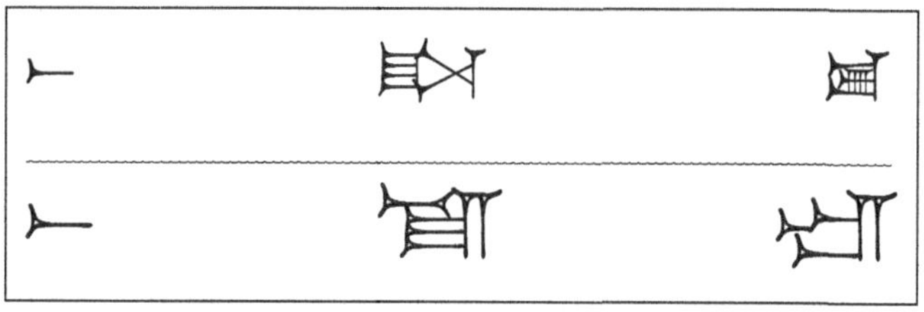

[12]*aššassu*

LH §133a XXIX (Rv. VI):13

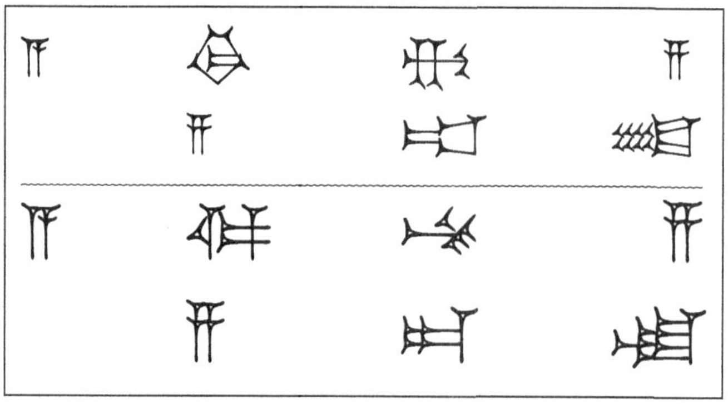

[13]*adi mussa ṣabtu*

LH §133a XXIX (Rv. VI):14

Note: The sign  in XXIX (Rv. VI):14 is *gàr*. This sign does not need to be learned.

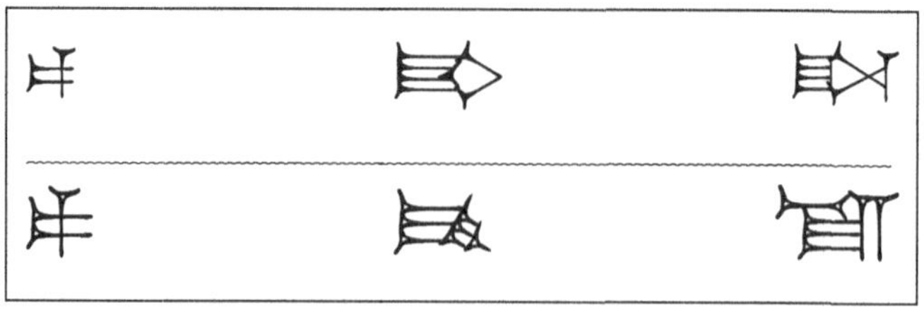

[14]*pagarša*

LH §133a XXIX (Rv. VI):15

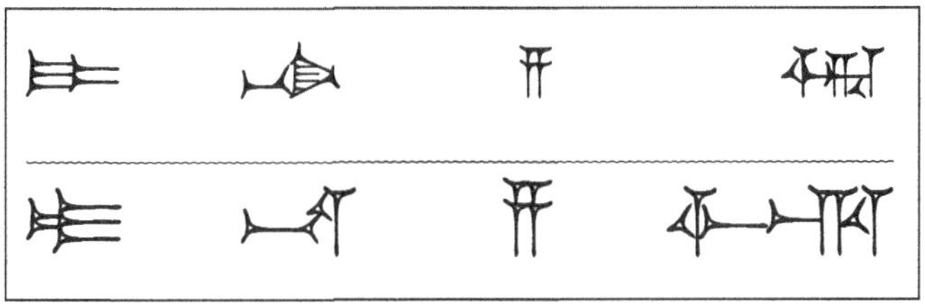

[15]*inaṣṣar*

LH §133a XXVIII (Rv. V):16

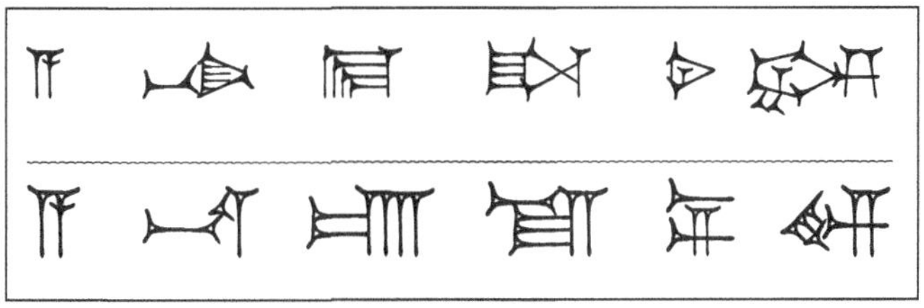

[16]*ana bît šanîm*

LH §133a XXIX (Rv. VI):17

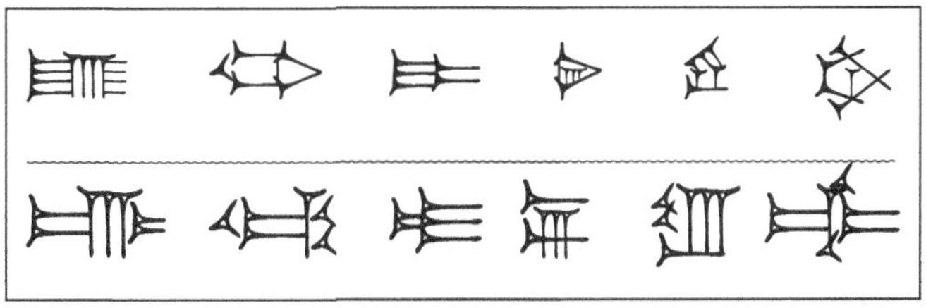

[17]*ul irrub*

1. Grammatical Analysis: Parse all verb forms. See the notes below for additional help and commentary.

Note: The verb *bašûm* (*i,i*), meaning "to exist, be (in the sense of, to exist)" and in the Š-stem "to produce," has a number of irregular features. First, it is nowhere attested in the perfect. Second, whenever it appears in a *šumma* clause in LH, it is in the durative (LH §§32, 48, 66, 133–135, 139, 151). Finally, *ibaššî* is used with both singular and plural subjects.[14]

Note: Some scholars, like S. R. Driver and John C. Miles and more recently Martha T. Roth, suggest that the idiomatic use of the verb and direct object in text boxes XXIX (Rv. VI):14–15 refers to guarding one's chastity.[15] This may find support in the present context, but the expression as it appears in other contexts can have the meaning "take care of (one's) self." For examples see *CAD*, P, under the word *pagru*.[16]

14. Cf. *CDA*, ad loc.; Borger, *Babylonisch-Assyrische Lesestücke*, 1:116
15. See Driver and Miles, *The Babylonian Laws*, 1:53, 216 and Roth, *Law Collections from Mesopotamia and Asia Minor*, 106.
16. See Streck, *Supplement to the Akkadian Dictionaries, Vol 1: B, P*, s.v. *pagru*, 56.

2. Translation: Translate LH §133a.

LH §133b, as reconstructed from other ancient copies of LH, sets a penalty of drowning for a wife who remarries (or cohabits with another man) without cause when her husband is missing due to being captured.

LH §133b XXIX (Rv. VI):18

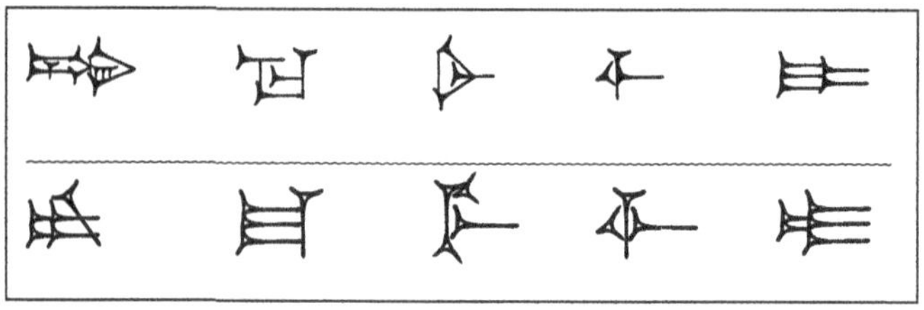

[18]*šumma sinništum šī*

LH §133b XXIX (Rv. VI):19

Note: The sign,  in XXIX (Rv. VI):19 is *gàr*. This sign does not need to be learned.

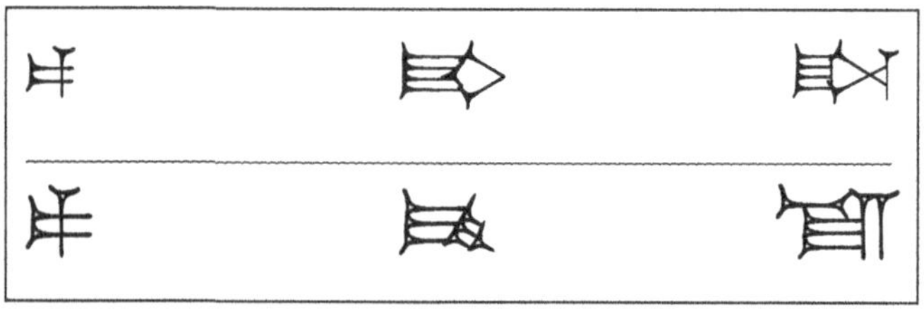

[19]*pagarša*

LH §133b XXIX (Rv. VI):20

Note: The sign, 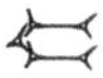 in XXIX (Rv. VI):20 is *ṣ ur*. This sign does not need to be learned.

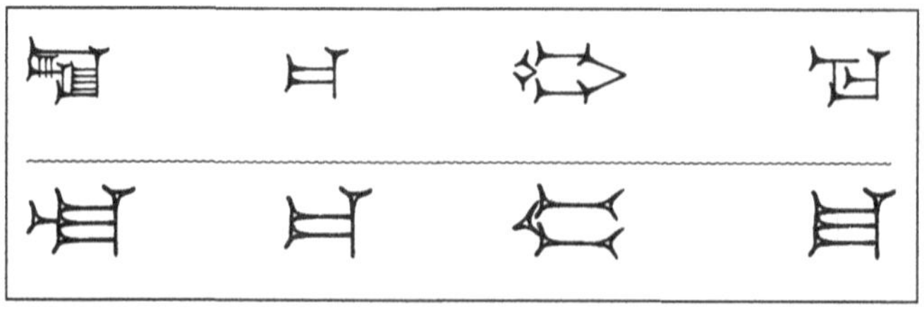

[20]*lâ iṣṣurma*

LH §133b XXIX (Rv. VI):21

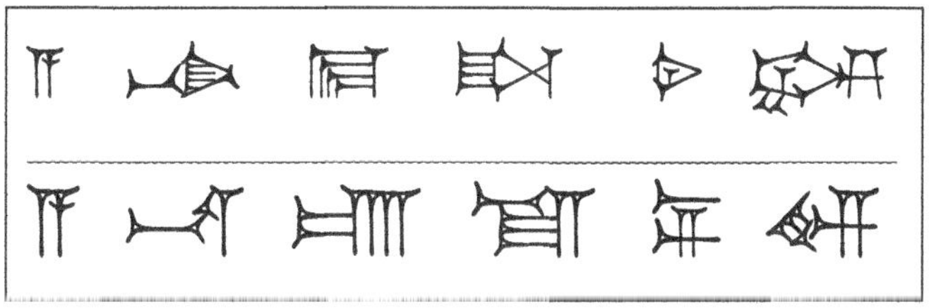

[21]*ana bît šanīm*

LH §133b XXIX (Rv. VI):22

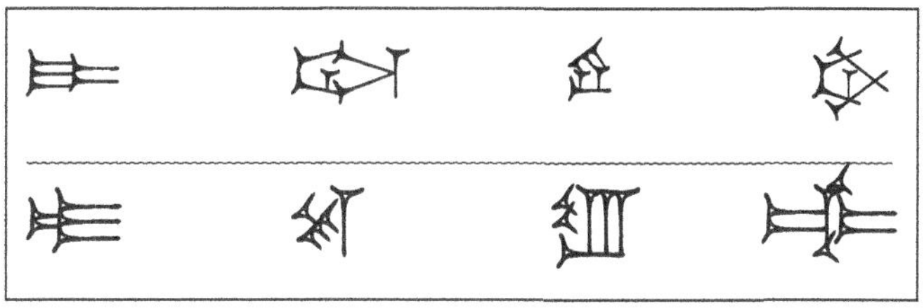

[22]*îterub*

LH §133b XXIX (Rv. VI):23

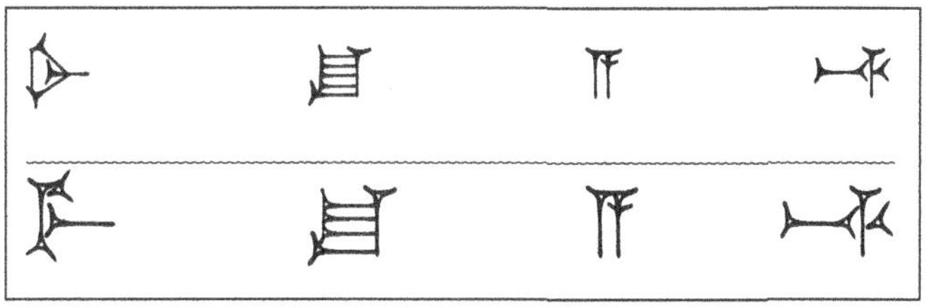

[23]*sinništam šu'āti*

LH §133b XXIX (Rv. VI):24

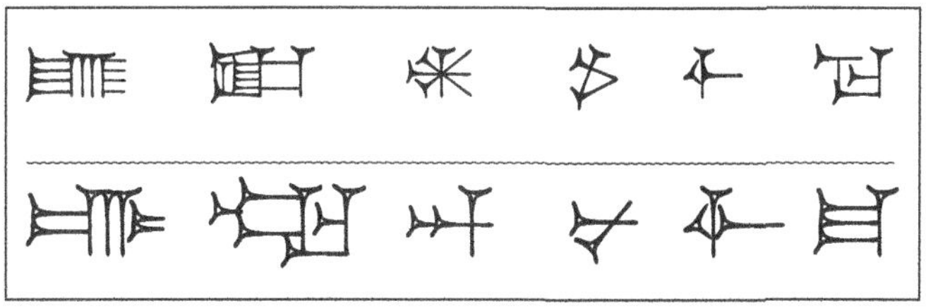

[24]*ukannūšīma*

LH §133b XXIX (Rv. VI):25

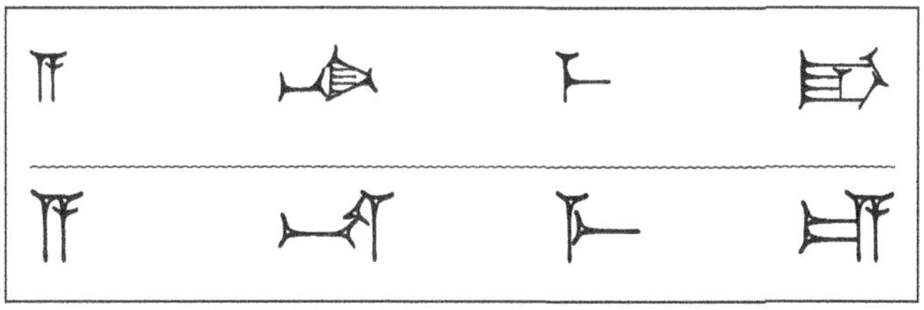

[25]*ana mē*

LH §133b XXIX (Rv. VI):26

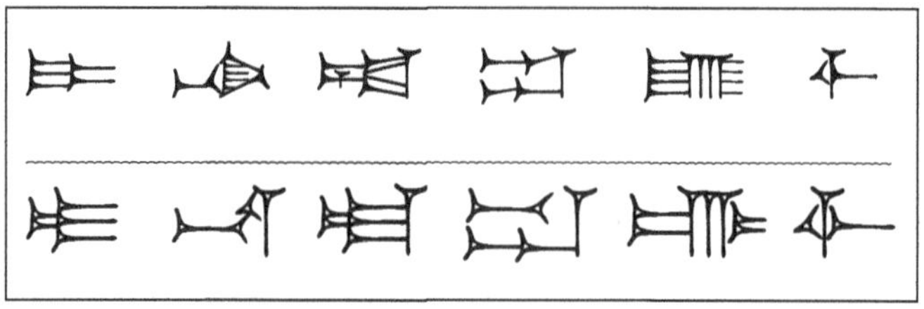

[26]*inaddūši*

1. Grammatical Analysis: Parse all verb forms.

2. Translation: Translate LH §133b.

LH §134 permits a wife to leave her husband's home if he has been captured and if there are not adequate provisions in her home by which she can sustain herself.

LH §134 XXIX (Rv. VI):27

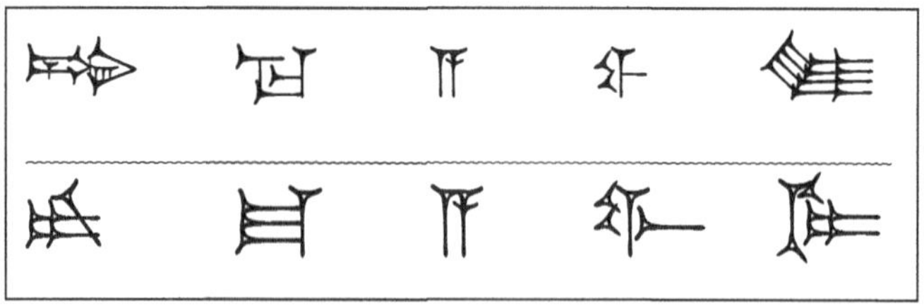

XXIX (Rv. VI):27 *šumma awīlum*

LH §134 XXIX (Rv. VI):28

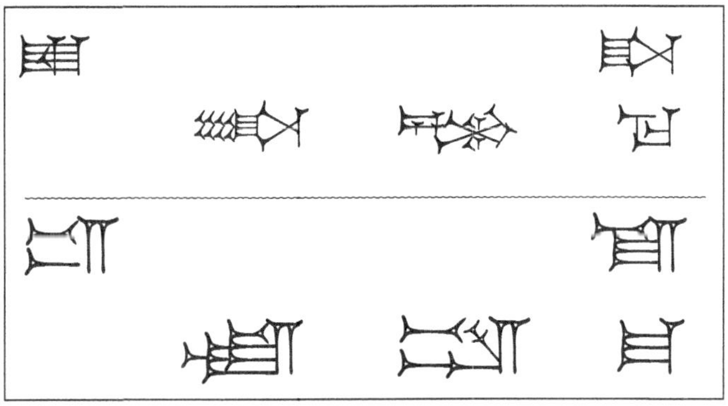

[28]*iššalilma*

LH §134 XXIX (Rv. VI):29

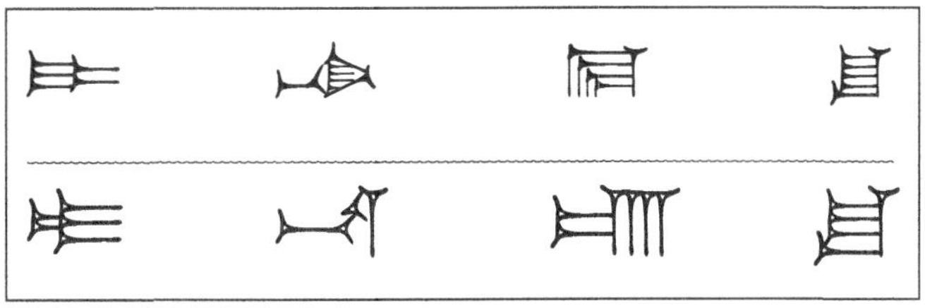

[29]*ina bîtišu*

LH §134 XXIX (Rv. VI):30

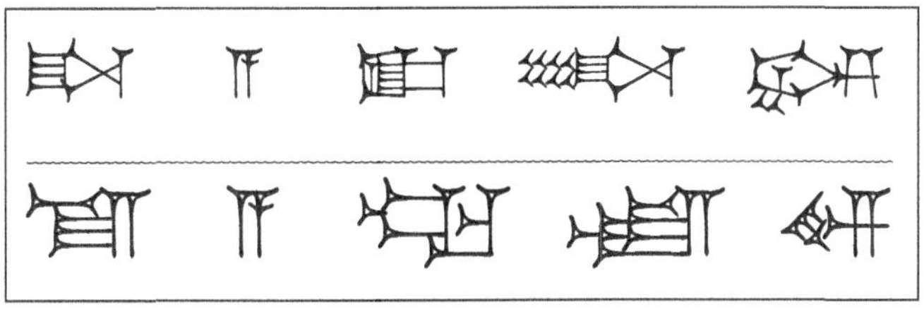

[30]*ša akālim*

LH §134 XXIX (Rv. VI):31

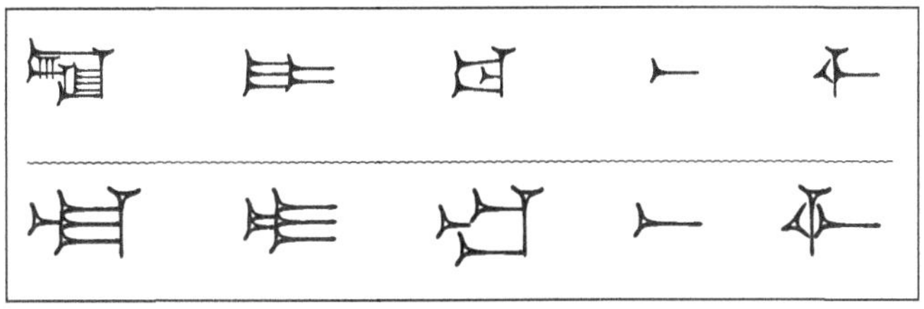

[31]*lâ ibaššî*

LH §134 XXIX (Rv. VI):32

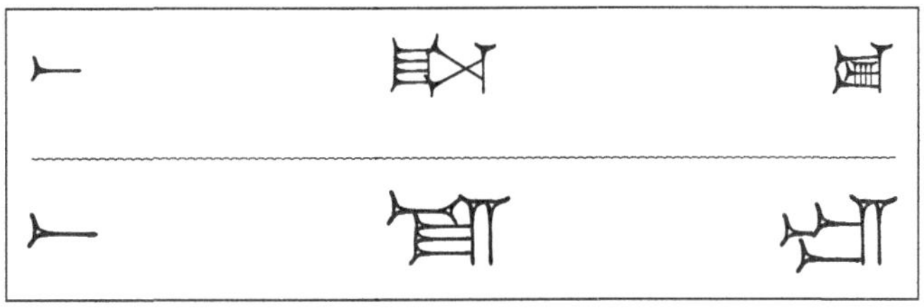

[32]*aššassu*

LH §134 XXIX (Rv. VI):33

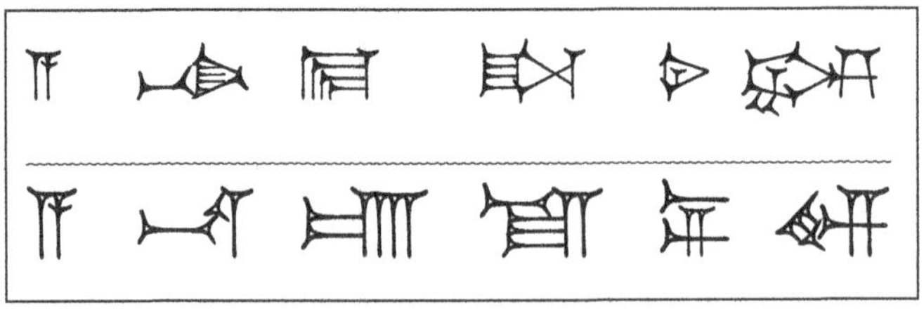

[33]*ana bît šanîm*

LH §134 XXIX (Rv. VI):34

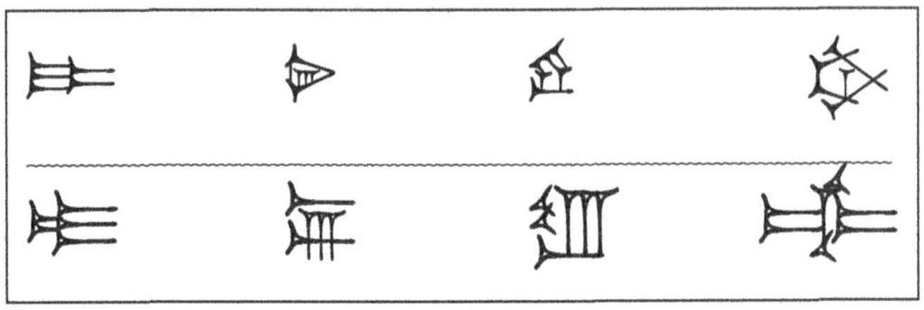

[34]*irrub*

LH §134 XXIX (Rv. VI):35

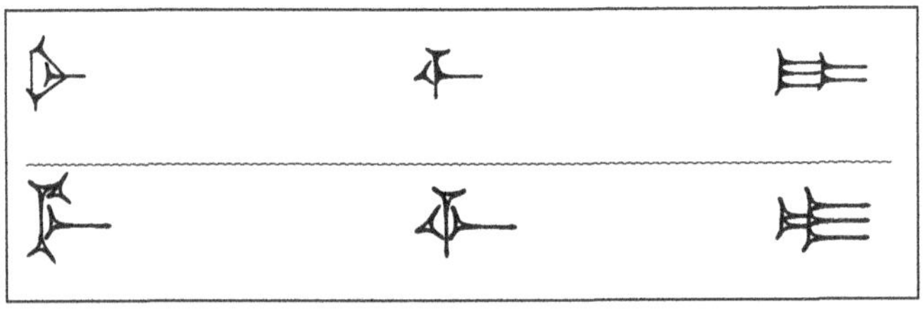

[35]*sinništum šî*

LH §134 XXIX (Rv. VI):36

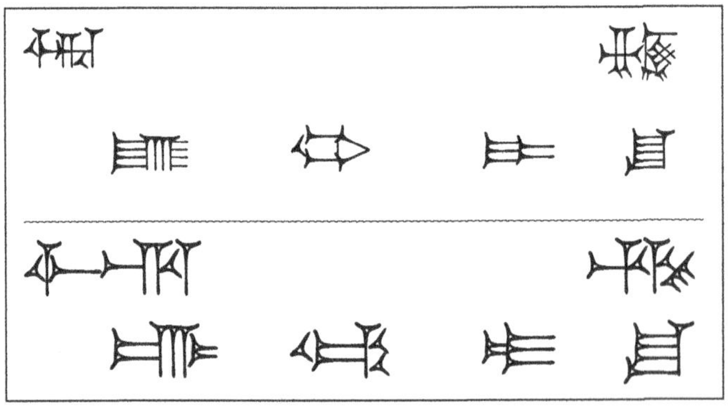

[36]*arnam ul îšû*

1. Grammatical Analysis: Parse all verb forms and answer the question below.

   a. Explain the unexpected tense of the verb in LH §134 XXIX (Rv. VI):36.

2. Translation: Translate LH §134.

LH §135 gives a husband who has returned home from captivity the right to reclaim his wife, but any sons go their respective fathers.

1. Transliterate and Normalize: See the note below for additional help.

LH §135 XXIX (Rv. VI):37

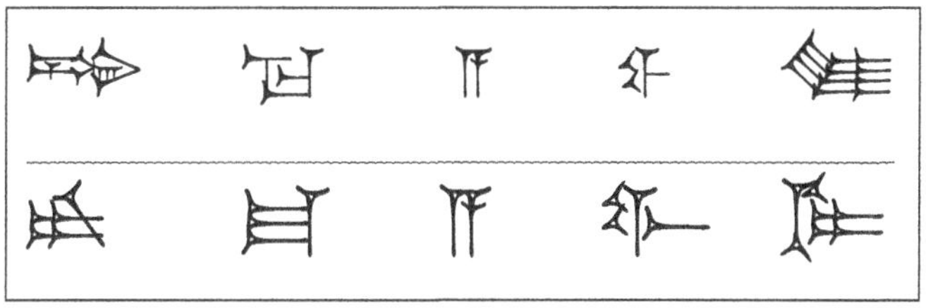

LH §135 XXIX (Rv. VI):38

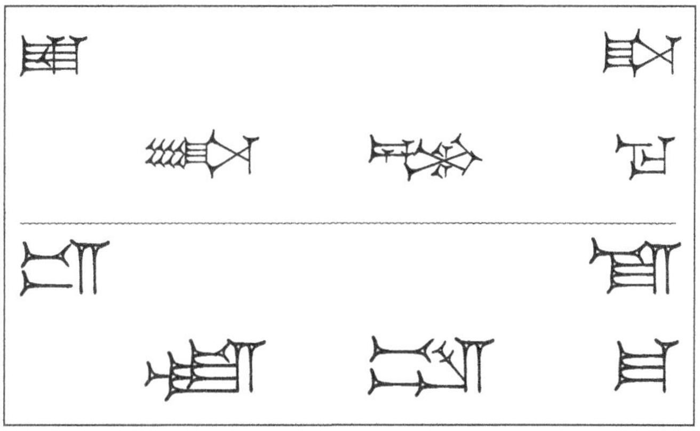

LH §135 XXIX (Rv. VI):39

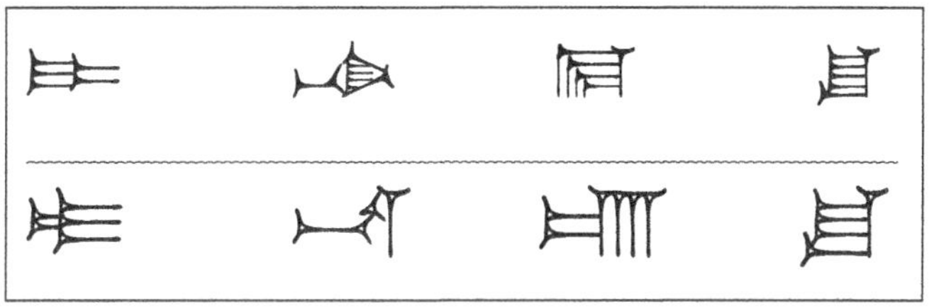

LH §135 XXIX (Rv. VI):40

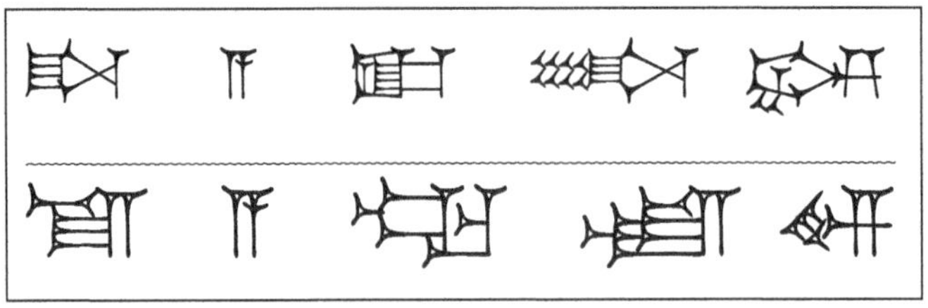

LH §135 XXIX (Rv. VI):41

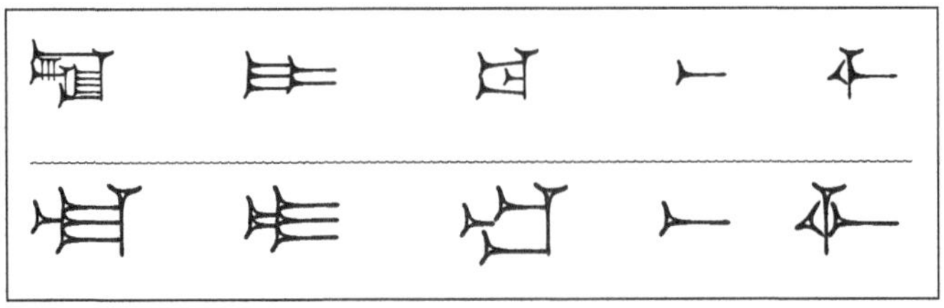

LH §135 XXIX (Rv. VI):42

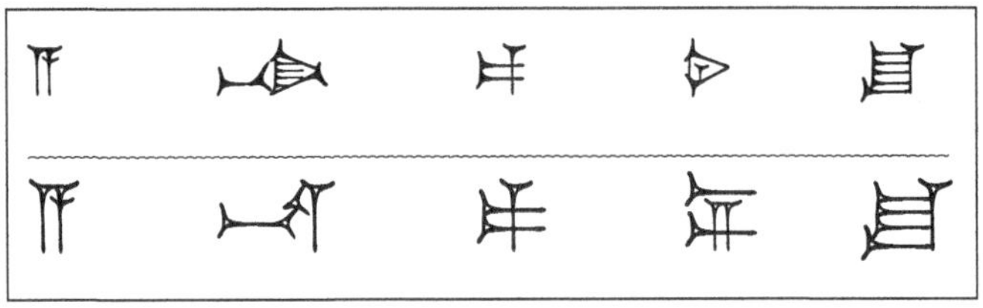

LH §135 XXIX (Rv. VI):43

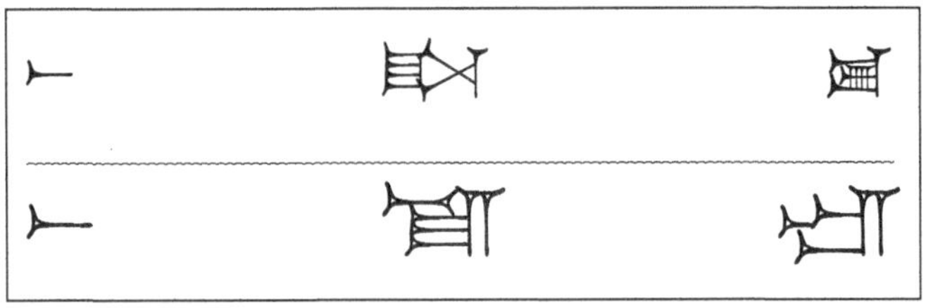

LH §135 XXIX (Rv. VI):44

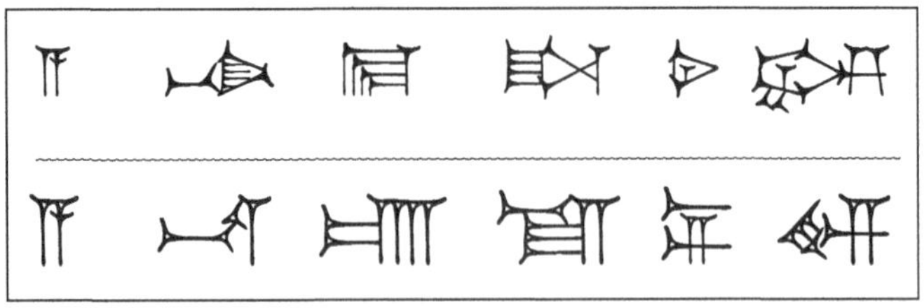

LH §135 XXIX (Rv. VI):45

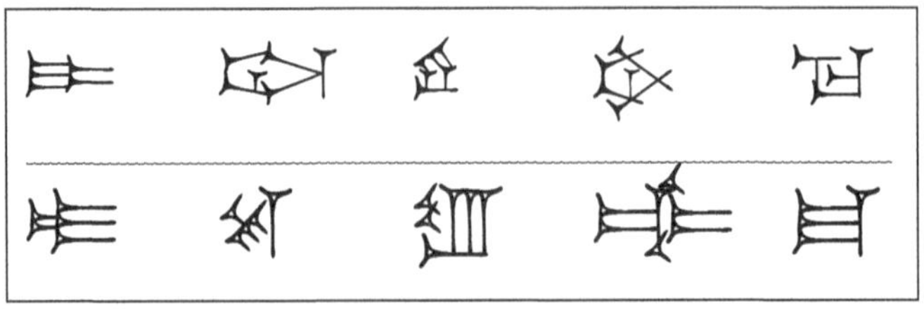

LH §135 XXIX (Rv. VI):46

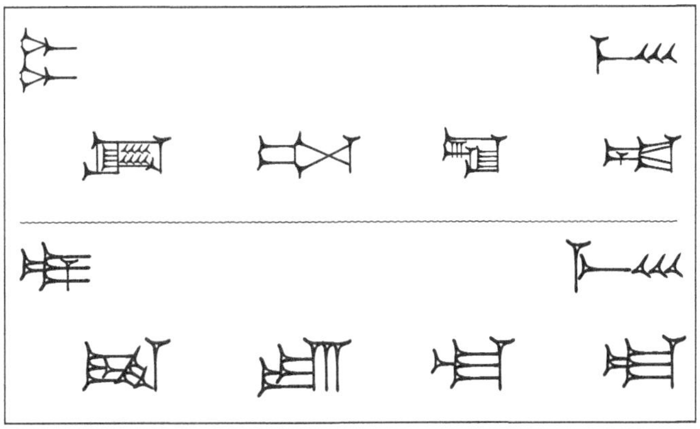

LH §135 XXIX (Rv. VI):47

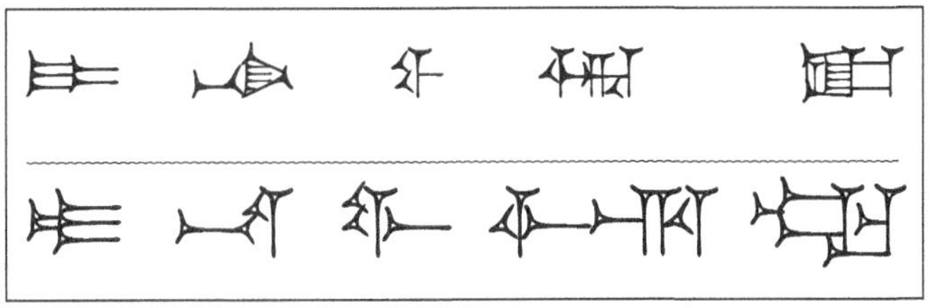

LH §135 XXIX (Rv. VI):48

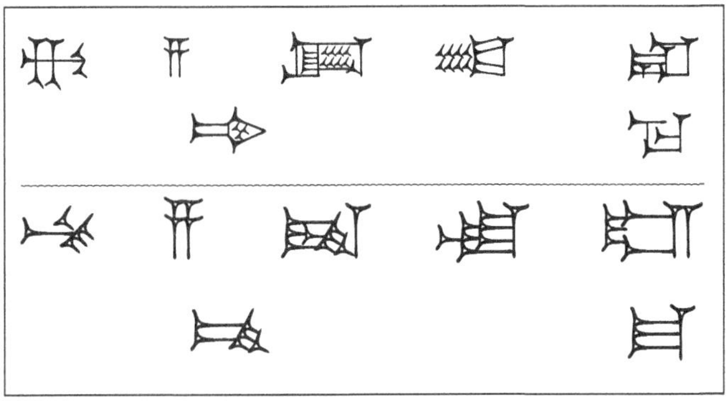

LH §135 XXIX (Rv. VI):49

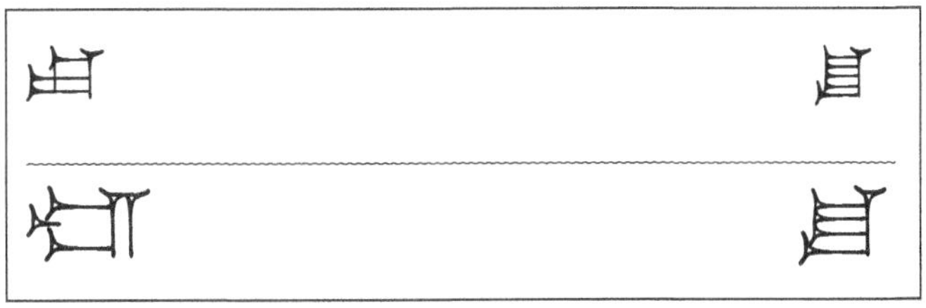

LH §135 XXIX (Rv. VI):50

Note: The sign  in XXIX (Rv. VI):50 is *dam*. This sign does not need to be learned.

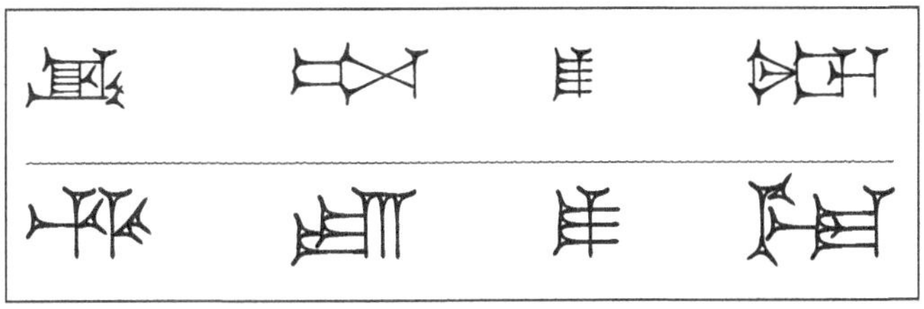

LH §135 XXIX (Rv. VI):51

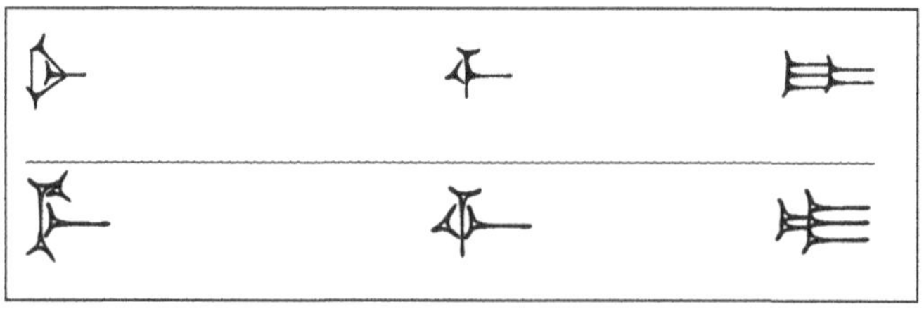

LH §135 XXIX (Rv. VI):52

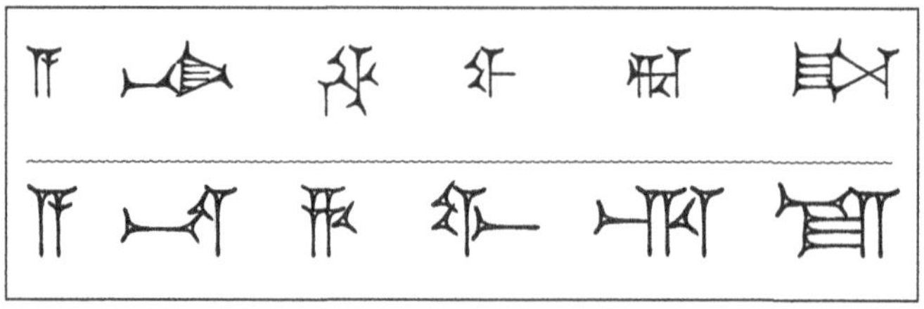

LH §135 XXIX (Rv. VI):53

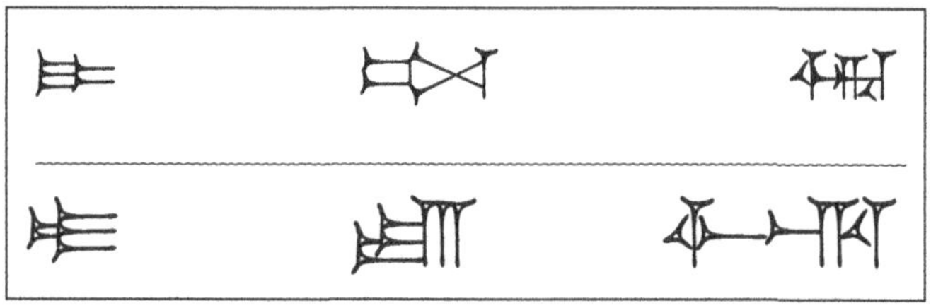

LH §135 XXIX (Rv. VI):54

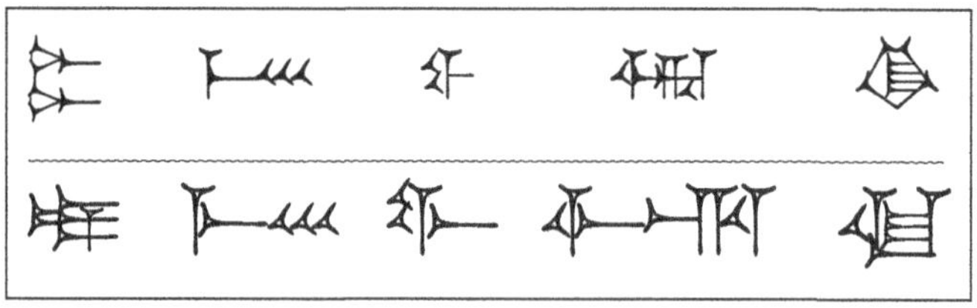

LH §135 XXIX (Rv. VI):55

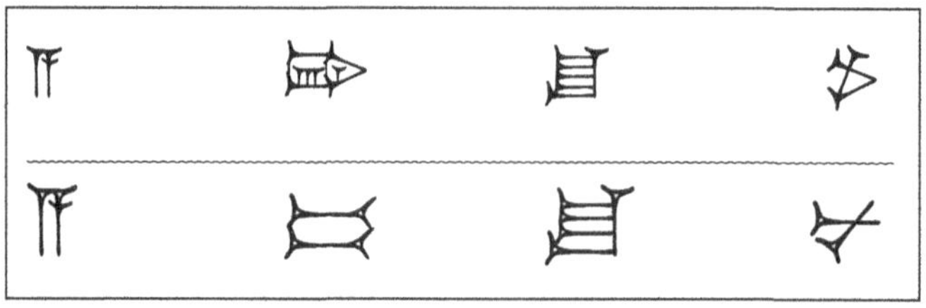

LH §135 XXIX (Rv. VI):56

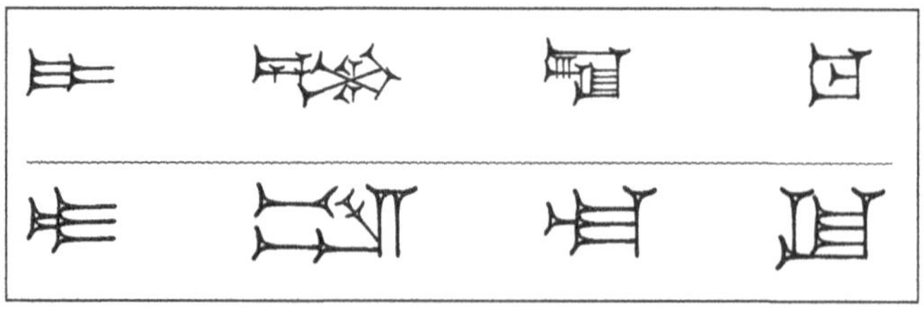

2. Grammatical Analysis: Parse all verb forms. See the note below for additional help.

Note: XXIX (Rv. VI):52 includes the word *ḫāwirum*, *ḫā'irum*, "(first) husband." It is a G-stem participle of *ḫārum*, "to choose (a mate), to select." This word does not need to be learned.

3. Translation: Translate LH §135.

LH §136 addresses the case of a husband's willful desertion of his wife.

1. Transliterate and Normalize.

LH §136 XXIX (Rv. VI):57

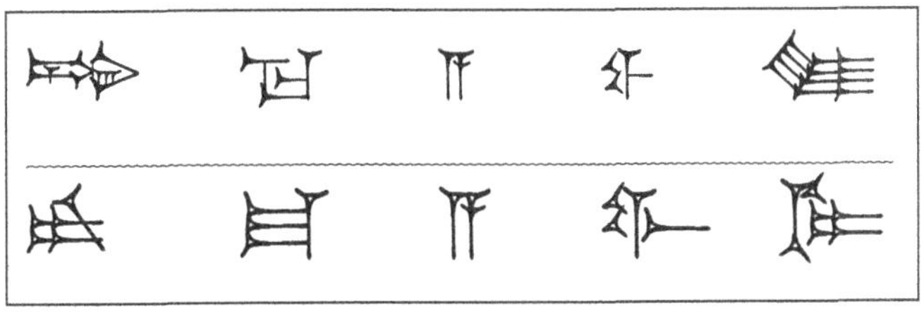

LH §136 XXIX (Rv. VI):58

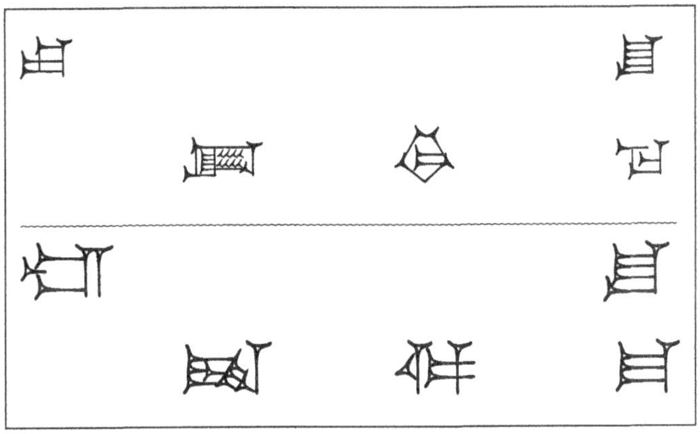

LH §136 XXIX (Rv. VI):59

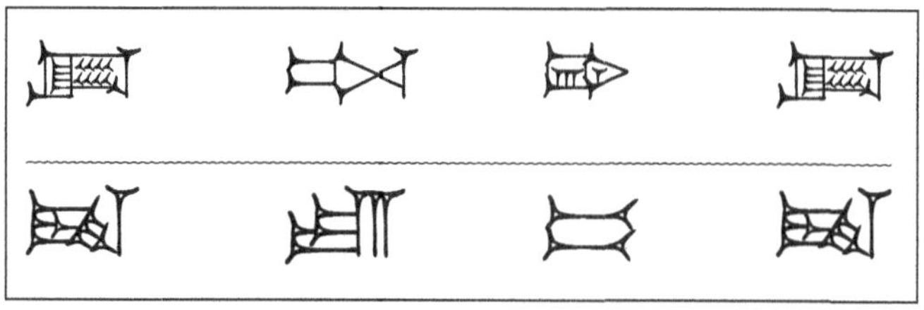

LH §136 XXIX (Rv. VI):60

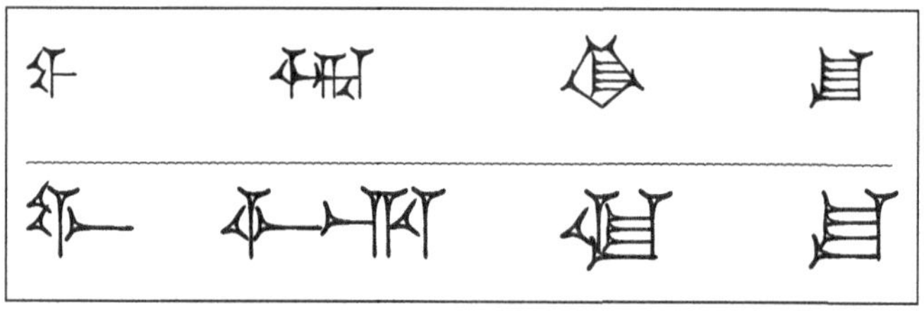

LH §136 XXIX (Rv. VI):61

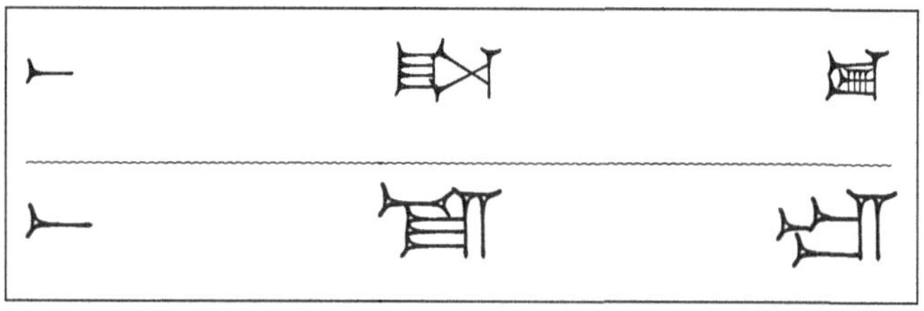

LH §136 XXIX (Rv. VI):62

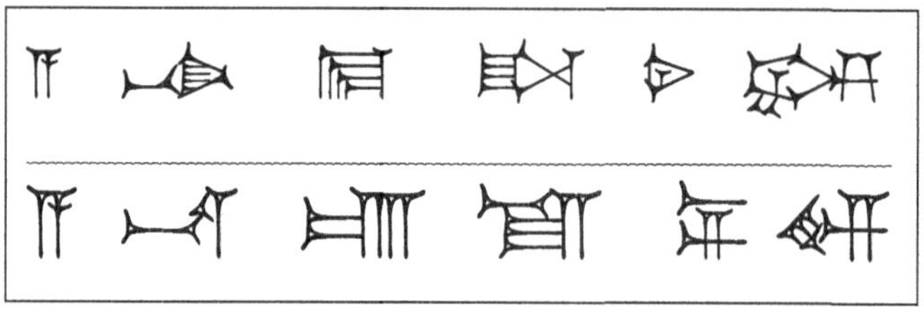

LH §136 XXIX (Rv. VI):63

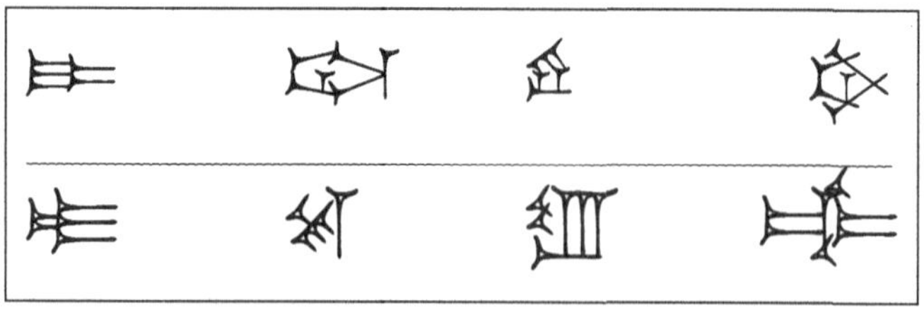

LH §136 XXIX (Rv. VI):64

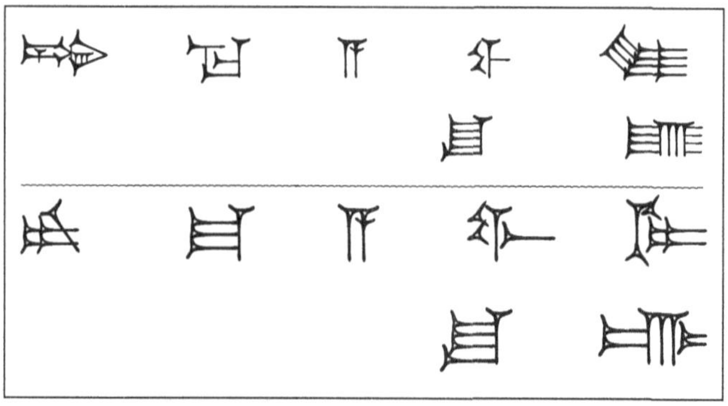

LH §136 XXIX (Rv. VI):65

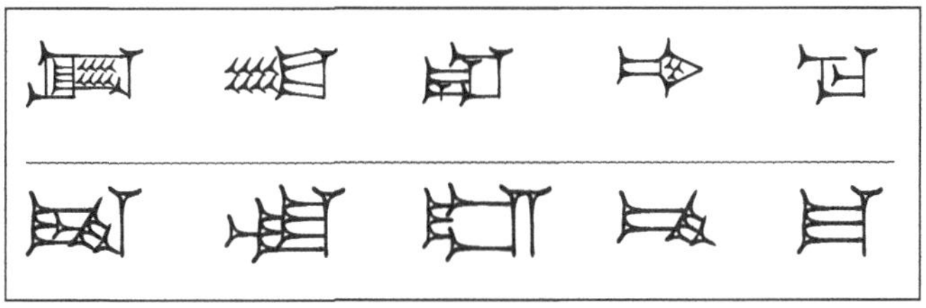

LH §136 XXIX (Rv. VI):66

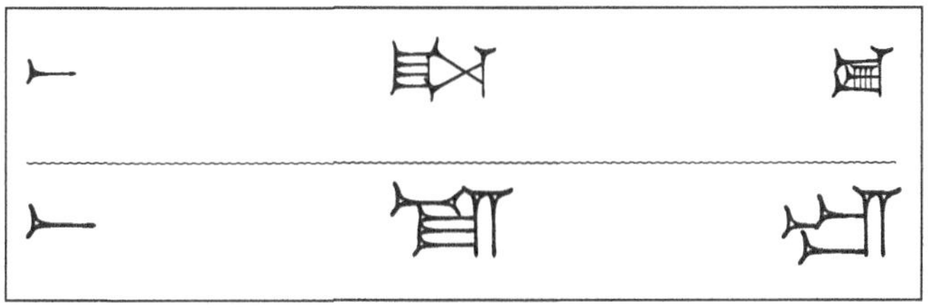

LH §136 XXIX (Rv. VI):67

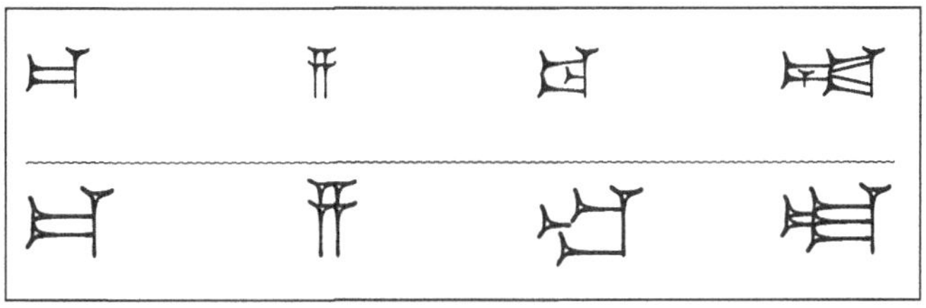

LH §136 XXIX (Rv. VI):68

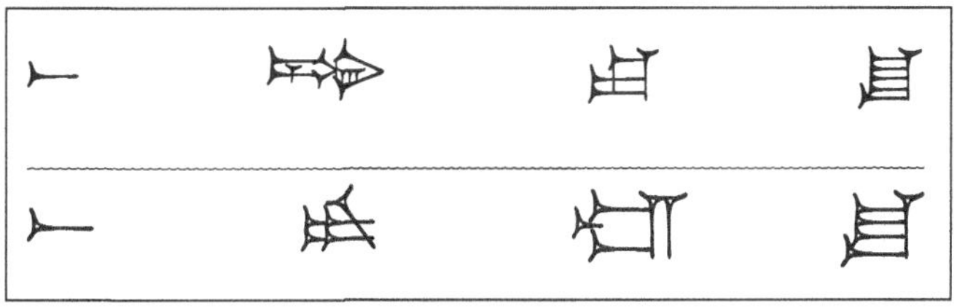

LH §136 XXIX (Rv. VI):69

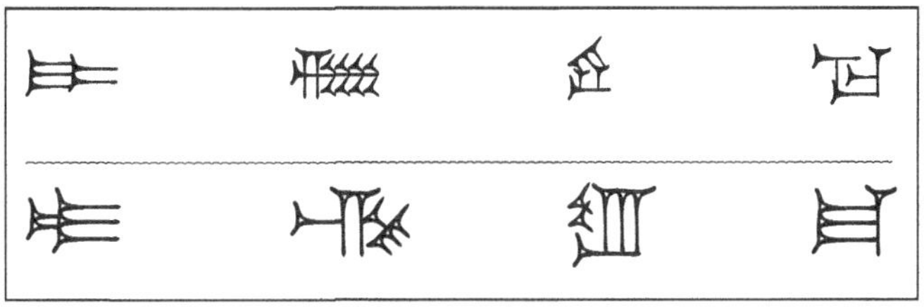

LH §136 XXIX (Rv. VI):70

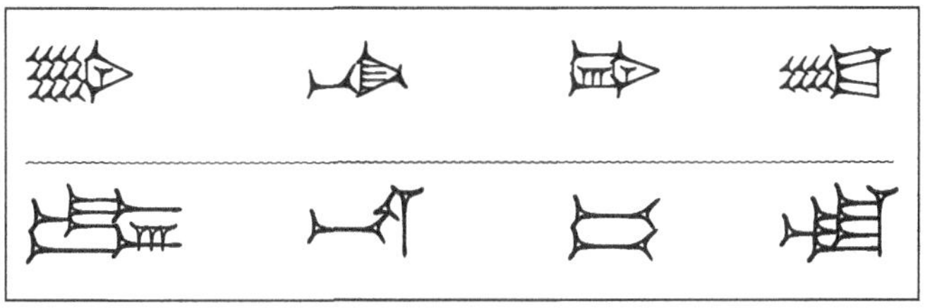

LH §136 XXIX (Rv. VI):71

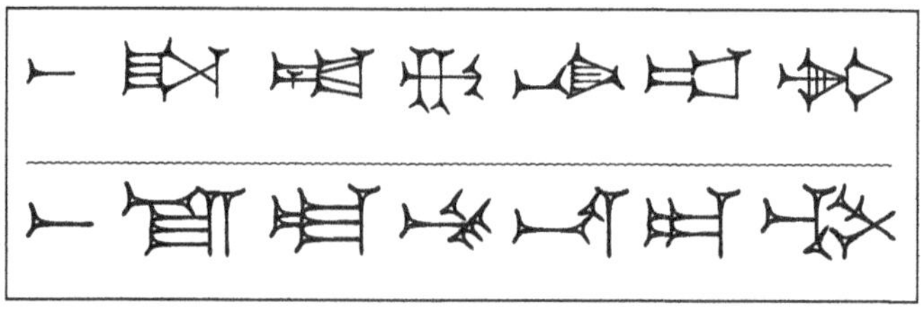

LH §136 XXIX (Rv. VI):72

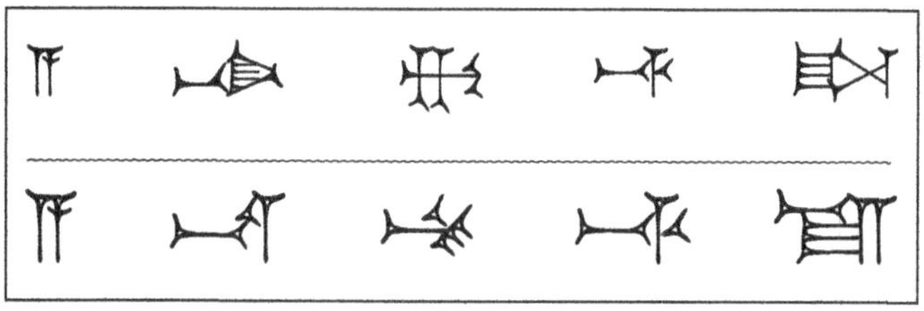

LH §136 XXIX (Rv. VI):73

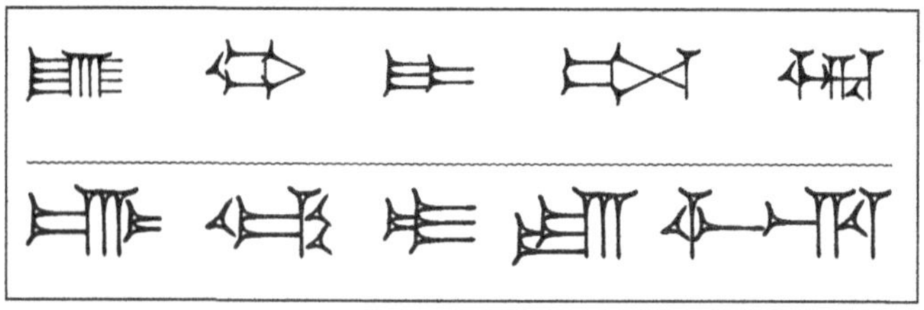

2. Grammatical Analysis: Parse all verb forms.

3. Translation: Translate LH §136.

18–

First- and Second-Person Forms and Cultural Background

The laws that will be translated in this chapter, LH §§137–140, continue the general theme of LH §§127–149, all of which involve laws regarding the family, especially women, sexual behavior, marriage, divorce, and inheritance. In the case of LH §§137–141 (LH §141 will be covered in Chapter 19), the focus is on issues related to abandonment and divorce. The full paradigms of pronominal forms of prefix and suffix tenses will also be reviewed. The so-called sandwich construction will also be addressed, as will the archaic *-u* construct suffix. Each of these grammatical points will find at least one example within LH §§137–141. Finally, some cultural background information regarding marriage will be provided in order to help understand the broader framework for the laws translated in this chapter.

18.1 Pronominal Forms of Prefix and Suffix Tenses

Casuistic laws like those in LH do not frequently employ second- and first-person pronominal references, as has been seen throughout the exercises, but there are a few exceptions. Moreover, any reading outside LH will require mastery of these forms. The full paradigm of the preterite (for prefix forms) is listed below. The full paradigm of the stative (for the suffix tense forms including the predicative state of nouns) is also below. These should now be learned in their entirety.

		Preterite	Stative
Singular	3m	*iprus*	*paris*
	3f	*iprus*	*parsat*
	2m	*taprus*	*parsāta*
	2f	*taprusī*	*parsāti*
	1c	*aprus*	*parsāku*
Plural	3m	*iprusū*	*parsū*
	3f	*iprusā*	*parsā*
	2m	*taprusā*	*parsātunu*
	2f	*taprusā*	*parsātina*
	1c	*niprus*	*parsānu*

18.2 The Sandwich Construction

One occasionally encounters a "sandwich construction" in LH. This refers to cases where a preposition is governing an infinitive, which is in the genitive case since it is the object of a preposition, but the direct object of the infinitive with perhaps other elements is "sandwiched" in between the preposition and the verb. This is especially common in purpose clauses introduced with *ana*. In such a situation, it occasionally happens that the expected accusative case for the direct object of the infinitive assimilates to the genitive, the case of the infinitive, since it is the actual object of the preposition.

For example, in LH §42 there is the expression, *ina eqlim šiprim lâ epēšim ukannūšūma*, "they would convict him for not doing work in the field." In this example the infinitive, *epēšim*, "to do," is in the genitive because it is the object of the preposition *ina*. Coincidentally, *ina* happens to be doing double duty since it is also modifying *eqlim*, "in a field." The noun *šiprim*, "work," should be in the accusative case since it is the direct object of *epēšim* "to do," but it is instead in the genitive case by assimilation, as if it were the object of the preposition as is the case of *eqlim*, "field."

18.3 The Archaic *-u* Construct Suffix

In §8.1 the common spelling options for construct forms of nouns were presented. The most challenging examples are nouns that are monosyllabic when the case ending is removed, some of which have more than one alternative spelling. For example, the construct state of *mutum*, "husband," may have a paragogic *-i*, resulting in *muti*, "husband of," or alternatively, it may appear without the paragogic *-i*, as happens with *mut*, "husband of," in LH §172.

In addition to these options, one more option needs to be noted. There are rare cases when an archaic construct ending *-u* appears on singular nouns in construct. For example, the construct form of *zikrum*, "name," is normally *zikir*, with the expected harmonizing anaptyctic vowel *-i*. On rare occasions, however, it is *zikru*, with the archaic *-u* construct suffix. This form appears in LH §Pro II:5–6, *zikru bâbilim*, "the name of Babylon."

18.4 Some Useful Cultural Background[1]

In this portion of LH there are some terms related to ancient Near Eastern marriage that are frequently misunderstood, the *šeriktum* and the *terḫatum*.

The *šeriktum*, or "dowry," was an amount given to a woman by her father upon her marriage. It had two sources. One source was the father himself, who gave it in order to provide economic protection for his daughter and ultimately as a means for passing on wealth to future grandchildren. The other source of a portion of the dowry was the husband.

A *terḫatum*, a "marriage present," often misleadingly translated "bride price," was given by a suiter to the father of his intended bride as a measure of his commitment to her. The marriage present was subsequently included with the dowry and passed along to his wife upon

1. See also footnote 10 in Chapter 16. For more details, cf. Greengus, "Redefining 'Inchoate Marriage' in Old Babylonian Contexts"; Hugenberger, *Marriage as a Covenant*, 240–49, 278. Greengus distinguishes five stages of marriage in the Old Babylonian period, not just two, while also noting that marriage remained somewhat "inchoate," at least in terms of the disposition of the dowry, until the birth of a first child. This is so because if a wife dies before giving birth, the wife's father or his heirs could reclaim the dowry. If, however, the wife has borne children, the dowry belongs to them as their inheritance (LH §162). While the analysis of Greengus is informative and largely persuasive, it seems possible to combine it with a more nuanced traditional two-stage view of OB marriage.

her change in domicile or the consummation of the marriage. The apparent reason that the groom did not give the marriage present directly to his bride was so that there would be an indisputable public record of the fact that after their marriage this portion of their shared wealth belonged, in particular, to his wife.

Once the bride moved into the home of her husband, the dowry was held in trust by the husband and could be used by the husband, especially it if included things like animals or even land. Ultimately, however, the marriage present and dowry belonged to the wife and would revert to her immediately if the husband divorced her for grounds other than marital infidelity (see LH §138) or if the husband died. Although the husband had use of the marriage present and dowry while married to his wife, if anything was spent, lost, or destroyed, the husband had to repay the full value of the marriage present and the dowry upon the dissolution of the marriage, if it was not for cause (see LH §138).

Apart from this important purpose of providing a degree of financial security for the wife in the event of an unjustified divorce or a life insurance policy in the event of her husband's death, there was an additional purpose for the dowry. It was also intended to provide a means for passing wealth down to one's grandchildren through a daughter's line.

Finally, it is likely that one practical motivation for such passage of wealth was the "contract of the generations." In other words, the dowry would help secure the assistance of the younger generation for the care of parents, especially a widowed mother. The passage of any inheritance to children was not unconditional, however. There is evidence that negligent or rebellious children could be and were in fact legally disinherited for cause. Undoubtedly, this potential threat provided a degree of leverage for an otherwise vulnerable older generation that helped secure needed care.

18.5 Homework

Before you move on, be sure to know the full paradigms for the preterite and stative forms. Facility with the prefixes and suffixes of both tenses will help you translate texts beyond LH. Also, be sure to understand the so-called sandwich construction and become comfortable with the use of the archaic *-u* construct suffix. Finally, make note of the cultural background information above so as to have a proper context for the translation exercises below.

18.5.1 *Signs*

 gi_4

 *ḫe, ḫi*

 LUKUR, *nadîtum* (<**nadīʾtum*) "devotee"; "high priestess" (< **nadīʾtum*)

 *en*

Congratulations! If you have learned the four cuneiform signs in this chapter and each of the preceding 113 signs, you will be able to read 98 percent of all the cuneiform signs in LH §§1–20, 127–149.

18.5.2 *Vocabulary*

aplum (< *apālum* = to declare an heir) = heir, son
ḫîrtum (< *ḫi'ārum* = to choose, select) = (first) wife
ištên (absolute with masc); *ište'at* (absolute with fem.) = one, individual
libbum = heart (cf. *lēb*, לֵב)
mala = all, as much as; full amount (cf. *mālē'*, מָלֵא, "full")
manûm = mina (≈ 1/2 kg.) (cf. *māneh*, מָנֶה)
manûm (*u,u*) = to count, reckon, recount (cf. *mānâ*, מָנָה)
nadîtum (<**nadī'tum*) = devotee; high priestess (one who must remain childless)[2]
rabûm (*i,i*) = to be great; D: to raise (cf. *rābâ*, רָבָה, "to be many, be great")
šeriktum (< *šarākum* = to give) = dowry
šugîtum= priestess; lay priestess[3]
terḫatum= marriage present, bride price (?)
-u = an archaic suffix found on some nouns that marks the construct
uzubbûm (< *ezēbum*) = divorce settlement (cf. *'āzab*, עָזַב, "to forsake, abandon")

18.5.3 *Exercises*

LH §137 begins a section of LH (LH §§137–141) that treats various legal issues related to divorce. The law establishes the rights of a wife who is a priestess and whose husband intends to divorce her. There is no mention of infidelity; instead, it is stated that she has borne or provided sons (children) for her husband. Under these circumstances, the husband must return to his wife her full dowry.

1. Transliterate and Normalize: See the notes below for additional help.

LH §137 XXIX (Rv. VI):74

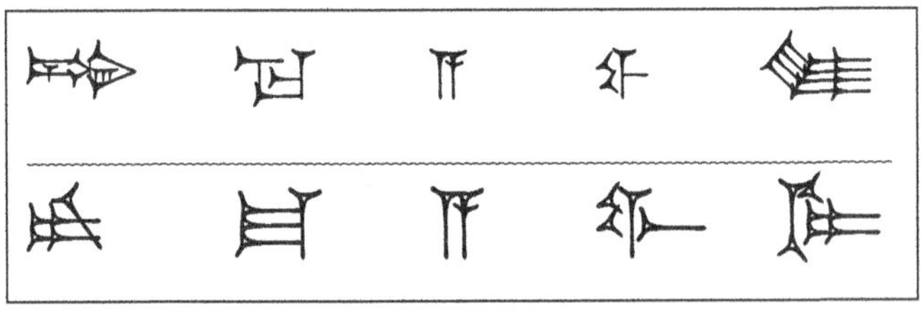

LH §137 XXIX (Rv. VI):75

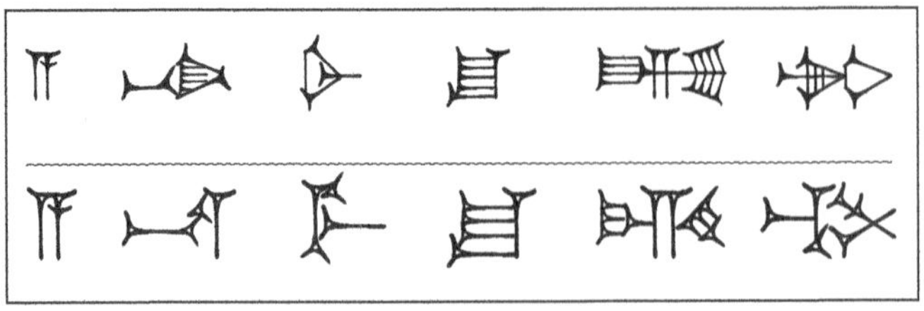

2. Lambert, "Class Notes."
3. Lambert, "Class Notes."

LH §137 XXIX (Rv. VI):76

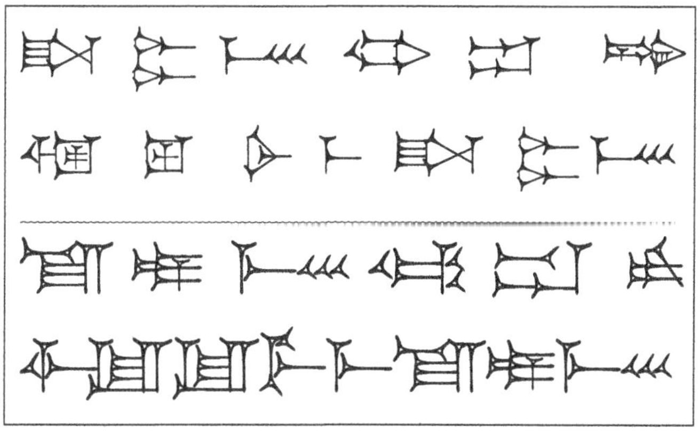

LH §137 XXIX (Rv. VI):77

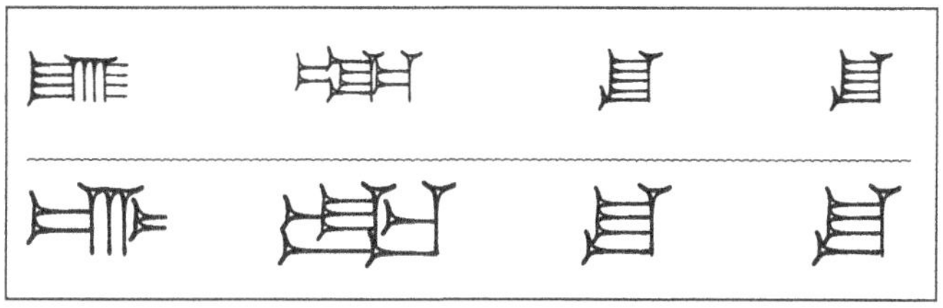

LH §137 XXIX (Rv. VI):78

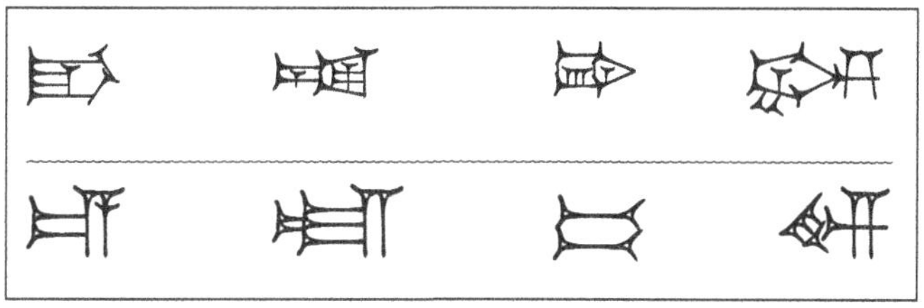

LH §137 XXIX (Rv. VI):79

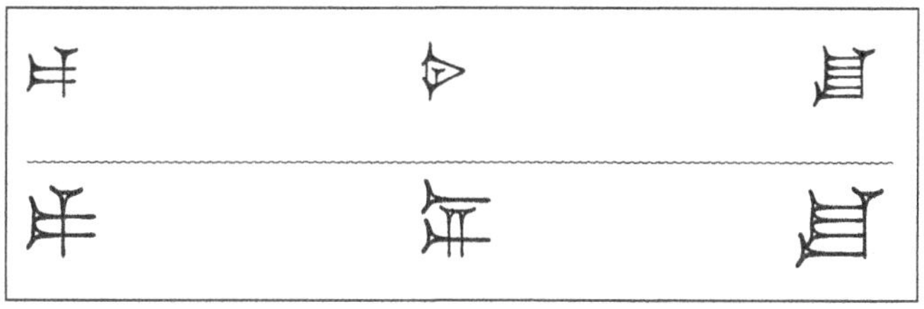

LH §137 XXIX (Rv. VI):80

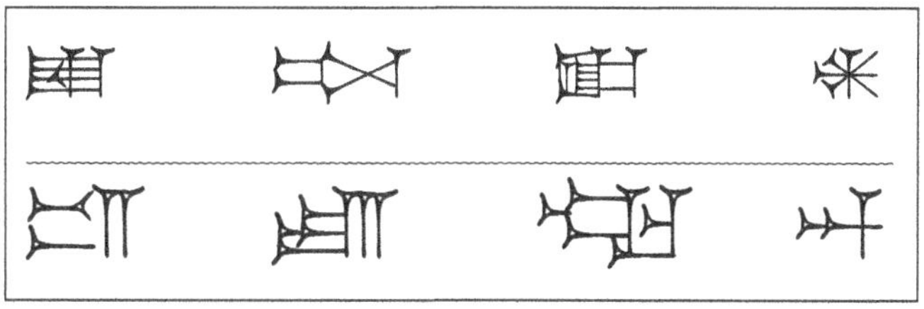

LH §137 XXIX (Rv. VI):81

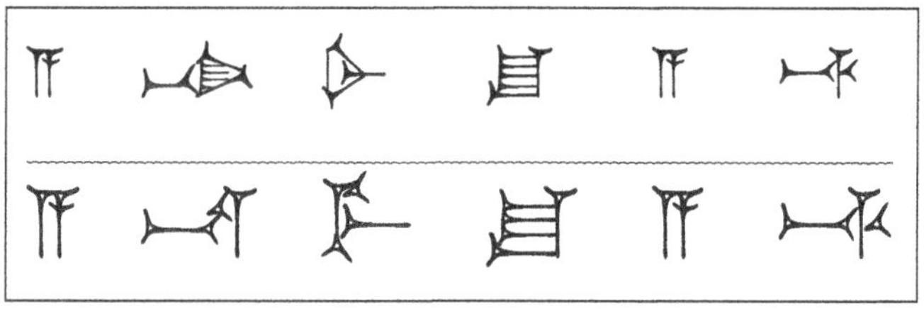

LH §137 XXIX (Rv. VI):82

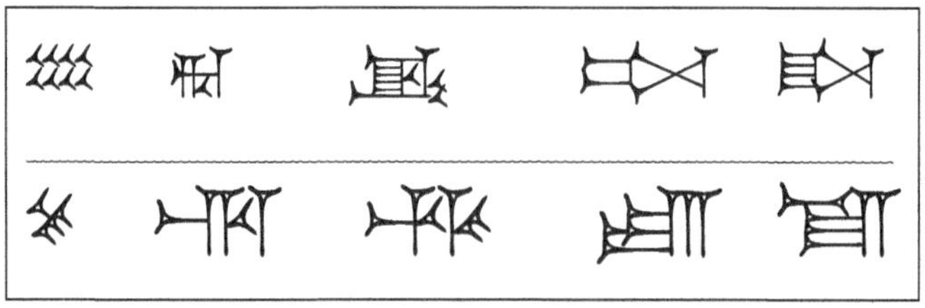

LH §137 XXIX (Rv. VI):83

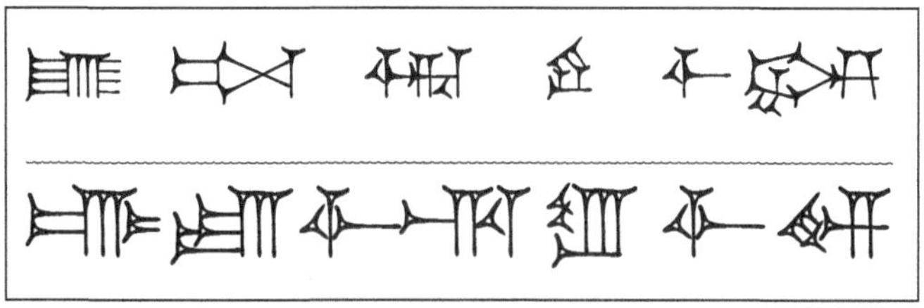

LH §137 XXIX (Rv. VI):84

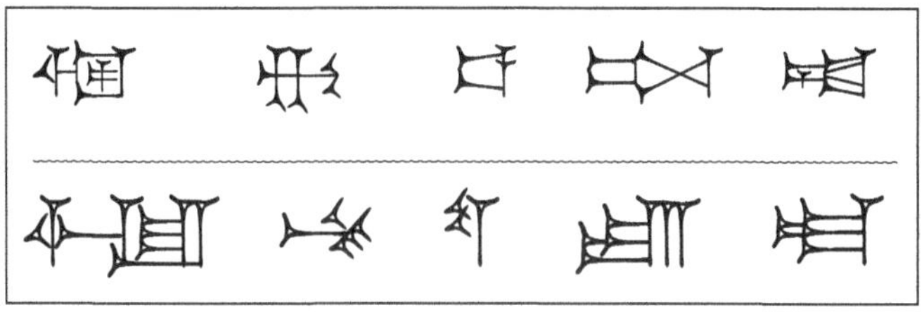

LH §137 XXIX (Rv. VI):85

Note: The sign in XXIX (Rv. VI):85 is A.ŠÀ, *eqlum*, meaning "field." This sign and word do not need to learned. This text box also includes the sign 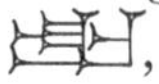, which is KIRI$_6$, *kirûm*, meaning "orchard." This sign, which also has the value *šar*, was learned in Chapter 12.

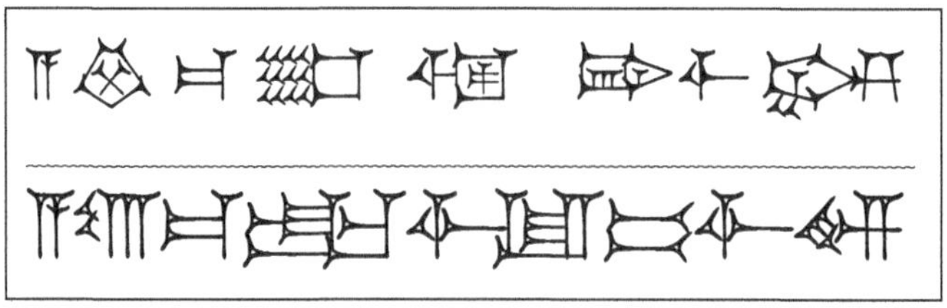

LH §137 XXX (Rv. VII):1

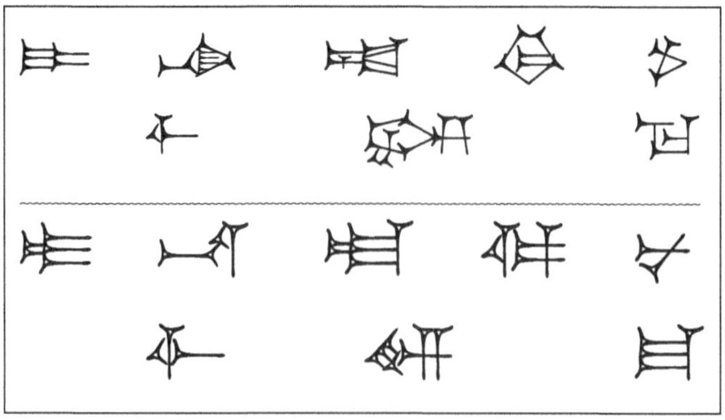

LH §137 XXX (Rv. VII):2

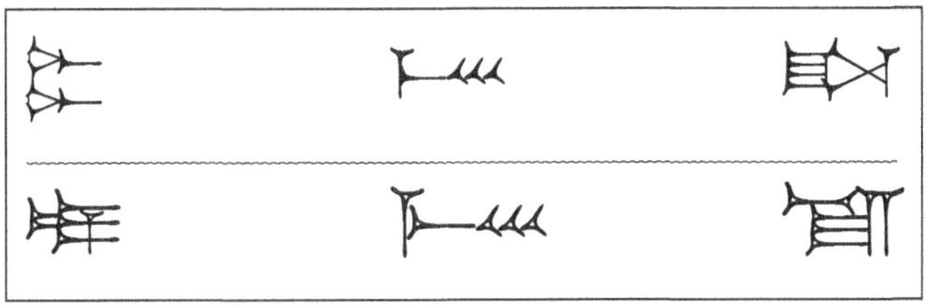

LH §137 XXX (Rv. VII):3

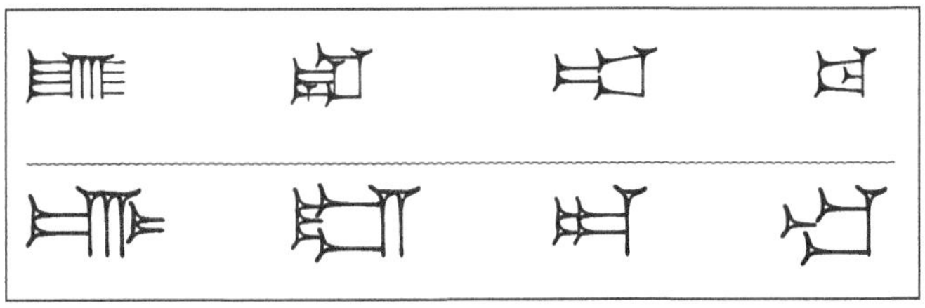

LH §137 XXX (Rv. VII):4

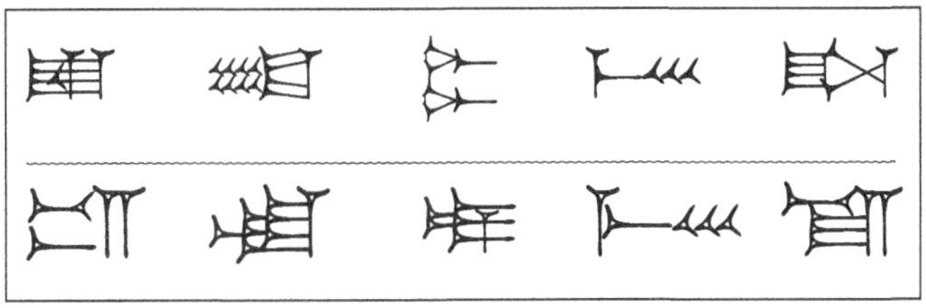

LH §137 XXX (Rv. VII):5

Note: The sign 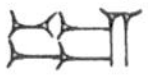 in XXX (Rv. VII):5 is *úr*. This does not need to be learned.

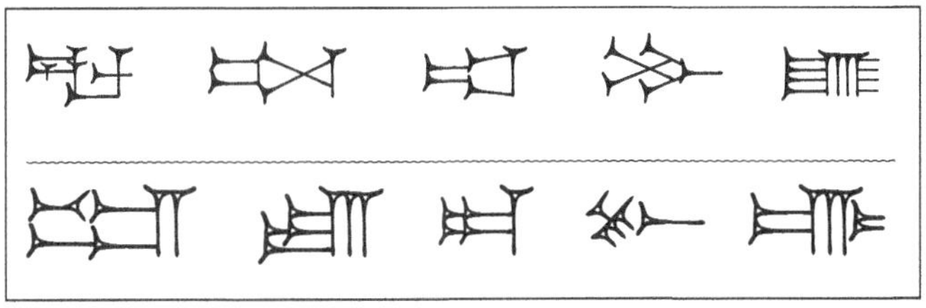

LH §137 XXX (Rv. VII):6

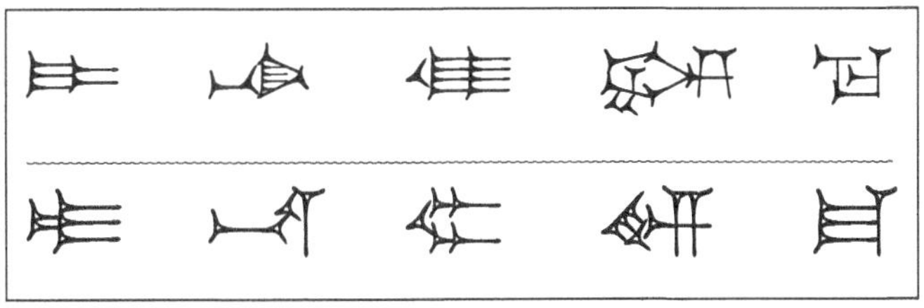

LH §137 XXX (Rv. VII):7

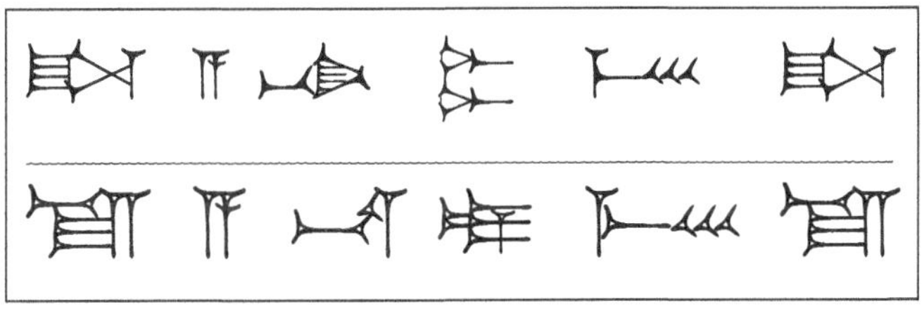

LH §137 XXX (Rv. VII):8

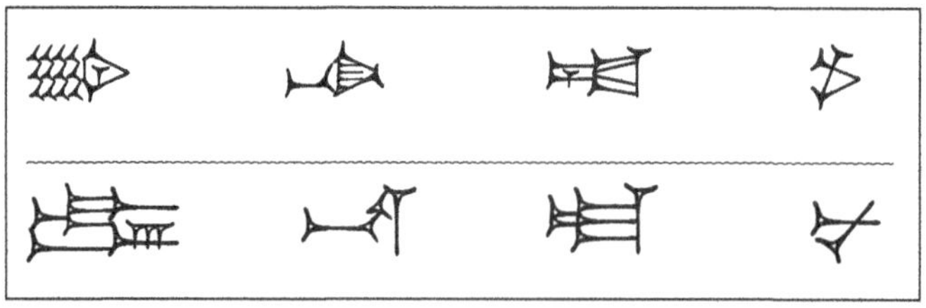

LH §137 XXX (Rv. VII):9

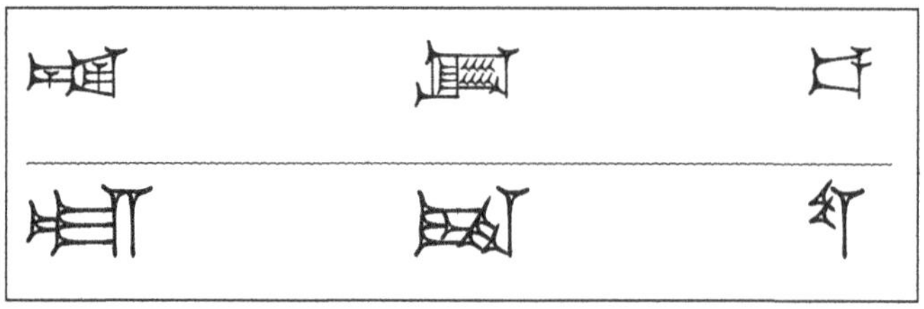

LH §137 XXX (Rv. VII):10

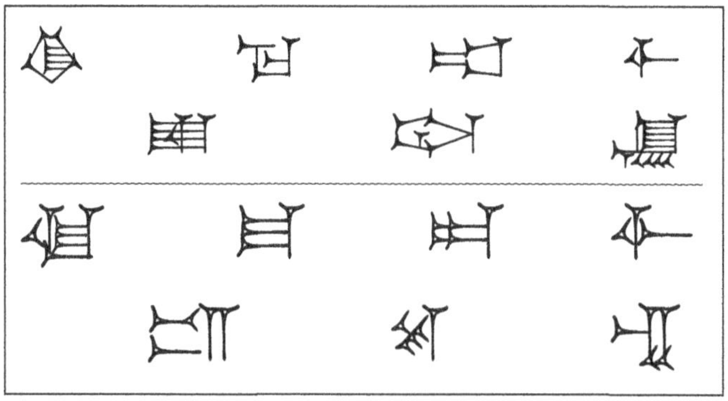

LH §137 XXX (Rv. VII):11

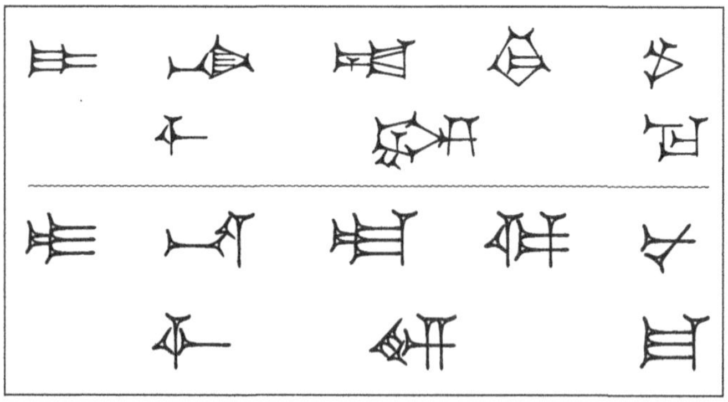

LH §137 XXX (Rv. VII):12

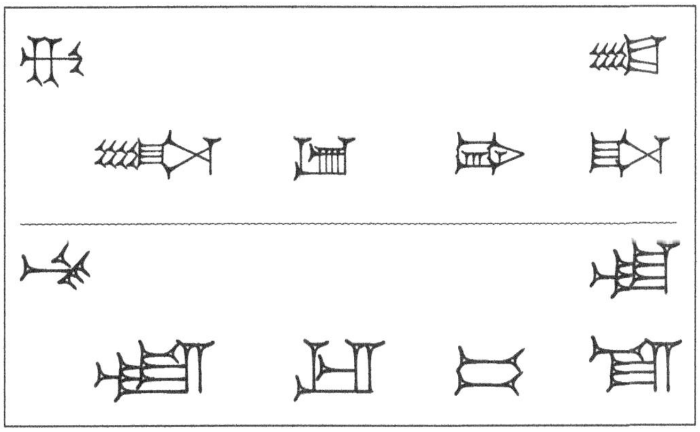

LH §137 XXX (Rv. VII):13

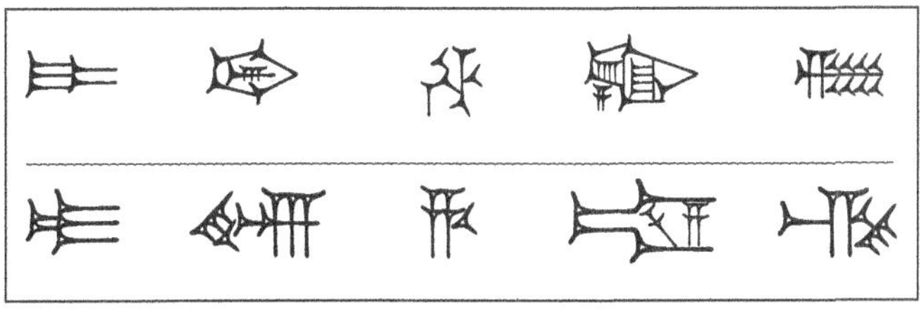

2. Grammatical Analysis: Parse all verb forms. See the notes below for additional help. Also answer the question below.

   a. How does the use of a "sandwich construction" explain an otherwise unexpected genitive case found in XXIX (Rv. VI):76?

Note: The word in XXIX (Rv. VI):77 is *rašûm* (*i,i*), meaning "to have, own, acquire." In the Š-stem, it means "to provide." This word does not need to be learned.

Note: The word in XXIX (Rv. VI):85 is *bîšum*, meaning "moveable property, possession." This word does not need to be learned.

Note: The word in XXX (Rv. VII):9 is *zîttum* (f), "portion, part, share" (< *zâzum*, "to divide"). Some authorities prefer *zittum*. This word does not need to be learned.

3. Translation: Translate LH §137 and answer the question below.

   a. As pointed out in §3.5, the enclitic *-ma* has two main alternative functions. Either it functions as a conjunction that connects clauses or as a topicalizing particle that emphasizes the word to which it is attached. As a conjunction, most of the time it is translated "and (then)" or "but." What other less common translation for *-ma*, also discussed in §3.5, is appropriate here in XXX (Rv. VII):1?

LH §138 stipulates the payments (equivalent of the marriage present and any dowry) that a husband must pay a wife if he leaves her though she did not bear him any children.

1. Transliterate and Normalize: See the note below for additional help.

LH §138 XXX (Rv. VII):14

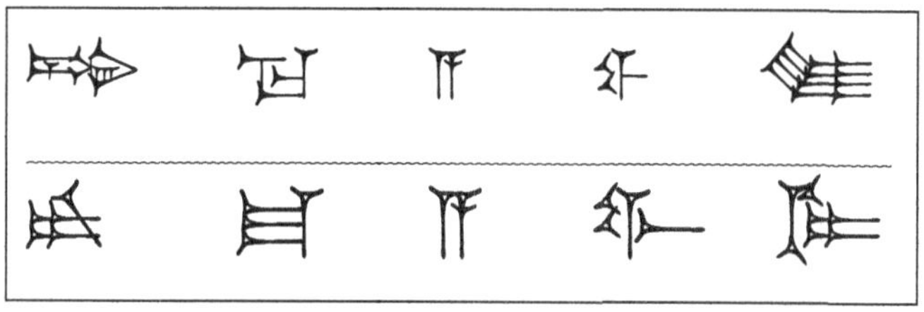

LH §138 XXX (Rv. VII):15

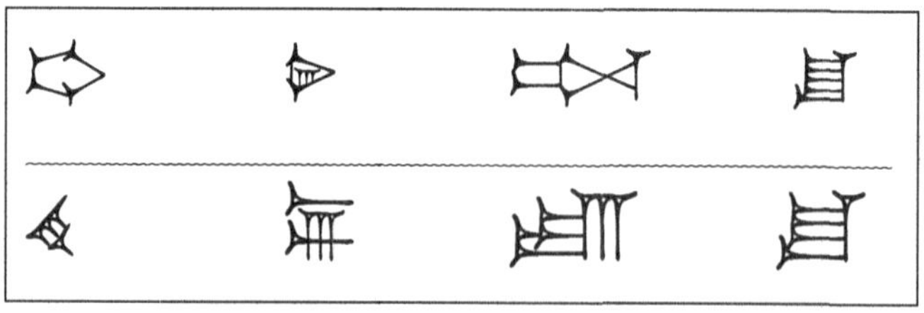

LH §138 XXX (Rv. VII):16

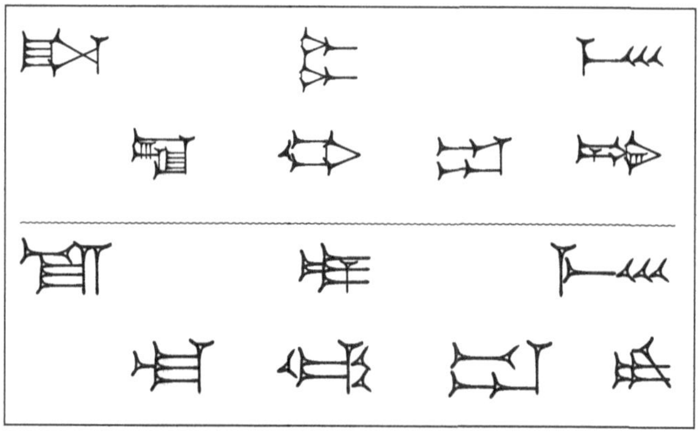

LH §138 XXX (Rv. VII):17

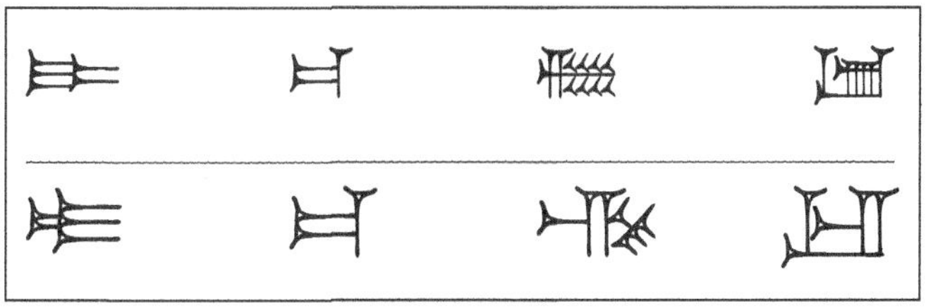

LH §138 XXX (Rv. VII):18

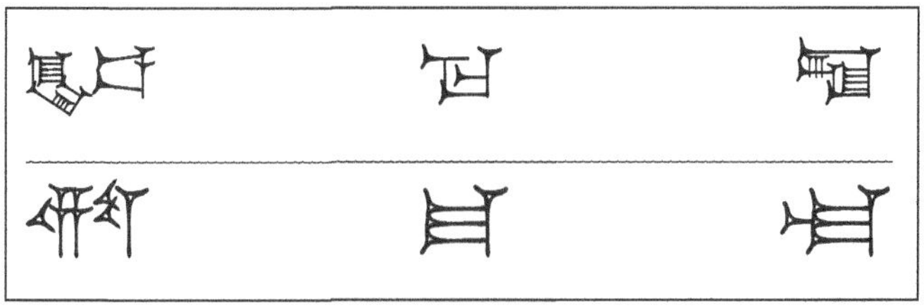

LH §138 XXX (Rv. VII):19

Note: The sign  in XXX (Rv. VII):19 is *ter*. This sign does not need to be learned.

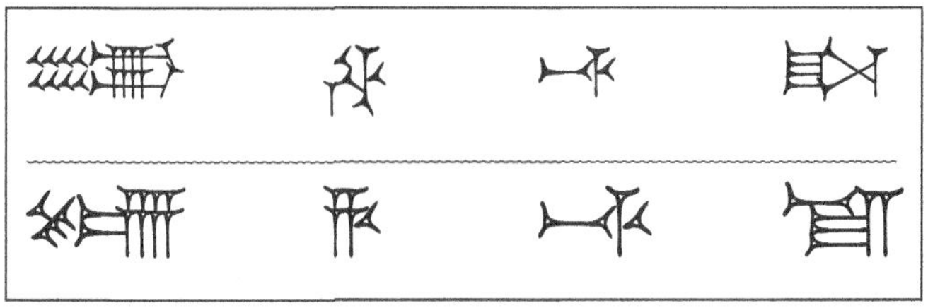

LH §138 XXX (Rv. VII):20

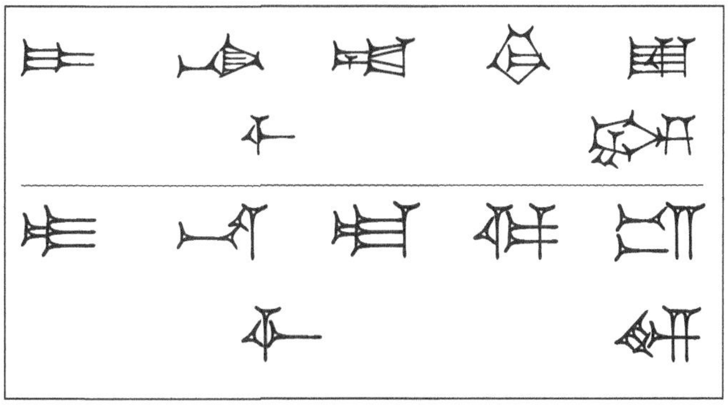

LH §138 XXX (Rv. VII):21

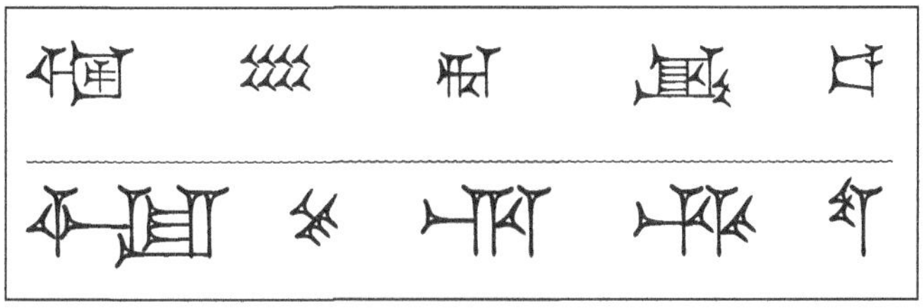

LH §138 XXX (Rv. VII):22

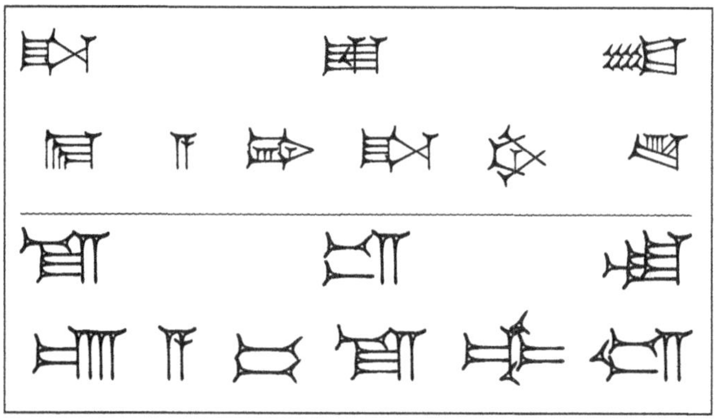

LH §138 XXX (Rv. VII):23

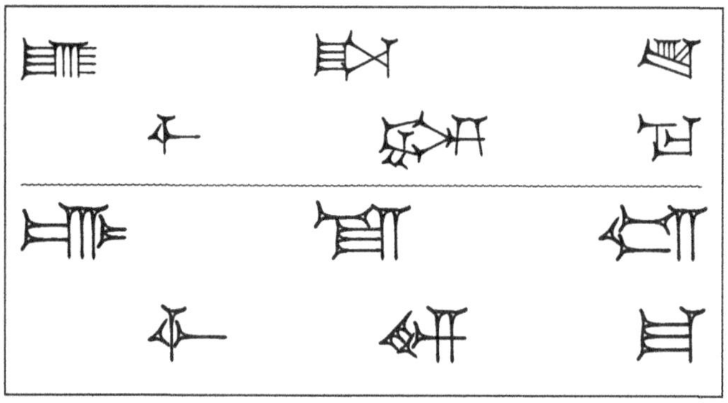

LH §138 XXX (Rv. VII):24

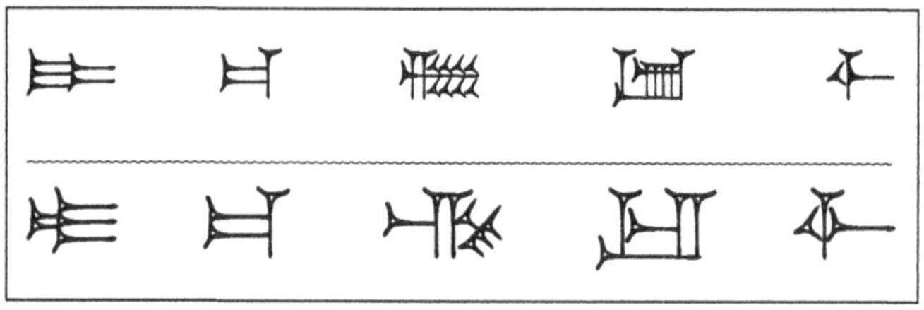

2. Grammatical Analysis: Parse all verb forms.

3. Translation: Translate LH §138.

LH §139 stipulates a minimum payment, in case there was no marriage present, that a husband must pay a wife who did not bear him any children if he leaves her.

1. Transliterate and Normalize: See the notes below for additional help.

LH §139 XXX (Rv. VII):25

Note: The signs  and  in XXX (Rv. VII):25 are *ter* and *tum* respectively. These signs do not need to be learned.

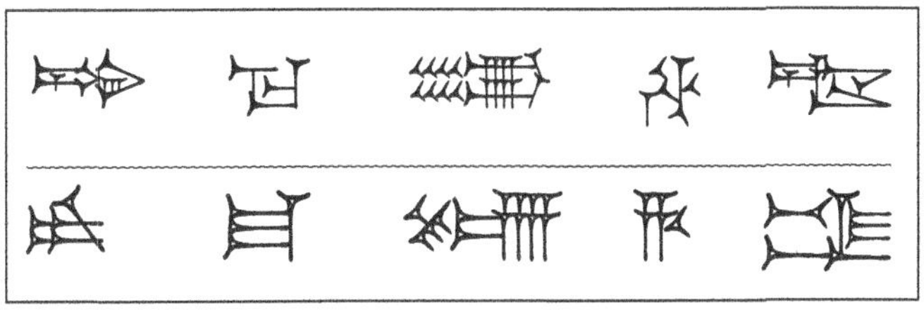

LH §139 XXX (Rv. VII):26

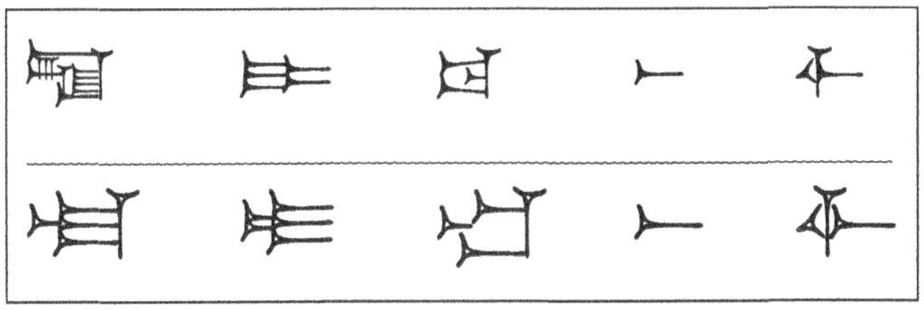

LH §139 XXX (Rv. VII):27

Note: The sign 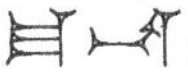 in XXX (Rv. VII):27 is MA.NA, *manūm*, meaning "mina" (≈ 1/2 kg.) (cf. *māneh*, מָנֶה). This sign, which combines elements that have been learned, and the word *manūm* are probably simple enough to remember, but they do not need to be learned.

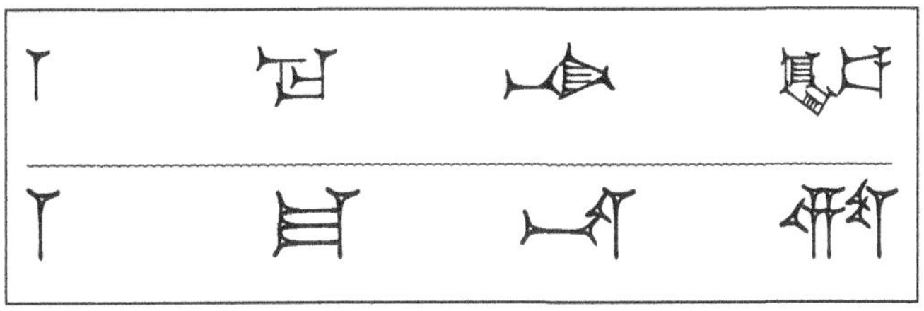

LH §139 XXX (Rv. VII):28

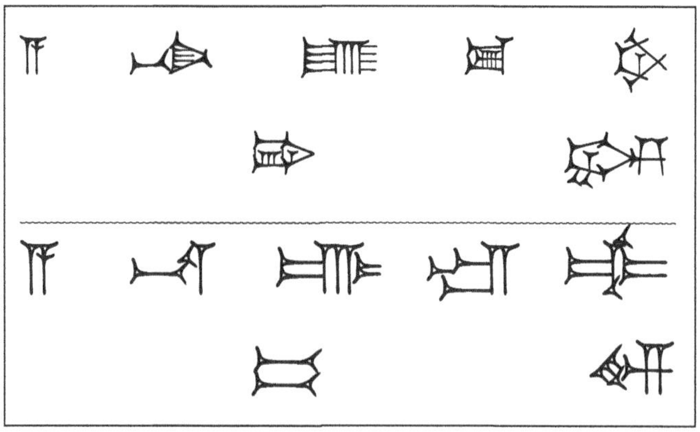

LH §139 XXX (Rv. VII):29

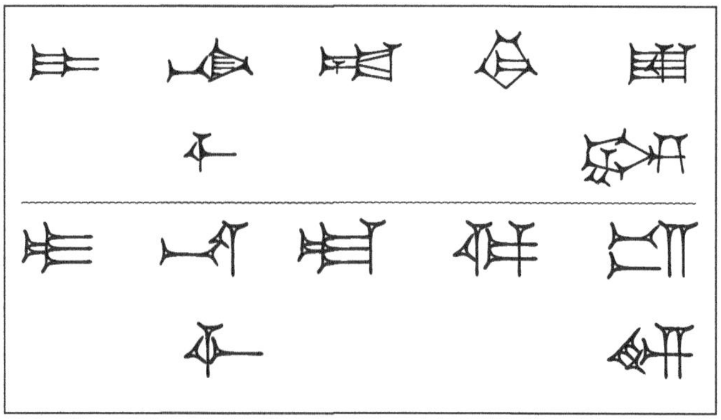

2. Grammatical Analysis: Parse all verb forms.

3. Translation: Translate LH §139.

LH §140 stipulates a minimum payment that a husband of more limited means (a civil servant) must pay his wife who did not bear him any children if he leaves her.

1. Transliterate and Normalize: See the note below for additional help.

LH §140 XXX (Rv. VII):30

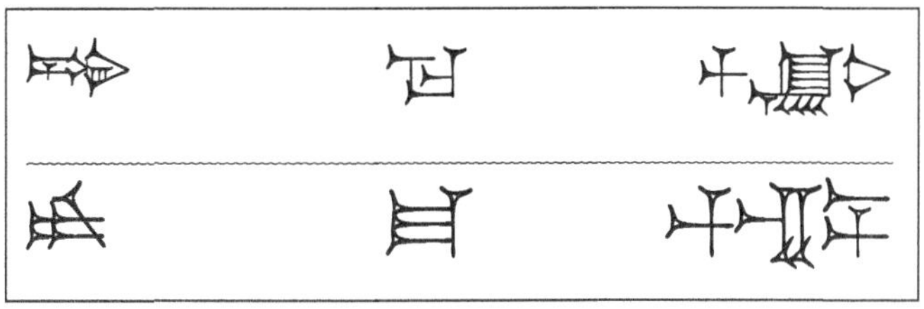

LH §140 XXX (Rv. VII):31

Note: The sign in XXX (Rv. VII):31 is ŠUŠANA, *šaluš(tum)*, meaning "1/3", or less often *šuššān*, literally "2/6." The sign in the same text box also appeared above in LH §139. It is MA.NA, *manûm*, meaning "mina" (≈ 1/2 kg.) (cf. *māneh*, מָנֶה).

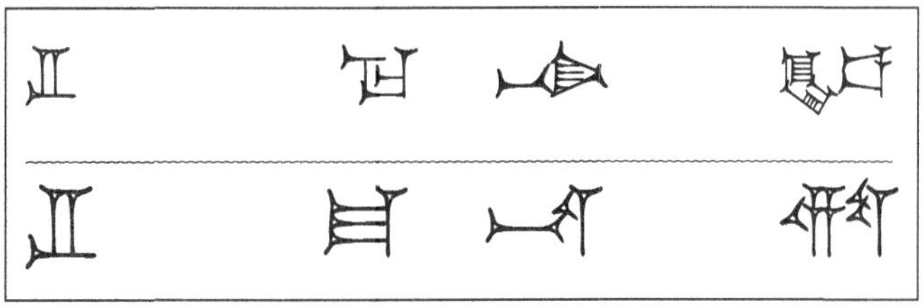

LH §140 XXX (Rv. VII):32

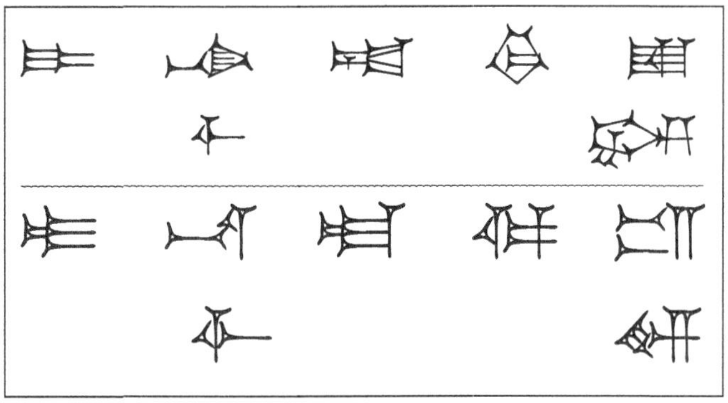

2. Grammatical Analysis: Parse all verb forms.

3. Translation: Translate LH §140.

The Mari Archive

Nancy L. Erickson

Mari, Tell *Ḥarīrī*, is located on the middle Euphrates River in Syria about 300 miles upstream from Babylon. The tell is situated at a strategic crossroads, controlling traffic down the river as well as across the northern plain toward Syria. Mari boasts a long history beginning in the Early Dynasty period (ca. 3150–2686) through the early eighteenth-century BCE, when it was destroyed by Hammurabi around 1760 BCE. Most of what is known about Mari comes from the last fifty years of the site's existence during the Lim dynasty, 1800–1750 BCE.

From the extensive excavations that have taken place at Mari, including remains of Zimri-Lim's enormous palace, are some twenty-five thousand Akkadian texts dating between the twenty-fourth and eighteenth centuries BCE. The majority of the texts, however, are from the final decades of the site, during the late nineteenth and early eighteenth centuries BCE. During this period Mari was the seat of an important Amorite kingdom, a West Semitic people group known primarily through their names found in Sumerian and Akkadian texts dating from the Ur III period (sometime after 2100 BCE) through the fall of Babylon (1600 BCE). The archive provides rich information about Syro-Mesopotamian history and culture through an Amorite lens during a particular timeframe, roughly the Middle Bronze Age.

The archive boasts an enormous array of written material, all in Old Babylonian. While some palace administrative texts detail important judicial matters and list royal records, others contain expense reports for food and drink, overhead concerning the palace temples, and gifts given, including lists of metal and fabric. Other texts relate treaties between important individuals (i.e., Zimri-Lim and Hammurabi), and still others contain ritual and omen texts, prophetic texts, and dream texts. The bulk of the extant tablets, however, are letters: letters from kings, administrators, diplomats from other regions, family members, priests, prophets, and a host of other individuals. The letters provide unique insight into life at Mari, detailing everyday activities. We get a glimpse of ancient life—how people lived, prayed, and did business. In this sense, the texts have proven indispensable for understanding the ancient world in Syro-Mesopotamia during this time.

Of particular interest for the study of the Hebrew Bible is the influence of the spoken language of the Amorite people group in the Mari texts. While the texts themselves are written in Old Babylonian, elements of the tablets reflect an underlying West Semitic dialect attributed to the West Semitic natives at Mari, the Amorites. Their spoken language, also labeled Amorite, may be observed throughout the Mari archive as distinct from Old Babylonian. For example, normally uncontracted vowels in Old Babylonian, such as *i'a*, *i'ā*, *e'a*, and *e'ā*, all contract in the Mari documents to *ē̃*. One example is the Akkadian form *iqbi'am* that shifts to *iqbē̃m* in the Mari archive. The shift is not reflected directly in Hebrew, per se, but as E. Knudsen notes, "it furnishes us with a parallel from the descendant of a closely related Northwest Semitic dialect."[1]

In addition to the regular *ē̃* contraction, numerous instances of non-Akkadian meanings of words

1. Ebbe Egede Knudsen, "The Mari Akkadian Shift ia > ê and the Treatment of ל״ה Formations in Biblical Hebrew," *Journal of Near Eastern Studies* 41 (1982): 35–43, quote on p. 43.

and uses of forms that reflect underlying West Semitic speech of the natives of Mari may be seen. To cite one example, the Mari term *nahālum/niḫlatum* ("inheritance, property") should be compared to Ugaritic *nḫlt* and Hebrew *naḥălâ* with the same meaning. Likewise, personal names in the Mari archive share West Semitic affinity.[2] For example, Mari attests the form *'qb,* corresponding to Hebrew *y'qb* (*ya'ăqōb*). Likewise, *binu-yamina,* the name of a tribal group from Mari, corresponds to Hebrew *binyāmîn,* the Israelite tribe of Benjamin.

Other West Semitic words in the Mari Archive exhibit shared etymology but not application. For example, *gā'um/gāwum* ("clan") from the archive seems closest in meaning *not* to Hebrew *gôy* but to *mišpāḥâ* (or perhaps *bêt 'āb*). Furthermore, Hebrew *gôy* seems to parallel the Mari term *ummatum.* Other parallels are not etymologically related at all but attest shared application. For example, the term *asakkum* from the Mari archive means "something set apart, taboo."[3] While *asakkum* is attested elsewhere in Akkadian religious documents and lexical lists, its nuanced use at Mari comes closest to the use of *ḥērem,* "ban," in the biblical texts.[4] The greatest similarity between the two words is regarding spoils of war. In the Mari archive, the expression "eating the taboo," *asakkam akālum,* meant violating a ban and was a serious violation (*ARM* 26 1.206).[5] In the Hebrew Bible, an object was in *ḥērem* either because of its uncleanness or because of its exalted sanctity.[6] Violation was also a serious offense, punishable even by death (Lev 27:28–29; Josh 6:18). Interestingly, in Mari, as in ancient Israel, the "ban" (Mari *asakkum;* Hebrew *ḥērem*) was not automatically operative in battle. Rather, it was "imposed by special decision taken for the particular occasion *ad hoc.*"[7] The striking difference between the "ban" in ancient Israel and in Mari is that *ḥērem* had a strictly religious function in Israel. The "ban" in the Hebrew Bible occurs only on behalf of the deity. In Mari, however, *asakkum* could be imposed by humans, including kings and even common soldiers.

The Mari archive not only provides insight into the Amorite language and its relationship to Hebrew and more broadly West Semitics, but it provides an unmatched view into shared practices of the Syro-Mesopotamian world, including those described in the Hebrew Bible. Notably, the Mari archive provides rich information regarding the role of prophets, their titles, and types of speeches; treaty and covenant-related texts; legal literature; and information about tribal society, nomadism, sedentary lifestyle and transhumance—all of which find expression in the Hebrew Bible.

The above summary is a small sample of the rich archive from Mari. If there is a reason to study and learn Akkadian, it is certainly, at least in part, because of the many texts from Mari and their unique importance for the study of the Hebrew Bible.

---

2. Though an older study, Herbert B Huffmon's important work, *Amorite Personal Names in the Mari Texts* (Baltimore: Johns Hopkins Press, 1965), continues to be a primary resource for studying personal names in the Mari archive.

3. "*asakku,*" CAD *A* 2:326.

4. Abraham Malamat, "The Ban in Mari and in the Bible," in *Biblical Essays—Proceedings of the 9th Meeting of Die Ou-Testamentliche Werkgemeenskap in Suid Africa* (Potchefstroom: Pro Rege, 1966), 40–49.

5. See Abraham Malamat, *Mari and the Bible,* Studies in the History and Culture of the Ancient Near East 12 (Leiden: Brill, 1998), 136–37.

6. See André Lemaire, "Mari, the Bible, and the Northwest Semitic World," *Biblical Archaeologist* (1984): 101–8.

7. Malamat, "The Ban in Mari and in the Bible," 46.

19–

Pronominal Suffixes Continued and Irregular *izuzzum*

This chapter continues explanation of the pronominal suffixes and introduces the irregular verb *izuzzum*. The chapter is otherwise light on grammatical instruction. The laws that will be translated in this chapter are LH §§141–145. LH §141 concludes the laws that relate to abandonment and divorce (LH §§137–141). LH §§142–143 are fascinating laws that pertain to the loss of a wife's affections. LH §§144–145 begin the section of laws that relate to marriage to the two main categories of priestesses, the *nadîtum*-priestesses and the *šugîtum*-priestesses (LH §§144–147).

19.1 Pronominal Suffixes Continued

In §4.3 it was necessary to learn the third-person pronominal suffixes because they are so common in LH. It will now be useful to memorize the remaining first- and second-person suffixes in order comfortably read texts beyond LH.

	Genitive (with nouns and prepositions)	**Dative (with verbs)**	**Accusative (with verbs)**
1cs	*-ī, -ya, 'a*[1]	*-am, -m, -nim*[2]	*-ni*
2ms	*-ka*	*-kum*	*-ka*
2fs	*-ki*	*-kim*	*-ki*
3ms	*-šu*	*-šum*	*-šu*
3fs	*-ša*	*-šim*	*-ši*
1cp	*-ni*	*-ni'āšim*	*-ni'āti*
2mp	*-kunu*	*-kunūšim*	*-kunūti*
2fp	*-kina*	*-kināšim*	*-kināti*
3mp	*-šunu*	*-šunūšim*	*-šunūti*
3fp	*-šina*	*-šināšim*	*-šināti*

1. The suffix *ya* is used for nouns that end in a vowel, as in *ḫulqiyami*, "my lost property," in LH §9. The suffix *'a* is used after the nominative plural suffix, *-ū*, as in *mârū'a*, "my children," in LH §170.

2. The suffix *-am* is used with verb forms that end with a consonant; *-m* is used with verb forms that end with *-ī*; and *-nim* is used with verb forms that end with *-ū* or *-ā*. When *-nim* is added to these verb forms, it causes the final long *-ū* or *-ā* to be preserved, just as happens when pronominal suffixes are added to words ending in these vowels (see §7.3).

19.2 The Irregular II-Weak Verb *izuzzum*

Although it only appears three times in LH (LH §Pro II:11; LH §253; LH §Epi L:91), the II-weak irregular verb, *izuzzum* (*a*), meaning "to stand (up)," is relatively common. Some Assyriologists interpret this verb as a highly irregular G-stem of the geminate root, *'-z-z*, or more likely of the II weak root, *z ' z* (< **z w z*), which in either case partially assimilates to the I-*n* paradigm. These assimilated forms make the verb look as if it were derived from *n-z-z*.[3]

More recent interpretation, however, views the paradigm as much less irregular since the most common forms of *izuzzum* are better understood as N-stem forms of the II-weak root *z-'-z* (< **z-w-z*), rather than as G-stem forms.[4] In this case, the only serious irregularity is with the N-stem infinitive, which would be expected to be *nazûzum* based on the strong verb paradigm (*naprusum*) but is instead *izuzzum* (in part explained by resolutory doubling) or, because of an assimilation of the *i*-vowel to the following *u*-vowels, *uzuzzum*.[5]

The following paradigm does not need to be memorized, but it should be understood well enough so that when *izuzzum/uzuzzum* is learned as a vocabulary item, its irregularity as an N-stem infinitive will be understood.

	Durative 3cs/3mp	Perfect 3cs/3mp	Preterite 3cs/3mp	Participle ms
Š	*ušapras/ušaprasū* *ušzâz/ušzazzū*	*uštapris/ uštaprisū* *uštazîz/uštazizzū*	*ušapris/ušaprisū* *ušzîz/ušzizzū*	*mušaprisum* *mušzizzum*
N	*ipparras/ipparrasū* *izzâz/izzazzū*	*ittapras/ittaprasū* *ittazîz/ittazizzū*	*ipparis/ipparsū* *izzîz/izzizū*	*mupparsum* *muzzazzum/muzzizzum*

	Verbal Adjective	Stative	Infinitive
Š	*šuprusum* *šuzuzzum*	*šuprus* *šuzûz*	*šuprusum* *šuzuzzum*
N	*naprusum* *i/uzuzzum*	*naprus* *nazûz*	*naprusum* *i/uzuzzum*

19.3 Homework

Before you move on, memorize the full pronominal suffix paradigm. The main rules for adding pronominal suffixes to nouns and substantivized adjectives were given in §8.2. These rules should be carefully reviewed so as to practice their application in the homework exercises below. Also, become comfortable with the forms of the irregular verb *izuzzum*.

3. Worthington (*Complete Babylonian*, 182) for example, calls *izuzzum* "ridiculously" irregular. Cf. also Richardson, *Hammurabi's Laws*, 364, 404, and later, Richardson, *A Comprehensive Grammar to Hammurabi's Stele*, 193, where he favors the view that this verb came from a mixture of the II-weak (*z-'-z*) and I-*n* (*n-z-z*) paradigms.

4. So, e.g., Kouwenberg, *The Akkadian Verb and Its Semitic Background*, §16.5.3.5.

5. Huehnergard (*A Grammar of Akkadian*, §37.2) favors the view that the posited N-stem forms were originally N-stem but later reinterpreted by ancient Akkadian speakers and modern grammars and lexica as G-stem forms.

19.3.1 *Signs*

 *ur* (this appeared in LH §7)

 *sa* (this appeared in LH §7 and §128)

 GÍN (= *šiqlum*, "shekel"), *ṭu* (this appeared in LH §17)

 *eš*, 30 (earlier seen as a part of the sign for *meš*, , a sign marking plurals, esp. of persons)

 *ṣu*

 *a'*, *'a*, *e'*, *'e*, *i'*, *'i*, *u'*, *'u* (discussed in §20.2.1)

19.3.2 *Vocabulary*

bâbtum (< *bâbum*, gate) = city quarter, community (cf. *bābāh*, בָּבָה, "apple [of the eye], pupil" in Zech 2:12 MT)[6]
ḫarrānum = travel, journey (cf. *ḥārān*, חָרָן, "Haran")
ḫiṭîtum = sin, fault (cf. *ḥāṭā'*, חָטָא, "to sin")
i/uzuzzum = N: to stand (up)
magal = greatly
magārum (*a,u*) = to agree, allow; to be willing
maṭûm (*i,i*) = to be small; Š: to humiliate, belittle, disparage (cf. *mə'aṭ*, מְעַט, "little, few")
sapāḫum (*a,u*) = to scatter, disrupt; D: to squander, disturb, neglect
šanîtum (fem. of *šanûm*) = another, a second (cf. *šənî*, שְׁנִי, "two")

Congratulations! If you learn the nine words above and have learned each of the 150 words in the vocabulary lists of the preceding chapters, you will be able to read 96 percent of all the words in LH §§1–20, 127–149.

19.3.3 *Exercises*

Answer the questions below.

1. The G-stem infinitive of the verb "to go" or "going" is *alākum*, "going." Write the Akkadian for "his going" in the nominative or accusative (attested in LH §26).

6. Supportive of the posited compensatory length of the *a*-vowel through metathesis of a lengthening consonant or metathesis of the two hypothesized earlier final root consonants (*b-b-'*). Cf. lexical texts and others that read *ba-a-bu*, *AHw*, ad loc., and Gelb, *Glossary of Old Akkadian*, ad loc. Cf. especially Huehnergard, *A Grammar of Akkadian*, §6.1(b) for a discussion of examples of compensatory lengthening like *mârum* < **mar'um*, "son."

2. The noun *nidîtum* means "uncultivated land." Write "your (ms) uncultivated land" in the genitive case (attested in LH §68).

3. The word for "daughter" in Akkadian is *mârtum*. Keeping in mind that there are three options for how to write "my," write "my daughter" in the accusative (attested in LH §161).

4. The word for "mother" in the nominative singular is *ummum*. Write the normalized Akkadian for "his mother" in the nominative (attested in LH §29).

5. The word for "missing property" is *ḫulqum*. The construct of *ḫulqum* is *ḫuluq*, "missing property of," with a harmonizing anaptyctic *u* vowel. Write the normalized Akkadian for "his missing property" in the accusative (attested in LH §9).

6. The word for "dowry" is *šeriktum*. The construct of *šeriktum* is *šerikti* with a paragogic *i*. Write the normalized Akkadian for "her dowry" in the accusative (attested in LH §137).

7. The feminine noun *šubtum*, "dwelling" (cf. *yāšab*, יָשַׁב) in the genitive-accusative plural is *šubātim*. Write "their (fp) dwellings" in the genitive-accusative (attested in LH §Pro IV:15).

LH §141 stipulates the various options of an aggrieved husband whose wife, though still living with him (and not guilty of any sexual infidelity), appears to be intent on leaving him. Confirming this intention, she is acting deceptively, deliberately mismanaging the household, and/or disparaging her husband.

Because of the substantial combined length of the laws covered in this chapter, normalized text is provided after each text box for LH §141, the longest of these laws. As time permits, students may find it helpful to use this combination of cuneiform and normalized text, once again, to practice more rapid recognition of the appropriate values for each combination of signs.

LH §141 XXX (Rv. VII):33

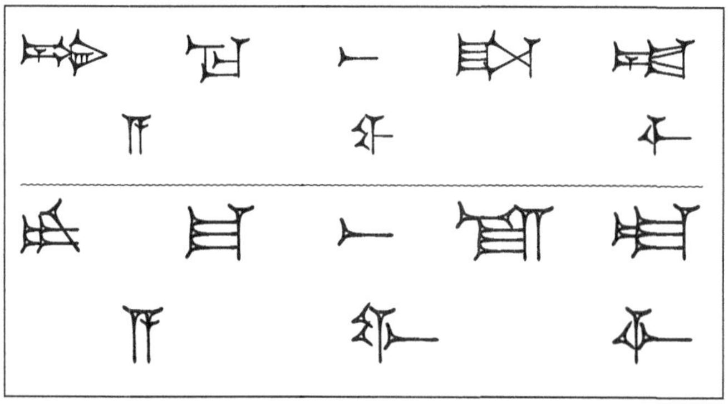

XXIX (Rv. VII):33*šumma aššat awīlim*

LH §141 XXX (Rv. VII):34

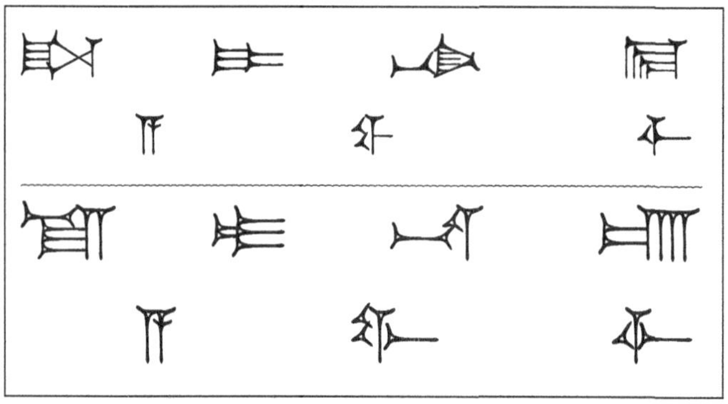

[34]*ša ina bît awīlim*

LH §141 XXX (Rv. VII):35

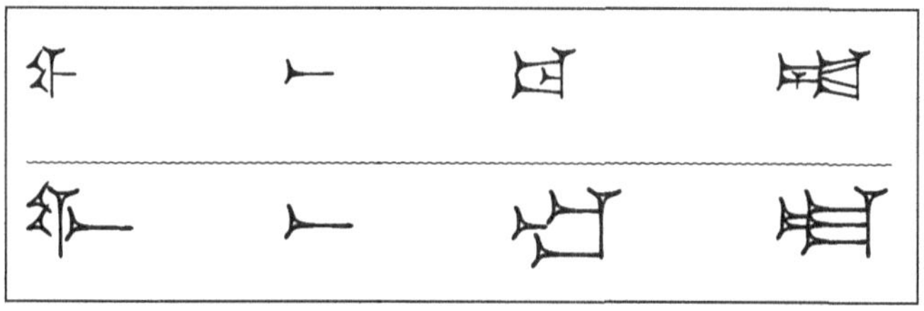

[35]*wašbat*

LH §141 XXX (Rv. VII):36

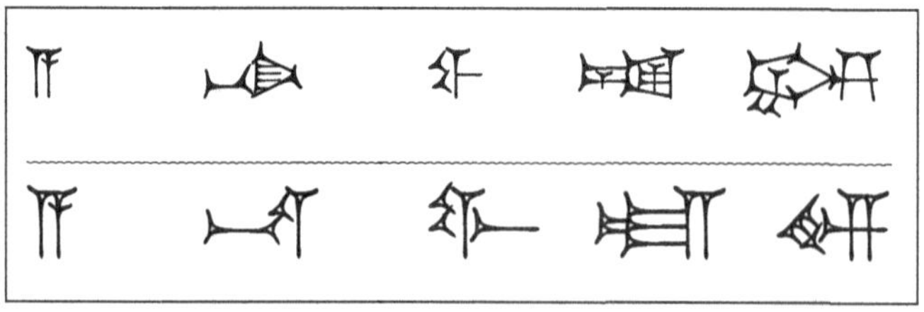

[36]*ana waṣēm*

LH §141 XXX (Rv. VII):37

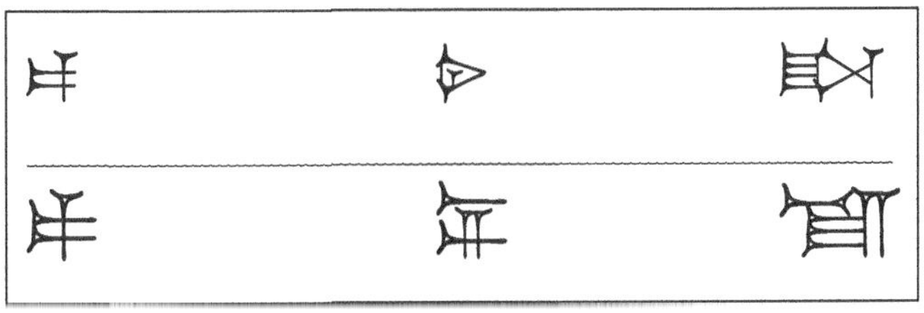

[37]*pânīša*

LH §141 XXX (Rv. VII):38

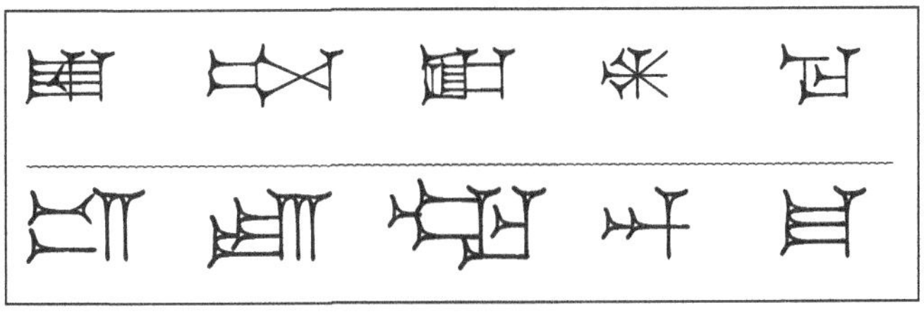

[38]*ištakanma*

LH §141 XXX (Rv. VII):39

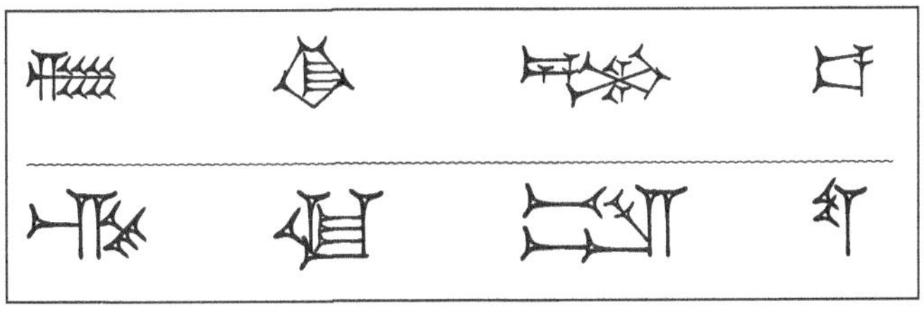

[39]*sikiltam*

LH §141 XXX (Rv. VII):40

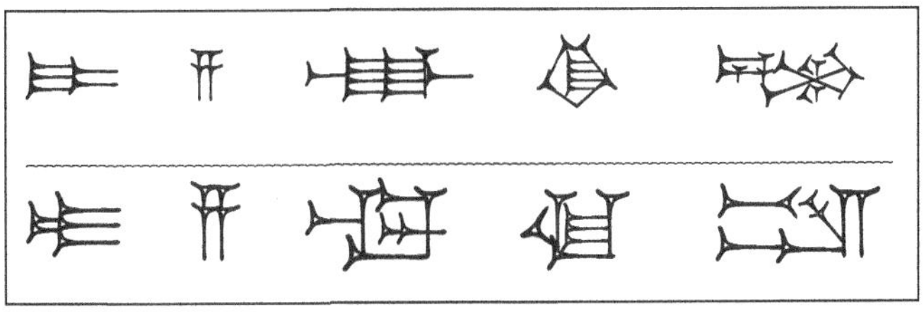

[40]*isakkil*

LH §141 XXX (Rv. VII):41

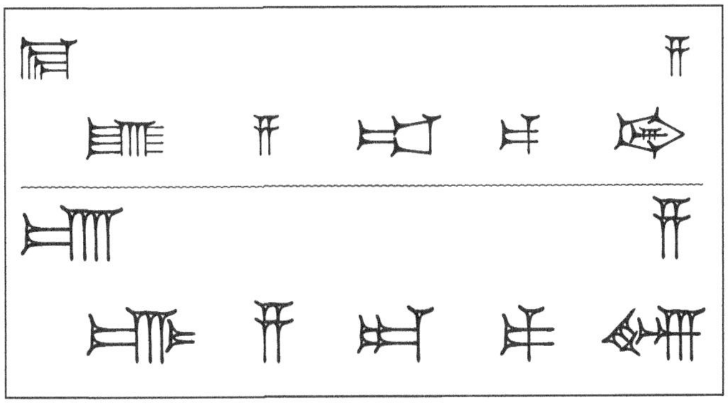

[41]*bîssa usappaḫ*

LH §141 XXX (Rv. VII):42

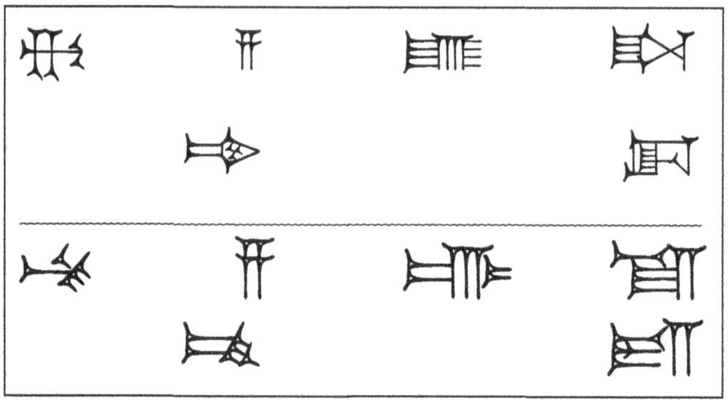

[42]*mussa ušamṭâ*

LH §141 XXX (Rv. VII):43

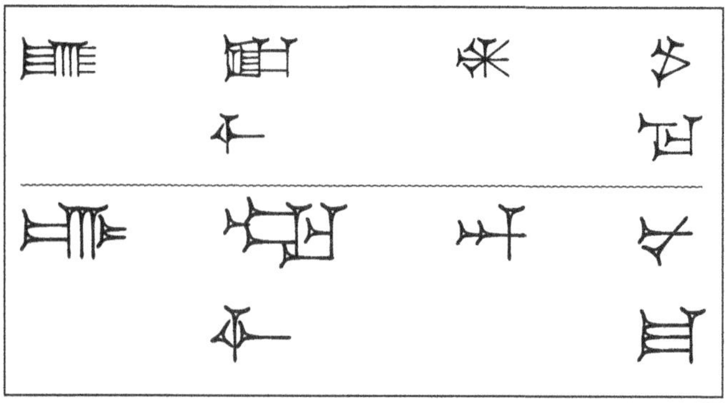

[43]*ukannūšīma*

LH §141 XXX (Rv. VII):44

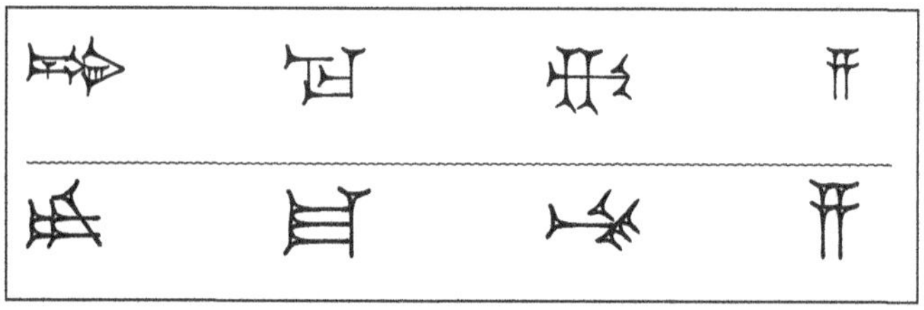

[44]*šumma mussa*

141 XXX (Rv. VII):45

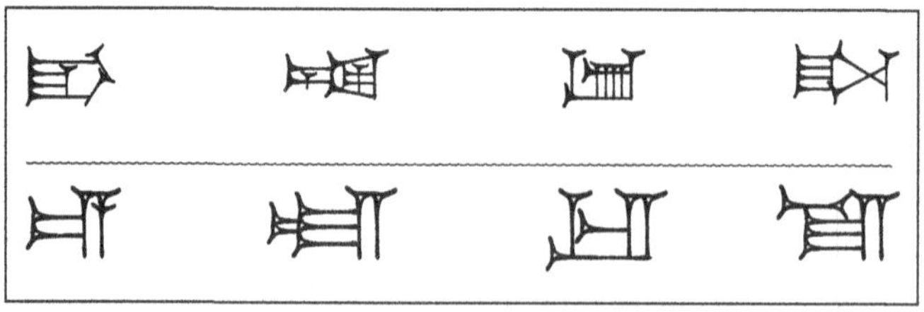

[45]*ezēbša*

LH §141 XXX (Rv. VII):46

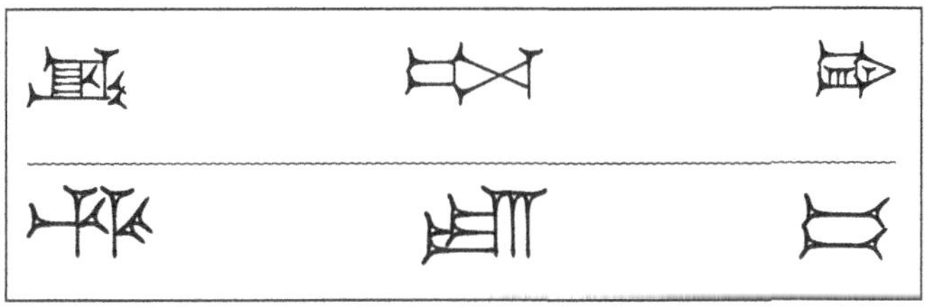

[46]*iqtabî*

LH §141 XXX (Rv. VII):47

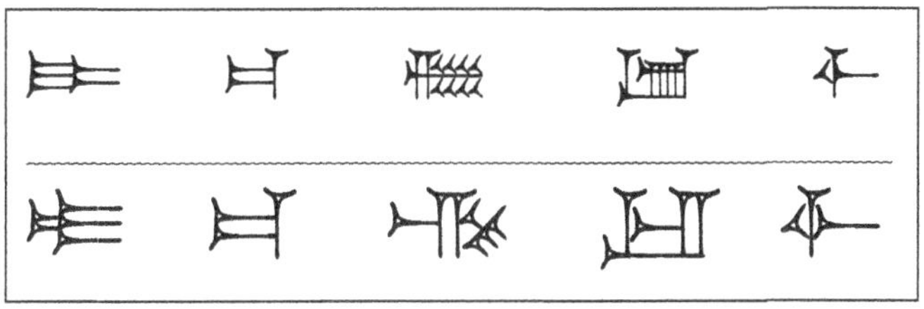

[47]*izzibši*

LH §141 XXX (Rv. VII):48

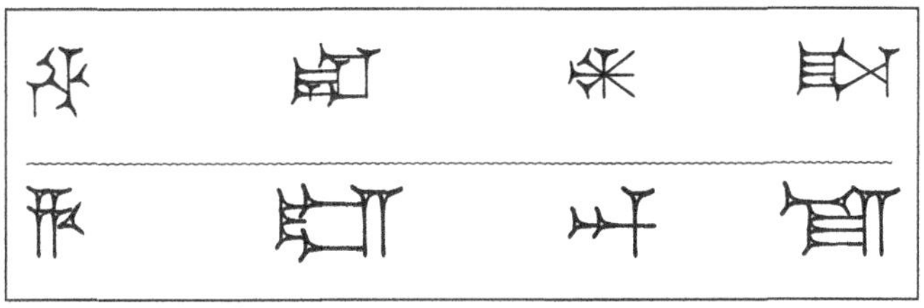

[48]*ḫarrānša*

LH §141 XXX (Rv. VII):49

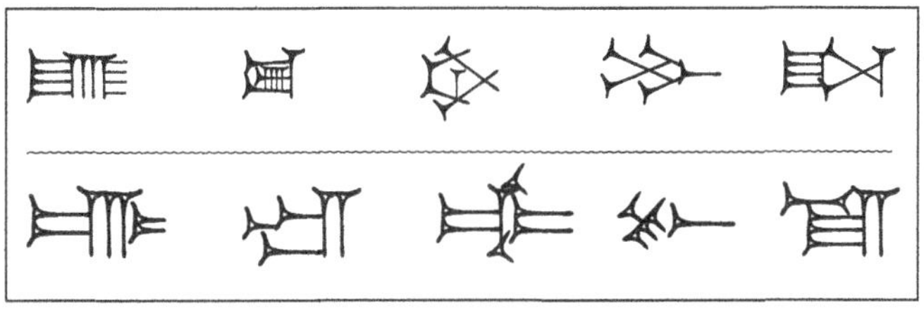

[49]*uzubbûša*

LH §141 XXX (Rv. VII):50

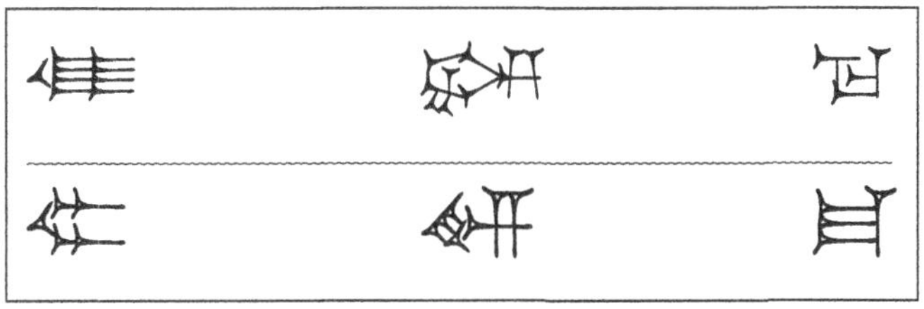

[50]*mimma*

LH §141 XXX (Rv. VII):51

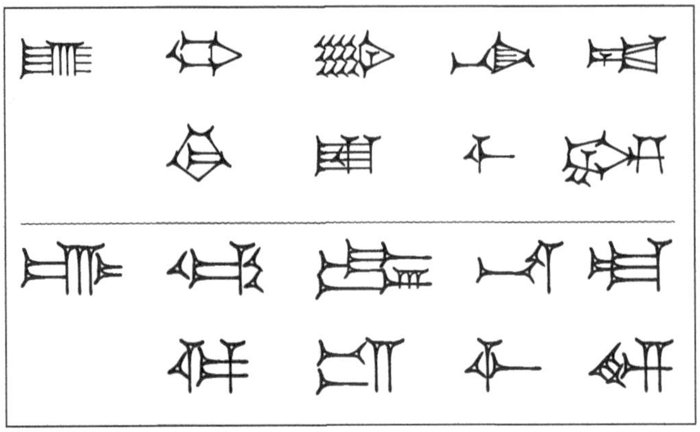

[51]*ul innaddiššim*

LH §141 XXX (Rv. VII):52

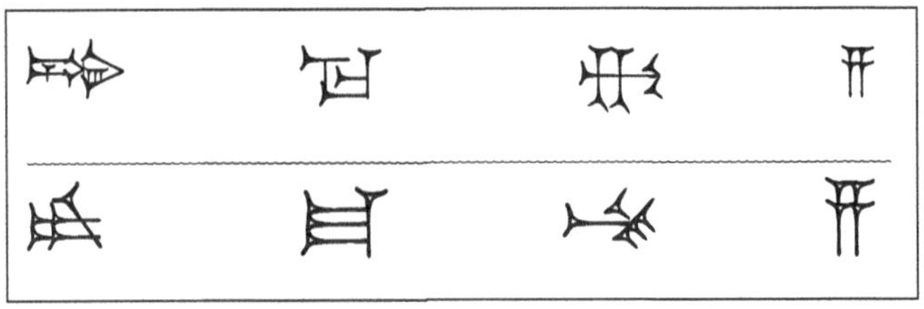

[52]*šumma mussa*

LH §141 XXX (Rv. VII):53

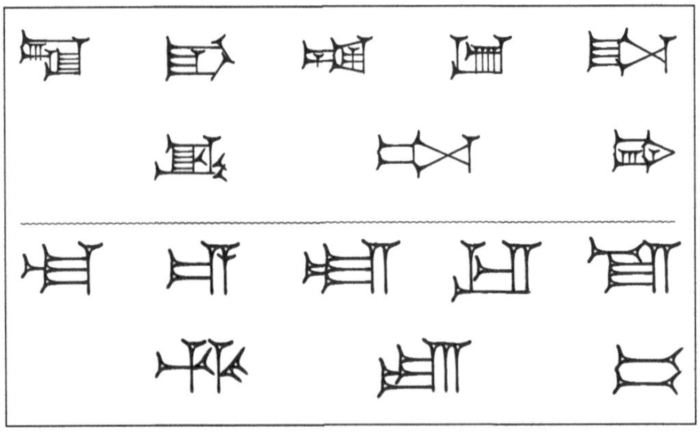

[53]*lâ ezēbša iqtabî*

LH §141 XXX (Rv. VII):54

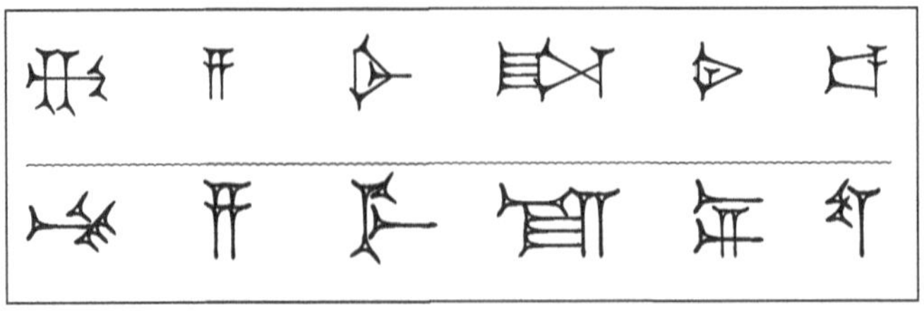

[54]*mussa sinništam šanîtam*

LH §141 XXX (Rv. VII):55

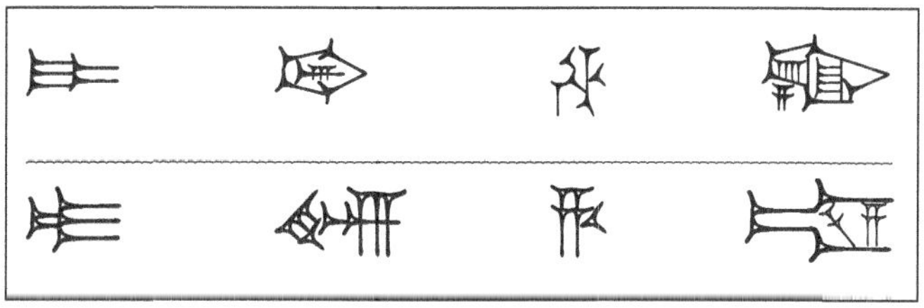

[55]*iḫḫaz*

LH §141 XXX (Rv. VII):56

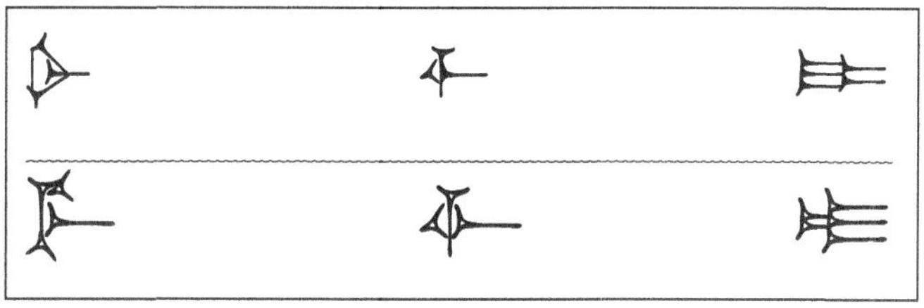

[56]*sinništum šī*

LH §141 XXX (Rv. VII):57

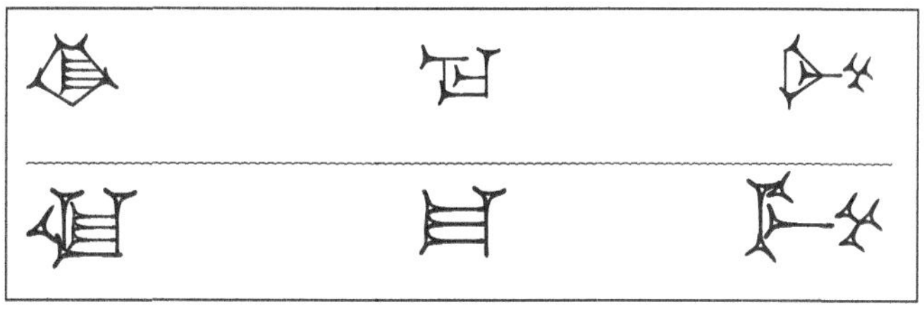

[57]*kīma amtim*

LH §141 XXX (Rv. VII):58

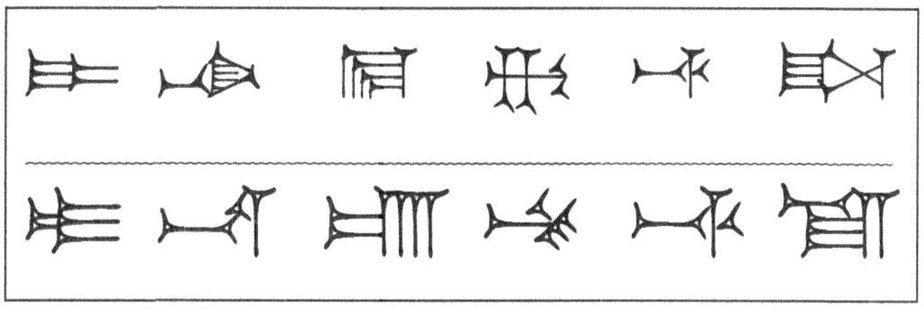

[58]*ina bît mutiša*

LH §141 XXX (Rv. VII):59

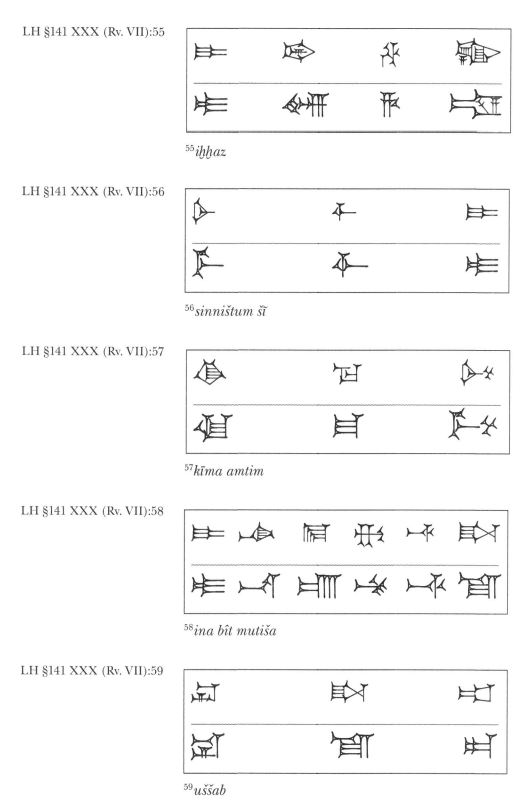

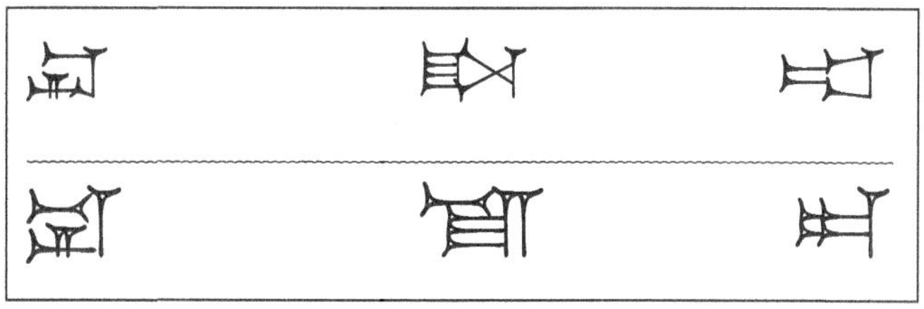

[59]*uššab*

1. Grammatical Analysis: Parse all verb forms and answer the question below. See the notes below for additional help.

a. Explain the spelling of the normalized form of the suffixed noun in XXX (Rv. VII):49.

b. In XXX (Rv. VII):51 one kind of negative particle is used and in XXX (Rv. VII):53 another kind of negative particle is used. What rules determine which particle is used in each situation?

Note: The word *sikiltum* (< *sakālum*) in XXX (Rv. VII):39 means "goods, property acquired illegally or fraudulently." This word does not need to be learned.

Note: The word *sakālum* (*i,i*) in XXX (Rv. VII):40 means "to acquire goods, property illegally or fraudulently." This word does not need to be learned.

2. Translation: Translate LH §141.

LH §142 considers the case of a wife who, for good reason, is refusing intimate relations with her husband. Once her own good conduct is confirmed by the community, as well as the husband's poor conduct, she is authorized to leave the marriage without guilt and with her marriage present/dowry returned to her.

1. Transliterate and Normalize: See the note below for additional help.

LH §142 XXX (Rv. VII):60

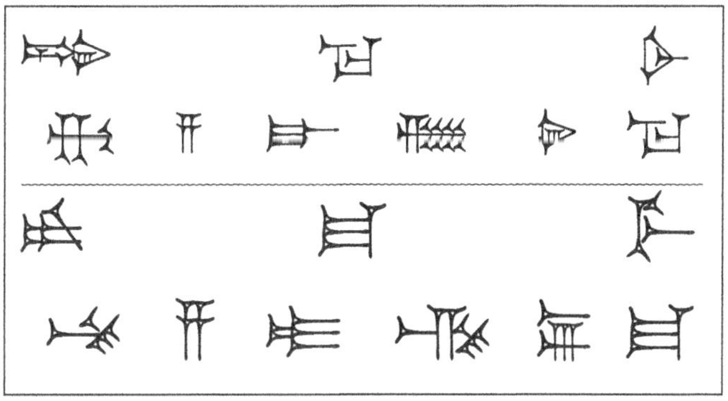

LH §142 XXX (Rv. VII):61

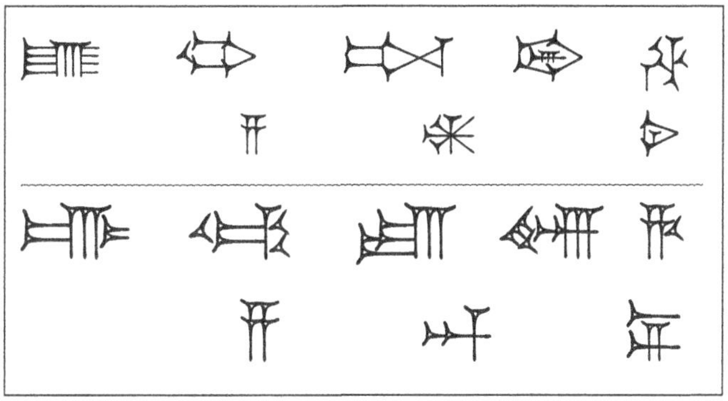

LH §142 XXX (Rv. VII):62

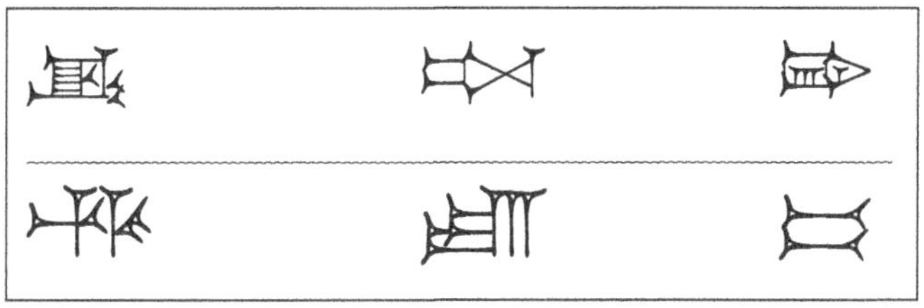

LH §142 XXX (Rv. VII):63

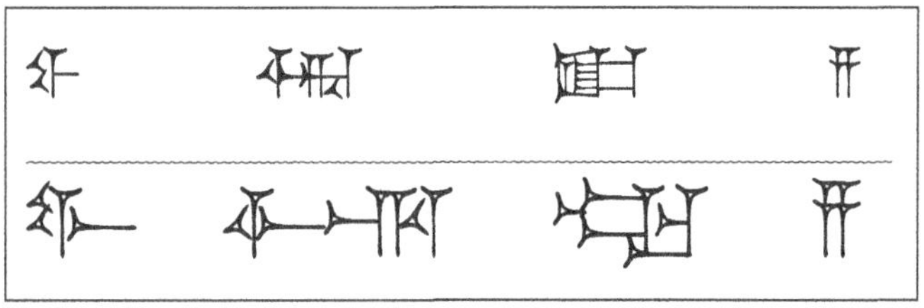

LH §142 XXX (Rv. VII):64

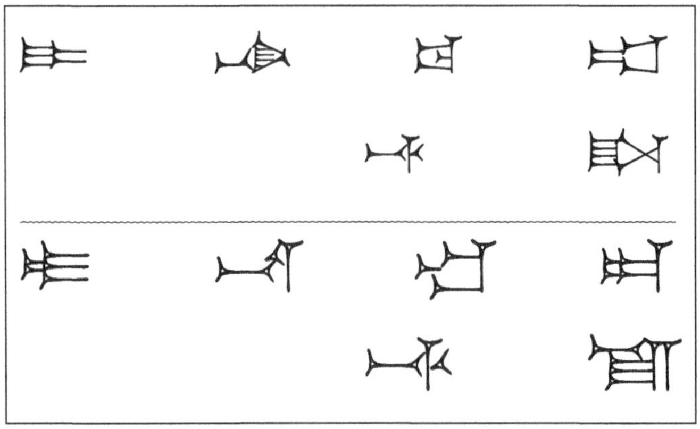

LH §142 XXX (Rv. VII):65

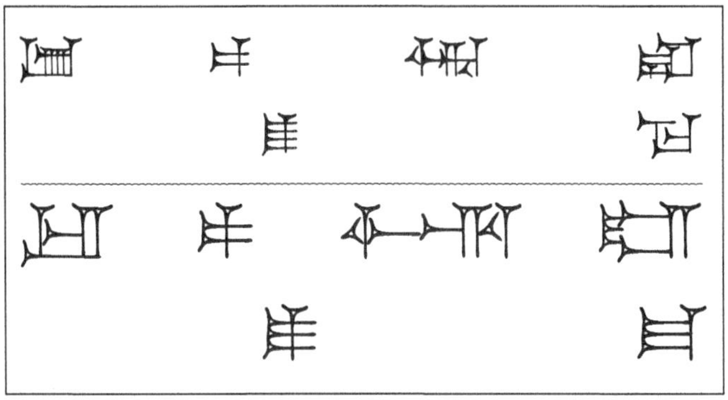

LH §142 XXX (Rv. VII):66

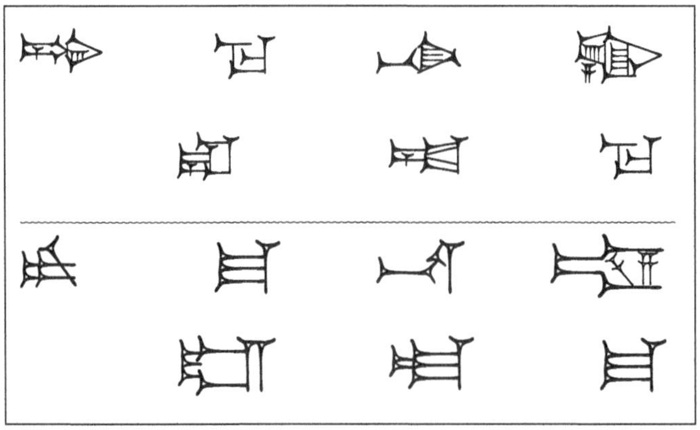

LH §142 XXX (Rv. VII):67

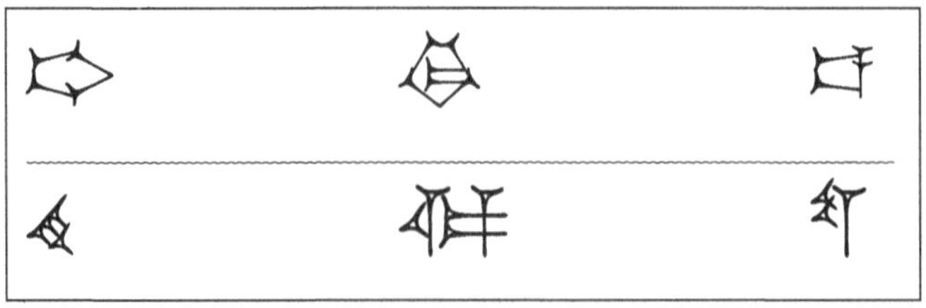

LH §142 XXX (Rv. VII):68

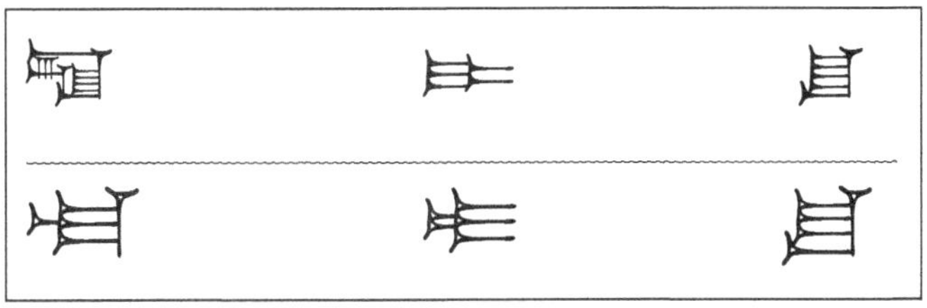

LH §142 XXX (Rv. VII):69

Note: The sign  in XXX (Rv. VII):69 is sa_6. This sign does not need to be learned.

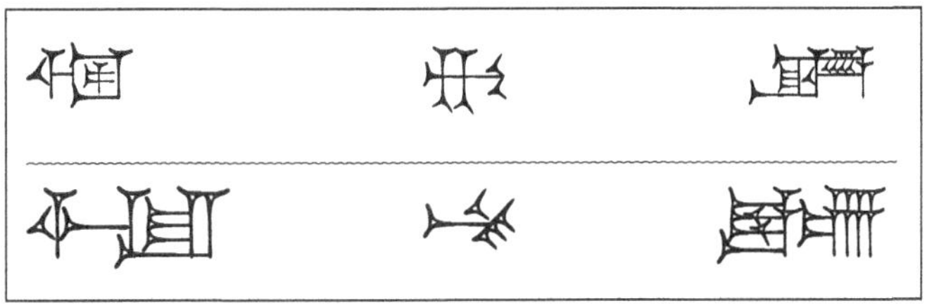

LH §142 XXX (Rv. VII):70

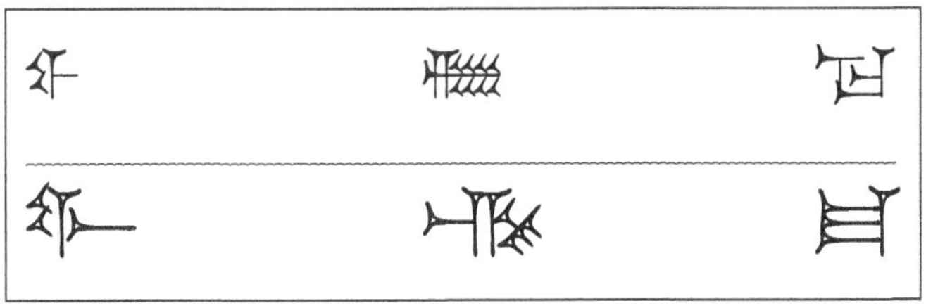

LH §142 XXX (Rv. VII):71

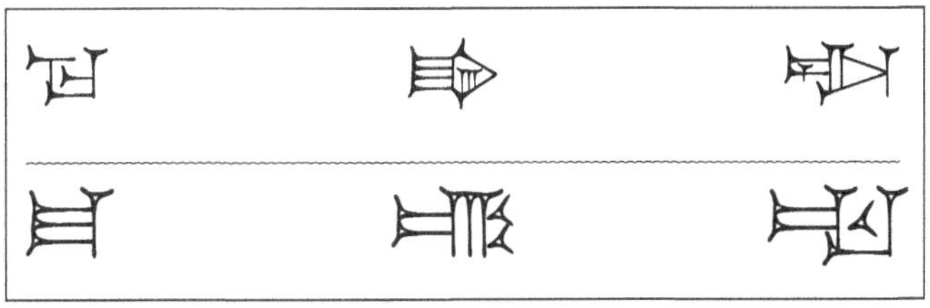

LH §142 XXX (Rv. VII):72

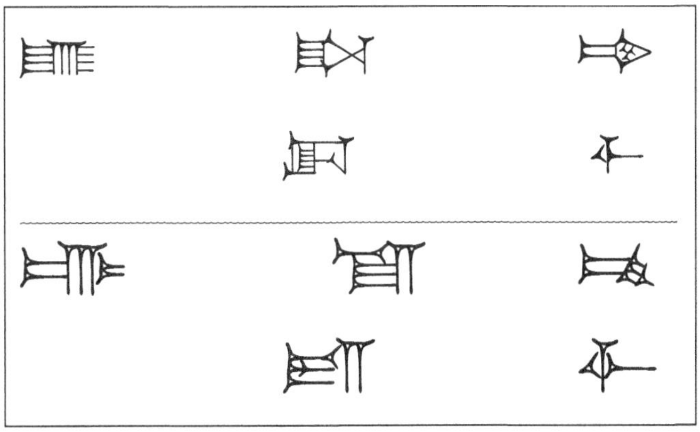

LH §142 XXX (Rv. VII):73

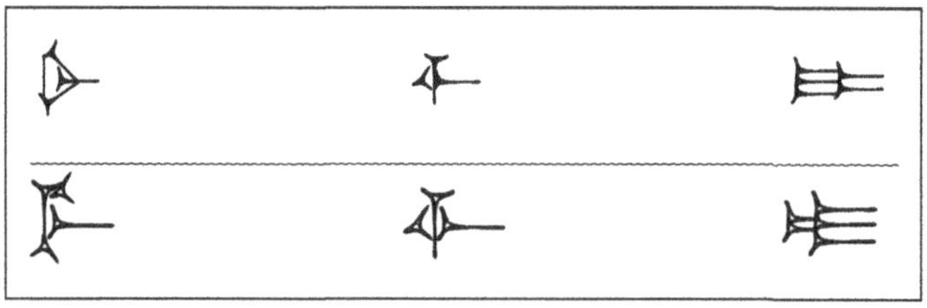

LH §142 XXXI (Rv. VIII):1

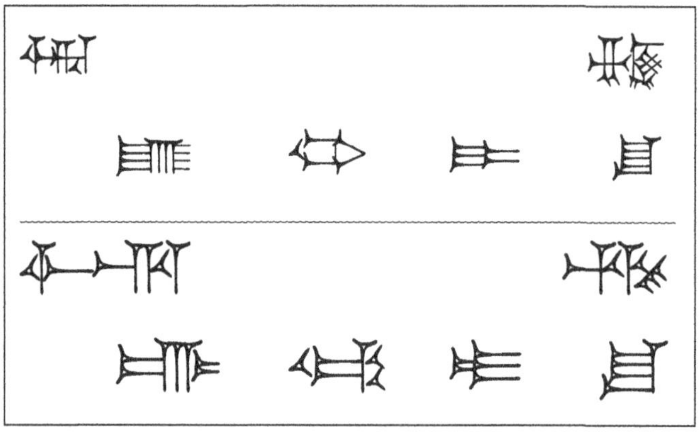

LH §142 XXXI (Rv. VIII):2

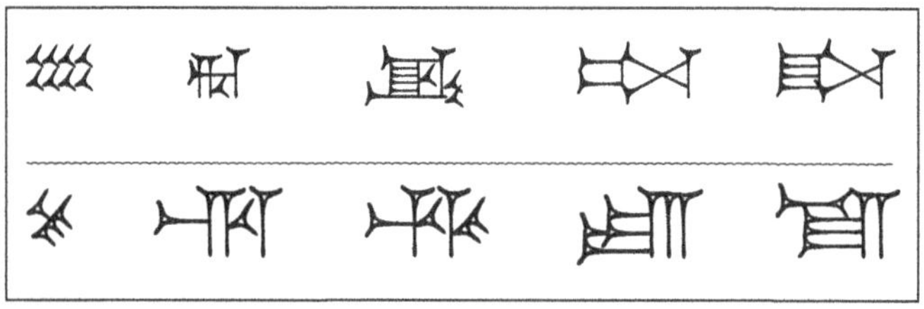

LH §142 XXXI (Rv. VIII):3

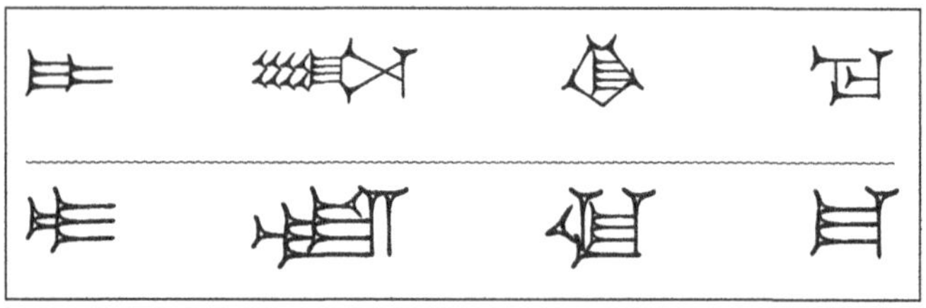

LH §142 XXXI (Rv. VIII):4

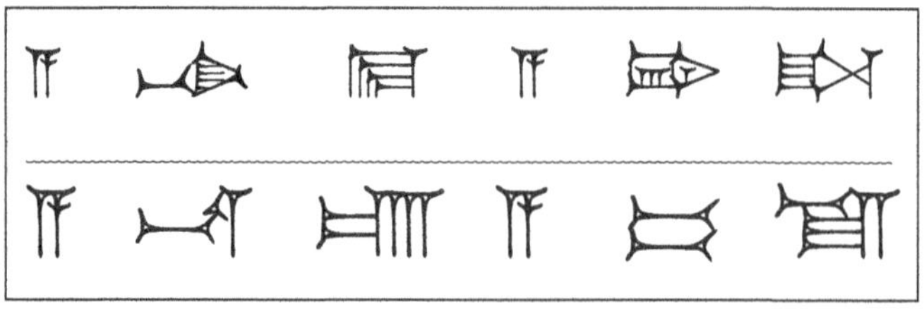

LH §142 XXXI (Rv. VIII):5

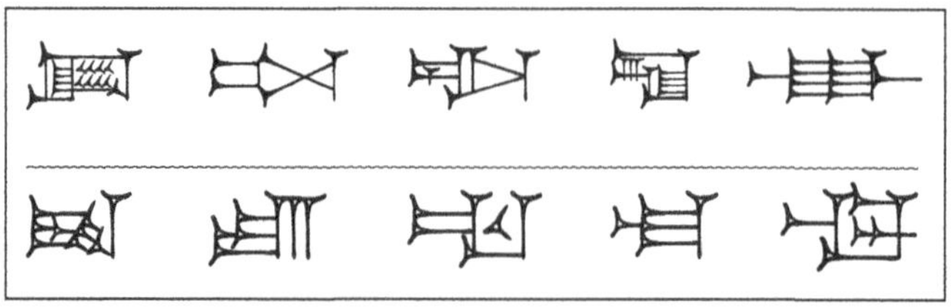

(Transliterate and normalize in the space provided here.)

2. Grammatical Analysis: Parse all verb forms and answer the question below.

   a. What is the significance of the stem of the verb in XXXI (Rv. VIII):5?

3. Translation: Translate LH §142.

LH §143 considers the alternative situation to that dealt with in LH §142. This time the wife is without just cause for her refusal of intimate relations. Instead, the community has confirmed that she herself has been acting reprehensibly, deliberately undermining the household, and/or (publicly?) disparaging her husband. LH §143 views this as a capital offense.

1. Transliterate and Normalize.

LH §143 XXXI (Rv. VIII):6

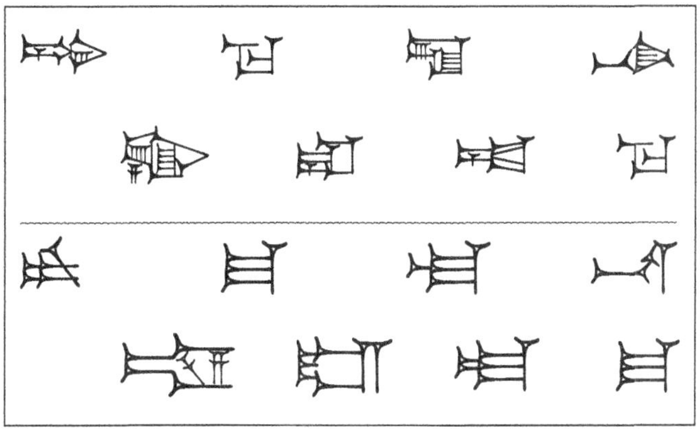

LH §143 XXXI (Rv. VIII):7

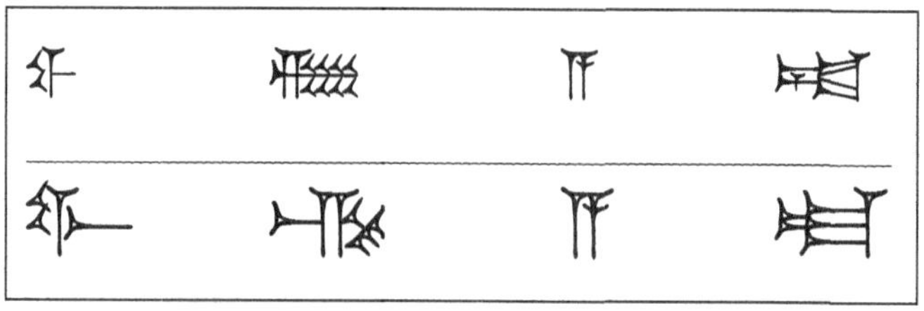

LH §143 XXXI (Rv. VIII):8

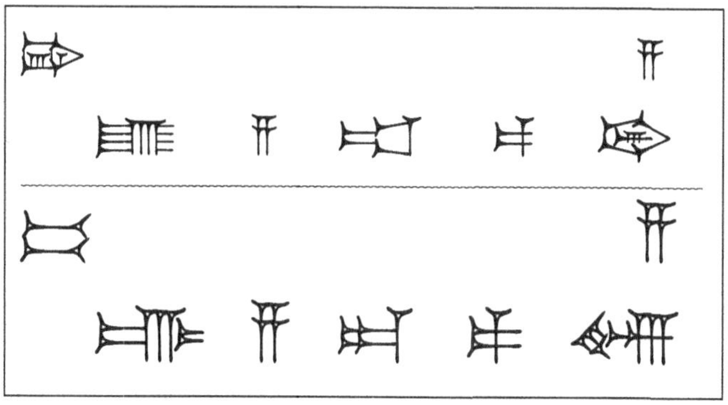

LH §143 XXXI (Rv. VIII):9

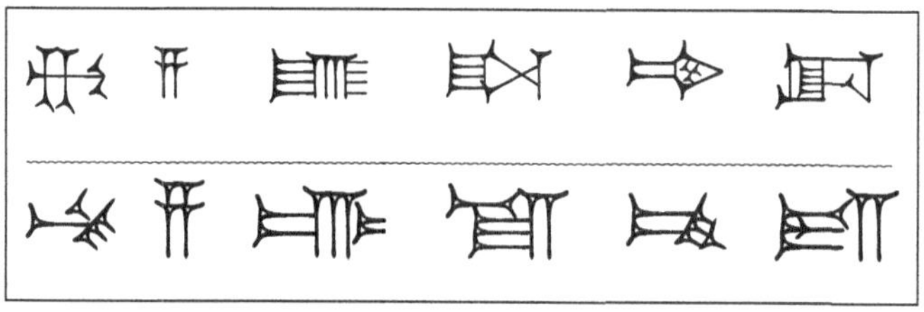

LH §143 XXXI (Rv. VIII):10

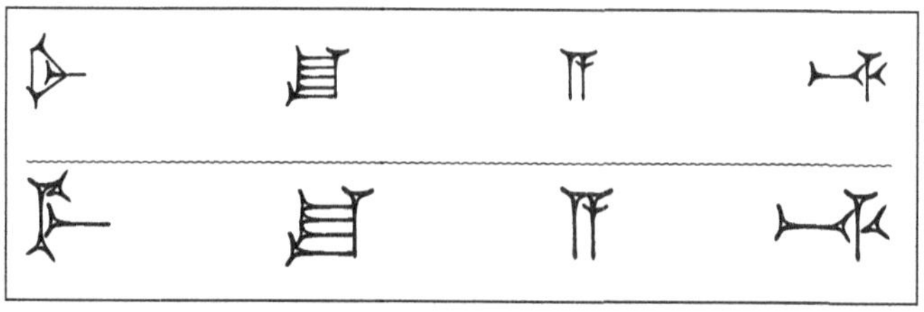

LH §143 XXXI (Rv. VIII):11

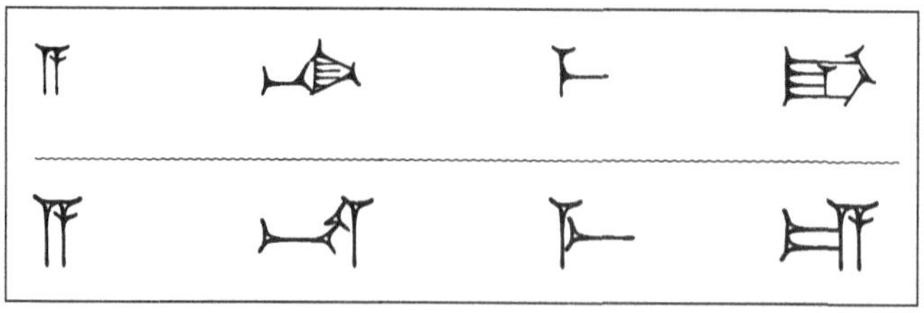

LH §143 XXXI (Rv. VIII):12

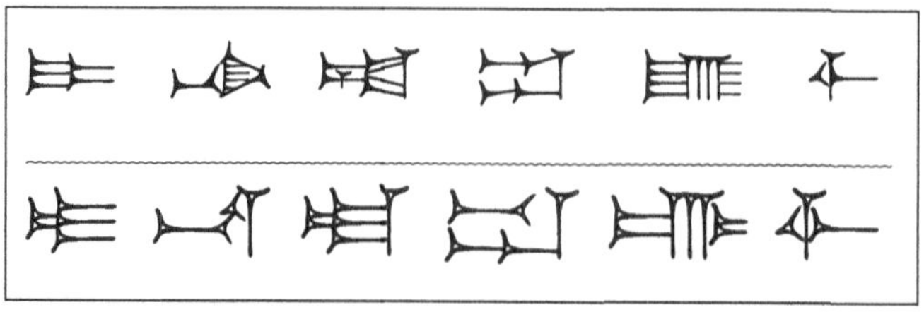

(Transliterate and normalize in the space provided here.)

2. Grammatical Analysis: Parse all verb forms.

3. Translation: Translate LH §143.

LH §144 considers the case of a man who married a high priestess (*nadîtum*), who provided her maidservant for her husband to have children. That husband is now planning to marry a lay priestess (*šugîtum*) anyway. LH §144 does not allow this. Note that high priestesses (*nadîtum*) were not allowed to bear children, whereas lay priestesses (*šugîtum*) were allowed.

1. Transliterate and Normalize.

LH §144 XXXI (Rv. VIII):13

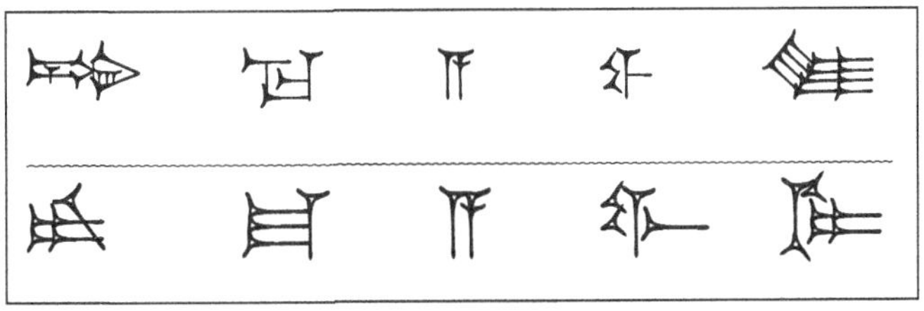

LH §144 XXXI (Rv. VIII):14

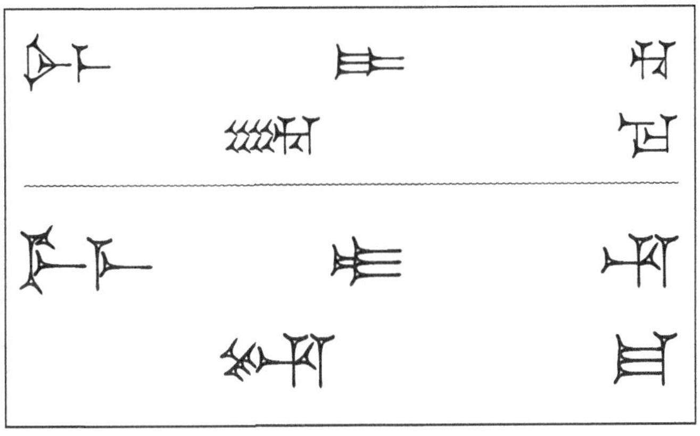

LH §144 XXXI (Rv. VIII):15

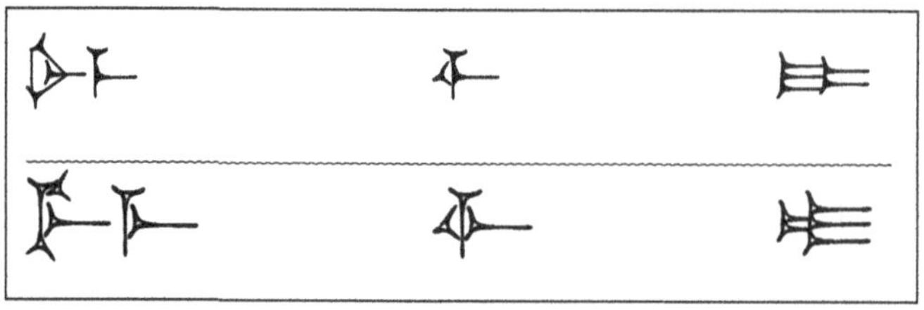

LH §144 XXXI (Rv. VIII):16

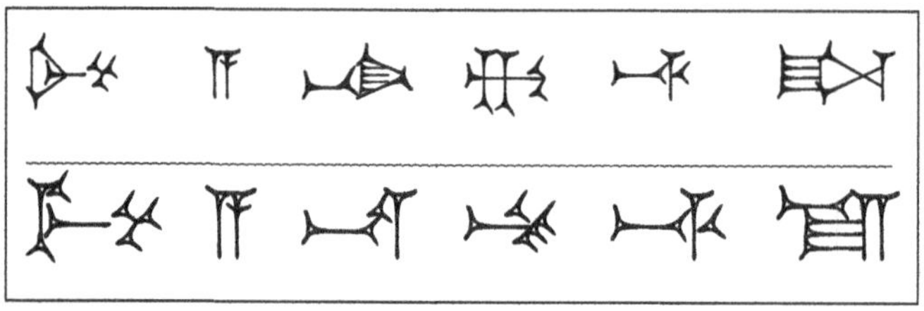

LH §144 XXXI (Rv. VIII):17

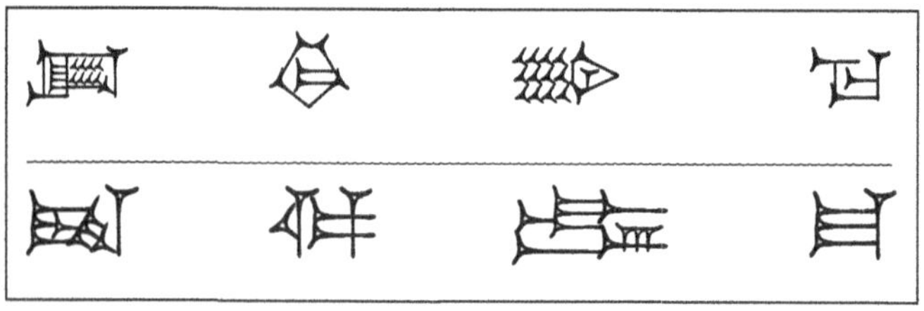

LH §144 XXXI (Rv. VIII):18

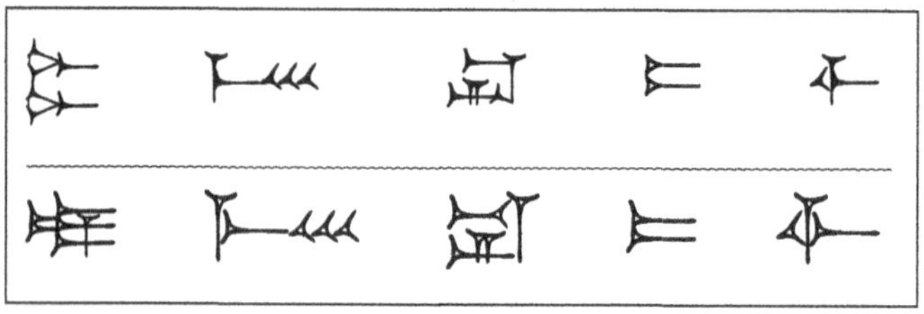

LH §144 XXXI (Rv. VIII):19

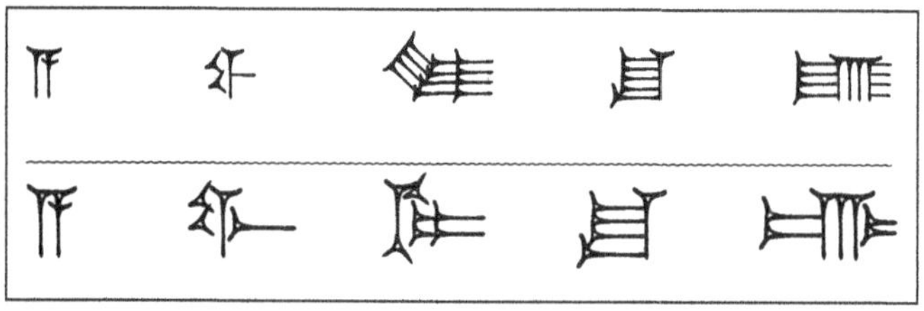

LH §144 XXXI (Rv. VIII):20

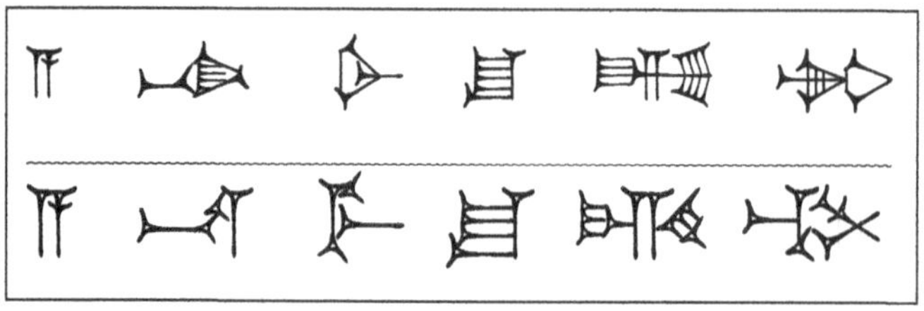

LH §144 XXXI (Rv. VIII):21

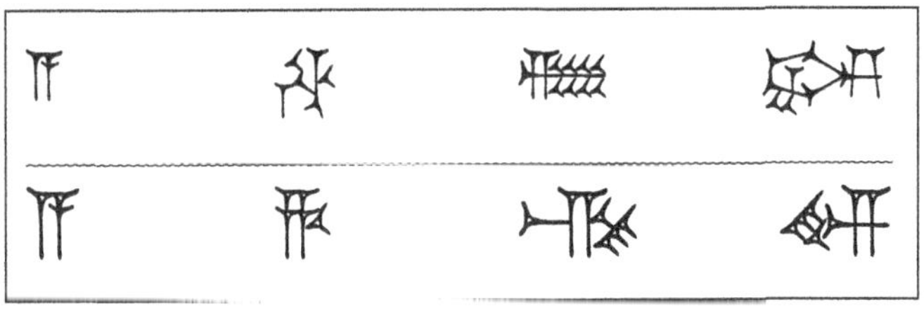

LH §144 XXXI (Rv. VIII):22

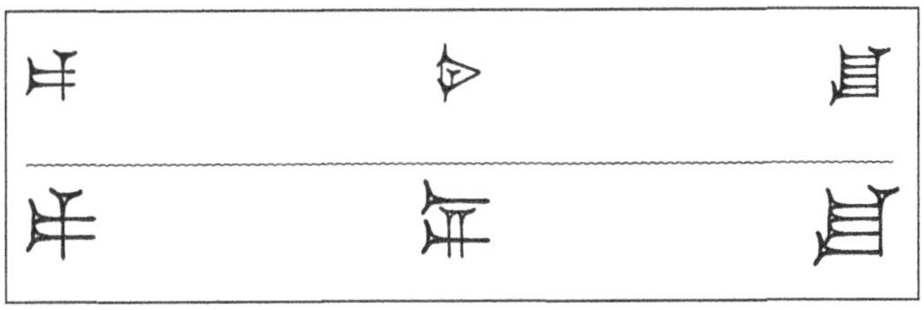

LH §144 XXXI (Rv. VIII):23

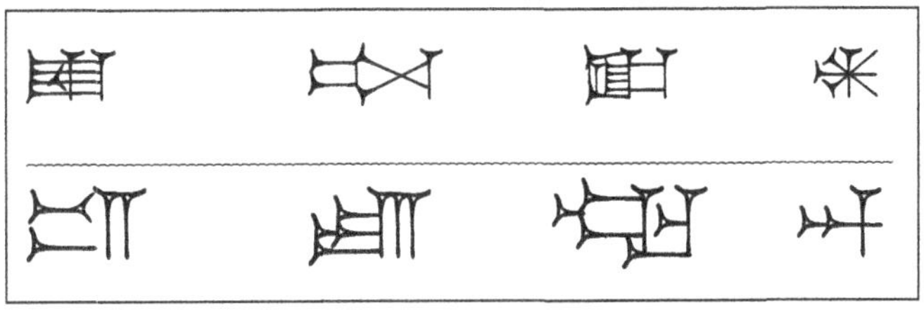

LH §144 XXXI (Rv. VIII):24

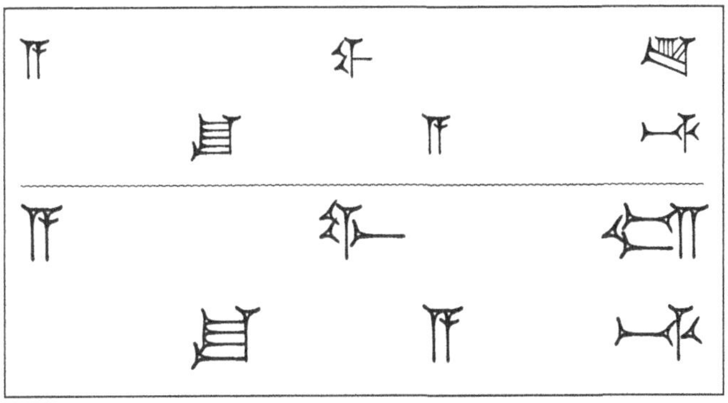

LH §144 XXXI (Rv. VIII):25

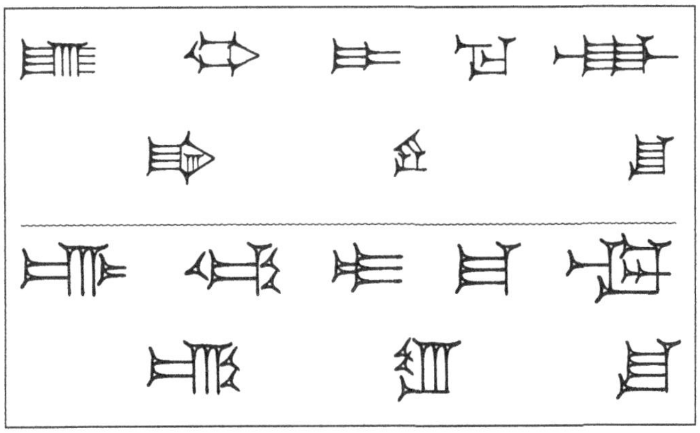

LH §144 XXXI (Rv. VIII):26

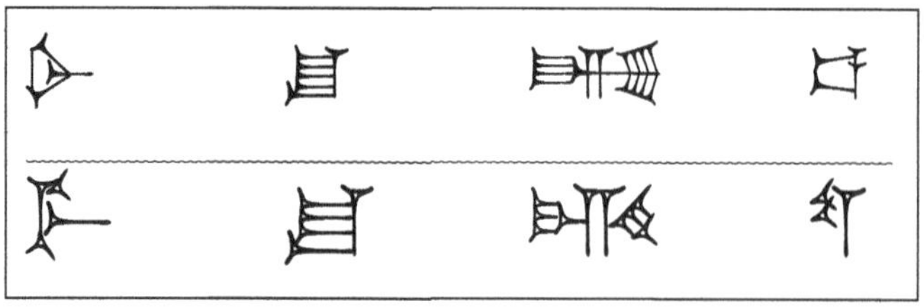

LH §144 XXXI (Rv. VIII):27

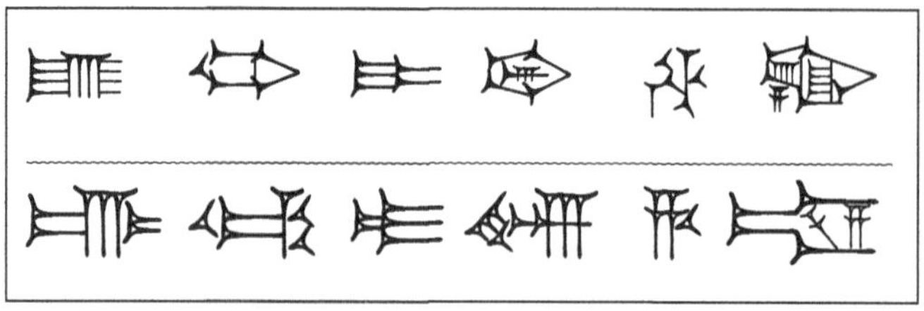

2. Grammatical Analysis: Parse all verb forms.

3. Translation: Translate LH §144.

LH §145 considers the case of a man who married a high priestess (*nadîtum*), but she was unwilling to provide a maidservant for her husband to have children. That husband then planned to a marry a lay priestess (*šugîtum*). LH §145 allows the husband to marry her and to bring her into their home. It insists, however, that the lay priestess is not allowed to usurp the primary position of the high priestess within the home.

1. Transliterate and Normalize: See the note below for additional help.

LH §145 XXXI (Rv. VIII):28

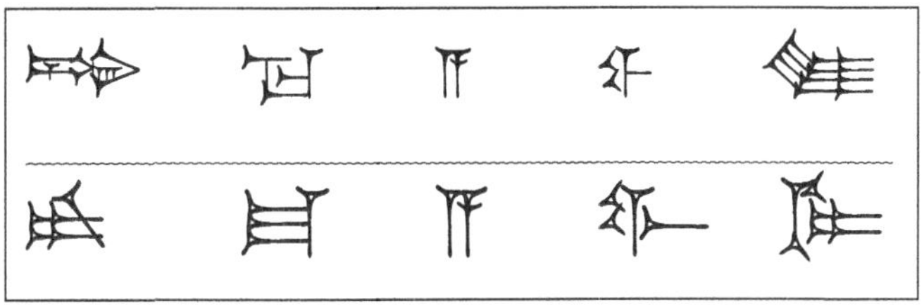

LH §145 XXXI (Rv. VIII):29

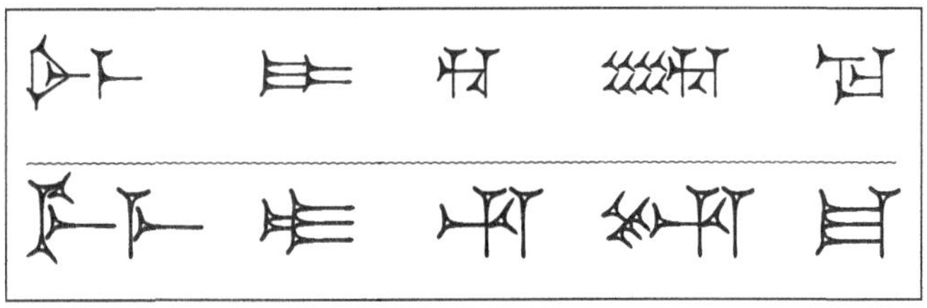

LH §145 XXXI (Rv. VIII):30

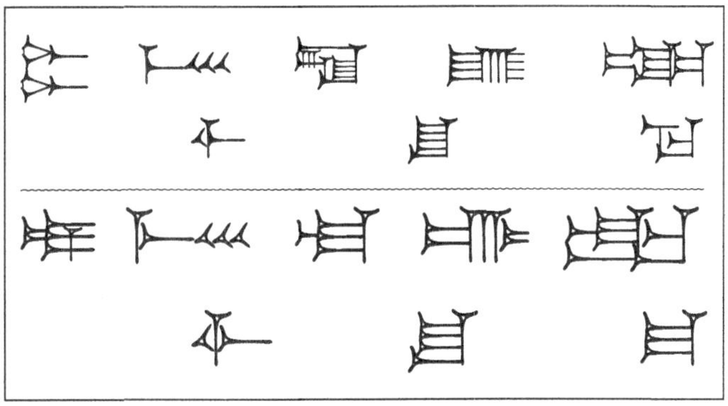

LH §145 XXXI (Rv. VIII):31

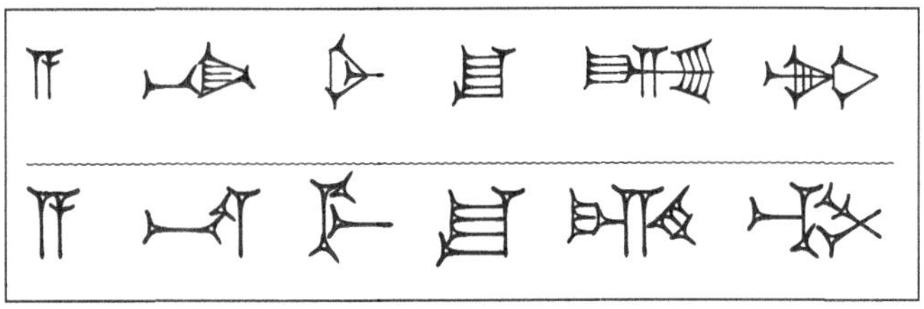

LH §145 XXXI (Rv. VIII):32

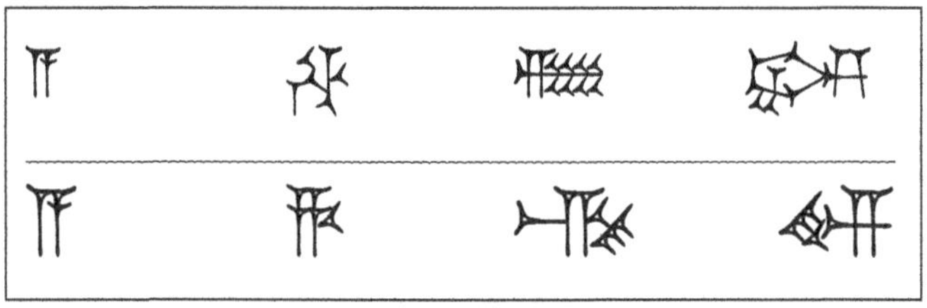

LH §145 XXXI (Rv. VIII):33

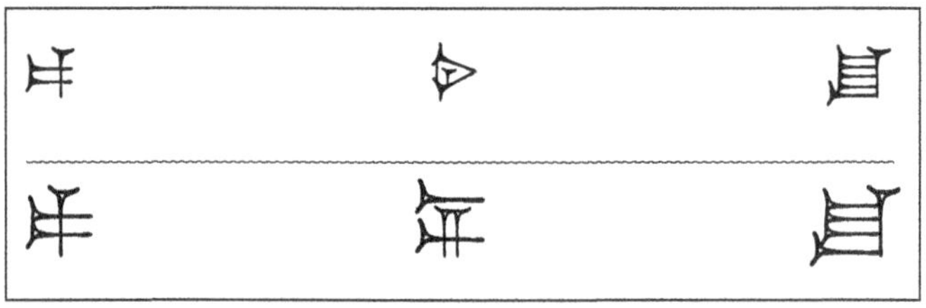

LH §145 XXXI (Rv. VIII):34

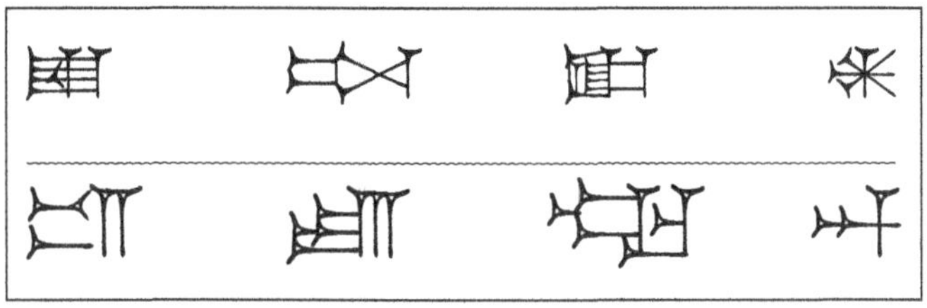

LH §145 XXXI (Rv. VIII):35

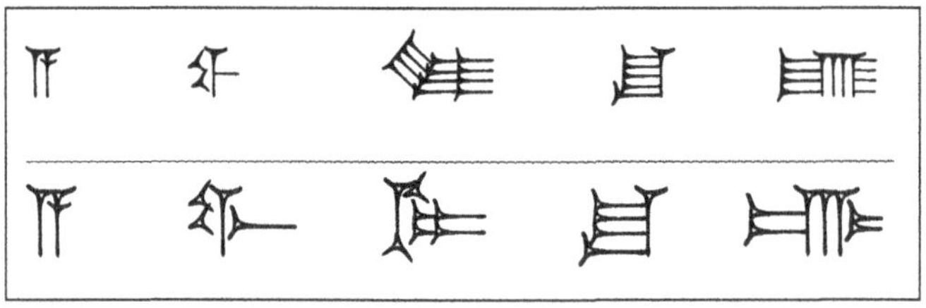

LH §145 XXXI (Rv. VIII):36

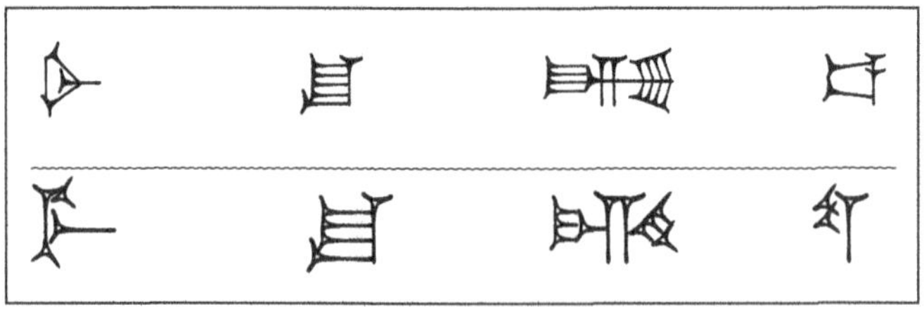

LH §145 XXXI (Rv. VIII):37

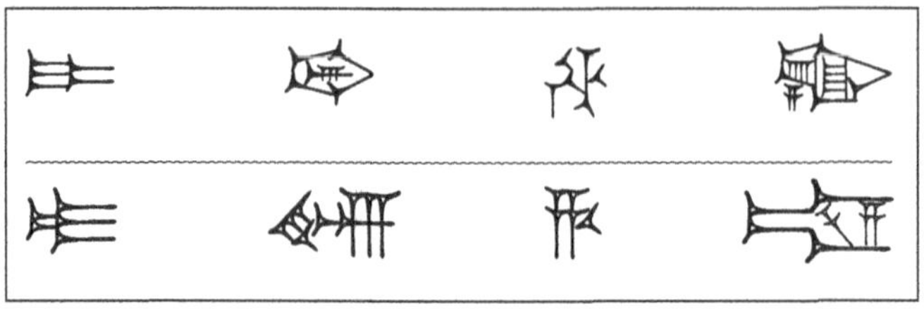

LH §145 XXXI (Rv. VIII):38

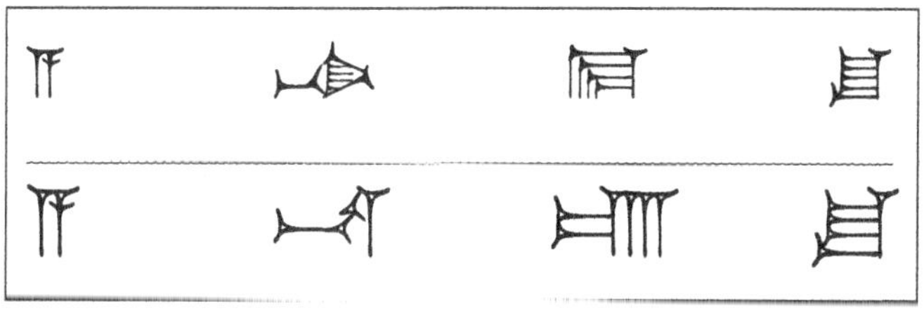

LH §145 XXXI (Rv. VIII):39

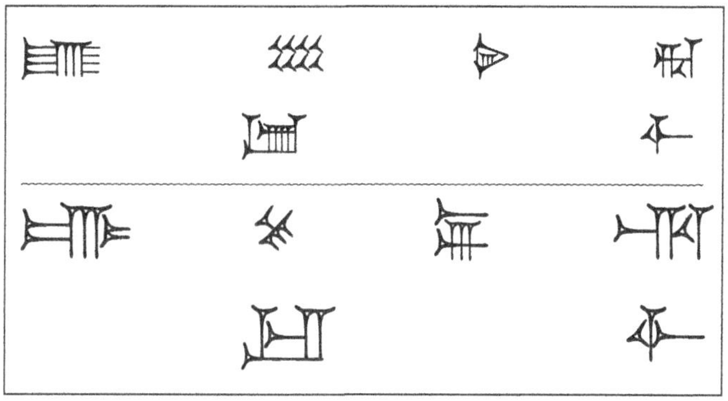

LH §145 XXXI (Rv. VIII):40

Note: The sign  in XXXI (Rv. VIII):40 is *tum*. This sign does not need to be learned.

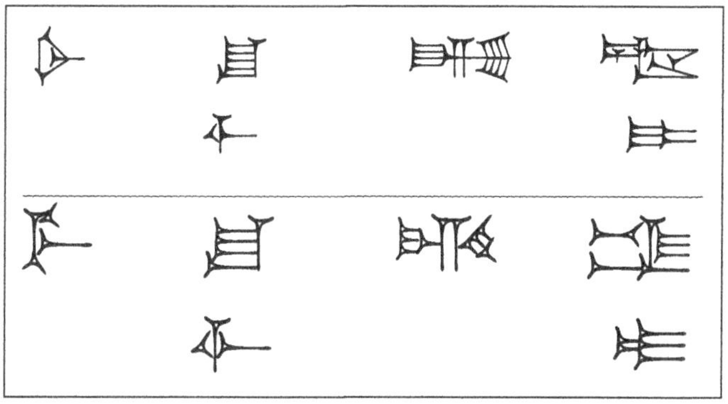

LH §145 XXXI (Rv. VIII):41

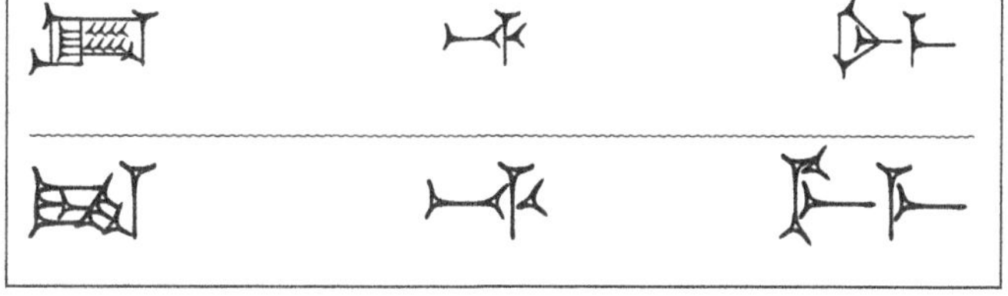

LH §145 XXXI (Rv. VIII):42

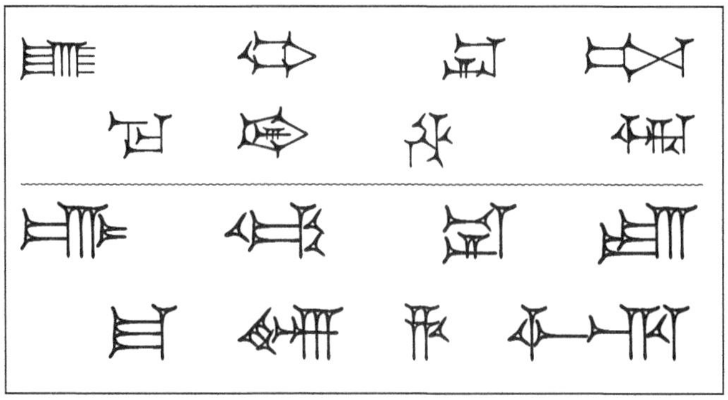

2. Grammatical Analysis: Parse all verb forms.

3. Translation: Translate LH §145.

Akkadian and the Book of Joshua

Richard S. Hess

The study of Akkadian impacts the Bible on many levels. One way is to examine an ancient Near Eastern text and note its applications to various biblical passages (e.g., LH to legal and related texts from the Bible). Another is to take a cognate expression and to trace it through its appearance in Akkadian and biblical Hebrew. The approach adopted here is to consider a biblical book, Joshua, and the manner in which Akkadian sources inform it on a variety of levels.

On a lexical level, there are the words found in Akkadian that occur in the text of Joshua, especially in the personal names. The non-Israelites in the book include several whose names are found elsewhere in Akkadian sources only from the second millennium BCE: Rahab (2:1, 3; 6:17, 23, 25; female at Mari [*ARM* 13 1.8.61; 1.9.46]), Japhia (at Lachish, 10:3; Gezer leader [EA 297.3; 298.4; 299.3; 378.3 (378.3 is a second figure associated with Byblos)]), Jabin (at Hazor, 11:1; *ARM* 8 19.14'; 13 38.13), Adoni-zedek (at Jerusalem, 10:3; EA 140.10 [*a-du-na*]; 170.37 [GAL-*ṣí-id-qí*]), Piram (at Jarmuth, 10:3; the *pir*- element occurs dozens of time at Nuzi [*NPN*, 245], Emar, Ekalte, et al.), Sheshai (at Hebron, 15:14; *NPN*, 256), and Talmai (at Hebron 15:14; *PRU* 3.37, Ras Shamra 15.81.9). While these are not necessarily Akkadian personal names, they are all found in Akkadian texts and come from the Middle and Late Bronze Ages (ca. 1500–1150 BCE).[1]

On the level of paragraphs and chapters, Akkadian texts inform the two major types of literature found in the book of Joshua: (1) battle accounts and (2) place name lists and boundaries. The former includes iterative accounts repeating verbs of battle, victory, and conquest as in Joshua 10:28–42. Babylonian and especially Middle and Neo-Assyrian accounts relate comparable successful conquest and destruction of cities and armies. There are also descriptions of divine intervention with hail and other heavenly assistance, as can be found in 10:11–14. Compare Sargon II's letter to Aššur, recounting the king's eighth campaign (*COS* 4.42, line 147): "the mighty god Adad, valiant son of Anu, let loose his immense thunder against them, and with his storm-cloud and hail finished off the remainder." While accounts also occur in Egyptian and Hittite records, a major focus appears in the Akkadian sources from Mesopotamia. Far from Martin Noth's Holy War theory with later scribal redactions in Israel, these accounts show that divine presence and intervention in battles occurs in virtually every battle account in the ancient Near East.[2]

The second area, that of boundary descriptions and place name lists, occurs in Joshua 13–19. There are nine Akkadian texts from Ugarit that preserve boundary descriptions, mostly concerning the border between this state and its northern neighbor, Mukish. As in the boundary descriptions of Joshua there are lists of towns that run along the border as well as intervening prepositions, verbs, and short narrative notes. They have introductions and conclusions identifying the lands that the border

1. See Richard S. Hess, "Non-Israelite Personal Names in the Book of Joshua," *Catholic Biblical Quarterly* 58 (1996): 205–14; Hess, "Personal Names in the Hebrew Bible with Second-Millennium B.C. Antecedents," *Bulletin for Biblical Research* 25 (2015): 5–12.

2. See K. Lawson Younger Jr., *Ancient Conquest Accounts: A Study in Ancient Near Eastern and Biblical History Writing* (Sheffield: Sheffield Academic, 1990); Richard S. Hess, *Joshua: An Introduction and Commentary*, Tyndale Old Testament Commentaries 6 (Downers Grove, IL: InterVarsity Press, 2008).

runs along. Further, duplicate descriptions of borders exist with similar names though different notes and, like the duplicate boundary between Benjamin and Judah in both Joshua 15:5–9 and 18:15–19, progressing in opposite directions.[3]

Finally, there is the level of the whole book of Joshua. Consider the Middle Bronze Age Akkadian tablet from Alalakh, describing the gift from Abbael to Yarimlim of some towns and lands. Both the tablet and the book of Joshua present, in the same sequence, (1) a narrative background explaining the circumstances leading to the allotment (lines 1–30; Josh 1–12); (2) the allotment itself with the mention of specific place names (lines 31–39a; Josh 13–21); (3) stipulations emphasizing loyalty toward the benefactor (lines 39b–61; Josh. 22:1–24:15); and (4) witnesses and oaths (lines 68–76; Josh. 24:16–33). Along with some examples of repeated terms functioning as literary inclusion for some of these sections, both texts function as land grants.[4]

3. Cf. PRU IV, 10–17; RS 17.340; RS 17.369A; RS 17.237; RS 17.62; RS 17.339A; RS 17.366; RS 17.368; and RS 19.81. See also Richard S. Hess, "Late Bronze Age and Biblical Boundary Descriptions of the West Semitic World" in *Ugarit and the Bible: Proceedings of the International Symposium on Ugarit and the Bible, Manchester, September 1992*, ed. George J. Brooke, Adrian H. W. Curtis, and John F. Healey, Ugaritisch-Biblische Literatur Band 11 (Münster: Ugarit-Verlag, 1994), 123–38; idem, "A Typology of West Semitic Place Name Lists with Special Reference to Joshua 13–21," *Biblical Archaeologist* 59/3 (September 1996): 160–70.

4. AT 456*. See Richard S. Hess, "The Book of Joshua as a Land Grant," *Biblica* 83 (2002): 493–506.

20–𒌋𒌋

Beyond Introductory Akkadian

This chapter will briefly treat some of the major differences in the various dialects of Akkadian, a language or language group that was spoken from the mid-third millennium BCE to at least the mid- to late-first millennium BCE, by which time at first Aramaic and later Greek took over as the lingua franca of the Fertile Crescent. Akkadian continued to be used as a written language in specialized scholarly settings (literary and religious works, especially astronomical/astrological texts) even until the late first century CE.

LH §§146–149 are the laws that will be translated in this final chapter. LH §§146–147 continue treating the issue of marriage to a priestess and permission for a secondary wife, in this case a slave, for the sake of bearing children. LH §§148–149 are also concerned with a potential polygynous marriage, but in this case, it is a permitted response to a wife who has contracted a serious, apparently incurable illness.

Students should focus on the main trends as they are sketched below, but it is not necessary to master every detail.

20.1 Differences in Akkadian over Time and Space[1]

It should not be surprising that the Babylonian family of dialects underwent many significant developments over the vast stretch of time during which Babylonian Akkadian was a spoken language (2500 BCE to perhaps 300 BCE), as well as the following four hundred years, during which it was primarily a scholarly written language employed by increasingly smaller groups of trained individuals.[2] In broad terms, these developments are reflected in the sequence of periods listed below (see §1.2).

Old Akkadian (OAkk) 2350–2000 BCE		
Old Babylonian (OB)	2000–1600 BCE	Old Assyrian (OA)
Middle Babylonian (MB)	1600–1000 BCE	Middle Assyrian (MA)
Neo-Babylonian (NB)	1000–600 BCE	Neo-Assyrian (NA)
Late Babylonian (LB)	600 BCE–100 CE	
Standard Babylonian (SB) 1500–100 BCE		

The fact that there would be a separation between the Babylonian and Assyrian branches of Akkadian is unsurprising based on the relative geographical separation of these regions of Mesopotamia. Assyria was centered in the highlands of the fast-moving Tigris river and its major tributaries in the mountainous northeast, while Babylonia was centered a couple of hundred

1. Cf. George, "Babylonian and Assyrian: A History of Akkadian," 31–71.

2. The approximate 2500 BCE date is based mostly on the evidence of Akkadian personal names, such as are attested in early Sumerian texts from Abu Salabiḫ and Fara.

miles to the south in the expansive alluvial plain created by the slow-moving Euphrates river and its tangled channels and estuaries.

The above listed periods are reasonably well defined by historical events, as well as by noticeable changes in the language. Old Babylonian, for example, begins after the fall of the last Sumerian dynasty (Ur III), and it ends with the destruction of Babylon by the Hittites in 1595 BCE. Middle Babylonian begins after the Kassite invasion of Babylonia about 1550 BCE.

Old Assyrian, on the other hand, begins around 1950 BCE with the settlement of trading colonies in central Anatolia, especially Kanesh (modern Kültepe, which is located almost in the exact center of modern Turkey), by merchants who travelled some 600 miles from Assur on the Tigris.

It is also the case that between each listed period, there is often a significant gap in the extant documentary evidence for each dialect. For example, there is a gap of at least two centuries between the youngest extant Old Assyrian texts (ca. 1700 BCE) and the oldest Middle Assyrian texts (ca. 1500 BCE).

Despite its helpful utility and apparent comprehensiveness, the above list could easily be augmented by the recognition of a number of important local (especially peripheral) dialects, such as those attested at Alalakh, Amarna, Emar, Hattusas (modern Boğazköy), Mari, Nuzi, Ugarit, etc. Many of these local dialects reflect the influence and mixing of other native languages (e.g., Amorite in the case of Mari; Hurrian in the case of Nuzi, Qatna, and Alalakh; Hittite in the case of Hattusas; Canaanite in the case of Amarna). As such, they are important witnesses not only to the rich diversity within the Akkadian language group but also to these other languages that are less well preserved.

It goes beyond the scope of an introductory grammar like this to do justice to the rich linguistic diversity represented by the above outline of the major phases in the development of Akkadian. What is offered here is only a sketch of some of the more salient developments.

20.2 Differences in Babylonian over Time

Entire books and major articles have been written to describe the unique characteristics of each of the major phases of Babylonian, as well as its local dialects.[3] Here is a sample of some of the more significant differences within Babylonian over time.

20.2.1 *Orthography*

1. One obvious difference between texts written in Old Babylonian, such as LH (about 1750 BCE), and those written in later periods, whether Middle Babylonian, Neo-Babylonian, Late Babylonian, or Standard Babylonian, are the differences in the shapes of many of the cuneiform signs and, often, differences also in their syllabic values.

For example, according to the classic (handwritten) and still useful manual on the history of Akkadian cuneiform produced by René Labat,[4] the pictographic sign for a ram's horn, as found on Sumerian tablets from Jemdet-Nasr from about 3000 BCE, was drawn as follows:

3. See the bibliography at the end of this book for some important examples.
4. Labat, *Manuel d'épigraphie akkadienne*, 90–91.

The Sumerian word for "ram's horn" is SI.

In third millennium BCE Sumerian and Akkadian tablets, this ram's horn sign became increasingly abstract and more linear (because of the demands of cuneiform writing), and over a period of time it was rotated 90 degrees counterclockwise. The following are examples:[5]

In the early second millennium BCE, the Old Babylonian period, this SI sign came to be written in the following four representative ways:

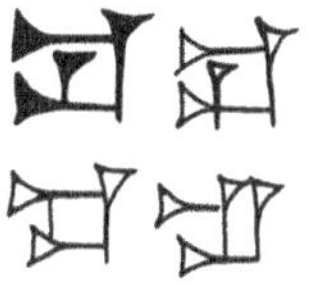

In the mid- to late-second millennium BCE, the Middle Babylonian period, this sign was written in one of the following five ways:

In the first millennium BCE, the Neo-Babylonian period, it was written in one of the following four options:

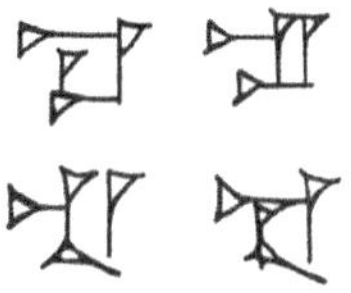

Labat records the various values that this sign had over this same lengthy period of use. At first its logographic value was SI, meaning "ram's horn" (in Akkadian, *qarnum*). In Sumerian, as well as in Old Babylonian, this sign was also used as a syllabogram for the syllable *si*. Babylonian continued to use this sign for *si* in all the subsequent periods. In the period of Middle Babylonian, however, it added *ší* as a possible alternative value, and in Standard Babylonian, which was not a spoken language but a special literary form of Akkadian invented in imitation of Old Babylonian and employed for literary works, added the value *ṣì*.

5. As mentioned in §1.1.3.5, the timing of this rotation, both in the lines of writing and the cuneiform signs in those lines, is uncertain and likely occurred over a long period of time. So, although there is evidence suggesting that the rotation occurred before the period of Old Babylonian, LH on the famous stele housed in the Louvre has all the signs and lines of writing oriented without that 90-degree rotation. In this book, however, the boxes of cuneiform text have all been rotated and with them the enclosed cuneiform signs because of the modern scholarly preference for ease of reading from left to right, rather than replicating the top to the bottom orientation that is on the stele.

Labat provides similar information for about 600 cuneiform signs for both Babylonian and Assyrian in all periods.

2. Another significant development in the orthography of Babylonian after the period of Old Babylonian is the invention of a sign for ', whether followed by or preceded by a vowel: . This sign was clearly based on 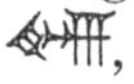, the sign for *aḫ*, *eḫ*, *iḫ*, *uḫ* (and before the creation of , also for *á'*, *é'*, *í'*, *ú'*).

3. A third significant development in the orthography of Babylonian after the period of Old Babylonian is a significant increase in the use of *cvc* cuneiform signs and sign values. In the latest period some *cvc* signs are used to represent two syllable combinations, *cvcv*.

20.2.2 ***Phonology.*** Babylonian also experienced a number of significant changes in phonology over time.

1. In Middle Babylonian and afterwards, when a sibilant (*s, ṣ, š, z*) appears before another sibilant or a dental (*d, t, ṭ*), it often changes into *l*. This phonological rule applies to Š-stem forms for any verb that has a sibilant or dental for its first root consonant.

For example, in Old Babylonian the Š-stem preterite first singular of the irregular verb *izuzzum*, "to stand," is *ušzîz*, meaning "I stationed." In subsequent forms of Babylonian, *ušzîz* becomes *ulzîz*.[6] Likewise, the noun *išdum*, "foundation," which appears in the prologue and epilogue of LH, is spelled *ildu* (the loss of the final *m* will be discussed in §20.2.3 below) when it appears in Middle Babylonian and Neo-Babylonian texts.

2. Another noticeable change is observed in Middle Babylonian and later. Whenever a second root consonant is doubled in a verb paradigm, if it is a *b, d, g,* or *z* (all voiced consonants), the first of them dissimilates into a nasal consonant, *m* or *n*.

For example, the G-stem durative 3cs *inaddin*, "he will give," in Old Babylonian becomes *inamdin* or *inandin* in Middle Babylonian and subsequently.

3. The *i'a* and *e'a* diphthongs or vowel sequences are the only vowel sequences that are maintained without contraction in Old Babylonian. In the dialect attested at Mari, however, they contract to *ẽ*. Elsewhere, toward the end of the Old Babylonian period these sequences of vowels contract so that *i'a* > *ã* and *e'a* > *ã*. This practice continues in Middle Babylonian and thereafter. For example, the Old Babylonian accusative ms form of the adjective *rabi'am*, "great," becomes *rabã(m)*.[7]

4. In Old Babylonian in verbal forms where a compensatorily lengthened vowel, *v̂*, occurs, it is sometimes shortened and replaced by resolutory doubling of the following consonant (§11.3.3). In the periods following Old Babylonian this often happens in nouns as well as verbal forms. For example, Old Babylonian *kûṣum*, which means "coldness, winter," in Middle Assyrian appears as *kuṣṣu*.

6. See §19.2. In Neo-Babylonian the G-stem preterite also appears as *ušazziz* and the durative as *ušazzaz*.
7. The loss of the final *m* is discussed in §20.2.3.

5. Starting toward the end of the Old Babylonian period and from then on, most words that begin with *w* in Old Babylonian drop the *w* without any lengthening. Because *CAD* lists most words in the form they have in Standard Babylonian, most words that start with *w* in Old Babylonian will be listed without the *w*.

For example, the verb *wašābum (a,i)*, meaning "to dwell, sit" (cf. *yāšab*, יָשַׁב, "to sit, dwell"), is listed in *CAD* under *ašab(u)*. Elsewhere, such as in *CDA*, the same verb is listed under the letter *w* but written as *(w)ašābu(m)*.

6. After Old Babylonian, any *w* inside a word also underwent significant changes. As mentioned in §4.5, any *w* at the end of a syllable was lost before the Old Babylonian period, unless it was followed by a syllable beginning with a *w*, as in *nuwwurim*, "to illumine," (D-stem infinitive of *nawārum*) in LH §Pro 1:44. A *w* that begins a syllable is sometimes preserved in Old Babylonian, as in the case of *awīlum*, "man, person, citizen (a free man)."

In many cases after Old Babylonian a *w* that begins a syllable appears as if it had become the consonant *m*. This is how it is written in terms of the cuneiform signs, and it is also how it should be normalized. There is reason to believe, however, that it may have continued to be pronounced as a *w*, at least when the *m* (the kind that represents an earlier *w*) appears between vowels. For example, *awīlum*, "man, person, citizen (a free man)," becomes *amīlu(m)* after Old Babylonian.[8]

20.2.3 ***Morphology.*** There are several significant changes in morphology that already began toward the end of the Old Babylonian period.

1. First and foremost is the loss of mimation (the *m* at the end of all singular nouns and feminine plural nouns, on all adjectives, on ventive endings, and on dative pronouns and pronominal suffixes). Because this loss of mimation happened so early in Akkadian, most Akkadian lexica list nouns, such as *šarrum*, "king," under a heading like *šarru(m)*, with parentheses around the final *m*. Similarly, they list verbs under G-stem infinitive forms, not like Old Babylonian *parāsum*, "to divide, separate, cut (off); to decide," but like *parāsu(m)*, indicating the absence of the final *m*, which was the norm following Old Babylonian.

2. A second significant change in morphology is the gradual mixing and ultimately erosion of the use of declension in Babylonian. This mixing begins around 1000 BCE, apparently because final short vowels were no longer being pronounced clearly. Interestingly, this loss of declension roughly coincides with the loss of declension in the Northwest Semitic languages, including Hebrew.[9]

At first the mixing is evident in the use of accusative forms where Old Babylonian would expect a nominative, or nominative forms where Old Babylonian expects an accusative. Subsequently, genitive forms are similarly confused or mixed. Often, plural forms are in the oblique case, ending with *ī* or *ē*, even if they are functioning as nominatives. These endings are also typical for bound forms.

8. The noun *amīlu* is often written with the normal sign for *me*, 𒈨, rather than the expected *mi*, 𒈪. Worthington (*Complete Babylonian*, in §7.2) plausibly explains this as a common alternative spelling that results from the fact that the sign for *me* is much easier to write.

9. An alternative explanation for this confusion of or apparent indifference toward vowels in the Neo-Babylonian period may be that it reflects the increasing influence of Aramaic, whose earliest orthography completely disregarded vowels and whose later orthography indicated only long vowels.

3. Related to the previous development, around the beginning of Neo-Babylonian (1000 BCE), not only are short vowel declensional endings no longer consistently used or spelled, the same is true for the subordinating *-u* suffix on verbs.

4. Plural suffixes for nouns with the stylistic *-ān* suffix (see §13.4), which are relatively rare in the Old Babylonian period (as in the plural of *ilum*: *ilānū*), become more common in later periods in the form of *ānū* and *ānī*.

5. Under the increasing influence of Aramaic starting from the early seventh century BCE, Neo-Babylonian in this later period acquired a distinct 3fs form (*t-*) for the prefix tenses.

20.3 Differences between Babylonian and Assyrian

The differences in vocabulary and grammar between Babylonian and Assyrian are sufficient that ancient speakers viewed them as two distinct languages, rather than as two dialects or branches of the same language, namely Akkadian, as is the dominant view of modern scholars.

The fact that Assyrian experienced many of the same developments as Babylonian over its history and at roughly the same time suggests that the two families of dialects were closely linked and directly influenced each other. The direction of influence, however, was mostly from Babylonian, the prestige language, to Assyrian.

After the period of Old Babylonian, for example, there was a loss of mimation in Assyrian at about the same time as mimation was lost in Babylonian. Likewise, starting around the beginning of Neo-Assyrian (1000 BCE) there was also the mixing of case endings (nominative and accusative) and later the erosion of declension in both branches of Akkadian at about the same time.

There is a shared development in the use of the perfect for the simple past tense, which, in both Middle Babylonian and Middle Assyrian, resulted in the preterite being mainly confined in its use to subordinate, negative, or interrogative clauses. Furthermore, after Old Babylonian both branches of Akkadian significantly reduced and later virtually eliminated the use of any of the derived *-t(a)-* stems and *-tan-* stems (other than *-tan-* duratives).

Finally, despite some differences in vocabulary between Babylonian and Assyrian, most of their vocabulary is shared by both branches of Akkadian with only minor spelling adjustments.

20.3.1 *Orthography*

1. Old Assyrian employs a greatly reduced syllabary as compared to Old Babylonian, using only about 130 signs, and it uses very few Sumerian logograms. Both practices are perhaps not surprising given that our principal sources for Old Assyrian are tablets that have been discovered at Assyrian trading colonies that were established in Anatolia, especially at Kanesh (located at modern Kültepe, which is almost the exact geographical center of modern Turkey), about 600 miles to the west of Assur. Assur was the original home for most of these traders and the center in Assyria for this trade.

A reduced number of syllabic signs facilitated greater practical literacy, as was required for these Assyrian merchants who used the written language of Old Assyrian for their work and also for letters to and from wives who, at least in the first generation, tended to remain back home in Assur. The relative lack of Sumerian logograms in Old Assyrian is perhaps also understandable because of the source of these documents. The centers of Sumerian culture and population were in southern-most Mesopotamia, far to the south of Assur, much less Kanesh.

2. Assyrian script evolved in similar ways over a similar period of time as did Babylonian script. The history of the SI sign is, again, illustrative of this development. Labat summarizes the historical development of the SI sign in his top entry on p. 90 in *Manuel d'épigraphie akkadienne*. The copy of Labat's entry is below. The far left column is for Sumerian around 3000 BCE. The second column is for developments in Sumerian and Old Akkadian. The top three boxes, starting in the third column and marked with an "A" represent the first signs used in Old Assyrian, then to its right, Middle Assyrian, and to the far right, the Neo-Assyrian sign 𒋛, as taught in Chapter 15 of this textbook. The three lower boxes marked with a B are for Old Babylonian, Middle Babylonian, and finally Neo-Babylonian.

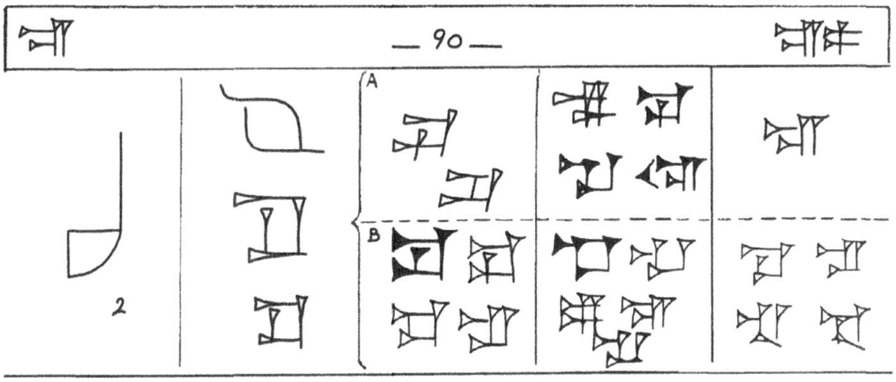

Assyrian almost immediately ceased as a spoken language with the fall of Nineveh in 612 BCE.

20.3.2 *Phonology*

1. In a number of instances, Assyrian preserves earlier practices of Old Akkadian that were lost in Babylonian. For example, the diphthong *ay* becomes *î* in Babylonian but *ê* in Assyrian, as it also did in earlier Old Akkadian. So *baytum, "house," became *bîtum* in Babylonian but *bêtum* in Assyrian.

2. Another illustration of this conservative tendency in Assyrian is that, unlike the normal contraction of vowels in Babylonian, vowel contraction does not occur in Assyrian until the Neo-Assyrian period. Accordingly, the II-weak and III-weak verbs of Babylonian are conjugated in Assyrian with the ' being treated as a strong consonant.

For example, whereas in Old Babylonian the G-stem durative 3cs of the hollow verb *târum* (*u*) (< *t-w-r*), "to return," is *itâr* (< *yitawwar), in Assyrian it is *itû'ar*, "he will return," a form that preserves the ' along with the uncontracted adjacent vowels. Similarly, with respect to G-stem infinitives of hollow verbs such as *kânum*, "to be firm"; D: "to establish, make secure, prove, have proof, convict," a hypothesized earlier form *kawānum became *kânum* in Old Babylon but Assyrian preserves an earlier form, *ku'ānum*.

3. When a consonantal cluster occurs in Babylonian (as may happen when creating a bound form of a noun), the cluster is broken up by adding a harmonizing anaptyctic vowel. In Assyrian,

however, rather than choosing a harmonizing vowel to be used for an anaptyctic vowel, the vowel *a* is generally chosen. For example, in Babylonian the noun *šiprum*, which means "work, job," has the bound form *šipir*, "the work of," which appears in LH §188. In Assyrian, however, the vowel *a* breaks up the consonantal cluster. Hence "the work of" in Assyrian is *šipar*.

4. Naturally, given its name, Babylonian vowel harmony does not occur in Assyrian. When the gutturals *ḥ*, ʿ, and sometimes *ǵ* were originally adjacent to an *a*-vowel, the *a* shifts to *e* in both Babylonian and Assyrian. If there is a second *a*-vowel in the word, however, that vowel will also shift to *e* in Babylonian (because of Babylonian vowel harmony), but it will remain in its more original form as an *a*-vowel in Assyrian. For example, the plural of the feminine noun *bêltum*, "mistress, lady," in Old Babylonian is *bêlētum*, but in Old Assyrian it is *bêlātum*.

5. On the other hand, Assyrian vowel harmony occurs when a short *a*-vowel in an open post-accented syllable assimilates to the vowel of a nominal suffix or a verbal suffix. For example, while *šarratum*, "queen," is how this feminine singular noun in the nominative case is spelled in Old Babylonian, in Old Assyrian it is *šarrutum*. Similarly, whereas in Old Babylonian the G-stem preterite 3mp of *ṣabātum* (*a*-class), "to seize, catch, find," is *iṣbatū*, in Old Assyrian, because of Assyrian vowel harmony, it is *iṣbutū*.

6. Assyrian tends to use an *e*-vowel in many situations where Babylonian uses an *i*-vowel, although by the time of Neo-Assyrian these vowels are mostly interchangeable in Assyrian. For example, mp obliques that end in *-ī* in Old Babylonian, such as the word for "gods," *ilī*, in Assyrian are spelled with the suffix *-ē*, such as *ilē*. Likewise, singular noun forms ending with *-im* in Old Babylonian end with *-e* in Assyrian after the period of Old Assyrian (when mimation was lost). For example, the Old Babylonian noun for "man, person, citizen (a free man)" in the genitive singular is *awīlim*, but in Middle Assyrian it is spelled *a'īle*. Similarly, prefix tense forms for I-' verbs that begin with an *i*-vowel in Old Babylonian begin with an *e*-vowel in Assyrian. For example, *îḫuz*, "he seized," in Old Babylonian will be *êḫuz* in Assyrian.

There are many other words that are not easily categorized where there is also a shift from what would be an *i*-vowel in Old Babylonian to an *e*-vowel in Assyrian. For example, the genitive Old Babylonian personal pronoun for "we" is *nīnu*, whereas the Assyrian form is *nēnu*.

7. Starting with Middle Assyrian an initial *wa*- becomes *u*-. For example, the Old Babylonian G-stem infinitive *wašābum*, "to dwell, sit" (cf. *yāšab*, יָשַׁב, "to sit, dwell"), becomes *ušābu(m)* starting with Middle Assyrian.

8. After Old Assyrian, a *-w-* that begins a syllable within a word appears as if it became the consonant *-m-* or *-b-*. This is how it is written in terms of the cuneiform signs, and it is also how it should be normalized. As in the case of Babylonian, it is possible that it continued to be pronounced as a *w*, at least when the *m* or *b* (the kind that represents an earlier *w*) appears between vowels. For example, the Old Babylonian noun for "word," *awātum*, is spelled in Middle Assyrian and Neo-Assyrian as *amātu*, or *abutu*.

Occasionally an intervocalic *w* becomes '. For example, the word for "man, person, citizen (a free man)," *awīlum*, is spelled as *a'ilu* in Middle Assyrian, as implied by the example offered in section 6. above.

9. When there are three short open non-final syllables in a row, the vowel of the second is apt to be elided in Babylonian (vowel syncope), whereas the vowel of the third syllable is apt to be elided in Assyrian. For example, the Gt-stem infinitive is *pitrusum* (> **pitarusum*) in Babylonian but *pitarsum* (> **pitarusum*) in Assyrian.

20.3.3 *Morphology*

1. Assyrian, like Babylonian, lost mimation and nunation after the Old Assyrian period.

2. Likewise, Assyrian began to lose the earlier case ending distinctions after Middle Assyrian (around 1000 BCE). At first, *-u* is used as both the nominative and accusative singular suffix, while *-i* or *-e* is used for genitive singular. Gradually, these case vowels were used almost randomly, as was the case in the Babylonian of the time, including Standard Babylonian.

3. Neo-Assyrian used its accusative pronominal suffixes for the dative as well.

4. After Old Assyrian, *lâ* is used as the only negative particle (*ul* is no longer used).

5. In Assyrian the subordinative suffix *-u* is normally an expanded form, *-u . . . ni*, where the *ni* follows any pronominal suffixes but comes before *-ma*. The subordinative suffix *-ni* often appears by itself, and it is also sometimes used to mark subordinate non-verbal sentences.

6. In Neo-Assyrian, the *-ma* suffix is no longer used as a conjunction indicating logical or temporal consecution.

7. Whereas Babylonian uses a 3cs verbal form in its prefix tenses, with the prefix *i-* or *u-*, Assyrian uses this form just for 3ms. It has a special 3fs form in its prefix tenses with the prefix *ta-* or *tu-*. This, too, may show the conservative tendency of Assyrian over Babylonian, since Old Akkadian definitely had this form, as is also assumed to be the case for Proto-Semitic.[10] For example, whereas the G-stem 3cs preterite of *parāsum* is *iprus* and the D-stem 3cs preterite is *uparris*, Assyrian can use an explicit 3fs prefix for each of these forms: *taprus* and *tuparris* respectively.

8. Finally, in the D-stem and Š-stem verbal adjective, stative, and infinitive where Babylonian uses a *u*-vowel between the first and second root consonants, Assyrian uses an *a*-vowel. For example, the D-stem infinitive for *parāsu(m)* is *purrusu(m)* in Babylonian, but it is *parrusu(m)* in Assyrian.

20.4 Homework

Before you move on, become comfortable with the grammatical nuances addressed above that exist throughout the Akkadian dialects. Familiarity will provide facility in any future study of the language.

10. Cf. Gelb, *Old Akkadian Writing and Grammar*, 157–67; Huehnergard, *A Grammar of Akkadian*, 62–63.

20.4.1 *Signs*[11]

 *qa*

 *qe, qi*

 *qu, qum*

Congratulations! If you learn the three signs in this chapter and the preceding 123 signs, you have learned not only 98 percent of all the cuneiform signs in LH §§1–20, 127–149, but also the signs for all the most common *cv* and *vc* syllables in Akkadian (Neo-Assyrian script). See Appendix D for an alphabetic listing of these signs.

20.4.2 *Vocabulary*

epēšum (*e,u* or *u,u*) = to do, make, build (cf., perhaps, *ḥāpaś*, חָפַשׂ, "to search")
bêltum = mistress, lady (cf. *ba'al*, בַּעַל)

Congratulations! If you have learned the 159 words in the vocabulary lists of each of the preceding chapters, and the two words you need to learn for this chapter, you will be able to read 96 percent of all the cuneiform words in LH §§1–20, 127–149.

20.4.3 *Exercises*

LH §146 continues a section of laws in LH that concern marriages to priestesses. In this law, a man marries a high priestess (*nadîtum*) who provides her maidservant through whom her husband can have children. If the maidservant bears children and then uses that fact to try to elevate her status over that of her mistress, her mistress cannot turn around and sell her off. Although it is implied that female slaves in this situation are automatically manumitted so that the children they bear will be free, because of this woman's presumptuous actions, her punishment is that she is made and treated as a slave once again.

LH §146 is often discussed in relation to Genesis 16, where Sarai offers her Egyptian maidservant Hagar to Abram in order to bear him a son, and Hagar's apparent attempt after Ishmael's birth to usurp Sarah.

1. Transliterate and Normalize: See the note below for additional help.

LH §146 XXXI (Rv. VIII):43

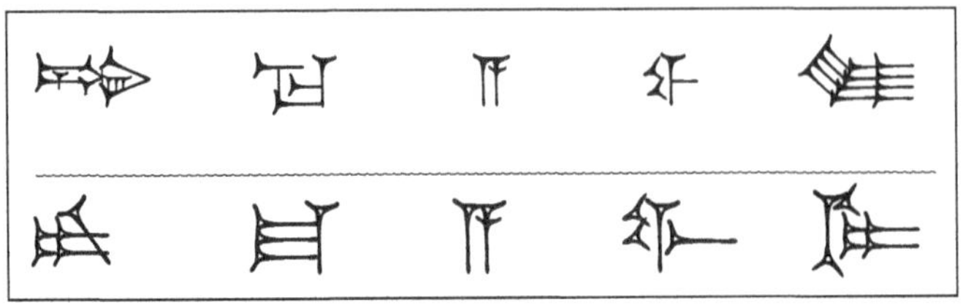

11. The signs below are not found in LH. Rather, the signs for the related non-emphatic *ga, ke, ki,* and *ku* are used. See §6.4.1 and §12.3.1.

LH §146 XXXI (Rv. VIII):44

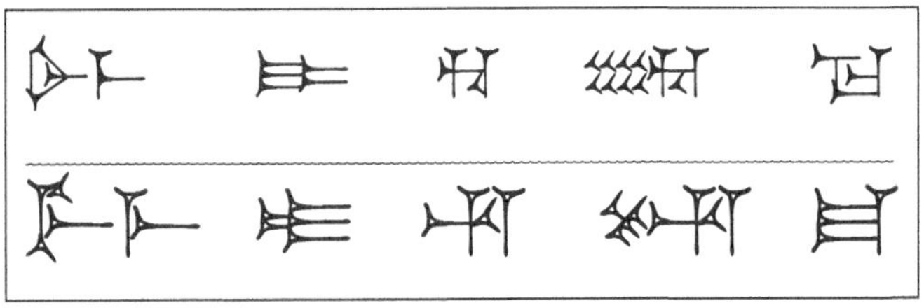

LH §146 XXXI (Rv. VIII):45

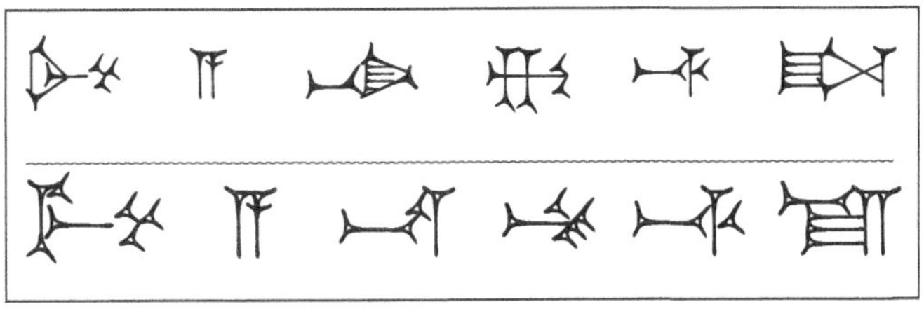

LH §146 XXXI (Rv. VIII):46

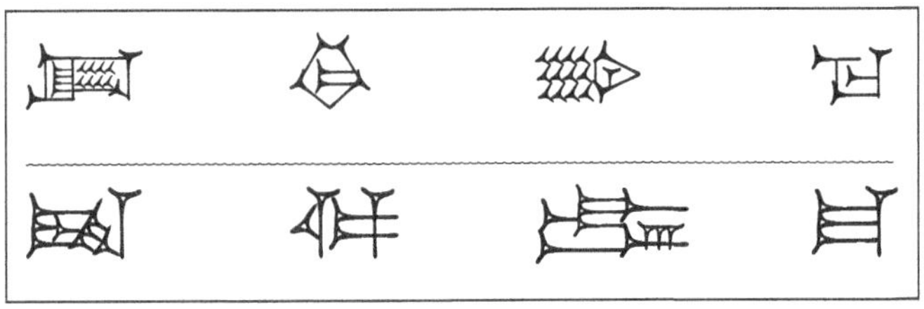

LH §146 XXXI (Rv. VIII):47

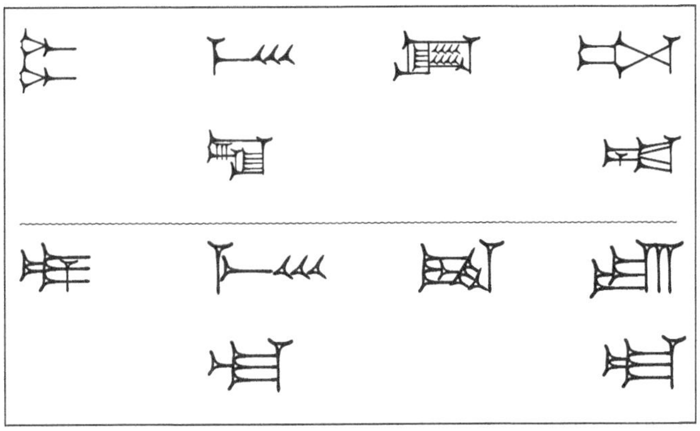

LH §146 XXXI (Rv. VIII):48

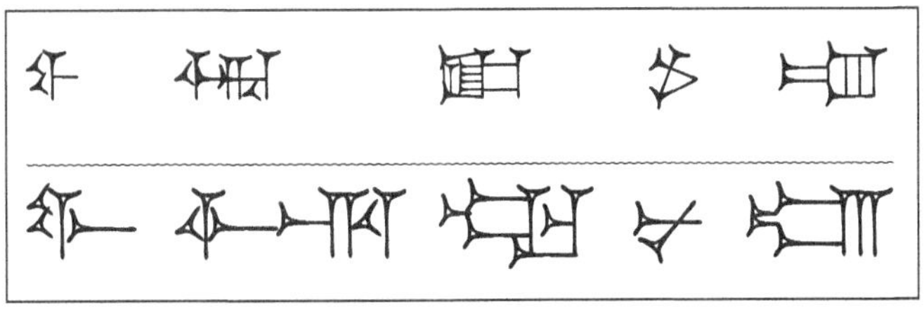

LH §146 XXXI (Rv. VIII):49

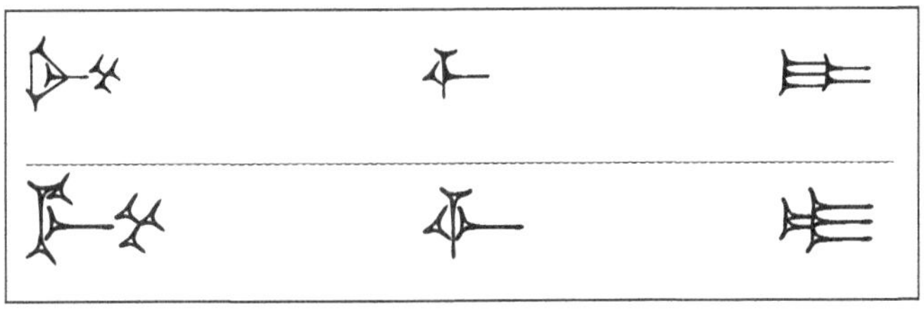

LH §146 XXXI (Rv. VIII):50

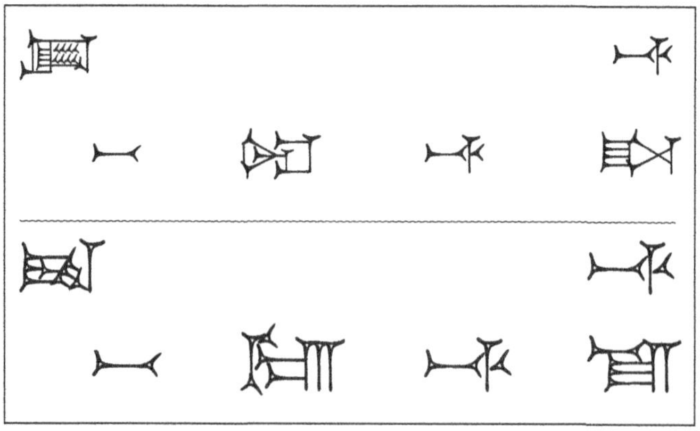

LH §146 XXXI (Rv. VIII):51

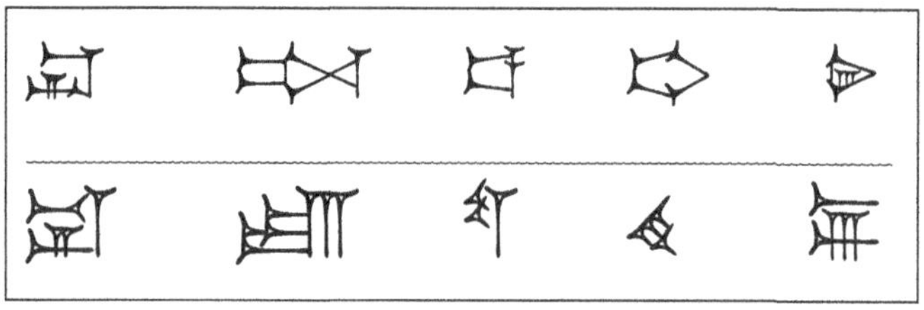

LH §146 XXXI (Rv. VIII):52

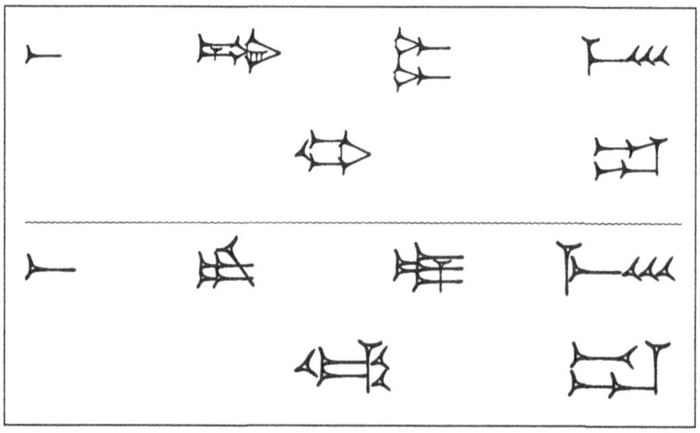

LH §146 XXXI (Rv. VIII):53

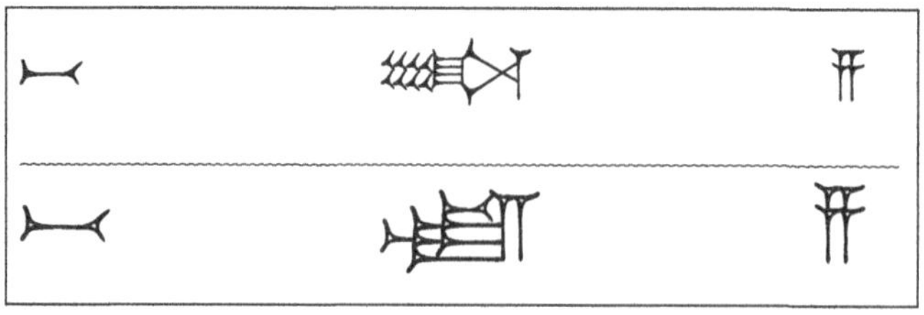

LH §146 XXXI (Rv. VIII):54

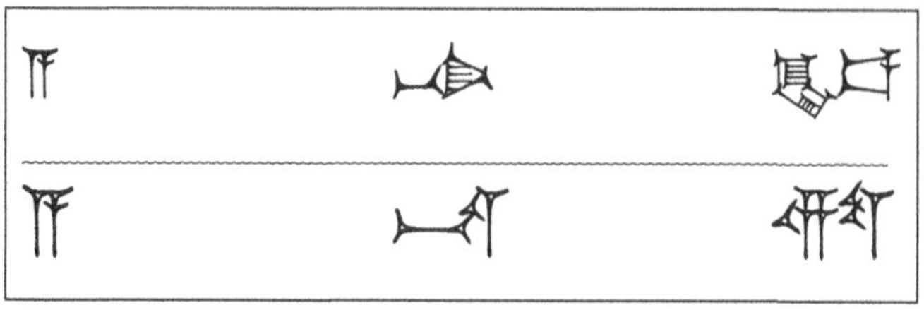

LH §146 XXXI (Rv. VIII):55

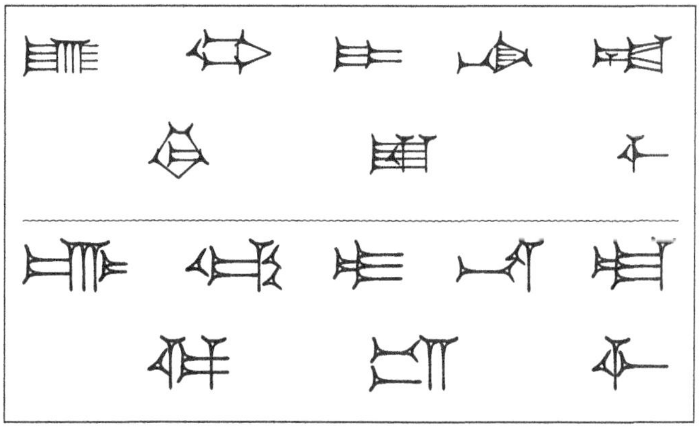

LH §146 XXXI (Rv. VIII):56

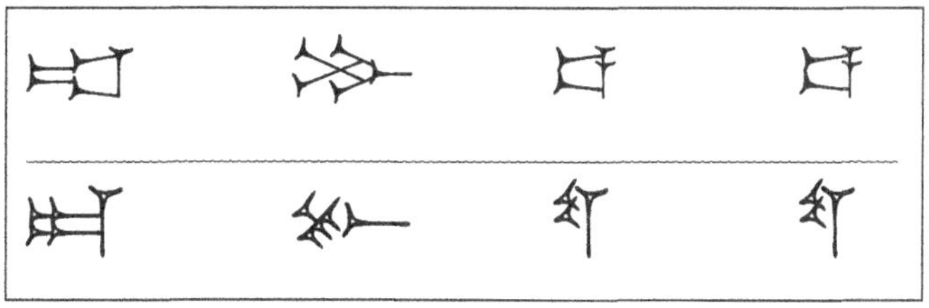

LH §146 XXXI (Rv. VIII):57

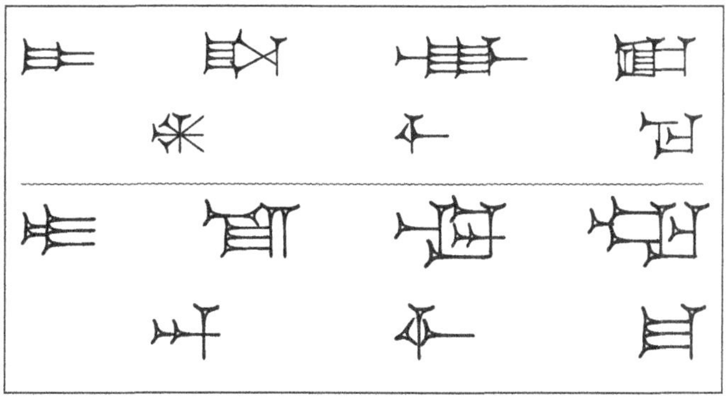

LH §146 XXXI (Rv. VIII):58

Note: The sign  in XXXI (Rv. VIII):58 is ^{ḪÁ}, a determinative for a plurality for objects. This sign does not need to be learned.

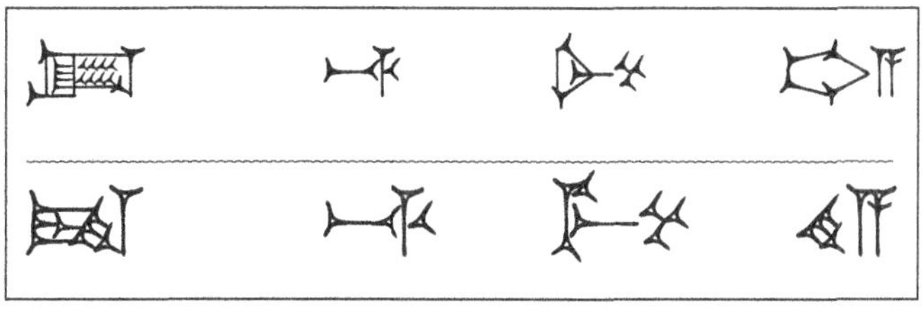

LH §146 XXXI (Rv. VIII):59

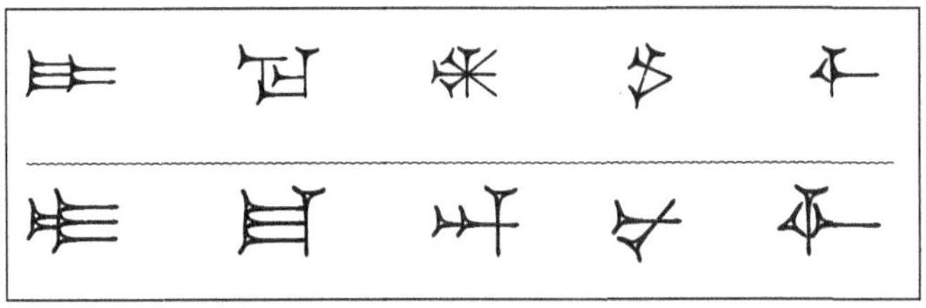

2. Grammatical Analysis: Parse all verb forms. See the note below for additional help.

   Note: XXXI (Rv. VIII):56 includes the word *abbuttum*, meaning "a special haircut that marks slaves." This word does not need to be learned.

3. Translation: Translate LH §146.

LH §147 completes the section of laws (LH §§144–147) regarding marriage to a priestess. It considers an alternative to that covered in LH §146. In this case, the overly ambitious maidservant has failed to bear any sons (children), so her mistress is permitted to sell her off.

1. Transliterate and Normalize.

LH §147 XXXI (Rv. VIII):60

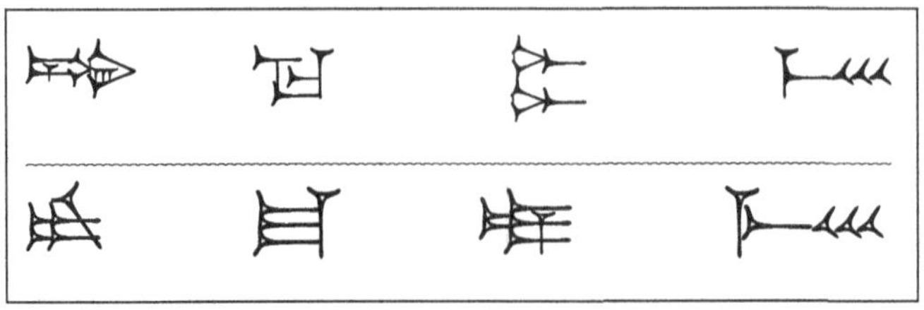

LH §147 XXXI (Rv. VIII):61

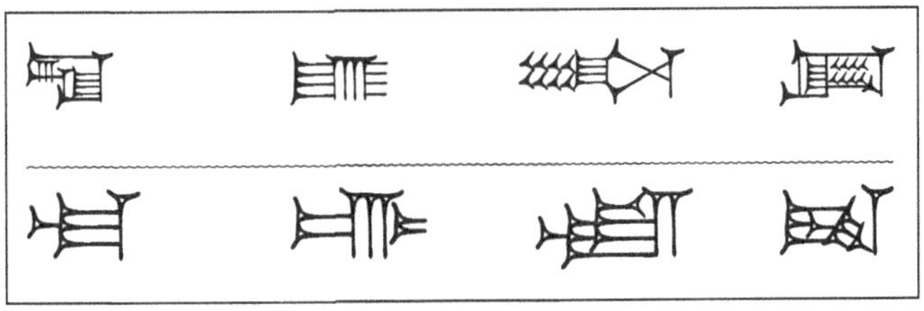

LH §147 XXXI (Rv. VIII):62

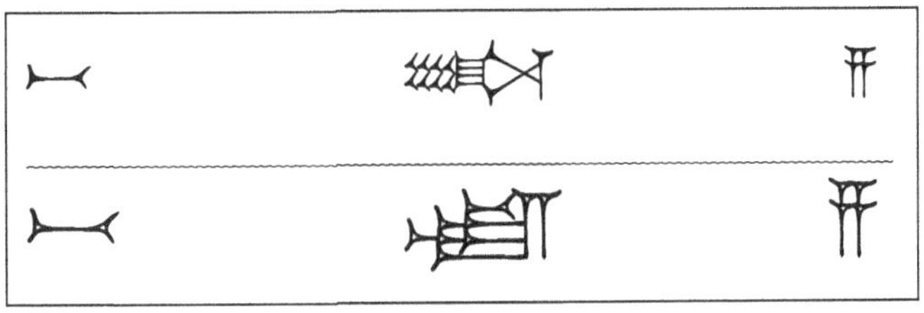

LH §147 XXXI (Rv. VIII):63

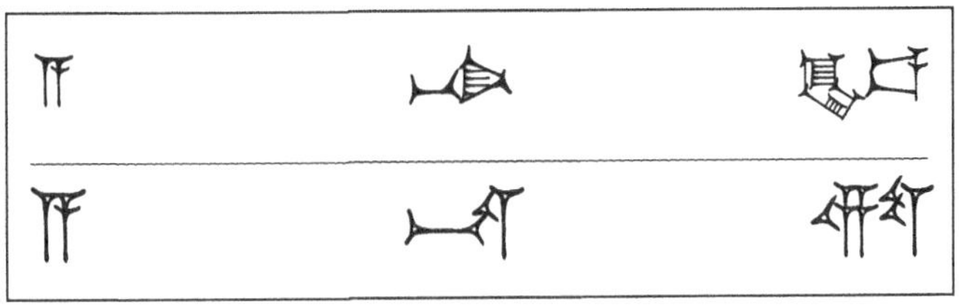

LH §147 XXXI (Rv. VIII):64

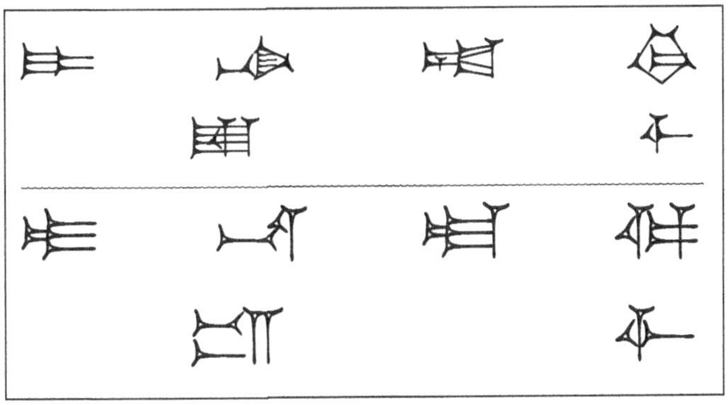

2. Grammatical Analysis: Parse all verb forms and answer the question below.

   a. Why is a plural surprising in XXXI (Rv. VIII):60? What, if any, implication might be drawn from this plural?

3. Translation: Translate LH §147.

LH §148 treats the challenge of marriage to a wife who contracts a serious, apparently incurable illness. Unlike LH §§144–147, the text nowhere states or implies that this wife is necessarily a priestess. Nevertheless, if the husband decides to marry another wife, he is not permitted to abandon the wife who is sick. He may marry the second wife, but his first wife will continue to live in her husband's house, and he will continue to support her as long as she lives.

1. Transliterate and Normalize.

LH §148 XXXI (Rv. VIII):65

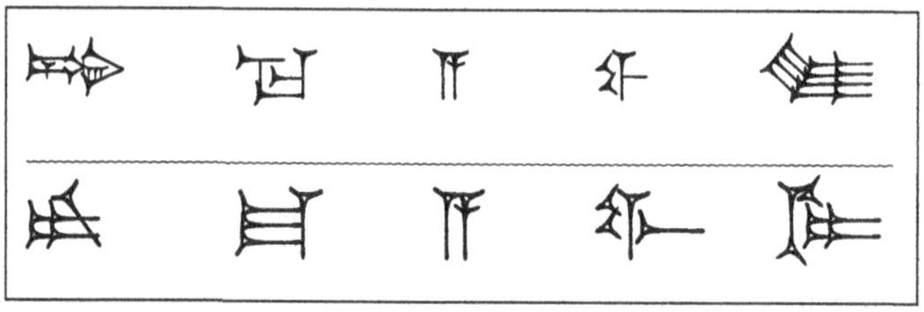

LH §148 XXXI (Rv. VIII):66

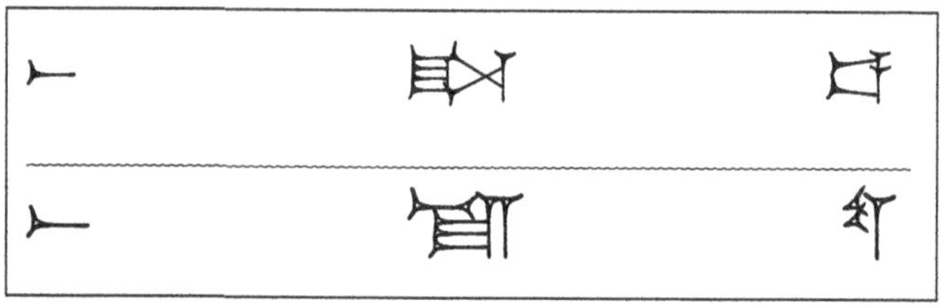

LH §148 XXXI (Rv. VIII):67

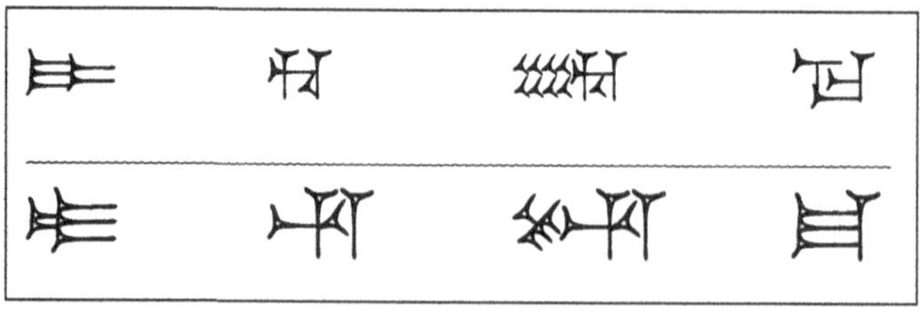

LH §148 XXXI (Rv. VIII):68

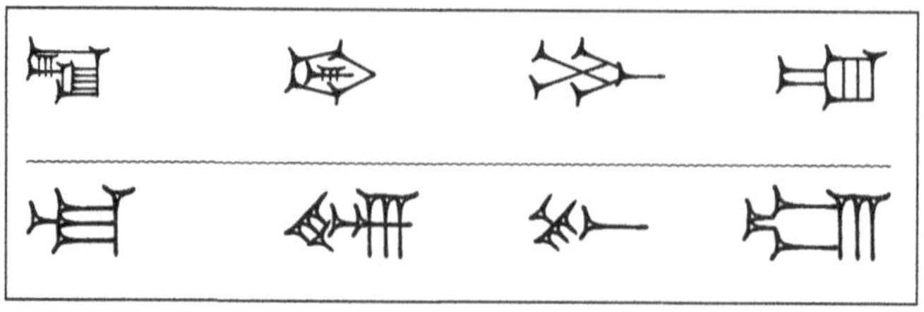

LH §148 XXXI (Rv. VIII):69

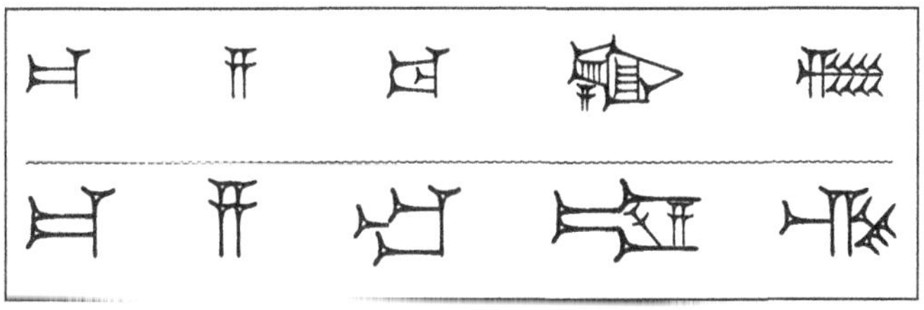

LH §148 XXXI (Rv. VIII):70

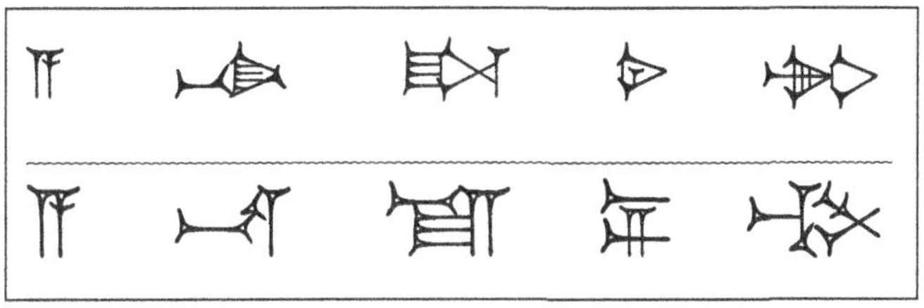

LH §148 XXXI (Rv. VIII):71

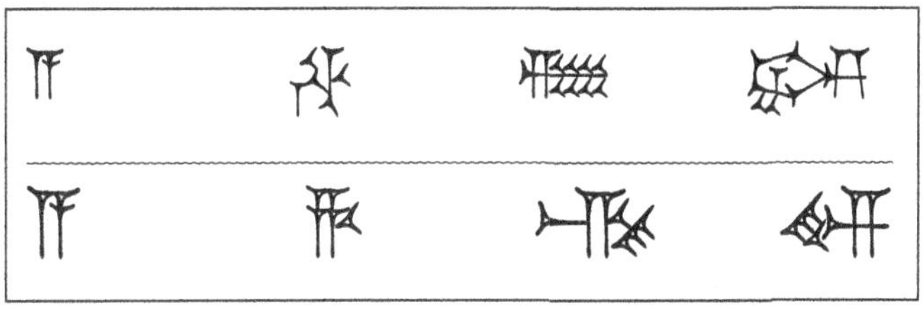

LH §148 XXXI (Rv. VIII):72

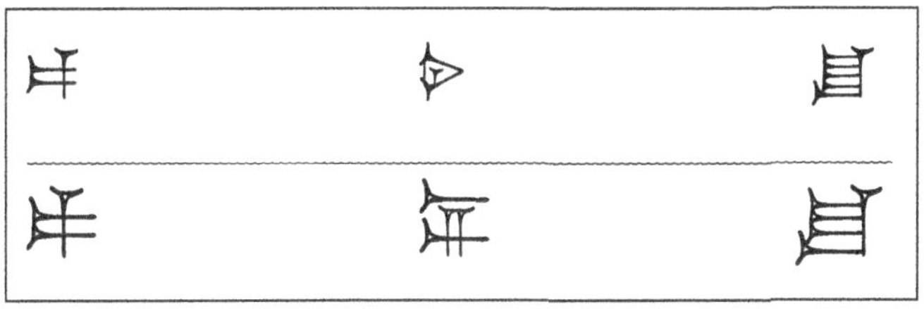

LH §148 XXXI (Rv. VIII):73

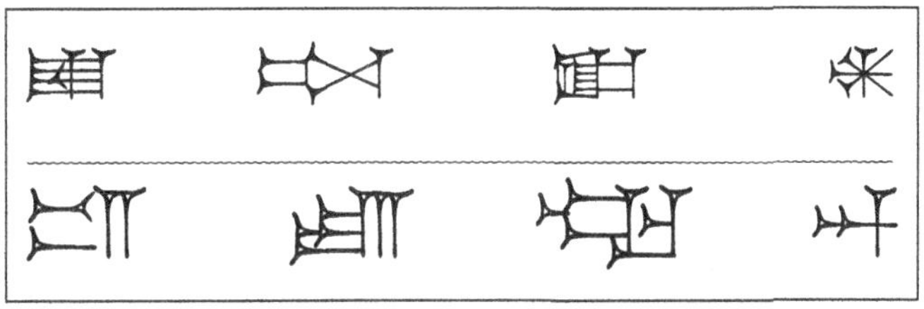

LH §148 XXXI (Rv. VIII):74

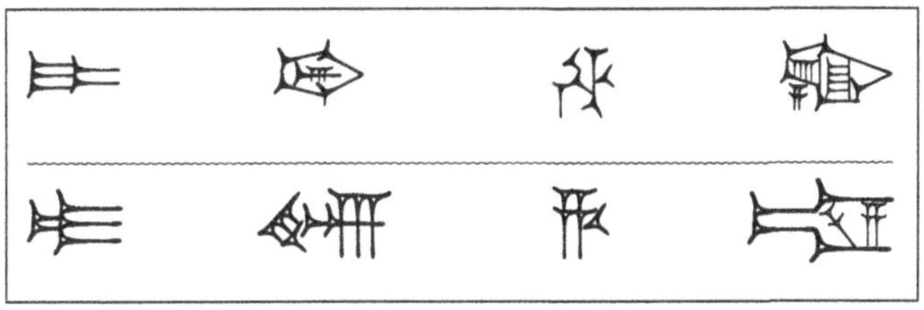

LH §148 XXXI (Rv. VIII):75

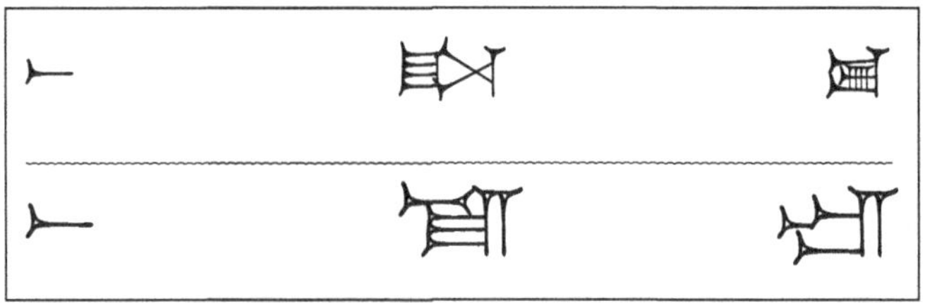

LH §148 XXXI (Rv. VIII):76

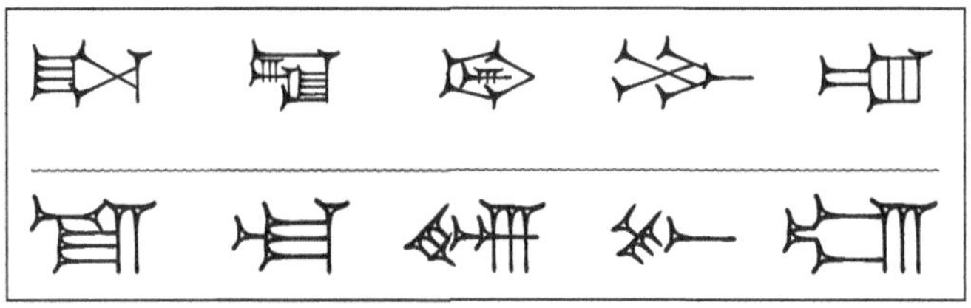

LH §148 XXXI (Rv. VIII):77

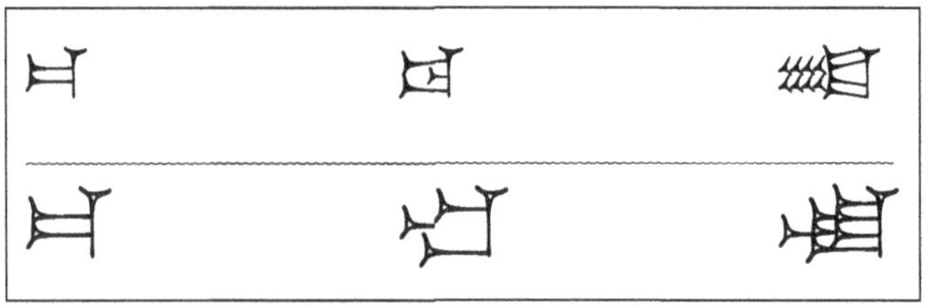

LH §148 XXXI (Rv. VIII):78

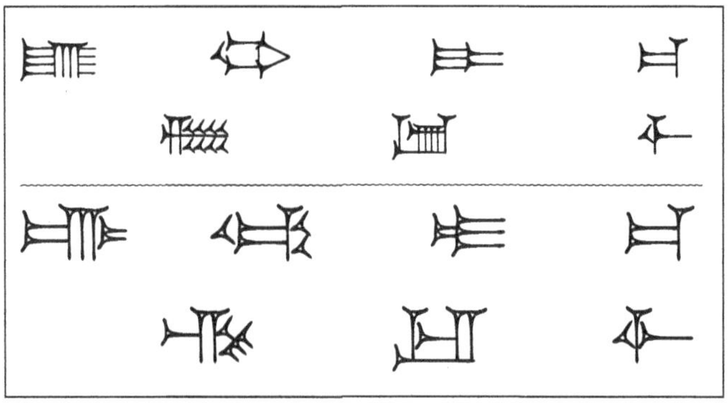

LH §148 XXXI (Rv. VIII):79

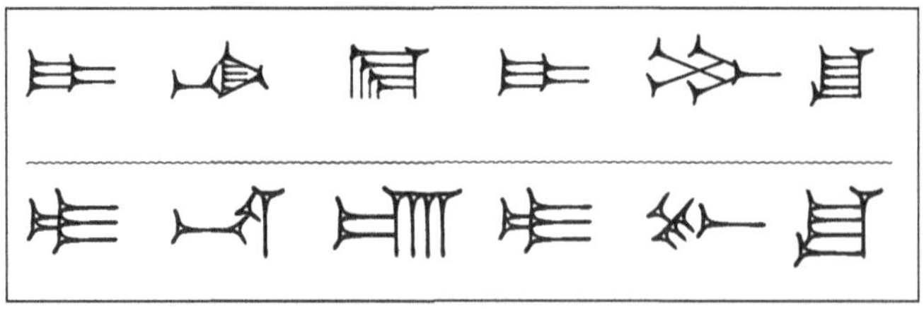

LH §148 XXXI (Rv. VIII):80

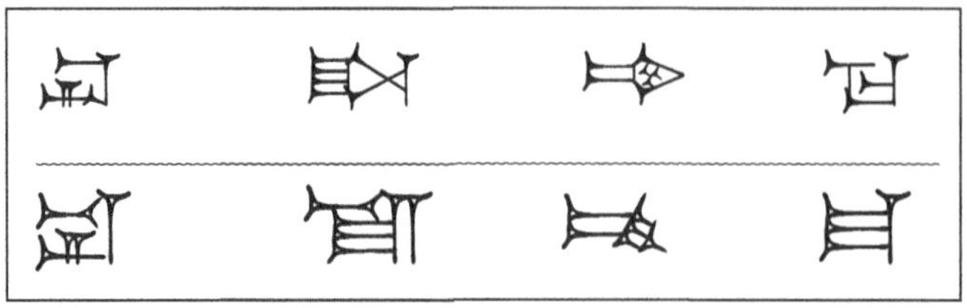

LH §148 XXXI (Rv. VIII):81

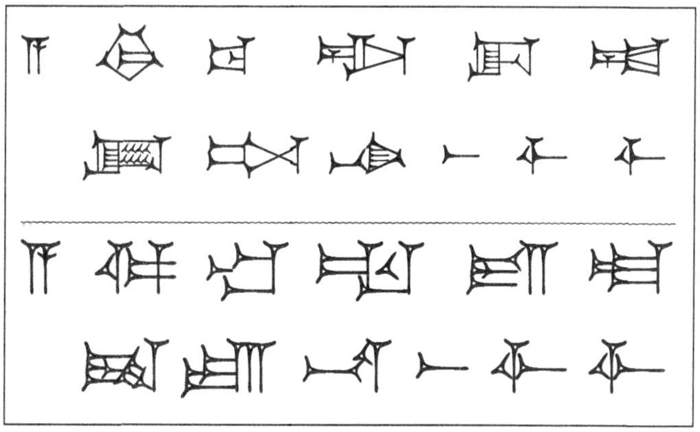

2. Grammatical Analysis: Parse all verb forms. See the notes below for additional help.

   Note: The word in XXXI (Rv. VIII):68 is from *la'bum*, meaning "a fever, serious illness" (cf. *lahab*, לַהַב, "flame"). This word does not need to be learned.

   Note: The final root consonant *b* in the form in XXXI (Rv. VIII):80 has assimilated to *m* immediately before the suffix *-ma*. Recall that the same assimilation sometimes occurs for a final root consonant *n* before the suffix *-ma*, and, far less often, for a final *p* before *-ma*.

3. Translation: Translate LH §148.

LH §149 builds on LH §148 and considers the possibility that his seriously ill wife may not wish to continue to live in her husband's house now that he has a second wife. If so, he must repay her dowry (the standard penalty for an unfaithful husband whose offended wife intends to leave him), and she can leave.

1. Transliterate and Normalize: See the notes below for additional help.

LH §149 XXXII (Rv. IX):1

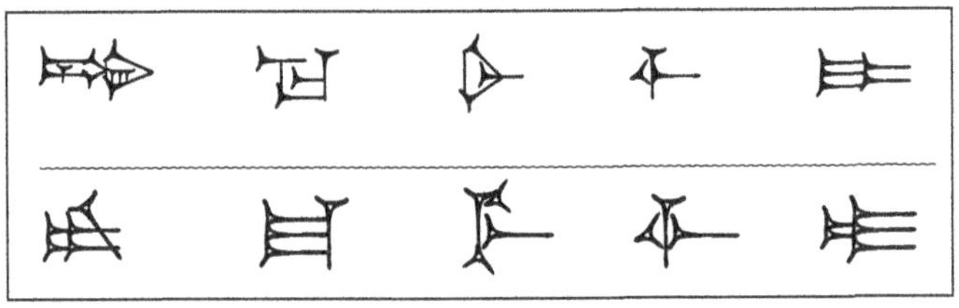

LH §149 XXXII (Rv. IX):2

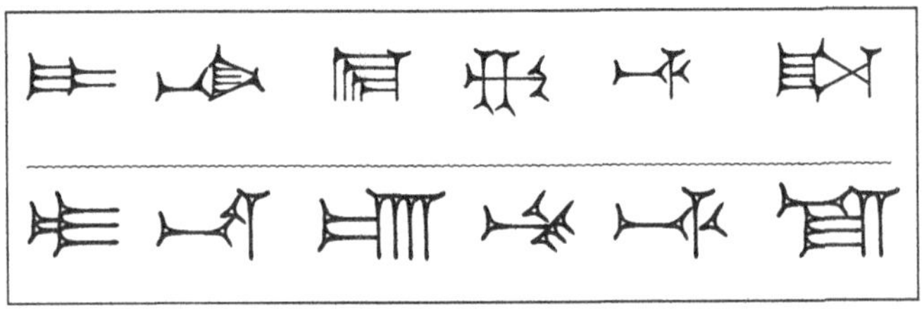

LH §149 XXXII (Rv. IX):3

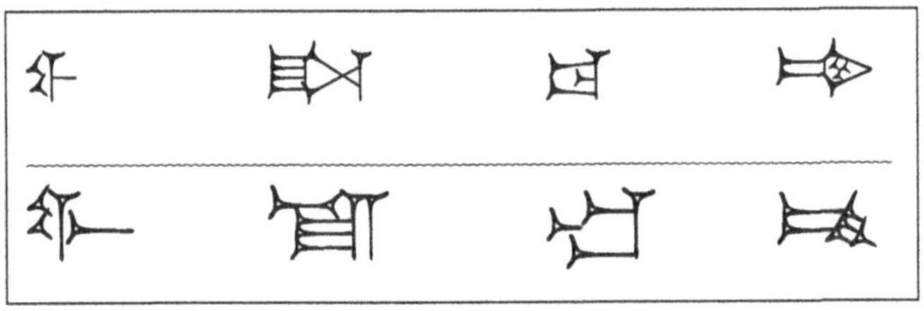

LH §149 XXXII (Rv. IX):4

Note: The sign  in XXXII (Rv. IX):4 is *gàr*. This sign does not need to be learned.

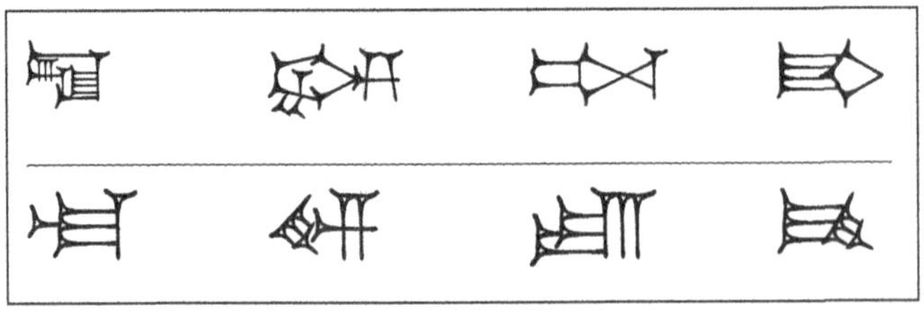

LH §149 XXXII (Rv. IX):5

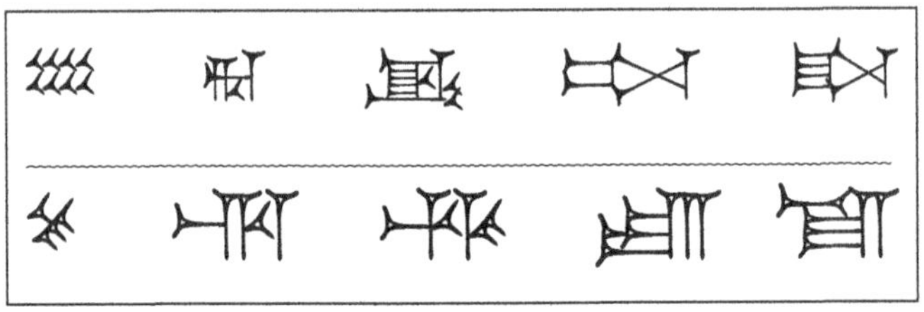

LH §149 XXXII (Rv. IX):6

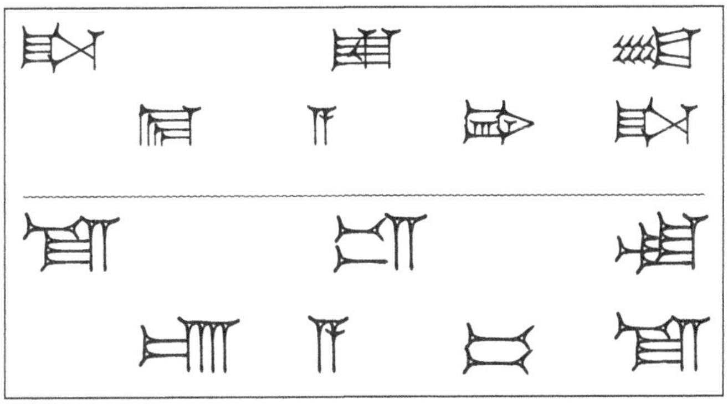

LH §149 XXXII (Rv. IX):7

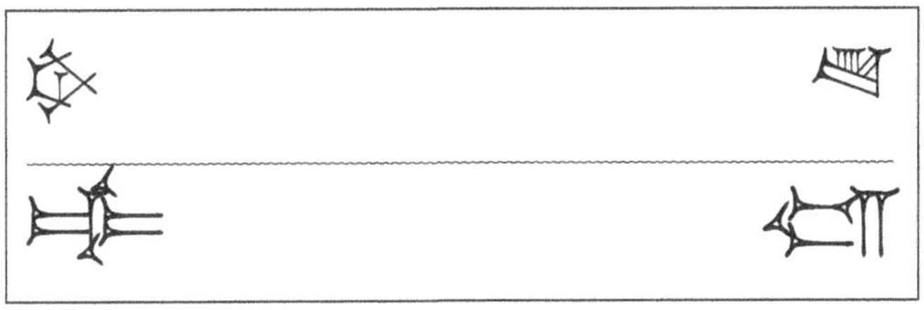

LH §149 XXXII (Rv. IX):8

Note: The sign  in XXXII (Rv. IX):8 is *šim*. This sign does not need to be learned.

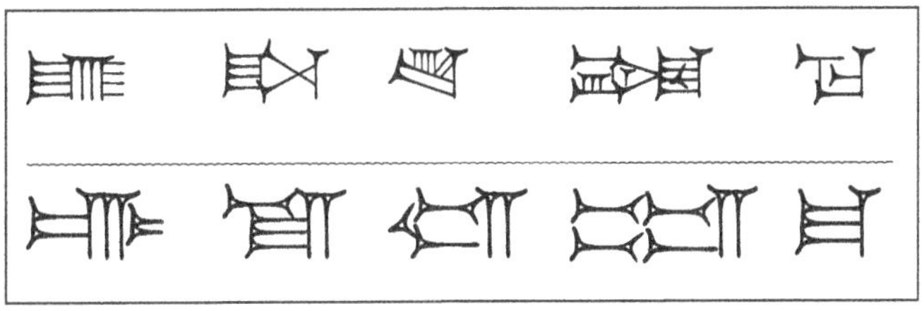

LH §149 XXXII (Rv. IX):9

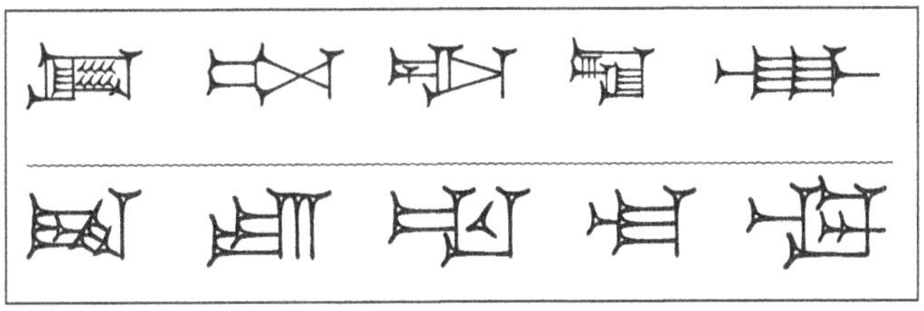

2. Grammatical Analysis: Parse all verb forms.

3. Translation: Translate LH §149.

APPENDIX A

Akkadian Phonology

Akkadian Vowels

Based on the evidence of cognate Semitic languages, it is clear that Proto-Semitic originally had only three vowels that are phonemic, *a*, *i*, and *u*, which could be either short or long. In Akkadian, however, there are four vowels, *a*, *e*, *i*, and *u*. Each of these also may be either short or long. Rules regarding the *e*-vowel are explained below. A chart for the pronunciation of vowels is also included below.

The *e*-vowel

The *e*-vowel is a secondary development, in some cases from an original *a* and in other cases from an original *i*.[1] There are five rules for its development:

1. An original *a* or *ā* vowel shifted to *ê* when in proximity to one of the following gutturals when the guttural quiesced: *ḥ*, ʿ, often *ǵ*, and sometimes *h*. This shift in vowel quality from *a* to *e* is called vowel attenuation (see §3.4.3). If the original guttural was word-initial, the *a* or *ā* vowel still shifted to *e* but without compensatory lengthening (see §3.4.4). For example, the Akkadian word for "lord, owner, master" was originally **baʿlum* (cf. *baʿal*, בַּעַל). The original *a*-vowel, however, shifted to *ê* when the guttural ʿ quiesced, resulting in *bêlum*.

2. The above rule applies also to cases when there is an intervening consonant between the *a*-vowel and the guttural consonant. For example, the Akkadian word for "seed" was originally **zarʿum* (cf. *zeraʿ*, זֶרַע). The original *a*-vowel, although separated from the guttural ʿ by the consonant *r*, nevertheless still shifted to *ê* when the guttural ʿ quiesced: *zêrum*.

3. In Babylonian according to the rule of Babylonian vowel harmony (see §3.4.3), if an *a*-vowel was in a syllable next to a syllable that had an *e*-vowel, the *a*-vowel shifted to an *e*-vowel. Babylonian vowel harmony, however, often does not apply to an *a*-vowel in a suffix, such as the ventive suffix *-am*.

4. Often, but inconsistently, an original *i*-vowel shifted to an *e*-vowel before an *r* or *ḫ* (*r* often acts like a guttural). The same word, however, may appear sometimes with one spelling and sometimes with the other. For example, the word for "dowry" is *širiktum* (< *šarākum* = "to give"), but it is far more frequently spelled *šeriktum*, as it is invariably spelled in LH.

Although Akkadian cuneiform often does not distinguish syllables with *i* over against those with *e*, it is preferable to assume that this *i* to *e* vowel shift has taken place since it is the norm.

1. See Kouwenberg, "The Interchange of *e* and *a* in Old Babylonian."

5. When *ā* + *i* contract because of the loss of an intervocalic ', the result is *ē̃* rather than the expected *ĩ* (see §3.4.5).

Pronunciation of Vowels

There is no indisputable way to determine the precise pronunciation of each vowel in any given period. As a matter of scholarly convention, however, these vowels may be pronounced as follows:

a	as the *a* in *hat*	*i*	as the *i* in *hit*
ā, â, ã	as the *a* in *father*	*ī, î, ĩ*	as the *i* in *machine*
e	as the *e* in *met*	*u*	as the *u* in *put*
ē, ê, ẽ	as the *e* in *they*	*ū, û, ũ*	as the *u* in *truth*

Akkadian Consonants

It is commonly proposed that in Proto-Semitic there were originally 29 (or 30) consonants that were phonemic (that is, each consonantal sound was meaningful and used to distinguish words).

Biblical Hebrew Preservation of Proto-Semitic Consonants

Akkadian is the earliest attested Semitic language. Interestingly, however, it preserves only 20 of the original 29 (or 30) Proto-Semitic consonants in its writing, while biblical Hebrew, which arose more than a millennium later, preserves 22 of the Proto-Semitic consonants in its writing, and in its spoken form Hebrew almost certainly preserved at least 25 of the 29 (or 30) Proto-Semitic consonants.

There is good evidence for the claim that Hebrew had a richer inventory of consonantal phonemes in its spoken language than in its written form because, as is widely known, the Masoretes (sixth-tenth centuries AD) preserved quite accurately the oral tradition of distinguishing the phonemes *ś* and *š* by means of adding a diacritical dot placed over the left or right vertical stroke in the Hebrew character ש. As a result, שׂ was used to represent *ś* and שׁ to represent *š*.

Furthermore, there is reasonable evidence that during the Old Testament period there were also two other consonantal graphemes, which likewise were used to represent two distinct phonemes each. The sign ח, depending on the word, could represent and be pronounced either as *ḥ* or as *ḫ*, while similarly the sign ע could represent and be pronounced as either ʿ or *ǵ*. It is unclear exactly when these alternative pronunciations of ח and ע were lost, but it is likely that they were still observed in the third and second centuries BCE based on evidence in the Septuagint. It appears, however, that they were lost not long thereafter, perhaps under the influence of increasing Hellenism.

Akkadian Preservation of Proto-Semitic Consonants

The following list follows the modern alphabetical order used in lexica for Akkadian. ' in Akkadian is ignored when alphabetizing. It is conventional, however, to list it first based on other Semitic languages such as Hebrew. In the case of Akkadian, as is evident below, its ' can reflect five different Proto-Semitic consonants and at times it may also derive from original *w* ($'_6$) or *y* ($'_7$). It is customary to number each of these seven *'aleph*'s with subscripts in order to indicate its origin.

The International Phonetic Alphabet (IPA) sounds for difficult consonants are indicated in the chart below in brackets. Using these symbols, the student can listen to a linguist pronounce each consonant online.[2]

Proto-Semitic	Akkadian	Hebrew	Aramaic
’ [ʔ]	$’_1$/∅	א	א
h [h]	$’_2$/∅	ה	ה
ḥ [ħ]	$’_3$/∅ or ḫ	ח (ḥ)	ח
‘ [ʕ]	$’_4$/∅	ע (‘)	ע
ǵ [ɣ]	$’_5$/∅ or ḫ	ע (ǵ)	ע
b	b	ב	ב
d	d	ד	ד
g	g	ג	ג
ḫ [x’]	ḫ	ח (ḫ)	ח
y	y/∅ ($’_7$)	י	י
k	k	כ	כ
l	l	ל	ל
m	m	מ	מ
n	n	נ	נ
p	p	פ	פ
q (ḳ) [k’]	q	ק	ק
r	r	ר	ר
s	s	ס	ס
ṣ [ts’]	ṣ	צ	צ
ṣ́ [ɬ’]	ṣ	צ	ע, ק
ṯ [θ’]	ṣ	צ	ט
ś [ɬ]	š [ʃ]	שׂ	ס
s (PS)/š (PNWS)[3]	š	שׁ	שׁ
ṯ [θ]	š	שׁ	ת
t	t	ת	ת
ṭ [t’]	ṭ	ט	ט
w	w/∅ ($’_6$)	ו/י	ו/י
^{d}z [dz]	z	ז	ז
ḏ [ð]	z	ז	ד

2. There are many such sites online including https://en.wikipedia.org/wiki/IPA_pulmonic_consonant_chart_with_audio.
3. PS = Proto-Semitic; PNWS = Proto-North-West Semitic.

In general, the consonants listed in the chart should be pronounced as they are in English, or better, as they are in biblical Hebrew rather than modern Hebrew.[4] Some consonants, however, are less familiar and deserve special comment.

ʾ is a glottal stop where the speaker holds his or her breath for just an instant—similar to the slight break one inserts between the first two words in the phrase "an ice man," in order to distinguish it from "a nice man."

ḥ is a voiceless pharyngeal fricative. Being voiceless means the vocal cords are not used. Instead, the sound that is produced is the sound of a sharp breath being forced through a constricted throat (like a person who is trying to exhale while being strangled).

ḫ is a voiceless velar fricative. Being velar means that the constriction that causes the sound, as an expulsion of air is forced through it, is produced by closing the back of the tongue against the back part of the roof of the mouth (its velar region). This results in a very brief rasping sound, like someone clearing his or her throat.

ʿ is a voiced pharyngeal fricative. Since it is voiced, it is accompanied by a sound produced by the vocal cords. Its sound, however, is shaped in the back of one's throat by the narrowing of the throat, accomplished by moving the tongue backward but not toward the roof of the mouth. The resulting expulsive sound is a grunt similar to the sound one might make when about to lift a very heavy weight.

ǵ is a voiced velar fricative. Since it is voiced, it too should be accompanied by a sound produced by the vocal cords. The shape of the sound, however, is produced by a constriction of the tongue against the back part of the roof of the mouth (the velar region) rather than the throat. This results in a sound that is similar to that which might be made when clearing the back of one's mouth of a small particle of food.

ṣ is an emphatic *s*. Consequently, the *s* should be articulated with a strong expulsion of air. Alternatively, the dot may be understood as indicating a velarized *s*. Velarized means simply that the consonant is pronounced with the tongue shifted slightly back into the mouth or the back of the tongue raised slightly into the velum at the back of the palate. This constricts the passage of air slightly so that the air has to be exhaled more forcibly. These two alternative descriptions apply to a dot placed under any letter, such as *ḥ*, *ṣ*, *ṣ́*, or *ṭ*.

ś is a lateralized voiceless *s* sound, which means it is pronounced like "sh," except that the tongue is pulled back a little so that the air is forced to go around both sides of the tongue.

Θ represents the voiceless *th* sound, like the *th* in the English word "thin" rather than the voiced *th*, as appears in the word "this."

ᵈz refers to a voiced alveolar affricate. Being voiced means that the sound is made by the vocal cords. Alveolar means the point of articulation is produced by the tip of the tongue being placed at or near the ridge of bone behind one's upper teeth. An affricate is a sound that starts with a stop, holding one's breath for an instant, which then instantly turns into a fricative with air passing through the point of articulation to shape the sound. The letter *z* in the English word "zebra" is an example.

ḏ is the voiced *d* sound, like the English *th* in the word "this" rather than the voiceless *th* found in the word "thin."

4. For a thorough treatment of the phonology of biblical Hebrew see Reymond, *Intermediate Biblical Hebrew Grammar.*

A hypothesized thirtieth Proto-Semitic consonant is a glottalic velar (or uvular) fricative, which may be represented by X'.[5] This proposed consonant merged with the *ḫ* in Akkadian and with the ח in Hebrew and Aramaic.

Akkadian Consonants and Cuneiform (§4.2)

There are several categories of Akkadian consonants that are useful to know.

	Voiced	Voiceless	Emphatic/Glottalic
Dentals	d	t	ṭ
Velars	g	k	q (= ḳ)
Sibilants	z	s	ṣ
Labials	b	p	

In the Old Babylonian cuneiform representation for these consonants, the same sign is often used to represent syllables that begin with a voiced, voiceless, or emphatic variant of the same type of consonant, and the same sign is invariably used with syllables that end with a voiced, voiceless, or emphatic variant of the same type of consonant. For example, although *ba* (𒁀) and *pa* (𒉺) are consistently distinguished, *bu* (𒁍) and *pu* (𒁍) are not. On the other hand, *ad* (𒀜), *at* (𒀜), and *aṭ* (𒀜) all employ the same sign.

5. See, e.g., Huehnergard, "Proto-Semitic," 49–79.

APPENDIX B

Major Paradigms

Nouns (§2.6)

		Masculine	Feminine
Singular	Nominative	*šarrum*	*šarratum*
	Genitive	*šarrim*	*šarratim*
	Accusative	*šarram*	*šarratam*
Dual	Nominative	*šarrān*	*šarratān*
	Genitive-Accusative	*šarrīn*	*šarratīn*
Plural	Nominative	*šarrū*	*šarrātum*
	Genitive-Accusative	*šarrī*	*šarrātim*

Adjectives (§5.2)

A participle is a verbal adjective. As such it uses the same set of suffixes as any other adjective. Likewise, the same set of suffixes is used for participles and all adjectives in any stem (G, D, Š, or N).

G-Stem Participle

		Masculine	Feminine
Singular	Nominative	*pārisum*	*pāristum*
	Genitive	*pārisim*	*pāristim*
	Accusative	*pārisam*	*pāristam*
Plural	Nominative	*pārisūtum*	*pārisātum*
	Genitive-Accusative	*pārisūtim*	*pārisātim*

Pronouns

Independent Personal Pronoun (§10.3)

	Nominative		Genitive-Accusative	Dative
1cs	*anāku*	I	*yâti*	*yâšim*
2ms	*atta*	you	*kâta*	*kâšim*
2fs	*atti*	you	*kâti*	*kâšim*
3ms	*šū*	he, it	*šu'āti, šu'ātu*	*šu'āšim*
3fs	*šī*	she, it	*šu'āti*	*šu'āšim*
1cp	*nīnu*	we	*ni'āti*	*ni'āšim*
2mp	*attunu*	you	*kunūti*	*kunūšim*
2fp	*attina*	you	*kināti*	*kināšim*
3mp	*šunu*	they	*šunūti*	*šunūšim*
3fp	*šina*	they	*šināti*	*šināšim*

Pronominal Suffixes (§4.3; §8.2.6)

	Genitive (with nouns and prepositions)	Dative (with verbs)	Accusative (with verbs)
1cs	*-ī, -ya, 'a*	*-am, -m, -nim*	*-ni*
2ms	*-ka*	*-kum*	*-ka*
2fs	*-ki*	*-kim*	*-ki*
3ms	*-šu*	*-šum*	*-šu*
3fs	*-ša*	*-šim*	*-ši*
1cp	*-ni*	*-ni'āšim*	*-ni'āti*
2mp	*-kunu*	*-kunūšim*	*-kunūti*
2fp	*-kina*	*-kināšim*	*-kināti*
3mp	*-šunu*	*-šunūšim*	*-šunūti*
3fp	*-šina*	*-šināšim*	*-šināti*

Verbs

Strong Verb Paradigm (§10.1.3)

Stem	Durative	Perfect	Preterite	Participle	Verbal Adjective	Stative	Infinitive
G	*iparras*	*iptaras*	*iprus*	*pārisum*	*parsum*	*paris*	*parāsum*
Gt	*iptarras*	*iptatras*	*iptaras*	*muptarsum*	*pitrusum*	*pitrus*	*pitrusum*
Gtn	*iptanarras*	*iptatarras*	*iptarras*	*muptarrisum*	*pitarrusum*	*pitarrus*	*pitarrusum*
D	*uparras*	*uptarris*	*uparris*	*muparrisum*	*purrusum*	*purrus*	*purrusum*
Dt	*uptarras*	*uptatarris*	*uptarris*	*muptarrisum*	*putarrusum*	*putarrus*	*putarrusum*
Dtn	*uptanarras*	*uptatarris*	*uptarris*	*muptarrisum*	*putarrusum*	*putarrus*	*putarrusum*
Š	*ušapras*	*uštapris*	*ušapris*	*mušaprisum*	*šuprusum*	*šuprus*	*šuprusum*
Št	*uštapras/ uštaparras*	*uštatapris*	*uštapris*	*muštaprisum*	*šutaprusum*	*šutaprus*	*šutaprusum*
Štn	*uštanapras*	*uštatapris*	*uštapris*	*muštaprisum*	*šutaprusum*	*šutaprus*	*šutaprusum*
N	*ipparras*	*ittapras*	*ipparis*	*mupparsum*	*naprusum*	*naprus*	*naprusum*
Nt	unattested or exceedingly rare						
Ntn	*ittanapras*	*ittatapras*	*ittapras*	*muttaprisum*	*itaprusum*	*itaprus*	*itaprusum*

Strong Verb Prefix and Suffix Tenses (§6.3)

		Durative	Perfect	Preterite	Stative
Singular	3m	*iparras*	*iptaras*	*iprus*	*paris*
	3f	*iparras*	*iptaras*	*iprus*	*parsat*
	2m	*taparras*	*taptaras*	*taprus*	*parsāta*
	2f	*taparrasī*	*taptarsī*	*taprusī*	*parsāti*
	1c	*aparras*	*aptaras*	*aprus*	*parsāku*
Plural	3m	*iparrasū*	*iptarsū*	*iprusū*	*parsū*
	3f	*iparrasā*	*iptarsā*	*iprusā*	*parsā*
	2m	*taparrasā*	*taptarsā*	*taprusā*	*parsātunu*
	2f	*taparrasā*	*taptarsā*	*taprusā*	*parsātina*
	1c	*niparras*	*niptaras*	*niprus*	*parsānu*

Four Main Vowel Classes (*a/u*, *a*, *i*, *u*) of Verbs (§4.4)

Stem	Class	Durative 3cs	Perfect 3cs	Preterite 3cs
G	*a,u*	*iparras*	*iptaras*	*iprus*
	a	*iṣabbat*	*iṣṣabat*	*iṣbat*
	i	*išallim*	*ištalim*	*išlim*
	u	*iballuṭ*	*ibtaluṭ*	*ibluṭ*
D		*uparras*	*uptarris*	*uparris*
Š		*ušapras*	*uštapris*	*ušapris*
N	*a,u*	*ipparras*	*ittapras*	*ipparis*
	a	*iṣṣabbat*	*ittaṣbat*	*iṣṣabit*
	i	*iššallim*	*ittašlim*	*iššalim*
	u	*ibballuṭ*	*ittabluṭ*	*ibbaliṭ*

I-*'aleph* Verbs (§14.1)

Stem	Class	Durative 3cs	Perfect 3cs	Preterite 3cs	Participle ms	Verbal Adjective ms	Stative 3ms	Infinitive ms
G	*a,u*	*iḫḫaz*	*îtaḫaz*	*îḫuz*	*āḫizum*	*aḫizum*	*aḫiz*	*aḫāzum*
	e,u	*ippeš/ ippuš*	*îtepeš/ îtepuš*	*îpuš*	*ēpišum*	*epišum*	*epiš*	*epēšum*
	a,i	*illak*	*ittalak*	*illik*	*ālikum*	*alikum*	*alik*	*alākum*
D		*uḫḫaz*	*ûtaḫḫiz*	*uḫḫiz*	*muḫḫizum*	*uḫḫuzum*	*uḫḫuz*	*uḫḫuzum*
Š		*ušaḫḫaz*	*uštâḫiz*	*ušâḫiz*	*mušâḫizum*	*šûḫuzum*	*šûḫuz*	*šûḫuzum*
N	*a,u*	*innaḫḫaz*	*ittanḫaz*	*innaḫiz*	*munnaḫzum*	*nanḫuzum*	*nanḫuz*	*nanḫuzum*
	e,u	*inneppeš*	*ittenpeš*	*innepiš*	*munnepšum*	*nenpušum*	*nenpuš*	*nenpušum*

I-*w* Verbs (§12.1)

Stem	Class	Durative 3cs	Perfect 3cs	Preterite 3cs	Participle ms	Verbal Adjective ms	Stative 3ms	Infinitive ms
G	Active	*uššab*	*ittašab*	*ušib (ûšib)*	*wāšibum*	*(w)ašbum*	*(w)ašib*	*(w)ašābum*
	Stative	*ittir*	*îtatir/îtetir*	*îtir*		*(w)atirum*	*(w)atar*	*(w)atārum*
D		*uwatter*	*ûtatter*	*uwaššir*	*muwašširum*	*(w)uššurum*	*(w)uššur*	*(w)ulludum*
Š		*ušabbal*	*uštâbil*	*ušâbil*	*mušâbilum*	*šûbulum*	*šûbul*	*šūbulum*
	e-type	*ušerred*	*uštêrid*	*ušêrid*	*mušêridum*	*šûrudum*	*šûrud*	*šûrudum*
N		*iwwallad*		*iwwalid*	*muwwaldum*			

II-Weak Verbs (§11.3)

Stem	Class	Durative 3cs/3mp	Perfect 3cs/3mp	Preterite 3cs/3mp	Infinitive ms
G	*u*	*ikān/ikunnū*	*iktûn/iktûnū*	*ikûn/ikûnū*	*kānum*
	i	*iqîʾaš/iqiššū*	*iqtîš/iqtîšū*	*iqîš/iqîšū*	*qiʾāšum*
	a	*irām/irammū*	*irtâm/irtâmū*	*irâm/irâmū*	*rāmum*
	e	*imēš/imeššū*	*imtêš/imtêšū*	*imêš/imêšū*	*mēšum*
D		*ukân/ukannū*	*uktîn/uktinnū*	*ukîn/ukinnū*	*kunnum*
Š		*ušmât/ušmattū*	*uštamît/uštamittū*	*ušmît/ušmittū*	*šumuttum*
N	*u*	*iddāk/iddukkū*	unattested	unattested	unattested
	i	*iqqîʾaš/iqqiššū*	unattested	*iqqîš* (rare)	unattested
	a	*irrām/irrammū*	unattested	*irrâm* (rare)	unattested
	e	*immēš/immeššū*	unattested	*immêš* (rare)	unattested

III-Weak Verbs[1] (§16.1)

Stem	Class	Durative 3cs	Perfect 3cs	Preterite 3cs/3mp	Participle ms	Verbal Adjective ms	Stative 3ms	Infinitive ms
G	*i*	*ibannî*	*ibtanî*	*ibnî/ibnû*	*bānûm*	*banûm*	*banî*	*banûm*
	u	*imannû*	*imtanû*	*imnû/imnû*	*mānûm*	*manûm*	*manî/û*	*manûm*
	a	*imallâ*	*imtalâ*	*imlâ/imlû*	*mālûm*	*malûm*	*malî*	*malûm*
	e	*ileqqê*	*ilteqê*	*ilqê/ilqû*	*lēqûm*	*leqûm*	*leqî*	*leqûm*
D		*ubannâ*	*ubtannî*	*ubannî*	*mubannûm*	*bunnûm*	*bunnû*	*bunnûm*
Š		*ušabnâ*	*uštabnî*	*ušabnî*	*mušabnûm*	*šubnûm*	*šubnû*	*šubnûm*
N	*i*	*ibbannî*	*ittabnî*	*ibbanî*	*mubbanûm*	*nabnûm*	*nabnû*	*nabnûm*
	u	*immannû*	*ittamnû*	*immanî*	*mummanûm*	*namnûm*	*namnû*	*namnûm*
	a	*immallâ*	*ittamlâ*	*immalî*	*mummalûm*	*namlûm*	*namlû*	*namlûm*
	e	*illeqqê*	*ittelqê*	*illeqî*	*mulleqûm*	*nelqûm*	*nelqû*	*nelqûm*

1. Although the particular verbs used in this chart are attested in some of the forms as indicated, they are not attested in all of them. Other III-weak verbs are, however.

APPENDIX C

List of Cuneiform Signs

The following is a complete list of cuneiform signs that are needed for the translations required in this textbook. The columns below are:

NA = Neo-Assyrian script
Values = values most common in LH
MZL = sign numbers in Borger's *Mesopotamisches Zeichenlexikon*
C = chapter in this textbook where presented (if in brackets then not required to be learned)
LH§ = the first law in which the sign appears in the translations in this textbook
OB = the sign in Old Babylonian Monumental (Lapidary) script

NA	Values	MZL	C	LH§	OB
	aš	1	8	2	
	ḫal	3	13	9	
	DINGIR, *ilum*, "god" (cf. *'ēl*, אֵל); ^{d}; an	10	1	2	
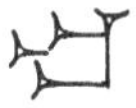	ba	14	8	2	
	sú, ṣú, zu	15	7	2	
	su	16	16	130	
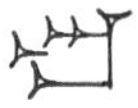	ÌR, *wardum*, "slave" (cf. *yārad*, יָרַד, "to descend")	18	12	7	
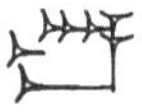	ITI, *warḫum*, "month"	20	14	13	
	ŠAḪA, *šaḫûm*, "pig"	22	[13]	8	
	ka	24	11	5	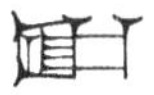
	URU, *âlum*, "city"	71	17	135	
	le, li	85	4	1	

(continued)

NA	Values	MZL	C	LH§	OB
	tu	86	13	9	
	la	89	5	1	
	maḫ	91	[13, 14]	9	
	mu	98	5	1	
	qa	99	20		
	na	110	6	2	
	ru	111	10	5	
	nu	112	10	3	
	be, bat	113	13	9	
	ti	118	5	1	
	MAŠ.EN.KA(K), *muškēnum*, "royal servant, civil servant"	120+164 +379	13	8	
	ag, ak, aq	127	5	1	
	ḫu	132	12	6	
	nam	134	10	5	
	eg, ek, eq, ig, ik, iq	136	7	2	
	sé, sí, ṣé, ṣí, ze, zi	140	9	5	
	ge, gi	141	15	16	
	re, ri	142	8	2	
	kab	148	[16]	130	
	en, EN	164	18	137	
	tim	167	9	3	
	sa	172	19	7	

NA	Values	MZL	C	LH§	OB
	se, si	181	15	16	
	MÁ, *eleppum*, "boat"	201	[13]	8	
	tab, tap	209	8	2	
	šum	221	2	1	
	KÁ.GAL, *abullum*, "city gate"	222+553	[15]	15	
	ab, ap	223	11	5	
	um	238	10	3	
	ta	248	7	2	
	i	252	6	2	
	DUMU, *mârum*, "son" (cf. Hebrew *mərîʾ*, מְרִיא, "fatling"; Aramaic *mārēʾ*, מָרֵא, "lord")	255	9	7	
	ad, at, aṭ	258	9	3	
	ṣe, ṣi, zé, zí	259	9	14	
	i'a, i'e, i'i, i'u, ya, ye, yi, yu	260	13	9	
	in	261	5	1	
	ug, uk, uq	296	5	1	
	as, aṣ, az	297	15	137	
	am	309	7	2	
	bíl	312	[16]	130	
	ne	313	4	1	
	qu, qum	339	[13] 20	9	
	úr	341	[12, 18]		

(continued)

NA	Values	MZL	C	LH§	OB
	il	348	6	2	
	du, ṭù, RÁ	350	1 [16]	2	
	ANŠE, *imērum*, "donkey" (cf. *ḥămôr*, חֲמוֹר)	353	[12]	7	
	tum	354	[18,19]	139	
	iš	357	6	2	
	bi, bé, pé, pí	358	2	1	
	šim	362	[20]	149	
	lí, ni	380	11	5	
	ús, uš	381	10	5	
	er, ir	437	3	1	
	pa	464	15	18	
	GIŠ, ⁱˢ < *iṣum*; determinative for wood (cf. *ʿēṣ*, עֵץ); is, iṣ, iz	469	11	5	
	GUD, *alpum*, "ox" (cf. *ʾelep*, אֶלֶף)	472	[12]	7	
	al	474	7	2	
	ú	490	2	1	
	ga, qá	491	12	6	
	É, *bîtum*, "house, household" (cf. *bayit*, בַּיִת)	495	1	2	
	É.GAL, *ekallum*, "palace" (lit. "great house") (cf. *hêkāl*, הֵיכָל)	495+553	7	6	
	e	498	4	1	
	un	500	16	128	
	ub, up	504	3	1	

NA	Values	MZL	C	LH§	OB
	gi_4	507	18	137	
	ra	511	9	3	
	šar	541	12	7	
	$KIRI_6$, *kirûm*, "orchard"	541	[12]	137	
	gàr	543	[17]	133	
	ás, áš	548	15	18	
	ma	552	1	1	
	MA.NA, *manûm*, "mina" (≈ 1/2 kg.) (cf. *māneh*, מָנֶה)	552+110	[18]	139, 140	
	gal, GAL	553	[16]	6	
	qer	558	[14]	13	
	ed, et, eṭ, id, it, iṭ (values with e or ṭ are less common)	560	4	1	
	da, ṭa (less often)	561	5	1	
	ša	566	6	2	
	šu	567	3	1	
	sa_6	571	[19]	142	
	ŠE, *še'um*, "barley" (perhaps cf. *šay*, שַׁי, "tribute," cf. KB, *DCH*, ad loc.); še	579	1	4	
	bu, pu	580	6	2	
	us, uṣ, uz	583	16	128	
	ter	587	[18]	138	
	te	589	8	2	
	kar	590	[15, 17]	18	

(continued)

NA	Values	MZL	C	LHS§	OB
	ud, ut, uṭ, tam, BABBAR	596	3	1	
	wa, wi (we, wu, pe, pi)	598	2	1	
	úḫ	611	[11]	5	
	ḫe, ḫi	631	18	138	
	ḪÁ (a determinative for a plurality for objects)	631+839	[20]	146	
	a', 'a, e', 'e, i', 'i, u', 'u (discussed in §20.2.1)	635	19		
	aḫ, eḫ, iḫ, uḫ, á', é', í', ú'	636	14	14	
	kam; KAM (postpositive determinative for numbers)	640	11	5	
	em, im	641	4	5	
	ḫar	644	[13, 16]	9	
	10, u	661	10	5	
	mi	681	9	7	
	nim	690	9	3	
	lam	693	3	1	
	ṣur	695	[17]	133	
	ul	698	11	5	
	eš, 30 (earlier seen as a part of the sign for meš, , a sign marking plurals, esp. of persons)	711	19	8	
	lim, ši	724	6	2	
	ar	726	9	3	
	ù	731	10	4	
	de, di, ṭe, ṭi (values with e or ṭ are less common)	736	4	1	

NA	Values	MZL	C	LH§	OB
	ke, ki, qé, qí	737	6	2	
	GUŠKIN, *ḫurāṣum*, "gold"; GUŠKIN is represented by KÙ.GI (logograms for "precious metal" and "yellow")	745+14	[12]	7	
	KÙ.BABBAR, *kaspum*, "silver"; KÙ means "pure, holy," referring to a precious metal, and BABBAR, means "white"; BABBAR is the same sign as UD, which means "day" (cf. *kesep*, כֶּסֶף)	745+596	3	4	
	60 (if located in the 60's column)	748	14	139	
	1 (if located in the 1's column)	748	1	139	
	me	753	14	12	
	MEŠ (postpositive determinative for plural, mostly of persons)	754	17	135	
	eb, ep, ib, ip	807	8	2	
	ku, qú	808	10	5	
	UDU, *immerum*, "sheep" (cf. *'immēr*, אִמֵּר); lu	812	12	7	
	qe, qi	815	20		
	2	825	2	5	
	ŠUŠANA, *šaluš(tum)*, "1/3"; or less often *šuššān*, lit. "2/6"	826	[18]	140	
	ur	828	19	7	
	3	834	3		
	GÍN, *šiqlum*, "shekel"; ṭu	836	[15] 19	17	
	a	839	1	1	
	A.RÁ, *adî* (< *'*adiy*; cf. *'ad*, עַד)	839+350	11	5	
	A.ŠÀ	839+599	[18]	137	

(continued)

NA	Values	MZL	C	LH§	OB
	ÍD (this sign begins with the A sign, which in Sumerian is a logogram for *nârum*, "river")	839+756	6	2	
	4, sà, ṣa, za	851	4	3	
	ḫa	856	17	135	
	NÍG.GA, *makkūrum*, "property" (cf. *mākar*, מָכַר, "to sell")	859+491	[12]	6	
	5	861	5	12	
	6	862	6	13	
	7	863	7		
	8	864			
	9	868			
	MÍ (a determinative for a female); MUNUS, *sinništum*, "woman"	883	16	137	
	LUKUR *nadîtum* (<**nadī'tum*) "devotee"; Lambert: "high priestess"	883+753	18	137	
	NIN.DINGIR, *ugbabtum*, "priestess"	887+10	[16]	127	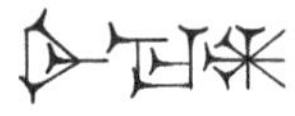
	ṣu	884	19		
	dam	889	[17]	135	
	GÉME, *amtum*, "female slave" (cf. *'āmâ*, אָמָה)	890	12	7	
	gu	891	11	5	
	GU.ZA, *kussûm*, "seat, throne"	891+851	[11]	5	
	el	899	13	9	
	lum	900	2	1	

Alphabetical List of *v*, *cv*, and *vc* Cuneiform Signs

a	𒀀	e	𒂊	i	𒄿	u	𒌑
						ú	𒌋
						ù	𒌗
				i'a,i'e,i'i,i'u,			
				ya,ye,yi,yu	𒅀		
a','a	𒀪	e','e	𒀪	i','i	𒀪	u','u	𒀪
ba	𒁀	be,bat	𒁁	bi,pí	𒁉	bu,pu	𒁍
		bé,pé	𒁽				
ab,ap	𒀊	eb,ep	𒅁	ib,ip	𒅁	ub,up	𒌒
da,ṭa	𒁕	de,ṭe	𒁲	di,ṭi	𒁲	du,ṭù,RÁ	𒁺
ad,at,aṭ	𒀜	ed,et,eṭ,Á	𒀉	id,it,iṭ,Á	𒀉	ud,ut,uṭ,tam	𒌓
ga,qá	𒂵	ge	𒄀	gi	𒄀	gu	𒄖
				gi₄	𒄄		
ag,ak,aq	𒀝	eg,ek,eq	𒂅	ig,ik,iq	𒅅	ug,uk,uq	𒊌
ḫa	𒄩	ḫe	𒄭	ḫi	𒄭	ḫu	𒄷
aḫ, á'	𒄴	eḫ	𒄴	iḫ	𒄴	uḫ	𒄴
ka	𒅗	ke,qé	𒆠	ki,qí	𒆠	ku,qú	𒆪
ak,ag,aq	𒀝	ek,eg,eq	𒂅	ik,ig,iq	𒅅	uk,ug,uq	𒊌
la	𒆷	le	𒇷	li	𒇷	lu	𒇻
				lí,ni	𒉌		

(continued)

al		el		il		ul	
ma		me		mi		mu	
am		em		im		um	
na		ne		ni,lí		nu	
an,DINGIR		en		in		un	
pa		pe,wa/e/i/u		pi,wa/e/i/u		pu,bu	
		pé,bé		pí,bi			
ap,ab		ep,eb		ip,ib		up,ub	
qa		qe		qi		qu,qum	
qá,ga		qé, ke		qí,ki		qú,ku	
aq,ag,ak		eq,eg,ek		iq,ig,ik		uq,ug,uk	
ra		re		ri		ru	
RÁ,du,ṭù							
ar		er		ir		ur	
						úr	
sa		se		si		su	
sà,ṣa,za		sé,ṣé,ze		sí,ṣí,zi		sú,ṣú,zu	
sa_6							
as,aṣ,az		es,eṣ,ez,[GIŠ]		is,iṣ,iz,[GIŠ]		us,uṣ,uz	
ás,áš						ús,uš	
ṣa,sà,za		ṣe,zé		ṣi,zí		ṣu	
		ṣé,sé,ze		ṣí,sí,zi		ṣú,sú,zu	
aṣ,as,az		eṣ,es,ez,[GIŠ]		iṣ,is,iz,[GIŠ]		uṣ,us,uz	
ša		še		ši,lim		šu	
aš		eš		iš		uš,ús	
áš,ás							

ta		te		ti		tu	
at,ad,aṭ		et,ed,eṭ		it,id,iṭ		ut,ud,uṭ,tam	
ṭa,da		ṭe,de		ṭi,di		ṭu	
						ṭù,du,RÁ	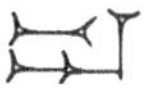
aṭ,at,ad		eṭ,ed,et		iṭ,id,it		uṭ,ud,ut,tam	
wa		we,pe		wi,pi		wu	
ya,i'a		ye,i'e		yi,i'i		yu,i'u	
za,sà,ṣa		ze,sé,ṣé		zi,sí,ṣí		zu,sú,ṣú	
		zé,ṣe		zí,ṣi			
az,as,aṣ		ez,es,eṣ,[GIŠ]		iz,is,iṣ,[GIŠ]		uz,us,uṣ	

APPENDIX E

Akkadian Glossary

Suffixes excluding pronominal suffixes are listed first, followed by all other words. Numbers in brackets following each entry indicate the chapter in this grammar where the word may be found.

Suffixes (Excluding Pronominal Suffixes)

-am = marks a ventive [7]
-ān = a stylistic suffix added to nouns or adjectives that does not change their meaning [13]
-iš = terminative adverbial suffix added to nouns with the meaning "to" or "toward," or with infinitives, "in order to"; when added to adjectives, it turns them into adverbs [11]
-ma = an enclitic particle when attached to a verb, "and (then), but, so"; when attached to a noun, it topicalizes the noun [3]
-mi = a suffix sometimes used to mark direct discourse that can be placed on any word within the discourse [13]
-šu = a suffix on some number x; "x-fold" [11]
-u = a subordinative suffix used on a final verb to mark a subordinate clause other than a protasis (a *šumma*, "if," clause); subordinative *-u* may be used on any verbal form ending in a consonant—not including a ventive *-am* or a 3fs stative suffix *-at*—or a vowel, but only if it is the root vowel of a III-weak verb. [6]
-u = an archaic suffix found on some nouns that marks the construct [18]
-ūm = locative-adverbial suffix added to a noun stripped of its case ending with the meaning "at" or "in" [11]
-ūt = a sufformative, feminine singular ending; when placed on a noun, it turns it into an abstract noun [14]

Words

abārum = D: to accuse (pin on), bind [2]
abātum (a,u) = to destroy; (cf. homologous forms of *'ābad*, אָבַד, which also means "to be lost, be a fugitive," as well as "to perish, to destroy"); *Note:* Many Assyriologists do not distinguish *abātum* from *nabātum*. [17]
abbuttum = a special haircut that marks slaves [20]
abullum = city gate [15]
abum = father (cf. *'āb*, אָב, "father") [3]
adânum (or *adannum*) = time limit [14]
adî = up to, until, so long as; *with numerals*: exactly, -times, -fold (< **'adiy*; cf. *'ad*, עַד) [10]
aḫāzum (a,u) = to take, take in marriage (used only of the man), take sexually (cf. *'āḥaz*, אָחַז, "to grasp, take") [16]

akālum (*a,u*) = to eat (cf. *'ākal*, אָכַל) [17]
alākum (*a,i*) = to go (cf. *hālak*, הָלַךְ) [6]
alpum = ox (cf. *'elep*, אֶלֶף) [12]
âlum = city (cf. *'ōhel*, אֹהֶל, "tent") [17]
amārum (*a,u*) = to see, examine (cf. *'āmar*, אָמַר, "to say") [13]
amtum = female slave (cf. *'āmâ*, אָמָה) [12]
ana = to, toward, into, for (the purpose of), at, in accordance with; *time*: for; *with verb*: in order to [4]
anāku = I (1cs) [10]
aplum = heir, son (< *apālum* = to declare an heir) [18]
arnum = penalty, guilt [8]
atta = you (2ms) [10]
atti = you (2fs) [10]
attina = you (2fp) [10]
attunu = you (2mp) [10]
aššatum (< *'-n-š*) = wife (cf. *'iššâ*, אִשָּׁה) [16]
aššum = because of, concerning; *with infinitive*: in order that (< **an[a] šum*, for the name of) [17]
awâtum = word (a feminine noun from the root *awûm*) [8]
awīlum = man, person, citizen (a free man) (cf. *'ĕwîl*, אֱוִיל, "citizen") [2]

bâbtum (< *bâbum*, gate) = city quarter, community (cf. *bābāh*, בָּבָה, "apple [of the eye], pupil" in Zech 2:12 MT) [19]
balāṭum (*u,u*) = to live; D: to let live, spare (through dissimilation, cf. *pālaṭ*, פָּלַט, "to escape") [16]
balūm = without (the *-ūm* suffix is an old locative suffix hence literally, "in lack of") (cf. *bal*, בַּל; *bəlî*, בְּלִי) [12]
bašûm (*i,i*) = to exist, be (in the sense of, to exist); Š: to produce (cf. *bə*, בְּ, "in" + *šû*, it) [10]
bêlum = lord, owner, master (cf. *ba'al*, בַּעַל) [13]
bîšum = moveable property, possession [18]
bîtum = house, household (cf. *bayit*, בַּיִת) [1]

dayyānum = a judge [9]
dayyānūtum = judgeship (cf. *dayyān*, דַּיָּן, "a judge") [11]
dâkum (< *d-w-k*) (*a,u*) = to kill, execute (outside LH also: to crush) (cf. *dûk*, דּוּךְ, "to pound"; *dākā'*, דָּכָא, *piel*: "to crush"; *dākâ*, דָּכָה, *piel*: "to crush") [4]
dânum (*dyn*) (*a,i*) = to try (conduct a trial), judge (cf. *dîn*, דִּין, "to judge"; *dān*, דָּן, "Dan") [9]
dekûm (*e,e*) = to stir up, raise [14]
dînum (m; plural is feminine: *dînātum*) = legal case, trial; decision (cf. *dîn*, דִּין; tribe of Dan, דָּן) [7]

ebēbum (*i,i*) = G: to be(come) clean; D: to clean, purify; to declare innocent [7]
ekallum = palace (cf. *hêkāl*, הֵיכָל) [7]
eleppum = boat [13]
elî = on, upon, over, against, beyond, than (in comparisons) (cf. *'al*, עַל, "on, upon, over, against," from the III-*y* and III-*h* verb *'ālâ*, עָלָה) [3]
enûm (*i,i*) (< *'-n-y*) = to change, exchange (cf. *'ānâ*, עָנָה, "to answer") [10]
epēšum (*e,u*; *u,u*) = to do, make, build (cf., perhaps, *ḥāpaś*, חָפַשׂ, "to search") [20]
eqlum = field [18]

erēbum (*u,u*) = to enter (cf. *ʿereb*, עֶרֶב, "evening") [17]
ezēbum (*i,i*) = G: to abandon, leave behind, divorce; Š: to cause to leave behind, deposit (cf. *ʿāzab*, עָזַב) [10]

galābum = D: to shave, cut off (cf. *gallāb*, גַּלָּב, "barber") [16]

ḫalaqum (*i,i*) = to lose, go/be missing [13]
ḫalqum = lost, missing [13]
ḫarrānum = travel, journey (cf. *ḥārān*, חָרָן, "Haran") [19]
ḫāwirum, ḫāʾirum = first husband (participle of *ḫārum*, to choose, to select) [17]
ḫīrtum = (first) wife (< *ḫiʾārum* = to choose, select) [18]
ḫiṭîtum = sin, fault (cf. *ḥāṭāʾ*, חָטָא, "to sin") [19]
ḫulqum = lost property [13]
ḫurāṣum = gold (cf. *ḥārûṣ*, חָרוּץ) [12]

dID = Id (god of the river ordeal); Id always has before it a determinative for deity, DINGIR (d) (cf. *ʾēd*, אֵד "stream, spring," in Gen 2:6); *nârum*, river (cf. *nāhār*, נָהָר) [6]
idûm (*edûm*) = to know (cf. *yādaʿ*, יָדַע)
i/uzuzzum = N: to stand (up) [19]
ilum = god (cf. *ʾēl*, אֵל) [1]
imērum = donkey (cf. *ḥămôr*, חֲמוֹר) [12]
immerum = "sheep" (cf. *ʾimmēr*, (אִמֵּר) [12]
ina = in, from, among, with, by (means of), some of; *time*: in, at; *with verb*: when, while, by (*ina* is never used as a conjunction) [5]
ištên (absolute with masculine); *ištēʾat* (absolute with feminine) = one, individual [18]
ištu = *place*: from, out of; *time*: since, after [14]
išûm (< *y/w-š-y*) (*u/i* alternates in preterite, *u* is older) = to have (cf. *yēš*, יֵשׁ, "there is") [13]
itti = with, from (cf. *ʾēt*, אֵת) [11]

kabālum = to be paralyzed; D: to bind, make immobile (cf. *kebel*, כֶּבֶל, "fetters") [16]
kalûm = to retain, detain, withhold (cf. *kālāʾ*, כָּלָא, "to withhold, keep back") [15]
kânum (< *k-w-n*) (*u,u*) = G: to be firm; D: to establish, make secure, prove, have proof, convict (cf. *kûn*, כּוּן, *niphal*: "to be firm"; *polel*: "to make firm, establish") [4]
kasûm (*u/i*) = to bind (cf. *kəsût*, כְּסוּת, "covering, clothing") [16]
kašādum (*a,u*) = to overcome, reach [6]
kaspum = silver (cf. *kesep*, כֶּסֶף) [3]
kīma = like, in the same way as (preposition); that (conjunction to introduce indirect discourse) (cf. *kə*, כְּ; *kî*, כִּי; *kəmô*, כְּמוֹ) [14]
kirûm = orchard [12]
kišpū (always plural) = witchcraft, sorcery (cf. *kāšap*, כָּשַׁף, *piel*: "to practice sorcery") [4]
kunukkum = seal; sealed clay tablet [9]
kussûm = seat (cf. *kissēʾ*, כִּסֵּא, "seat, throne") [11]

lâ = not (a negative particle used only in subordinate clauses) (cf. *lōʾ*, לֹא, "not") [2]
laʾbum = a fever, serious illness (cf. *lahab*, לַהַב, "flame") [20]
leqûm (*e,e*) = to take, receive (cf. *lāqaḥ*, לָקַח) [13]

libbum = heart (cf. *lēb*, לֵב) [18]
lû = either, or (cf. *lû*, לוּ, "if only") [12]

magal = greatly [19]
magārum (*a,u*) = to agree, allow; to be willing [19]
maḫārum (*a,u*) = to receive, acquire, be comparable; Št: to make oneself equal to (cf. *məḥîr*, מְחִיר, "money, recompense") [6]
maḫrum = front, presence; *construct*: before (cf. *maḫārum*; *məḥîr*, מְחִיר, "equivalent value, price, recompense") [13]
makkūrum = property (cf. *mākar*, מָכַר, "to sell") [12]
maṣṣarūtum (< *n-ṣ-r*) = watch, guard, safekeeping (cf. *nāṣar*, נָצַר) [12]
mala = all, as much as; full amount (cf. *mālē'*, מָלֵא, "full") [18]
manûm = mina (≈ 1/2 kg.) (cf. *māneh*, מָנֶה) [18]
manûm (*u,u*) = to count, reckon, recount (cf. *mānâ*, מָנָה) [18]
mârum = son (cf. Hebrew *mərî'*, מְרִיא, "fatling"; Aramaic *mārē'*, מָרֵא, "lord") [9]
maṭûm (*i,i*) = to be small; Š-stem: to humiliate, belittle, disparage (cf. *mə'aṭ*, מְעַט, "little, few") [19]
mimma = something, anything, whatever, all that; property (cf. *mə'ûmâ*, מְאוּמָה) [12]
mimmûm = whatever; property (the form of *mimma* used with pronominal suffixes) (cf. *mə'ûmâ*, מְאוּמָה) [12]
mûdûm (<**mûde'um*) = knowing, wise; knower, expert [13]
mûdûtum = knowledge (cf. *yāda'*, יָדַע) [13]
mûm (*plurale tantum*); *oblique and construct*: *mê* [< **ma'i*] = water (cf. *mayim*, מַיִם) [16]
muškēnum (< *m-š-k-'*) = royal servant, civil servant (cf. *miskēn*, מִסְכֵּן, "poor") [13]
muttatum = half [of hair] [16]
mutum = husband (cf. *mətîm*, מְתִים, "men"; *mətûšelaḥ*, מְתוּשֶׁלַח, "Methuselah") [17]

nabātum (*i,i*) (< **n-'-b-t*) = N: to flee, escape; to be a fugitive (cf. homologous forms of *'ābad*, אָבַד, which also means "to be lost, be a fugitive," as well as "to perish, destroy") [17]
nadānum (*i,i*) = to give, pay; to sell (cf. *nātan*, נָתַן) [10]
nadîtum [LUKUR] = devotee; high priestess (one who must remain childless (< **nadī'tum*) [18]
nadûm (< *n-d-y*) (*i,i*) = to throw, hurl, accuse (lay a charge of), leave (cf. *nādâ*, נָדָה, *piel*: "to throw out, to exclude") [4]
nāgirum = herald, (town) crier [15]
napištum = life (cf. *nepeš*, נֶפֶשׁ, "life") [8]
nârum = river (cf. *nāhār*, נָהָר). [6]
naṣārum (*a,u*) = to watch over, guard, keep; *stative*: to be careful (cf. *nāṣar*, נָצַר) [17]
našûm (*n-š-'*) (*i*) = to lift, carry, bear; to support (cf. *nāśā'* נָשָׂא, "to bear") [9]
naṭûm (*i,i*) (*u,u*) = to beat [16]
nêrtum = (f) murder [3]
ni'ālum (*i*)/*nâlum* (*a*) = to lie down, sleep; Gt: to lie down together, sleep together (cf. possible cognates with dissimilation: *lîn*, לִין, "to spend the night"; *laylâ*, לַיְלָה, "night") [16]
nīnu = we (1cp) [10]
nîšum = life (cf. *nāšîm*, נָשִׁים, "women") [15]

pagrum = body, self (cf. *peger*, פֶּגֶר) [17]

pânum = face; *ina pâni* = because of, in front of; *ana pâni* = previously, in front of, before (cf. *pānîm*, פָּנִים) [17]
parāsum (*a,u*) = to divide, separate, cut (off); to decide (cf. *pāras*, פָּרַס, *qal*: "to break [bread]"; *hiphil*: "to divide, split [hoofs]") [3]
puḫrum = assembly, council [11]
purussûm = decision (common noun type with doubled final consonant, called R-stem, followed by -*a*'; cf. *pāras*, פָּרַס, "to break [bread]"; "to divide [hoof]") [9]

qabûm (*qby*) (*i,i*) = to speak, declare, order [8]
qadūm = besides, together with (locative -*ūm*) (cf. *qedem*, קֶדֶם)
qâtum = hand [5]
qerbūm = within (cf. *qerbum*, inside) (cf. *qereb*, קֶרֶב) [10]
qerēbum (*i,i*) (irregular stative ms is *qerub*) = to be near, draw near; to be available (cf. *qārab*, קָרַב) [14]

rābum (or *ri'ābum*) (*a,i*) = to compensate, make restitution [13]
rabûm (*i,i*) = to be great; D: to raise (cf. *rābâ*, רָבָה, "to be many, be great") [18]
raqûm (*i,i*) = to hide, give refuge to [15]
rašûm (*i,i*) = to have, own, acquire; Š: to provide [18]
redûm (*e,e*)/(*i,i*) [(*e,e*) is more likely for LH] = to lead, send; ventive:"to bring (cf. *rādâ*, רָדָה, "to rule") [14]
riksum (fp: *riksātum*) = contract, covenant (cf. *rākas*, רָכַס, "to bind") [12]
rugummûm = complaint [10]

sakālum (*i,i*) = to acquire goods, property illegally or fraudulently [19]
sikiltum (< *sakālum*) = goods, property acquired illegally or fraudulently [19]
sapāḫum (*a,u*) = to scatter, disrupt; D: to squander, disturb, neglect [19]
sarārum (*a,u*) = to lie, be criminally dishonest [14]
sarrātum (always plural) = lies, deception, fraud (cf. *sārar*, סָרַר, "to be stubborn") [7]
sarrum = false, dishonest; *substantive use:* liar [14]
sinništum [MUNUS] = woman, female; MÍ, a determinative for a female [16]
sûnum = loin, lap, genital area [16]

ṣabātum (*a,a*) = to seize, catch, find; N: to be found, be captured (cf. *ṣābaṭ*, צָבַט, "to reach, hold") [13]
ṣābitānum = one who finds, captor [15]
ṣeḫrum = small, young (cf. *ṣā'îr*, צָעִיר) [15]
ṣêrum = open country (beyond cultivated areas) [15]

ša = who, whom, which, he who, the one who, that which, of; *ša* is an undeclined determinative relative pronoun (cf. *ša*, שֶׁ + doubling, "which") [6]
šaḫûm = pig [13]
šayyāmānum (< *šâmum*) = buyer [13]
šakānum (*a,u*) = to set, appoint, arrange, provide (cf. *hiphil* of *kûn*, כּוּן) [14]
šalālum (*a,u*) = to take captive; N: to be captured (cf. *šālal*, שָׁלַל, "to plunder") [17]
šalāmum (*i,i*) = G: to be well, whole, safe; D: to make whole, make restitution; to heal; to pay back in full (cf. *šālēm*, שָׁלֵם, "to be complete, sound") [4]

šalūm (< *š-l-y*) (*i,i*) = to plunge, immerse [5]
šaluš(tum) [ŠUŠANA] = "1/3"; or less often *šuššān*, lit. "2/6" [18]
šāmum (*a,a*) (< *š-y-m*) = to purchase, buy [12]
šanītum (feminine of *šanūm*) = another, a second (cf. *šənî*, שְׁנֵי, "two") [19]
šanūm = another, a second (cf. *šēnî*, שֵׁנִי, "second") [16]
šaqālum (*a,u*) = to weigh out (cf. *šāqal*, שָׁקַל) [13]
šarāqum (*i,i*) = to steal [12]
šarrāqum = thief [12]
šarratum = queen [2]
šarrum = "king (cf. *śar*, שַׂר, "prince, commander, officer, suzerain"; cf. "Sarai," שָׂרָי, or "Sarah," שָׂרָה, both of which mean "princess") [2]
še'um = barley (perhaps cf. *šay*, שַׁי, "tribute"; see *KB*, *DCH*, ad loc.) [1]
šeriktum (< *šarākum* = to give) = dowry [18]
šī = that, this (nom fs); she, it (3fs) [8, 10]
šībum = old man; witness (cf. *śêbâ*, שֵׂיבָה, "old age") [7]
šībūtum = testimony [7]
šīmtum = destiny, fate (literally, "that which is appointed or set") (cf. *śîm*, שִׂים) [14]
šīmum (< *šāmum*) = purchase [13]
šina = those, these (nom fp); they (3fp) [8, 10]
šināti = those, these (gen-acc fp) [8]
šiqlum [GÍN] = shekel (cf. *šeqel*, שֶׁקֶל) [15]
šisītum = summons, call [15]
šū = that, this (nom ms); he, it (3ms) [8, 10]
šu'āti = that, this (gen-acc cs) [8]
šugītum = priestess; lay priestess [18]
šumma = if [2]
šumum = name (cf. *šēm*, שֵׁם) [7]
šunu = those, these (nom mp); they (3mp) [8, 10]
šunūti = those, these (gen-acc mp) [8]
šurqum = stolen property [12]

tabālum (*a,a*) (related to *wabālum*) = to take, remove, confiscate, bring (away) [5]
tarāṣum (*a,u*) = to extend, stretch out; Š: to point [16]
tārum (*t-w-r*) (*u*) = to return; *in hendiadys*: to do again (intransitive in G and transitive in D) (cf. תור, *t-w-r*, "to explore") [11]
tebūm (*i,i*) = to rise up, depart; Š: to remove [11]
terḫatum = marriage present, bride price (?) [18]
tuššum = slander, calumny, malicious talk [14]

u = and, but (cf. *wə/û*, וְ/וּ) [3]
û (< *'u*) = or (cf. *'ô*, אוֹ) [10]
û lû = or (cf. *lû*, לוּ, "if only") [12]
ubānum (< *'-b-h-n*) = finger (cf. *bōhen*, בֹּהֶן) [16]
ugbabtum = priestess, often a daughter of a king or other socially ranked person [16]
ul = not (independent clauses) (cf. *'al*, אַל) [5]

uzubbûm (< *ezēbum*) = divorce settlement (cf. *ʿāzab*, עָזַב, "to forsake, abandon") [18]

wabālum (*a,i*) = to bring (away), carry [5]
walādum (*a,i*) = to bear, give birth to (cf. *yālad*, יָלַד,) [12]
wardum = slave (cf. *yārad*, יָרַד, "to descend") [12]
warḫum = month (cf. *yeraḥ*, יֶרַח) [14]
warka = after, afterwards (see *warki*; cf. *yərēkâ*, יְרֵכָה, "rear [portion], most distant part") [15]
warkānūm (< **warki* + *ān* [common noun ending] + *-ūm* [locative/adverbial ending]) = afterwards (cf. *yərēkâ*, יְרֵכָה, "rear [portion], most distant part") [10]
warkatum = back, inheritance, background (cf. *yərēkâ*, יְרֵכָה, "rear [portion], most distant part") [15]
warki = after (preposition and conjunction) (cf. *yərēkâ*, יְרֵכָה, "rear [portion], most distant part") [10]
waṣûm (*i,i*) = to go out (cf. *yāṣāʾ*, יָצָא) [7]
wašābum (*a,i*) = to dwell, sit (cf. *yāšab*, יָשַׁב) [11]
wašārum = to be free; D: to prove innocent; Dt: to be proved innocent, exonerated, allowed to go free (cf. *yātar*, יָתַר, *niphal*: "to be left over") [15]
watārum (*i,i*) = to be exceeding, be much; D: to exceed; Š: to make supreme (cf. *y- t- r*, יתר , *niphal*: "to be left over")

zakārum (*a,u*) = to speak, say, name, swear + *nîš ilim* = to swear by a god (cf. *zākar*, זָכַר, "to mention, remember") [15]
zêrum (*e,e*) = to hate, dislike; to reject [17]
zikarum = man, a male (cf. *zākār*, זָכָר) [16]
zîttum = portion, part, share (< *zâzum*, to divide) [18]

APPENDIX F

Answer Key to Select Questions

Chapter 3

1. *ú-[ub/up]-[bi/bé/pé/pí]-[er/ir]-ma*
   Note: The sign numbers (in MZL) for this sequence of signs are 490–504–358–437–552.
   Note: The extra cuneiform sign ú is a "historical spelling." In this case it reflects the fact that this word at an earlier period began with an ʾ (and before that with a *y*). See §2.5.1.4 and §2.5.1.5.
2. *ubbirma*
3. D-stem preterite 3cs from *abārum* + *-ma*; "and/but he accused"
4. "If a man accused a man and/but"
   Note: The verb *abārum* in the G-stem means "to embrace" and in the D-stem means "to bind magically" or, in legal contexts, "to pin blame on," or "to accuse." We know that the implied initial ʾ of this verb is an $ʾ_3$, that is, one that originated in the Proto-Semitic consonant *ḥ*, based on the cognate Hebrew verb *ḥbr*, חבר (II), found in Deuteronomy 18:11, Isaiah 47:9, and Psalm 58:6 [MT], where it refers to one who "binds by magic." In Akkadian the verb *abārum* is attested mostly in the D-stem, and in LH, it only has the meaning "to accuse."

Chapter 4

1. *ne-[er/ir]-[ud/ut/uṭ/tam] e-[le/li]-šu*
   [ed/id/et/it/eṭ/iṭ]–[de/di/ṭe/ṭi]–ma
2. *ne-er-tam e-li-šu id-di-ma*
   - G-stem preterite 3cs of *parāsum* = *iprus*
   - Hypothetical G-stem preterite 3cs of *nadūm* = **induʾ*
   - Assimilation of consonant *n* to juxtaposed consonant = **idduʾ*
   - Replace vowel class = **iddiʾ*
   - Quiescing ʾ lengthens vowel = *iddî*
   - Adding the enclitic *-ma* = *iddîma*
3. *nêrtam elīšu iddîma*
4. "he hurled (made a charge of) murder against him and/but"
   "If a man accused another man, and he made a charge of murder against him and/but"

Chapter 5

1. *la [ug/uk/uq]-ti-in-šu*
   mu-[ub/up]-[bi/bé/pé/pí]-[er/ir]-šu
   [ed/id/et/it/eṭ/iṭ]-[da/ṭa]-[ag/ak/aq]

2. *la uk-ti-in-šu mu-ub-bi-ir-šu id-da-ak*
   D-stem perfect 3cs of *parāsum* = *uptarris*
   Hypothetical D-stem perfect 3cs of *kānum* = **uktawwin*
   Diphthong *aw* contracts = **uktûwin*
   II-w reduction to ' = **uktû'in*
   Vowel contraction = *uktīn*
   Add the 3ms object suffix *šu* = *uktīnšu*

   N-stem durative 3cs of *parāsum* = *ipparras*
   Hypothetical N-stem durative 3cs of *dākum* = **iddawwak*
   Diphthong *aw* contracts = **iddûwak*
   II-w reduction to ' = **iddû'ak*
   Vowel contraction = *iddāk*
3. *lâ uktînšu mubbiršu iddāk*
4. "he did not convict him, the one who was accusing him will/would be executed"
   "If a man accused another man, and he made a charge of murder against him, but he did not convict him, his accuser would be executed."
   Note: It is traditional to translate LH with present tense translations for preterites and perfects and future tense translations for duratives, since this reflects the practice of modern legislation. Nevertheless, based on the prologue and epilogue, these laws are presented not just as models for future legal cases but as a supposed (even if unlikely) summary of the legal decisions that Hammurabi made by which he hopes to commend himself to the deity and secure the approbation of future generations. So, translating the preterites and perfects with past tenses (their normal meaning in OB) and the duratives with "would," rather than "will" or "shall," is grammatically and contextually justified if not preferable.

Chapter 6

1. *šum-ma a-[wa/we/wi/wu/pe/pi]-lum*
   [ke/ki/qé/qí]-iš-[bé/bi/pé/pí]
   e-[le/li] a-[wa/we/wi/wu/pe/pi]-[lim/ši] [ed/id/et/it/eṭ/iṭ]-[de/di/ṭe/ṭi]-ma
   la [ug/uk/uq]-ti-in-šu
   ša e-[li/le]-šu
   [ke/ki/qé/qí]-iš-[bu/pu] na-[du/ṭù]-ú
   a-na [an/^{d}*/*DINGIR*(=ilum)]-*ÍD*(=nârum)*
   i-il-la-[ag/ak/aq]
2. *šum-ma a-wi-lum ki-iš-pí e-li a-wi-lim id-di-ma la uk-ti-in-šu ša e-li-šu ki-iš-pu na-du-ú a-na* ^{d}ÍD *i-il-la-ak*
3. *šumma awīlum kišpī elî awīlim iddîma lâ uktînšu ša elîšu kišpū nadû ana Id/nârim illak*
4. a. G-stem preterite 3cs + *-ma* from *nadûm*; D-stem perfect 3cs + *šu* from *kânum*; G-stem stative 3mp from *nadûm*; G-stem durative from *alākum*
   Note: The *-u* suffix on *nadû* is the 3mp ending of the G-stem stative rather than a subordinative *-u* suffix, since the subject of *nadû* is *kišpū*, the masculine plural term for "sorcery, witchcraft."

b. *awīlum*=nominative ms; *kišpī*=genitive mp; *awīlim*=gentive ms; *kišpū*=nominative mp; Id(=*nârim*)=ms genitive

5. "If a man, sorcery (witchcraft) against a man has hurled (made charges of) and/but he did not convict him, which, against him sorceries were hurled (charged), into Id (the river) he would go."

Chapter 7

1. *Id/nârum išalli'amma šumma Id/nârum iktašassu*

Bibliography

Alstola, Tero. "Judeans in Babylonia. A Study of Deportees in the Sixth and Fifth Centuries BCE." PhD diss., The University of Helsinki, 2018.

Andersen, Francis I. *The Sentence in Biblical Hebrew.* Janua Linguarum. Series Practica, vol. 231. The Hague: Mouton, 1974.

Aruz, Joan, Kim Benzel, and Jean Evans, eds., *Beyond Babylon: Art, Trade, and Diplomacy in the Second Millennium B.C.* The Metropolitan Museum of Art Symposia. New Haven: Yale University Press, 2008.

Aruz, Joan, Sarah B. Graff, and Yelena Rakic, eds., *Cultures in Contact: From Mesopotamia to the Mediterranean in the Second Millennium B.C.* The Metropolitan Museum of Art Symposia. New Haven: Yale University Press, 2013.

Bloch, Yigal, "Judeans in Sippar and Susa during the First Century of the Babylonian Exile: Assimilation and Perseverance under Neo-Babylonian and Achaemenid Rule," *Journal of Ancient Near Eastern History* 1 (2014): 119–72.

Borger, Rykle, *Babylonisch-Assyrische Lesestücke.* 3rd ed. 2 vols. Rome: Pontifical Biblical Institute, 2006.

———. *Mesopotamisches Zeichenlexikon*, 2nd ed. AOAT 305. Münster: Ugarit-Verlag, 2010.

Bottéro, Jean. *Mesopotamia: Writing, Reasoning, and the Gods.* Translated by Z. Bahrani et al. Chicago: University of Chicago Press, 1992.

Buccellati, Giorgio. *A Structural Grammar of Babylonian.* Wiesbaden: Harrassowitz, 1996.

Caplice, Richard. *Introduction to Akkadian.* 4th ed. Rome: Pontifical Biblical Institute, 2002.

Cavigneaux, Antoine. "Le nom akkadien du grain." *NABU* 1989.3 §52.

Chavalas, Mark W. and K. Lawson Younger Jr., eds. *Mesopotamia and the Bible: Comparative Explorations.* Grand Rapids: Baker Academic, 2002.

Davies, Graham I. *Ancient Hebrew Inscriptions: Corpus and Concordance.* 2 vols. Cambridge: Cambridge University Press, 2007.

Driver, S. R. and John C. Miles. *The Babylonian Laws.* 2 vols. Oxford: Oxford University Press, 1968.

Finkel, Irving L. *The Ark Before Noah: Decoding the Story of the Flood.* New York: Anchor Books, 2015.

Finkel, Irving and Jonathan Taylor. *Cuneiform.* London: The British Museum Press, 2015.

Fitzgerald, Madeleine. "pisan dub-ba and the Direction of Cuneiform Script." *Cuneiform Digital Library Bulletin* (2003): 2.

Foxvog, Daniel A. *Introduction to Sumerian.* Cuneiform Digital Library Preprints, 2. http://cdli.ucla.edu/pubs/cdlp/cdlp0002_20160104.pdf, 2016.

Garr, R. Randall. "On Voicing and Devoicing in Ugaritic." *Journal of Near Eastern Studies* 45.1 (1986): 45–52.

Gelb, Ignace J. *Glossary of Old Akkadian.* Chicago: University of Chicago Press, 1957.

———. *Old Akkadian Writing and Grammar.* 2nd ed. Chicago: University of Chicago Press, 1961.

George, Andrew. "Babylonian and Assyrian: A History of Akkadian." Pages 31–71 in *Languages of Iraq, Ancient and Modern*. Edited by J. N. Postgate, ed. London: British School of Archaeology in Iraq, 2007.

Goetze, Albrecht. "The *t*-Form of the Old Babylonian Verb." *JAOS* 56 (1936): 297–334.

Greengus, Samuel. "Redefining 'Inchoate Marriage' in Old Babylonian Contexts." Pages 123–40 in *Riches Hidden in Secret Places: Ancient Near Eastern Studies in Memory of Thorkild Jacobsen*. Edited by Tzvi Abusch. University Park: Pennsylvania State University Press, 2002.

Hasselbach, Rebecca. "Barth-Ginsberg Law." Pages 258–59 in *Encyclopedia of Hebrew Language and Linguistics*. Edited by Geoffrey Khan. Leiden: Brill, 2013.

Hayes, John L. *A Manual of Sumerian Grammar and Text*. 3rd ed. rev. expanded. Malibu, CA: Undena, 2018.

Huehnergard, John. *A Grammar of Akkadian*. 3rd ed. Harvard Semitic Studies 45. Winona Lake, IN: Eisenbrauns, 2011.

———. "Proto-Semitic." Pages 49–79 in *The Semitic Languages*. 2nd ed. Edited by John Huehnergard and Na'ama Pat-El. New York: Routledge, 2019.

Huehnergard, John and Christopher Woods. "Chapter 8: Akkadian and Eblaite." Pages 218–87 in *The Cambridge Encyclopedia of the World's Ancient Languages*. Edited by Roger D. Woodard. Cambridge: Cambridge University Press, 2004.

Hugenberger, Gordon P. *Marriage as a Covenant: Biblical Law and Ethics as Developed from Malachi*. Supplements to Vetus Testamentum 52. Leiden: Brill, 1994. Repr. in Biblical Studies Library. Eugene, OR: Wipf and Stock, 2014.

Jagersma, Abraham H. *Descriptive Grammar of Sumerian*. Leiden: Universiteit Leiden, 2010.

Joüon, Paul, and T. Muraoka. *A Grammar of Biblical Hebrew*. 2nd ed. Rome: Biblical Institute Press, 2006.

Koppen, Frans van. "The Scribe of the Flood Story and His Circle." Pages 140–66 in *The Oxford Handbook of Cuneiform Culture*. Edited by Karen Radner and Eleanor Robson. Oxford: Oxford University Press, 2011.

Kouwenberg, N. J. C. *The Akkadian Verb and Its Semitic Background*. Languages of the Ancient Near East 2. Winona Lake, IN: Eisenbrauns, 2010.

———. "The Interchange of *e* and *a* in Old Babylonian." Pages 225–49 in *Veenhof Anniversary Volume: Studies Presented to Klaas R. Veenhof on the Occasion of his Sixty-Fifth Birthday*. Edited by W. H. van Soldt et al. Leiden: Nederlands Instituut voor het Nabije Oosten, 2001.

———. "Nouns as Verbs: The Verbal Nature of the Akkadian Stative." *Orientalia* (*NS*) 69:1 (2000): 21–71.

———. Review of *A Grammar of Akkadian*, by John Huehnergard. *Bibliotheca Orientalis* 55:5/6 (1998): 814–15.

Labat, René and Florence Malbran-Labat. *Manuel d'épigraphie akkadienne, signes, syllabaire, idéogrammes*. 6th ed. Paris: Geuthner, 2002.

Lambert, Wilfred G., "Class Notes." The University of Birmingham, 1985–1986.

———. "Introduction to Akkadian." Pages 91–99 in *Horizons in Semitic Studies: Articles for the Student*. Edited by J. H. Eaton. Birmingham: University of Birmingham, 1980.

Mansfield, Daniel F. and Norman J. Wildberger. "Plimpton 322 is Babylonian Exact Sexagesimal Trigonometry." *Historia Mathematica* 44:4 (2017): 395–419.

Marcus, David. *A Manual of Akkadian*. New York: University Press of America, 1978.

Merwe, Christo H. J. van der, Jacobus A. Naudé, and Jan H. Kroeze. *A Biblical Hebrew Reference Grammar*. 2nd ed. London: Bloomsbury, 2017.

Miller, Cynthia Lynn, ed. *The Verbless Clause in Biblical Hebrew, Linguistic Approaches*. Linguistic Studies in Ancient West Semitic 1. Winona Lake, IN: Eisenbrauns, 1999.

Miller, Douglas B. and R. Mark Shipp. *An Akkadian Handbook*. 2nd ed. Winona Lake, IN: Eisenbrauns, 2014.

Moran, William L. *The Amarna Letters*. Baltimore: Johns Hopkins University Press, 2000.
Parpola, Simo. *Letters from Assyrian and Babylonian Scholars*. State Archives of Assyria 10. Helsinki: Helsinki University Press, 1993.
Patterson, R. D. "Old Babylonian Parataxis as Exhibited in the Royal Letters of the Middle Old Babylonian Period and in the Code of Hammurapi." PhD diss. University of California, Los Angeles, 1970.
Pearce, Laurie E. and Cornelia Wunsch. *Documents of Judean Exiles and West Semites in Babylonia in the Collection of David Sofer*. Cornell University Studies in Assyriology and Sumerology 28. Bethesda, MD: CDL, 2014.
Pope, Marvin H. *Song of Songs*. Anchor Bible. Garden City, NY: Doubleday, 1970.
Provan, Iain, V. Philips Long, and Tremper Longman III. *A Biblical History of Israel*. Louisville: Westminster John Knox, 2015.
Reiner, Erica. *A Linguistic Analysis of Akkadian*. Janua Linguarum. Series Practica XXI. The Hague: Mouton, 1966.
Reymond, Eric D. *Intermediate Biblical Hebrew Grammar: A Student's Guide to Phonology and Morphology*. Atlanta: SBL Press, 2018.
Richardson, M. E. J. *A Comprehensive Grammar to Hammurabi's Stele*. Piscataway, NJ: Gorgias, 2008.
———. *Hammurabi's Laws: Text, Translation and Glossary*. Sheffield: Sheffield Academic, 2000.
Riemschneider, Kaspar K. *Lehrbuch des Akkadischen*. 6th ed. Leipzig: Langenscheidt, 1992; *An Akkadian Grammar: A Translation of Riemschneider's Lehrbuch des Akkadischen*. Translated by Thomas A. Caldwell, John N. Oswalt, and John F. X. Sheehan. Marquette: Marquette University Press, 1978.
Roth, Martha T. *Law Collections from Mesopotamia and Asia Minor*. Atlanta: Scholars Press, 1995.
———. "Mesopotamian Legal Traditions and the Laws of Hammurabi." *Chicago-Kent Legal Review* 71, Article 3 (1995): 13–39.
Seri, Andrea. "Adaptation of Cuneiform to Write Akkadian." Pages 85–98 in *Visible Language: Inventions of Writing in the Ancient Middle East and Beyond*. Edited by Christopher Woods with Emily Teeter and Geoff Emberling. 2nd printing. Oriental Institute Museum Publications 32. Chicago: Oriental Institute of the University of Chicago, 2015.
Stein, Gil J. Foreword to *Visible Language: Inventions of Writing in the Ancient Middle East and Beyond*, edited by Christopher Woods with Emily Teeter and Geoff Emberling. 2nd printing. Oriental Institute Museum Publications 32. Chicago: Oriental Institute of the University of Chicago, 2015.
Streck, Michael P. Review of *Letters in the British Museum*, by W. H. van Soldt. *Bibliotheca Orientalis* 54 (1997): 143–48.
Streck, Michael P. et al., eds. *Supplement to the Akkadian Dictionaries, Vol 1: B, P*. Leipziger Altorientalistische Studien 7,1. Wiesbaden: Harrassowitz, 2018.
———. *Supplement to the Akkadian Dictionaries, Vol 2: D, T, and Ṭ*. Leipziger Altorientalistische Studien 7,2. Wiesbaden: Harrassowitz, 2019.
———. *Supplement to the Akkadian Dictionaries, Vol 3: G, K, and Q*. Leipziger Altorientalistische Studien 7,2. Wiesbaden: Harrassowitz, 2022.
Studevent-Hickman, Benjamin. "The Ninety-Degree Rotation of the Cuneiform Script." Pages 485–513 in *Ancient Near Eastern Art in Context: Studies in Honor of Irene J. Winter by Her Students*. Edited by Jack Cheng and Marian H. Feldman. Culture & History of the Ancient Near East 26. Leiden: Brill, 2007.
Tawil, Hayim ben Yosef. *An Akkadian Lexical Companion for Biblical Hebrew: Etymological-Semantic and Idiomatic Equivalents with Supplement on Biblical Aramaic*. New York: Ktav, 2017.
Ungnad, Arthur. *Akkadian Grammar*. Revised by Lubor Matouš. Translated by Harry A. Hoffner. 5th ed. Atlanta: Scholars Press, 1992.

Weeden, M. "The Akkadian Words for 'Grain' and the God 'Ḫaya.'" *Die Welt des Orients* 39 (2009): 77–107.

Woods, Christopher with Emily Teeter and Geoff Emberling, eds. *Visible Language: Inventions of Writing in the Ancient Middle East and Beyond.* 2nd printing. Oriental Institute Museum Publications 32. Chicago: Oriental Institute of the University of Chicago, 2015.

Worthington, Martin. *Complete Babylonian.* 2nd ed. London: John Murray Learning, 2018.

Wright, David P. *Inventing God's Law: How the Covenant Code of the Bible Used and Revised the Laws of Hammurabi.* Oxford: Oxford University Press, 2013.

Young, Ian. *Diversity in Pre-Exilic Hebrew.* Forschungen zum Alten Testament 5. Tübingen: Mohr Siebeck, 1993.

Zólyomi, Gábor. *An Introduction to the Grammar of Sumerian.* Budapest: Eötvös University Press, 2016.

Index

Zondervan Language Basics

Basics of Ancient Ethiopic

A Complete Grammar, Workbook, and Lexicon

Archie T. Wright

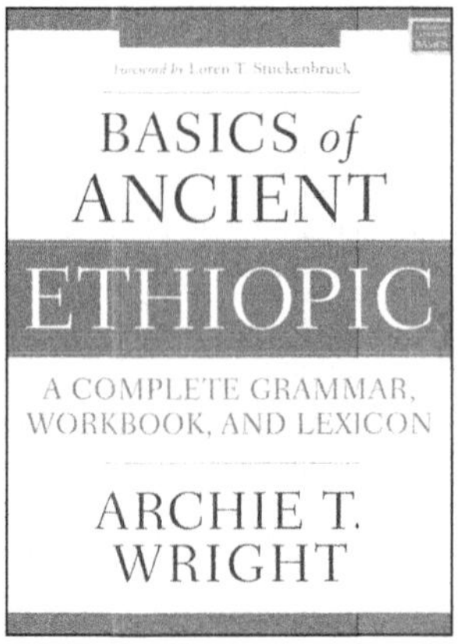

Basics of Ancient Ethiopic by Archie Wright introduces students to the basic grammar of ancient Ethiopic (Ge'ez) while approaching the language through its wider cultural and literary context, and its historical legacy.

As part of the widely-used Zondervan Language Basics series of resources, Wright's Ethiopic grammar is a student-friendly introduction. It helps students learn by:

- Minimizing technical jargon
- Providing only the information needed to learn the basics
- Breaking the grammar of language down into manageable and intuitive chunks
- Illustrating the grammar in question by its use in rich selections from ancient Christian and the Second Temple Jewish books of 1 Enoch and Jubilees
- Providing grammar, readings, exercises, and a lexicon all in one convenient volume

Basics of Ethiopic provides an ideal first step into this important language and focuses on getting the student into texts and translation as quickly as possible.

Basics of Arabic

A Complete Grammar, Workbook, and Lexicon

Ayman S. Ibrahim

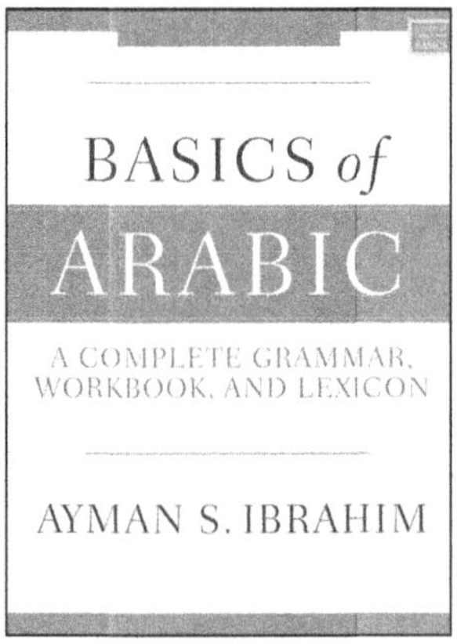

Basics of Arabic by Ayman Ibrahim is an introductory grammar, workbook, and lexicon for learning Modern Standard Arabic. Designed for students approaching Arabic for the first time the book provides them with all the tools necessary to develop skills in reading and writing Arabic. Students will learn Arabic grammar and vocabulary and be able to translate key Arabic passages from biblical and qur'anic texts.

Each lesson includes:

- A thorough and understandable introduction to a particular grammatical feature in Arabic
- List of vocabulary to be memorized
- Exercises for practice and reinforcement of key concepts

Basics of Arabic will help readers:

- Recite the Arabic alphabet
- Read and pronounce Arabic words
- Learn the Arabic noun and verbal system
- Understand syntax for writing and reading sentences

Additional translation exercises and a complete lexicon are included at the back of the book. Ideal for students, missionaries, independent learners, and homeschoolers this accessible guide give readers a clear and understandable introduction to this important language.

ZondervanAcademic.com/LanguageBasics